The Singapore Convention on Mediation

Global Trends in Dispute Resolution

VOLUME 8

Series Editor

Nadja Alexander is Director of the Singapore International Dispute Resolution Academy and Professor of Law at Singapore Management University. Professor Alexander is an award-winning author and educator in the field of negotiation and dispute resolution. She is known for the passion, energy and creativity she brings to her various roles as scholar, policy adviser, mediation practitioner and trainer. She has been identified by *Who's Who Legal* as a global thought leader in mediation.

Introduction

Global Trends in Dispute Resolution offers readers a garden rich in ideas and insights into contemporary dispute resolution principles, processes, and practices. The series leads the way in first-class debate and analysis of dispute resolution trends across our rapidly globalising world. More particularly, its volumes analyse dispute resolution developments in various geographical regions around the world and in relation to diverse transnational practice areas. These practice areas include not only well-established legal categories such as intellectual property, construction, and resources law, but also emerging dispute resolution trends ranging from dispute systems design to cross-border mediation in private and public law.

Objective

With a particular focus on new initiatives and dispute resolution practices, the *Global Trends in Dispute Resolution* series aims to provide practitioners, scholars, policymakers, and 'pracademics' (that elusive yet rapidly emerging category of practical academics and academically-oriented practitioners – you know who you are) with the resources both to cultivate the dispute resolution gardens of the world and to explore new paths within and beyond them.

Frequency of Publication

A volume is published whenever an interesting topic presents itself.

The titles published in this series are listed at the end of this volume.

The Singapore Convention on Mediation

A Commentary

Second Edition

Nadja Alexander
Shouyu Chong
Vakhtang Giorgadze

SINGAPORE CONVENTION ON MEDIATION

Wolters Kluwer

Published by:
Kluwer Law International B.V.
PO Box 316
2400 AH Alphen aan den Rijn
The Netherlands
E-mail: lrs-sales@wolterskluwer.com
Website: www.wolterskluwer.com/en/solutions/kluwerlawinternational

Sold and distributed by:
Wolters Kluwer Legal & Regulatory U.S.
7201 McKinney Circle
Frederick, MD 21704
United States of America
E-mail: customer.service@wolterskluwer.com

ISBN 978-94-035-2825-0

e-Book: ISBN 978-94-035-2823-6
web-PDF: ISBN 978-94-035-2824-3

About the Authors

Nadja Alexander, BA, LLB *Hons* (Qld), Dip. International Studies (Vienna), LLM (Tübingen), D jur *summa cum laude* (Tübingen). Nadja is a Professor of Law and Director of the Singapore International Dispute Resolution Academy (SIDRA) at Singapore Management University (SMU) with honorary academic appointments in the United States and Australia. Consistently recognised as a global thought leader in mediation (*Who's Who Legal*), Nadja is a professional mediator and has extensive experience advising corporations and governments on designing mediation and dispute resolution systems. In 2018 Nadja joined the Singapore delegation to the UNCITRAL Working Group II for the drafting of what became the Singapore Convention on Mediation and has spearheaded research and capacity-building on the Convention since. Further, she is a foundation member of the International Advisory Board of the United Nations (UN) Global Mediation Panel established by the UN Office of the Ombudsman, and a lead academic for the Asia-Pacific Economic Cooperation (APEC) Online Dispute Resolution Collaborative Framework. Nadja's books include the award-winning *International and Comparative Mediation*, *Global Trends in Mediation*, and *EU Mediation Law Handbook*; she is the co-editor of the *Kluwer Mediation Blog*.

Shouyu Chong, LLM (National University of Singapore). Shouyu Chong is a Research Fellow at the Singapore International Dispute Resolution Academy (SIDRA), Singapore Management University, Singapore. He is a PhD Research Student with the Centre of Construction Law and Dispute Resolution, King's College London. He is also a Visiting Lecturer at The Dickson Poon School of Law, King's College London. He researches on Private International Law and Cross-Border Alternative Dispute Resolution Mechanisms and has been awarded a number of competitive grants for his research. His PhD research is funded by the Centre of Construction Law and Dispute Resolution on a Nash Research Scholarship, and by the Society of Construction Law on a Frances Paterson Scholarship. In 2022 he was awarded the Singapore Management University's Fellowship for Social Science Graduate Research. He has written extensively about the Singapore Convention on Mediation.

Vakhtang Giorgadze, LLB (Free University of Tbilisi), LLM (IHEID/UNIGE). Vakhtang is a qualified lawyer and a Singapore International Mediation Institute (SIMI) accredited mediator. He specialises in international dispute resolution including mediation, arbitration, investor-State and State-State dispute settlement processes. His experience includes working for the Singapore International Dispute Resolution Academy (SIDRA), the World Trade Organization (WTO), the Singapore International Arbitration Centre (SIAC) and the Ministry of Justice of Georgia. He has authored or co-authored several publications, including peer-reviewed papers. He holds an LLB from the Free University of Tbilisi and an LLM from the Graduate Institute of International and Development Studies (IHEID)/University of Geneva (UNIGE), Switzerland.

Table of Contents

Foreword

Recent years have witnessed growing recourse to mediations as an alternative method of solving disputes in the area of international commercial and investment relations. A long-standing and well-known alternative means of dispute settlement, mediation offers multiple and flexible avenues for solving disputes, in a manner that allows for the enforcement of contracts, preserves long-term business relationships, and facilitates the administration of international transactions by parties.

Having fully recognised the benefits of mediation, the United Nations Commission on International Trade Law (UNCITRAL), the core legal body of the United Nations in the field of international trade law, has been a pioneer in providing rules and model legislative provisions on mediation. As early as 1980, UNCITRAL adopted Conciliation Rules for use by disputing parties and, in 2002, the Model Law on International Commercial Conciliation (the 'Model Law') to further strengthen the adoption of mediation.

In 2018, UNCITRAL contributed to the international mediation framework by adopting the United Nations Convention on International Settlement Agreements Resulting from Mediation, also known as the Singapore Convention on Mediation, and amended the Model Law accordingly. The Singapore Convention on Mediation provided for the enforcement of settlement agreements, the requirements for reliance on settlement agreements, and the grounds for refusing to grant relief. By unifying the rules related to the enforcement of settlement agreements, the Convention reduced the risk of refusal to enforce such agreements, strengthened predictability and certainty in the use of mediation, and encouraged the resolution of cross-border disputes in a non-confrontational, cost-effective and efficient manner, in line with the United Nations Sustainable Development Goals, more specifically SDG 16 on access to justice.

The Convention was negotiated by States and international stakeholders within UNCITRAL Working Group II (Dispute settlement), through a decision-making process based on consensus, taking account of experience with mediation in different jurisdictions. It was then finalised by UNCITRAL at its fifty-first session in 2018 and adopted by a resolution of the United Nations General Assembly on 20 December 2018. The legal framework established by the Convention was therefore acceptable to States with different legal traditions and different levels of development.

Since its last Commission session, UNCITRAL has adopted various new instruments in the mediation framework. First, the UNCITRAL Mediation Rules, which offer an internationally harmonised set of procedural rules for the conduct of Mediation proceedings, second, the UNCITRAL Notes on Mediation which is an explanatory text and seeks to assist parties in better understanding mediation. Finally, the Model Law on International Commercial Mediation and International Settlement Agreement has been complemented by a Guide to Enactment and Use, which provides a detailed explanation of each article of the Model Law. Thereby, UNCITRAL developed by now a complete Mediation framework at the disposal of States, disputing parties and other interested stakeholders, akin to the UNCITRAL Arbitration framework.

The change of the UNCITRAL framework and the attention mediation gained in the past years around the globe with numerous discussions, events and articles triggered by the adoption of the Singapore Convention made it necessary to update the Commentary on the Singapore Convention by Nadja Alexander, Shouyu Chong and Vakhtang Giorgadze in a very short period.

This Commentary, though not representing an official interpretation of the Convention, contributes deeply to the understanding of the Convention's main terms. It also provides clarity and fosters a wider acceptance of mediation. Furthermore, it complements the efforts by the UNCITRAL Secretariat to encourage countries to become members of the Convention.

The Commentary starts out with a succinct overview of UNCITRAL, its work in the area of dispute resolution and its methods of work. It then follows with the inception of the Convention and its development by Working Group II of UNCITRAL. The article-by-article commentary with practical illustrations will be useful for practitioners and disputing parties and provide valuable references for users in the years to come.

The sustainable growth of international trade and investment requires reliable ways to solve disputes. To further increase the potential of mediation as a tool for effective dispute settlement, I invite the reader to follow the authors in their exploratory journey of the international mediation framework and enjoy the comprehensive and clear Commentary on the Singapore Convention on Mediation.

Anna Joubin-Bret
The Secretary, UNCITRAL
Director, International Trade Law Division

Preface

In the second decade of the twenty-first century, mediation is emerging as a cross-border dispute resolution mechanism with the capacity to navigate cultures, borders, and legal categories with greater fluidity than arbitration and litigation. Dubbed the pandemic-proof process, online applications of mediation have proved helpful in addressing cross-border disputes efficiently and effectively, particularly during the height of the 2020 global health pandemic when international travel and face-to-face meetings were restricted.

But mediation's fresh image belies its significant history. As a traditional dispute resolution mechanism, anthropologists confirm that mediation is as old as human existence itself. It is simply part of the success story of *homo sapiens* as communicators and collaborators. As a professionalised dispute resolution procedure, mediation developed in the 1970s in the United States and has since become an integrated element of court and private dispute resolution systems in many common law and civil law jurisdictions. In the 50 years since contemporary mediation first appeared in practice, we have seen the development of domestic mediation legislation and jurisprudence worldwide. This collective body of mediation law provides an essential reference point for the international legal context in which the Singapore Convention on Mediation is placed.

In the second edition of the *Singapore Convention on Mediation: A Commentary*, Nadja Alexander and Shouyu Chong are joined by Vakhtang Giorgadze to update and extend the article-by-article commentary of the Singapore Convention. In addition to updates on ratifications and new State signatories, this new edition includes many more jurisprudential and legislative illustrations from diverse legal regimes. Insights from domestic mediation laws and, where appropriate, arbitration laws have been extended. A new section on confidentiality is included in the commentary to Article 5 and new tables of cases and legislation, treaties and other instruments have also been prepared for this second edition. The appendices have also been updated and serve as a comprehensive reference for readers.

It takes a village to raise a child, and so it is with a book.

We wish to acknowledge the contributions of Terence Yeo, Clarissa Chern, Aziah Hussin, Janet Checkley, Alexandra Piscionere, Samantha Choo and Alan Limbury to the first and second editions of this work. A special thank you to Judith Knieper for her insightful feedback on the manuscript. For research and editorial assistance, we are grateful to Joshua Phang and Sarah Lim.

To our colleagues at the Singapore International Dispute Resolution Academy, Singapore Management University and the Ministry of Law in Singapore, we have benefited from your wisdom and insights in countless ways. Thank you for your generosity and ongoing support.

To Eleanor Taylor at Wolters Kluwer, our heartfelt thanks for recognising the importance of this project and supporting us from its beginning and now into the second edition! To Sudha Elango and Pritha Nirmalraj thank you for your patience and precision in taking us from manuscript to book. It has been such a pleasure to work with the team.

To the Secretary of UNCITRAL, Anna Joubin-Bret, our sincere gratitude for contributing the Foreword to this second edition.

To our families and friends, thank you for your love and understanding as we meticulously and persistently worked on this commentary, through a global pandemic while living across territorial borders. This book would never have been possible without you. Nadja would like to especially thank Mia for her indefatigable singing and cheering whenever Mum descended from the 'writing room', each time believing that the book was 'really, truly finished'. Shouyu is grateful for the kindness of his friends, Douglas, Adam, Sebastian, Plicca, Sara, Maureen, Katerina, Omar, Ronan, Maxime, Basil, Alan and Samantha, Nicole, Francine and Irina, as well as touched by the love of his family and his late grandmother, Mdm Yuen Yoke Chan. Vakhtang would like to thank his mother, Mzia Giorgadze, for her unconditional love and sacrifice.

The manuscript takes into account developments up to 31 May 2022.

All errors are our own.

Nadja Alexander, Shouyu Chong, Vakhtang Giorgadze
Singapore, July 2022

The Singapore Convention on Mediation: An Introduction

0.01 The United Nations Convention on International Settlement Agreements Resulting from Mediation,[1] also known as the Singapore Convention on Mediation, is a multilateral treaty which offers a legal framework facilitating the circulation of international mediated settlement agreements (iMSAs) across national borders. The Singapore Convention achieves this by elevating iMSAs to the status of a new type of legal instrument recognised in international law: neither a contract nor a consent arbitral award, iMSAs that fall within the scope of, and that satisfy the conditions within, the Singapore Convention enjoy a unique status. As outlined below, the new Convention establishes a system for the recognition[2] and enforcement of commercial iMSAs.

0.02 The Singapore Convention promises to leave a significant impact on international dispute resolution practices and, beyond that, on trade and investment flows.[3] It has

1. United Nations Convention on International Settlement Agreements Resulting from Mediation (2018), https://uncitral.un.org/sites/uncitral.un.org/files/media-documents/EN/Texts/UNCITRAL/Arbitration/mediation_convention_v1900316_eng.pdf (Accessed 18 February 2022). The articles of the Convention are reproduced in Appendix B of this book.
2. The Singapore Convention on Mediation does not expressly use the term 'recognition'. Instead, Art. 3(2) of the Convention provides a functional description of the process of recognition – the invocation of a settlement agreement as a complete defence. For more on this issue, see the commentary to Art. 3.
3. For example, Sussman has observed that the Singapore Convention has so far inspired 'the proposed changes to the ICSID rules on conciliation [which] specifically suggests that the parties sign a settlement agreement [which may be embodied in a conciliation Report] so that parties in ICSID conciliation proceedings can benefit from the enforcement regime for mediated settlements contemplated by the Singapore Convention': Edna Sussman, *The Singapore Convention – Promoting the Enforcement and Recognition of International Mediated Settlement Agreements*, 3 ICC Disp. Resol. Bull. 42 (2018), at 54, citing ICSID Secretariat, *Proposals for Amendment of the ICSID Rules – Synopsis*, Volume 1 (2 August 2018) https://icsid.worldbank.org/sites/default/files/publications/Synopsis_English.pdf (Accessed 18 February 2022), at para. 95. See also the Centre for Effective Dispute Resolution (CEDR)'s survey, according to which mediation can save commercial parties GBP 4.6 billion per annum in the United Kingdom. CEDR, The Nineth Mediation Audit – A Survey of Commercial Mediator Attitudes and Experience in the United

the capacity to enhance the attractiveness of mediation within regional initiatives, such as the Belt and Road Initiative[4] and to support the regulatory robustness of cross-border online dispute resolution (ODR) initiatives.[5] This capacity will, in turn, enhance access to justice and the efficacy of dispute resolution for users across borders. From a user perspective, the Singapore Convention offers a risk management mechanism accessible in terms of its flexibility and affordability to cross-border business players, whether they are multi-national corporations, publicly listed corporations, traditionally incorporated limited entities, sole traders, or start-ups.

0.03 In this introduction to the article-by-article commentary that follows, we offer a background to the Singapore Convention and to the body responsible for its drafting,

---

Kingdom, https://www.cedr.com/wp-content/uploads/2021/05/CEDR_Audit-2021-lr.pdf (Accessed 18 February 2022). In the context of the European Union, see also The Cost of Non ADR – Surveying and Showing the Actual Costs of Intra-Community Commercial Litigation, implemented by ADR Center in cooperation with European Association of Craft, Small and Medium-Sized Enterprises – UEAPME, and European Company Lawyers Association – ECLA, June 2010. Available at https://www.adrcenterfordevelopment.com/wp-content/uploads/2018/06/Survey-Data-Report.pdf (Accessed 18 February 2022).

4. According to the World Bank, the Belt and Road Initiative (BRI) is an effort initiated by China to improve regional cooperation and connectivity between continents, endeavouring to build robust infrastructure, trade and investment ties between China and at least 65 other countries which, together, account for over 30 per cent of global Gross Domestic Product (GDP) and over 60 per cent of the world's population. See the World Bank website at https://www.worldbank.org/en/topic/regional-integration/brief/belt-and-road-initiative (Accessed 18 February 2022). Regarding the use of mediation in BRI disputes, see Allison Goh, *Framework for the Resolution of Disputes Under the Belt and Road Initiative,* in Stavros Brekoulakis (ed.), Arbitration: The International Journal of Arbitration, Mediation and Dispute Management, Kluwer Law International (2021); Volume 87 Issue 2 at 243-267; Mark McLaughlin, *Investor–State Mediation and the Belt and Road Initiative: Examining the Conditions for Settlement,* 24(3) J. Int'l Econ. L. (September 2021), at 609–629; Guiguo Wang, Yuk-Lun Lee and Mei-Fun Leung, *Dispute Resolution Mechanism for the Belt and Road Initiative,* Springer Singapore (2020). See also initiatives of mediation service provider organisations regarding the use of mediation in BRI disputes: a memorandum of understanding between the Singapore International Mediation Centre (SIMC) and the Mediation Center of the China Council for the Promotion of International Trade (CCPIT)/China Chamber of International Commerce (CCOIC) https://simc.com.sg/blog/2017/09/29/simc-and-ccpit-ccoic-mou-19-september-2017/ (Accessed 18 February 2022); a memorandum of understanding between the SIMC and the Permanent Forum of China Construction Law (PFCCL) for the promotion of mediation in infrastructure-related disputes https://simc.com.sg/blog/2019/10/12/simc-inks-mou-with-the-permanent-forum-of-china-construction-law-pfccl-to-promote-mediation-for-infrastructure-related-disputes/ (Accessed 18 February 2022); International Chamber of Commerce (ICC) Guidance on Mediation of Belt and Road Disputes https://iccwbo.org/publication/icc-guidance-mediation-belt-road-disputes/ (Accessed 18 February 2022); the establishment of the Malaysia-China Business Mediation Centre by Malaysian Bar Council, the Mediation Center of CCPIT and the CCOIC for the resolution of disputes arising under the BRI http://www.malaysianmediationcentre.org/malaysia-china-business-mediation-centre-2/ (Accessed 18 February 2022).

5. See, for example, the proposed Asia Pacific Economic Council (APEC)-wide ODR framework that is set to provide access to commercial justice for micro, small and medium enterprises (MSMEs) in cross-border B2B disputes. APEC Draft Collaborative Framework for Online Dispute Resolution of Cross-Border E-Commerce Business to Business Disputes, (2018). ODR is discussed in the commentary to Art. 2(2). See also Report of the Colloquium on Possible Future Work on Dispute Settlement held during the 75th Session of Working Group II (New York, 28 March-1 April 2022), A/CN.9/1091 (2022). Available at https://uncitral.un.org/sites/uncitral.un.org/files/media-documents/uncitral/en/a_cn9_1091_advance_copy.pdf (Accessed 16 May 2022).

the United Nations Commission on International Trade Law (UNCITRAL). We examine the object and purpose of the Convention before introducing its main themes and presenting an overview of how it works. Given the impact that the Singapore Convention will have on private international law, we briefly explain the elements in this area of law and the role that the Convention plays within it. We conclude with some reflections on the future of the Singapore Convention on Mediation.

0.04 At this point, it is useful to make some comments about the geographical scope of this work. This commentary is international in nature and illustrations and references are drawn from around the world. As appropriate, reference has been made to regulatory instruments of States that have signed or ratified the Singapore Convention.

INTRODUCTION TO UNCITRAL AND ITS WORK

0.05 Here we present an overview of UNCITRAL and the nature of model laws, rules and conventions that are a central part of its work.

What is UNCITRAL?

0.06 UNCITRAL was established in 1966 as a subsidiary body of the General Assembly of the United Nations (UN).[6] The Secretariat of UNCITRAL is the International Trade Law division of the Office of Legal Affairs of the UN. Whereas the General Assembly comprises representatives of all 193 Member States,[7] the Commission comprises a smaller number of elected Member States representing the various geographical regions, including Africa, Asia, Eastern Europe, North America, Latin America and the Caribbean, and Western Europe.[8]

0.07 Its mandate is to advance and modernise the regulation of international trade, *inter alia*, through the 'harmonisation' and 'unification' of relevant national laws on the subject. 'Harmonisation' refers to attempts to ensure that different legal systems generate transactions with similar effects across jurisdictions. 'Unification' goes further and involves the adoption of the same laws in different legal systems, a process which typically requires countries to repeal their existing relevant laws and replace them with a unified version. In contrast, UNCITRAL's mandate reflects the belief that increased international trade, which expands interdependence and interpersonal interaction among countries and their citizens, contributes to world peace – an integral part of the UN's overall mission.[9] Accordingly, UNCITRAL's work aims to ensure that the voices

6. For more information on the General Assembly of the United Nations (UN), see www.un.org under the heading *Main Bodies* (Accessed 18 February 2022).
7. For a list of the Member States of the UN and the dates on which they joined the organisation see https://www.un.org/en/member-states/ (Accessed 18 February 2022). This information is accurate at the time of writing.
8. For a list of the Member States representing each regional group, see the UNCITRAL website at www.uncitral.org or https://uncitral.un.org/en/about (Accessed 18 February 2022).
9. For more information on UNCITRAL's mandate, see Resolution 2205(XXI) at https://undocs.org/en/A/RES/2205(XXI) (Accessed 18 February 2022).

and interests of developing countries are considered. It does this by preparing and promoting the adoption of new international conventions and model laws that serve as an equaliser.[10]

0.08 In fulfilling its mandate, UNCITRAL Member State delegates have debated, drafted and adopted a range of legislative instruments relating to commercial and trade law, including model laws and conventions, which impact international trade and cross-border commercial transactions.[11] Model laws and conventions are intended for voluntary enactment by domestic legislatures of nation States, irrespective of their membership in the UN.[12] Decisions at UNCITRAL are typically taken by consensus, reflecting the desire of the Commission to produce texts that are acceptable to, and therefore likely to be adopted by, the maximum number of participating countries, regardless of their membership. To that end, participation in preparing legislative texts is not limited to Member States. Non-Member States and interested inter-governmental organisations (IGOs) or non-governmental organisations (NGOs) may also participate in the proceedings of the Commission and its working groups as observers.[13] In this capacity, they may participate actively in the discussion and drafting of legislative texts and other instruments. The rationale behind this practice is found in UNCITRAL's international mandate and the potential worldwide application of UNCITRAL instruments.[14]

What are UNCITRAL Model Laws and Rules?

0.09 UNCITRAL model laws are legislative texts which have been adopted by the resolution of the UN General Assembly as a model for members and other States to adopt as domestic legislation. Understanding that domestic legislatures have the ability

10. *General Assembly Resolution on the Establishment of the United Nations Commission on International Trade Law*, GA Res 2205, UN GAOR, Twenty-First Session, UN Doc A/Res/2205 (1966).
11. UNCITRAL texts relate to International Commercial Arbitration; International Commercial Mediation; International Sale of Goods (CISG) and Related Transactions; Procurement and Public-Private Partnerships; Micro, Small and Medium-Sized Enterprises; Electronic Commerce; Insolvency; Security Interests; Online Dispute Resolution; International Payments; and International Transport of Goods. See the UNCITRAL website at https://uncitral.un.org/en/texts (Accessed 18 February 2022).
12. The only 'independent' country that is not a member of the UN is the Vatican City. However, the number of non-members is largely dependent on whether or not a political entity is recognised as independent or not. At the time of writing the following countries are political entities but not UN members: Kosovo, Palestine and Taiwan.
13. Working groups are organisational groups within UNCITRAL designated to work on particular topics such as conciliation. There are six working groups in total focusing on: (I) Micro, Small and Medium-sized Enterprises; (II) Dispute Settlement; (III) Investor-State Dispute Settlement Reform; (IV) Electronic Commerce; (V) Insolvency Law; and (VI) Judicial Sale of Ships. See https://uncitral.un.org/en/working_groups (Accessed 18 February 2022).
14. A list of Non-Member States, IGOs, NGOs and other entities with observer status can be found in a Note by the Secretariat of the 59th Session of the UN General Assembly: *List of Non-Member States, entities and organisations having received a standing invitation to participate as observers in the sessions and the work of the General Assembly*, UN Doc A/INF/59/4/Add.1 (14 December 2004).

to amend their provisions, UN model laws are flexible instruments. Model laws may be adopted with or without amendment by enacting States. Some enacting States may elect to amend parts of a model law so that it better suits local substantive and procedural legal requirements. While desirable, complete uniformity among national provisions is not expected. Where amendments are made, however, enacting States are encouraged to maintain the basic principles of the law and to make as few changes as possible to the provisions. National laws are more likely to be interpreted consistently across different jurisdictions where similar terms are used. From the disputing parties' perspectives, consistent interpretation of national laws on mediation may increase clarity and certainty with respect to their meaning, application and implementation. At the same time, the flexible nature of model laws allows States to make adjustments to comply with national public policy and procedural law.

0.10 For the purposes of this work, the UNCITRAL Model Law on International Commercial Mediation and International Settlement Agreements Resulting from Mediation 2018 (amending the UNCITRAL Model Law on International Commercial Conciliation 2002) (Model Law on Mediation) and the UNCITRAL Model Law on International Commercial Arbitration 1985 with amendments as adopted in 2006 (Model Law on Arbitration) are the relevant model laws.[15]

0.11 UNCITRAL also drafts non-legislative texts, such as its Arbitration Rules (UAR) and its Mediation Rules (2021) (UMR)[16], which are directed at parties, rather than States, to use as part of their dispute resolution procedures.[17] The UNCITRAL arbitration and mediation rules may be incorporated into dispute resolution clauses in commercial contracts, as part of an agreement to mediate or arbitrate. They may also

15. UNCITRAL Model Law on International Commercial Mediation and International Settlement Agreements Resulting from Mediation, 2018 (amending the UNCITRAL Model Law on International Commercial Conciliation, 2002), https://uncitral.un.org/sites/uncitral.un.org/files/media-documents/uncitral/en/annex_ii.pdf (Accessed 18 February 2022); UNCITRAL Model Law on International Commercial Conciliation With Guide to Enactment and Use 2002, https://uncitral.un.org/sites/uncitral.un.org/files/media-documents/uncitral/en/03-90953_ebook.pdf (Accessed 18 February 2022); Model Law on International Commercial Arbitration (1985), with amendments as adopted in 2006 https://uncitral.un.org/sites/uncitral.un.org/files/media-documents/uncitral/en/19-09955_e_ebook.pdf (Accessed 18 February 2022). These Model Laws have been instrumental in shaping and modernising arbitration and mediation laws across jurisdictions. Laws based on the Model Law on Arbitration have been adopted in 85 States in a total of 118 jurisdictions, see https://uncitral.un.org/en/texts/arbitration/modellaw/commercial_arbitration/status (Accessed 18 February 2022). Laws based on or influenced by the Model Law on Mediation and its predecessor Model Law on Conciliation have been adopted in 33 States in a total of 46 jurisdictions, see https://uncitral.un.org/en/texts/arbitration/modellaw/commercial_conciliation/status (Accessed 18 February 2022).
16. The UNCITRAL Mediation Rules (2021) (UMR) updated the UNCITRAL Conciliation Rules (1980) (UCR). The UMR is reproduced in Appendix F of this book. UNCITRAL texts use the terms 'conciliation' and 'mediation' interchangeably. See footnote 2 of the Model Law on Mediation.
17. There are three different versions of UNCITRAL Arbitration Rules: the 1976 version; the 2010 revised version; and the 2013 version which incorporates the UNCITRAL Rules on Transparency for Treaty-based Investor-State Arbitration and UNCITRAL Expedited Arbitration Rules 2021; UNCITRAL adopted the UMR in 2021, the idea of which is to ensure consistency between the UMR and the Model Law on Mediation.

be adopted by dispute resolution organisations as part of their recommended procedural rules for dispute resolution processes.[18] As an illustration, the Singapore International Arbitration Centre (SIAC) provides an UNCITRAL model clause on its website; contracting parties may incorporate in their international commercial contracts the model rules governing a breach or dispute. Similarly, the Australian Centre for International Commercial Arbitration (ACICA) and the Hong Kong International Arbitration Centre (HKIAC) refer parties to provisions from the UAR as part of their recommended procedures for international arbitration.[19] The American Arbitration Association (AAA), one of the country's leading arbitration centres, lists the UAR among its active rules and regularly administers international cases in adherence to them.[20]

0.12 Additionally, numerous institutions have adopted the wording of the UNCITRAL Conciliation Rules (1980) (UCR), which is the predecessor of the UMR, for their own institutional rules. For example, ACICA recommends that parties engaging in mediation and conciliation use the UCR. The Optional Conciliation Rules of the Permanent Court of Arbitration (PCA) are closely modelled upon the UCR; other institutional rules, including the Netherlands Mediation Institute (NMI) Mediation Rules, draw upon the UCR as well.[21] In addition, Article 10 of the UCR, which provides that conciliators must disclose the substance of all actual information received from one party to the other party unless expressly requested not to do so by the informing party, has been adopted by the Indian Council of Arbitration (ICA) in Article 10 of its Rules of Conciliation and by the PCA in Article 10 of its Optional Conciliation Rules. As another example, Article 9 of the UCR, which states that the conciliator may meet or communicate with each of the parties separately, can be found in Article 12 of the Mediation Rules of the World Intellectual Property Organisation (WIPO) (2002), Article 9 of the Rules of Conciliation of the ICA and Article 3(d) of the Model Mediation Procedure Rules (1998) of the International Institute for Conflict Prevention and Resolution (CPR).

0.13 UNCITRAL rules may be used by public entities or private parties whether or not they are nationals of Member States. While the Model Law on Mediation, or at least its predecessor, the Model Law on International Commercial Conciliation, 2002, was designed to dovetail with the UCR, both texts operate independently of each other and can interact with different dispute resolution laws and rules. While the UCR and UMR can operate as a set of ad hoc procedural guidelines or as the basis for institutional

18. UNCITRAL's website provides a non-exhaustive list of arbitration centres which (i) have institutional rules based on, or inspired by, the UAR, (ii) administer arbitral proceedings or provide administrative services under the Rules, and/or (iii) act as an appointing authority under the Rule. See https://uncitral.un.org/en/texts/arbitration/contractualtexts/arbitration/centres (Accessed 18 February 2022).
19. See ACICA's website at https://acica.org.au/uncitral-arbitration-clause/ (Accessed 18 February 2022).
20. See AAA's active rules at https://www.adr.org/active-rules (Accessed 18 February 2022).
21. See Permanent Court of Arbitration (PCA) Optional Conciliation Rules (1996) at https://docs.pca-cpa.org/2016/01/Permanent-Court-of-Arbitration-Optional-Conciliation-Rules.pdf (Accessed 18 February 2022); see also the Netherlands Mediation Institute's Mediation Rules (2001).

rules, the Model Law on Mediation is designed as a template for the construction and incorporation of international commercial mediation into national laws.

0.14 However, UNCITRAL also adopted the UNCITRAL Notes on Mediation (2021) (Notes), the idea of which is to assist mediation practitioners, parties to a dispute and mediators in better understanding the mediation process, including the wide and flexible range of possible outcomes.[22] The Notes do not impose an obligation upon the parties or the mediator and can be used at their discretion. The Notes explain the main features of mediation, commencement and termination of the mediation, selection and appointment of a mediator, preparatory steps and conduct of the mediation, and a settlement agreement.

0.15 As a result, UNCITRAL offers States, mediation practitioners, parties to a dispute and mediators a complete package of legal instruments applicable to the mediation process: the Singapore Convention on Mediation for the enforcement and recognition of international mediated settlement agreements; the Model Law on Mediation (and its predecessor the Model Law on Conciliation with Guide to Enactment and Use 2002) for the enactment of legislation on mediation; the Mediation Rules (and its predecessor the Conciliation Rules) for conducting the mediation process; and the Notes on Mediation for better understanding the mediation process and its main features.

What are UNCITRAL Conventions?

0.16 A convention is a legislative text binding under international law on States and other entities with treaty-making capacity that choose to become a party to that instrument. In general, departures from a convention are only permitted if the convention permits reservations to be taken to its provisions. Some conventions may also contain customary international law, which are norms binding States and entities regardless of whether they are party to the convention. The fact that conventions are binding instruments differentiates them from model laws, which serve only as a suggested guide for States if they so choose to adopt them as domestic legislation. UNCITRAL has developed numerous conventions on various topics relating to international trade law. These conventions include: the UN Convention on Contracts for the International Sale of Goods (Vienna, 1980); the UN Convention on the Assignment of Receivables in International Trade (New York, 2004); and the UN Convention on the Use of Electronic Communications in International Contracts (New York, 2005).[23]

---

22. The text of the UNCITRAL Notes on Mediation (2021) is available at https://uncitral.un.org/sites/uncitral.un.org/files/media-documents/uncitral/en/v2107071_mediation_notes.pdf (Accessed 18 February 2022). The UNCITRAL Notes on Mediation is reproduced in Appendix G of this book.
23. In addition to these conventions, we note that UNCITRAL's mandate extends to the UN Convention on the Recognition and Enforcement of Foreign Arbitral Awards (the New York Convention). The New York Convention was adopted on 10 June 1958 prior to the establishment of UNCITRAL. However, UNCITRAL, since its establishment, has been working on the promotion and worldwide adoption of the New York Convention. As an example, UNCITRAL adopted the Recommendation regarding the interpretation of article II, paragraph 2, and article VII,

0.17 Typically, a UNCITRAL working group comprising of Member State delegations takes on the role of drafting the legislative text of a convention. After the finalisation of the draft, it must be presented before the General Assembly, which decides whether to adopt the text. If the convention is ratified as a treaty, the General Assembly passes a resolution to that effect.

0.18 A State may sign a convention; however, it is not immediately bound by it. The State must take further action expressing its consent to be bound by the convention, namely through 'ratification' or 'accession' once the treaty itself has entered into force.[24]

0.19 The Convention on the Recognition and Enforcement of Foreign Arbitral Awards (the New York Convention) has arguably become the most influential instrument adopted by the General Assembly. At the time of writing, it has 170 State Parties, with 167 of the 193 UN Member States as signatories, together with the Cook Islands, the Holy See and the State of Palestine.[25] Renaud Sorieul, former Secretary of UNCITRAL, has referred to the New York Convention as 'the cornerstone of the international arbitration system'. In furtherance of UNCITRAL's mandate of the harmonisation and unification of international trade laws, the primary objective of the New York Convention was to render arbitral awards and arbitration agreements enforceable among State parties to the Convention, legitimising arbitration as an alternative dispute resolution forum which provides legally binding solutions across borders. Not only has the New York Convention proven to be essential to the adjudication and enforcement of transnational disputes but it is also said to have contributed to an exponential increase in world trade. The Singapore Convention on Mediation sets out similar aspirations.[26]

BACKGROUND TO THE SINGAPORE CONVENTION ON MEDIATION

0.20 On 20 December 2018, the UN General Assembly voted to adopt the UNCITRAL Convention on International Settlement Agreements Resulting from Mediation (also known as the Singapore Convention on Mediation).[27] This is the first international

---

paragraph 1, of the Convention on the Recognition and Enforcement of Foreign Arbitral Awards, done in New York, 10 June 1958 (2006); and the UNCITRAL Secretariat Guide on the Convention on the Recognition and Enforcement of Foreign Arbitral Awards. The texts are available at https://uncitral.un.org/ (Accessed 18 February 2022).

24. For more information on what 'ratification' or 'accession' entails, refer to the commentary in Art. 11. Depending on the domestic laws that govern a state, domestic legislation may also be required for the convention to be legally implemented into the state's body of laws.
25. The UN Convention on the Recognition and Enforcement of Foreign Arbitral Awards (1958) (referred to in subsequent commentaries as the 'New York Convention' or the 'Convention on the Recognition and Enforcement of Foreign Arbitral Awards'). The status of the New York Convention is at https://uncitral.un.org/en/texts/arbitration/conventions/foreign_arbitral_awards/status2 (Accessed 18 February 2022).
26. See the preamble of the Singapore Convention and the Resolution adopted by the General Assembly on 20 December 2018, A/73/496.
27. Press Release: General Assembly Adopts the United Nations Convention on International Settlement Agreements Resulting from Mediation, https://uncitral.un.org/en/news/general-assembly-adopts-united-nations-convention-international-settlement-agreements-resulting (Accessed 18 February 2022).

treaty which provides private contractual agreements (that is, iMSAs) with a legal status comparable to foreign arbitral awards under the New York Convention,[28] foreign court judgments under the 2005 Hague Convention on Choice of Court Agreements and the Convention of 2 July 2019 on the Recognition and Enforcement of Foreign Judgments in Civil or Commercial Matters.[29]

0.21 A proposal from the US delegation at UNCITRAL prompted the creation of an instrument on the enforcement of iMSAs.[30] Subsequently, in 2015, Working Group II (WG II) commenced deliberations to draft an instrument (or, possibly, several instruments) which would facilitate the enforcement of international commercial settlement agreements arising from mediation (referred to in this Introduction as iMSAs).[31] In February 2018, during its 68th Session in New York, WG II concluded its work, having reached a consensus on two prepared instruments: a Convention and a Model Law.[32]

0.22 The decision to proceed with the drafting of two instruments rather than one (that is, either Convention or Model Law) is a result of the determination and creativity of WG II. Upon receiving its mandate, the initial discussions of WG II had presented a number of challenges as there were divergent views on the need for an instrument to begin with, let alone the choice between a Model Law and a Convention. Despite these challenges, WG II found a common commitment to move forward to draft both a Model Law and Convention in tandem. Moving past any differences in technical detail, the desired fulfilment of the mandate was achieved.[33]

0.23 On 25 June 2018, UNCITRAL, at its 51st session, recommended the final draft of the Convention for submission to the UN General Assembly for its consideration.[34] Also, at that session, the Model Law was adopted and a resolution to name the Convention the 'Singapore Convention on Mediation' was recommended, which was eventually approved by the General Assembly. On 20 December 2018, the Convention

28. UN Convention on the Recognition and Enforcement of Foreign Arbitral Awards (1958) (New York Convention).
29. Hague Convention of 30 June 2005 on Choice of Court Agreements. Readers should note that the foreign judgment which may be rendered enforceable under the Convention must be delivered by a court from a Contracting State to the Convention, where that court has seized jurisdiction through an exclusive choice of court agreement in respect to a civil or commercial dispute after the Convention enters into force in that Contracting State. Convention of 2 July 2019 on the Recognition and Enforcement of Foreign Judgments in Civil or Commercial Matters, otherwise known as the Hague Judgments Convention, has not entered into force.
30. Note by the Secretariat, Proposal by the Government of the United States: future work for Working Group II, 47th Session (New York, 7-18 July 2014), A/CN.9/822 (2014).
31. Report of Working Group II (Arbitration and Conciliation) on the Work of its 63rd Session (Vienna, 7-11 September 2015), A/CN.9/861 (2018).
32. Report of Working Group II (Dispute Settlement) on the Work of its 68th Session (New York, 5–9 February 2018), A/CN.9/934 (2018).
33. Khory McCormick and Sharon S.M. Ong, *Through the Looking Glass: An Insider's Perspective into the Making of the Singapore Convention on Mediation*, 31 SAcLJ 520 (2019).
34. Report of the United Nations Commission on International Trade Law, 51st Session (25 June–13 July 2018), A/73/17 (2018).

was adopted by the UN General Assembly.[35] This brought a close to three years of energetic debate, in which 85 UN Member States and 35 international governmental and non-governmental organisations participated.

0.24 The signing ceremony for the Singapore Convention on Mediation was held on 7 August 2019 in Singapore. On that day, 46 States, including the world's two largest economies – the US and China – as well as three of the four largest economies in Asia – China, India and South Korea – signed the Singapore Convention on Mediation, a historically unprecedented number of first-day signings for an UNCITRAL treaty.[36] On 25 February 2020, Singapore and Fiji became the first two States to deposit their respective instruments of ratification of the Convention at the UN Headquarters in New York. With the third instrument of ratification deposited by Qatar on 12 March 2020, the Convention entered into force on 12 September 2020. At the time of writing, the Convention has been signed by 55 States, out of which ten States have ratified/approved it.[37]

ON THE OBJECT AND PURPOSE OF THE SINGAPORE CONVENTION

0.25 Before exploring the object and purpose of the Singapore Convention, we first consider the meaning and significance of 'object and purpose' according to the law of treaties.

Meaning and Significance of 'object and purpose'

0.26 In public international law, a fundamental principle of the law of treaties is *pacta sunt servanda*,[38] which rules that treaties are binding and must be performed in good faith.[39] Its importance is enshrined in the Preamble to the Charter of the UN.[40]

0.27 While the motif of good faith applies throughout international relations, it is especially significant in the law of treaties. This is reiterated in Article 31 of the Vienna

35. Press Release: General Assembly Adopts the United Nations Convention on International Settlement Agreements Resulting from Mediation, https://uncitral.un.org/en/news/general-assembly-adopts-united-nations-convention-international-settlement-agreements-resulting (Accessed 18 February 2022).
36. Nadja Alexander and Shouyu Chong, UN Treaty on Mediation Signed in Singapore, 23(2-3) Nederlands-Vlaams tijdschrisft voor Mediation en conflict management 71 (2019).
37. At the time of writing, the following States have ratified/approved the Convention: Belarus, Ecuador, Fiji, Georgia, Honduras, Kazakhstan, Qatar, Saudi Arabia, Singapore and Turkey. For the status of the Singapore Convention, see https://uncitral.un.org/en/texts/mediation/conventions/international_settlement_agreements (Accessed 26 May 2022). A list of signatories and ratifiers are available in Appendices C and D respectively.
38. Latin for 'agreements must be kept'.
39. Vienna Convention on the Law of Treaties (1969) (VCLT), Art. 26.
40. In addition, Art. 2(2) of the Charter expressly provides that Members are to 'fulfill in good faith the obligations assumed by them in accordance with the present Charter'.

Convention on the Law of Treaties 1969 (VCLT), which establishes the context of the interpretation of treaties.[41] VCLT Article 31(1) states that:

> [a] treaty shall be interpreted in good faith in accordance with the ordinary meaning to be given to the terms of the treaty in their context and in the light of its object and purpose.

0.28 VCLT Articles 31(2) and 31(3) set out what the 'context' of the treaty is to comprise for the purpose of interpretation and what may be taken into account: this includes subsequent agreements between the parties on the interpretation, subsequent practice in the application of the treaty and relevant rules of international law applicable in the relations between the parties.

0.29 The principle in VCLT Article 31(1) relating to the 'object and purpose' of the treaty is founded on both common sense and good faith: the ordinary meaning of a term in the treaty is not to be determined in the abstract, but in the context of the treaty and in light of its object and purpose.[42]

0.30 According to the International Law Commission, in its Guide to Practice on Reservations to Treaties 2011:

> The object and purpose of the treaty is to be determined in good faith, taking account of the terms of the treaty in their context, in particular the title and preamble of the treaty. Recourse may also be had to the preparatory work[43] of the treaty and the circumstances of its conclusion and, where appropriate, the subsequent practice of the parties.[44]

0.31 Applying the principles of interpretation in Article 31(1), jurists may differ on the emphasis placed on the object and purpose of the treaty or the primacy of the text. Some may give greater weight to the object and purpose, and are more ready to admit teleological interpretations of the text which go beyond the original intentions of the parties as expressed in the text. The majority emphasises the primacy of the text as the basis of interpretation, while giving a certain place to extrinsic evidence of the intentions of the parties as a means of interpretation.[45]

41. Oliver Corten and Pierre Klein (eds), *The Vienna Conventions on the Law of Treaties: A Commentary*, OUP (2010), at 823–829.
42. Richard Gardiner, *Treaty Interpretation* (2nd Ed.), OUP (2015), at 212 et seq.
43. The preparatory work, also known as *travaux préparatoires*, of the Singapore Convention on Mediation is available at https://uncitral.un.org/en/texts/mediation/conventions/international_settlement_agreements/travaux (Accessed 16 May 2022). The preparatory work consists of reports adopted by WG II and the Commission. These reports are organised by article and, where relevant, by paragraph or issue within the article.
44. Guide to Practice on Reservations, Report of the International Law Commission, 63rd Session (2011), at para. 3.1.5.1.
45. Oliver Corten and Pierre Klein (eds), *The Vienna Conventions on the Law of Treaties: A Commentary*, OUP (2010), at 804 et seq.

0.32 The issue of the interpretation of the 'object and purpose' of the treaty most commonly arises in multilateral treaties, with respect to the making of and objecting to a reservation.[46]

Object and Purpose of the Singapore Convention on Mediation

0.33 To explore the 'object and purpose' of the Singapore Convention, we turn, first, to its Preamble, which states:

> ***Preamble***
>
> *The Parties to this Convention,*
>
> *Recognizing* the value for international trade of mediation as a method for settling commercial disputes in which the parties in dispute request a third person or persons to assist them in their attempt to settle the dispute amicably,
>
> *Noting* that mediation is increasingly used in international and domestic commercial practice as an alternative to litigation,
>
> *Considering* that the use of mediation results in significant benefits, such as reducing the instances where a dispute leads to the termination of a commercial relationship, facilitating the administration of international transactions by commercial parties and producing savings in the administration of justice by States,
>
> *Convinced* that the establishment of a framework for international settlement agreements resulting from mediation that is acceptable to States with different legal, social and economic systems would contribute to the development of harmonious international economic relations [...].[47]

0.34 Beyond being an instrument to facilitate the recognition and enforcement of iMSAs, the Preamble to the Singapore Convention reveals a deeper objective, namely to provide a regulatory foundation to help springboard mediation into the main dispute resolution arena alongside arbitration.

0.35 The Preamble begins by acknowledging the value of mediation 'for international trade'. In terms of the benefits of mediation, it refers to preserving business relationships, facilitating international business and saving costs for State justice systems – all well-recognised features of mediation.[48]

---

46. It has been State practice to object to reservations made in multilateral treaties on the basis that such reservations are not within the object and purpose of the treaty. For example, Germany, the United Kingdom and the US reacted to an interpretative declaration by Yugoslavia concerning the 1971 Seabed Treaty by considering it first as an actual interpretative declaration (which they rejected) and then as a reservation (which they considered to be late and inconsistent with the object and purpose of the treaty. See Guide to Practice on Reservations, Report of the International Law Commission, 63rd Session (2011), at footnote 149.
47. Similar language is found in the Resolution adopted by the General Assembly on the 2002 Model Law on 19 November 2002 at its 57th Session, U.N. Doc. A/RES/57/18.
48. Klaus J. Hopt and Felix Steffek, *Mediation: Comparison of Laws, Regulatory Models, Fundamental Issues*, in Klaus J. Hopt and Felix Steffek (eds), Mediation Principles and Regulation in Comparative Perspective, OUP (2013), at 8-10.

0.36 WG II took note of evidence showing that MSAs generally enjoy high compliance rates, referring to the low rates of litigation seeking relief in relation to MSAs.[49] The increasing use of mediation in international and domestic dispute resolution settings is also noted in the Preamble.[50] At the same time, feedback from users indicated that they often faced challenges convincing other parties to mediate international commercial disputes in the absence of a trust mark of legitimacy, such as a multilateral convention.[51] These views are reflected in empirical research. For example, the findings of a 2014 survey among members of the international business and legal communities indicated that 74 per cent of respondents believed a multilateral treaty providing for the international enforcement of commercial iMSAs would increase the number of mediations in their home jurisdictions.[52] While repeat player commercial dispute resolution users typically were familiar with the New York Convention on the Recognition and Enforcement of Foreign Arbitral Awards, and therefore, with arbitration procedures, many were less familiar with mediation. This highlighted the need to address issues of visibility, credibility and sustainability of mediation as a stand-alone dispute resolution process in international commercial settings.

0.37 At the same time, WG II was mindful that any instrument or instruments it produced should not increase litigation about iMSAs. This shared understanding informed the deliberations of the Working Group and shaped the final concept and drafting for an essentialist and efficient framework that is reflected by the text of the Singapore Convention. As contemplated by the final paragraph of the Preamble, it was

49. Report of Working Group II (Arbitration and Conciliation) on the Work of its 63rd Session (17 September 2015), UN Doc. A/CN.9/861 (2015), at para. 33. See also Report of Working Group II (Arbitration and Conciliation) on the Work of its 62nd Session, (11 February 2015), UN Doc. A/CN.9/832 (2015), at para. 33, where '[i]t was stated that very few settlement agreements required enforcement as most parties would abide by the terms of the settlement agreement'; Timothy Schnabel, *The Singapore Convention on Mediation: A Framework for the Cross-Border Recognition and Enforcement of Mediated Settlements*, 19 Pepp. Disp. Resol. L.J. 1 (2019), at 4 ('Ideally, the Convention will rarely need to be invoked in court, as in most cases, parties will abide by the mediated settlements they conclude.'); and Klaus J. Hopt and Felix Steffek, *Mediation: Comparison of Laws, Regulatory Models, Fundamental Issues*, in Klaus J. Hopt and Felix Steffek (eds), Mediation Principles and Regulation in Comparative Perspective, OUP (2013), at 105 et seq. Furthermore, consider Craig A. McEwen and Richard J. Maiman, *Small Claims Mediation in Maine – An Empirical Assessment*, 33 Maine Law Review 237 (1981), at 261 et seq.

50. In relation to international disputes, empirical research shows a significant shift in user preferences from arbitration to arbitration plus ADR (alternative dispute resolution). This suggests that the increase in international mediation is at least partly due to the growing use of mediation in international arbitration settings: White & Case, 2021 International Arbitration Survey: Adapting arbitration to a changing world https://arbitration.qmul.ac.uk/media/arbitration/docs/LON0320037-QMUL-International-Arbitration-Survey-2021_19_WEB.pdf (Accessed 18 February 2022). See also Singapore International Dispute Resolution Academy (SIDRA) International Dispute Resolution Survey: 2020 Final Report, https://sidra.smu.edu.sg/sites/sidra.smu.edu.sg/files/survey/index.html (Accessed 18 February 2022).

51. Roland Schroeder, *The Singapore Convention: New York Convention for Mediation?*, Panel Presentation at the Fordham Arbitration and Mediation Symposium, New York (2019).

52. Stacie Strong, *Realizing Rationality: An Empirical Assessment of International Commercial Mediation*, 73 Wash. & Lee L. Rev. 1973 (2016), at 2031.

considered that such a framework for commercial iMSAs would further the 'development of harmonious international economic relations'.[53]

ON LAW AND PRIVATE INTERNATIONAL LAW

0.38 Aside from the public international law considerations discussed above, the Singapore Convention, like all multilateral treaties, contributes to a body of law known as private international law. As indicated previously, the Convention brings into consideration a new type of legal instrument in the realm of private international law, namely the iMSA. Accordingly, the basic definitions of the terms 'private international law' and 'law', in the context of mediation, are examined here.

0.39 Private international law generally governs how private law disputes between parties that contain a foreign element are managed. For instance, the rules of private international law would be relevant:

(1) when a consumer makes an online purchase from a website that offers to deliver consumer goods from another State,[54]
(2) when cargo on board a ship on the high seas is damaged and its consignees attempt to arrest the ship with judicial assistance to assert claims for damages,
(3) when a tourist is injured while on holiday in a foreign land by a tortfeasor whom he attempts to sue in the state courts of his residence,[55] or
(4) when parties proceed to a neutral jurisdiction to resolve their disputes, whether through litigation, arbitration or mediation.

0.40 In countries with a federal structure, such as in Australia and the US, private international law would apply to disputes with interstate elements.[56]

0.41 The study of private international law addresses three key areas set out below:[57]

(1) questions relating to the *jurisdiction* or *competence* of dispute resolution forums (such as courts, arbitral tribunals and mediation), concerning legal issues such as:
   (a) personal jurisdiction (for example, whether, according to the forum's rules of procedure, one can indeed pursue a case in that forum against the other party) and subject-matter jurisdiction (that is, whether the object of the

53. Preamble to the UN Convention on International Settlement Agreements Resulting from Mediation (2019), at para. 4.
54. Consider Regulation (EC) No. 593/2008 of the European Parliament and of the Council of 17 June 2008 on the law applicable to contractual obligations (Rome I).
55. See *Boys v Chaplin* [1971] AC 356. Also consider Regulation (EC) No 864/2007 of the European Parliament and of the Council of 11 July 2007 on the law applicable to non-contractual obligations (Rome II).
56. See Symeon C. Symeonides, *Choice of Law*, OUP (2016), at 6-8.
57. Paul Torremans et al. (eds), *Cheshire, North & Fawcett: Private International Law* (15th Ed.), OUP (2017), at 3; Lord Collins of Mapesbury (Gen ed.), *Dicey, Morris and Collins on the Conflict of Laws* (15th Ed.), Sweet & Maxwell (2012), at para. 1-003.

dispute – for instance, immovable property rights – can be disposed of by that forum) of the forum;[58] and

(b) enforceability of choice of court,[59] arbitration[60] or mediation[61] agreements;

(2) questions in relation to the *choice of law* governing obligations subsisting between parties, concerning issues such as:

(a) the characterisation of whether a private law dispute in a cross-border context is of a contractual, tortious or proprietary nature;[62]

(b) the determination of the proper law of a contractual relationship between parties;[63]

(c) the scenarios where parties fail to make a choice of law, or when they make a choice of law that fails to be recognised[64] under the law;[65] and

(d) what is the relevant law applicable to parties who are acquainted with each other outside of a contractual relationship (for instance, in a vehicular accident);[66] and

(3) issues in relation to the *recognition and enforcement of dispute resolution outcomes across territorial borders*, such as:

(a) court judgments;[67]

(b) international arbitral awards;[68] and

(c) iMSAs – which become relevant in this area upon the Singapore Convention on Mediation coming into force.

58. Cf. *Burgundy Global Exploration Corp v Transocean Offshore International Ventures Ltd* [2014] 3 SLR 381, at paras 79-83. The issue of personal jurisdiction deals with whether a party (that is, legal or natural persons) lies amenable to the jurisdiction of the forum concerned (e.g., court or arbitral tribunal) when they are brought before it. The issue of subject matter jurisdiction deals with the substantive powers a forum may possess and yield over the parties before them to regulate their conduct, pegged in respect to territorial limits (in the case of cross-border litigation) or terms of reference (*vis-à-vis* written and signed arbitration clauses in the case of international arbitration).
59. Consider Adrian Briggs, *Agreements on Jurisdiction and Choice of Law*, OUP (2008); Adrian Briggs, *Jurisdiction Clauses and Judicial Attitudes*, 109 L. Q. Rev. 382 (1993); Yock Lin Tan, *Choice of Court Agreement: From a Viewpoint of Anglo-Commonwealth Law* in Akira Saito (ed.), Evolution of Party Autonomy in International Civil Disputes, LexisNexis (2005); and Tiong Min Yeo, *The Contractual Basis of the Enforcement of Exclusive and Non-Exclusive Choice of Court Agreements*, 17 SAcLJ 306 (2005).
60. Consider Gary Born, *International Commercial Arbitration* (2nd Ed.), Wolters Kluwer (2014).
61. Nadja Alexander, *International Comparative Mediation*, Wolters Kluwer (2009), at 171 et seq.
62. *Macmillan Inc v Bishopsgate Investment Trust plc (No 3)* [1996] WLR 387.
63. Consider Regulation (EC) No. 593/2008 of the European Parliament and of the Council of 17 June 2008 on the law applicable to contractual obligations (Rome I).
64. *Dubai Electricity Co and ors v Islamic Republic of Iran Shipping Lines (The Iran Vojdan)* [1984] 2 Lloyd's Rep 380, at 385; and *Shanghai Turbo Enterprises Ltd v Liu Ming* [2018] SGHC 172, at paras 27 et seq.
65. Consider: Tiong Min Yeo, *The Effective Reach of Choice of Law Agreements*, 20 SAcLJ 723 (2008); and Yock Lin Tan, *Good Faith Choice of a Law to Govern a Contract*, Sing. J. Legal Stud 307 (2014).
66. See *Boys v Chaplin* [1971] AC 356. Also consider Regulation (EC) No. 864/2007 of the European Parliament and of the Council of 11 July 2007 on the law applicable to non-contractual obligations (Rome II).
67. Consider Adeline Chong (ed.), *Recognition and Enforcement of Foreign Judgments in Asia*, Asian Business Law Institute (2017).
68. Consider Gary Born, *International Commercial Arbitration* (2nd Ed.), Wolters Kluwer (2014).

0.42 The study of private international law is also undergirded by the sometimes competing notions of, on the one hand, party autonomy and, on the other, State sovereignty over regulation of private law dealings and disputes that occur within territorial limits.[69] Here 'party autonomy' refers to considerations such as:

(1) the freedom of parties in commercial transactions to bargain and choose the forum to which they may submit their disputes;
(2) the freedom of parties in commercial transactions to choose the law which applies to their dispute; and
(3) the enforcement mechanisms which they may agree to administer to enforce dispute resolution outcomes across borders.

0.43 While the private international law of mediation has been the subject of previous academic investigation,[70] it is not as widely recognised as the private international law relevant to arbitration and litigation. This is, in part, due to the still-nascent role that mediation plays in the resolution of international commercial disputes. It is also a consequence of a broader and contextual understanding of what the content of law engenders within mediation circles, owing to the extensive use of soft law regulation in this field.[71]

0.44 The contextual perspective of law administered in mediation shifts the focus from positivist notions of law focusing on government-made statutory law to one of law as part of a dynamic order embracing regulatory content (the subject matter of regulation), regulatory actors (stakeholders) and regulatory form (a diverse range of regulatory instruments). This contextual approach also highlights connections between law, ethics, policy, professions, organisations, civil society and governments. In relation to the law of mediation, there is a significant amount of soft law that is being continually shaped and moulded by diverse stakeholders.[72] By way of example, commentators noted the high number of mediation stakeholders[73] who played an active observer role

69. See Alex Mills, *Party Autonomy in Private International Law*, CUP (2018). It bears emphasis that Yeo observes that in cross-border contracts, parties' agreement is *almost always* conclusive in respect of both their choice of litigation forum and their choice of the law governing the contractual relationship: Tiong Min Yeo, *The Effective Reach of Choice of Law Agreements*, 20 SAcLJ 723 (2008).
70. Nadja Alexander, *Harmonisation and Diversity in the Private International Law of Mediation: The Rhythms of Regulatory Reform*, in Klaus J. Hopt and Felix Steffek (eds), Mediation – Principles and Regulation in Comparative Perspective, OUP (2013).
71. See Klaus J. Hopt and Felix Steffek, *Mediation: Comparison of Laws, Regulatory Models, Fundamental Issues*, in Klaus J. Hopt and Felix Steffek (eds), Mediation Principles and Regulation in Comparative Perspective, OUP (2013); and Nadja Alexander, *International Comparative Mediation*, Wolters Kluwer (2009).
72. Nadja Alexander, *Through the Looking Glass: Exploring the Regulatory Ethical Eco-system for Mediation*, in Maria-Frederica Moscati, Michael Palmer and Marian Roberts (eds), Comparative Dispute Resolution: A Research Handbook, Edward Elgar Publishing (2019).
73. Mediation stakeholders may include courts, mediation provider organisations, mediators, professional advisors such as lawyers, repeat users of mediation such as insurers and corporates, dispute resolution service providers, professional organisations such as bar associations and law societies, industry groups with an interest in mediation for their B2B and/or B2C

in the WG II meetings that led to the Singapore Convention.[74] In terms of the role of soft law, mediator professional codes of conduct and ethics, mediator practice standards and procedural rules that govern the mediation process will be relevant to the proper law and other aspects of private international law as they play out in the interpretation of the Singapore Convention. This is most evident in the administration of mediator standards in relation to the mediator misconduct grounds for refusal of relief under Articles 5(1)(e) and 5(1)(f) of the Convention.

HOW THE SINGAPORE CONVENTION WORKS?

0.45 With its 16 Articles, the drafters of the Singapore Convention intended to create a minimalist and efficient framework for the recognition and enforcement of iMSAs internationally. Here we present a summary of the Convention's direct enforcement mechanism.[75] Then we outline five points of compromise that underpin the Convention, which are essential to understanding its formulation.

A Summary of the Direct Enforcement Mechanism of the Convention

0.46 In most cases, once parties have reached an iMSA, they comply with their obligations. Where this is not the case, the Singapore Convention offers to parties of iMSAs that fall within its scope (Article 1) the possibility to proceed to a relevant court or any other competent authority of a State to seek relief (Article 3). The party seeking relief will file an application before that court and submit as evidence the iMSA containing the parties' signatures and an attestation by the mediator or mediation institution or the mediator's signature on the iMSA that the settlement resulted from mediation[76] (Article 4). Provided the iMSA does not fall foul of any of the grounds for refusal defined in Article 5, it will be directly enforced. Alternatively, issues resolved and contained in the iMSA may be administered as a complete defence to the commencement of litigation or arbitral proceedings where parties seek to contest issues already resolved and contained in the iMSA. The key to the direct enforcement method is that there is no requirement for an iMSA to undergo a review process at the place where it was concluded (the State of origin) as a pre-condition for enforcement. In other words, the Singapore Convention does not prescribe a *double executor* process, which would defeat the purpose of the Convention to establish an efficient, expedited

disputes such as telecommunications and banking, policy makers such as government departments of justice, politicians and legislators: Klaus J. Hopt and Felix Steffek, *Mediation: Comparison of Laws, Regulatory Models, Fundamental Issues*, in Klaus J. Hopt and Felix Steffek (eds), Mediation Principles and Regulation in Comparative Perspective, OUP (2013).

74. See, for example, Stacie Strong, *Clash of Cultures: Epistemic Communities, Negotiation Theory, and International Lawmaking*, 50(3) Akron L. Rev. 495 (2017).
75. Here it is assumed that the state at which enforcement is sought has not lodged an Art. 8(1)(b) reservation, requiring that parties who endeavour to enforce their iMSAs under the Singapore Convention opt in to its applicability if it is brought to its competent authorities for enforcement.
76. Art. 4 further provides that other forms of suitable evidence may be submitted in the absence of the mediator's signature on the iMSA or an attestation by the mediator or mediation institution that the settlement agreement resulted from mediation: see commentary to Art. 4.

and direct enforcement mechanism for iMSAs. Further, as there is no 'seat' of mediation in the sense that there is a 'seat' of arbitration, any court review in terms of the Convention can only occur in the State of enforcement.

Five Points of Compromise

0.47 As indicated previously, the WG II delegates began their work on the topic of enforcement of iMSAs with very different views, including with respect to the type of instrument (convention or model law) that they would draft. A five-point compromise paved the way for consensus.[77] Understanding the basis of the compromise is important as it explains the decisions made by WG II, not only about what the Singapore Convention contains but also about what it does not.

0.48 Five key issues were negotiated during what has become known as the 'Breakthrough Session' of WG II. First, while members of WG II were generally aligned in relation to the enforcement of iMSAs, there were divergent views on the use of the term 'recognition' in relation to iMSAs being used as a defence to legal or arbitral proceedings on the same issues. Much of the debate centred on the meaning of the term 'recognition' in different legal systems. The solution reached by WG II was to avoid the use of the term 'recognition' altogether and instead describe it in a functional manner. The extent and basis of the compromise will be addressed in the commentary to Article 3 of the Singapore Convention.

0.49 Second, there was much debate about the extent to which iMSAs are enforceable as court judgments or consent arbitral awards ought to be included in a possible convention or model law. Certain WG II members sought to exclude iMSAs already subject to expedited enforcement opportunities through existing multilateral treaties, such as the Hague Convention on Choice of Court Agreements and the New York Convention. Other members of WG II considered that any potential overlap would simply provide parties seeking relief with greater choices, in terms of the number of enforcement mechanisms available to them, and that not excluding these types of iMSAs would not lead to any inconsistency with existing treaties. Eventually, the argument for exclusion prevailed. The exclusions are examined in the commentary to Article 1(3).

0.50 The third contentious issue relates to the degree of consent required of parties to an iMSA to trigger the applicability of a multilateral convention or model law. In line with the New York Convention, one view was that the application of the proposed Convention should be mandatory regardless of the parties' choice, as this would minimise potential disputes between parties about the applicable enforcement regime. The other view was more consonant with the principle of party autonomy: parties to an

77. Khory McCormick and Sharon S.M. Ong, *Through the Looking Glass: An Insider's Perspective into the Making of the Singapore Convention on Mediation*, 31 SAcLJ 520 (2019). The following five points are drawn from this article.

iMSA ought to have a choice about the applicability of the proposed convention or model law. In the second view, it was proffered that parties may choose an opt-in or opt-out approach.[78] In the final compromise, both opt-in and opt-out approaches were accommodated. Recognising that an opt-out approach would lead to more widespread application of the proposed Convention and thereby align with its object and purpose to encourage the use of international commercial mediation, an opt-out approach was accepted as part of the compromise. As a result, while the Convention may be administered by default, parties to an iMSA may expressly opt-out of the enforceability regime under the Convention. This is examined in the commentary to Article 5(1)(d). At the same time, States preferring an opt-in regime may declare a reservation to this effect in accordance with Article 8(1)(b). The implications of reservations made pursuant to the Singapore Convention will be further examined in the commentary to Article 8.

0.51 The fourth compromise point relates to the grounds for refusal of relief in relation to an iMSA brought to a relevant competent authority for enforcement. However, WG II agreed to identify an exhaustive and limited list of grounds for refusal that would be permissive in nature, meaning that courts may choose to provide enforcement relief despite the fact that an Article 5 defence has been proven. Further, the defences would be broadly worded to accommodate diverse interpretations in different legal systems. There was, however, considerable disagreement in relation to the mediator misconduct defences in Articles 5(1)(e) and 5(1)(f). These provisions focus on the impact of a mediator's conduct on the resulting iMSA. One view was that these issues were adequately covered by other defences, such as the 'null and void' defence (Article 5(1)(b)(i)) and the public policy defence (Article 5(2)) and were therefore unnecessary. Furthermore, it was felt by some that the inclusion of these defences would encourage additional disputes related to mediator conduct. However, the prevailing view was that the mediator-related defences were worthwhile as they drew attention to the critical importance of ethical mediation practice and provided a review mechanism to protect parties. The compromise involved framing these two defences narrowly and also setting a very high bar[79] to prove either of them. These defences are explored in the commentary to Article 5.

0.52 Finally, the form of the instrument to be drafted to address enforcement of iMSAs was the source of some debate. Some delegations were in favour of a model law as they considered it more suitable for States with less developed mediation systems; others considered that a multilateral convention would more effectively and efficiently serve to facilitate the international circulation of iMSAs and promote the use of cross-border commercial mediation. The compromise was a first in UNCITRAL's history, with the Working Group electing to move forward with the parallel drafting of a convention (which became the Singapore Convention), as well as a model law which would amend

78. See the Point of Interest discussion on opt-in and opt-out approaches in the commentary to Art. 8.
79. For example, a causal link between the mediator's conduct and the decision by at least one party to enter into the iMSA must be established.

the 2002 Model Law on Conciliation. Both instruments were prepared to be complementary to each other.

0.53 Understanding the five issues of compromise achieved during its drafting helps us better appreciate the overall function of the Singapore Convention.

AN ISSUE NOT COVERED BY THE SINGAPORE CONVENTION: MEDIATION AGREEMENTS

0.54 As set out at the start of this chapter, the Singapore Convention endeavours to regulate the expedited enforcement of iMSAs across borders. However, it does not regulate contractual agreements to enter into mediation – these are referred to as mediation agreements or agreements to mediate.[80] In this aspect, the Singapore Convention diverges from the New York Convention, which regulates both arbitration agreements and arbitral awards.

0.55 The reasons for this were varied, including the desire to maintain the momentum behind the drafting effort and produce an instrument that would be better-focused on the primary issue of iMSA enforcement. The pathways to mediation are diverse:[81] in addition to mediation agreements and mediation clauses, other triggering mechanisms include court referrals[82] and triggering legislation which provides for mediation with respect to certain types of disputes.[83] As a result, regulation and enforcement measures directed towards mediation agreements will not always be relevant to how parties enter the mediation process in the first place.[84] Furthermore, while some mediation agreements may contain terms of reference that limit the scope of issues to be negotiated in mediation, it is widely accepted that the nature of the mediation forum, with its focus on flexibility and party decision-making, means that disputing parties may agree to negotiate on issues beyond those envisaged in their mediation agreement. In other words, once at the mediation table, they may effectively vary the terms of their mediation agreement.

80. Cf. Stacie Strong, *Beyond International Commercial Arbitration? The Promise of International Commercial Mediation*, 45 Wash. U. J. L. & Pol'y 11 (2014), at 32-34. Strong had appealed to the drafters of the Singapore Convention to address mediation agreements.
81. On different pathways to mediation, see the commentary to Art. 2(3).
82. Consider, for instance, the mandatory court mediation referrals regime in the courts of New South Wales, Australia: see David Spencer, *Mandatory Mediation Litigation Begins in NSW*, 4(4) ADR Bull. 52 (2001). Also see Vicki Waye, *Mandatory Mediation in Australia's Civil Justice System*, 45(2-3) Common L. World Rev. 214 (2016).
83. For instance, in Australia, note that pre-litigation mediation is mandated (under s 86B) for disputes in relation to the Native Title Act 1993 (No. 110, 1993). Also consider the Canadian Farm Debt Mediation Act (S.C. 1997, c. 21).
84. See James R. Coben, *Evaluating the Singapore Convention Through a U.S.-Centric Litigation Lens: Lessons Learned from Nearly Two Decades of Mediation Disputes in American Federal and State Courts*, 20 Cardozo J. Conflict Resol. 1063 (2019); Edna Sussman, *The Singapore Convention: Promoting the Enforcement and Recognition of International Mediated Settlement Agreements*, 3 ICC Disp. Resol. Bull. 42 (2018), at 49.

0.56 For the purposes of the Singapore Convention, therefore, the scope of a mediation agreement is not relevant. The terms of an iMSA may lie beyond the scope of a mediation agreement that triggered the mediation. This practice aligns with settled mediation principles, namely that once parties are at the mediation table, they may address any differences between themselves and are not contrived by the terms of a mediation clause, agreement or referral.

WHAT HAPPENS AFTER THE INK HAS DRIED?

0.57 The international mediation community now has its very own 'New York Convention' in addition to a Model Law – an international treaty that promises to put mediation on the global map and change the landscape of international dispute resolution. But this is just the beginning. The New York Convention has been in force for more than 60 years and continues to attract new signatories. Today with 170 Contracting States, it is important to remember that it began with ten ratifying States. As indicated previously, empirical evidence highlights the widespread perception that the use of international mediation will increase with the introduction of a multilateral treaty on enforcement.[85] The Singapore Convention will certainly lend to cross-border mediation practice the regulatory robustness, visibility and credibility needed for it to become a long-term player in the international dispute resolution arena. At the same time, experience with the New York Convention caveats against the expectation that this will occur overnight.

0.58 What happens, therefore, after the ink has dried on the paper of this new Convention?[86] The Singapore Convention is likely to encourage States to develop their regulatory and institutional capacity to serve as an international hub for the mediation of commercial disputes. Developing capacity for international mediation practice requires an engagement that goes beyond the minimalist requirements of becoming a State or party to the Singapore Convention. It could, for instance, involve consultation with the professional mediation community and other stakeholders to further develop institutional mediation in a coordinated manner. Attention would wisely be directed towards reviewing and clarifying norms and standards for mediator credentialing and ethical practice, especially given the focus of Articles 5(1)(e) and 5(1)(f) of the Singapore Convention on mediator (mis)conduct as grounds for refusal of relief. In addition, States desiring to enact comprehensive mediation legislation may look to the UNCITRAL Model Law on Mediation for inspiration. Other considerations include the establishment of institutional frameworks for mediation service providers, professional mediator associations and the development of mediation infrastructure, including the appropriate integration of technology into mediation services, specifically with respect

85. Stacie Strong, *Realizing Rationality: An Empirical Assessment of International Commercial Mediation*, 73 Wash. & Lee L. Rev. 1973 (2016), at 2031.
86. This question is inspired by Michelle LeBaron's work on the implementation of multilateral agreements: *After the Ink is Dry*, International Round Table, Peter Wall Institute, UBC, Vancouver, October 2017. See also, Nadja Alexander, *The Singapore Convention: What Happens after the Ink Has Dried?*, 30(2) Am. Rev. Int'l Arb. (2020).

to ODR platforms as anticipated by the Singapore Convention. In this regard, both the UMR and the Notes are important instruments. Mediation service providers can administer mediations under or draft their own mediation rules on the basis of the UMR. The Notes offer a useful guide for mediation practitioners and interested parties to have a better understanding of the process of mediation.

0.59 Looking forward, the Singapore Convention represents the dawn of a new era. It is an invitation to shift the culture of dispute resolution and, with it, business practices at an international level. In the commentary, we seek to advance this significant development by offering a comprehensive examination of the 16 Articles of the Singapore Convention on Mediation.

ARTICLE 1

Scope of Application

1. This Convention applies to an agreement resulting from mediation and concluded in writing by parties to resolve a commercial dispute ('settlement agreement') which, at the time of its conclusion, is international in that:

(a) At least two parties to the settlement agreement have their places of business in different States; or
(b) The State in which the parties to the settlement agreement have their places of business is different from either:
    (i) The State in which a substantial part of the obligations under the settlement agreement is performed; or
    (ii) The State with which the subject matter of the settlement agreement is most closely connected.

2. This Convention does not apply to settlement agreements:

(a) Concluded to resolve a dispute arising from transactions engaged in by one of the parties (a consumer) for personal, family or household purposes;
(b) Relating to family, inheritance or employment law.

3. This Convention does not apply to:

(a) Settlement agreements:
    (i) That have been approved by a court or concluded in the course of proceedings before a court; and
    (ii) That are enforceable as a judgment in the State of that court;
(b) Settlement agreements that have been recorded and are enforceable as an arbitral award.

COMMENTARY

1.01 This commentary will address the following issues:

(1) scope of the Singapore Convention;
(2) use of the terminology 'international mediated settlement agreement';
(3) meaning of key terms such as 'international' and 'commercial';
(4) the absence of a seat in international mediation;
(5) meaning of 'parties to the settlement agreement';
(6) exclusions to the scope of the Singapore Convention; and
(7) differences in enforcement between the Singapore Convention and the New York Convention.

Scope of Application of the Convention

1.02 The Convention's scope encompasses agreements resulting from mediation[1] that have been concluded in writing[2] by parties to resolve a commercial dispute ('settlement agreements'), and that are international in character.[3]

1.03 A careful consideration of the key terms, 'international', 'commercial', 'mediation' and 'settlement agreement' is essential. The 'in writing' requirement is considered in the commentary of Article 2(2), as well as in the commentary of Article 4 in relation to form requirements for settlement agreements.

Mediated Settlement Agreement (MSA)

1.04 In the Convention, agreements in writing resulting from mediation are referred to as 'settlement agreements' (Article 1(1)). In this work, we refer to them as 'mediated settlement agreements' or MSAs as it highlights the connection between the mediation process and the settlement agreement. Moreover, it is a term widely recognised in mediation circles. To the extent that MSAs meet the criteria of 'international', they are referred to as 'international mediated settlement agreements' or iMSAs.

About MSAs Generally

1.05 In most jurisdictions, MSAs may take the form of standard contracts. In common law, this means that the basic elements of contract formation - offer, consideration, acceptance and intention to create legal relations - must be present.[4] By way of

1. United Nations Convention on International Settlement Agreements Resulting from Mediation (2019), Art. 1(1).
2. *Ibid.*
3. *Ibid.*
4. Daniel Spencer and Michael Brogan, *Mediation Law and Practice*, Cambridge University Press (2006), at 356-357.

example, in the American case of *Helmericks v Peak Trust Co.*, the court stated that a settlement agreement is contractual in nature and must satisfy all essential criteria of contract formation, specifically, an offer that encompasses all essential terms, unequivocal acceptance by the offeree, consideration and an intention to be bound.[5] Similarly, in civil law jurisdictions, there must be compliance with the general law on contracts and any additional legal requirements applicable to the category of contract being established. In many jurisdictions, MSAs, much like standard contracts, can be made orally and free from formal requirements.[6] However, formal written requirements for contract formation can be found in numerous categories of contracts, such as the transfer of land.[7] An increasing number of jurisdictions require an MSA to be made in writing. Formal requirements applicable to MSAs can be found in Georgia,[8] Vietnam,[9] Cyprus,[10] Luxembourg[11] and Sri Lanka.[12] In other jurisdictions, concluding an MSA in writing may determine whether it is enforceable as a court judgment or not.[13]

1.06 In the absence of a legislative mechanism like that envisaged by the Singapore Convention, MSAs can take a number of different legal forms. These include ordinary contracts, various categories of settlement deeds,[14] court orders[15] and arbitral

5. *Helmericks v Peak Trust Co.*, 2020 Alas. LEXIS 123, *1 (Alaska 30 September 2020).
6. On the enforcement of an oral mediated settlement which was confirmed by a letter from the mediator, see the case of *Joseph v Edison Control Corp* N° A-3856-04T1, 2006 WL 2033666 (NJ Super Ct App. Div. 2006).
7. By way of example, according to Art. 183 of the Civil Code of Georgia, a transaction on immovable property shall be made in writing and the ownership right shall be registered in the Public Registry.
8. According to Art. 9(3) of the Law of Georgia on Mediation, a settlement reached at a mediation shall be concluded in writing and signed by the parties and the mediator.
9. According to Art. 15(1) of the Decree No. 22/2017/ND-CP on Commercial Mediation of Vietnam, upon attaining a successful mediation result, the parties shall make a written record thereof, which is binding on the parties in accordance with the civil law. According to Art. 15(2), a written settlement agreement shall contain the following: grounds for conducting mediation; basic information about the parties; circumstances of the dispute; the agreement reached and solution; other contents as agreed upon by the parties in accordance with law. According to Art. 15(3), a written record of a successful mediation result must bear the signatures of the parties and the commercial mediator.
10. According to Art. 30 of the Law on Certain Aspects of Mediation in Civil Matters of 2012, Law No. 159(I)/2012 of Cyprus, if the parties reach a settlement, the mediator shall draft an agreement in writing, which shall reflect the contents of the settlement arrived at by the parties.
11. According to Art. 1251-10 of the New Code of Civil Procedure (NCCP), when the parties reach a mediated settlement agreement, this agreement is recorded in writing, dated and signed by the parties.
12. According to s. 11 of the Mediation Boards Act No. 72 of 1988, where the disputants agree to a settlement, the terms of the settlement shall be reduced to writing and be signed by the Chief Mediator and the disputants.
13. By way of example, according to Art. 47 of the Arbitration and Mediation Act of Ecuador, a mediated settlement agreement which is drawn up in writing has the effect of a court judgment.
14. Settlement deeds and other special forms of settlement are agreements that have particular form requirements and a special legal status in terms of enforceability. In terms of enforceability, settlement deeds usually engender expedited enforcement by courts, provided there has been compliance with the relevant form requirements and the deed does not embody an illegal agreement. They are a popular legal form for mediated settlements in civil law jurisdictions and in this section are referred to collectively as settlement deeds, although the forms and legal

awards.[16] Depending on the jurisdiction, parties may have different procedural paths to enforceability available to them. Here are some examples of enforcement pathways that go beyond the enforcement of MSAs as ordinary contracts. In the Philippines, parties may record an MSA as a court order[17] or request the mediator to take on the role of an arbitrator and to issue the settlement agreement as an arbitral award;[18] in India, an MSA may be enforced as an arbitral award under several statutes;[19] and in Turkey, an MSA may be enforced as a court order.[20] In Singapore, in addition to direct enforcement under the Singapore Convention on Mediation Act 2020, parties may enforce an MSA as a court order under the Mediation Act 2017 and as a consent order of the court in court-referred mediation.[21]

1.07 Where the contents of MSAs are disputed, this may lead to litigation requiring a review of what occurred in the mediation. Here, tensions arise between the accountability of the mediation participants (including mediators, parties and legal advisers) and the confidentiality of the mediation process. These topics are considered in the commentary to Article 5, which deals with the grounds for a refusal to enforce an iMSA.

---

natures of the various categories of *transaction* (France), *Vaststellingsovereenkomst* (Norway), *Vergleich* (Germany) and notarial deeds are different. On settlement deeds in a variety of jurisdictions, see the relevant chapters in Nadja Alexander, Sabine Walsh and Martin Svatos (eds), EU Mediation Law Handbook – Regulatory Robustness Ratings for Mediation Regimes, Kluwer Law International (2017); Nadja Alexander, *Harmonisation and Diversity in the Private International Law of Mediation: The Rhythms of Regulatory Reform*, in Klaus Hopt and Felix Steffek (eds), Mediation – Principles and Regulation in Comparative Perspective, OUP (2013), at 179 et seq. Note that in Greece, if an iMSA is signed by the mediator it may be enforceable by application of any party to it before the competent court: Law No. 4512/2016, Art. 184(5).

15. See the commentary to Art. 1(3) below.
16. See the commentary to Art. 1(3) below.
17. According to s. 17(c) of the Alternative Dispute Resolution Act of 2004, if the parties so desire, they may deposit such a settlement agreement with the appropriate Clerk of a Regional Trial Court of the place where one of the parties resides.
18. According to s. 17(d) of the Alternative Dispute Resolution Act of 2004, the parties may agree in the settlement agreement that the mediator shall become a sole arbitrator for the dispute and shall treat the settlement agreement as an arbitral award which shall be subject to enforcement. Also, according to s. 36 of the Alternative Dispute Resolution Act of 2004, the parties may agree in writing that, following a successful mediation, the mediator shall issue the settlement agreement in the form of an arbitral award.
19. Under the Micro, Small, and Medium Enterprises Development Act 2006, the Facilitation Council delivers a settlement arrived at by a buyer and a seller in the form of an award, which has the same status and effect as an arbitral award. Further, the Commercial Courts Act 2015 mandates pre-institution mediation. Under this Act, a settlement reached at a mediation is enforceable as an award on agreed terms. See Shraddha Bhosale and Sahil Kanuga, *Chapter 6: Mediating Commercial Disputes*, in Gracious Timothy (ed.), Mediation and Conciliation in India, Kluwer Law International (2021), at 151-168.
20. According to Art. 18(2) of the Law on Mediation in Civil Disputes No. 6325, should the parties reach an agreement at the end of the mediation process, they may submit such an agreement to an enforcement court and may demand for the issuance of a commentary regarding its enforceability. The agreement containing such commentary shall be considered as a document with the force of a court order.
21. Nadja Alexander and Shouyu Chong, *Leading the Way for the Recognition and Enforcement of International Mediated Settlement Agreements: The Singapore Convention on Mediation Act 2020*, 34 SAcLJ 1 (2021).

Case Illustrations

Illustration [A]: In the American case of *Singer v Neven*,[22] the plaintiff made an objection that the settlement agreement was not binding, on the ground that the plaintiff and the opposing party neither shook their hands nor signed a formal contract. The court did not agree with the plaintiff and stated that these actions were not necessary for concluding a binding settlement agreement. The court opined, 'there was an offer, acceptance, meeting of the minds, and consideration. Having placed their oral agreement on the record, there is a binding and enforceable settlement agreement regardless of any dispute as to later terms to include or exclude from a written agreement'.[23]

Illustration [B]: In another American case of *Adamson v Adamson*,[24] a party made an objection that an MSA was unenforceable, on the ground that it was a contract for the sale of real estate and such a contract had to be made in writing and signed by the parties. The Court of Appeals of Kentucky did not agree with the objection and stated that the mediation agreement was not a specific contract for the sale of real estate and '[t]he mediation agreement was merely a contractual, written agreement to resolve outstanding issues between the parties in a civil dispute'. Therefore, the Court of Appeals of Kentucky found that the settlement agreement did not need to be made in writing.[25]

Illustration [C]: In *Helmericks v Peak Trust Co.*, the Supreme Court of Alaska opined: '[a]nd even if an oral settlement agreement contemplates that the agreement will be reduced to writing, the parties are free to agree that the oral settlement is final and binding. Such an oral agreement remains final and binding even if the parties do not later draft a written document'.[26]

Illustration [D]: In *Martz v Webb*, the US District Court for the Western District of Arkansas made an important reasoning about the enforcement of an oral settlement agreement. According to the court, '[a] valid oral settlement agreement is binding and the parties' signature on a written agreement is not essential to finalize the contract'.[27] The court went on and opined that '[a] court should keep in mind two legal principles when deciding whether a valid contract exists: (1) a court cannot make a contract for the parties, but can only construe and enforce the contract that they have made; and (2) to make a contract, there must enforce the contract that they have made; and (2) to make a contract, there must be a meeting of the minds as to all terms, using objective indicators. A party to a

22. *Singer v Neven*, 2020 U.S. Dist. LEXIS 24836 (D. Nev. 23 January 2020).
23. *Id.*, at 4-5.
24. *Adamson v Adamson*, 2020 Ky. App. Unpub. LEXIS 228 (Ky. Ct. App. 27 March 2020).
25. *Id.*, at 5.
26. *Helmericks v Peak Trust Co.*, 2020 Alas. LEXIS 123, *12 (Alaska 30 September 2020).
27. *Martz v Webb*, 2020 U.S. Dist. LEXIS 80349, *6, 2020 WL 2214427 (W.D. Ark. 7 May 2020).

valid settlement agreement cannot avoid the agreement simply because the agreement ultimately proves to be disadvantageous or because he later feels that the amount of the settlement is unsatisfactory'.[28]

'[I]n writing'

1.08 An iMSA must be in writing.[29] This requirement is explored in the commentary to Article 2(2).

'[I]nternational'

1.09 The application of the Convention is limited to iMSAs that, at the time of their conclusion, possess an international character. The international requirement reflects the cross-border nature of UNCITRAL's[30] mandate and its desire not to interfere in the domestic law of enacting States.[31] Working Group II made the practical decision to confine the scope of the Convention to iMSAs, which are of an international nature, to make it simpler for States to sign on to it without having to make significant reforms or amendments to their current law on the enforcement of purely domestic MSAs.[32] Article 1(1) generally defines what constitutes an international dispute, where:

(a) At least two parties to the settlement agreement have their places of business in different states; or
(b) The State in which the parties to the settlement agreement have their places of business is different from either:
   (i) The State in which a substantial part of the obligations under the settlement agreement is performed; or
   (ii) The State with which the subject matter of the settlement agreement is most closely connected.[33]

1.10 An MSA may still be international even if the parties have their place of business in the same State, provided the MSA itself relates to another jurisdiction according to Article 1(1)(b). The internationality of an iMSA is benchmarked against the identity of

28. *Ibid.*
29. See Intervention of Norway, in UNCITRAL Audio Recordings: Working Group II (Arbitration and Conciliation), 63rd Session, 8 September 2015, 9:30-12:30.
30. The United Nations Commission on International Trade Law.
31. Report of Working Group II (Arbitration and Conciliation) on the Work of its 63rd Session, A/CN.9/861 (2015), https://documents-dds ny.un.org/doc/UNDOC/GEN/V15/065/85/PDF/V 1506585.pdf?OpenElement (Accessed 25 March 2018), at paras 36-39.
32. See Intervention of Israel, in UNCITRAL Audio Recordings: Working Group II (Arbitration and Conciliation), 63rd Session, 7 September 2015, 14:00-17:00; and Timothy Schnabel, *The Singapore Convention on Mediation: A Framework for the Cross-Border Recognition and Enforcement of Mediated Settlements*, 19(1) Pepp. Disp. Resol. L.J. 1 (2019), at 20.
33. United Nations Convention on International Settlement Agreements Resulting from Mediation (2019), Art. 1(1).

the parties in dispute: in other words, it depends on their place of business.[34] The following cases are illustrative.

Case Illustrations

Illustration [A]: In *Fung Sang Trading Limited v Kai Sun Sea Products and Food Company Limited,*[35] the High Court of Hong Kong ruled, albeit in the context of international commercial arbitration,[36] that, although the dispute involved parties based in the same State (that is, Hong Kong), the dispute was international in nature as the contract involved a supply of soybeans to the People's Republic of China (which was at that time considered a different territory from Hong Kong). This was because a substantial part of the obligations of the commercial relationship and the contract (that is, the supply of goods to China) had taken place outside of Hong Kong.

Illustration [B]: In *D Heung and Associates, Architects and Engineers v Pacific Enterprises (Holdings) Company Limited,*[37] the Hong Kong High Court in 1995 held that the dispute between two Hong Kong companies was international in nature, as the subject matter of the dispute was found to be most closely connected with the design and supervision of a project in Dongshan Island, China (which was at that time considered a different territory from Hong Kong). Furthermore, a substantial part of the defendant's duties was related to the design and supervision of a project in Dongshan Island, China.

Illustration [C]: In *Mitsui Engineering & Shipbuilding Co Ltd v PSA Corp Ltd,*[38] the High Court of Singapore, in the context of international commercial arbitration, opined that 'a place where substantial part of the obligations performed' refers to any place where a substantial part of the obligations takes place and not the place of substantial performance. For the court, this meant that even if the place of substantial performance was in Singapore, a substantial part of the obligations could still take place in Japan and vice versa.[39]

1.11 The meaning of 'place of business' in situations where the party has more than one place of business – or, in the case of natural persons, has no place of business – is set out in Article 2(1) and examined in the commentary thereto.

34. See Interventions of the United States and Thailand, in UNCITRAL Audio Recordings: Working Group II (Arbitration and Conciliation), 63rd Session, 7 September 2015, 14:00-17:00.
35. *Fung Sang Trading Limited v Kai Sun Sea Products and Food Company Limited* [1992] HKLR 40.
36. The case involved a ruling as to whether an arbitration was international for the purposes of Art. 1(2)(b)(ii) of the Model Law on International Commercial Arbitration (1985).
37. *D Heung and Associates, Architects and Engineers v Pacific Enterprises (Holdings) Company Limited* 04.05.1995, CLOUT case No. 108.
38. *Mitsui Engineering & Shipbuilding Co Ltd v PSA Corp Ltd and another* [2002] SGHC 170.
39. *Id.*, paras 27-30.

1.12 For the purposes of the Singapore Convention, the international character of the MSA must exist at the time of the conclusion of the MSA.[40] Therefore, if one of the parties changes its place of business after the conclusion of an MSA, this, in itself, would not impact the international character of the settlement agreement.

1.13 Finally, the location of the mediation is irrelevant to the determination of the international character of the MSA.[41]

The Absence of a Seat in Mediation

1.14 The Singapore Convention does not conceive of a 'seat of mediation'.[42] This reflects the broad consensus reached by Working Group II in support of the notion that direct enforcement of iMSAs means to control at the State of enforcement and not of origin.[43] As Schnabel explains:

---

40. See Intervention of China, in UNCITRAL Audio Recordings: Working Group II (Dispute Settlement), 65th Session, 19 September 2016, 14:00-17:00.
41. Timothy Schnabel, *Implementation of the Singapore Convention: Federalism, Self-Execution, and Private Law Treaties*, 30 Am. Rev. Int'l Arb. 265 (2020).
42. The relevance of the seat is fundamental in international arbitration because it is crucial in the determination of whether the award sought to be enforced is a foreign or domestic award (see Art. I of the New York Convention). In addition, it is commonly understood that the courts of the seat of arbitration have been traditionally entrusted with the powers by the drafters of the New York Convention through Art V(1)(e) of the Convention to engage in a principal review of awards made by the tribunal (see Nadia Darwazeh, *Article V(1)(e)*, in Herbert Kronke et al. (eds), Recognition and Enforcement of Foreign Arbitral Awards: A Global Commentary on the New York Convention, Kluwer Law International (2010), at 327. For further information on how the seat of arbitration is determined and a perusal of the function of courts at the seat before it is taken abroad for enforcement, see Alexander J. Bělohlávek, *Seat of Arbitration and Supporting and Supervising Function of Courts*, 5 Czech (& Central European) Yearbook of Arbitration 21 (2015). In jurisdictions that follow the common law tradition, such as in the United Kingdom (see *Carillion Construction Limited v Devonport Royal Dockyard Limited* [2005] EWCA Civ 1358 at para. 53), Singapore (see *Soh Beng Tee & Co Pte Ltd v Fairmount Development Pte Ltd* [2007] 3 SLR(R) 86, paras 29, 42-65) and New Zealand (see *Trustees of Rotoaira Forest Trust v Attorney-General* [1999] 2 NZLR 452, 463), it may be usual for the courts at the seat to examine whether rules of natural justice have been breached by the arbitral tribunal during the determinative process and set it aside if any breach has occurred: for instance, the court may examine whether the parties have been sufficiently appraised of the justifications by arbitrators when rendering their award (see for an illustration from Singapore, *TMM Division Maritima SA de CV v Pacific Richfield Marine Pte Ltd* [2013] 4 SLR 972, at para. 99; and for an illustration from England, *Pilon Limited v Breyer Group Plc* [2010] 1 BLR 452, at para. 22). It follows that there is no need to discern the seat of mediation as it is not a determinative process as is arbitration – the nature of the natural justice considerations is fundamentally different, because, in mediation, parties are not compelled to arrive at their dispute resolution outcome. Accordingly, the power of the competent authority of the State to refuse to enforce an iMSA based on the fairness of the mediation process resulting in an iMSA is strictly confined to cases where mediator misconduct is so egregious that it *materially influences* parties to enter into it inadvertently (see Arts 5(1)(e) and 5(1)(f) of the Singapore Convention). See Shouyu Chong and Nadja Alexander, *Singapore Convention Series: Why Is There No 'Seat' of Mediation?*, Kluwer Arbitration Blog (2019), available at http://mediationblog.kluwerarbitration.com/2019/02/01/singapore-convention-series-why-is-there-no-seat-of-mediation/ (Accessed 21 February 2022).
43. See Intervention of the United States, in UNCITRAL Audio Recordings: Working Group II (Dispute Settlement), 65th Session, 16 September 2016, 14:00-17:00; and Norel Rosner, *The New*

> Because no particular state of origin is designated, the scope of the Convention could not be delineated by referring to whether relief is sought in a jurisdiction other than the mediated settlement's state of origin. Many jurisdictions may be involved in one cross-border mediation. A particular dispute may involve parties that do business in two jurisdictions but are physically present in two other jurisdictions at the time of the mediation, with the mediator in a fifth jurisdiction, and with the applicable law from a sixth state. Such a situation would provide no obvious answer to the question of which state the settlement is 'from'. Thus, identifying a 'seat' of the mediation, especially if the settlement is developed via email, would be unnecessarily difficult. [...] [T]he Working Group expressed a desire to avoid replicating the 'artificial' concept of the place of the arbitration and its consequences in terms of applicable law. [...] Thus a mediated settlement is essentially made a stateless instrument that is generally not subject to domestic law requirements, except insofar as the Convention permits a state to apply some domestic concepts and procedures when relief is requested (e.g., its rule of procedure for administering the request for relief, and the grounds for refusal in Article 5(2)).[44]

Therefore, unlike arbitral awards, there is no single jurisdiction that has the power to set aside an iMSA. Furthermore, iMSAs and the mediation processes from which they result, are not required to comply with the prerequisites of the domestic law or rules of an originating State, for the purposes of relief pursuant to the Convention.[45]

1.15 Thus, while the internationality of a 'foreign' judgment or arbitral award enforced under the Hague Convention of 30 June 2005 on Choice of Court Agreements (HCCCA) and the 1958 New York Convention on the Recognition and Enforcement of Foreign Arbitral Awards respectively is clear,[46] the internationality of an MSA must be defined because it is a non-starter to describe that agreement as 'foreign'. For this reason, it is only meaningful to refer to MSAs as being of 'international' character, in contrast to those of 'domestic' character, which fall outside of the Article 1(1) definition.

1.16 Finally, it should be noted that the issue of reciprocal enforcement of iMSAs under the Singapore Convention does not arise at all. Without a 'seat' of mediation, it is impossible to define any form of reciprocity from the perspective of the enforcing competent court. Consider the following case illustration.

UNCITRAL Instruments on International Commercial Settlement Agreements Resulting from Mediation – An Insider's View, 22(4) Nederlands-Vlaams tijdschrift voor Mediation en conflict management 30 (2018), at 33.

44. Timothy Schnabel, *The Singapore Convention on Mediation: A Framework for the Cross-Border Recognition and Enforcement of Mediated Settlements*, 19(1) Pepp. Disp. Resol. L.J. 1 (2019), at 21-22. Also see Natalie Y. Morris-Sharma, *Constructing the Convention on Mediation – The Chairperson's Perspective*, 31 SAcLJ 487 (2019), at para. 31.
45. Timothy Schnabel, *The Singapore Convention on Mediation: A Framework for the Cross-Border Recognition and Enforcement of Mediated Settlements*, 19(1) Pepp. Disp. Resol. L.J. 1 (2019), at 22.
46. Take for example, Art. I of the New York Convention on the Recognition and Enforcement of Foreign Arbitral Awards provides, 'This Convention shall apply to the recognition and enforcement of arbitral awards made in the territory of a State [that is, the "seat"] *other than the State where the recognition and enforcement of such awards are sought* [...].' [*emphasis added*]

Case Illustration

Donatella, who runs a sole proprietorship in Jakarta, Indonesia, selling clothes, becomes entangled in a dispute with her supplier, *Gianni Sdn Bhd* (Gianni), which is based in Kuala Lumpur, Malaysia. Both parties agree to mediate their dispute by turning to a novel online dispute resolution toolkit offered by an international mediation service provider based in Singapore (whose servers are also housed in Singapore). In this situation, it is contrived to force parties to choose a seat, let alone allocate one for them. Under the Singapore Convention, regulation of the enforcement of iMSAs is left to the competent courts of the States. Assuming that Singapore, Malaysia and Indonesia are Parties to the Singapore Convention, the competent courts of each jurisdiction have an equal stake in regulating the iMSA, which materialises from the online dispute resolution process undertaken by *Donatella* and *Gianni*.[47]

'[C]ommercial'

1.17 The restriction of the application of the Convention to commercial disputes is the result of two factors, namely that commercial matters have been the traditional mandate of UNCITRAL, and that non-commercial matters are more likely to clash with public policies specific to legal cultures and national circumstances.[48] The term 'commercial' is not defined in the Convention.[49] It is noteworthy that it has been broadly defined in footnote 1 of the Model Law on International Commercial Mediation.[50] This definition may be useful for countries without a discrete body of commercial law:

> The term 'commercial' should be given a wide interpretation so as to cover matters arising from all relationships of a commercial nature, whether contractual or not. Relationships of a commercial nature include, but are not limited to, the following transactions: any trade transaction for the supply or exchange of goods or services; distribution agreement; commercial representation or agency; factoring; leasing; construction of works; consulting; engineering; licensing; investment; financing; banking; insurance; exploitation agreement or concession; joint venture and other

47. In relation to electronic communications and iMSAs, see the commentaries to Arts 2(2) and 4(2).
48. Report of Working Group II (Arbitration and Conciliation) on the Work of its 63rd Session, A/CN.9/861 (2015), https://documents-dds-ny.un.org/doc/UNDOC/GEN/V15/065/85/PDF/V1506585.pdf?OpenElement (Accessed 19 May 2022), at para. 42. Also consider Intervention of the Chair, in UNCITRAL Audio Recordings: Working Group II (Arbitration and Conciliation), 63rd Session, 8 September 2015, 9:30-12:30.
49. See Intervention of Israel, in UNCITRAL Audio Recordings: Working Group II (Arbitration and Conciliation), 63rd Session, 7 September 2015, 14:00-17:00.
50. UNCITRAL Model Law on International Commercial Mediation and International Settlement Agreements Resulting from Mediation (2018).

forms of industrial or business cooperation; and carriage of goods or passengers by air, sea, rail or road.[51]

1.18 According to the Guide to Enactment[52] to the Model Law on Mediation, the purpose behind the insertion of the broad definition in the Model Law was to overcome any inconsistencies or difficulties relating to the definition of the term 'commercial' that might exist in national laws as to which transaction was commercial.[53] The Model Law on Mediation does not provide a strict definition in order to allow States to construe the term broadly and to subject all relationships of commercial nature to the Model Law on Mediation, whether contractual or not.[54] The definition of the term 'commercial' in the Model Law on Mediation does not depend on what an individual State considers as commercial.[55] In this regard, the drafting history of the Model Law on Arbitration is also illustrative, which provides the same broad definition of the term. It is suggested that the term 'commercial' in the Model Law on Arbitration should not be construed in accordance with national laws, as in some States, the qualification of whether a certain transaction is to be considered commercial depends on the status of the parties involved in the transaction.[56] Similarly, the qualification of whether an iMSA is commercial in nature does not depend on the national laws of Contracting

51. See footnote 1 of the UNCITRAL Model Law on International Commercial Mediation and International Settlement Agreements Resulting from Mediation (2018) (amending the UNCITRAL Model Law on International Commercial Conciliation, 2002), www.uncitral.org/pdf/english/commissionsessions/51st-session/Annex_II.pdf (Accessed 1 May 2019). This definition of 'commercial' would seem to extend to certain investor-State disputes (see Timothy Schnabel, *The Singapore Convention on Mediation: A Framework for the Cross-Border Recognition and Enforcement of Mediated Settlements*, 19(1) Pepp. Disp. Resol. L.J. 1 (2019), at 22). Some jurisdictions provide a similar broad and illustrative definition of the term 'commercial'. By way of example, according to s. 2(c) of the Commercial Courts Act 2015 of India, a 'commercial dispute' includes, among others, ordinary transactions of merchants, bankers, financiers and traders such as those relating to mercantile documents, including enforcement and interpretation of such documents, export or import of merchandise or services, issues relating to admiralty and maritime law, construction and infrastructure contracts, including tenders, agreements relating to immovable property used exclusively in trade or commerce. Importantly, the same section explains that a commercial dispute shall not cease to be commercial in nature just because one of the parties is the state, a state agency, or a private body carrying out public functions.
52. Guide to Enactment and Use of the UNCITRAL Model Law on International Commercial Mediation and International Settlement Agreements Resulting from Mediation (2018). Available at https://undocs.org/en/A/CN.9/1073 (Accessed 25 May 2022). See also UNCITRAL Model Law on International Commercial Conciliation with Guide to Enactment and Use 2002, footnote 2. The Model Law on International Commercial Mediation amends and updates the Model Law on International Commercial Conciliation (2002). Available at https://uncitral.un.org/sites/uncitral.un.org/files/media-documents/uncitral/en/03-90953_ebook.pdf (Accessed 25 May 2022).
53. *Ibid.*
54. *Ibid.*
55. *Ibid.*
56. UNCITRAL Model Law, Chapter I, Article 1 – original version [Scope of application], in Howard M. Holtzmann and Joseph Neuhaus, A Guide to the UNCITRAL Model Law on International Commercial Arbitration: Legislative History and Commentary, Kluwer Law International (1989), at 33-34.

Parties[57] to the Singapore Convention on Mediation. The nature of iMSAs should be construed broadly in light of the illustrative definition provided in the Model Law on Mediation.

1.19 Consistent with the focus on 'commercial' transactions, disputes arising from transactions entered into by consumers[58] 'for personal, family or household purposes' are expressly excluded by Article 1(2). Working Group II excluded these issues because they wanted to avoid consumer protection issues.[59] Matters in relation to 'family, inheritance or employment law' are also excluded.[60] This exclusion allows Working Group II to steer clear of the areas of private international law (particularly on matters of cross-border *family law* disputes), which are traditionally associated with the Hague Conference on Private International Law.[61] The exclusion relating to transactions entered into 'for personal, family or household purposes' has the same meaning as used in the United Nations Convention on Contracts for the International Sale of Goods (CISG).[62] However, unlike the CISG, Article 1(2) of the Singapore Convention on Mediation does not refer to whether a party neither knew nor ought to have known that the transaction at issue was 'for personal, family or household purposes'. Whether a transaction was made 'for personal, family or household purposes' has to be decided objectively. A court seized with the question of whether an iMSA falls within the scope of the exclusions set out in Article 1(2) of the Singapore Convention on Mediation may take into account any applicable substantive law designated in the iMSA.

Case Illustrations

Illustration [A]: In *R.M. Investment & Trading Co. v Boeing Co.*,[63] the Supreme Court of India addressed the question of whether a consultancy agreement on promoting the sale of certain types of aircraft in India was a commercial

57. The term 'Party' with a capital 'P' refers to a Contracting Party to the Singapore Convention. The term 'p' with a small 'p' refers to a party to an iMSA. See the commentary to Art. 3, paras 3.03-3.08.
58. The reference to consumers is drafted into Art. 1(2)(a) to clarify the scope of 'personal, family or household purposes': see interventions of Colombia, Argentina, Israel, and Germany, in UNCITRAL Audio Recordings: Working Group II (Dispute Settlement), 65th Session, 14 September 2016, 14:00-17:00.
59. See Intervention of Canada, in UNCITRAL Audio Recordings: Working Group II (Arbitration and Conciliation), 63rd Session, 7 September 2015, 14:00-17:00.
60. See Intervention of Finland, in UNCITRAL Audio Recordings: Working Group II (Arbitration and Conciliation), 63rd Session, 7 September 2015, 14:00-17:00; and Intervention of Egypt, in UNCITRAL Audio Recordings: Working Group II (Arbitration and Conciliation), 64th Session, 1 February 2015, 10:30-13:00.
61. Timothy Schnabel, *The Singapore Convention on Mediation: A Framework for the Cross-Border Recognition and Enforcement of Mediated Settlements*, 19(1) Pepp. Disp. Resol. L.J. 1 (2019), at 24.
62. Ellen E. Deason, *What's in a Name? The Terms 'Commercial' and 'Mediation' in the Singapore Convention on Mediation*, 20(4) Cardozo J. Conflict Resol. 1149 (2018-2019), at 1149.
63. *R.M. Investments & Trading Co. PVT. LTD. v Boeing Co.*, on 10 February 1994, 1994 AIR 1136, 1994 SCC (4) 541.

transaction. The court was of the view that the transaction at issue was commercial in nature and stated '[t]rade and commerce do not mean merely traffic in goods, i.e., exchange of commodities for money or other commodities. In the complexities of modern conditions, in their wide sweep are included carriage of persons and goods by road, rail, air and waterways, contracts, banking, insurance, transactions in the stock exchanges and forward markets, communication of information, supply of energy, postal and telegraphic services and many more activities – too numerous to be exhaustively enumerated – which may be called commercial inter-course'.[64]

Illustration [B]: In *European Grain & Shipping Ltd. v Bombay Extractions Private Ltd.*,[65] the Bombay High Court relied on the Black's Law Dictionary and stated that the term 'commercial' 'relates to or is connected with trade and traffic or commerce in general' and it is a 'generic term for almost all aspects of buying and selling'.[66]

Illustration [C]: In *R v Wah Kee*, the Alberta Supreme Court, in deciding whether a laundry was a commercial business, opined: '[I] read the word "commercial" in the sense of relating to commerce partly on the ejusdem generis principle and partly because that is its ordinary and generally understood meaning. [...] The word "commercial" conveys to the mind the idea of dealing or trading in some article of commerce [...]. In a sense, of course, every business which has profit for its object [...] is a commercial business [...].'[67]

Illustration [D]: In *Carter v McLaughlin*,[68] the Ontario Court addressed the question of whether an arbitration that dealt with a transaction involving the purchase and sale of a residential property was a commercial transaction. The court made the following statement:

'In my view, the arbitration agreement between the parties to this application and the resulting award should be viewed as being "commercial" within the meaning of that term as used in the International Commercial Arbitration Act of Ontario and the UNCITRAL Model Law it implements in this Province. While the sale of the home by the McLaughlins to the Carters was unconnected to the regular business activity of either party, that, in my view, is insufficient to remove the transaction from the scope of what is meant by the term "commercial" in the legislation. The transaction was done in a business-like way, with the assistance of professional realtors and within a legal framework appropriate for a transaction involving a large sum of money. It bears all the earmarks of what goes on in trade and commerce except that the parties were not "commercial

64. *Id.*, para. 13.
65. AIR 1983 Bom 36, (1982) 84 BOMLR 246.
66. *Id.*, para. 22.
67. *R v Wah Kee* [1920] 3 WWR 656.
68. *Carter v McLaughlin* [1996] OJ No 328, 27 OR (3d) 792, 61 ACWS (3d) 11.

persons" or merchants in regards to that transaction. It was not part of their usual business. Nevertheless, the relationship of the parties was commercial in nature. Indeed, they had no other relationship. Their relationship had only one dimension, involving the sale of property.'

Illustration [E]: In the Australian case of *Re Ku-ring-gai Co-operative Building Society (No 12) Ltd,*[69] the Federal Court of Australia, in the context of the Trade Practices Act 1974, made the following statement with respect to the terms 'trade' and 'commerce':

'The terms "trade" and "commerce" are not terms of art. They are expressions of fact and terms of common knowledge. While the particular instances that may fall within them will depend upon the varying phases of development of trade, commerce and commercial communication, the terms are clearly of the widest import: see, generally, *W & A McArthur Ltd v State of Queensland* (1920) 28 CLR 530 at 546ff; *Bank of New South Wales v Commonwealth* (1948) 76 CLR 1 at 284ff and 381ff. They are not restricted to dealings or communications which can properly be described as being at arm's length in the sense that they are within open markets or between strangers or have a dominant objective of profit-making. They are apt to include commercial or business dealings in finance between a company and its members which are not within the mainstream of ordinary commercial activities and which, while being commercial in character, are marked by a degree of altruism which is not compatible with a dominant objective of profit-making. I have already expressed the conclusion that, notwithstanding the particular nature of the applicants and the particular character of their activities, their lending to their members are commercial or business dealings in finance. In my view, that lending is, for the purposes of s 47 of the Act, in trade or commerce.'

Illustration [F]: The Australian case of *Rinehart v Rinehart (No 3)*[70] interpreted the term 'commercial' for the purposes of the commercial arbitration legislation. According to the court, 'a commercial dispute may arise from the terms of a contract between parties even though the parties do not have a pre-existing commercial relationship, although not every contractual dispute is also a commercial dispute'.[71] The court went on and explained that 'a dispute is aptly described as a commercial dispute where it concerns ownership of commercially valuable assets and entitlements to profits generated by those assets. Typically, such disputes will arise from a relationship based on shared ownership of the relevant assets or contractual agreements concerning entitlements to profits generated by the assets. However, as this case illustrates, a dispute may arise

69. *Re Ku-ring-gai Co-operative Building Society (No 12) Ltd* (1978) 22 ALR 621.
70. *Rinehart v Rinehart (No 3)* (2016) 337 ALR 174.
71. *Id.*, at 65.

over ownership of valuable commercial assets where those assets form part of a deceased estate or a family trust'.[72]

1.20 Article 1(2) excludes employment relationships from the scope of the Singapore Convention on Mediation, as employment relationships are not considered commercial in nature. However, in some cases, a question arises whether a particular relationship is an employment relationship or a service contract that is commercial in nature. By way of example, in some jurisdictions, a contract between a company and its director may be considered commercial in nature depending on the functions that the director in question performs. Another grey area regarding the characterisation of a relationship as commercial is observed in the relationship between a client and a law firm. Even though in some jurisdictions, the relationship between a client and a law firm is considered a professional activity, disputes that arise out of a service contract between a law firm and a client may be considered commercial in other jurisdictions.

Case Illustrations

In *M/S Comed Chemicals Ltd v C.N. Ramchand*,[73] the Supreme Court of India addressed the issue of whether a contract concluded between a company and its director was a commercial contract. The court deemed that a director of a company has a dual capacity: first as an employee of the company and second as a director of the company. The court opined that in the case at hand, the director was performing supervisory functions relating to policymaking decisions in the affairs of the company and was looking after all operational matters.[74] For these reasons, the court deemed that the dispute between the company and its director was commercial in nature and covered by the provisions of the Arbitration and Conciliation Act, 1996.

In *Spentex Industries Ltd v Quinn Emanuel Urquhart & Sullivan*,[75] the High Court of Delhi deemed that the relationship between an Indian client and a foreign law firm was commercial in nature and covered by the provisions of the Arbitration and Conciliation Act, 1996. The court stated that the term 'commercial' should be interpreted liberally in accordance with its grammatical and literal meaning.[76]

72. *Id.*, at 66.
73. *M/S Comed Chemicals Ltd v C.N.Ramchand* AIR 2009 SC 494 (judgment from the Supreme Court of India, delivered on 6 November 2008). Similarly, in Georgia, according to Art. 45(1) of the Law on Entrepreneurs, a contract between directors/supervisory members and a company is considered as a service contract and is not subject to employment regulations.
74. *Id.*, para. 32.
75. *Spentex Industries Ltd v Quinn Emanuel Urquhart & Sullivan*, the High Court of Delhi at New Delhi, 12 May 2020.
76. *Id.*, para. 34.

The court relied on the definition of the term 'commerce' provided in the Collins Concise Dictionary and opined that 'clearly transactions relating to services for valuable consideration would be a commercial legal relationship'.[77] The case at hand was not related to professional issues. Rather, the proceedings were initiated to recover an outstanding sum of money, which was a commercial matter.[78]

1.21 An interesting illustration to consider in relation to Article 1(2) is whether iMSAs derived from sports-related mediation may be considered commercial in nature and, as a result, be enforced under the provisions of the Singapore Convention on Mediation. Sports-related disputes may bring about various issues, including commercial disputes such as sponsorship-related disputes, contractual disputes between athletes and clubs, and disciplinary disputes. Such disputes are commonly resolved under the Rules of the Court of Arbitration for Sport (CAS). The CAS also provides the mediation rules for the resolution of contractual disputes and, in certain circumstances, for the resolution of disciplinary disputes as well.[79] The relationship between athlete and club is normally recognised as an employment relationship, and it is unlikely that an iMSA derived from such a mediation will be enforceable under the Singapore Convention on Mediation. Similarly, an iMSA that resolves a disciplinary dispute between an athlete and a club or an organisation is highly unlikely to be considered commercial in nature. The case below is illustrative in this regard.

Case Illustration

In the Australian case of *ASADA v 34 Players and One Support Person*,[80] the court had to determine whether a dispute that involved an alleged violation of doping rules by 34 current and former players and one former support person at the Essendon Football Club was commercial in nature and consequently, covered by the provisions of Commercial Arbitration Act 2011. The court noted that even though the definition of the term 'commercial' was very broad under the Model Law on Arbitration, the term was not boundless. According to the court, this term does not encompass labour or consumer-related relationships. The court stated that a professional athlete enjoys rights analogous to those of employees. The court emphasised that the involvement of a professional athlete in a competition is under 'a contract of service' and not 'contract for service'. Consequently, the

77. *Id.*, para. 36.
78. *Id.*, para. 38.
79. Art. 1 of the CAS Mediation Rules.
80. *Chief Executive Officer of Australian Sports Anti-Doping Authority Australian Football League (ASADA) v 34 Players and One Support Person* [2014] VSC 635.

court deemed that the dispute was not commercial in nature and did not fall within the scope of Commercial Arbitration Act 2011.[81]

'[C]ommercial' and Investor-State Disputes

1.22 The term 'commercial' may include investor-State disputes if the nature of such disputes is commercial itself.[82]

1.23 The Singapore Convention on Mediation generally applies to commercial iMSAs to which States are a party. This issue was raised and discussed during the negotiations at Working Group II. It was noted that government entities are normally involved in commercial activities and might be willing to use mediation and conciliation for the resolution of commercial disputes.[83] The exclusion of iMSAs that States and government entities are a party to would deprive them of the opportunity to enforce such iMSAs under the new enforcement regime of the Singapore Convention on Mediation against their commercial partners. However, Contracting Parties to the Singapore Convention have the right to make a reservation under Article 8 and exclude iMSAs to which Contracting Parties are a party, or to which any governmental agencies or any person acting on behalf of a governmental agency is a party.[84]

1.24 The term 'commercial' used in UNCITRAL instruments includes investor-State disputes. Footnote 1 of the Model Law on Mediation, which provides an illustrative list of matters that are considered commercial, suggests that the term 'commercial' includes investment. The same illustrative list of commercial relationships is provided in the Model Law on Arbitration. During the negotiations at Working Group II, a suggestion was made that the commercial nature of iMSAs be determined on the basis of the parties involved, the subject matter of the dispute being resolved and the obligations to be performed under the iMSA.[85] It was suggested that while the nature of obligations in an iMSA might be commercial in nature, the parties involved and the dispute itself might have arisen from a non-commercial relationship.[86] Further, an investor-State dispute can be considered commercial in nature even if the dispute itself involves a regulatory relationship. Schnabel suggests that the scope of the Convention should cover at least some investor-State disputes in the field of natural resource

81. *Id.*, paras 52-56.
82. Nadja Alexander and Shouyu Chong, *The Singapore Convention on Mediation: Origins and Application to Investor-State Disputes*, in Mahdev Mohan and Chester Brown (eds), The Asian Turn in Foreign Investment, Cambridge University Press (2021), at 340-360; and see Romesh Weeramantry et al., *Conciliation and Mediation in Investor-State Dispute Settlement Provisions: A Quantitative and Qualitative Analysis*, 37 ICSID Review (2022), at s. III.
83. Report of Working Group II (Arbitration and Conciliation) on the work of its 63rd Session (Vienna, 7-11 September 2015), A/CN.9/861, para. 46.
84. For more on the reservations, see the commentary to Art. 8.
85. United Nations Commission on International Trade Law Working Group II (Arbitration and Conciliation) 64th Session New York, 1-5 February 2016, A/CN.9/WG.II/WP.195, para. 14.
86. *Ibid.*

extraction and construction.[87] Finally, had the drafters of the Convention intended to exclude investor-State disputes from the scope of the application of the Convention, they would have expressly prescribed that in the exclusions under Article 1(2) of the Convention.

Case Illustrations

Illustration [A]: In *The United Mexican States v Metalclad Corporation,*[88] the Supreme Court of British Columbia addressed the issue of whether an award rendered under the North American Free Trade Agreement was commercial for the purposes of the International Commercial Arbitration Act that is based on the Model Law on Arbitration. In response to the objection put forward by Mexico that the relationship between Mexico and Metalclad was a regulatory relationship instead of a commercial relationship, the court stated that '[i]t is true that the dispute between Metalclad and the Municipality arose because the Municipality was purporting to exercise a regulatory function. However, the primary relationship between Metalclad and Mexico was one of investing and the exercise of a regulatory function by the Municipality was incidental to that primary relationship. The arbitration did not arise under an agreement between Metalclad and the Municipality in connection with regulatory matters. Rather, the arbitration was between Metalclad and Mexico pursuant to an agreement dealing with the treatment of investors'.[89] Eventually, the court deemed that the award was commercial in nature, and consequently, the International Arbitration Act was applicable to the proceedings.

Illustration [B]: In *Anatolie Stati, Gabriel Stati, Ascom Group SA and Terra Raf Trans Traiding Ltd v Republic of Kazakhstan,*[90] the US District Court for the District of Columbia addressed whether an award rendered under the Energy Charter Treaty was commercial in nature for the purposes of the New York Convention. The US made a reservation under Article I(3) of the New York Convention, according to which, a Contracting Party may apply the New York Convention only to the awards that are considered commercial according to its national law. The court, in this case, stated that the term 'commercial' generally refers to 'matters or relationships, whether commercial or not, that arise out of or

87. Timothy Schnabel, *The Singapore Convention on Mediation: A Framework for the Cross-Border Recognition and Enforcement of Mediated Settlements*, 19(1) Pepp. Disp. Resol. L.J. 1 (2019), at 22-23. For the application of the Singapore Convention on cross-border construction disputes, see Shouyu Chong, *The Singapore Convention on Mediation: Its Impact on International Construction Disputes*, in Renato Nazzini (ed.), Construction Arbitration and Alternative Dispute Resolution – Theory and Practice Around the World, Informa Law (2021), at 29-49.
88. *The United Mexican States v Metalclad Corporation* [2001] BCSC 664.
89. *Id.*, para. 46.
90. *Stati v Republic of Kaz.*, 2016 U.S. Dist. LEXIS 103357, *1, 199 F. Supp. 3d 179, 181 (D.D.C. 5 August 2016).

in connection with commerce'.[91] The court deemed the award commercial and opined that '[i]n the transactions underlying this case, respondent Kazakhstan granted and revoked petitioners' rights to develop oil and gas fields within its borders, so the relationship between the parties clearly "arise[s] out of or in connection with commerce"'.[92]

Illustration [C]: In another American case of *Belize Soc. Dev. Ltd. v Government of Belize,*[93] the Court of Appeals for the District of Columbia opined that an award derived from a dispute relating to an accommodation agreement, by which Belize Telemedia Limited obtained various tax reliefs, was commercial in nature for the purposes of the New York Convention. The court stated that a 'government is a party to a transaction does not destroy its commercial character; indeed, the fact that an agreement to arbitrate is in the contract between a government and a private person may confirm its commercial character. A matter or relationship may be commercial even though it does not arise out of or relate to a contract, so long as it has a connection with commerce, whether or not that commerce has a nexus with the United States'.[94]

Point of Interest

In the context of investor-State arbitration, certain multilateral treaties expressly provide that awards rendered under these treaties should be considered commercial for the purposes of enforcement under the New York Convention. By way of example, Article 26(5)(b) of the Energy Charter Treaty provides that claims submitted to arbitration under this treaty shall be considered to arise out of a commercial relationship for the purposes of Article I of the New York Convention. A similar wording is provided under Article 1136(7) of the North American Free Trade Agreement. Article I(3) of the New York Convention allows the Contracting States to make a commercial reservation according to which only those awards will be subject to the New York Convention that are considered commercial according to the domestic law of the enforcing State. If awards derived from the Energy Charter Treaty and the North American Free Trade Agreement are considered to arise out of a commercial transaction, the same proposition should be true in the case of iMSAs derived from the same treaties for the purposes of enforcement under the Singapore Convention on Mediation.

91. *Ibid.*
92. *Id.*, at 16.
93. *Belize Soc. Dev., Ltd. v Gov't of Belize,* 2015 U.S. App. LEXIS 12531, 794 F.3d 99, 417 U.S. App. D.C. 257 (D.C. Cir. 21 July 2015).
94. *Id.*, at 11.

The use of mediation for the resolution of investor-State disputes is slowly but surely on the rise. The Singapore International Dispute Resolution Academy (SIDRA) International Dispute Resolution Survey: 2020 Final Report reveals that between the years 2016-2018, 14 per cent of user respondents used ad hoc mediation and 7 per cent of the respondents opted for institutional mediation for the resolution of investor-State disputes.[95] In response to the demand to provide dispute resolution processes that offer an alternative to international arbitration, a number of international organisations and institutions have developed mediation rules for the resolution of investor-State disputes. On 21 March 2022, the Member States of the International Centre for Settlement of Investment Disputes (ICSID) approved mediation rules for the resolution of Investor-State disputes. The new mediation rules have come into force on 1 July 2022.[96] In 2016, the Energy Charter Secretariat adopted the Guide on Investment Mediation, the idea of which is to provide an explanatory document to assist governments and companies to make decisions on whether to engage in mediation for the resolution of disputes that arise out of the Energy Charter Treaty.[97] In 2012, the International Bar Association adopted the Rules for Investor State Mediation.[98]

Bilateral and multilateral investment treaties increasingly provide for mediation and conciliation provisions for the resolution of investor-State disputes. By way of illustration, Article 8(3) of the Hong Kong-United Arab Emirates investment protection agreement provides for mandatory conciliation for the resolution of investor-State disputes.[99] Similarly, Article 14.23(1) of the Indonesia-Australia Comprehensive and Economic Partnership Agreement contains mandatory conciliation for the resolution of investor-State disputes.[100] The EU's investment

95. Nadja Alexander, Vakhtang Giorgadze and Allison Goh, Singapore International Dispute Resolution Academy International Dispute Resolution Survey: 2020 Final Report, at 16. Available at https://sidra.smu.edu.sg/sites/sidra.smu.edu.sg/files/survey/index.html (Accessed 21 February 2022).
96. News Release, ICSID Administrative Council Approves Amendment of ICSID Rules. 21 March 2022. Available at https://icsid.worldbank.org/news-and-events/communiques/icsid-administrative-council-approves-amendment-icsid-rules (Accessed 17 May 2022).
97. Available at https://www.energycharter.org/fileadmin/DocumentsMedia/CCDECS/2016/CCDEC201612.pdf (Accessed 21 February 2022).
98. Available at https://www.ibanet.org/Document/Default.aspx?DocumentUid=8120ED11-F3C8-4A66-BE81-77CB3FDB9E9F (Accessed 21 February 2022).
99. According to this provision, when required by the Contracting Party, if the dispute cannot be settled amicably within six months from the date of receipt of the written notice, it shall be submitted to the competent authorities of that Contracting Party or arbitration centres thereof, for conciliation.
100. Conciliation is mandatory for the investor. According to this provision, if the dispute cannot be resolved within 180 days from the date of receipt by the disputing Party of the written request for consultations, the disputing Party may initiate a conciliation process, which shall be mandatory for the disputing investor, with a view towards reaching an amicable settlement. Such a conciliation process shall be initiated by a written request delivered by the disputing Party to the disputing investor. According to this treaty, 'disputing Party' with a

protection agreements with Singapore and Vietnam contain a detailed procedure for the use of mediation in the resolution of investor-State disputes. Further, Article 30 of the ASEAN Comprehensive Investment Agreement 2012 states that the disputing parties may at any time agree to resort to conciliation, including during an arbitration procedure. In other words, this treaty expressly provides the disputing parties with an opportunity to resort to a hybrid dispute resolution process either in the form of *arb-med, med-arb* or a simultaneous *arb-med.*[101]

'parties to the settlement agreement'

1.25 The term 'parties to the settlement agreement' first appears in Articles 1(1)(a) and 1(1)(b). The terms 'party' and 'parties' (with a small 'p')[102] also appear in Article 4(1) in the context of a 'party relying on' an iMSA to seek relief and an iMSA 'signed by the parties'.

1.26 On a plain reading of Articles 1(1)(a) and 1(1)(b), the reference made to 'parties to the settlement agreement' may refer to the disputants (including co-disputants) that have agreed to resolve their disagreements at the mediation table through an iMSA. However, depending on the governing law of the iMSA,[103] it may be possible to understand and interpret the reference to 'parties to the settlement agreement' expansively, in the context of complex cross-border commercial transactions, to embrace entities (or persons) that may have derivative interests in such transactions, for instance, by means of a trust.

Case Illustration

Sarah Pte Ltd (Sarah) is a real estate investment trust (REIT) created to hold and manage land titles on trust for *Jessica Pte Ltd's* (Jessica) benefit. Both Sarah and Jessica are incorporated in Rustica. *Parker Sdn Bhd* (Parker) is a company that specialises in demolition works and is incorporated in Mediterra. In one of Parker's demolition projects, their workers had negligently rigged explosives to a building scheduled for demolition, causing it to collapse onto one of Sarah's properties located in Rustica, resulting in serious damage. Sarah and Parker

capital 'P' means a Party against which a claim is made and 'disputing party' with a small 'p' means a disputing investor or a disputing Party.

101. For more information on mixed mode dispute resolution processes, see paras 1.49-1.53 below.

102. The term 'party' with a small 'p' is to be distinguished from 'Party' with a capital 'P' (Party to the Convention), which is discussed in the commentary to Art. 3.

103. For instance, if Singapore law governs the agreement, it may be possible for third parties to an iMSA to rely on it and seek its recognition and enforcement, applying the Contract (Rights of Third Parties) Act (Cap 53B, 2002 Rev Ed) (namely, s. 2 of the Act). The relevant conditions under the Act need to be satisfied: see *VKC v VJZ* [2021] 2 SLR 753.

agree to proceed to mediation in a neutral jurisdiction, Singland. The mediation, which takes place at the Singland International Mediation Centre results in a settlement. Sarah and Parker agreed to endorse the terms that are recorded in an iMSA, under which Parker has agreed to pay a sum of money to Sarah in instalments. In the context of the Singapore Convention, could Jessica be considered a party to the iMSA for the purposes of seeking enforcement of the iMSA signed by Sarah and Parker?

Point of Interest

Referring to the case illustration above, it is arguable from a private law perspective that Jessica may be considered a party to the iMSA, on the supposition that the iMSA had been concluded as part of Sarah's trust duties (that is, which involves the handling of trust assets) in its capacity of trustee in favour of the former's benefit.

Such an interpretation should be considered in light of the phrasing of Article 4(1) of the Singapore Convention, which establishes the mandatory form requirements in order for relief to be granted *vis-à-vis* the iMSA under the Singapore Convention. For relief to be granted, parties have to produce the following as evidence to the competent court: (1) the iMSA *signed by the parties*;[104] and (2) proof[105] that the iMSA resulted from mediation.[106]

Whether Jessica may be considered a party to the iMSA will hinge on how Article 4(1)(a) of the Singapore Convention is interpreted. Normally under a trust arrangement, it is unlikely that the beneficiary (that is, Jessica) would be involved in the mediation, let alone in the endorsement of the resulting iMSA concluded between the tortfeasor (that is, Parker) and the trustee (that is, Sarah). Approaches to this question are likely to vary across jurisdictions, and must turn on the governing law of the iMSA. A traditional common law approach would permit a beneficiary to bring enforcement proceedings on an iMSA, but only in circumstances where the trustee cannot or will not.[107] Further, in such

104. United Nations Convention on International Settlement Agreements Resulting from Mediation, Art. 4(1)(a).
105. *Id.*, Art. 4(1)(b).
106. The specific requirements pursuant to Art. 4(1) are examined in the commentary to Art. 4.
107. See the '*Vandepitte* procedure': *Vandepitte v Preferred Accident Insurance Corp of New York* [1933] AC 70; Tham succinctly explains: '[I]f A refused to bring the action at law against B on C's request, C may sue in equity to compel A to do so, joining such suit inequity against A to A's common law action against B.': Chee Ho Tham, *Joinder of Equitable Assignors of Equitable and Legal Choses in Action*, 4 LMCLQ 537 [2017], at 538. The '*Vandepitte* procedure' is accepted in many jurisdictions, including in England – see *Harmer v Armstrong and Others;*

circumstances, the beneficiary would typically join the trustee as a co-defendant.[108] The Australian case of *Global Partners Fund v Babcock & Brown*[109] offers a different approach. The case provides precedence that a third party to a contract (Party C) may hold a party (Party A) bound, if it may prove that the other party to the contract (Party B) is a trustee of that promise for itself (that is, Party C).[110] This may be shown if Party C establishes that its claims against Party A are so closely related or even identical to Party B's, providing Party C with the ability to sue Party A *in their own right*.[111] In this illustration, it seems that the required nexus would certainly be established between Sarah and Jessica because of their clearly constituted trustee-beneficiary relationship. Such an inclusive approach to interpreting the word 'parties' *per* Articles 1 and 4 would seem to align with the overarching aim of the Singapore Convention to encourage the use of mediation for a range of commercial disputes, including complex trust matters, such as the illustration highlighted here. Furthermore, such an interpretation of the term 'parties' would likely embrace rights under an iMSA which have been assigned to third-party assignees. It remains to be seen which approach the competent courts of States and other Parties to the Singapore Convention will adopt.

An iMSA for the Benefit of a Third Party

Depending on its governing law,[112] an iMSA may encompass terms that confer benefits on a non-signatory. Complex commercial arrangements between parties might have an impact not only on the parties present at the mediation table but also on different commercial entities or individuals behind the curtains. An iMSA may expressly state that a party to an iMSA has to transfer a certain amount of money to a person(s) that is not a signatory to the iMSA. While parties to an iMSA cannot impose obligations on non-signatories, they may have the right to give

Same v Same (Cross-Appeal) [1933] All ER Rep 778; in Singapore – see *Motor Insurers' Bureau of Singapore and another v AM General Insurance Bhd* [2018] SGHC 39; in India – *Indian Mutual General Insurance Society Limited Madras v Himalaya Finance and Construction Company Daryaganj Delhi Lnind* 1973 DEL 25, *Snow White Food Product Pvt Ltd v Sohanlal Bagla and Ors*. AIR 1964 Cal 209; in Hong Kong – *Wong Yu-Shi (No 1) v Wong Ying Kuen* [1957] HKCU 38; in Australia – *Lidden and another v Composite Buyers and Others* (1996) 139 ALR 549, *Pearson (as a beneficiary of the Jancy Trust) v CMR of Taxation* (2001) 116 FCR 357; in Canada – *Fraser River Pile & Dredge Ltd v Can-Dive Services Ltd* [1999] 3 S.C.R. 108, 176 D.L.R. (4th) 257.

108. See *Harmer v Armstrong* [1934] Ch 65 (CA), at 84; *Barbados Trust Co Ltd v Bank of Zambia* [2007] 1 Lloyd's Rep 495, at para. 45.
109. *Global Partners Fund Ltd v Babcock & Brown Ltd (in liq)* [2010] NSWA 196.
110. Cf. Adeline Chong, *The 'Party Scope' of Exclusive Jurisdiction Clauses: Global Partners Fund v Babcock & Brown*, 4 LMCLQ 470 (2011), at 474-475.
111. *Global Partners Fund Ltd v Babcock & Brown Ltd (in liq)* [2010] NSWA 196, at para. 73.
112. The determination of the governing law is usually left to the competent authorities, and it may be in and of itself the subject of vigorous litigation: see *Kabab-Ji SAL (Lebanon) v Kout Food Group (Kuwait)* [2021] UKSC 48, [2022] 1 Lloyd's Rep 24, as an illustration of how the issue of

benefits to a third non-signatory party provided that the applicable substantive law allows it. By way of illustration, a seller and a shipping company might sign an iMSA, according to which the shipping company will be obliged to deliver the goods agreed in the iMSA to a non-signatory. Will the non-signatory have the right to enforce the iMSA? In this case, if the applicable substantive law allows such a possibility, the non-signatory may be able to enforce the iMSA.

Some jurisdictions provide a third non-signatory party with the possibility to enforce a contract if the contract confers benefits on this non-signatory. By way of illustration, section 328(1) of the German Civil Code (BGB) provides that performance to a third party may be agreed by contract with the effect that the third party acquires the right to demand the performance directly. Even if a contract does not expressly provide the right of performance to the third party, section 328(2) states that in the absence of a specific provision, it may be inferred from the circumstances, in particular from the purpose of the contract, whether the third party is to acquire the right, whether the right of the third party is to come into existence immediately or only under certain conditions, and whether the power is to be reserved for the parties to the contract to terminate or alter the right of the third party without his approval. Article 6:110(1) of the Principles of European Contract Law states that a third party may require performance of a contractual obligation when its right to do so has been expressly agreed upon between the promisor and the promisee, or when such agreement is to be inferred from the purpose of the contract or the circumstances of the case. Importantly, the same article specifies that the third party need not be identified at the time the agreement is concluded. The same right is provided in Article 5.2.1 of the UNIDROIT Principles on International Commercial Contract, which puts an emphasis on the autonomy of parties to a contract to determine the scope of a third party's rights. Article 349 of the Civil Code of Georgia also allows beneficiary third parties to enforce a contract. In the judgment dated 13 January 2015, No. 2b/5180-14, the Tbilisi Appellate Court opined that while a contract can only give rights and obligations to the parties, the parties are free to confer benefits on a third party. In this case, the non-signatory will be entitled to enforce the contract, provided that the contract does not specify otherwise. For the court, if a contract gives benefits to a third party, it is assumed that this third party can enforce the contract if the contract does not specify otherwise.[113]

Even though common law traditionally does not allow the enforcement of a contract by a non-signatory, there are some exceptions to this approach.[114] In

whether a third party may be bound by an arbitral agreement turned on the contention of whether English law was the applicable law.

113. The judgment dated 13 January 2015, No. 2b/5180-14, the Tbilisi Appellate Court. The case is available on http://www.tbappeal.court.ge/.

114. According to the doctrine of privity, a contract can only confer rights and impose obligations on parties and a third party cannot enforce a contract. See *Tweddle v Atkinson* (1861) 25 JP 517 for

England, section 1 of the Contracts (Rights of Third Parties) Act 1999 (UK) sets out the circumstances when a non-signatory can enforce a term of a contract: first, when the contract expressly provides that a non-signatory may do so and second, the term purports to confer a benefit on the non-signatory. Singapore follows the same approach, where section 2(1) of the Contracts (Rights of Third Parties) Act provides the same possibility to a third non-signatory party. In the US, the Supreme Court of Illinois in *Olson v Etheridge* opined that 'if a contract is entered into for the direct benefit of a third person, the third person may sue for a breach of the contract in his or her own name, even though the third person is a stranger to the contract and the consideration'.[115] The court emphasised that this principle is widely accepted in the US.[116]

Exclusions to Scope of Application of the Convention

1.27 The Convention aims to fill a gap in the cross-border enforcement of iMSAs. To this end, it features two sets of exclusions.

1.28 It was discussed earlier that Article 1(2) excludes certain types of disputes. Article 1(2)(a) excludes disputes arising from transactions entered into by consumers 'for personal, family or household purposes'. Article 1(2)(b) excludes disputes in relation to 'family, inheritance or employment law'. These exclusions pre-empt concerns about

the English law approach, which is also the position taken by the contract law of many Commonwealth countries adopting the common law. There are a number of exceptions to the common law doctrine of privity, and they will vary in different jurisdictions. Two notable exceptions which appear in the contract law of India include circumstances when a family arrangement confers benefits on a third party who can enforce the contract, as discussed in *Lakshmiammal v Sundararaja Aiyangar and another* (1915) ILR 38 Mad 788; and when a beneficiary third party is treated as privy to a contract by the conduct of parties, as discussed in *Smt. Narayani Devi v Tagore Commercial Corporation Ltd* AIR 1973 Cal 401. In the English common law, one notable instance where the rule of privity does not apply is when an agency relationship exists (see Edwin Peel, Tritel: The Law of Contract (15th Ed.), Sweet & Maxwell (2020), at [14-087]). In Australia, an exception to the doctrine of privity was confirmed in *Trident General Insurance Co Ltd v McNiece Bros Pty Ltd* (1988) 165 CLR 107, where the court allowed a contractor to sue for indemnity against an insurer based on the insurance policy between the insurer and the assured. Even though the contractor was a third party to the insurance policy, the court allowed the suit and stated: 'the injustice which would flow from the application of the old rules to an insurance policy arose not only from its failure to give effect to the expressed intention of the person who took out the insurance but also from the common intention of the parties and the circumstances that others, aware of the existence of the policy, would order their affairs accordingly. [...] In the nature of things the likelihood of some degree of reliance on the part of the third party in the case of a benefit to be provided for him under an insurance policy was so tangible that the common law rules should be shaped with that likelihood in mind'.

115. *Olson v Etheridge*, 177 Ill. 2d 396, 404, 686 N.E.2d 563, 566, 1997 Ill. LEXIS 438, *10, 226 Ill. Dec. 780, 783 (Ill. 25 September 1997).

116. *Ibid.*

potential power imbalances and the need to put protections in place for vulnerable parties in certain situations. They are consistent with UNCITRAL's mandate to focus on commercial matters, which are more likely to be at arm's length and not invoke public policy considerations. Furthermore, family law disputes and iMSAs are already addressed by the Hague Conference on Private International Law.[117]

1.29 The next set of exclusions examined here relate to iMSAs that are enforceable as judgments or awards. Article 1(3) provides that the Convention does not apply to iMSAs that:[118]

(1) have been approved by a court or have been concluded in the course of court proceedings, *and* are enforceable as a judgment in the State of that court; or
(2) have been recorded and are enforceable as an arbitral award.

1.30 The carve-out provisions deconflict the administration of the Singapore Convention from that of other international instruments,[119] such as the New York Convention and the HCCCA, which contain mechanisms that specifically govern the enforcement of those forms of iMSAs that fall within Article 1(3).[120]

1.31 In this regard, the Singapore Convention intends to operate as a 'gap-filler' when other treaty frameworks do not apply.[121] Next, the two exclusions in Article 1(3) will be examined in detail.

117. Hague Conference on Private International Law, *Family Agreements Involving Children*, https://www.hcch.net/en/projects/legislative-projects/recognition-and-enforcement-of-agreements (Accessed 9 November 2018).
118. Art. 1(3) of the Singapore Convention.
119. See, for example, intervention of the European Union, in UNCITRAL Audio Recordings: Working Group II (Arbitration and Conciliation), 64th Session, 2 February 2016, 15:00-18:00; intervention of the European Union, in UNCITRAL Audio Recordings: Working Group II (Dispute Settlement), 66th Session, 8 February 2017, 10:00-13:00; Also see Timothy Schnabel, *The Singapore Convention on Mediation: A Framework for the Cross-Border Recognition and Enforcement of Mediated Settlements*, 19 Pepp. Disp. Resol. L.J. 1 (2019), at 25.
120. Consider, for instance, Art. 12 of the HCCCA. Additionally, it should be noted that the applicability of the Singapore Convention must also be de-conflicted with the Convention of 2 July 2019 on the Recognition and Enforcement of Foreign Judgments in Civil or Commercial Matters (the Hague Judgments Convention), which was concluded on 2 July 2019 but has not come into force at the time of writing (see Francisco J. Garcimartín Alférez and Geneviève Saumier, *Fourth Meeting of the Special Commission on the Recognition and Enforcement of Foreign Judgments 24-29 May 2018, Judgments Convention: Revised Preliminary Explanatory Report* (May 2018)).
121. Schnabel observes that not permitting an overlap between Conventions may result in some iMSAs not being covered by any convention at all, owing to the fact that not all states will be Parties to the Hague Convention on Choice of Court Agreements, the New York Convention, and the Singapore Convention. Nevertheless, Schnabel concludes that 'this exclusion in the Convention was worthwhile because it will be relevant only in marginal cases, and it enabled a compromise on much more significant issues': Timothy Schnabel, *The Singapore Convention on Mediation: A Framework for the Cross-Border Recognition and Enforcement of Mediated Settlements*, 19 Pepp. Disp. Resol. L.J. 1 (2019), at 25.

iMSAs Enforceable as Court Judgments or Orders

1.32 This exclusion contained in Article 1(3)(a) has two parts:

(1) the iMSA has been approved by a court or alternatively has been concluded in the course of court proceedings, *and*
(2) the iMSA is enforceable as a judgment in the State of that court.

1.33 The exclusion extends to a range of situations in which iMSAs are enforceable as court judgments or orders, for example, by operation of the HCCCA, the Hague Judgments Convention[122] and similar instruments.[123] For the purposes of Article 1(3)(a) of the Convention, the relevant jurisdiction is the State of origin; that is, the State where the iMSA has been approved by a court or concluded in court proceedings as described in Article 1(3)(a)(i) *and* is enforceable (Article 1(3)(a)(ii)). It is possible that a court may approve and, therefore, recognise an iMSA as a judgment, but that it may not be *enforceable* as a judgment or no longer be enforceable; for example, in the

122. For more information on the Convention of 2 July 2019 on the Recognition and Enforcement of Foreign Judgments in Civil or Commercial Matters, see Francisco J Garcimartín Alférez and Geneviève Saumier, *Fourth Meeting of the Special Commission on the Recognition and Enforcement of Foreign Judgments 24-29 May 2018, Judgments Convention: Revised Preliminary Explanatory Report* (May 2018).

123. The HCCCA establishes rules for the enforcement of choice of court (CoC) agreements in international commercial transactions and certain international civil matters. Under the HCCCA, Contracting States may declare that their respective courts will recognise and enforce judgments given by courts of other Contracting States designated in a non-exclusive CoC agreement (Art. 22). Judicial settlements resulting from such agreements approved by the court of a Contracting State shall be enforced under the Convention in the same manner as judgments (Art. 12). The same regime is provided under Art. 11 of the Hague Judgments Convention, which enforces judicial settlements as judgments.

Within the EU, settlements sanctioned by courts in the form of court orders fall within Art. (1)(3)(a). According to Art. 6 of the 2008 EU Mediation Directive, where express consent is provided, a mediated settlement agreement may be made enforceable by a court or other competent authority in the form of a judgment if such enforcement were sought within the jurisdiction between Member States, and the relevant terms of the Directive are complied with (Directive 2008/52/EC of the European Parliament and of the Council of 21 May 2008 on certain aspects of mediation in civil and commercial matters. Available at https://eur-lex.europa.eu/legal-content/EN/TXT/?uri=CELEX%3A32008L0052 (Accessed 8 November 2018). Chapter IV of the EU Regulation (EU) No. 1215/2012 of the European Parliament and of The Council of 12 December 2012 (Brussels I Recast Regulation) is entitled *Authentic Instruments and Court Settlements* and provides that mediated settlements sanctioned by the court in the original country may be recognised as 'authentic foreign instruments' throughout the European Union (Regulation (EU) No. 1215/2012 of the European Parliament and of the Council of 12 December 2012 on jurisdiction and the recognition and enforcement of judgments in civil and commercial matters. Available at https://eur-lex.europa.eu/legal-content/EN/ALL/?uri=celex%3A32012R1215 (Accessed 17 May 2018), Arts 58 et seq.). In addition, the European Regulation on Enforcement Order for uncontested claims would seem to include mediated settlements of disputes which have not been the subject of litigation (Arts 3(1)(a) and (d), 24 and 25 of Regulation EC No. 805/2004 of the European Parliament and of the Council of 21.04.2004 creating a European Enforcement Order for uncontested claims).

case where a limitation period for enforcement has passed.[124] To the extent that both of these conjunctive requirements in Article 1(3)(a) are not fulfilled, the iMSA may still be capable of falling within the scope of the Singapore Convention.

1.34 In relation to the first part of the exclusion in Article 1(3)(a)(i), it envisages a situation where courts have already approved an iMSA. For example, where courts have referred a case to mediation with an external (non-court) mediator, and after a settlement has been reached, the parties may submit the iMSA back to the court for approval and that approval is granted. If approval is not granted, the Singapore Convention may be applied to recognise and enforce the iMSA, if it does not otherwise fall within the other exclusions.

1.35 Across jurisdictions, there may be a wide variety of domestic laws available to record mediated settlements in court. In France, for example, parties may apply to a court for a ruling that mediated settlements by compromise (*transaction*) – as defined in Article 2044 of the Civil Code – are immediately enforceable.[125] In England, litigating parties reaching a mediated settlement may apply for a Tomlin Order,[126] which provides expedited court enforcement of the terms of settlement as if embodied in a judgment.[127] In another illustration of a court-approved iMSA, section 12 of the Singapore Mediation Act 2017[128] provides that an iMSA procured privately[129] between parties may be recorded by the Singapore Courts in accordance with the procedures laid out in sections 12(1) to 12(4).[130] Where the iMSA is recorded in compliance with the Act, it would appear to fall within the terms of Article 1(3)(a)(i).

---

124. Timothy Schnabel, *The Singapore Convention on Mediation: A Framework for the Cross-Border Recognition and Enforcement of Mediated Settlements*, 19(1) Pepp. Disp. Resol. L.J. 1 (2019), at 26.
125. See Art. 1441-4 of the New Code of Civil Procedure, Decree No. 98-1231 of 28 December 1998.
126. See *Dashwood v Dashwood* [1927] WN 276; (1926) 64 LJNC 431.
127. For a Tomlin Order precedent, see the CEDR model mediation settlement, www.cedr.co.uk/library/documents/settlement_agreement.pdf (Accessed 22 May 2019).
128. Mediation Act 2017 (No. 1 of 2017). Specifically, s. 12(5) provides, 'A mediated settlement that is recorded under this section as an order of court may be enforced in the same manner as a judgment given or an order made by a court.'
129. Dorcas Quek Anderson, *Comment – A Coming of Age for Mediation in Singapore? Mediation Act 2016*, 29 SAcLJ 275 (2017), at para. 5.
130. The Mediation Act applies to iMSAs procured from any mediation wholly or partly conducted in Singapore, or if the terms of reference for the mediation stipulate that Singapore law or the Singapore Mediation Act 2017 shall be administered: s 6 of the Mediation Act 2017 (No. 1 of 2017). At the time of writing, the expedited enforcement mechanism under the Singapore Mediation Act is available only to mediations administered by the Singapore International Mediation Centre and Singapore Mediation Centre, or conducted by a mediator accredited by the Singapore International Mediation Institute (SIMI); see also s. 12(3)(a) of the Mediation Act 2017 (No. 1 of 2017), read with s. 7; see also Ministry of Law, *Responses to Feedback Received From Public Consultation on the Draft Mediation Bill*, https://www.mlaw.gov.sg/news/public-consultations/responses-to-feedback-received-from-public-consultation-on-the-d/ (Accessed 11 March 2022), at 8. Also see Dorcas Quek Anderson, *Comment – A Coming of Age for Mediation in Singapore? Mediation Act 2016*, 29 SAcLJ 275 (2017), who summarises at para. 34:
    These other conditions also have to be fulfilled:
    (a) all the parties to the agreement (excluding the mediator) must consent to making the application: s 12(1);

1.36 In some jurisdictions, it is a requirement that all parties to a mediated settlement apply to the court to ratify the settlement.[131] This leaves open a potential risk that one party may unilaterally refuse to do so. Where this occurs, the party seeking to enforce the settlement may still do so by suing for breach of the contractual settlement. Here, the contract will not be subject to expedited enforcement as it would have been if sanctioned by the court. In *Environmental Abatement Inc v Astrum,*[132] the judge refused to enter a consent decree on the grounds that one party had withdrawn consent prior to the order, and the agreement was neither in written form nor had it been presented in open court. Coben and Thompson suggest that, although in this case the consent decree was refused, the agreement may still be enforceable as a contract.[133] In this type of situation, it is conceivable that an iMSA might not be excluded from the application of the Singapore Convention, provided that it satisfies the formal requirements, such as the in-writing requirement.

1.37 Courts may have powers of review in relation to approving iMSAs, though these vary according to jurisdiction; and, in commercial matters, they are generally restricted to a few areas. For example, in France, if all the parties to a pre-litigation (non-contentious) mediated settlement agree, the court may review and confirm the agreement.[134] Here, the review of the mediated settlement is typically limited to factors such as the *bona fides* of the agreement, the informed consent of the parties, clarity in relation to the interpretation of the agreement, the ability of the agreement to be performed, the legality of the terms of the agreement, and whether it injures third party rights.[135]

1.38 Note that granting a request for relief from a court or other competent authority pursuant to the Convention does not equate to 'approval' in the sense of Article

(b) the mediated settlement agreement must be in writing and signed by all the parties to the agreement: s 12(3)(*b*); and

(c) the application must be made within eight weeks after arriving at the settlement agreement. Any other longer duration has to be approved by the court: s 12(2).

131. By way of example, Art. 6(1) of the 2008 EU Mediation Directive states that Member States shall ensure that it is possible for the parties, or for one of them with the explicit consent of the others, to request that the content of a written agreement resulting from mediation be made enforceable.

132. *Environmental Abatement Inc v Astrum RE Corp* 27 SW 3d 530 (Tenn Ct App 2000), at 541-542.

133. James Richard Coben and Peter N. Thompson, *Disputing Irony: A Systematic Look at Litigation About Mediation*, 11 Harvard Negot. L. Rev. 43 (2006), at 78. However, in *JN Intern Inc v MS Transgene Biotek Ltd* Nos 8:05CV67, 8:05CV158, 2006 WL 1559709 (D Neb 2006), the court refused to consider the enforceability of a mediated settlement as the parties had not submitted it to the court for approval before asking the court to enforce it.

134. See Art. 131-12 C pr civ.

135. These are summarised by Katrin Deckert, *Mediation in Frankreich – Rechtlicher Rahmen und praktische Erfahrungen*, in Klaus J. Hopt and Felix Steffek (eds), Mediation – Rechtstatsachen, Rechtsvergleich, Regelungen, Mohr Siebeck (2008), at 205-206. Also see generally, Delphine Wietek, *France*, in Nadja Alexander et al. (eds), EU Mediation Law Handbook – Regulatory Robustness Ratings for Mediation Regimes, Wolters Kluwer (2017), at 341-344.

1(3)(a)(i).[136] As Schnabel explains, '"approved by a court" does not cover instances in which the mediated settlement is presented for recognition or enforcement under this Convention'.[137] To do so would effectively mean that an iMSA could only be presented before a court in one jurisdiction, after which time it could no longer circulate under the Singapore Convention.[138] This runs counter to the object and purpose of the Singapore Convention and the provision must be interpreted with this in mind.[139]

1.39 In addition to the examples of court-approved iMSAs set out above, the first part of this exclusion (Article 1(3)(a)(i)) also envisages a situation where an iMSA has been concluded in the course of court proceedings. This may occur, for example, where as part of court proceedings, a judge-mediator or internal court mediator conducts a mediation that leads to an iMSA concluded between the parties. To illustrate, in the Singapore State Courts, matters are routinely referred from the trial judge to specially trained mediator judges.[140] Settlements resulting from these mediations will be recorded by the mediator judge in the form of either a settlement agreement or consent order,[141] embodied in the form of an order of court.[142]

1.40 To sum up, where a court has approved an iMSA or the iMSA has been concluded in the course of court proceedings, the first part of the exclusion set out in Article 1(3)(a)(i) is fulfilled.

1.41 For an iMSA to be excluded under Article 1(3)(a), there is an *additional* requirement, namely that the iMSA is enforceable as a judgment in that jurisdiction's

136. See UNCITRAL Working Group II (Arbitration and Conciliation), *Settlement of Commercial Disputes, International Commercial Conciliation: Enforceability of Settlement Agreements*, Note by the Secretariat, A/CN.9/WG.II/WP.202 (2-6 October 2017), at para. 28.
137. Timothy Schnabel, *The Singapore Convention on Mediation: A Framework for the Cross-Border Recognition and Enforcement of Mediated Settlements*, 19(1) Pepp. Disp. Resol. L.J. 1 (2019), at 26. For example, under Singapore's implementing legislation, the Singapore Convention on Mediation Act 2020 (the SCMA 2020), a party to an iMSA may apply to the relevant to court to record the iMSA as an order of the court for the purposes of enforcement. The use of the regulatory vehicle of a court order for the purposes of direct enforcement under the SCMA will not deprive the iMSA of the legal effect in another Contracting Party to the Singapore Convention on Mediation based on Art. 1(3) of the Singapore Convention on Mediation. See s. 4 of the SCMA 2020 and Nadja Alexander and Shouyu Chong, *Leading the Way for the Recognition and Enforcement of International Mediated Settlement Agreements: The Singapore Convention on Mediation Act 2020*, 34 SAcLJ 1 (2021), at para. 44.
138. It may, however, possibly circulate under another Convention or international instrument, particularly when we consider the example of a regional economic integration organisation in the context of its internal rules. Take, for instance, an iMSA brought into a Member State of the European Union for enforcement (assuming its Member States become a Party to the Convention) and that State issues judgment granting the enforcement under the Singapore Convention, the other Member States of the EU may be obliged to recognise that judgment *per* their internal recognition rules of foreign judgments (namely, through the Brussels I Recast Regulation). Cf. Art. 12 of the Singapore Convention.
139. On the object and purpose of the Singapore Convention, see the Introduction to this book.
140. Speech by Hon Justice Andrew Phang, *Mediation and the Courts – The Singapore Experience*, 4th Asian Mediation Association Conference, Beijing, China, 20 October 2016, www.supremecourt.gov.sg/Data/Editor/Documents/Keynote%20Speech%20-%204th%20Asian%20Mediation%20Conference.pdf (Accessed 22 March 2019).
141. *Lock Han Chng Jonathan v Goh Jessiline* [2008] 2 SLR(R) 455, at para. 30.
142. *Id.*, at para. 34.

court (Article 1(3)(a)(ii)). Therefore, the requirements of court approval and being concluded in the course of court proceedings are insufficient to trigger this exclusion. The iMSA concerned must *also* be enforceable.[143]

1.42 Inevitably, different legal traditions may possess a disparate understanding of what constitutes a judgment of a court, in the context of MSAs or judicial settlements. Without a proper appreciation of the nuances and debates in the study of the conflict of laws, the administration of Article 1(3)(a)(ii) (read with Article 1(3)(a)(i)) may run the risk of over-inclusivity in some jurisdictions and under-inclusivity in others.

1.43 It is useful to consider the notion of a 'judgment of a court' from an *autonomous* perspective. In the study of private international law, the autonomous method of interpreting terms of art found in an international instrument (for example, a Convention) is applied to derive the meaning of such a term as far as possible from within the instrument itself, independent of other external considerations.[144] The implicit assumption is that the instrument, which is a subject of interpretation, subsists on its own as a comprehensive set of rules.

1.44 The reality is that courts of different legal traditions are likely to approach this issue from the perspective of their own legal system and culture. For the purposes of interpreting this Convention, it is suggested that courts of States, as a matter of practice, peruse terms of art within this Convention with the cognisance that the Convention concerns itself with international transactions intricately woven by webs of diverse perspectives. In this manner, courts may determine the issue of what constitutes a judgment of a court autonomously. A possible comparator to be administered would be to focus on the functional characteristics of a judgment from a comparative perspective.[145]

iMSAs as Consent Awards

1.45 Article 1(3)(b) provides that the Singapore Convention does not apply to iMSAs that have been recorded and are enforceable as arbitral awards. Such awards are called

143. For example, according to Art. 6 of the 2008 EU Mediation Directive, where express consent is provided a mediated settlement agreement may be made enforceable by a court or other competent authority in the form of a judgment if such enforcement were sought within the jurisdiction between Member States, and the relevant terms of the Directive are complied with: Directive 2008/52/EC of the European Parliament and of the Council of 21 May 2008 on certain aspects of mediation in civil and commercial matters, https://eur-lex.europa.eu/legal-content/EN/TXT/?uri=CELEX%3A32008L0052 (Accessed 8 November 2018). In Spain, where a judicial process is pending prior to mediation, mediated settlement agreements will be rendered enforceable by way of judicial approval according to Art. 25(4) of the Act 5/2012, read with Art. 19(2) of the Civil Procedure Act, see Mercedes Tarrazón and Marian Gili Saldaña, *Spain*, in Nadja Alexander *et al* (eds), EU Mediation Law Handbook – Regulatory Robustness Ratings for Mediation Regimes, Wolters Kluwer (2017), at 758.
144. Maren Heidemann, *The Autonomous Interpretation Method in International Law with Particular Reference to the Proposed European Sales Law I*, 93 Amicus Curiae 21 (2013), at 22.
145. For instance, a possibility for consideration would be how the instrument examined may engender *res judicata*.

'consent awards' and may also be referred to as 'awards on consent' or 'awards on agreed terms'. In this commentary, they are referred to as 'consent awards'.

1.46 Before examining the second exclusion in Article 1(3)(b) in detail, we begin with an exploration of the variety of mixed mode dispute resolution situations in which Article 1(3)(b) may be relevant.[146]

1.47 Mixed mode dispute resolution processes (MDRs), also known as hybrid alternative dispute resolution (hybrid ADR), may include formal or informal mediation windows within arbitration processes and other mixed mode dispute resolution processes.[147] The idea behind MDR is to provide several possible avenues to dispute settlement within one dispute resolution procedure. The result is a mechanism that combines various dispute resolution methods such as mediation and arbitration in different ways. In mixed mode settings, where the parties settle through mediation, it is not uncommon for MSAs to be recorded as consent arbitral awards.

1.48 Clauses incorporating MDR are a recent development in commercial and cross-border contexts. Yet, in some parts of the world, such as China[148] and other civil law countries such as Germany,[149] it remains standard practice for judges and arbitrators to attempt to facilitate settlement in the course of trial and arbitration.[150] In other words, the extent to which mediation and informal settlement attempts take place in international arbitration varies according to legal culture. Further, the extent to which settlement processes within an arbitration can be defined as mediation, in line with Article 2(3) of the Singapore Convention, is an important consideration. This is illustrated by the cautionary comments made by Justice Reyes in *Gao HaiYan v Keeneye*

146. Parts of the commentary to Art. 3(1)(b) are drawn from the previous work: Nadja Alexander, International and Comparative Mediation: Legal Perspectives, Kluwer Law International (2009); Nadja Alexander, *Opening the Mediation Window in the Arbitration House*, 20(2) Can. Arbit. & Med. J. 37 (2011); Nadja Alexander, Joel Lee and Lum Kit-Wye, Singapore Mediation Handbook, LexisNexis (2019).

147. See the types of situations introduced at the *Inaugural summit, International Task Force on Mixed Mode Dispute Resolution*, International Task Force on Mixed Mode Dispute Resolution at The Straus Institute for Dispute Resolution, Pepperdine University School of Law (2016).

148. *Inaugural summit, International Task Force on Mixed Mode Dispute Resolution*, The Straus Institute for Dispute Resolution, Pepperdine University School of Law (2016) at Scenario 3, 16. Cf. the concept of 'litigation-mediation' in the People's Republic of China in local courts: Zhi Wu, *Litigation Mediation for Intellectual Property Disputes in Chinese Local Courts: Experiences and Contradictions*, 17(1) A.P.L.R. 117 (2009). Also see Bac Arb. Rules Art. 42 (Beijing Arbitration Commission, 2014); CIETAC Arbitration Rules, Art. 47, China Council for the Promotion of International Trade, China Chamber of International Commerce, 2014.

149. Christian Bühring-Uhle, Kirchhoff and Gabriele Scherer, *Arbitration and Mediation in International Business* (2nd Ed.), Kluwer Law International (2006), at 128. See, Dis Arbitration Rules 32.1 (German Institution or Arbitration 1998), which states: 'At every stage of the proceedings, the arbitral tribunal should seek to encourage an amicable settlement of the dispute or of individual issues in dispute'.

150. Thomas Stipanowich and Véronique Fraser, *The International Task Force on Mixed Mode Dispute Resolution: Exploring the Interplay Between Mediation Evaluation and Arbitration in Commercial Cases*, Pepperdine University School of Law, Legal Studies Research Paper Series 2017/4 (2017).

Holdings Ltd.[151] In that case, serious questions were raised about whether a settlement attempt amounted to a mediation under the Xi'an Arbitration Commission Rules: see the case illustration in the commentary to Article 2(3).[152]

Point of Interest

Four Categories of Dispute Resolution Processes

There are four primary categories of dispute resolution, namely facilitative, transformative, advisory and determinative processes.

Facilitative processes feature assisted negotiation, party autonomy and consensus-based outcomes. The facilitative model of mediation is an example of a process in which third-party interveners function as process experts with skills in structuring and facilitating negotiations. Facilitative mediation is the dominant mediation model in training and policy worldwide and it is widely used in practice. Facilitative dispute resolution processes represent the classic mediation model and fall within the Convention's definition of mediation.

Transformative processes are similarly consensus-based, leaving substantive decision-making to the parties. They also encourage the parties' input into the process itself. Generally, transformative processes enable a broader understanding of the conflict as compared with other categories of dispute resolution, which tend to focus on the issues in the dispute rather than the broader implications of a conflict. In addition, they are less focused on a specific form of outcome, be it a decision, recommendation or an agreement. Rather, the focus is on the relational dynamics among parties to the mediation. Transformative processes include some forms of mediation. In cross-border contexts, transformative dispute resolution processes have typically been used in public interest disputes with the environment, urban planning and pollution issues. The Vienna International Airport (VIA) mediation is illustrative in this regard: the issue of whether, and if so, how to add an additional runway to the VIA became the subject of an international mediation as it affected local Austrian communities as well as those across the border in the Czech Republic and Bratislava.[153] Transformative dispute resolution processes fall within the Convention's definition of mediation.

151. *Gao HaiYan and another v Keeneye Holdings Ltd and another* [2011] HKCFI 240, [2011] 3 HKC 157, where Justice Reyes refused to allow the enforcement of a foreign arbitral award as a matter of public policy. It should be noted that refusal for enforcement was overturned on appeal: *Gao HaiYan and another v Keeneye Holdings Ltd and another* [2011] HKCA 459, [2012] 1 HKC 335, [2012] 1 HKLRD 627. However, the Court of Appeal did not disturb Justice Reyes' observations on the issues over whether the settlement attempt amounted to mediation.
152. See also the discussion on the inapplicability of the Convention to settlement agreements concluded outside of mediation in the commentary to Art. 4.
153. Horst Zillessen, *The Transformative Effect of Mediation in the Public Arena*, 7 ADR Bull. 82 (2004).

In *advisory processes*, third-party interveners move beyond facilitation and consensus-based processes to include evaluative or advice-giving elements, but fall short of imposing a decision on the parties involved. Advisory processes include neutral evaluation, case appraisal, conciliation and advisory forms of mediation. Third-party interveners are usually lawyers or technical experts who are limited to providing recommendations and advice. The advisory nature of the process varies. For example, case appraisers formulate the likely judicial outcome of the dispute should the matter proceed to court. Other processes such as neutral evaluation contemplate the intervener making proposals for settlement. Conciliators may advise the parties about the merits of issues and a range of suitable outcomes. While roles and functions vary, advisory processes all feature the intervener's input on substantive issues. It would be reasonable to interpret advisory processes as within the Convention's definition of mediation.

Determinative processes involve decision-making by a third party, such as a judge or an arbitrator. In modern States, determinative processes tend to be legalistic, focusing primarily on legal and positional arguments. Decisions are usually based on legal criteria, although there may be scope for the application of industry benchmarks and equitable principles. Determinative processes include court adjudication, private judging, construction adjudication and arbitration. Determinative processes do not fall within the Convention's definition of mediation.

Aside from these four categories, there are numerous processes that traverse classifications. As indicated previously, we refer to these as mixed mode dispute resolution or MDRs as they involve a number of procedural stages. MDR mechanisms often favour facilitative processes as the initial interventions to encourage flexibility, party-driven negotiation and collaborative solutions. If a dispute remains live after facilitative interventions, advisory and evaluative mechanisms can be introduced. Advisory and evaluative dispute resolution is usually more formal, costlier and may be more time-consuming than facilitative dispute resolution. MDR mechanisms involving mediation and arbitration are relevant to Article 1(3)(b).

Mixed Mode Forms of Dispute Resolution

1.49 MDRs can take many forms. Here, we examine some of the more frequently used forms of MDRs. Issues relating to procedural fairness and potential bias become acutely relevant in mixed mode contexts, particularly where the same third-party neutral acts as both mediator and arbitrator. Ethical issues that arise in MDRs are examined in the context of mediator misconduct in the commentary to Article 5.

1.50 *Med–arb* generally takes one of the following two forms:

(1) the matter first goes to mediation - and, if the issues in dispute are not resolved by the mutual agreement of the parties, the matter proceeds to arbitration; or
(2) the parties agree to mediate certain issues in dispute and to arbitrate the others. In other words, there is a division of the issues according to whether mediation or arbitration is considered to be the more suitable process.

1.51 Conversely, *arb–med* is an example of a hybrid process, which begins with a determinative element and then moves to a facilitative mode to explore the possibility of agreement between the parties. Here, an arbitral decision is made, but usually is not communicated to the parties and will only be made known in the form of an award if the ensuing mediation does not result in an agreement. There are, however, some forms of *arb–med* in which the arbitrator's decision is communicated to the parties directly after the arbitration phase but without an award being issued. Aware of their default position (the arbitral decision), the parties then have an opportunity to reach a resolution on terms preferable to the arbitral award.

1.52 *Mediation windows* are an increasingly common feature in arbitration proceedings. Here, a metaphorical window may be opened in the course of arbitration in an attempt to resolve the dispute through mediation. As long as the mediation window is open, the arbitration procedure is suspended.[154] If the matter is settled through mediation, then the MSA can be recorded as an arbitral award and thus attract the operation of the New York Convention.[155] This process has become embodied in the SIAC-SIMC Arb-Med-Arb (AMA) Protocol administered by the Singapore International Mediation Centre (SIMC) in partnership with the Singapore International Arbitration Centre (SIAC).[156]

1.53 Alternatively, mediation windows may open alongside the arbitration, where different representatives are available for each process. The *Centre de Médiation et*

154. On mediation windows in the form of arb–med–arb, see Bobette Wolski, *Arb–Med–Arb (and MSAs): A Whole Which Is Less Than, Not Greater Than, The Sum Of Its Parts?*, 6(2) Contemp. Asia Arb. J. 249 (2013); the 2009 Report of the CEDR (Centre for Effective Dispute Resolution) Commission on Settlement in International Arbitration at 3 and 10-17, available at CEDR Arbitration Commission, www.cedr.com/about_us/arbitration_commission/Arbitration_Commission_Doc_Final.pdf (Accessed 23 January 2019); I Yang, *Med–Arb in Mainland China: A Bold Chinese Invention or a Recipe for Disaster?*, Session II International Arbitration Conference Proceedings 1-3 (2008); Lijun Cao, *Combining Conciliation and Arbitration in China: Overview and Latest Developments*, Int'l Arb. L. Rev. (2006), at 89 et seq.; Klaus Berger, *Integration of Mediation Elements into Arbitration: 'Hybrid' Procedures and 'Intuitive' Mediation by International Arbitrators*, 19 Arb. Int'l 3 (2003).
155. Joel Lee, *Singapore Developments – The Singapore International Mediation Institute and the Singapore International Mediation Centre* (14 November 2014) Kluwer Mediation Blog.
156. See the SIMC website, *Singapore International Mediation Centre*, http://simc.com.sg (Accessed 23 January 2019) and specifically on this protocol http://simc.com.sg/siac-simc-arb-med-arb-protocol/ (Accessed 23 January 2019). See also Aziah Hussin, Claudia Kück and Nadja Alexander, *SIAC–SIMC's Arb-Med-Arb Protocol*, 11(2) N. Y. Disp. Res. Lawyer 85 (2018).

d'Arbitrage de Paris (CMAP) in France has developed a specific hybrid procedure called *med–arb simultanés* where an arbitration process runs simultaneously with, and independently from, a mediation process. If the mediation does not result in a mediated settlement within an agreed time frame, then the arbitration will result in an award binding on the parties eight days after the mediation deadline has expired. During the parallel processes, the mediator and arbitrator are not permitted to communicate with each other about the case. However, at the end of each day or during breaks, the parties may consult with their legal representatives in each process in relation to the progress that has been made. *Med–arb simultanés* aims to do away with the concerns associated with the same dispute resolution professional(s) acting as mediator and arbitrator. At the same time, it offers clients the finality of an arbitral award should the mediation not result in a settlement.[157]

Consent Awards

1.54 Consent awards may occur in three ways:

(1) as a settlement in the course of an arbitral process;
(2) as a settlement between parties to an arbitral agreement prior to arbitration; or
(3) where the law provides that an MSA can be treated as an award, provided there is compliance with certain conditions.

1.55 As with the first exclusion examined previously, there are two parts to this exclusion, namely:

(1) iMSAs must be recorded as an arbitral award; and
(2) iMSAs must be capable of enforcement as an arbitral award.

iMSA Recorded as an Arbitral Award

1.56 Any one of the above MDRs could lead to an iMSA. To fall within the scope of the exclusion of Article 1(3)(b) of the Singapore Convention, the iMSA must be recorded in the form of a (consent) arbitral award.[158] Although the New York Convention is silent

157. See the CMAP website, Centre de Médiation et d'Arbitrage de Paris, *Le Centre Créateur De Solutions*, http://www.cmap.fr/ (Accessed 23 January 2019).

158. In the German civil procedure law (*Zivilprozessordnung*, ZPO), §. 1053 provides, 'A consent award must indicate that it is an award. It will have the same effect as any other award.' This would seem to require the MSA to be recorded as an arbitral award. See, for example, the following jurisprudence:

(1) *Rechtsprechung der Oberlandesgerichte in Zivilsachen* (OLGZ) (Higher Regional Court of Frankfurt), 3 Sch 01/99, 28 June 1999: a settlement agreement recorded by a tribunal in the form of a consent award is enforceable under the ZPO, as long as it expressly states that it is a consent award (statutory requirement).

on consent awards, Article 30 read with Article 31 of the UNCITRAL Model Law on International Commercial Arbitration (2006) recognises consent awards and sets out requirements as to form.[159] Generally, arbitral tribunals have the power to review an MSA, and even to refuse to record it in the form of an award.[160] Importantly, where an MSA is treated as an arbitral award but is not recorded as such, it will not fall within this exclusion.[161]

Case Illustration

Barry from Dreamland and *Edna* from Edenville (both States are Parties to the Singapore Convention) begin arbitration proceedings to resolve their dispute. During the arbitration, the parties and arbitrator elect to stay arbitration proceedings and attempt to resolve the dispute through mediation.

The parties are able to resolve the dispute and arrive at a settlement during the mediation window. Now they may record their settlement as an iMSA and walk away from the arbitration proceeding by withdrawing from arbitral proceedings unilaterally or by consent. The iMSA in this scenario will not trigger the exception of Article 1(3)(b) and the Singapore Convention will still apply. Alternatively, the parties may elect to have the iMSA recorded as an arbitral

(2) *Rechtsprechung der Oberlandesgerichte in Zivilsachen* (OLGZ) (Higher Regional Court of Frankfurt), 20 Sch 01/02, 14 March 2003: same.
(3) *Bundesgerichtshof* (BGH) [Federal Court of Justice], III ZB 55/99, 2 November 2000.

Also see similar legislation in England: 1996 Arbitration Act (UK), s. 51(3) states, 'An agreed award shall state that it is an award of the tribunal and shall have the same status and effect as any other award on the merits of the case.'

159. See Gary Born, *International Commercial Arbitration* (2nd Ed.), Wolters Kluwer (2014), at 3021-3027.
160. See, for example, UNCITRAL Model Law on International Commercial Arbitration (2006), Arts 30 and 31.
161. Consider the following examples. In China, Art. 51 of the Arbitration Law of the People's Republic of China provides that conciliation may be conducted by an arbitral tribunal and if settlement occurs the tribunal may document it as either a written conciliation statement or an arbitration award in accordance with the settlement agreement: see '中华人民共和国仲裁' ('Arbitration law of the People's Republic of China'), http://www.npc.gov.cn/wxzl/wxzl/2000-12/05/content_4624.htm. (Accessed 20 November 2018). In Hong Kong, parties to an arbitration agreement may appoint a conciliator to assist them settle their dispute, with the advantage that any resulting settlement is treated as an award on an arbitration agreement and, with the leave of the court, may be enforced *domestically* in the same manner as a judgment to the same effect: s. 66 of the Hong Kong Arbitration Ordinance (Cap. 609). The law in Bermuda is also the same as in Hong Kong: see ss 20 and 48 of the Bermuda International Conciliation and Arbitration Act 1993. Finally, it is noteworthy that some US states have legislation which provides for iMSAs to be treated as arbitral awards; he refers to legislation in California (Cal. Civ. Pro. § 1297.401), Texas (Tex. Civ. Prac. & Rem. Code Ann. § 172.211), Ohio (Ohio Rev. Code § 2712.87), North Carolina (N.C. Gen. Stat. § 1-567.84) and Oregon (Or. Rev. Stat. § 36.546).

award in which case Article 1(3)(b) of the Singapore Convention may come into play.

iMSA Consent Award is 'capable of enforcement'

1.57 The Singapore Convention makes it clear that not only must the iMSA be recorded as an arbitral award if it is to be an exception, but it must also be capable of enforcement. This wording is based on the premise that consent awards are enforceable under the New York Convention.[162]

1.58 At the same time, there may be circumstances in which a consent award may not be capable of enforcement under the New York Convention.[163] As Meidanis notes, such circumstances do not refer to grounds for non-enforcement under Article V of the New York Convention; rather, they refer to the legal nature of the consent award being incapable of enforcement.[164] From an international enforcement point of view, there may be a number of situations in which such an award might be considered to be incapable of enforcement.

1.59 Where the iMSA deals with matters not covered by the arbitration agreement or the submission to arbitration, then it is unlikely that the tribunal has jurisdiction to render the award, unless an agreement between the parties and arbitrators is made to extend the terms of the arbitration agreement or to introduce the matters covered in the settlement into the arbitration submission. However, where part of a consent award lies outside the jurisdiction of the arbitral tribunal, it may be possible to sever that part from the rest of the consent award that has been validly issued, thereby saving the latter part of the award.[165] It is conceivable that the former, now severed, part of the award may be enforceable under the Singapore Convention.

162. This position represents the leading opinion on the matter. However, it is certainly not without its critics. Consent awards are called 'awards'; they are issued by arbitrators, and they are contemplated under most arbitration rules. Yet a consent award is different from what is usually referred to as an award, and has little in common with an adjudicatory act. A consent award also raises the question of whether typical grounds for non-enforcement or annulment are well adapted to consent awards. For example, the French *Cour de cassation* annulled the judgment of the Versailles Court of Appeal and held that a consent award did not qualify as an adjudicatory act that can be enforced as such, stating that '[t]he mere act of recording a settlement without any reasoning is not an adjudicative act'. Cour de Cassation (Cass civ 1e, 14 November 2012, M A c Societe B-C).
163. UNCITRAL Working Group II (Dispute Settlement) 67th Session, Settlement of Commercial Disputes International Commercial Conciliation: Preparation of an Instrument on Enforcement of International Commercial Settlement Agreements Resulting from Conciliation, Note by the Secretariat, A/CN.9/WG.II/WP.202 (2-6 October 2017).
164. Haris Meidanis, *International Enforcement of Mediated Settlement Agreements: Two and a Half Models – Why and How to Enforce Internationally Mediated Settlement Agreements*, 85(1) Arbitration 49 (2019), at 62.
165. New York Convention on the Recognition and Enforcement of Foreign Arbitral Awards (1958), Art V(c).

1.60 In relation to partial consent awards, where a consent award does not contain the entirety of the terms of the iMSA but only certain terms which the parties wished to have recorded as an arbitral award, then a question arises as to how those iMSA terms not contained in the consent award may be enforced. We suggest that, insofar as this iMSA representing a partial settlement of the dispute between the parties meets the requirements of the Singapore Convention, then it is covered by the Convention and is capable of direct enforcement.

1.61 In relation to *med-arb* situations, there is the question as to whether parties are entitled to settle their dispute through mediation and then commence arbitration for the purpose of converting the settlement agreement into a consent award. Arguably, as the parties no longer have a dispute, they cannot commence an arbitration.[166]

1.62 Article 30 of the Model Law on International Commercial Arbitration applies where the dispute is settled *during* – and *not before* the initiation of – arbitral proceedings and could be seen to support this view. Commentators are divided on this point, with some pointing out that the New York Convention does not impose a temporal requirement in relation to the appointment of the arbitrator.[167] While a number of jurisdictions, such as Hong Kong[168] and Bermuda,[169] have legislated to permit such arrangements (albeit in a domestic[170] arbitration setting), the acceptance of this approach is far from uniform.

Case Illustrations

Illustration [A]: In the US case of *Castro v Tri Marine Fish Co.*,[171] the US Court of Appeals for the Ninth Circuit opined that an order issued by an arbitrator in the Philippines was not a foreign arbitral award for the purposes of the New York

166. Gary Born, *International Commercial Arbitration* (2nd Ed.), Wolters Kluwer (2014), at 3023. Born reports, 'An arbitral tribunal [must have] the authority to make [the] consent award [which accrues] only if the parties commenced an arbitration regarding an actual dispute. The authority to make a consent award does not extend to cases where the parties settle a dispute and then subsequently commence an arbitration solely for the purpose of recording the settlement as a consent award.'
167. Edna Sussman, *The Final Step: Issues in Enforcing the Mediation Settlement Agreement*, in Arthur W. Rovine (ed.), The Fordham Papers 2008, Volume 2 (Martinus Nijhoff, 2008) 343, at 358; Ellen E. Deason, *Enforcement of Settlement Agreements in International Commercial Mediation: A New Legal Framework?*, 22 Disp. Res. Mag. 32 (2015), at 33; and see Haris Meidanis, *International Enforcement of Mediated Settlement Agreements: Two and a Half Models – Why and How to Enforce Internationally Mediated Settlement Agreements*, 85(1) Arbitration 49 (2019), at 62.
168. Hong Kong Arbitration Ordinance (Cap. 609), s 66.
169. Bermuda International Conciliation and Arbitration Act 1993, ss 20 and 48.
170. That is, such an award may not be enforced internationally under the terms of the 1958 New York Convention on Recognition and Enforcement of Foreign Arbitral Awards. See John Cheong and J Romesh Weeramantry (Gen eds), *The Hong Kong Arbitration Ordinance: Commentary and Annotations*, Thomson Reuters (2011), at para. 66.17.
171. *Castro v Tri Marine Fish Co. LLC*, 921 F.3d 766, 2019 U.S. App. LEXIS 10961, 2019 AMC 931 (9th Cir. Wash. 15 April 2019).

Convention. The court stated, 'the parties had already agreed to settle their dispute, and so there was no outstanding dispute to arbitrate when they brought the matter to the arbitrator'.[172] For the court, the timing of recording a settlement agreement as an order was of crucial importance because a 'consent award becomes possible after a tribunal has been constituted. Otherwise, the tribunal will have no right to render a consent award'.[173]

However, where the settlement was reached during arbitral proceedings, courts have reached a different decision. In *Albtelecom SH.A v UNIFI Communs., Inc.*,[174] the US District Court for the Southern District of New York addressed the issue of whether a settlement agreement that the parties arrived at during the arbitral proceedings and converted into an arbitral award was a foreign arbitral award for the purposes of the New York Convention. The court rejected the argument that consent awards are outside the scope of the New York Convention and opined 'the opposite rule would discourage resolution of disputes in mid-arbitration. Parties who initiate arbitration under the [arbitral court] might be less willing to settle, were the implication of a settlement that the resulting Award would lose its enforceability under the New York Convention'.[175]

Illustration [B]: In yet another US case, *Transocean Offshore Gulf of Guinea VII Ltd v Erin Energy Corp.*,[176] the court affirmed the enforceability of consent awards, recorded during arbitral proceedings, under the New York Convention. The court opined, '[n]o binding or persuasive statutory language or case law requires a court to hold that a tribunal must reach its own conclusions, separate from the parties' agreement, to make a valid, binding award subject to the Convention'. For the court, the opposite conclusion 'would dissuade parties from seeking arbitration in the first place or benefitting from the efficiencies it is meant to provide'.[177]

1.63 Some jurisdictions strictly require compliance with formal requirements in order for a settlement agreement arrived at during arbitral proceedings to be converted into an arbitral award. By way of illustration, section 1053(2) of the Code of Civil Procedure (ZPO) of Germany prescribes that an award on agreed terms shall be made in accordance with section 1054 and shall state that it is an award. Case law shows that a court will not declare an award enforceable in case of failure to adhere to the formal requirements. The Higher Regional Court of Frankfurt, in the case dated 14 March 2003, refused to declare the settlement enforceable, on the ground that the settlement

172. *Id.*, at 1.
173. *Id.*, at 16.
174. *Albtelecom SH.A v UNIFI Communs., Inc.*, 2017 U.S. Dist. LEXIS 82154 (S.D.N.Y. 30 May 2017).
175. *Id.*, at 14.
176. *Transocean Offshore Gulf of Guinea VII Ltd. v Erin Energy Corp.*, 2018 U.S. Dist. LEXIS 39494, 2018 WL 1251924 (S.D. Tex. 12 March 2018).
177. *Id.*, at 12.

failed to mention that it was an award on agreed terms.[178] It was considered irrelevant whether the failure to specify that the settlement agreement was in fact an award was due to error or was intentional.

Practical and Legal Considerations of Enforcement under the New York Convention and the Singapore Convention on Mediation

1.64 With the entry into force of the Singapore Convention, parties have two options if they arrive at a mediated settlement during arbitral proceedings to resolve a cross-border commercial dispute: they may either draft and sign off on an iMSA and enforce it under the new enforcement regime of the Singapore Convention on Mediation, or convert it into an arbitral award and enforce it under the New York Convention. The consideration of whether to enforce an iMSA under the Singapore Convention or a consent arbitral award under the New York Convention requires an examination of practical and legal differences that exist in the application of these two Conventions. This section reviews six main considerations that may have an impact on parties' decision on whether to convert an iMSA and enforce it under the New York Convention, namely:

(1) the geographical coverage of the Singapore Convention on Mediation compared to the New York Convention;
(2) the restricted scope of a consent arbitral award, being limited to the scope of the arbitration agreement under the New York Convention;
(3) the non-existence of a supervisory court under the Singapore Convention;
(4) the existence of contractual defences in the Singapore Convention;
(5) different standards for refusing to grant relief in relation to an iMSA and an arbitral award, respectively (in the context of mediators and arbitrators' ethical standards); and
(6) the opportunity to opt out of the Singapore Convention.[179]

Geographical Coverage of the New York Convention

1.65 The Singapore Convention on Mediation entered into force on 12 September 2020. At the time of writing, the Singapore Convention on Mediation has been signed by 55 States out of which ten States have ratified/approved it. By comparison, the New York Convention has been in force for more than 60 years and has become one of the most influential instruments in private international law. At the time of writing, the New York Convention has 170 Contracting States. It will take some years before the Singapore Convention on Mediation achieves a geographical coverage similar to that of the New York Convention. Accordingly, parties to an iMSA wishing to avail themselves

178. Oberlandesgericht Frankfurt a.M., Germany, 20 Sch 01/02, 14 March 2003, reported in UNCITRAL 2012 Digest of Case Law on the Model Law on International Commercial Arbitration, at 125, footnote 568.
179. Some of these points are considered elsewhere in the book, as indicated.

of a larger geographical area for enforcement purposes might prefer enforcement under the New York Convention. In this case, they may choose to record their iMSA as a consent arbitral award. Consent arbitral awards may be enforced under the New York Convention in 170 jurisdictions.[180]

A Consent Arbitral Award is Limited to the Scope of the Arbitration Agreement

1.66 According to the New York Convention, consent arbitral awards are limited to the scope of the arbitration agreement. Article II(3) of the New York Convention states that the court of a Contracting State to the New York Convention, when seized of an action in a matter in respect of which the parties have made an agreement within the meaning of this article, shall, at the request of one of the parties, refer the parties to the arbitration. One of the implications of this provision is that, in principle, the tribunal cannot make decisions that go beyond the scope of the arbitration agreement between the parties. If the tribunal renders an award that goes beyond the scope of the arbitration agreement, the award may not be enforced according to Article V(1)(c) of the New York Convention.[181]

1.67 By contrast, the Singapore Convention on Mediation does not regulate mediation clauses[182] or mediation agreements.[183] There are many paths that lead to mediation, including mediation clauses, mediation agreements, court referrals and legislation that triggers mediation processes.[184] Parties to a mediation have a possibility to tailor their settlement agreement according to their needs and, if necessary, to go beyond the scope of an agreement/clause that may have triggered the mediation. Therefore, if parties to an arbitration agreement commence mediation and wish to go beyond the scope of the arbitration agreement in terms of their settlement, they may not record their iMSA as a consent arbitral award.[185] Such a consent arbitral award may not be

180. This possibility is subject to the limitation discussed in paras 1.57-1.63.
181. This Article states that the recognition and enforcement of the award may be refused if: 'The award deals with a difference not contemplated by or not falling within the terms of the submission to arbitration, or it contains decisions on matters beyond the scope of the submission to arbitration, provided that, if the decisions on matters submitted to arbitration can be separated from those not so submitted, that part of the award which contains decisions on matters submitted to arbitration may be recognized and enforced.'
182. A mediation clause refers to parties' agreement to mediate *before* a dispute arises.
183. A mediation agreement refers to parties' agreement to mediate *after* a dispute arises.
184. Nadja Alexander, *International and Comparative Mediation: Legal Perspectives*, Kluwer Law International (2009), at 95-96, 171-214.
185. In this regard, it should be noted that arbitrators normally have the power to refuse to record a settlement agreement as an arbitral award. By way of example, according to Art. 30(1) of the Model Law on Arbitration, if, during arbitral proceedings, the parties settle the dispute, the arbitral tribunal shall terminate the proceedings and, if requested by the parties and *not objected to by the arbitral tribunal*, record the settlement in the form of an arbitral award on agreed terms [*emphasis added*]. It is conceivable that if the settlement terms go beyond the scope of the arbitration agreement, the tribunal may not record such a settlement agreement as an arbitral award.

enforced according to Article V(1)(c) of the New York Convention.[186] It could, however, be enforced under the Singapore Convention on Mediation.

1.68 Therefore, parties to an arbitration agreement who find themselves settling their dispute via mediation, must be mindful of the scope of their iMSA before electing whether or not to record it as a consent arbitral award.

A Supervisory Court

1.69 It was explained in paragraph 1.14 above that the Singapore Convention does not prescribe a seat of mediation. The absence of a seat of mediation plays a significant role, as there is no single State with the exclusive jurisdiction to set aside an iMSA. Consequently, Article 5 of the Singapore Convention on Mediation, which prescribes the grounds for refusing to enforce and recognise an iMSA, does not contain a ground pertaining to the non-enforcement of an iMSA that was set aside by the competent authority in the country where the iMSA was made. As a result, even if an iMSA was set aside in a Contracting Party to the Singapore Convention,[187] this fact itself will not have any decisive impact on the enforcement of this iMSA in other Contracting Parties to the Singapore Convention on Mediation.[188]

1.70 The New York Convention provides a different framework for the enforcement of foreign arbitral awards, which corresponds to the functions of a seat of arbitration. The court in *Karaha Bodas Co., L.L.C. v Perusahaan Pertambangan Minyak Dan Gas Bumi Negara*[189] summed up the structure for the review and enforcement of foreign arbitral awards under the New York Convention. Only a court with primary jurisdiction over an arbitral award can annul the award. All other Contracting States to the New York Convention are considered as secondary jurisdictions and their power is limited to the enforcement of foreign arbitral awards.[190] Primary jurisdiction is designated by a seat of arbitration, which is enshrined in Article V(1)(e) of the New York Convention as 'the country in which, or under the law of which, that award was made'. If an award is annulled in the primary jurisdiction, then the enforcement of such an award will be doubtful in the other Contracting States to the New York Convention, as Article V(1)(e) of the New York Convention states that the competent authority may refuse to enforce an award if the award has been set aside or suspended by a competent authority of the country in which, or under the law of which, that award was made.[191]

---

186. For situations where there is no arbitration agreement and a mediated settlement agreement is recorded as a consent arbitral award, see para. 1.62 above.
187. The term 'Party' with a capital 'P' refers to a Contracting Party to the Singapore Convention. See the commentary to Art. 3, paras 3.03-3.08.
188. In this regard, see also the commentary to Art. 6, paras 6.03-6.06, which considers whether Art. 6 of the Singapore Convention provides an implied ground for refusal to enforce iMSAs.
189. *Karaha Bodas Co., L.L.C. v Perusahaan Pertambangan Minyak Dan Gas Bumi Negara*, 364 F.3d 274, 2004 U.S. App. LEXIS 5445 (5th Cir. Tex. 23 March 2004).
190. *Id.*, at 1.
191. Some Contracting States provide a more favourable regime for the enforcement of arbitral awards and their competent authorities may still enforce awards, that were set aside, under a more favourable enforcement regime, which is allowed according to Art. VII of the New York

1.71 Even though the Singapore Convention and the New York Convention take a different approach in the review and enforcement of iMSAs and foreign arbitral awards, the practical application of the difference in approach may not be significant. The successful application of the defence under Article V(1)(e) of the New York Convention has not been reported in great numbers.[192] In practice, it seems unlikely that parties, that voluntarily negotiate and agree to an iMSA and convert it into an award, would challenge the validity of the award. However, such a scenario is not inconceivable, as there are reported cases of parties having a change of heart after concluding a mediated settlement.[193]

1.72 In short, if parties wish to subject the validity of an iMSA in the form of a consent arbitral award to one specific jurisdiction, then converting an iMSA into an arbitral award might be the best course of action. Conversely, the Singapore Convention on Mediation does not prescribe a seat of mediation. Therefore, in principle, the annulment of an iMSA in one jurisdiction may not necessarily lead to non-enforcement in other jurisdictions under the Singapore Convention on Mediation.[194]

Contractual Defences under the Singapore Convention

1.73 MSAs result from a meeting of the minds between the parties. They are creatures of contract. As a result, Article 5(1)(a) – (d) of the Singapore Convention set out a number of defences drawn from contract law principles.[195] By contrast, arbitral awards are the result of arbitrators' decisions and not agreements between the parties. Therefore, it is logical that Article V of the New York Convention does not contain similar contract-based grounds to refuse enforcement of arbitral awards;[196] this appears to extend to consent arbitral awards on the basis that the New York Convention does not make a distinction between consent arbitral awards and awards that are derived through normal arbitral proceedings. The grounds for refusal prescribed in Article V of the New York Convention generally relate to procedural irregularities of

Convention. By way of example, the enforcement of awards that were set aside in primary jurisdiction is allowed under the laws of France and there have been a number of cases in which the courts of France allowed the enforcement of such awards. See UNCITRAL Secretariat Guide on the Convention on the Recognition and Enforcement of Foreign Arbitral Awards (New York, 1958) (2016), footnote 992.

192. UNCITRAL Secretariat Guide on the Convention on the Recognition and Enforcement of Foreign Arbitral Awards (New York, 1958) (2016), at 221.
193. See, as an illustration from Singapore, the case of *Chan Gek Yong v Violet Netto* [2019] 3 SLR 1218.
194. It has to be noted that an iMSA may provide for a dispute resolution clause according to which any dispute arising out of the iMSA will be resolved, for instance, either by litigation, arbitration or any other dispute resolution means agreed by the parties.
195. More on the available defences under Art. 5 of the Singapore Convention, see the commentary to Art. 5.
196. The only contractual defence in the New York Convention is found in Art. V(1)(a), which relates to the invalidity of the arbitration agreement. It reads as follows: 'The parties to the agreement referred to in article II were, under the law applicable to them, under some incapacity, or the said agreement is not valid under the law to which the parties have subjected it or, failing any indication thereon, under the law of the country where the award was made.'

arbitration proceedings. It has been established that 'judicial review of arbitral awards is extremely limited, and a court does not sit to hear claims of factual or legal error by an arbitrator in the same manner that an appeals court would review the decision of a lower court'.[197]

1.74 Accordingly, should parties to an iMSA wish to keep the option to avail themselves of contractual defences to enforcement, they ought not to record the iMSA as a consent arbitral award. Rather, they may be better off seeking relief under the Singapore Convention on Mediation.

Ethical Standards of Arbitrators and Mediators

1.75 The Singapore Convention on Mediation puts the spotlight on mediators' ethical standards, as Article 5(1)(e) – (f) of the Singapore Convention provides two mediator misconduct-related grounds for refusing to grant relief. According to Article 5(1)(e) of the Singapore Convention, the competent authority may not grant relief if there was a serious breach by the mediator of standards applicable to the mediator or the mediation, without which breach that party would not have entered into the iMSA. Further, according to Article 5(1)(f), relief may not be granted if there was a failure by the mediator to disclose to the parties circumstances that raise justifiable doubts as to the mediator's impartiality or independence and such failure to disclose had a material impact or undue influence on a party without which failure that party would not have entered into the iMSA. Even though the New York Convention does not expressly provide similar grounds for refusing to enforce and recognise foreign arbitral awards, it has been established that the public policy defence under Article V(2)(b) of the New York Convention can be relied on to oppose the enforcement and recognition of arbitral awards that were tainted with arbitrators' lack of impartiality or independence.[198]

1.76 While both arbitrators and mediators must comply with the obligations of applicable ethical standards, particularly the obligations of impartiality and independence, a breach of such standards may have different consequences under the Singapore Convention and the New York Convention. According to Article 5(1)(e) – (f) of the Singapore Convention: (1) there must be a breach of the applicable obligations of impartiality or independence; (2) such a breach must be serious/material; and (3)

---

197. *Int'l Trading & Indus. Inv. Co. v DynCorp Aero. Tech.*, 763 F. Supp. 2d 12, 15, 2011 U.S. Dist. LEXIS 5954, *1 (D.D.C. 21 January 2011). Justice of the Singapore Court of Appeal, Judith Prakash, has also opined, 'It is well established that the grounds for curial intervention in arbitration proceedings are narrowly circumscribed: parties to an arbitration do not have the right to a "correct" decision from an arbitral tribunal that can be vindicated by the courts, but only the right to a decision that is within the ambit of their agreement to arbitrate, and that is arrived at following a fair process. Furthermore, in ascertaining whether that has been the case, the courts accord a margin of deference to the tribunal, which is generally expected to have some independence in controlling the arbitral proceedings and considering the issues before it.' (*CJA v CIZ* [2022] SGCA 41).
198. UNCITRAL Secretariat Guide on the Convention on the Recognition and Enforcement of Foreign Arbitral Awards (New York, 1958) (2016), at 253.

without such a breach, a party would not have entered into the iMSA.[199] The wording of Article 5(1)(e) – (f) of the Singapore Convention makes it clear that even though a mediator may be in breach of his/her ethical obligations, impartiality or independence, if such a breach did not impact a party's decision to enter into the iMSA, the competent authority will not refuse to grant relief.

1.77 The standard under the New York Convention is different. A court, seized with the issue of whether or not the award was tainted by the arbitrator's breach of impartiality or independence, will not assess whether such a breach *actually* had an impact on the final award. A court, in relation to a breach of impartiality,[200] will normally examine 'whether the fair-minded and informed observer, having considered the facts, would conclude that there was a real possibility that the tribunal was biased'[201] and in relation to a breach of independence,[202] the court will objectively assess 'whether a fair-minded and informed observer might view the arbitrator as having "a personal or pecuniary interest in the outcome, however small"'.[203] As indicated above, there is no requirement to show that an arbitrator's breach of impartiality or independence influenced his or her arbitral decision.[204] While a court will only refuse to grant relief under Article 5(1)(e) – (f) of the Singapore Convention if a breach of the applicable ethical standards, the obligations of impartiality or independence had a material impact on the parties' decision to enter into an iMSA, there is no equivalent requirement under the New York Convention. This may lead to a scenario where a breach of impartiality or independence results in refusing to enforce a consent arbitral award under the New York Convention, while such a breach might not be enough for a refusal of enforcement under the Singapore Convention.

Possibility of Opting Out

1.78 Party autonomy played an important role in the negotiation and drafting process of the Singapore Convention. Working Group II concluded that parties to an iMSA would have the possibility of opting out of the Singapore Convention.[205] Therefore, where parties to an iMSA effectively opt out of the application of the Singapore Convention, the competent authority will not enforce the iMSA under the terms of the Singapore Convention. In terms of the mechanics of opting out, Article 5(1)(d) of the

199. Michel Kallipetis, *Singapore Convention Defences Based On Mediator'sMisconduct: Articles 5.1(e) & (f)*, in Harold Abramson (ed.), Singapore Mediation Convention Reference Book, 20(4) Cardozo J. Conflict Resol. 1149 (2018-2019), at 1197-2003. For more on the defences under the Singapore Convention see the commentary to Art. 5 of the Singapore Convention.
200. See *Halliburton Co v Chubb Bermuda Insurance Ltd* [2020] UKSC 48, [2021] 1 Lloyd's Rep 1; and *Newcastle United Football Co v Football Association* [2021] EWHC 349, [2022] 1 Lloyd's Rep 183.
201. *Porter v Magill* [2002] 2 AC 357, at para. 103, *per* Lord Hope.
202. See *Halliburton Co v Chubb Bermuda Insurance Ltd* [2020] UKSC 48, [2021] 1 Lloyd's Rep 1.
203. LCIA Reference Mo. 81160, Decision Rendered 28 August 2009, reported in Arbitration International, Volume 27, Issue 3, 1 September 2011, at 315-474.
204. See *Halliburton Co v Chubb Bermuda Insurance Ltd* [2020] UKSC 48, [2021] 1 Lloyd's Rep 1.
205. Report of Working Group II (Dispute Settlement) on the Work of its 68th Session, A/CN.9/934 (2018), para. 78.

Singapore Convention provides that the competent authority may not grant relief if granting relief would be contrary to the terms of the iMSA. It follows that parties to an iMSA must expressly specify that the iMSA is not subject to the provisions of the Singapore Convention. Parties to an iMSA may also consider inserting a dispute resolution clause in the iMSA, which, in turn, may lead to the non-application of the Singapore Convention. In these circumstances, the competent authority would likely uphold party autonomy by recognising or enforcing the relevant dispute resolution provision, which could take the form of a mediation, arbitration or jurisdiction clause, or a mixed mode dispute resolution clause.[206]

1.79 Unlike the Singapore Convention, the New York Convention provides no options for parties to opt out of its application. This reflects the fact that arbitral awards and iMSAs are fundamentally different in nature. As previously discussed, arbitral awards are based on third-party binding decisions, while iMSAs are based on contractual principles, voluntarily agreed and signed by parties. As part of the parties' agreement, they may choose to opt out of the Singapore Convention. Further, iMSAs can be subject to limited review on contractual grounds if challenged, whereas arbitral awards usually are only subject to procedural review.

1.80 In short, party autonomy means that parties to an iMSA have choices. As canvassed earlier, parties may, in certain circumstances, convert the iMSA into an arbitral award to bring it within the scope of the New York Convention. Further, parties may expressly exclude the application of the Singapore Convention, or they may provide for a dispute resolution provision in the iMSA so that in case of a dispute pertaining to the iMSA, the case will be adjudicated according to the forum chosen by the parties.

Table 1[207] *A Comparison Table on the Enforcement of an iMSA under the Singapore Convention and Enforcement of a Consent Arbitral Award under the New York Convention*

	The Singapore Convention	*The New York Convention*
Enforcement of an agreement to submit disputes to mediation/arbitration.	No. The Singapore Convention does not prescribe an enforcement regime for an agreement to mediate.	Yes. Article II enforces an agreement to arbitrate that is made in writing.

206. Vakhtang Giorgadze, *Dispute Resolution Clauses and the Enforcement of International Mediated Settlement Agreements under the Singapore Convention on Mediation*, TDM 3 (2021).
207. This table provides the differences discussed in this chapter. The table on all differences between enforcement under the Singapore Convention and the New York Convention is provided in Appendix A.

	The Singapore Convention	*The New York Convention*
Commercial Nature.	Yes. The Singapore Convention only applies to commercial iMSAs. The definition of the term 'commercial' does not depend on the domestic law of a Contracting Party to the Singapore Convention.	No. Article I(1) of the New York Convention states that it applies to foreign arbitral awards. However, according to Article I(3), Contracting States can make a reservation and declare that they apply the New York Convention only to awards that are considered 'commercial' according to their domestic laws.
Seat.	No. The Singapore Convention does not provide a seat of mediation.	Yes. A seat of arbitration determines the 'foreign' nature of arbitral awards under Article I(1) of the New York Convention. Also, Article V(1)(e) contains a ground for refusing to enforce an award if that award was set aside or suspended in the jurisdiction where the award was made.
A supervisory court with exclusive jurisdiction over a set-aside procedure.	No. The Singapore Convention does not provide a concept of the seat. As a result, no court has exclusive jurisdiction to set aside an iMSA. However, an iMSA may provide for a dispute resolution clause for the resolution of disputes arising out of the iMSA.	Yes. A seat of arbitration determines a court with exclusive jurisdiction to set aside an award. Article V(1)(e) of the New York Convention contains a reference to the seat of arbitration.

	The Singapore Convention	*The New York Convention*
Contractual defences to enforcement and recognition.	Yes. Article 5(1)(a) – (d) of the Singapore Convention contains grounds for refusing to grant relief that are contractual in nature.	No. The New York Convention does not provide such grounds. The only contractual defence in the New York Convention is found in Article V(1)(a), which relates to the invalidity of the arbitration agreement.
Defences relating to ethical standards.	Yes. Article 5(1)(e) – (f) of the Singapore Convention expressly provides two novel grounds for refusing to enforce iMSAs relating to mediators' misconduct.	Yes. Even though the New York Convention does not expressly provide a defence relating to arbitrators' misconduct, a party has the possibility to raise this defence under the public policy ground according to Article V(2)(b). However, the standard of review under the New York Convention may be different as compared to the Singapore Convention.
Possibility to opt out by parties.	Yes. Parties to an iMSA can opt out of the application of the Singapore Convention.	No. The New York Convention does not contain such a possibility.

ARTICLE 2

Definitions

1. For the purposes of article 1, paragraph 1:

(a) If a party has more than one place of business, the relevant place of business is that which has the closest relationship to the dispute resolved by the settlement agreement, having regard to the circumstances known to, or contemplated by, the parties at the time of the conclusion of the settlement agreement;
(b) If a party does not have a place of business, reference is to be made to the party's habitual residence.

2. A settlement agreement is "in writing" if its content is recorded in any form. The requirement that a settlement agreement be in writing is met by an electronic communication if the information contained therein is accessible so as to be useable for subsequent reference.
3. "Mediation" means a process, irrespective of the expression used or the basis upon which the process is carried out, whereby parties attempt to reach an amicable settlement of their dispute with the assistance of a third person or persons ("the mediator") lacking the authority to impose a solution upon the parties to the dispute.

COMMENTARY

2.01 This commentary will address the following issues which arise from Article 2:

(1) the definition of the term 'place of business';
(2) the definition of the term 'in writing'; and
(3) the definition of the term 'mediation'.

Article 2(1): For the Purposes of Article 1, Paragraph 1

2.02 Article 2(1) of the Singapore Convention serves to elucidate the definition provided in Article 1(1) as to how an international mediated settlement agreement (iMSA) may be considered 'international' for the purposes of the Convention. Working Group II thought that it was important to set out a definition of 'international' to reduce the risk of abuse of process by the parties.[1] As explained by Schnabel, 'Although the Model Law enables parties to a mediation to opt into being covered even if the "international" criterion is not otherwise met, that approach was seen as too broad for the Convention [by the drafters in Working Group II].'[2] First, Article 2(1) provides guidance on what is to be considered a party's 'place of business', for the purposes of Article 1(1), where a party has more than one place of business. Second, Article 2(1) acknowledges and provides for the possibility that parties to iMSAs may not have entered into iMSAs in the capacity of non-natural legal persons (that is, parties entering into iMSAs in their personal capacities). In doing so, it provides further clarification on the definition of 'place of business' in respect of natural persons.

Article 2(1)(a): Parties with More Than One Place of Business

2.03 Article 2(1)(a) provides a general framework for determining a party's place of business, where it has more than one place of business. The place of business which yields the relationship closest to that of the dispute resolved by the iMSA will be prioritised. A relevant indicator in determining a party's place of business is where a substantial part of the obligations under the commercial relationship which forms the subject matter of the dispute resolved by the iMSA is fulfilled.[3] The fact that the subject matter of the dispute itself is most closely connected to one jurisdiction may also be another relevant indicator.[4]

2.04 Article 2(1)(a) is also grounded by a temporal clause: the parties' relevant places of business have to be determined with regard to the circumstances known to, or contemplated by, the parties *at the time of the conclusion of the settlement agreement*. If circumstances such as a cross-border acquisition of a party or a simple migration of their place of business into another jurisdiction are made known (actual knowledge or objective knowledge)[5] to the parties at the time the iMSA is concluded, the test applied under Article 2(1)(a) may be administered to determine the affected party's place of business. This is because in light of the existence of an older and newer place of business (that is, more than one place of business), the most relevant one *vis-à-vis* the affected party may need to be ascertained to ensure that the iMSA sought to be enforced satisfies the international scope of the Singapore Convention. However, if, at the time

1. See Intervention of the Chair, in UNCITRAL Audio Recordings: Working Group II (Dispute Settlement), 65th Session, 14 September 2016, 9:30-12:30.
2. Timothy Schnabel, *The Singapore Convention on Mediation: A Framework for the Cross-Border Recognition and Enforcement of Mediated Settlements*, 19(1) Pepp. Disp. Resol. L.J. 1 (2019), at 21.
3. See *Fung Sang Trading Limited v Kai Sun Sea Products and Food Company Limited* [1992] HKLR 40. See the case illustration in commentary to Art. 1(1).
4. *D Heung and Associates, Architects and Engineers v Pacific Enterprises (Holdings) Company Limited* 04.05.1995, CLOUT case No. 108. See the case illustration in commentary to Art. 1(1).
5. The notion of 'Nelsonian blindness' may also be considered as relevant knowledge: see Michael P. Furmston, *Some Themes and Thoughts*, 17 SAcLJ 141 (2005), at 141-147.

of the conclusion of the iMSA, parties have no such knowledge, the question of whether parties have more than one place of business does not arise.[6]

2.05 The Singapore Convention takes a different approach in determining the place of business when parties have more than one place of business as compared to the UNCITRAL Model Law on International Commercial Mediation and International Settlement Agreements Resulting from Mediation (2018) (Model Law on Mediation). While Article 3(3)(a) of the Model Law on Mediation puts an emphasis on 'the closest relationship to the agreement to mediate', Article 2(1)(a) of the Singapore Convention focuses on the dispute that was resolved by, and documented in, the iMSA. The drafting history of Article 2(1)(a) shows that Working Group II initially considered the suggestion that the definition should focus on the conciliation process rather than the settlement agreement, which would be consistent with the UNCITRAL Model Law on International Commercial Conciliation (2002) (Model Law on Conciliation), as Article 1(4) of the Model Law on Conciliation referred to 'an agreement to conciliate'.[7] However, the suggestion was eventually rejected, on the ground that: there were situations where parties would reach a settlement agreement without an agreement to conciliate; parties to an agreement to conciliate might be different from parties to a settlement agreement, and parties' places of business could differ at the time of conclusion of the agreement to conciliate and at the formation of the settlement agreement.[8]

2.06 Reference can be made to jurisprudence on Article 10 of the United Nations Convention on Contracts for the International Sale of Goods (CISG) as to what constitutes 'the closest relationship' for determining parties' place of business.[9] In *S.A. Isocab France v E.C.B.S*, the court deemed that a party's relevant place of business was in Belgium and not in the US, on the ground that the invoice was addressed to the place in Belgium and issued in Dutch. Therefore, the contract had the closest relationship to the place of business in Belgium.[10] In another *Floor tiles case*,[11] the court found that the

6. The same temporal clause can be found in Art. 10(a) of the United Nations Convention on Contracts for the International Sale of Goods (CISG), which makes reference to 'the circumstances known to or contemplated by the parties at any time before or at the conclusion of the contract' for determining a party's place of business. It is suggested that in the context of the CISG, if the relevant circumstances are not known to parties at the latest of the conclusion of the contract, they will not be taken into account. In addition, reference shall not be made to the argument that 'parties ought to have known' relevant circumstances. See Fritz Enderlein and Dietrich Maskow, *International Sales Law: United Nations Convention on Contracts for the International Sale of Goods Convention on the Limitation Period in the International Sale of Goods*, Oceana Publications (1992), at 71.
7. Report of Working Group II (Dispute Settlement) on the Work of its 65th Session (Vienna, 12-23 September 2016), A/CN.9/896 (2016), at para. 158. Available at http://undocs.org/A/CN.9/896 (Accessed 17 May 2022).
8. *Id.*, para. 159.
9. Art. 10(a) of the CISG states that if a party has more than one place of business, the place of business is that which has the closest relationship to the contract and its performance, having regard to the circumstances known to or contemplated by the parties at any time before or at the conclusion of the contract.
10. Belgium 2 June 1999 District Court Hasselt (*Isocab France v E.C.B.S.*), available at https://cisgw3.law.pace.edu/cases/990602b1.html (Accessed 28 January 2021).

contract had the closest relationship to a party's place of business in Germany and not to the party's representative office in Spain because of 'control over the formation and performance of the contract, which the [buyer] was well aware of'. In *Asante Techs. v PMC-Sierra, Inc.*,[12] the court found that the contract at issue had the closest relationship to the place of business in Canada based on several factors, including that the claims were related to breaches of representations made by the defendant from Canada, the products in question were manufactured in Canada and the purchase orders were sent directly to Canada.

Case Illustrations

Illustration [A]: *Calvin Pte Ltd* (Calvin) and *Jimmy Pte Ltd* (Jimmy) are companies registered in Saltsfield. They have reached an MSA under the auspices of the Saltsfield Mediation Centre to resolve a non-payment issue in respect of the sale and exchange of goods. It was public knowledge to both parties that Jimmy was in the final stages of moving its operations into Ruritania because tariffs imposed by the Saltsfield government on raw material imports, which came into effect 24 months earlier, severely drove up its operational costs. If Calvin and Jimmy wish to enforce the terms of their settlement agreement in accordance with the Singapore Convention, Article 2(1)(a) must be applied to determine if the 'international' requirement established by Article 1(1) of the Singapore Convention has been satisfied: that is, parties need to show that Jimmy's place of business is more closely connected with Ruritania, possibly by showing how a substantial part of the obligations under the commercial relationship which forms the subject matter of the dispute resolved by the iMSA is performed there.

Illustration [B]: *Emma Pte Ltd* (Emma) and *Roberts Pte Ltd* (Roberts), companies registered in Saltsfield, have reached an MSA under the auspices of the Saltsfield Mediation Centre to resolve a non-payment issue in respect of the sale and exchange of goods. Subsequently, Roberts experienced unexpected cash flow problems and was sold off to an angel investor from Ruritania in a 'fire sale'. The investor decided to immediately shut down Roberts' premises in Saltsfield and move its operations to Ruritania. For the purposes of enforcing the terms of the settlement agreement under the Singapore Convention, Roberts would not be taken to have more than one place of business according to Article 2(1)(a) because the changes in its circumstances were not within the actual or objective contemplation of the parties at the time of the conclusion of the settlement agreement. Consequently, it will be difficult for Emma and Roberts to prove that

11. Germany 28 February 2000 Appellate Court Stuttgart (*Floor tiles case*), reported in UNCITRAL Digest of Case Law on the United Nations Convention on Contracts for the International Sale of Goods (2016 Edition), at 69-70.
12. *Asante Techs. v PMC-Sierra, Inc.* 164 F. Supp. 2d 1142, 2001 U.S. Dist. LEXIS 16000 (N.D. Cal. 27 July 2001).

their settlement agreement is 'international' *per* Article 1(1) of the Singapore Convention, as, at the time of the settlement agreement's conclusion, only one place of business was apparent (that is, in Saltsfield).

Article 2(1)(b): Habitual Residence of Natural Persons

2.07 Article 2(1)(b) establishes that parties who enter into iMSAs in their personal capacity will have their place of habitual residence considered for the purposes of determining if the 'international' requirement under Article 1(1) of the Singapore Convention is satisfied.

Case Illustration

Anthia runs a humble baking business from her home in Greenwood. She receives small catering orders online but has a long-term commercial deal with *Lucas Sdn Bhd* (Lucas) to supply an endless flow of chocolate chip cookies for all of Lucas's offices in Ruritania. Unfortunately, both parties had a dispute because Anthia threatened to repudiate the supply contract, hoping to raise the prices of her delicious cookies, but Lucas refused to budge. Both parties proceed for mediation at the Greenwood International Mediation Centre, and a settlement agreement is concluded. For the purposes of enforcing the settlement agreement under the Singapore Convention, the parties must show that it is 'international' *per* Article 1(1), with reference to the places of their business. Applying Article 2(1)(b), Anthia's place of business would be her place of habitual residence, which is in Greenwood.

2.08 A question might arise with respect to how to determine a person's habitual residence. Even though the term 'habitual residence' has been consistently used in UNCITRAL instruments, including in Article 1(5)(b) of the Model Law on Conciliation, Article 3(3)(b) of the Model Law on Mediation and Article 1(4)(b) of the Model Law on Arbitration, no definition or guiding principle is provided as to how to define a person's habitual residence. This question might be of practical importance, as the determination of one's habitual residence may lead to the non-application of the Singapore Convention.

2.09 The term 'habitual residence' plays a key role in the application of the Convention of 25 October 1980 on the Civil Aspects of International Child Abduction, as the purpose of this Convention is to establish a procedure to ensure children's prompt return to the State of their habitual residence. While the drafters of this Convention deliberately chose not to provide any strict definition of 'habitual residence' in order to avoid a formalistic approach in the interpretation of the term,[13] courts, particularly in the US and England, have frequently interpreted this term in child abduction cases. By way of example, the Family Division of the High Court of Justice in England opined that the child's habitual residence was in New York because the parents rented a place in New York for three months and the child was receiving therapy in New York.[14] In *Feder v Evans-Feder*,[15] the US Court of Appeals for the Third Circuit opined that the child's habitual residence was in Australia, on the ground that the child lived in Australia for six months, attended preschool and was enrolled in a kindergarten and the parents purchased a flat in Australia.[16] The Bombay High Court in *Sandip Shankarlal Kedia v Pooja Kedia* stated that the wife's habitual residence was in Dubai because she was a director of three companies and had businesses in Dubai.[17]

2.10 While these cases illustrate how 'habitual residence' is defined in the context of family law and child abduction disputes, they can be relevant to the interpretation of 'habitual residence' for the purposes of UNCITRAL instruments and the Singapore Convention. The case below is illustrative in this regard, in which the Bombay High Court addressed the issue of what constitutes 'habitually resident' for the purposes of the Arbitration and Conciliation Act, 1996 of India, which is based significantly on the UNCITRAL Model Law on Arbitration.[18]

Case Illustration

In *Aslam Ismail Khan Deshmukh v Asap Fluids Pvt. Ltd.*,[19] the Bombay High Court addressed whether the applicant's habitual residence was outside India. This issue was of significant importance, as the answer to this question would determine the international nature of the arbitral proceedings at issue.[20] The applicant submitted that the arbitral proceedings were not international, as the applicant was domiciled in India and held an Indian passport. In addition, the

13. Jeff Atkinson, *The Meaning of 'Habitual Residence' under the Hague Convention on the Civil Aspects of International Child Abduction and the Hague Convention on the Protection of Children*, 63(4) Oklahoma L. Rev. 647 (2011), at 649.
14. *Re Bates* [1989] 2 WLUK 293 (High Court of Justice, Family Division, Royal Courts of Justice, London WC2, United Kingdom, No. CA 122/89 (Fam. 1989)).
15. *Feder v Evans-Feder* 63 F.3d 217, 1995 U.S. App. LEXIS 21443 (3d Cir. Pa. 8 August 1995).
16. *Id.*, at 23.
17. *Sandip Shankarlal Kedia v Pooja Kedia* on 29 April 2013, WP.2636/2013-judgment.
18. The list of states that adopted arbitration laws on the basis of the UNCITRAL Model Law on Arbitration, available at https://uncitral.un.org/en/texts/arbitration/modellaw/commercial_arbitration/status (Accessed 27 January 2021).
19. *Aslam Ismail Khan Deshmukh v Asap Fluids Pvt. Ltd. and another*, 22 February 2019, the Bombay High Court.
20. According to s. 11(12)(a) of the Arbitration and Conciliation Act, 1996 of India, the Supreme Court has exclusive jurisdiction on appointing arbitrators in international arbitration cases.

applicant was residing in Dubai only for work and frequently visiting his family in India.[21]

The court made a number of important conclusions in this case. First, the court did not see any distinction between the terms 'ordinary residence' and 'habitual residence' and stated, '[t]he expression ordinarily carries on business would mean regularly or habitually not casually. It obviously cannot mean "always". The plain and popular meaning of the word "ordinarily" means usually, normally and exceptionally as contrasted with extraordinarily'.[22] For the court, 'ordinary residence' did not mean that a person uses a particular place always or on a permanent and uninterrupted basis. Whether a person habitually resides in a particular place depends on the specific case and surrounding circumstances. The court listed some of the factors and tests that can have an impact on determining a person's habitual residence: (1) the quality and not duration of residence; (2) residence must be actual and there must be an actual physical presence; (3) the purposes may be one or several but it has to be a settled purpose; (4) the reasons why a person may reside in a place include education, business or profession, employment, health, family or merely love of the place; (5) the specific factors for determining one's habitual residence include location of bank accounts, location of movable objects, purchase of a house, obtaining licences and residential status; (6) residence must be something more than casual.[23] The court, based on these factors, stated that the applicant was habitually residing in Dubai because the applicant's address was in Dubai, where he was working and residing and the applicant was receiving his remuneration in USD in a bank in Dubai.[24]

2.11 The concept of 'habitual residence' plays an important role in cross-border insolvency. The UNCITRAL Model Law on Cross-Border Insolvency (1997) refers to the concept of 'habitual residence' in several provisions, particularly in relation to the determination of a debtor's centre of interests.[25] Reference to a debtor's habitual residence can be found in Regulation (EU) 2015/848 on Insolvency Proceedings. However, similar to the other instruments, no definition of habitual residence is provided in the UNCITRAL Model Law on Cross-Border Insolvency (1997) and in Regulation (EU) 2015/848 on Insolvency Proceedings. A recent judgment below of the Federal Court of Australia summarises what constitutes a person's habitual residence for the purposes of the UNCITRAL Model Law on Cross-Border Insolvency (1997).

21. *Aslam Ismail Khan Deshmukh v Asap Fluids Pvt. Ltd. and another*, 22 February 2019, the Bombay High Court, at para. 8.
22. *Id.*, para. 27.
23. *Id.*, para. 30.
24. *Id.*, para. 32.
25. Art. 16(3) states that in the absence of proof to the contrary, the debtor's registered office, or habitual residence in the case of an individual, is presumed to be the centre of the debtor's main interests.

Case Illustration

In the Australian case of *Meng v Mackellar (A Bankrupt)*,[26] the court addressed whether the debtor was 'habitually resident' in Australia for the purposes of the UNCITRAL Model Law on Cross-border Insolvency (1997). In determining a debtor's 'habitual residence', a court can consider 'a wide variety of circumstances that bear upon where a person is said to reside and whether that residence is to be described as habitual' and 'past and present intentions will often bear upon the significance that is to be attached to particular circumstances such as the duration of a person's connections with a particular place of residence'.[27] The court explained that even though it is unlikely, a person might habitually reside in more than one place. Eventually, the court did not find that the debtor was habitually residing in Australia, on the ground that there was 'no evidence as to the duration of his residency, the permanence or otherwise of it, his modality of living or of his intentions'.[28]

Article 2(2): Meaning of 'in writing' Includes Electronic Communications

2.12 The 'in writing' requirement is the most fundamental one that parties must fulfil, if they would like to have their iMSAs enforced under the Singapore Convention. A settlement agreement that is set out in writing contains the necessary information, proving and demonstrating to the enforcing competent authority the enforceable obligations which are covered by the settlement agreement.[29] It should be noted that there is no requirement that the contents of the iMSA have to be drafted into a single document.[30] This is because the drafters of the Convention are well aware that, in practice, mediation may take place under flexible conditions and the outcome of mediation may be contained in an exchange of communications (for instance, over a series of emails and text messages).[31] Furthermore, it is simply common practice in contract drafting that the resulting iMSA may contain clauses which refer to other

26. *Meng (as joint and several trustees of the property of Mackellar (a Bankrupt)) v Mackellar (a bankrupt)* [2020] FCA 1151.
27. *Id.*, at 52.
28. *Id.*, at 54.
29. See Intervention of Norway, in UNCITRAL Audio Recordings: Working Group II (Arbitration and Conciliation), 63rd Session, 8 September 2015, 9:30-12:30.
30. See Intervention of the Chair, in UNCITRAL Audio Recordings: Working Group II (Dispute Settlement), 65th Session, 21 September 2016, 9:30-12:30.
31. See Interventions of Argentina, Canada, the UNCITRAL Secretariat, Mexico, Kuwait, and the United States, in UNCITRAL Audio Recordings: Working Group II (Dispute Settlement), 65th Session, 14 September 2016, 14:00-17:00; Interventions of the United States, Switzerland, and the International Academy of Mediators (IAM), in UNCITRAL Audio Recordings: Working Group II (Dispute Settlement), 65th Session, 20 September 2016, 14:00-17:00; and Intervention of Italy, in UNCITRAL Audio Recordings: Working Group II (Dispute Settlement), 65th Session, 21 September 2016, 9:30-12:30.

documents, contracts or communications, validly incorporating them into the agreement.[32] According to Article 2(2), the 'in writing' requirement for an iMSA is fulfilled 'if its content is recorded in any form [...] [including] an electronic communication if the information contained therein is accessible so as to be usable for subsequent reference'.[33]

2.13 This provision acknowledges the possibility of disputes settled through online dispute resolution (ODR) mechanisms administered through various channels of electronic communication (such as emails, text messages and online forums),[34] and other forms of online settlement interactions (such as those administered by ODR service providers)[35] to be amenable to enforcement under the Convention.[36] Parties would remain obliged to conclude their iMSA by endorsing it in a manner recognised by Article 4(2),[37] and providing the enforcement authority with evidence that the iMSA was a result of mediation.[38] There is no requirement that the iMSA be contained in a single document. It could, for example, comprise an exchange of emails.[39]

2.14 A question might arise as to what constitutes an 'electronic communication'. While the Singapore Convention itself does not provide a definition of an 'electronic communication', an analogy can be drawn from the United Nations Convention on the Use of Electronic Communications in International Contracts. According to this Convention, 'electronic communications' include any statement, declaration, demand, notice or request by means of data messages, that is, information generated, sent, received or stored by electronic, magnetic, optical or similar means, including, but are not limited to, electronic data interchange, electronic mail, telegram, telex or telecopy; of data messages.[40] Due to the fact that the Singapore Convention does not require the contents of an iMSA to be recorded in one document,[41] there will be compliance with Article 2(2) if a part of an iMSA is documented by means of electronic communication and the other part is recorded on paper, provided that the party relying on the iMSA can identify the relevant contents of the iMSA.

32. *Ibid.*
33. United Nations Convention on International Settlement Agreements Resulting from Mediation (Singapore Convention), Art. 2(2).
34. See United Nations Commission on International Trade Law, Report on the Work of its 51st Session, UN Doc A/73/17 (2018), at para. 23.
35. See, for example, such services as provided by the online dispute resolution provider Fairway, https://www.fairwayresolution.com, which provides online dispute resolution software and services including online facilitated negotiations, access to an online mediator, and an adjudicated decision should mediation fail. See also the case illustration in the commentary to Art. 1(1).
36. See Michael G. Bowers, *Implementing an Online Dispute Resolution Scheme: Using Domain Name Registration Contracts to Create a Workable Framework*, 64(4) Vanderbilt Law Review 1265 (2011).
37. Singapore Convention, Art. 4(1)(a) read with Art. 4(2).
38. *Id.*, Art. 4(1)(b).
39. See the commentary to Art. 4(2).
40. Art. 4.
41. Report of Working Group II (Arbitration and Conciliation) on the Work of 64th Session (New York, 1-5 February 2016), A/CN.9/867 (2016) at para. 134. Available at http://undocs.org/A/CN.9/867 (Accessed 16 February 2021).

2.15 A similar provision is not found in the New York Convention on Recognition and Enforcement of Foreign Arbitral Awards (1958) (New York Convention), perhaps not surprisingly given that the New York Convention was adopted in 1958. This was well before the information technology (IT), ODR and artificial intelligence (AI) revolutions. The potential limitations of not explicitly embracing electronic communications within the definition of 'writing' are evident in jurisprudence addressing this point in the New York Convention.[42] However, on 7 July 2006, the UNCITRAL adopted a recommendation regarding the interpretation of Article II(2) and Article VII(1) of the New York Convention, according to which States are encouraged to apply a more-favourable-form requirement in relation to arbitration agreements and arbitral awards as compared to what is provided under the New York Convention.[43] Specifically, States are recommended to rely on Article 7(3) of the Model Law on Arbitration, which states that an arbitration agreement is in writing if its content is recorded in any form, whether the arbitration agreement or contract has been concluded orally, by conduct, or by other means.

Point of Interest

Article 2(2) of the Singapore Convention establishes that the writing requirement for a settlement agreement may be met by electronic communication so long as the information in the electronic communication is accessible for subsequent reference.

This article gives particular effect to the emerging field of ODR in cross-border mediation. ODR refers to any form of dispute resolution which occurs in part or in whole through online communications or proceedings. Therefore, ODR proceedings may be entirely ad hoc, as in the case of parties settling their dispute through an exchange of emails and Skype calls with the assistance of a mediator. Alternatively, they may be entirely institutionalised, as in the case of parties submitting to a set of institutional mediation rules, selecting a mediator from a pre-determined panel, and participating in remote sessions hosted by a centralised platform on the dispute resolution provider's server.

42. See, for example, *Sphere Drake Insurance plc v Marine Towing, Inc.* 16 F.3d 666 (5th Cir. 1994), 1994 A.M.C. 1581, cert. denied, 513 U.S. 87, 1115 S.Ct. 195 (Mem), 130 L.Ed.2d at 127; *Kahn Lucas Lancaster, Inc. v Lark Intern. Ltd.* 186 F.3d 210 (2nd Cir. 1999), at 215. In both cases the courts struggled to interpret the writing requirement in Art. II(2) of the New York Convention when faced with electronically concluded arbitration agreements and outcomes. Art. II(2) of the New York Convention provides, 'The term "agreement in writing" shall include an arbitral clause in a contract or an arbitration agreement, signed by the parties or contained in an exchange of letters or telegrams.' Also see David N. Baquero, *Problemáticas del arbitraje virtual y algunas reflexiones a la luz del estatuto arbitral internacional colombiano,* 14(2) Revista e-Mercatoria 3.
43. Recommendation regarding the interpretation of Art. II, para. 2, and Art. VII, para. 1, of the Convention on the Recognition and Enforcement of Foreign Arbitral Awards, done in New York, 10 June 1958 (2006). Available at https://uncitral.un.org/sites/uncitral.un.org/files/media-documents/uncitral/en/a2e.pdf (Accessed 16 February 2021).

Whatever the case, the prevalence and use of ODR methods are expanding rapidly. ODR is relatively affordable for parties in cross-border disputes because it eliminates the need for participants to travel and reduces the costs associated with using physical meeting rooms. The relative affordability of ODR compared to traditional forms of cross-border dispute resolution for some jurisdictions presents a valuable opportunity to expand access to commercial justice for micro, small, and medium enterprises in cross-border disputes. Within the Asia Pacific Economic Cooperation (APEC), for example, member economies are considering the adoption of a regional ODR platform for resolving commercial cross-border disputes. The platform would include a set of opt-in ODR procedures and rules, taking guidance from the UNCITRAL Technical Notes on Online Dispute Resolution. In Singapore, the Singapore Mediation Centre launched its Online Dispute Resolution Platform in 2019.[44] In the EU, the Regulation (EU) No 524/2013 established the European Online Dispute Resolution (ODR), the idea of which is to provide an independent and cost-effective out-of-court dispute resolution means to traders and consumers with the help of a neutral third party.[45]

Mediation laws in some jurisdictions expressly provide the possibility of conducting mediation by using electronic means of communication. By way of illustration, Article 18(3) of the Law on Certain Aspects of Mediation in Civil Matters of 2012 of Cyprus provides that the mediation process may be conducted via the use of modern technologies of communication.[46] In Spain, Article 24 of the Royal Decree-Law 5/2012, of 5 March, Mediation in Civil and Commercial Matters states that parties may agree to conduct mediation partially or wholly via the use of electronic means, which shall guarantee the identity of parties.[47] In Singapore, section 3(3) of the Mediation Act 2017 specifies that a meeting with a mediator includes a meeting conducted by electronic communication, video conferencing or other electronic means. The same rule is provided under section 4(3) of the Mediation Ordinance of Hong Kong. UNCITRAL Notes on Mediation (2021) also makes reference to the use of electronic communication tools.[48]

44. Singapore Mediation Centre's Online Dispute Resolution Platform, https://smc.resolvedisputes.online/#/access/login (Accessed 18 May 2019).
45. Regulation (EU) No. 524/2013 of the European Parliament and of the Council of 21 May 2013 on online dispute resolution for consumer disputes and amending Regulation (EC) No. 2006/2004 and Directive 2009/22/EC (Regulation on consumer ODR).
46. Victoria - Zoi Papagiannis & George Mountis, *Cyprus*, in Nadja Alexander et al. (eds), EU Mediation Law Handbook - Regulatory Robustness Ratings for Mediation Regimes, Wolters Kluwer (2017), at 150.
47. Arts 30-38 of the Royal Decree 980/2013 implements a simplified mediation process conducted online.
48. By way of example, the document notes that a preparatory meeting with the parties can take place in person or remotely through a video conference call. It is also noted that the parties and mediator can agree to submit mediation documents electronically. The use of electronic documents can make mediation more efficient and expeditious. It is also noted that the use of

Mediation institutions' rules also provide parties with the possibility of conducting mediation by using electronic means of communication. By way of example, Article 6.5 of the Rules of the Singapore International Mediation Centre (SIMC) states that the pre-mediation conference may take place in person, by teleconference, or by other electronic means. In addition, according to Article 6.7 of the same Rules, the mediator may communicate with the parties orally, in writing, in person, electronically, or otherwise, and may do so jointly or separately before and during the scheduled mediation. Article 6.2 of the Mediation Rules of the London Court of International Arbitration (LCIA) states that the mediator may communicate with the parties orally or in writing, together or individually, and may convene a meeting or meetings in person at a venue to be determined by the mediator, or virtually by conference call, videoconference or using other communications technology (or in a combined form) after consultation with the parties. Section M7(ii) of the American Arbitration Association (AAA)'s Commercial Arbitration Rules and Mediation Procedure states that the mediator may have separate or *ex parte* meetings with parties and their representatives via telephone, in writing, via email, online, in person or otherwise. Article 9(3) of the Mediation Rules 2018 of the Vienna International Arbitration Centre (VIAC) authorises the mediator to conduct the mediation process online or in person. Article 8(3) of the Mediation Rules of the Vietnam Mediation Centre (VMC) provides the same possibility. Article 4(4) of the UNCITRAL Mediation Rules (2021) states that in conducting the mediation, the mediator may, in consultation with the parties and taking into account the circumstances of the dispute, utilise any technological means as he or she considers appropriate, including to communicate with the parties and to hold meetings remotely. Even where institutional rules do not explicitly consist of a possibility to conduct the mediation process online, a mediator usually has the right to conduct the process in a manner he or she deems appropriate, which includes conducting the mediation process by using electronic means of communication in consultation with parties.

Institutional rules provide parties with the possibility to record settlement terms in an electronic form, which is in compliance with the Singapore Convention on Mediation and the Model Law on Mediation. Article 8.3 of the LCIA Mediation Rules states that unless the parties agree otherwise, the settlement agreement may be signed electronically and/or in counterparts and assembled into a single instrument. Similarly, pursuant to Article 8.2 of the SIMC Mediation Rules, a settlement agreement may take the form of an electronic record and be signed by

---

electronic means of communication requires 'to consider whether all parties have access to, or are familiar with, such means. The parties and the mediator may need to consider issues of compatibility, storage, access, data security as well as related costs when deciding on electronic means of communication'. See UNCITRAL Notes on Mediation (2021), paras 58-66.

an electronic signature. The same provision can be found in the rules of the Singapore Mediation Centre (SMC). In light of the requirements set out in the Singapore Convention, Article 8(3) of the UNCITRAL Mediation Rules (2021) states that the parties can sign a settlement agreement electronically.[49]

In many jurisdictions, MSAs take the form of a private contract. Therefore, even without the Singapore Convention, parties still have the possibility to sign an MSA electronically, provided that parties comply with the requirements of the applicable national law. By way of example, in *Waddle v Elrod*,[50] the Supreme Court of Tennessee deemed the settlement agreement valid, on the ground that the parties intended to finalise the settlement by electronic means. The court also stated that an exchange of emails by the counsels satisfied the writing requirements for the purposes of the Statute of Frauds. Similarly, in *Kluver v PPL Mont.*,[51] the Supreme Court of Montana deemed the settlement agreement concluded and signed electronically as an enforceable instrument. In *Powell v City of Newton*,[52] the Supreme Court of North Carolina stated that electronic signatures have the same legal force as traditional signatures as long as the requirements of the statute of frauds are satisfied. In this case, the applicable requirements were not met because the parties did not intend to sign the settlement agreement electronically.

ODR and mediation via electronic means of communication were particularly on the rise in 2020 when the world faced unprecedented challenges due to the COVID-19 pandemic.[53] The massive shutdown of businesses across countries forced dispute resolution institutions to switch to online processes and to provide special COVID-19 protocols. By way of example, the SIMC adopted the SIMC COVID-19 Protocol, which allows parties to enjoy reduced fees and online processes in response to the global pandemic.[54] Hong Kong's COVID-19 Online Dispute Resolution Scheme, which was introduced in 2020, is especially focused

49. According to Art. 8(3) of the UNCITRAL Mediation Rules (2021): The requirement that a settlement agreement shall be signed by the parties is met in relation to an electronic communication if: (a) A method is used to identify the parties and to indicate the parties' intention in respect of the information contained in the electronic communication; (b) The method is used either: (i) As reliable as appropriate for the purpose for which the electronic communication was generated or communicated, in the light of all the circumstances, including any relevant agreement; or (ii) Proven in fact to have fulfilled the functions described in subparagraph (a) above, by itself or together with further evidence.
50. *Waddle v Elrod* 2012 Tenn. LEXIS 290, 367 S.W.3d 217, 2012 WL 1406451 (Tenn. 24 April 2012).
51. *Kluver v PPL Mont.* LLC, 2012 Mont. LEXIS 382, 2012 MT 321, 368 Mont. 101, 293 P.3d 817 (Mont. 31 December 2012).
52. *Powell v City of Newton* 2010 N.C. LEXIS 1078, 364 N.C. 562, 703 S.E.2d 723 (N.C. 20 December 2010).
53. Noam Ebner and Daniel Rainey, *ODR and Mediation*, in Daniel Rainey, Ethan Katsh and Mohamed Abdel Wahab (eds), Online Dispute Resolution: Theory and Practice (2nd Ed.), Eleven Intl. Publishing (2021).
54. See https://simc.com.sg/simc-covid-19-protocol/ (Accessed 9 March 2021).

on micro, small and medium-sized enterprises (MSMEs) that may be adversely affected or hard hit by the pandemic with claim amounts capped at HK$ 500,000.[55] The VIAC also adopted a special 'Mediation Initiative', the idea of which is to restore the business relationships affected by the global pandemic. Therefore, ODR processes, including mediation, will most likely continue to rise, particularly in cross-border disputes, given the reduced cost of mediating online and the growing familiarity of dispute resolution users with the technology.

Therefore, in the scenario that a party seeks to enforce a mediated settlement agreement resulting from online mediation in a Contracting Party to the Singapore Convention, the agreement being electronic in nature is unlikely to present an issue to its enforcement, thanks to Article 2(2). As indicated previously, this distinguishes the Singapore Convention from the New York Convention, which contains a writing requirement in Article II(2) thought by scholars not to anticipate the advent of electronically concluded arbitration agreements or e-arbitration proceedings. Courts such as the US Fifth and Second Circuits have at times struggled to interpret the New York Convention's writing requirement in light of its narrow wording. Unlike in the case of MSAs, institutional rules or arbitration laws based on the Model Law on Arbitration rarely provide for the possibility of recording an arbitral award electronically. The Arbitration Rules of the LCIA represent one of the very few examples, if not the only example, which contains the possibility of rendering an arbitral award electronically.[56] In 2020, the International Chamber of Commerce (ICC) adopted the ICC Guidance Note on Possible Measures Aimed at Mitigating the Effects of the COVID-19 Pandemic, which states that subject to the mandatory requirements of the applicable law, the parties may agree that an award be signed by the tribunal in counterparts and all such counterparts be assembled in a single electronic file. With respect to national arbitration laws, while Article 31 of the Model Law on Arbitration requires an award to be made in writing, section 52(1) of the Arbitration Act 1996 of England gives freedom to parties to agree on the form of an award. Similarly, according to Article 189(1) of Chapter 12 of the Swiss Private International Law Statute, parties have the freedom to agree on the form of an award. However, practice regarding recording an arbitral award electronically is not uniform and parties may face challenges in the enforcement of such an award under the New York Convention. In contrast, competent authorities or courts are unlikely to face these interpretation challenges when reviewing electronically concluded MSAs under the Singapore Convention.

Article 2(3) and Definitions of Mediation

2.16 The various ways in which mediation has been defined by scholars, policymakers, legislatures, courts and dispute resolution organisations have influenced its practice. Conceptual definitions of mediation draw upon the objectives and values of the process. They frequently attempt to identify the underlying philosophy of mediation and set theoretical parameters, objectives and criteria for conducting the process.

2.17 In many cases, the detailed mediation policies of mediation institutions shape their practice. A legislative illustration of a conceptual definition of mediation may be found in Article 1(1) of the Austrian Law on Mediation in Civil Cases 2001, which refers to the principles of neutrality, voluntariness, systematic communication methods and self-determination. The definition also refers to the specialist qualifications required of mediators.[57] Another is located in section 4 of the Mediation Ordinance of Hong Kong,[58] which defines mediation in terms of the nature of the process, the role of the mediator and the activities that attach to mediation. The definition promotes a facilitative approach to mediation but without insisting on it. It highlights the impartiality of the mediator and defines the core mediator functions as assisting parties to communicate with each other, identifying the issues in dispute between them, exploring the terrain of those issues, generating options for resolution of the dispute and reaching an agreement.

2.18 Conversely, there is also evidence that definitions of mediation have been influenced by practice, making them more descriptive than conceptual in nature. Early proponents of action-based mediation theory are Kressel and Pruitt, who used an inductive approach to develop their research on, and theories of, mediation from practice.[59] Della Noce presents the view that where mediation values are not prescribed in conceptual definitions, the way mediation is practised is a result of the worldviews and personal theories of mediators themselves. She argues that the differences in

55. eBRAM, *COVID-19 Online Dispute Resolution (ODR) Scheme*, https://www.ebram.org/covid_19_odr.html.
56. Art. 26.2 states that unless the parties agree otherwise, or the Arbitral Tribunal or LCIA court directs otherwise, any award may be signed electronically and/or in counterparts and assembled into a single instrument.
57. Zivilrechts-Mediations-Gesetz 2001 (ZivMediatG) (the Austrian Law on Mediation in Civil Cases 2001). For an analysis of the Austrian definition of mediation see: Markus Roth and David Gherdane, *Mediation in Österreich – Zivilrechts-Mediations-Gesetz: Rechtlicher Rahmen und Praktische Erfahrungen*, in Klaus J. Hopt and Felix Steffek (eds), Mediation – Rechtstatsachen, Rechtsvergleich, Regelungen, Mohr Siebeck (2008), at 108-112.
58. 2012 Hong Kong Mediation Ordinance (Cap. 620).
59. See Peter T. Coleman, Katharina G. Kugler and Ljubica Chatman, *Adaptive Mediation: An Evidence-Based Contingency Approach to Mediating Conflict*, 28(3) Int'l J. Conflict Mngt 383 (2017); Peter T. Coleman et al., *Putting the Peaces Together: A Situated Model of Mediation*, 26(2) Int'l J. Conflict Mngt 145 (2015), at 163; E. Patrick McDermott, *Discovering the Importance of Mediator Style – An Interdisciplinary Challenge*, 5(4) Negot. & Conflict Mngt Research 340 (2012); Kenneth Kressel and Howard Gadlin, *Mediating among Scientists: A Mental Model of Expert Practice*, 2 Negot. & Conflict Mngt Research 308 (2009); Lucinda E. Sinclair and William D. Stuart, *Reciprocal-Influence Mediation Model: A Guide for Practice and Research*, 25 Conflict Resol. Q. 185 (2007), at 186-188; E. Patrick McDermott and Ruth Obar, *What's Going on in Mediation: An Empirical Analysis of the Influence of a Mediator's Style on Party Satisfaction and Monetary Benefit*, 9 Harvard Negot. L. Rev. 75 (2004); Kenneth Kressel et al., Mediation Research: The Process and Effectiveness of Third-Party Intervention, Jossey-Bass Publishers (1989).

mediation practice matter significantly, and that the values which in fact underpin practice must be recognised by policymakers.[60]

2.19 Descriptive definitions of mediation are often found in the general legislation on mediation and court-annexed mediation statutes. In the US, the Uniform Mediation Act[61] (UMA) has a descriptive definition of mediation: it refers to mediation as a process in which a mediator facilitates communication and negotiation between parties to assist them in reaching a voluntary agreement regarding their dispute. The Reporters' Working Notes explain that the definition has been framed to exclude determinative dispute resolution processes, as well as interventions such as counselling. However, the definition remains broad and seems to include negotiation-based processes where the mediator plays an advisory role.[62] Similarly, the definition of mediation in the European Directive on Mediation (EU Directive) (Articles 3(a) and 3(b))[63] is characterised by inclusive wording but draws the line at determinative processes. It explicitly excludes situations where trial judges attempt to facilitate settlement in matters before them and where, in the absence of settlement, they would proceed to hear and determine the matter. This type of intervention is often referred to as judicial settlement. By contrast, dispute resolution processes in which judges mediate cases over which they have no determinative power, so that in the event of no settlement, the case would be referred to another judge for a hearing, are typically referred to as judicial mediation, and fall within the definition of mediation pursuant to the EU Directive.

2.20 The Model Law on Mediation[64] offers a descriptive definition of mediation, recognising the diversity in mediation practice.[65] It is formulated in such a way as to extend to most mediation models and even to other dispute resolution processes such as neutral evaluation. It simply describes mediation as a process by any name, whereby parties request a third person to assist them in their attempts to reach an amicable settlement of their dispute.

60. Dorothy J. Della Noce, Robert A. Baruch Bush and Joseph P. Folger, *Clarifying the Theoretical Underpinnings of Mediation: Implications for Policy and Practice*, 3 Pepp. Disp. Resol. L. J. 39 (2002); Dorothy J. Della Noce, *Mediation Policy: Theory Matters* (1999), available at www.mediate.com.
61. The Uniform Mediation Act is a Model Law which has been adopted in approximately 13 states in the United States. Hawaii, Idaho, South Dakota, District of Columbia, Vermont, Utah, Ohio, Washington, New Jersey, Iowa, Illinois, Nebraska and Georgia. For more information, visit the website of The Uniform Law Commission, www.uniformlaws.org/committees/community-home?CommunityKey=45565a5f-0c57-4bba-bbab-fc7de9a59110w, www.uniformlaws.org/Act.aspx?title=Mediation%20Act.
62. See Reporter's Notes to the UMA in National Conference of Commissioners on Uniform State Laws, *Uniform Mediation Act with Prefatory Note and Comments*, NCCUSL (2001).
63. *Directive 2008/52/EC of the European Parliament and of the Council on certain aspects of mediation in civil and commercial matters*, Official Journal of the European Union L 136/3, (21 May 2008).
64. The UNCITRAL Model Law on International Commercial Mediation and International Settlement Agreements Resulting from Mediation, 2018 (amending the UNCITRAL Model Law on International Commercial Conciliation, 2002).
65. *Id.*, Art. 1(3).

2.21 The Singapore Convention also relies on a descriptive definition of mediation.[66] Descriptive definitions in mediation regulation tend to be broadly framed and encourage diverse mediation practices ranging from interest-based and relational approaches to settlement and advisory models of mediation.[67]

2.22 The definition of 'mediation' in the Singapore Convention is adapted from the definition of 'conciliation' found in Article 1(3) of the Model Law on Conciliation, which reads:

> For the purposes of this Law, 'conciliation' means a process, whether referred to by the expression conciliation, mediation or an expression of similar import, whereby parties request a third person or persons ('the conciliator') to assist them in their attempt to reach an amicable settlement of their dispute arising out of or relating to a contractual or other legal relationship. The conciliator does not have the authority to impose upon the parties a solution to the dispute.

2.23 The above definition was adopted almost word-for-word in the Model Law on Mediation, although the latter Model Law was deliberated upon at the same time as the Singapore Convention and conceivably could have adopted the same definition as the Convention for better uniformity. In any event, Article 1(3) of the Model Law on Mediation reads:

> For the purposes of this Law, 'mediation' means a process, whether referred to by the expression mediation, conciliation or an expression of similar import, whereby parties request a third person or persons ('the mediator') to assist them in their attempt to reach an amicable settlement of their dispute arising out of or relating to a contractual or other legal relationship. The mediator does not have the authority to impose upon the parties a solution to the dispute.

2.24 While Working Group II pointed out that the change in terminology is not intended to have any conceptual or substantive implications,[68] reference will be made to the other differences in the wording of Article 2(3) of the Singapore Convention and Article 1(3) of the current Model Law on Mediation in examining the meaning and scope of the terms 'mediator' and 'mediation'.

66. See Intervention of the Chair, in UNCITRAL Audio Recordings: Working Group II (Arbitration and Conciliation), 63rd Session, 7 September 2015, 10:00-12:30.
67. On different mediation practice models see Michal Alberstein, *Forms of Mediation and Law: Cultures of Dispute Resolution*, 22 Ohio State J. Disp. Resol. 321 (2007); Nabil N. Antaki, *Cultural Diversity and ADR Practices in the World*, in Jean-Claude Goldsmith, Arnold Ingen-Housz and Gerald H. Pointon (eds), ADR in Business: Practice and Issues across Countries and Cultures I, Kluwer Law International (2006), at 265; Nadja Alexander, *The Mediation Metamodel: Understanding Practice*, 26 Conflict Resol. Q. 97 (2008), at 97.
68. See UNCITRAL Working Group II (Arbitration and Conciliation), *Settlement of Commercial Disputes, International Commercial Mediation: Draft Convention on International Settlement Agreements Resulting From Mediation*, Note by the Secretariat, A/CN.9/942 (25 June-13 July 2018), at para. 5.

Meaning of 'mediation' and 'mediator'

2.25 It is clear from discussions by Working Group II that the Singapore Convention on Mediation applies only to *mediated* settlement agreements, and *not* to negotiated settlement agreements which are *not a result of mediation.*[69] The Singapore Convention does not define 'mediator'. The definition of mediator, however, may be discerned from the definition of 'mediation' in Article 2(3). Here 'mediation' is defined broadly to be 'a process, irrespective of the expression used or the basis upon which the process is carried out, whereby parties attempt to reach an amicable settlement of their dispute with the assistance of a third person or persons ("the mediator") lacking the authority to impose a solution upon the parties to the dispute'.[70] It should be noted that while the Working Group II was engaged in substantial discussions over whether 'mediation' for the purposes of the Singapore Convention should be confined to processes which are well-structured or institutional,[71] the drafters ultimately decided not to do so[72] because it is widely accepted that mediation is a flexible process which may manifest in diverse shapes and forms.[73]

2.26 The definition of mediation in Article 2(3) covers both facilitative and advisory dispute resolution processes, but not determinative systems such as arbitration. Such

69. See Intervention of the Chair, in UNCITRAL Audio Recordings: Working Group II (Arbitration and Conciliation), 63rd Session, 7 September 2015, 10:00-12:00.
70. United Nations Convention on International Settlement Agreements Resulting from Mediation (2019), Art. 2(3). Irrespective of different styles of mediation that may potentially fall within the scope of this definition, the mediator does not have the power to impose an outcome on the parties. Reference can be made to the Malaysian case of *Sabah Forest Industries Sdn Bhd v Mazlan bin Ali* [2012] 5 MLJ 382, which refers to two different models of mediation: 'There are mainly two types of mediation and they are known as facilitative and evaluative mediation. In facilitative mediation, the mediator only facilitates the sessions between the parties and at no time gives any evaluation of the merit of the dispute. He or she may of course suggest options for settlement for parties to consider. In evaluative mediation, the mediator expresses his views on the merit of the case in caucus or private to the respective parties and may even suggest to one of the parties that it would be in their interests to settle rather than have the matter litigated in court. The mediator can be said to be in control of the manner in which the mediation is conducted and is very much a solution driven exercise. If I may add here, irrespective of which method of mediation is used, it is a voluntary process of negotiation between two parties and if at any time of the process one of the parties feel that it does not wish to continue with the process, he or she has the right to withdraw from it be it conducted by a judge or an non judicial mediator.' See also the Mediation Meta Model, which outlines six mediation models and is summarised in a Point of Interest section in the commentary to Art. 2.
71. See Intervention of the International Law Association (ILA), the United States, Canada and Thailand, in UNCITRAL Audio Recordings: Working Group II (Arbitration and Conciliation), 64th Session, 3 February 2016, 10:00-13:00; and Intervention of the Russian Federation, in UNCITRAL Audio Recordings: Working Group II (Dispute Settlement), 65th Session, 20 September 2016, 09:30-12:30.
72. See Intervention of the Chair, in UNCITRAL Audio Recordings: Working Group II (Dispute Settlement), 65th Session, 20 September 2016, 09:30-12:30.
73. See Intervention of Canada, in UNCITRAL Audio Recordings: Working Group II (Dispute Settlement), 65th Session, 14 September 2016, 09:30-12:30; and Intervention of Mexico, in UNCITRAL Audio Recordings: Working Group II (Dispute Settlement), 65th Session, 14 September 2016, 09:30-12:30.

a broad descriptive definition recognises the diversity of mediation practice internationally.[74]

2.27 There are many models of mediation practice. They vary according to factors such as the goals for the mediation, the types of mediator intervention and the nature of the interaction between the parties. The parties' goals in mediation will vary from case to case. For some parties, a confidential, cost and time-efficient settlement is their primary aim. For others who are contemplating a continuing commercial relationship, the need to make strategic and long-term business decisions will be a priority. In other situations, where personal, professional or business relationships have broken down, the goal of mediation might be focused on restoring the relationship among parties. These objectives can be served by different mediator approaches. A systematic approach to mediation practice models is presented below.

Point of Interest

The Mediation Meta Model

The Mediation Meta Model comprises six models that reflect the diverse mediation practices around the world. Most mediators find their practice style reflected in one or a combination of these models. Brief descriptions of each model follow:

Expert Advisory Mediation

The primary objective of this form of mediation is to provide quick delivery of settlements and speedy access to justice. It supports both legally and technically focused disputes, which in turn encourages positional negotiation between the parties and advice-giving mediators. Expert advisory mediators are often senior lawyers or specific professionals selected on the basis of their expertise on the subject matter of the dispute. This allows them to provide useful advice on the technical aspects of each dispute.

Settlement Mediation

The goal of settlement mediation is to provide efficient access to justice, efficient delivery of settlement agreements and party autonomy. Settlement mediators are responsible for creating a suitable environment for settlement negotiations to occur between the parties. It is common for parties to separate into individual sessions and not reconvene until much later in settlement mediations. The settlement mediator will shuttle back and forth, facilitating the negotiations by carrying back-and-forth offers, counter-offers, concessions, agreements and draft documents.

74. See, generally, the IMI Model Mediation Rules and Clauses which are expressly 'designed to be applicable to any mediation style': www.imimediation.org.

Facilitative Mediation

Facilitative mediation values place a premium on parties' self-determination and client satisfaction. The process aims to offer parties access to a participatory justice forum. Facilitative mediators are responsible for creating an optimal environment for interest-based negotiation between the parties. They do not provide advice or legal information to the parties, and are often selected for their process and communication skills, rather than their subject-matter expertise.

Wise Counsel Mediation

The primary objectives of wise counsel mediation are access to justice, efficient conflict management and solutions that address the long-term interests of the parties. Wise counsel mediators often provide input in terms of identifying interests, priorities, strategies, options, walk-away alternatives and solutions. While the final decision remains with the parties, the mediator assumes a certain level of responsibility for the issues discussed, the options generated and the shape of the final mediated outcome. Wise counsel mediators are often selected for their high standing in the community or relevant experience in a certain industry.

Transformative Mediation

The primary goals of transformative mediation include party autonomy, perspective and relational shifting and, depending on the context, restorative justice. In transformative mediation, the mediator's role is to create an environment in which the parties can engage in dialogue, through which they are empowered to articulate their needs and values, and to recognise and acknowledge those of the other party. These mediators are selected on the basis of their process and relationship skills and their knowledge of causes of conflict dynamics and behavioural science.

Diagnostic Mediation

Diagnostic mediation prioritises the goals of party autonomy and perspective-shifting. Mediators guide parties through a diagnostic inquiry and explore sources of the conflict with a view to enhancing relational understanding among parties, providing opportunities for resolution. Parties are encouraged to engage in dialogue with each other and to extend their discussion beyond interests and priorities in the immediate dispute to include reflections on fundamental needs, values, identity and other underlying causes of conflict.

Case Illustration

A dispute among multiple corporate parties, who had been in business together for close to 30 years, had been festering for a long time and had become a legendary part of the corporate storytelling culture in the respective organisations. The dispute escalated, lawyers were consulted and litigation proceedings commenced. After numerous interim applications and hearings, amendments to pleadings and other submissions made along the way, close to a decade had passed.

Eventually, the matter was referred to mediation; the mediator appointed was a legal expert with an excellent reputation as an expert advisory mediator. One day was set aside for the mediation. At the mediation table, negotiations focused on the legal issues. All lawyers and parties were present, with the lawyers playing an active role, engaging directly with the mediator and one another and consulting with their clients as needed. The clients generally adopted a passive role and sat in the chairs furthest away from the mediator. From time to time, one or the other party would leave the room to take a business call. The mediator made extensive use of separate sessions with the parties and their legal advisers to reality test the parties' positions, offering her advice on the merits of the case and the likely outcome of the matter should it go to court. Despite best endeavours, no settlement was reached.

Some ten months later, a suggestion was made to design a different type of mediation process with a mediator, who was a negotiation process expert, but not a subject-matter expert. Despite initial reluctance, the lawyers were eventually persuaded by their clients – business people who were so fatigued with the past ten years of adversarial engagement that they were highly motivated to try something different. Given the history of the dispute, the clients were well-versed in the claims and counterclaims previously made; it was agreed that all parties (11 people in total) would physically attend mediation and their lawyers would be available by phone as required. The appointed mediator held a meeting with all legal advisers to brief them on their role in the mediation and his role as mediator. The mediator explained that he intended to expand the issues under discussion to include business, relational and other issues not reflected in the legal pleadings. Should an agreement be reached at mediation, the lawyers would be contacted to draw up the terms of a legally binding contract.

The mediation took two and a half days. At lunchtime of the third day, the parties had reached an agreement in principle, after a decade of battle. Relief was written on their faces. But in fact, they were not finished yet. They took a break to contact their lawyers and email a summary of the heads of agreement. The lawyers called in that afternoon on a conference call with all parties still in the room, and the mediator summarised the agreement reached. All parties agreed that the current document was not legally binding upon them and that their lawyers would draft and finalise a legally binding contract within five days. In the following days, the mediator shepherded the documentation and finalisation process for the MSA. All parties returned for a final mediation session with their lawyers to formally sign off on the MSA.

This case illustration highlights two different approaches to mediation. Depending on the case dynamics, either approach may be suitable. In the case presented here, the long 'festering' history of the conflict suggests that the legal issues were symptoms of a dysfunctional business partnership. In the circumstances such as these, facilitative and transformative approaches to mediation may be appropriate.

A Process, Irrespective of the Expression Used

2.28 The Singapore Convention's definition of 'mediation' refers to a process, 'irrespective of the expression used', thereby highlighting that it is the substance of the process and not the label attached to it that is important. This differs from the phrase used in the Model Law on Mediation, 'whether referred to by the expression conciliation, mediation or an expression of similar import'. The difference may be explained as follows. Given:

(1) the binding legal nature of a Convention, compared to the non-binding nature of the Model Law, and the fact that jurisdictions adopting such Model Law may choose to vary its terms;[75]
(2) a recognition that legal systems may use different terms for dispute resolution processes intended to be covered by the provision and may potentially interpret the above phrase referring to mediation and conciliation in a more limiting manner than intended; and
(3) a desire to encourage States from diverse legal systems, cultures and languages to commit themselves to the Convention.

2.29 The Model Law phrasing does not add anything to the intended meaning of the provision. Accordingly, it was deleted from the Singapore Convention wording and the broader phrasing, 'irrespective of the expression used' was inserted.

2.30 The result of the nuanced phrasing in the Singapore Convention is that parties need not specifically refer to the term 'mediation' – neither in their agreement to pursue means to settle their dispute at alternative dispute resolution forums nor in the eventual (and final) settlement agreements reached – for the Convention to apply. As

75. On the nature of model laws, see the introductory chapter to this book.

a result, advisory dispute resolution processes such as neutral evaluation[76] and mini-trial[77] conceivably would fall within the definition of mediation.[78] In future, as and when technology advances in such a sophisticated manner that AI algorithms could be administered and function to provide mediation services to parties on an online platform, the question arises as to whether the definition provided of 'the mediator' would be refined accordingly to accommodate such innovations, particularly if we begin to accept the possibility of bestowing legal personality on AI software systems.[79]

2.31 The importance of looking behind the label of dispute resolution processes is highlighted in situations where parties may possess a different understanding of the nature of the dispute resolution process in which they are engaged. While this is less likely to occur in institutional mediation, the intention of the parties may be less clear in ad hoc mediation.[80] By way of example, parties may engage in a mediation-like process without being aware that they could potentially fall within the scope of the Singapore Convention. The question as to the applicable law may only come into cognisance later, for example, at the stage where an iMSA is sought to be enforced.

2.32 Another type of situation arises where parties engage in a dispute resolution process with a very different understanding of its purpose. This was the case in *Acorn Farms Ltd v Schnuriger*[81] where the plaintiff thought it was engaged in a mediation process and not, as was found to be the case, arbitration (*see* the case illustration below). The implications that flow from the definition of a dispute resolution process can be significant. In a cross-border context, it could potentially determine the applicability of the Singapore Convention itself.

76. On neutral evaluation see Nadja Alexander, *Through the Looking Glass: Exploring the Regulatory Ethical Eco-system for Mediation*, in Maria-Frederica Moscati, Michael Palmer and Marian Roberts (eds), Comparative Dispute Resolution: A Research Handbook, Edward Elgar Publishing (2019); and Tania Sourdin, Alternative Dispute Resolution (5th Ed.), Thomson Reuters (2016).
77. *Ibid.*
78. Nadja Alexander and Shouyu Chong, *An Introduction to the Singapore Convention on Mediation – Perspectives from Singapore*, 22(4) Nederlands-Vlaams tijdschrift voor Mediation en conflict management 37 (2018), at 41. For functional definitions of common dispute resolution mechanisms, see Felix Steffek, *Principled Regulation of Dispute Resolution: Taxonomy, Policy, Topics*, in Felix Steffek and Hannes Unberath (eds), in (cooperation with Hazel Genn, Reinhard Greger and Carrie Menkel-Meadow), Regulating Dispute Resolution: ADR and Access to Justice at the Crossroads, Hart Publishing (2013), at 36-43. Chong and Steffek have additionally suggested that 'ombud proceedings would commonly comply with this definition [of "mediation" *per* the Singapore Convention] (except in those cases where they are unilaterally binding)': Shouyu Chong and Felix Steffek, *Enforcement of International Settlement Agreements Resulting from Mediation under the Singapore Convention – Private International Law Issues in Perspective*, 31 SAcLJ 448 (2019).
79. Paulius Čerka, Jurgita Grigiene and Gintare Sirbikyte, *Is It Possible to Grant Legal Personality to Artificial Intelligence Software Systems?*, 33 Computer L. & Sec. Rev. 685 (2017).
80. On institutional and ad hoc mediation, see below.
81. *Acorn Farms Ltd v Schnuriger* [2003] 3 NZLR 121.

2.33 When determining whether a dispute resolution process falls within the definition of Article 2(3) of the Singapore Convention, it is suggested that courts take into account the specific circumstances of the case, factoring in the understanding and expectations of the parties regarding the nature of the process they have entered.[82] By way of comparison, the UMA in the US provides a set of criteria – which also includes reference to parties' expectations – to assist in the determination of whether or not a process may be defined as a 'mediation' for the purposes of the act.[83] However, international policy differences and intercultural considerations steered UNCITRAL away from adopting such an approach.

2.34 It is important to note that the term 'mediation' under the Singapore Convention does not refer to a process, which necessarily takes place in formal settings. During the negotiation process at Working Group II, some delegates made a suggestion that 'mediation' should refer to a 'structured/organised' process in order to make an iMSA derived from mediation legitimate and trustworthy.[84] It was argued that this approach would rule out informal processes. Also, it would help to ensure that the mediation process was governed by a legal framework, administered by an institution, or regulated in some manner.[85] Working Group II eventually disregarded this suggestion, on the basis that: the requirement of a 'structured/organised' process would be understood differently in different jurisdictions; it would likely introduce domestic requirements that would diminish the attractiveness of the instrument; and it would go against the spirit of party autonomy on which the Model Law on Conciliation and UNCITRAL Conciliation Rules were based.[86]

---

82. Jernej Sekolec and Michael B. Getty, *The UMA and the UNCITRAL Model Rule: An Emerging Consensus on Mediation and Conciliation*, J. Disp. Resol. 175 (2003).
83. UMA 2001, s. 3.
84. Report of Working Group II (Dispute Settlement) on the Work of its 65th Session (Vienna, 12-23 September 2016), A/CN.9/896 (2016), at para. 42. Available at https://undocs.org/en/A/CN.9/896 (Accessed 9 March 2021). Some national laws define the term 'mediation' as a structured process. By way of example, in Austria, §. 2(1) of the EU-Mediationsgesetz defines mediation as a structured process, however named or referred to, whereby two or more parties to a dispute attempt by themselves, on a voluntary basis, to reach an agreement on the settlement of their dispute with the assistance of a mediator. Similarly, in Germany, §. 1 of the Mediationsgesetz defines mediation as a confidential and structured process in which the parties strive, on a voluntary basis and autonomously, to achieve an amicable resolution of their conflict with the assistance of one or more mediators. Also, Art. 1251-2 of the New Code of Civil Procedure (NCCP) of Luxembourg defines mediation as a structured process. According to Art. 2(1)(b) of the Law on Mediation in Civil Disputes No. 6325 of Turkey, mediation means the method used for the resolution of disputes, employing systematic techniques, carried out voluntarily and with the participation of an impartial and independent third person with specialty training, bringing the parties together to discuss and negotiate, and establishing a communication process between the parties in order to help them to understand each other and thus enabling them to work out their own solutions.
85. *Ibid.*
86. *Id.*, para. 43.

Case Illustration

The Importance of Looking Behind the Label: *Acorn Farms Ltd v Schnuriger*[87]

This dispute involved Acorn Farms, the Schnurigers and a very costly miscommunication between the parties. Acorn Farms owned a dairy farm and they entered into a share milking agreement with the Schnurigers. The agreement provided that in the event of any dispute, parties will first refer to conciliation to resolve the dispute. After 21 days, they can consider arbitration if the matter is still unresolved.

When the parties did enter into a dispute, Schnuriger advisers sent a proposal letter to the Van der Helms (Acorn's representatives) suggesting that the parties should move straight to 'mediation/arbitration' since they had little chance of agreeing by conciliation methods. They also explained that someone will be appointed as 'mediator/arbitrator' and that if mediation does not work out they will proceed to arbitration. At the end of the proposal letter, the Schnuriger representatives expressly recommended Mr Stewart as the chosen arbitrator to hear their dispute. The Van der Helms accepted the proposal.

During the arbitration, Mr Van der Helm tried to admit an important farm-consultant report as evidence. Unfortunately, Mr Stewart refused to take that report into account as the author was not present at the proceeding and at the end of the arbitration, an arbitral award was issued in favour of the Schnurigers.

The Acorn representatives now argue that the arbitral award should not be enforced as Mr Van der Helm had mistakenly assumed that he was taking part in a mediation and not an arbitration. This mistake occurred because, according to Acorn, the proposal was ambiguous, and the label to proceeding to 'mediation/arbitration' was confusing. This ambiguity was exacerbated since English was not Mr Van der Helm's first language.

As a result of that mistake, Mr Van der Helm was not aware that the rules of evidence were to apply, preventing him from calling upon a critical witness. He also believed that since he was only in mediation, he would have another chance to call upon that critical witness again during 'the next stage of arbitration'.[88]

This case illustration highlights how important it is for parties and their legal advisers to clarify and comprehend the dispute resolution process(es) in which they engage.

87. *Acorn Farms Ltd v Schnuriger* [2003] 3 NZLR 121.
88. *Ibid.* Eventually Fisher J ruled that the objective test for procedural fairness in an arbitration was not satisfied and in any case, Acorn had not established that subjectively, it was mistaken about the nature of the proceedings.

2.35 *Gao HaiYan v Keeneye Holdings Ltd*[89] highlights the cultural confusion that may arise in relation to defining mediation, especially where it is linked to other dispute resolution processes such as arbitration. There was no settlement in this case. Rather, an arbitral award based on the Tribunal's decision was involved, and so the nature of the dispute resolution outcome would not fall within the scope of the Singapore Convention. Nevertheless, the facts of this case are instructive. As His Honour Mr Justice Reyes (as he then was) commented in his judgment, '... *labelling a process as mediation does not mean that anything goes. There are appropriate and inappropriate ways of conducting mediations*'. The case is discussed further in the Case Illustration.

Case Illustration

Gao HaiYan v Keeneye Holdings Ltd[90]

The case concerned the validity of a share transfer agreement and was brought to arbitration under the Xi'an Arbitration Commission (XAC) rules in the People's Republic of China. The XAC Rules contained a clause granting the arbitrators broad authority to act as conciliators (or mediators) and propose settlement agreements. During an adjournment in arbitration proceedings, a member of the tribunal contacted a lawyer for the respondent and invited him and a friend of the respondent, Zeng, to a meeting. Over dinner at the Shangri-La Hotel, the Secretary-General of the XAC conveyed that the tribunal took the respondent's position and regarded the share transfer agreement to be valid, but that the tribunal wanted the respondent to consider compensating the claimant by a certain amount to settle the dispute. Zeng agreed to convey the tribunal's view to the respondent. Though the respondent was satisfied that the tribunal took its view of the share transfer agreement, it ultimately disagreed with the proposed compensation. The arbitration resumed, and – much to the respondent's surprise, given the information relayed after the Shangri-La meeting – the tribunal issued an award favourable to the claimant that the share transfer agreement was not valid.

When the claimant proceeded to enforce the award in Hong Kong, the respondent challenged the enforcement on the grounds of bias, pointing to the informal dinner meeting at the Shangri-La. The claimant contended that the meeting amounted to a mediation under the XAC Rules.

89. *Gao HaiYan and another v Keeneye Holdings Ltd and another* [2011] HKCFI 240, [2011] 3 HKC 157 (Court of First Instance). The parties appealed and the outcome from the Court of First Instance was overturned, but for reasons unrelated to the mediation point that is to be discussed below: see *Gao Haiyan and another v Keeneye Holdings Ltd and another* [2011] HKCA 459, [2012] 1 HKC 335, [2012] 1 HKLRD 627.

90. *Gao HaiYan and another v Keeneye Holdings Ltd and another* [2011] HKCFI 240, [2011] 3 HKC 157. This case illustration is adapted from Nadja Alexander, *Try as You May, You Can't Hide Behind the Label*, Kluwer Mediation Blog (2011).

However, in his judgment, Justice Reyes expressed reservations about whether the so-called mediation complied with the Rules, pointing to numerous 'unusual' aspects of the process, including the:

(1) venue and timing, namely dinner in a hotel rather than a formal venue;
(2) fact that parties did not appear to consent to the time and place of the mediation;
(3) fact that parties also did not appear to consent to a third-party 'mediator', namely the Secretary-General;
(4) fact that mediation was conducted by a non-presiding member of the Tribunal and the Secretary-General of the XAC, an unusual combination;
(5) fact that parties did not attend the mediation; rather, a non-party who was thought to have influence over the respondents was asked to attend;
(6) fact that the claimant did not appear to have been consulted about the proposal put to the respondents and it is unclear how the compensation figure in the proposal (RMB 250 million) was calculated; and
(7) fact that the 'mediators' asked the person in attendance, Zeng, to 'work on' the respondents to accept the proposal. This seems to amount to more than neutral communication of a message.

Therefore, despite the mediation label, Justice Reyes seemed to doubt whether the process was indeed mediation.

2.36 The *Keeneye* case sends a strong signal to dispute resolution practitioners. Despite being highly flexible in nature, mediation is not an 'anything goes' process. Combining facilitative processes, such as mediation, with determinative processes, such as arbitration, must be done in a manner that maintains the integrity of both processes and ensures procedural fairness and the perception thereof.

2.37 In this case, Justice Reyes concluded that the events at the Shangri-La Hotel would have given the fair-minded observer 'a palpable sense of unease' and would have caused the apprehension of a real risk of bias. As a matter of public policy, therefore, he refused enforcement of the award. Ultimately, the decision to refuse enforcement of the award was overturned on appeal.[91] Nevertheless, the court's comments about looking beyond the label remain relevant and reflect the approach of the Singapore Convention.

91. *Gao Haiyan and another v Keeneye Holdings Ltd and another* [2011] HKCA 459; [2012] 1 HKC 335, [2012] 1 HKLRD 627.

Case Illustrations

In *Mahindra Lifespace Developers Ltd v The New Great Eastern Spinning & Weaving Company Ltd*,[92] the Bombay High Court addressed the issue of whether Mr Rozal Mehta, who was named as the sole arbitrator in the dispute resolution clause, acted as an arbitrator or as a mediator.

The dispute resolution clause at issue provided: '[a]ll disputes and differences between the parties hereto including interpretation of any clause herein contained arising out of or under this Agreement shall be referred to the sole arbitration of Mr Rozal Mehta, or in the event of his non-availability Mr ... whose decision shall be final and binding on the parties hereto'. After concluding the contract, the parties tried to negotiate certain terms but without any success. Mr Rozal Mehta was attending the discussions and negotiations between the parties. The applicant took the view that Mr Rozal Mehta was acting as a mediator in this process and, therefore, he should be disqualified to act as an arbitrator in subsequent proceedings.

The court, in deciding whether Mr Rozal Mehta acted as a mediator or an arbitrator, examined the functions he performed during the discussions and negotiations between the parties. The court made reference to a letter, which stated that Mr Rozal Mehta should meet the parties separately in order to bridge the gap between them. Mr Rozal Mehta even anticipated the potential profit from the execution of the contract between the parties. The court also made reference to another letter, in which Mr Rozal Mehta noted that mediation would be commenced between the parties by submitting their claims in a sealed envelope. The court pointed out that in the same letter, Mr Rozal Mehta noted he could not wear two hats, i.e., one of an arbitrator and the other of a mediator. On the basis of these facts, the court concluded that Mr Rozal Mehta never acted as an arbitrator and he performed the functions of a mediator. According to the court, Mr Rozal Mehta was meeting the parties individually, putting forth proposals of one party to another and helping them find a solution. According to the court, these functions were of a mediator and not of an arbitrator.

The Australian case of *Ku-ring-gai Council v Ichor Constructions Pty Ltd*[93] involved the issue of whether the arbitrator acted as a mediator in the course of the arbitral proceedings and, therefore, the arbitrator required the consent of the parties to resume the arbitral proceedings. In this case, on the last hearing day,

92. *Mahindra Lifespace Developers Ltd v The New Great Eastern Spinning & Weaving Company Ltd*, 16 April 2009, the Bombay High Court.
93. *Ku-ring-gai Council v Ichor Constructions Pty Ltd* [2018] NSWSC 610. The case was appealed but the court dismissed the appeal. See *Ku-ring-gai Council v Ichor Constructions Pty Ltd* (2019) 364 ALR 728.

the arbitrator asked the parties whether they would consent if the arbitrator put forward a proposal for settlement under the cloak of mediation. In a breakout room with the parties, the arbitrator made a number of statements, expressed concerns about the complexity of the case and stated that the parties would unlikely be happy about the outcome of the case. He also put forward a proposal for settlement. The proposal was not accepted and the arbitrator resumed the proceedings. The respondent argued that considering that the arbitrator acted as a mediator, he required the consent of both parties to resume the arbitration as per the applicable law. The applicant took the position that the arbitrator did not act as a mediator in the course of the arbitration.

The primary judge opined that the arbitrator acted as a mediator in this case. The primary judge stated that the concept of a mediator includes a conciliator and other non-arbitral intermediaries. According to the primary judge, 'the essential contrast between the function of an arbitrator and that of the mediator is that the latter is acting in a "non-arbitral" capacity'. The primary judge stated that when the arbitrator put forward a proposal, he was acting in a non-arbitral capacity. The main functions of an arbitrator do not include helping parties arrive at a settlement by compromise.[94]

Irrespective of the Basis upon Which the Process is Carried Out

2.38 The Singapore Convention is not focused on how parties enter the mediation process, but rather on the outcome of a mediation – an MSA. There are many pathways to mediation and, subject to the exclusions in Article 1(3),[95] the path the parties take is irrelevant. At the same time, it is useful to be aware of the primary pathways to mediation for commercial parties. These are set out below.

2.39 Commercial parties frequently insert mediation clauses (or dispute resolution clauses with a mediation element) into their commercial contracts. Generally, mediation clauses regulate the manner in which all future disputes arising out of subsisting obligations are to be managed, but they may also deal with specific disputes only. International mediation clauses may include information about the way the mediation is to be conducted, how the mediator is to be appointed, the venue, costs and fees, the State or national law to be applied, the impact of mediation on litigation limitation periods and the language to be used.[96] Agreements to enter into a mediation process

94. *Id.*, paras 25-30. Note that in some jurisdictions, for example, Germany, arbitrators may as a matter of course assist parties to explore opportunities for settlement. See, for example, Christian Bühring-Uhle, Lars Kirchhoff and Gabriele Scherer, Arbitration and Mediation in International Business (2nd Ed), Kluwer Law International (2006), at 100 ff.
95. See the commentary to Art. 1(3).
96. Mediation institutions provide model mediation clauses that parties can insert in a contract. For instance, model mediation clauses can be found on the websites of the International Chamber of Commerce (ICC), Singapore International Mediation Centre (SIMC) and Japan International Mediation Center (JIMC).

(mediation agreements) can also be concluded between parties after a dispute has arisen. Post-dispute agreements typically define the specific dispute to be mediated and may take the form of an appointment contract between the mediator and parties.

2.40 The trend in many countries, including Australia,[97] Singapore, [98] Hong Kong,[99] the US, [100] England, [101] Germany,[102] Georgia[103] and France is to recognise and enforce

97. See, for example, *Computershare Ltd v Perpetual Registrars Ltd (No 2)* [2000] VSC 233, at para. 6. In Australia, courts will generally enforce a dispute resolution clause. By way of example, see the following cases *Huddart Parker Ltd v Ship Mill Hill and Her Cargo* (1950) 81 CLR 502, *Straits Exploration (Australia) Pty Ltd v Murchison United NL* [2005] WASCA 241, *Hooper Bailie Associated Ltd v Natcon Group Pty Ltd* (1992) 28 NSWLR 194, *Zeke Services Pty Ltd v Traffic Technologies Pty Ltd* [2005] QSC 135. The position of Australian courts is that a dispute resolution clause postpones a party's right to access the court rather than completely abolishes it. See *Freshwater v Western Australian Assurance Co Ltd* [1933] 1 KB 51. However, a court may not grant a stay if a party seeks a remedy in the form of rectification or construction of a contract (*Zeke Services Pty Ltd v Traffic Technologies Pty Ltd* [2005] QSC 135, at para. 21), or when a dispute relates to misleading and deceptive conduct (*Zeke Services Pty Ltd v Traffic Technologies Pty Ltd* [2005] QSC 135, at para. 21), or granting a stay will result in the multiplication of proceedings (*Savcor Pty Ltd v State of NSW* (2001) 52 NSWLR 587), or if the disclosure was required to justly resolve the dispute (*Dance with Mr D Ltd v Dirty Dancing Investments Pty Ltd* [2009] NSWSC 332). In the case of *Hooks Enterprises Pty Ltd v Sonnenberg Pty Ltd* [2017] QSC 69, the Supreme Court of Queensland enforced the following dispute resolution clause: 'If a party asserts that a dispute exists between the parties arising out of or in connection with this Agreement, the party *can* give a Notice of Dispute to the other party...' [*emphasis added*]. Even though the court agreed with the respondent that the language of the clause was not mandatory, it came to the conclusion that the clause 'does not require an initial claim to be made by one party, nor does it state that a party must be the first to agitate the dispute in order to provide a notice of dispute; clause 12 does not reserve the right to serve the notice of dispute so narrowly'.
98. *Haribo Asia Pacific Pte Ltd v Aquarius Corp* [2021] SGHC 278, at para. 160. Also see *International Research Corp PLC v Lufthansa Systems Asia Pacific Pte Ltd and another* [2014] 1 SLR 130; *Ling Kong Henry v Tanglin Club* [2018] 5 SLR 871, para. 25; and *EXXA Network Pte Ltd v SQ2 Fintech Pte Ltd* [2021] SGHCR 9.
99. See, for example, *Hyundai Engineering and Construction Co Ltd v Vigour Ltd* [2005] HKEC 258, [2005] 1 HKC 579, [2005] 3 HKLRD 723, at para. 29.
100. However, this was not always the case. See, for example, a number of US cases where the courts refused to enforce mediation and other non-binding dispute resolution clauses on the basis that it would be a futile exercise: *In re Estate of Ferdinand Marcos Human Rights Litigation* 94 F 3d 539 (9th Cir 1996), citing *Virginian Ry Co v System Fed'n* No. 40, 300 US 515, 550, 57 S Ct 592, 601 (1937). Other courts refused to issue what they referred to as a 'vain order' to enforce such clauses: *Lorch Inc. v Bessemer Hall Shopping Center Inc* 294 Ala 17, 310 So 2d 872 (1975) and *Livoti v Elston* 52 AD 2d 444, 384 NYS 2d 484 (App Div 1976). The breakthrough was made with *AMF Inc v Brunswick Corp* 621 F Supp 456, 462 (EDNY 1985) where an advisory dispute resolution clause was recognised and enforced. For an overview of the development of US case law on this topic see Peter Tochtermann, *Agreements to Negotiate in the Transnational Context – Issues of Contract Law and Effective Dispute Resolution*, Uniform L. Rev. 685 (2008), at 696-706.
101. See, *Ohpen Operations UK Ltd v Invesco Fund Managers Ltd* [2019] BLR 576, at para. 58; and *Wah (aka Alan Tang) and another v Grant Thornton International Ltd and others* [2012] EWHC 3198.
102. Peter Tochtermann, *Mediation in Germany: The German Mediation Act – Alternative Dispute Resolution at the Crossroads*, in Klaus J. Hopt and Felix Steffek (eds), Mediation – Principles and Regulation in Comparative Perspective, OUP (2013), at 549. Tochtermann has reported that in Germany, while mediation clauses '[d]epending on its particular wording, ... may be binding on the parties in the sense that a claim may not be brought before a mediation session has been conducted', § 307 of the *Bürgerliches Gesetzbuch* (BGB) could render mediation

mediation clauses provided certain conditions are met. Deckert explains that in France, mediation clauses are recognised as legally valid and *prima facie* enforceable. They are covered by contract law principles according to Article 1134 of the French Civil Procedure Code (C pr civ) and the duties contained in them are legally binding on the parties; in other words, they are imbued with *force obligatoire*.[104] Conversely, in jurisdictions such as Austria, the existence of a mediation clause in a commercial contract does not prevent the institution of legal proceedings in relation to a dispute covered by the terms of the clause.[105]

2.41 Apart from mediation clauses, many jurisdictions encourage participation in mediation by means of so-called triggering mechanisms. For instance, Article 1(1) of the EU Directive[106] specifies its objective as being, *inter alia*, to 'facilitate access to alternative dispute resolution'. Article 5 sets out different mediation triggering mechanisms that Member States may consider in their regulation policy, including court information sessions on mediation and voluntary and mandatory referrals by courts and other competent authorities.

2.42 Various forms of incentive, including requirements to attempt mediation and cost sanctions imposed against parties who unreasonably refuse to participate in mediation, are found in different regulatory forms, including legislation and practice directions, in England,[107] Singapore,[108] Hong Kong,[109] Australia,[110] Germany,[111] the US[112] and other

clauses null and void 'where the clause does not sufficiently clarify that mediation is a non-binding procedure and may be broken off at every stage of the negotiations'.

103. According to Art. 7(4) of the Law of Georgia on Mediation: 'In the case of a mediation agreement, in which the parties agree not to apply to the court or arbitration until the expiration of a certain time frame or until the occurrence of certain circumstances, the court or arbitration shall not review the dispute until the fulfilment of the conditions of the mediation agreement, unless a claimant confirms that the claimant will suffer an irreparable damage without the court or arbitration proceedings. A respondent shall submit an application on the mediation agreement before the expiration of the time frame established for filing a statement of defence. The application of a party to the court or arbitration shall not be considered as a waiver of a mediation agreement or a termination of initiated mediation.'
104. Katrin Deckert, *Mediation in Frankreich*, in Klaus J. Hopt and Felix Steffek (eds), Mediation – Rechtstatsachen, Rechtsvergleich, Regelungen, Mohr Siebeck (2008), at 196. Deckert refers to French literature supporting the approach including L. Cadiet, *L'Effet processuel des clauses de médiation* RDC (2003) 182, at 184 et seq. and X. Lagarde, *L'Éfficacité des clauses de médiation ou de conciliation* (2000) Rev arbitrage 376, at 377. See also Cass civ 2ème, 06.07.2000, N° 98–17827 in relation to Art. 1134 C pr civ and Cass (ch mixte) 14.02.2003 N° 00–19423 00–19424 where a court recognised mediation clauses for their full obligatory force and held that a 'friendly solution' must be sought before judicial intervention is actioned.
105. In relation to Austria, see Christina Lenz and Martin Risak, *Austria*, in Nadja Alexander et al. (eds), EU Mediation Law Handbook – Regulatory Robustness Ratings for Mediation Regimes, Wolters Kluwer (2017), at 42.
106. See, *Directive 2008/52/EC of the European Parliament and of the Council on certain aspects of mediation in civil and commercial matters*, Official Journal of the European Union L 136/3, (21 May 2008).
107. See, for example, Practice Direction to the Pre-action Protocols (UK), at para. 8; Civil Procedure Rules (UK) (1998), r. 1.4; and the case of *Halsey v Milton Keynes General NHS Trust* [2004] 1 WLR 3002 and *Steel v Joy and Halliday* [2004] EWCA Civ 576. See also Civil Procedure Rules (UK), r. 44.3 providing that, in imposing costs orders, courts 'must have regard to all the circumstances, including (a) the conduct of all the parties' before and during the proceedings and especially in relation to pre-action protocols.

jurisdictions. Court referral schemes are varied and include referrals to mediation only with all parties' consent,[113] referrals to mediation at the request of at least one of the parties[114] and mandatory referral to mediation at the discretion of a referring body irrespective of the parties' wishes.[115] Furthermore, court mediation schemes vary in

---

108. See, for example, Singapore Rules of Court (Chapter 322, R 5), Order 59 r. 5(c), which provides: 'The Court in exercising its discretion as to costs shall, to such extent, if any, as may be appropriate in the circumstances, take into account – […] the parties' conduct in relation to any attempt at resolving the cause or matter by mediation or any other means of dispute resolution.'
109. See, for example, Hong Kong Practice Direction – 31 (on Mediation). See also Nadja Alexander, *Hong Kong Mediation Manual*, Lexis Nexis (2014), Chapter 9.
110. See, for example, Australia Civil Dispute Resolution Act 2011, ss 6-11. Consider, for instance, that pre-litigation mediation is mandated (under s 86B) for disputes in relation to the Native Title Act 1993 (No. 110, 1993).
111. See Kristina Osswald and Gustav Flecke-Giammarco, *Germany*, in Nadja Alexander et al. (eds), EU Mediation Law Handbook – Regulatory Robustness Ratings for Mediation Regimes, Wolters Kluwer (2017), at 381.
112. See, for example, the mandatory consideration ADR rule in Minnesota: Minnesota General Rules of Practice, r. 114.
113. Illustrations of this approach can be found in France: Code of Civil Procedure C pr civ, Art. 131-1; in Germany: Code of Civil Procedure, § 278a; in Australia: Federal Court Rules (Amendment) 1991 N° 461, r. 4(1); in Croatia: Mediation Act, Art. 19; in Cyprus: Law on Certain Aspects of Mediation in Civil Matters (2012), Art. 15; in Ireland: Rules of the Superior Court (Commercial Proceedings), r. 6(1)(xiii) of Order 63 A states that the court on its own initiative or on the application of any of the parties may suggest that the parties consider alternative forms of dispute resolution including mediation. Practice shows that commercial judges usually ask parties to consider mediation under this provision and parties normally do not ignore such a request in light of possible adverse cost sanctions. The case of *Kay-El (Hong Kong) v Musgrave ltd* [2005] IEHC 418 is an example of the application of this provision. See Sabine Walsh, *Ireland*, in Nadja Alexander et al. (eds), EU Mediation Law Handbook – Regulatory Robustness Ratings for Mediation Regimes, Wolters Kluwer (2017), at 445-446; in Latvia: Civil Procedure Law of Latvia, s. 149(4^1).
114. Illustrations of this approach can be found in United States: Florida Statutes 2008, s. 44.102(2)(a); and in Australia: Farm Debt Mediation Act (SA) (2018), s. 9(1).
115. Illustrations of this approach can be found in the United States: California Rules of Court – Civil Rules in relation to disputes not over USD50 000, r. 3.891; Florida Statues 2008, § 44.102, and in relation to appellate mediation § 44.1011(2)(a); Texas Civil Practice and Remedies Code, § 154.021 and § 154.022. In Queensland, Australia for example, where a mandatory referral model exists, it is also possible for litigating parties to obtain a consent order for mediation: Supreme Court of Queensland Act 1991 (Qld), s. 102; and r. 320 of the Uniform Civil Procedure Rules 1999, allows the court to refer the party to mediation where a party asks the court for an Order. Additionally, consider the mandatory court mediation referrals regime in the courts of New South Wales, Australia: see David Spencer, *Mandatory Mediation Litigation Begins in NSW*, 4(4) ADR Bull. 52 (2001). In the European Union, the European Court of Justice in the case of *Rosalba Alassini and Others v Telecom Italia SpA and Others*, Judgment of the Court (Fourth Chamber) of 18 March 2010, found that Italy's mandatory mediation did not breach Art. 6(1) (Right to A Fair Trial) of the Convention for the Protection of Human Rights and Fundamental Freedoms. Greece introduced mandatory mediation by adopting the Law 4640/2019 on 30 November 2019. Mediation is mandatory for the following types of disputes: (1) family disputes filed as of 15 January 2020; (2) disputes falling within the Single-Member Court of First Instance, value of which exceeds EUR 30,000; and (3) contractual disputes with a valid mediation clause. See Vassiliki Koumpli, *Greece: Institutionalizing Mediation Through Mandatory Initial Mediation Session* (Law 4640/2019), Kluwer Mediation Blog, 20 January 2020, available at http://mediationblog.kluwerarbitration.com/2020/01/20/greece-institutionalizing-mediation-through-mandatory-initial-mediation-session

terms of whether referrals are made to external private mediators or internal court-based mediators, including judges. Judicial mediation seems to fall within the definition of mediation, provided the mediating judge is not in a position to hear the dispute between the parties should they not reach an agreement.[116] Ultimately, while the parties may be nudged by regulation to proceed to mediate their disputes, what is of utmost importance is that they should enter into a settlement agreement *voluntarily*.[117]

2.43 In international dispute resolution settings, it is usual to also distinguish between institutionalised and ad hoc mediation. Institutionalised mediation refers to mediation administered by an institutional service provider such as the SIMC or the ICC. Mediation is conducted in accordance with a set of procedural rules, usually of the administering institution, such as the SIMC Mediation Rules[118] or the ICC Mediation Rules,[119] which clarify the parties' intentions on the nature and characteristics of the process in which they are engaging. Alternatively, mediation rules from another body may be used. By way of example, the International Mediation Institute (IMI) has produced a set of model mediation rules, although IMI is not an administering institution or service provider.[120] Similarly, the UNCITRAL Mediation Rules (2021) can be adopted and adapted by mediation parties, although UNCITRAL does not administer mediations.[121]

2.44 In an ad hoc mediation, parties, with the help of their legal advisers, select a mediator. The mediator is responsible for setting up the mediation in consultation with the parties and their advisers. There is a greater capacity to customise the procedural rules of the mediation, although parties often make use of institutional rules.

-law-4640-2019/#: ~ :text = The%20Greek%20Mandatory%20Mediation%20Scheme,court%20judgment%20for%20its%20resolution. (Accessed 3 March 2021). Art. 187[3] of the Civil Procedural Code of Georgia states that a judge *may*, after examining all the relevant factors and circumstances, refer parties to mediation *without their consent* in the following types of disputes: (1) family disputes with certain exceptions; (2) inheritance disputes; (3) disputes between neighbours; (4) employment disputes with the exception of collective employment disputes; (5) disputes relating to the realisation of shared rights; (6) property disputes if the subject matter does not exceed GEL 20,000; (7) disputes relating to loan contracts concluded by financial institutions if the subject matter does not exceed GEL 10,000; and (8) non-property disputes.

116. See the commentary to Art. 1(3).
117. Timothy Schnabel, *The Singapore Convention on Mediation: A Framework for the Cross-Border Recognition and Enforcement of Mediated Settlements*, 19(1) Pepp. Disp. Resol. L.J. 1 (2019), at 17, noting the Intervention of Canada, in UNCITRAL Audio Recordings: Working Group II (Arbitration and Conciliation), 63rd Session, 9 September 2015, 09:30-12:30.
118. SIMC Mediation Rules: http://simc.com.sg/mediation-rules/, reproduced in the Appendix F of this book.
119. ICC Mediation Rules: https://iccwbo.org/dispute-resolution-services/mediation/mediation-rules/.
120. IMI Model Mediation Rules and Clauses: https://www.imimediation.org/resources/online/rules-and-clauses/.
121. UNCITRAL Mediation Rules (2021): https://uncitral.un.org/sites/uncitral.un.org/files/media-documents/uncitral/en/uncitral_mediation_rules_advance_copy.pdf.

Parties Attempt to Reach an Amicable Settlement of Their Dispute

2.45 This phrase highlights the consensual nature of mediation. As the previous discussion shows, parties may, in certain circumstances, be required to attend mediation by virtue of a mediation clause or a court referral. However, parties cannot be compelled to reach a settlement.

2.46 It is noteworthy that the Singapore Convention does not contain a phrase that appears in both the Model Law on Mediation and its predecessor, the Model Law on Conciliation: the words 'arising out of or relating to a contractual or other legal relationship'. This phrase, which appears in both Model Laws, goes to the scope of the dispute that can be the subject of mediation and does not appear in the Convention definition. The references in the Model Laws to a 'dispute arising out of or relating to a contractual or other legal relationship' make clear that these instruments do not only apply to the mediation of contractual claims. It is sufficient if there is a connection between the dispute at mediation and any legal relationship that exists between the parties. In this way, disputes that are related in fact but not in law can be addressed and resolved at the same mediation, an illustration of mediation's flexibility as a dispute resolution mechanism. At the same time, this phrase seems to suggest that a mediator's 'jurisdiction' is only invoked if there is a legal dispute.

2.47 The Singapore Convention simply refers to the parties' dispute without a qualifying phrase. Consistent with the core principles of mediation and Working Group II's choice not to address mediation agreements in the Convention,[122] the words of this provision remove any limitations as to the scope of the disputed issues that can be addressed at mediation. One could, for example, envisage a cross-border dispute among business partners, where the legal issues relate to an alleged breach of contract, but the real obstacle preventing the parties from reaching a settlement is linked to interpersonal differences between them. Experienced mediators will recognise that this is not an uncommon situation in mediation settings. Article 2(3) makes it clear that mediation can potentially cover any differences between parties.[123] However, pre-emptive forms of dispute resolution such as transactional mediation may fall outside the scope of the Singapore Convention.[124]

122. On the decision not to include mediation agreements in the Convention, see the introductory chapter to this book.
123. In this regard, see the IMI Model Mediation Rules and Clauses which, as indicated previously, are designed for any mediation practice model. The Rules refer to an 'Issue', rather than a 'Dispute' in order to capture the widest scope possible for mediation: www.imimediation.org.
124. Transactional mediation is also known as deal mediation. It is a process used to facilitate the making of complex transactions and partnership arrangements. While there is not a dispute at the commencement of transactional mediation, the process anticipates that differences will emerge among the parties in the course of the mediation. It is a form of preventative or pre-emptive dispute resolution. On transactional mediation see Scott R. Peppet, *Contract Formation in Imperfect Markets: Should we use Mediators in Deals*, 19 Ohio St. J. Disp. Resol. 283 (2004).

With the Assistance of a Third Person or Persons ('the mediator')

2.48 Mediators are variously referred to as third parties, neutrals, dispute resolution interveners and dispute resolution practitioners. Here they are referred to as third persons, highlighting their impartial and independent role.[125] The involvement of a third-party mediator in the production of a settlement agreement enforceable under the Singapore Convention distinguishes such iMSAs from regular negotiated contracts and settlement agreements.[126]

2.49 There is no indication in the Singapore Convention as to the extent of 'assistance' a mediator must offer in the dispute. Given the broad descriptive definition of mediation and the diversity of mediation practice models, we suggest that the term 'assistance' and the requirement for the mediator's involvement be interpreted in an equally broad and flexible manner. This aspect of the definition of mediation is linked to Article 4(1)(b), which requires parties seeking relief to provide evidence that the settlement agreement had 'resulted' from mediation.[127] Here Schnabel suggests that in order to prove that a settlement agreement did not result from mediation, 'the party would need to demonstrate fraud or collusion in attempting to portray a link between a dispute and an entirely unrelated mediation'[128] or, we would add, between a negotiated (*not* mediated) settlement agreement and an entirely unrelated mediator.

2.50 The *travaux préparatoires* of Article 2 shows that the idea of the insertion of the phrase 'with the assistance of a third person or persons' was to distinguish an MSA from other types of contracts, to provide for legal certainty and to prevent abuse in the enforcement process of iMSAs.[129] Delegates at Working Group II made various suggestions as to how to show that parties came to a settlement with the help of a mediator, including the requirement for a mediator to sign a settlement agreement or to provide a separate attestation signed by the mediator.[130] Other suggestions included

125. On the duties of mediators associated with impartiality and independence, see the commentary to Arts 5(1)(e) and 5(1)(f).
126. See Intervention of China, in UNCITRAL Audio Recordings: Working Group II (Dispute Settlement), 65th Session, 12 September 2016, 14:00-17:00; and Intervention of France, in UNCITRAL Audio Recordings: Working Group II (Dispute Settlement), 67th Session, 3 October 2017, 14:00-17:00.
127. Section 3(1) of the Mediation Act 2017 of Singapore expressly sets out the type of 'assistance' parties may get from the mediator: identifying the issues in dispute, exploring and generating options, communicating with one another and voluntarily reaching an agreement. If the mediator is involved in any of the mentioned processes, without assessing the degree of his/her involvement, a settlement agreement reached by the parties should be considered as one derived with the 'assistance' of the mediator. A similar provision can be found under s. 4 of the Mediation Ordinance of Hong Kong.
128. Timothy Schnabel, *The Singapore Convention on Mediation: A Framework for the Cross-Border Recognition and Enforcement of Mediated Settlements*, 19 Pepp. Disp. Resol. L.J. 1 (2019), at 18.
129. Report of Working Group II (Dispute Settlement) on the Work of its 65th Session (Vienna, 12-23 September 2016), A/CN.9/896 (2016), at para. 70. Available at https://undocs.org/en/A/CN.9/896 (Accessed 9 March 2021).
130. *Id.*, paras 71-72.

the mere submission of a mediation clause/agreement to mediate, which was not supported by the delegates of Working Group II.[131]

2.51 The reference to 'third person or persons' in the Convention definition of mediation reflects the reality of commercial mediation practice. International commercial mediators tend to work solo. At the same time, co-mediation involving two or more mediators is practised in relation to complex international commercial disputes involving multiple parties, referred to as multi-party disputes.[132]

2.52 The Singapore Convention does not require a person who assists parties at a mediation in coming to a settlement to be accredited or otherwise credentialed by a professional mediation organisation. Mediation parties have the freedom to choose any individual, whether a professional mediator recognised by a credentialing body or any other person with the skills and knowledge to perform the functions of a mediator. As long as a person selected by parties at a mediation assists the parties in coming to a settlement, the iMSA is likely to fall within the scope of the Singapore Convention, provided that the other requirements of the Singapore Convention are met. By way of contrast, in some jurisdictions, the use of the title 'mediator' is linked to credentialing or registration.[133] In other jurisdictions, the availability of an expedited enforcement

131. For more on this issue see the commentary to Art. 4.
132. For an illustration of a multi-party mediation with an international team of three mediators, see the analysis of the Vienna Airport mediation: Horst Zillessen, *The Transformative Effect of Mediation in the Public Arena*, 7 ADR Bull. 82 (2004). Co-mediation is used in international family mediation: Christoph Paul and Sybille Kiesewetter (eds), Cross-Border Family Mediation: International Parental Child Abduction, Custody and Access Cases, Metzner Verlag (2014). International family mediation is, however, beyond the scope of the Singapore Convention and this commentary.
133. In Turkey, Art. 2(1)(a) of the Law on Mediation in Civil Disputes No. 6325 states that a mediator means a natural person carrying out the mediation activity, who is entered in the register of mediators maintained by the Ministry of Justice. According to Art. 6(1) of the same law, registered mediators can use the title 'mediator'. According to Art. 20(1), an applicant must comply with the following requirements to be registered at the registry of mediators: being a Turkish citizen; having at least five years experience and undergraduate law degree; being fully competent; having no criminal record; completing the mediator training and passing the written and practical examination carried out by the Ministry of Justice. In Georgia, Art. 2(e) of the Law of Georgia on Mediation states that a mediator is a natural person registered with the Unified Register of Mediators who meets the requirements of this Law and agrees to conduct mediation, regardless of his/her status and selection/appointment procedure. Art. 14(4) of the same Law prescribes that a legally competent natural person with no criminal record, who has completed a mediation training/training for mediators in accordance with a certification programme for mediators and who holds a certificate issued by the Association of Mediators, may be registered with the Unified Register of Mediators. In Austria, §. 3(2) of the Austrian Law on Mediation in Civil Cases 2001 (ZivMediatG) states that the term 'mediator' refers to a registered mediator. According to §. 9, an applicant has to comply with the following requirements: has reached the age of 28; is professionally qualified; is trustworthy and has taken out liability insurance in accordance with §. 19. In Luxembourg, a mediator can be licensed or non-licensed. According to Art. 1251-3 of the New Code of Civil Procedure (NCCP), an applicant who wishes to be licensed as a mediator has to: present guarantees of good reputation, competence, training, independence and impartiality; produce an extract from the Luxembourg criminal record or a similar document issued by the competent authorities of the country of residence in which the applicant has resided for the past five years; have the enjoyment of civil rights and the exercise of political rights; and have specific training in mediation.

regime for MSAs may depend on whether the mediator in question is appropriately credentialed or approved.[134]

2.53 While mediator credentialing is not required for the purposes of enforcement of an iMSA under the Convention, credentialing and other standards may be relevant to the applicability of other aspects of mediation law, such as the law on mediator confidentiality.[135] Further credentialing may be relevant to the identification of the applicable standards in Article 5(1)(e) of the Singapore Convention.[136]

Case Illustrations

United States Fid. & Guar. Co. v Dick Corp.[137] pertains to whether certain settlement documents were entitled to the protection of mediation privilege. The case is of practical importance for Article 2 of the Singapore Convention, as it deals with the issue of whether a settlement agreement arrived at by the parties and any negotiations conducted for the purposes thereof resulted from mediation and with the assistance of a mediator.

In this case, the parties attempted to settle a dispute before a mediator. The mediation session was not successful. After one unsuccessful mediation session, the parties continued to negotiate the matter. During these subsequent negotiations, the mediator had some communication with the parties. The parties eventually reached a settlement. After signing a formal settlement agreement, an insurance company attempted to obtain the settlement documents. The parties took the position that the settlement documents were protected under mediation privilege.

The court established the following facts: the parties had one unsuccessful mediation session; they discussed the possibility of a second mediation session but whether it occurred was not clear; after the unsuccessful mediation session, the parties continued to negotiate without the help of the mediator; the parties eventually arrived at a settlement; and the mediator had no further contact with the parties involving the settlement negotiations. The court, in rejecting the position that the settlement documents were entitled to protection under mediation privilege, opined, 'the mediation process requires the presence, or at least

134. By way of example, s. 12(3) of the Mediation Act 2017 of Singapore states that a court may record a settlement agreement as a court order only if, among the other applicable requirements, the mediation was administered by a designated mediation service provider or conducted by a certified mediator.
135. By way of example, the confidentiality provisions of the Mediation Act 2017 of Singapore apply only where the mediation was administered by a designated mediation service provider or conducted by a certified mediator.
136. See the commentary to Arts 5(1)(e) and 5(1)(f), the mediator misconduct provisions.
137. *United States Fid. & Guar. Co. v Dick Corp.* 215 F.R.D. 503, 2003 U.S. Dist. LEXIS 9444 (W.D. Pa. 28 May 2003).

the active participation, of a mediator'.[138] Based on the facts available on the record, the court deemed that the mediator did not have 'any significant involvement in helping to reach the ultimate terms and structure of the settlement reached by the parties'.[139] The court concluded that there was not any nexus between the mediation process and the settlement agreement arrived at by the parties.

The Australian case of *Cook v Taing*[140] usefully distinguishes between unassisted negotiation and mediator-assisted negotiation. In this case, the parties executed a mediation agreement, which included a term that the mediation would be terminated upon the execution of a written settlement agreement in respect of the dispute between the parties and no oral settlement or handshake would be binding on the parties. The mediation took place on 27 May 2014. The parties and the mediator left the mediation without executing any formal settlement and the mediation was not adjourned or refixed. On 30 May 2014, the mediator notified the court that the parties had reached a settlement, subject to the parties executing a deed of settlement. Following 30 May 2014, however, the parties exchanged several emails for the purposes of settling the dispute, which lasted until the end of June 2014. No formal settlement deed was executed. One of the parties took the position that the parties had settled the matter and they did not need to sign a formal settlement deed, as the parties were negotiating outside the mediation agreement. The court addressed whether the negotiations of the parties' solicitors after 27 May 2014 were subject to the terms of the mediation agreement.

The court held that after 27 May 2014, the parties' negotiations were not conducted under the framework of the mediation agreement between the parties for the following reasons:

(1) the parties and the mediator did not have any communications regarding the extension of the mediation timeline beyond 27 May 2014. The mediation was not adjourned or refixed. It was simply abandoned;
(2) the parties had extensive communications between each other, which did not include the mediator;
(3) the court stated that following 27 May 2014, the parties themselves were not involved in the negotiation process. The negotiations were conducted between the solicitors. For the court, this made a fundamental difference as mediated negotiations actively involve parties;

138. *Id.*, at 6.
139. *Id.*, at 8.
140. *Cook v Taing* [2014] VSC 428.

(4) the communications between the solicitors did not suggest that the parties thought that the mediation agreement was still applicable to the negotiation process; and
(5) lastly, the communication from the mediator was an indication that the mediator did not have any plans to continue mediating the negotiation between the parties.

Lacking the Authority to Impose a Solution upon the Parties to the Dispute

2.54 These words draw the definitional boundary of mediation. Settlement agreements resulting from dispute resolution processes where third-party interveners have the authority to impose a decision that binds the parties are not covered by the Singapore Convention. Third parties leading determinative processes such as court (and private) adjudication and the arbitration will fall outside the definition of 'mediator' because they have the authority to impose a solution upon parties.[141] These words also appear to exclude some mixed mode dispute resolution processes from the definition of mediation, especially where *the same individual* (*or individuals*) conducts the non-determinative *and* determinative parts of the mixed-mode procedure; for example, in judicial settlements (referred to previously)[142] and in mediation windows in arbitration where the same person conducts both the mediation and arbitration parts. Another mixed mode procedure, which would fall outside the scope of the Singapore Convention, is so-called binding mediation – utilised mostly in the US and particularly in the State of California.[143] 'Binding mediation' begins with parties negotiating, discussing, and having private sessions with a mediator. If the parties reach a consensus, the mediator will execute an MSA. If no consensus is reached at the end of the mediation, the mediator will render a binding decision. However, unlike the med-arb procedure, the mediator will not conduct evidentiary hearings or review submissions. The following case from the US shows the process of 'binding mediation' in practice.

141. Consider Intervention of the Chair, in UNCITRAL Audio Recordings: Working Group II (Dispute Settlement), 68th Session, 5 February 2018, 10:00-13:00.
142. *Directive 2008/52/EC of the European Parliament and of the Council on certain aspects of mediation in civil and commercial matters*, Official Journal of the European Union L 136/3, (21 May 2008), at Art. 3, which expressly excludes judicial settlement from the definition of mediation.
143. Damon Thayer and MacKenzie L. Smith, *Binding Mediation – A Trap for the Unwary*, 136(31) The Recorder (30 July 2012).

Case Illustration

In *Bowers v Raymond J. Lucia Companies, Inc.*,[144] during arbitral proceedings, the parties came to a settlement and signed a settlement agreement. The settlement agreement contained an unusual dispute resolution provision: in the event of a dispute, the parties shall participate in a full day mediation. If the parties fail to reach a settlement, the plaintiffs and defendants shall provide the mediator with their final offers in the amount of between USD 100,000.00 and USD 5,000,000.00. The mediator shall render a binding judgment in favour of the plaintiffs by choosing either the plaintiffs' demand or the defendants' offer.

Based on this clause, the mediator made the final decision in the amount of USD 5,000,000.00 in favour of the plaintiffs. The mediator did not conduct traditional arbitral proceedings relating to evidentiary hearings. The Court of Appeal stated that the parties mutually consented to the process of binding mediation and rejected the argument that mediation should have been followed by arbitration, which would have necessitated an evidentiary hearing. The court also rejected another argument that the term 'binding mediation' was inherently uncertain, on the ground that the parties clearly elaborated the dispute resolution procedure in the contract and the defendant never objected to binding mediation. Subsequently, the Court of Appeal affirmed the decision of the mediator.

144. *Bowers v Raymond J. Lucia Companies, Inc.* 206 Cal. App. 4th 724, 142 Cal. Rptr. 3d 64, 2012 Cal. App. LEXIS 635, 2012 WL 1939722 (Cal. App. 4th Dist. 30 May 2012).

ARTICLE 3
General Principles

1. Each Party to the Convention shall enforce a settlement agreement in accordance with its rules of procedure and under the conditions laid down in this Convention.
2. If a dispute arises concerning a matter that a party claims was already resolved by a settlement agreement, a Party to the Convention shall allow the party to invoke the settlement agreement in accordance with its rules of procedure and under the conditions laid down in this Convention, in order to prove that the matter has already been resolved.

COMMENTARY

3.01 Article 3 deals with the principles of enforcement and, implicitly, the recognition of international mediated settlement agreements (iMSAs). This commentary focuses on these two themes. It also addresses the meaning of 'in accordance with its rules of procedure' and 'under the conditions laid down in this Convention'.

3.02 With its entry into force, the Singapore Convention has changed the law on recognition and enforcement of dispute resolution outcomes and expanded the number (and nature) of legal instruments susceptible to recognition and enforcement under private international law rules. In this way, Article 3 has a significant impact on private international law.[1]

Meaning of 'Party'

3.03 The term 'Party' with a capital 'P' is distinct from 'party' with a small 'p' throughout the Singapore Convention. This is a list of terms used in the Convention to describe relevant entities in the Convention:

(1) 'party' in Articles 1, 2 and 4;
(2) 'Party to the Convention' or 'Parties to the Convention' in Articles 3, 5, 7-8, 12-13 and 15-16; and

1. For private international law, see the introduction to this book.

(3) 'State' or 'States' in Articles 1, 11-12 and 14.

In this Convention, the term 'party' refers to the parties to an MSA.

3.04 The terms 'Party to the Convention' and 'Parties to the Convention' refer to States[2] and regional economic integration organisations (REIOs) that have consented to be bound by the treaty and for which the treaty is in force. This is consistent with the definition of the term 'Party' in the Vienna Convention on the Law of Treaties (VCLT): 'a State which has consented to be bound by the treaty and for which the treaty is in force'.[3] Article 12(3) of this Convention confirms that the terms 'Party to the Convention' and 'State' are to apply equally to REIOs, where the context requires.

3.05 Similarly, the use of the term 'State' and 'States' in this Convention is consistent with the definition of 'Contracting States' in the VCLT: 'a State which had consented to be bound by the treaty, whether or not the treaty has entered into force'.[4] The Singapore Convention also uses the term 'State' in Article 1(1)(a) to refer to a party's place of business.

3.06 The usage of these terms, and counter-suggestions for the use of other terms such as 'Parties', 'State Parties' or 'Contracting Parties', were raised in discussions in Working Group II. A comment made in those discussions was that the use of the term 'Parties' could be confusing as the draft convention often referred to 'parties' to the settlement agreement.[5]

3.07 A suggestion deliberated on in the 68th Session was to use the term 'Contracting Parties'. It was noted that 'the term might be more confusing and not known in the treaty law context'.[6] Working Group II ultimately decided that the Singapore Convention could tentatively use the terms 'Parties to the Convention' or 'a Party to the Convention', and further clarified that the draft convention would continue to refer to 'States' where appropriate[7].

3.08 A textual interpretation of the usage of the terms in the Singapore Convention shows they are consistent with the definitions in the VCLT and maintain the intended meaning and purpose of the relevant Articles in the Convention. Given the content of Article 12(3) of the Convention, this suggests that States and REIOs were contemplated by Working Group II as the only entities to which the Convention is open for ratification, acceptance, approval or accession.

---

2. The term 'state' here bears its plain and ordinary meaning. This is to be distinguished from the term 'State', defined in the Vienna Convention on the Law of Treaties (1969) (VCLT), Art. 2(1)(f).
3. VCLT (1969), Art. 2(1)(g).
4. VCLT (1969), Art. 2(1)(f).
5. Report of Working Group II on the Work of its 68th Session, (5-9 February 2018), A/CN.9/934 (2018) at paras 116-117.
6. *Id.*, para. 117.
7. *Id.*, para. 118.

Meaning of 'shall enforce' and 'shall allow the party to invoke'

3.09 Article 3 of the Singapore Convention imposes the obligation on Contracting Parties to recognise and enforce iMSAs provided that the conditions prescribed in the Convention are met. The Singapore Convention employs the word 'shall' in relation to the enforcement and invocation of iMSAs, which means that the competent authority of a Contracting State does not have any discretionary power to refuse the enforcement or invocation of iMSAs unless the opposing party proves one of the grounds under Article 5 of the Convention.[8] Article 31(1) of the VCLT states that '[a] treaty shall be interpreted in good faith in accordance with the ordinary meaning to be given to the terms of the treaty in their context and in the light of its object and purpose'. The ordinary meaning of the word 'shall' is 'a word of command' and '[i]t has the invariable significance of excluding the idea of discretion'.[9] For comparison, Article 5 of the Singapore Convention employs the word 'may' in relation to the non-enforcement and non-recognition of iMSAs, which is an indication of the competent authority's discretionary power to grant relief irrespective of whether the opposing party proves one of the grounds under Article 5. The usage of 'shall' in Article 3 and 'may' in Article 5 clearly shows the drafters' intention to choose a pro-recognition and pro-enforcement approach. The competent authority shall not have any discretion to refuse to grant relief in relation to an iMSA unless the other party proves one of the grounds under Article 5 of the Singapore Convention.

3.10 In the context of international arbitration, courts across different jurisdictions have established that Article III of the New York Convention takes the same pro-recognition and pro-enforcement approach in relation to foreign arbitral awards. The first sentence of Article III of the New York Convention, which reads as follows '[e]ach Contracting State shall recognize arbitral awards as binding and enforce them', has been interpreted by different courts as a pro-enforcement bias.[10] In the English case of *Yukos Oil Company v Dardana Limited*,[11] the Court of Appeal rejected an interpretation of Article III, according to which a party wishing to enforce an award has to prove the existence of a valid arbitration agreement. The court opined that Article III gives a party a 'prima facie right to recognition and enforcement'.[12] The court explained that a two-stage process of recognition and enforcement under the New York Convention means that a party wishing to enforce or recognise an award only needs to provide two documents as per Article IV of the New York Convention. It is for the opposing party to prove one of the grounds under Article V at the second stage under the structure set out in the New York Convention, including the invalidity or non-existence of an arbitration

8. See the commentary to Art. 5.
9. *People v O'Rourke* 124 Cal. App. 752, 13 P.2d 989, 1932 Cal. App. LEXIS 907 (Cal. App. 18 July 1932).
10. UNCITRAL Secretariat Guide on the Convention on the Recognition and Enforcement of Foreign Arbitral Awards (New York, 1958) (2016), at 78-79.
11. *Yukos Oil Company v Dardana Limited* [2002] EWCA Civ 543.
12. *Id.*, para. 10.

agreement. In *Glencore Grain Rotterdam B.V. v Shivnath Rai Harnarain Co.*,[13] the court stated that the New York Convention has a pro-enforcement bias, which has been long recognised by courts in the US. Furthermore, the mandatory language employed under Article III of the New York Convention leaves practically no discretion to the competent authority in the enforcement of foreign arbitral awards unless one of the grounds under Article V is present.[14] The pro-enforcement bias of the New York Convention has been confirmed in other cases and by commentators in literature.[15]

Meaning of 'in accordance with its rules of procedure'

3.11 Part of the balancing act contemplated by Working Group II was how to facilitate direct enforcement, on the one hand, without interfering with the civil procedure of States, on the other. This is in accordance with the trite rule in private international law that the *lex fori* (law of the forum) is applied in relation to procedural rules. Working Group II decided that States would rely on their own procedural rules[16] to give effect to direct enforcement in circumstances in which the conditions set out in the Singapore Convention were met.[17] As Sussman comments, the drafters 'deftly circumvented the fact that enforcement mechanisms for mediated settlement agreements vary across jurisdictions, a fact which had stymied the earlier efforts to achieve an enforcement

13. *Glencore Grain Rotterdam B.V. v Shivnath Rai Harnarain Co.* 284 F.3d 1114, 2002 U.S. App. LEXIS 4853, 2002 Cal. Daily Op. Service 2696, 2002 Daily Journal DAR 3263, 194 A.L.R. Fed. 755 (9th Cir. Cal. 26 March 2002).
14. *Ibid.*
15. UNCITRAL Secretariat Guide on the Convention on the Recognition and Enforcement of Foreign Arbitral Awards (New York, 1958) (2016), footnotes 368-374 refer to the following cases: *Gouvernement de la région de Kaliningrad (Fédération de Russie) v République de Lituanie* Court of Appeals of Paris, France, 18 November 2010, 09/19535; *Sojuznefteexport (SNE) (Russian Federation) v Joc Oil Ltd. (Bermuda)* Court of Appeal of Bermuda, Bermuda, 7 July 1989, XV Y.B. Com. Arb. 384 (1990); *AO Techsnabexport (Russian Federation) v Globe Nuclear Services and Supply, Limited (United States of America)* District Court, District of Maryland, US, 28 August 2009, AW-08-1521, XXXIV Y.B. Com. Arb. 1174 (2009); *WTB – Walter Thosti Boswau Bauaktiengesellschaft (Germany) v Costruire Coop. srl (Italy)* Court of Cassation, Italy, 7 June 1995, 6426; *ECONERG Ltd. (Croatia) v National Electricity Company AD (Bulgaria)* Supreme Court of Appeal, Civil Collegium, Fifth Civil Department, Bulgaria, 23 February 1999, XXV Y.B. Com. Arb. 641 (2000); *S.a.S. Wieland K. G. (Austria) v Società Industriale Meridionale (S.I.M.) (Italy)* Court of Appeal of Messina, Italy, 19 May 1976, V Y.B. Com. Arb. 266 (1980); *Gater Assets Ltd. v Nak Naftogaz Ukrainiy* Court of Appeal, England and Wales, 17 October 2007, A3/2007/0738, para. 11; *Claimant (UK) v Defendant (Germany)* Oberlandesgericht, Rostock, Germany, 22 November 2001, 1 Sch 03/00, XXIX Y.B. Com. Arb. 732 (2004).
16. See the following Working Group II documents regarding the application of rules of procedure of a State where enforcement or recognition is sought: Report of Working Group II (Dispute Settlement) on the Work of its 67th Session (Vienna, 2-6 October 2017), A/CN.9/929 (2017), at paras 46-48, 61. Available at http://undocs.org/A/CN.9/929; Report of Working Group II (Dispute Settlement) on the Work of its 66th Session (New York, 6-10 February 2017), A/CN.9/901 (2017), at paras 52, 55. Available at http://undocs.org/A/CN.9/901; Report of Working Group II (Dispute Settlement) on the Work of its 65th Session (Vienna, 12-23 September 2016), A/CN.9/896 (2016), at paras 81, 152, 155, 182. Available at http://undocs.org/A/CN.9/896 (Accessed 12 May 2022).
17. See the commentary to Art. 4.

mechanism for cross-border mediated settlement agreements'.[18] A similar approach is taken by the New York Convention, which subjects recognition and enforcement of arbitral awards to the relevant State's procedural rules.[19]

3.12 The case below illustrates matters that may be determined 'in accordance with rules of procedure' of the Contracting Party where the enforcement or recognition of an iMSA is sought.

Case Illustration

In the US case of *Artemis Shipping & Navigation Co. SA v TorMar Shipping AS*,[20] the court addressed the issue of the applicable law to the ranking of six different claims against the defendant for the purposes of the New York Convention. Each claim was based on the defendant's breach of its contractual obligations to pay to six claimants under six separate charter parties. The claimants commenced the enforcement process of the awards, rendered in England, on US territory.

First, the court rejected the argument that the ranking of six claims should be determined by referring to the substantive law, English law in this case, specified in each charter contract. The court opined that the ranking of six different claims for the purposes of enforcement was not a contractual issue. Therefore, the court stated that English law, the applicable substantive law to the charter contracts, was not relevant for enforcing the award.

Second, the court referred to Article III of the New York Convention and opined that 'the territory where the award is relied upon' clearly means the US, i.e., where the enforcement of the award is sought, and not England, i.e., where the award was rendered. The court determined that the ranking of claims was an issue of procedure and, therefore, governed by the procedural law of the US. The court stated, '[t]he contracts and the Convention provide the remedies of damages and an arbitral award. How the claims should be ranked has no effect on the claimants' substantive right to recover from' the defendant.[21] The court added that in case a lower-ranking claimant was not able to satisfy its claims, this would not extinguish any rights under the award, as this claimant could take the award to a different jurisdiction and enforce it there.

3.13 An important question might arise whether the competent authority is entitled to refuse to grant relief, based on the procedural law of the Contracting Party where enforcement is sought. The commentary to Article 5 of the Singapore Convention deals

18. Edna Sussman, *The Singapore Convention: Promoting the Recognition and Enforcement of International Mediated Settlement Agreements*, 3 ICC Disp. Resol. Bull. (Paris) 42 (2018), at 51.
19. Marike Paulsson, The 1958 New York Convention in Action, Wolters Kluwer (2016), at 20.
20. *Artemis Shipping & Navigation Co. SA v TorMar Shipping AS* 2003 U.S. Dist. LEXIS 22314, 2003 WL 22928792 (E.D. La. 9 December 2003).
21. *Id.*, para. 17.

with the grounds for refusing to grant relief. The grounds under Article 5 are exhaustive and the drafting history of the Singapore Convention suggests that the competent authority may not refuse to grant relief based on a ground, which is not envisaged under Article 5.[22] However, Article 3, which states that the competent authority grants relief 'in accordance with its rules of procedure', may contain an implicit ground of refusal based on the rules of procedure of the Contracting Party where enforcement or recognition is sought. The case below, albeit in the context of international arbitration, is illustrative, as Article III of the New York Convention provides the same stipulation.

Case Illustration

In the US case of *Zeevi Holdings Ltd. v Republic of Bulg.*,[23] the forum selection clause provided for the following stipulation: '[t]he execution of an award against the Seller may be conducted only in Bulgaria in accordance with the provisions of Bulgarian law'. After the tribunal rendered an award, the petitioner tried to enforce it in the US. The court addressed the issue of whether the enforcement of the award should be denied, based on the forum selection clause mentioned above.

The court referred to Article III of the New York Convention and stated, 'while the defences articulated in Article V are the exclusive substantive grounds for refusing enforcement of an arbitral award, a Court is not necessarily barred from refusing to enforce such an award on procedural grounds'.[24] The court opined that Contracting States to the New York Convention are free to apply their procedural rules to the enforcement process of an award, provided that such procedural rules or conditions are not more onerous than the ones that are applicable to domestic arbitral awards. Based on this reasoning, the court stated that a forum selection clause is a procedural rule rather than a substantive one. Therefore, for the court, the enforcement of a forum selection clause and, consequently, the rejection or confirmation of the award would not go against the spirit of the New York Convention.[25]

22. Working Group II noted that 'defences to be provided in the instrument should be *limited* and not cumbersome to implement in order to allow for a simple and efficient verification by the enforcing authority of the grounds for refusing enforcement. It was widely felt that the grounds for refusing enforcement under the instrument should also be *exhaustive* and stated in general terms, giving flexibility to the enforcing authority with regard to their interpretation' (*emphasis added*). See Report of Working Group II (Arbitration and Conciliation) on the Work of its 63rd Session (Vienna, 7-11 September 2015), A/CN.9/861 (2015), at para. 93. Available at https://undocs.org/en/A/CN.9/861 (Accessed 11 May 2022).
23. *Zeevi Holdings Ltd. v Republic of Bulg.* 2011 U.S. Dist. LEXIS 38556 (S.D.N.Y. 29 March 2011).
24. *Id.*, para. 9.
25. In this case, the petitioner tried to enforce the same award in Israel and the US. The court in the US noted that the courts of Israel took a different approach and enforced the award in accordance with the laws of Israel despite the forum selection clause. In another US case of *Monegasque De Reassurances S.A.M. (monde Re) v Nak Naftogaz of Ukr.*, the court refused to confirm an arbitral award based on the doctrine of forum non conveniens. The court rejected the argument that Art.

3.14 Another question that may arise in relation to Article 3 of the Singapore Convention is whether the limitation period applicable to the recognition and enforcement of iMSAs is a procedural rule. In the context of international arbitration, national courts normally interpret the statute of limitation applicable to the recognition and enforcement of foreign arbitral awards as a rule of procedure of the place where enforcement is sought. The case provided below is illustrative in this regard.

Case Illustration

In *Yugraneft Corp. v Rexx Management Corp.*, the Supreme Court of Canada addressed the issue of the applicable limitation period to the enforcement of foreign arbitral awards. The court made the following statement:

'The Convention allows Contracting States to impose local time limits on the recognition and enforcement of foreign arbitral awards if they so wish. While limitation periods are not included in the list of grounds upon which a Contracting State may refuse to recognize and enforce a foreign arbitral award, the Convention stipulates that recognition and enforcement shall be "in accordance with the rules of procedure of the territory where the award is relied upon". If the competent legislature intended to subject recognition and enforcement proceedings to a limitation period, the limitation period in question will be construed as a "rule of procedure" as that term is understood under the Convention. *The domestic characterization of limitation periods as substantive or procedural is immaterial*' [*emphasis added*].[26]

3.15 If a Contracting Party to the Singapore Convention subjects the recognition and enforcement of iMSAs to a limitation period, it is likely that such a limitation period will be applicable to the recognition and enforcement of iMSAs in accordance with Article 3 of the Singapore Convention, notwithstanding any substantive law applicable to the iMSA. However, the domestic law of a Contracting Party to the Singapore Convention may not contain any specific limitation period to the recognition and enforcement of iMSAs. In this case, the competent authority may determine the applicable limitation period by referring to its rules of private international law. By way of example, in Singapore, according to section 3 of the Foreign Limitation Periods Act 2012, the

V of the New York Convention lists the only grounds for refusing to enforce an award and stated: '[t]he signatory nations simply are free to apply differing procedural rules consistent with the requirement that the rules in Convention cases not be more burdensome than those in domestic cases. If that requirement is met, whatever rules of procedure for enforcement are applied by the enforcing state must be considered acceptable, without reference to any other provision of the Convention.' *Monegasque De Reassurances S.A.M. (monde Re) v Nak Naftogaz of Ukr.*, 311 F.3d 488, 496, 2002 U.S. App. LEXIS 23681, *19, 2002 AMC 2782, 161 Oil & Gas Rep. 976 (2d Cir. N.Y. 15 November 2002).

26. *Yugraneft Corp v Rexx Management Corp.* [2010] 1 SCR 649.

limitation period will be determined by referring to the substantive law to an iMSA.[27] The same approach is taken in the Foreign Limitation Periods Act 1984 (England).

3.16 Interestingly, Article 3 of the Singapore Convention does not specify whether a Contracting Party can impose more burdensome procedural conditions or fees on the recognition and enforcement of iMSAs as compared to the recognition and enforcement of domestic settlement agreements. In the context of international arbitration, Article III of the New York Convention prescribes that '[t]here shall not be imposed substantially more onerous conditions or higher fees or charges on the recognition or enforcement of arbitral awards to which this Convention applies than are imposed on the recognition or enforcement of domestic arbitral awards'. The absence of the same stipulation in Article 3 of the Singapore Convention might be an indication that Contracting Parties may impose different procedural requirements on the recognition and enforcement of iMSAs and domestic MSAs. For instance, a requirement that a party to an iMSA is required to pay a higher fee for the enforcement of the iMSA than for the enforcement of a domestic settlement agreement would not seem to fall foul of the provisions of the Singapore Convention.

Meaning of 'under the conditions laid down in this Convention'

3.17 Not only shall Parties to the Convention give effect to iMSAs under Articles 3(1) and 3(2) in accordance with their rules of procedure, they must do so under the conditions that have been set out in the other Articles of the Singapore Convention. Essentially, this clause elucidates that the effect of Articles 3(1) and 3(2) is subject to the iMSA:[28]

(1) falling within the scope and definition requirements of Articles 1 and 2;
(2) not being barred by any exclusions established by Articles 1(2) and 1(3);
(3) satisfying the procedural requirements set out in Article 4 (this will be analysed in the commentary under Article 4);
(4) not falling foul of any of the Article 5 grounds for refusal of relief (this will be analysed in the commentary under Article 5); and
(5) subject to any Article 8 reservations lodged *vis-à-vis* the Party to the Convention in which it is sought to be enforced (*see* the commentary to Article 8).

27. Singapore adopted the Singapore Convention on Mediation Act 2020, which implements the Singapore Convention on Mediation in Singapore. At the time of writing, this Act or other relevant acts do not contain any specific limitation period applicable to the recognition and enforcement of iMSAs.
28. Timothy Schnabel, *The Singapore Convention on Mediation: A Framework for the Cross-Border Recognition and Enforcement of Mediated Settlements*, 19 Pepp. Disp. Resol. L.J. 1 (2019), at 39-41.

Enforcement

3.18 Article 3 sets out the Singapore Convention's expedited enforcement mechanism. It is helpful to employ the metaphors of 'sword' and 'shield' to elucidate the operation of Articles 3(1) and 3(2). States and other parties to the Convention, that is, States and REIOs,[29] must give effect to the mechanisms in Article 3 and may modify their own laws and rules of civil or court procedure as they see fit in order to comply with Article 3.[30]

3.19 The enforcement mechanism of Article 3(1) enables parties to administer iMSAs as a 'sword' against another party that dishonours its terms, through the initiation of proceedings in the jurisdiction of the relevant competent authority of a Contracting State or other Party to the Singapore Convention. The enforcement mechanism is typically triggered when parties seek, through judicial means, to enforce dishonoured obligations by compelling the dishonouring party to perform its end of the bargain. Sometimes, this may also involve seizing assets held by the dishonouring party to set off those dishonoured obligations. It should be emphasised that the proceedings are to be conducted in accordance with the rules and procedure of the relevant jurisdiction. Enforcement would typically be granted by the competent authority if the essential conditions laid down by the Convention with regard to scope (Article 1) and form and evidence (Article 4) are fulfilled, and the parties are unable to prove the existence of one or more of the grounds for refusal in Article 5.[31]

3.20 The expedited enforcement mechanism promotes predictability, certainty and conclusiveness of dispute resolution outcomes reflected in an iMSA. This enables the iMSA to be uniformly executed across jurisdictions that are States or other Parties to the Singapore Convention. Outside of the Singapore Convention, whenever the obligations pursuant to an iMSA are dishonoured, parties would normally proceed to court to enforce the agreement as a binding contract, assuming there were no other expedited enforcement mechanisms accessible within the jurisdiction. However, the enforcement of such obligations in the courts of one jurisdiction may yield different results from another. The availability of specific performance in common law jurisdictions is one source of this inconsistency, and this is explored in the Point of Interest below. By way of comparison, civil law jurisdictions are more open to granting specific performance for a breach of a contractual obligation.[32]

29. See the commentary to Art. 12.
30. On how States amend their domestic law to comply with treaty obligations, see the commentary to Art. 11.
31. We note that the ability for courts of the Parties to the Convention to review the obligations enshrined within the iMSA are strictly and exhaustively confined to those found in Art. 5 of the Singapore Convention: see the commentary to Art. 5.
32. By way of example, see Art. 1221 of the Code Civil in France and Art. 1453 of Codice Civile in Italy.

Point of Interest

Enforcement: Specific Performance or Damages

It is the trite position of common law courts that specific performance of contractual obligations will not be awarded if damages would sufficiently compensate the 'innocent' party for losses accrued given any breach of contract.[33] This applies to MSAs as well.[34] Even if the obligations enshrined in the iMSA are of unique character (for instance, articulating the conveyance of land), parties may nevertheless be barred from obtaining specific performance if they are deemed not to have come to court with 'clean hands'[35] – a doctrine unique to the equitable jurisdiction of common law courts.[36] There is a risk that shrewd negotiation tactics adopted by one party may be interpreted as deceitful, cunning or dishonest in the eyes of the court. These parties may be dismissed as approaching the court with 'unclean hands' *vis-à-vis* the specific performance sought through the iMSA. Consequently, the work put into painstakingly negotiated iMSAs may become all for naught, especially where parties mediated with the reasonable expectation of mending and preserving a cross-border business relationship built upon compromise over compensation.

3.21 The *travaux préparatoires* of the Singapore Convention suggests that the remedies available under Article 3 are not limited to pecuniary obligations and a party to an iMSA can request specific performance. Working Group II discussed that iMSAs may contain both, pecuniary and non-pecuniary, obligations and 'the enforcement of only pecuniary obligations would be overly limitative and create an imbalance between the

33. *Beswick v Beswick* [1968] AC 68; and Mindy Chen-Wishart, Contract Law (6th Ed.), OUP (2018), at 546 et seq.
34. *Turf Club Auto Emporium Pte Ltd and others v Yeo Boong Hua and others and another appeal and other matters* [2017] 2 SLR 12, [2017] SGCA 21, at para. 156: the Singapore Court of Appeal ruled that non-compliance of a settlement agreement, which was subsequently recorded as a consent order by the High Court in 2006, 'had the effect of *prospectively* terminating the parties' agreement and releasing the parties from *future* obligations'; consequently, the Court of Appeal awarded compensatory damages to the 'innocent' parties owing to the breach of settlement agreement: see *Turf Club Auto Emporium Pte Ltd & 4 Ors v Yeo Boong Hua & 2 Ors* [2018] 2 SLR 655, [2018] SGCA 44. It is imperative to note that the mediated settlement agreement was recorded before the Singapore Mediation Act 2017 came into effect: had it been recorded in accordance with the Singapore Mediation Act 2017, the High Court may have enforced the resulting consent order 'in the same manner as a judgment given or an order made by a court' (s. 12(5) of the Mediation Act 2017).
35. *E C Investment Holding Pte Ltd v Ridout Residence Pte Ltd* [2012] 1 SLR 32, at para. 103.
36. In Singapore, Menon JC (in his capacity at the time) had explained what a hypothetical plaintiff must do in order to be viewed as to have approached the court with clean hands, in *Hong Leong Singapore Finance Ltd v United Overseas Bank Ltd* [2007] 1 SLR(R) 292, at paras 225-226. The Hong Kong position was similarly set out by Lord Brightman in *Sang Lee Investment Co Ltd v Wing Kwai Investment Co Ltd* [1983] HKLR 197, at 208. The English position has been elucidated in Ian C.F. Spry, Equitable Remedies (9th Ed.), Sweet & Maxwell (2014), at 253-256.

parties'.[37] In response to possible complications that may occur in the enforcement of non-pecuniary obligations, Working Group II noted that the competent authority could handle such issues in accordance with the applicable law.[38] Jurisprudence across different common law countries shows that the remedy of specific performance is available in the enforcement of an MSA, including in the US,[39] Hong Kong,[40] England,[41] Canada[42] and New Zealand,[43] provided that certain requirements for granting specific performance are met.

3.22 Ultimately, the Singapore Convention provides a convenient and effectual solution, ensuring direct enforcement of obligations enshrined within iMSAs across jurisdictions, securing conclusive dispute resolution outcomes for parties who agree to mediate their cross-border commercial disputes.

Case Illustration

Jack Pty Ltd ('Jack') and *Jill Pte Ltd* ('Jill')[44] have concluded a settlement agreement after a mediation session. The resulting iMSA falls within the scope of the Singapore Convention's application *per* Article 1, and satisfies the Article 4 evidential requirements for reliance on iMSAs. However, Jill fails to comply with the terms of the iMSA. Jack, knowing that Jill has liquid assets in Utopia (a Party

37. Report of Working Group II (Arbitration and Conciliation) on the Work of its 63rd Session (Vienna, 7-11 September 2015), A/CN.9/861 (2015), at para. 47. Available at https://undocs.org/en/A/CN.9/861 (Accessed 2 March 2022).
38. *Ibid.*
39. In the case of *Lype v Watkins*, the Court of Appeals of Texas stated, '[a] party seeking specific performance of a settlement agreement must plead and prove the agreement and provide adequate notice and opportunity to be heard. Provided these safeguards are met, a trial court properly enforces the agreement, despite post agreement withdrawal of consent by one party'. *Lype v Watkins* 1998 Tex. App. LEXIS 6626, *1, 1998 WL 734429 (Tex. App. Houston 1st Dist. 22 October 1998). In the case of *Torske v Torske Farms, Inc.*, the District Court of Montana opined, 'as long as there is an unconditional offer and an unconditional acceptance and the agreement is signed by the parties or their attorneys, an agreement reached during the course of mediation is enforceable by an order of specific performance.' *Torske v Torske Farms, Inc.* 2003 ML 1324, 16, 2003 Mont. Dist. LEXIS 2448, *11-12 (Mont. Dist. Ct. 2 April 2003). See also *Fontenot v Hanus* 2011 Tex. App. LEXIS 7234; *Exp. Worldwide, Ltd. v Knight* 2007 U.S. Dist. LEXIS 13294.
40. *Yeung Chi Wang (楊智宏) v Yeung Chi Wing (楊志榮)* [2018] HKCU 3010. Contrarily, in the case of *Yau Simon Shik Man & Ors v Yau Shik Yin & Anor*, the Court of First Instance of Hong Kong refused to grant specific performance, on the ground that it would not be equitable for the party who did not adhere strictly to the contractual obligations to request for specific performance. *Yau Simon Shik Man & Ors v Yau Shik Yin & Anor* [2018] HKCFI 1733.
41. *Vision Express (UK) Ltd v Wilson and another* [1998] BCC 173. In this case, the court granted specific performance for the enforcement of a Tomlin order, even though there was a significant delay from entering into the Tomlin order to requesting the specific performance of the Tomlin order.
42. *Diniro v Diniro* [2008] OJ No. 5902; *Beier v Proper Cat Construction Ltd* [2013] AJ No. 707.
43. *McGRATH v SIMSON (as Executor and Trustee of the Estate of SIMSON)* [2015] NZHC 2644.
44. Note that Pty Ltd is the abbreviation for a proprietary limited company in Australia and Pte Ltd is the abbreviation for a private limited company in Singapore.

to the Singapore Convention), applies to the High Court of Utopia (the relevant competent authority) to enforce the iMSA under Article 3(1) of the Singapore Convention, to seize those assets. Jill does not challenge the proceedings. The settlement agreement will be enforced under Article 3(1) of the Singapore Convention.

Alternative scenario: Jill challenges the enforcement proceedings by arguing in the High Court of Utopia that it did not grant any express or implied authority to its representative at the mediation table to conclude the iMSA with Jack. Assuming that Jill was able to prove the facts claimed to the court's satisfaction, the High Court rules that Jill has proven a defence under Article 5(1)(a). The settlement agreement will not be enforced under Article 3(1). This is because, under the conditions of the Singapore Convention, the court may refuse to enforce an iMSA if an Article 5 defence (that is, Article 5(1)(a)) has been proven.

Recognition of iMSAs

3.23 The 'recognition' mechanism of Article 3(2) enables parties to administer iMSAs as a 'shield' in the courts of Contracting Parties to the Singapore Convention.[45] An iMSA may be invoked in dismissal, or striking out, proceedings as evidence of having resolved those discrete issues – which are being raised for a second time in court or arbitration – at mediation, concluded through the signing of the written iMSA.[46] Here an iMSA that falls within the scope of the Singapore Convention can be relied upon as a complete defence.

Case Illustration

In *Rakna Arakshaka Lanka Ltd v Avant Garde Maritime Services (Pte) Ltd*,[47] the Court of Appeal of Singapore confirmed the invocation of a settlement agreement as a complete defence against legal proceedings in court or arbitration. In this case, the dispute at issue is related to a private-public partnership arrangement between the parties. Avant Garde Maritime Services (AGMS) commenced arbitration at the Singapore International Arbitration Centre (SIAC) against Rakna Arakshaka Lanka Ltd (RALL) over a contractual dispute. RALL counterclaimed

45. See the Point of Interest below on the recognition of mediated outcomes in different legal forms.
46. For an illustration of an MSA being used as a shield where one party attempted to continue litigation in relation to issues resolved at mediation, see the Singapore case of *Chan Gek Yong v Violet Netto (practising as L F Violet Netto) and another and another matter* [2019] 3 SLR 1218, [2018] SGHC 208.
47. *Rakna Arakshaka Lanka Ltd v Avant Garde Maritime Services (Pte) Ltd* [2019] 2 SLR 131. The case is discussed in Nadja Alexander and Shouyu Chong, *Mediation and Appropriate Dispute Resolution*, 20 SAL Ann. Rev. 614 (2019), at paras 22.7-22.12.

in separate judicial proceedings, on the basis of an alleged loss of reputation. The parties eventually came to a settlement, which was recorded and documented as a memorandum of understanding. According to the memorandum of understanding, the parties had to discontinue and withdraw the legal proceedings against each other. However, AGMS did not consent to withdraw the arbitration claim and eventually, obtained an award against RALL. As a result, RALL sought to set aside the award.

The Court of Appeal came to the conclusion that the parties executed a valid and binding settlement agreement that precluded them from taking any legal action regarding the issues that were resolved and documented in the memorandum of understanding. The Court of Appeal confirmed that the settlement agreement put an end to the dispute between the parties. As a result, the Court of Appeal deemed that the arbitral tribunal did not have jurisdiction to render an award because the parties had already settled the issues between them. Therefore, the court set aside the award.

3.24 It should be emphasised that issues discussed and negotiated during the mediation which were *not* recorded or reflected in the written and signed settlement agreement may not be recognised for the purposes of Article 3(2).[48] In other words, if parties reach a partial settlement in relation to their dispute that resolves a number, but *not all* of the matters of difference between them, then the outstanding issues may still be subject to other dispute resolution proceedings, such as litigation and arbitration.[49] It bears further note that if parties were misled (perhaps, by reason of misrepresentation or material non-disclosure of fact,[50] depending on the applicable law) into concluding a settlement agreement, such that they would have settled for less than what they would have obtained as a settlement sum, the parties may proceed to court under a separate cause of action to pursue the difference. The New Zealand Court of Appeal, in *Southern Response Earthquake Services Ltd v Dodds*,[51] allowed a homeowner's claim against their insurer for the difference in what they have received under a settlement agreement for damaged real estate, compared to what they would have actually received had the insurer disclosed all the material facts that they were privy to, in assessing the damages which would have been paid out under the relevant home insurance policy. The insurers persuaded the homeowner to settle their claims for NZ$894,937.78 by reference to an abridged Detailed Rebuild/Repair Analysis Report. However, the full Detailed Rebuild/Repair Analysis Report, which was *not disclosed* to

48. *Jumaiah bte Amir and Another v Salim bin Abdul Rashid* [2019] SGHC 63, at paras 16-17; and see for a case note, Nadja Alexander and Shouyu Chong, *Singapore Case Note: Interpretation of MSAs and Inadmissibility of Evidence from Mediation*, Kluwer Mediation Blog (17 March 2019).
49. See the commentary to Art. 1 on partial iMSAs.
50. Consider *Navin Jatia v Ram Niranjan* [2020] 1 SLR 1098 as an illustration from Singapore jurisprudence.
51. *Southern Response Earthquake Services Ltd v Dodds* [2020] NZCA 395, [2021] Lloyd's Rep IR 426.

the homeowner at the time of settlement, projected the cost of the damage suffered on the piece of real estate to be NZ$1,186,920.75. The New Zealand Court of Appeal allowed the homeowner's claim for the difference of more than NZ$ 200,000 against the insurers, ruling that the insurers were liable for misrepresentation which induced the homeowner to enter into the settlement agreement. The fact that the settlement agreement contained a clause which stated that it represented the full and final settlement between the parties did not preclude the homeowner's claims of misrepresentation.

3.25 In line with the analysis of Article 3(1), recognition under Article 3(2) of the Singapore Convention would prima facie be granted by the courts, unless the requirements in relation to scope, form and/or evidence are not fulfilled, or if a party successfully proves that one or more of the Article 5 grounds for refusal exist.

Case Illustration

Jack Pty Ltd ('Jack') and *Jill Pte Ltd* ('Jill')[52] have concluded an iMSA after a mediation session. The terms of the agreement involve Jill paying Jack USD 50,000 in compensation for losses suffered as a result of late delivery of a batch of Goods H, in exchange for the latter's forbearance to file a lawsuit in the High Court of Utopia with respect to the dispute. During the mediation, Jack's representative, who also relies on Jill to supply Goods J, mentions in passing that Jack hopes the supply of Goods J would not be affected, and that it would consider reaching a favourable compromise if guarantees were made for the delivery of Goods J. There was, however, no follow-up to the discussion, and no mention of Goods J in the iMSA. The iMSA falls within the scope of the Convention's application *per* Article 1, and easily satisfies the Article 4 evidential requirements for reliance on iMSAs. Shortly after signing the iMSA document, Jill encounters difficulty delivering Goods J. Jack files a suit for damages in the High Court of Utopia (a Party to the Singapore Convention). In this scenario, it is unlikely that Jill can rely on the settlement agreement under Article 3(2) of the Singapore Convention to apply for a striking out of the suit because the discussions during the mediation on the delivery of Goods J were not recorded or reflected in the written and signed settlement agreement. It is unlikely that the High Court of Utopia would rule that the issues arisen with respect to the delivery of Goods J have been resolved by the iMSA.[53]

This case illustration highlights the importance of drafting comprehensive terms in iMSAs. The flexibility of negotiating tailor-made outcomes in mediation is only beneficial if such terms are incorporated into the final iMSA.

52. Note that Pty Ltd is the abbreviation for a proprietary limited company in Australia and Pte Ltd is the abbreviation for a private limited company in Singapore.
53. Cf. *Jumaiah bte Amir and Another v Salim bin Abdul Rashid* [2019] SGHC 63, at paras 16-17.

Point of Interest

Recognition of Mediated Outcomes in Different Legal Forms

A mediated outcome can take different forms, including a consent arbitral award, court judgment and settlement deed.[54] The issue of whether a mediated outcome recorded as a consent award, judgment, or settlement deed, are capable of recognition in the same way as court judgments, is not uniform across jurisdictions and depends on the jurisdiction and the applicable legal instruments. An awareness of the international landscape on recognition of instruments containing settlements, is useful in understanding the drafting and operation of Article 3(2) of the Singapore Convention.

Recognition of Consent Awards

The New York Convention applies to both 'recognition' and 'enforcement' of foreign arbitral awards.[55] The use of these terms calls for clarification. While the term 'enforcement' refers to the forced execution of arbitral awards, the term 'recognition' refers to a court's determination of arbitral awards' preclusive effect.[56] The 'recognition' of an arbitral award occurs when a party institutes formal proceedings on the same dispute, which was decided in the arbitral award between the same parties. In this situation, the opposing party can ask a court or tribunal to recognise the binding force of the arbitral award by invoking the effect of *res judicata.*[57] The Supreme Court of India, in *Brace Transport Corporation of Monrovia v Orient Middle East Lines Ltd,*[58] elaborated on the difference between the recognition and enforcement of arbitral awards for the purposes of the New York Convention. The court reasoned, '[r]ecognition alone may be asked for as a shield against re-agitation of issues with which the award deals. Where a court is asked to enforce an award, it must recognise not only the legal effect of the award but must use legal sanctions to ensure that it is carried out'.[59] Therefore,

---

54. For more on this topic see the commentary to Art. 1.
55. Art. I(1) of the New York Convention states that it shall apply to the recognition and enforcement of arbitral awards made in the territory of a State other than the State where the recognition and enforcement of such awards are sought. The terms 'recognition' and 'enforcement' are also used in other provisions, particularly in Art. III that imposes the obligation on Contracting States to recognise awards as binding and enforce them in accordance with their procedural rules and the requirements of the Convention; Art. IV that prescribes the items that shall be submitted to the competent authority for the recognition and enforcement of arbitral awards; and Art. V that deals with the non-recognition and non-enforcement of foreign arbitral awards.
56. Andreas A. Frischknecht, Yasmine Lahlou and Gretta L. Walters, Enforcement of Foreign Arbitral Awards and Judgments in New York, Kluwer Law International (2018), at Chapter 8: Basic Principles Governing Recognition and Enforcement of Foreign Arbitral Awards in the United States and New York.
57. Albert Jan van der Berg, The New York Arbitration Convention of 1958, Towards a Uniform Judicial Interpretation, Kluwer Law and Taxation Publishers (1981), at 244.
58. AIR 1994 SC 1715.
59. *Id.*, para. 13.

these two concepts are different but closely intertwined – while a party can ask for recognition without enforcement of an award, the enforcement of an award necessarily implies the recognition of the same award. The court went on and explained that a party generally needs to ask a court to recognise an award when formal proceedings are instituted on the matter that was decided by the arbitral tribunal. Courts from various jurisdictions, including the US and Portugal, agree that parties could separately request the recognition of an arbitral award by invoking its preclusive effect.[60] Furthermore, German legislation expressly distinguishes these two concepts.[61]

A question arises whether MSAs arrived at *during* arbitral proceedings and converted into consent arbitral awards enjoy the same status as any other arbitral awards on the merits. The answer to this question, as shown by an examination of arbitration laws of various jurisdictions, is in the affirmative. By way of illustration, Article 30(2) of the UNCITRAL Model Law on International Commercial Arbitration (1985)[62] states that awards on agreed terms[63] have the same status and effect as any other awards on the merits of the case.[64] Article 51(3) of the Arbitration Act 1996 of England also states that an award on agreed terms shall have the same status and effect as any other award on the merits of the case. Furthermore, section 18(b) of the International Arbitration Act 1994 of Singapore explicitly states that awards on agreed terms may be enforced in the same manner as a judgment or an order to the same effect. Similar provisions can be found in other jurisdictions, including in Germany,[65]

60. UNCITRAL Secretariat Guide on the Convention on the Recognition and Enforcement of Foreign Arbitral Awards (New York, 1958) (2016), at 13-14, referring to the Evora Court of Appeal, Portugal [31 January 2008, Case No. 1141/06-2] and the United States [*Yusuf Ahmed Alghanim & Sons, W.L.L v Toys 'R' Us, Inc.*, Court of Appeals, Second Circuit, United States of America, 10 September 1997, 126 F.3.d 15].
61. Section 1055 of the Code of Civil Procedure (ZPO) deals with the recognition of awards, which states that an arbitration award has the effect of a final and binding judgment handed down by a court. Sections 1060-1061 deal with the enforcement of domestic and foreign arbitral awards. Concerning the distinction between 'recognition' and 'enforcement' in German legislation, see Stefan Kröll, *Chapter VII – Recognition and Enforcement of Awards*, in Karl-Heinz Böckstiegel et al. (eds), Arbitration in Germany – The Model Law in Practice, Wolters Kluwer (2007), at 481-483.
62. As at 11 May 2022, legislation based on the UNCITRAL Model Law on International Commercial Arbitration (1985) has been adopted in 85 States in a total of 118 jurisdictions. The status of the Model Law is available at www.uncitral.org (Accessed 11 May 2022).
63. The terms 'awards on agreed terms' and 'consent awards' are used interchangeably.
64. See also the drafting history of the Model Law on Arbitration, which shows that arbitral awards on agreed terms shall be treated the same way as any other awards. The Report of the Working Group on International Contract Practices on the Work of its 3rd Session (New York, 16-26 February 1982), A/CN.9/216 (1982). Available here https://undocs.org/en/A/CN.9/216 (Accessed 2 March 2022).
65. Section 1053 of the Code of Civil Procedure (ZPO) states that settlement agreements arrived at during arbitral proceedings and converted into arbitral awards have the same effect as any other arbitral awards. Reference to the 'same effect' shows that consent arbitral awards have the effect

Hong Kong,[66] Canada[67] and India.[68] These laws show that MSAs arrived at *during* arbitral proceedings and converted into consent arbitral awards enjoy the same preclusive effect, or in other words, the *res judicata* effect, as any other awards on the merits.

The question remains whether settlements arrived at *before* the commencement of arbitral proceedings, by way of illustration in the *med-arb* procedure and rubber-stamped as 'awards', can have the same effect as settlement agreements that are arrived at *during* arbitral proceedings and converted into consent arbitral awards. As discussed elsewhere in this book,[69] it is unlikely such awards will have the same status as awards on the merits. Article I(1) of the New York Convention applies to foreign arbitral awards arising out of 'differences' between parties and 'differences' would not exist if parties settled a dispute before the commencement of arbitral proceedings.[70]

Recognition of Court Orders

It is universally recognised that court judgments produce the *res judicata* effect, that is to say, the preclusive effect of a judgment prevents a party from instituting formal proceedings on the matter that has been adjudicated and resolved in that judgment between the same parties.[71] But do MSAs that have been approved and recorded as court orders enjoy the same status and effect as any other court judgments? While consent arbitral awards usually enjoy the same status and effect as normal court judgments, the situation is less clear in relation to

of *res judicata* between the same parties regarding the same dispute. See Gino Lörcher, *Enforceability of Agreed Awards in Foreign Jurisdictions*, 17(3) Arb. Int'l (1 September 2001), at 279.

66. Section 66(1) of the Arbitration Ordinance incorporates Art. 30 of the UNCITRAL Model Law on Arbitration, which deals with settlements arrived at *during* arbitral proceedings and converted into consent arbitral awards. Such awards enjoy the same effect as any other awards. However, s. 66(2) goes even further and states that settlement agreements that are not arrived at *during* arbitral proceedings can also be treated as arbitral awards. However, s. 66(2) does not specify whether such awards enjoy the same status as any other awards on the merits, which raises doubts about the *res judicata* effect of such awards and particularly for the purposes of the New York Convention.
67. Most of the arbitration laws in the provinces of Canada are based on the UNCITRAL Model Law on Arbitration.
68. Section 30(4) of the Arbitration and Conciliation Act, 1996 of India states that awards on agreed terms, arrived at during arbitral proceedings, have the same effect as any other awards on the merits.
69. This is also discussed in the commentary to Art. 1-Art. 1(3), at paras 1.54-1.63.
70. The timing of converting a settlement agreement into an arbitral award is crucial. If parties settle a dispute before the commencement of arbitral proceedings, there will not be any dispute to settle in arbitration. *See Castro v Tri Marine Fish Co. LLC* 916 F.3d 1191, 2019 U.S. App. LEXIS 5864, 2019 WL 1592282 (9th Cir. Wash. 27 February 2019).
71. See Jacob B. van de Velden, Finality in Litigation: The Law and Practice of Preclusion: *Res Judicata* (Merger and Estoppel), Abuse of Process and Recognition of Foreign Judgments, Kluwer Law International BV (2017) and Peter R. Barnett, *Res Judicata*, Estoppel, and Foreign Judgments, OUP (2001).

settlements approved by a court as 'judicial settlements',[72] 'court settlements',[73] 'consent orders or judgments',[74] or 'Tomlin orders'.[75]

Chapter III of the Hague Convention of 30 June 2005 on Choice of Court Agreements (HCCCA) deals with the recognition and enforcement of foreign court judgments. Article 8, titled as 'Recognition and Enforcement', imposes the obligation on Contracting States to 'recognise' and 'enforce' a judgment given by a court of a Contracting State designated in an exclusive choice of court agreement. This provision expressly distinguishes the process of recognition from the process of enforcement and ensures that foreign court judgments enjoy both in Contracting States to the HCCCA. However, Article 8 of the HCCCA does not encompass MSAs recorded as court orders. The enforcement of MSAs recorded as court orders is regulated under Article 12. Article 12 of the HCCCA states that judicial settlements (*transactions judiciaires*) which a court of a Contracting State designated in an exclusive choice of court agreement has approved, or which have been concluded before that court in the course of

72. By way of example, Art. 12 of the Hague Convention of 30 June 2005 on Choice of Court Agreements (HCCCA) employs the term 'judicial settlement', which refers to settlements that have been approved, or which have been concluded before a court in the course of proceedings, and which are enforceable in the same manner as a judgment.
73. By way of example, according to Art. 2(b) of the EU Regulation (EU) No. 1215/2012 of the European Parliament and of The Council of 12 December 2012 (Brussels I Recast Regulation), the term 'court settlement' means a settlement which has been approved by a court of a Member State or concluded before a court of a Member State in the course of proceedings.
74. By way of example, s. 40.6 of the Civil Procedure Rules 1998 (UK) regulates consent judgments and orders where the parties agree on the terms in which a judgment should be given or an order should be made. According to s. 40.6(3)(a), a consent judgment or order is possible for: the payment of an amount of money (including a judgment or order for damages or the value of goods to be decided by the court); or the delivery up of goods with or without the option of paying the value of the goods or the agreed value. According to s. 40.6(3)(b), a consent order is possible for: the dismissal of any proceedings, wholly or in part; the stay of proceedings on agreed terms, disposing of the proceedings, whether those terms are recorded in a schedule to the order or elsewhere; the stay of enforcement of a judgment, either unconditionally or on condition that the money due under the judgment is paid by instalments specified in the order; the setting aside under Part 13 of a default judgment which has not been satisfied; the payment out of money which has been paid into court; the discharge from liability of any party; the payment, assessment or waiver of costs, or such other provision for costs as may be agreed.
75. A Tomlin order in the English Civil Justice System is a type of consent order. *Vanden Recycling Ltd v Kras Recycling BV* [2017] EWCA Civ 354, at 45, distinguishes a 'consent order' from a 'Tomlin order': '[a] court will not make a consent order unless satisfied that it has power to do so, whilst it has no right to disapprove a Tomlin order and such an order can include matters that the court has no power to order. A breach of a consent order may be punishable as a contempt in appropriate circumstances, whilst the remedy for breach of the scheduled terms of a Tomlin order is a claim for breach of contract. In terms of enforcement, the remedies in CPR [Civil Procedure Rules] Part 83 are available for breach of a consent order but not for breach of a Tomlin order. A variation of a consent order is possible in the interests of justice, whilst rectification would be necessary to vary the contractual terms of a Tomlin order. Confidentiality for a consent order requires CPR 39.2 to be satisfied, whilst it can be contractually agreed for a Tomlin order. An appeal of a consent order is possible subject to the usual permission test,

proceedings and which are enforceable in the same manner as a judgment in the State of origin, shall be enforced under this Convention in the same manner as a judgment. Contrary to Article 8, Article 12 employs only the term 'enforcement'. It is suggested that Article 12 requires only the enforcement of judicial settlements and matters of recognition are not governed by the Convention.[76] The recognition of judicial settlements is left to the national laws of Contracting States.[77] While the HCCCA imposes the obligation on Contracting States to 'recognise' and 'enforce' foreign court judgments, Contracting States have the obligation only to 'enforce' judicial settlements. The HCCCA does not require Contracting States to 'recognise' the preclusive effect, or in other words, the *res judicata* effect, of judicial settlements. The same approach has been retained in the Convention of 2 July 2019 on the Recognition and Enforcement of Foreign Judgments in Civil or Commercial Matters, otherwise known as the Hague Judgments Convention.[78]

Article 59 of the EU Regulation (EU) No 1215/2012 of the European Parliament and of The Council of 12 December 2012 (Brussels I Recast Regulation) states that a court settlement, which is enforceable in the Member State of origin shall be enforced in the other Member States under the same conditions as authentic instruments.[79] It is suggested that Article 59 regulates only the enforcement of court settlements and does not deal with their recognition. Court settlements are generally not attributed to the *res judicata* effect because they are derived from parties' agreement rather than a court's determination.[80] In *Solo Kleinmotoren GmbH v Emilio Boch,*[81] the European Court of Justice explained the difference between court judgments and court settlements. The court stated that a judgment refers 'solely to judicial decisions actually given by a court or tribunal of a

---

whilst there is no appeal from the agreed terms of a Tomlin order. These differences reflect the fact that a consent order is an order of the court whilst the scheduled terms to a Tomlin order are a contractual agreement'.

76. Ronald A. Brand and Paul Herrup, *The 2005 Hague Convention on Choice of Court Agreements*, Cambridge University Press (2009), at 130-132.
77. *Ibid.*
78. Art. 11 of the Hague Judgments Convention, titled as 'Judicial settlements (transactions judiciaires)' reads as follows: '[j]udicial settlements (transactions judiciaires) which a court of a Contracting State has approved, or which have been concluded in the course of proceedings before a court of a Contracting State, and which are enforceable in the same manner as a judgment in the State of origin, shall be enforced under this Convention in the same manner as a judgment.'
79. The enforcement of authentic instruments is regulated in Art. 58, which reads as follows: '[a]n authentic instrument which is enforceable in the Member State of origin shall be enforceable in the other Member States without any declaration of enforceability being required. Enforcement of the authentic instrument may be refused only if such enforcement is manifestly contrary to public policy (ordre public) in the Member State addressed.'
80. Xandra Kramer, *Art. 59*, in Ulrich Magnus and Peter Mankowski (eds), Brussels Ibis Regulation - Commentary, Otto Schmidt KG, Verlag (2016), at 988.
81. *Solo Kleinmotoren GmbH v Emilio Boch* Judgment of the Court (Sixth Chamber) of 2 June 1994.

Contracting State'.[82] A judgment emanates from a judicial body deciding on its own authority, while a settlement is essentially contractual in nature, and it depends on the will and autonomy of parties.[83] Therefore, while judgments enjoy the effect of *res judicata*, court settlements do not produce the same preclusive effect for the purposes of the Brussels I Recast Regulation in the EU.[84]

In England, a distinction is drawn between judgments by consent and Tomlin orders. A consent order has the same effect as a court judgment.[85] A Tomlin order involves a contractual settlement agreement between parties and allows for proceedings to be continued in order to implement that agreement.[86] While the court has the power not to make a consent order, it does not have the right to disapprove a Tomlin order.[87] In *Zurich Insurance Co plc v Hayward*,[88] the Court of Appeal opined that a judgment by consent is capable of creating the preclusive effect and the effect of a judgment by consent is the same as that of a judgment entered after a trial.[89] However, the court said that a Tomlin order is different because a Tomlin order terminates proceedings without any decision of a court on the substance of the claim and it may not produce the same effect.[90] In another case of *Spire Healthcare Ltd v Brooke*,[91] the court confirmed that while consent judgments are capable of creating a preclusive effect, the position on Tomlin orders is not clear. However, in the context of English law, Spenser Bower and Turner note that at the request of the parties, a court or tribunal converts a mere agreement into a judicial decision, which is capable of producing the *res judicata* effect and such decisions are no less effective than any other judgments on the merits.[92] The situation in the US is clearer: the dismissal of a suit based on a settlement agreement is capable of creating the *res judicata* effect.[93] The position

82. *Id.*, para. 15.
83. *Id.*, paras 17-18.
84. One commentator on this issue cautioned that some decisions are on the borderline between judgments and settlements, especially English consent judgments and French *Jugements d'expedient*. See Xandra Kramer, *Art. 59*, in Ulrich Magnus and Peter Mankowski (eds), Brussels Ibis Regulation – Commentary, Otto Schmidt KG, Verlag (2016), at 987.
85. *Vanden Recycling Ltd v Kras Recycling BV* [2017] EWCA Civ 354, at para. 47.
86. *Ibid.*
87. *Id.*, para. 45.
88. *Zurich Insurance Co plc v Hayward* [2011] EWCA Civ 641.
89. *Id.*, para. 47.
90. *Id.*, para. 78.
91. *Jellett v Brooke and Another* [2017] 1 WLR 1177.
92. George Spenser Bower and Alexander Kingcome Turner, *The Doctrine of Res Judicata*, Butterworths (1969), at 37.
93. *Brown v One Beacon Ins. Co. Inc.* 317 F. App'x 915, 918 (11th Cir. 2009). See also *Stone v Potter* No. 1:08-CV-1139-VEH, 2009 WL 10694953, at *6 (N.D. Ala. 15 October 2009) and *United States v Ameritrade Terminals, Inc.* 177 Fed. Appx. 855, 856, 2006 U.S. App. LEXIS 7928, *1 (11th Cir. Fla. 31 March 2006).

on whether consent judgments enjoy the effect of *res judicata* is not clear in Singapore, as the courts have rendered conflicting decisions in this regard.[94]

Recognition of Settlement Deeds

While consent arbitral awards are capable of creating the *res judicata* effect and court settlements may have the preclusive effect depending on the jurisdiction, it is unlikely that settlement deeds enjoy an equivalent status.

The Brussels I Recast Regulation represents the main international legal instrument that regulates the circulation of settlement deeds, which are referred to as 'authentic instruments' within the EU. According to Article 58, an authentic instrument which is enforceable in the Member State of origin shall be enforceable in the other Member States without any declaration of enforceability being required. This Article goes on and states that enforcement may be refused if such enforcement would be contrary to the public policy of the State where enforcement is sought. This Article does not use the term 'recognition' because authentic instruments do not enjoy the effect of *res judicata* similar to that of court judgments or arbitral awards.[95] For the purposes of enforcement, the contents of authentic instruments are 'accepted', which means that an authentic instrument has the same evidentiary effects in another EU Member State as in the EU Member State of origin.[96] One commentator notes that notarial deeds are incapable of producing *res judicata* because such deeds are of indeterminate legal effect and they lack finality.[97] The finality of a foreign judgment allows a court to identify the *res judicata* effect of that judgment and this is not possible in the case of authentic instruments.[98] As an authentic instrument can be challenged even after its enforcement, it is impossible to attribute an authentic instrument with finality similar to that of a judgment; therefore, it is impossible for an authentic instrument to produce *res judicata*. This position is shared in other studies,

94. See the following cases: *Low Heng Leon Andy v Low Kian Beng Lawrence (administrator of the estate of Tan Ah Kng, deceased)* [2013] 3 SLR 710; *Cost Engineers (SEA) Pte Ltd and another v Chan Siew Lun* [2016] 1 SLR 137; *Jaidin bin Jaiman v Loganathan a/l Karpaya and another* [2013] 1 SLR 318; *Soh Lay Lian Cherlyn v Kok Mui Eng* [2015] 5 SLR 53 and *Kok Mui Eng v Cherlyn Soh Lay Lian* [2014] SGDC 419. The cases are discussed in Dorcas Quek Anderson, *Issue Estoppel Created by Consent Judgments: Dissonance Between the Principles Underlying Settlement and Court Decisions*, Sing. J. Legal Stud. 100 (2017), at 100-123.
95. Xandra Kramer, *Art. 59*, in Ulrich Magnus and Peter Mankowski (eds), Brussels Ibis Regulation - Commentary, Otto Schmidt KG, Verlag (2016), at 984.
96. Art. 59 of Regulation (EU) No. 650/2012 of the European Parliament and of the Council of 4 July 2012 on jurisdiction, applicable law, recognition and enforcement of decisions and acceptance and enforcement of authentic instruments in matters of succession and on the creation of a European Certificate of Succession.
97. Jonathan Fitchen, *Authentic Instruments and European Private International Law in Civil and Commercial Matters: Is Now the Time to Break New Ground?*, 7(1) J. Priv. Int'l L. (2011), at 83.
98. *Ibid.*

which confirm that the term 'recognition' with the meaning of *res judicata*, does not exist in relation to authentic instruments.[99]

A Functional Approach to Recognition

3.26 On its face, it appears that Article 3(1) provides for an enforcement mechanism for iMSAs, while Article 3(2) provides for a recognition mechanism. It is important to note that iMSAs and settlement agreements, in general, are not obtained from an adjudicative (or determinative) forum. This characteristic of iMSAs has led some commentators to ask the question: on what premise may iMSAs be 'recognised' by courts in the private international law sense? The notion of 'recognition' in private international law occasions a consideration of overlapping principles generally falling within the concept of *res judicata*:[100] for instance, the cause of action estoppel,[101] issue estoppel[102] and the *Henderson v Henderson*[103] estoppel.

3.27 During the drafting stages of the Singapore Convention, representatives from the EU (representing predominantly civil law traditions) opposed the insertion of the term 'recognition' (as understood in private international law) into Article 3. In justification, they argued that *res judicata* should be employed only over matters stemming from acts of State, such as court judgments.[104] The concern raised by the EU delegates may not be apparent to lawyers who practise under the common law tradition, as it is possible to justify the consequences of 'recognition' of a dispute resolution outcome arising

99. Comparative Study on Authentic Instruments – National Provisions of Private Law, Circulation, Mutual Recognition and Enforcement, Possible Legislative Initiative by the European Union (United Kingdom, France, Germany, Poland, Romania, Sweden), available at https://www.europarl.europa.eu/thinktank/en/document.html?reference=IPOL-JURI_ET(2008)408329 (Accessed 2 March 2022) (*Comparative Study on Authentic Instruments*). The examination of six jurisdictions in this study, namely the United Kingdom, France, Germany, Poland, Romania, and Sweden shows that authentic instruments have two main effects: establishing conclusive proof of their contents and enforcing their contents by operation of law. In all these jurisdictions, authentic instruments can be challenged either in the same procedure where the authentic instrument was used as a proof or through a special procedure. See *Comparative Study on Authentic Instruments*, at 63-73. An examination of these jurisdictions indicates that authentic instruments do not enjoy the same status and effect as those of court judgments and arbitral awards.

100. Dorcas Quek Anderson, *Issue Estoppel Created by Consent Judgments: Dissonance Between the Principles Underlying Settlements and Court Decisions*, Sing. J. Legal Stud. 100 (2017), at 101.

101. See *Thoday v Thoday* [1964] 1 All ER 341, (*per* Lord Diplock) at 197.

102. See *Lee Tat Development Pte Ltd v Management Corporation of Strata Title Plan No. 301* [2005] 3 SLR(R) 157, at paras 14-15.

103. *Henderson v Henderson* [1843-60] All ER Rep 378, at 115.

104. See, for example, Intervention of the European Union, in Audio Recording: Working Group II, 64th Session (United Nations 2016), 4 February 2016, at 10:00-13:00, http://www.uncitral.org/uncitral/audio/meetings.jsp (Accessed 31 December, 2018); this was also reported by Schnabel: Timothy Schnabel, *The Singapore Convention on Mediation: A Framework for the Cross-Border Recognition and Enforcement of Mediated Settlements*, 19 Pepp. Disp. Resol. L.J. 1 (2019), at 35 et seq.; and see Norel Rosner, *The New UNCITRAL Instruments on International Commercial Settlement Agreements Resulting from Mediation – an Insider's View*, 22(4) Nederlands-Vlaams tijdschrift voor Mediation en conflict management 30 (2018), at 33.

from mediation as a means to avoid abuse of the court's process.[105] In civil law traditions, the notion of 'recognition' of dispute resolution outcomes is tied tightly to the principle of *res judicata excluding* [*emphasis added*] the *Henderson v Henderson* estoppel referred to previously. In this context, concerns arising from re-litigation to abuse court processes are tenuous and marginalised.[106] In addition to the issue raised by the EU, the delegates who were opposing the inclusion of 'recognition' in the Singapore Convention noted that 'recognition would not have any practical effect. It was also said that the recognition procedure could have a negative impact on the expeditious enforcement of settlement agreements as, at the recognition stage, the validity of the conciliation procedure and its outcome might be examined. It was further said that settlement agreements might become void, be terminated or amended by the parties at any time including after the recognition of the agreement by a court, which could raise legal difficulties. It was pointed out that inclusion of a recognition procedure would generally require formalities in relation to settlement agreements, which were usually not required in relation to ordinary contracts'.[107]

3.28 A compromise was reached among the drafters to reflect the functional description of 'recognition' in Article 3(2) without explicitly referring to it.[108] In this way, they were able to circumvent the risk of the irreconcilability of potentially discordant interpretations of the private international law concept of 'recognition' under domestic conditions.

3.29 The Singapore Convention, therefore, has broken new ground because a new instrument for dispute resolution outcomes acquired from a non-adjudicative process – namely iMSAs – may be 'recognised' and enforced within the private international law framework. MSAs with an international character have thereby been elevated to a new status recognised by international law.[109]

105. *Chan Gek Yong v Violet Netto (practising as L F Violet Netto) and another and another matter* [2019] 3 SLR 1218, [2018] SGHC 208.
106. See Michael Bogdan, *Concise Introduction to EU Private International Law*, Europa Law Publishing (2006), at 74 et seq.
107. Report of Working Group II (Arbitration and Conciliation) on the Work of its 63rd Session (Vienna, 7-11 September 2015), A/CN.9/861 (2015), at para. 76. Available at http://undocs.org/A/CN.9/861. See also: Report of Working Group II (Arbitration and Conciliation) on the Work of its 64th Session (New York, 1-5 February 2016), A/CN.9/867 (2016), at para. 146. Available at http://undocs.org/A/CN.9/867; Report of Working Group II (Dispute Settlement) on the Work of its 65th Session (Vienna, 12-23 September 2016), A/CN.9/896 (2016), at paras 76-83. Available at http://undocs.org/A/CN.9/896; Report of Working Group II (Dispute Settlement) on the Work of its 66th Session (New York, 6-10 February 2017), A/CN.9/901 (2017), at paras 16-24. Available at http://undocs.org/A/CN.9/901 (Accessed 11 May 2022).
108. Report of Working Group II (Dispute Settlement) on the Work of its 66th Session (New York, 6-10 February 2017), A/CN.9/901 (2017), at paras 51-52. Available at http://undocs.org/A/CN.9/901 (Accessed 11 May 2017).
109. Note that iMSAs that fall within the scope of the Singapore Convention, while enjoying special status under the Convention, do not lose their character as iMSAs in contract. They can be both.

Table 2[110] *A Comparison Table on the Enforcement of an iMSA under the Singapore Convention and Enforcement of a Consent Arbitral Award under the New York Convention*

	The Singapore Convention	*The New York Convention*
Enforcement.	Yes. Article 3(1) of the Singapore Convention provides a direct enforcement mechanism for iMSAs.	Yes. Article III of the New York Convention provides a direct enforcement mechanism for foreign arbitral awards. Regarding the limitations on the enforcement of consent arbitral awards under the New York Convention, *see* commentary to Article 1.
Recognition.	Yes. Even though the Singapore Convention does not expressly mention the term 'recognition', Article 3(2) provides a functional description of the process of recognition and Contracting Parties to the Singapore Convention have an obligation to recognise the effect of iMSAs.	Yes. Article III imposes the obligation on the Contracting States to the New York Convention to recognise foreign arbitral awards. Regarding the preclusive effect of consent arbitral awards, *see* above Point of Interest – Recognition of Mediated Outcomes in Different Forms.
Rules of procedure of the State where enforcement/ recognition is sought.	Yes. Article 3(1)-(2) of the Singapore Convention prescribes that each Contracting Party shall enforce and recognise iMSAs in accordance with its rules of procedure.	Yes. Article III of the New York Convention prescribes that each Contracting State shall recognise foreign arbitral awards as binding and enforce them in accordance with its rules of procedure.

110. This table provides the differences discussed in this chapter. The table on all differences between enforcement under the Singapore Convention and the New York Convention is provided in Appendix A.

	The Singapore Convention	*The New York Convention*
Prohibition of imposing different conditions in relation to domestic and international iMSAs/awards.	No. There is no provision restricting Contracting Parties to the Singapore Convention from imposing more onerous conditions and higher fees on the enforcement and recognition of iMSAs than what they impose on the recognition and enforcement of domestic mediated settlements.	Yes. Article III of the New York Convention states that there shall not be imposed substantially more onerous conditions or higher fees or charges on the recognition or enforcement of arbitral awards to which this Convention applies than are imposed on the recognition or enforcement of domestic arbitral awards.

ARTICLE 4

Requirements for Reliance on Settlement Agreements

1. A party relying on a settlement agreement under this Convention shall supply to the competent authority of the Party to the Convention where relief is sought:

(a) The settlement agreement signed by the parties;
(b) Evidence that the settlement agreement resulted from mediation, such as:
  (i) The mediator's signature on the settlement agreement;
  (ii) A document signed by the mediator indicating that the mediation was carried out;
  (iii) An attestation by the institution that administered the mediation; or
  (iv) In the absence of (i), (ii) or (iii), any other evidence acceptable to the competent authority.

2. The requirement that a settlement agreement shall be signed by the parties or, where applicable, the mediator is met in relation to an electronic communication if:

(a) A method is used to identify the parties or the mediator and to indicate the parties' or mediator's intention in respect of the information contained in the electronic communication; and
(b) The method used is either:
  (i) As reliable as appropriate for the purpose for which the electronic communication was generated or communicated, in the light of all the circumstances, including any relevant agreement; or
  (ii) Proven in fact to have fulfilled the functions described in subparagraph (a) above, by itself or together with further evidence.

3. If the settlement agreement is not in an official language of the Party to the Convention where relief is sought, the competent authority may request a translation thereof into such language.
4. The competent authority may require any necessary document in order to verify that the requirements of the Convention have been complied with.

5. When considering the request for relief, the competent authority shall act expeditiously.

COMMENTARY

4.01 If a party to an international mediated settlement agreement (iMSA) which falls within the scope of the Singapore Convention seeks relief from a court, that party must comply with minimal formality requirements in Article 4. The reason why formality requirements are still in place is because unlike the Convention on the Recognition and Enforcement of Foreign Arbitral Awards (New York Convention), settlement agreements can be arrived at after mediation, negotiation, or other means of informal discussion.[1] Essentially, the party seeking relief must submit to the relevant court or authority:

(1) the iMSA in writing with the parties' signatures (Article 4(1)(a)); and
(2) evidence showing that the iMSA document did result from a mediation process (Article 4(1)(b)).

4.02 The above formalities are exhaustive and minimal and are intended to reduce obstacles to obtaining relief. Competent courts may not impose additional requirements to prove that a settlement agreement resulted from mediation,[2] such as notarisation, requirements to use locally licensed mediators or the like. Moreover, it was considered that minimal requirements would promote the circulation of iMSAs and reduce the likelihood of satellite litigation.[3]

4.03 Article 4 goes on to provide examples of what might amount to sufficient evidence that a settlement agreement resulted from mediation. Finally, Article 4 addresses electronic communications in relation to iMSAs and parties' signatures and the powers and duties of the competent court or authority.

1. Eunice Chua, *The Singapore Convention on Mediation — A Brighter Future for Asian Dispute Resolution*, 9(2) Asian J. Int'l L. 195 (2019), at 199. We note that UNCITRAL texts use the terms 'mediation' and 'conciliation' interchangeably. See footnote 2 of the UNCITRAL Model Law on International Commercial Mediation and International Settlement Agreements Resulting from Mediation (2018) in Appendix E. For more on the definition of the term 'mediation', see the commentary to Art. 2.
2. Schnabel points out that Art. 4 does not do away with legal form requirements that might attach to the subject matter of the iMSA (and not the iMSA itself), citing the transfer of real estate as an example: Timothy Schnabel, *The Singapore Convention on Mediation: A Framework for the Cross-Border Recognition and Enforcement of Mediated Settlements*, 19 Pepp. Disp. Resol. L.J. 1 (2019), at 28.
3. See, for example, intervention of the Chair, in Audio Recording: Working Group II, 64th Session (United Nations 2016), 3 February 2016, 10:00-13:00, http://www.uncitral.org/uncitral/audio/meetings.jsp (Accessed 20 May 2019).

4.04 The commentary to Article 4 focuses on the following topics:

(1) iMSAs in writing with the parties' signatures;
(2) the meaning of 'competent authority' and the use of the term 'relief';
(3) what amounts to evidence that the settlement agreement resulted from mediation; and
(4) electronic communications and parties' signatures.

iMSAs in Writing with the Parties' Signatures

4.05 As set out in Articles 1(1) and 2(2), iMSAs falling under the scope of the Singapore Convention must be in writing which includes forms of electronic communication. There is no requirement that the iMSA be contained in a single document,[4] as it could comprise an exchange of emails.[5] Schnabel points out that the requirement for parties' signatures may in certain circumstances be met by signatures from their counsel, citing interventions in Working Group II meetings from Israel, Canada, Germany and the Chair,[6] but subject to the counsel obtaining the necessary capacity to do so (see the commentary of Article 5(1)(a)).[7] Requirements for parties' signatures on the iMSA where emails and other forms of electronic communications are involved are set out in Article 4(2), examined below. The requirement that parties sign their settlement agreement reflects the principle of party autonomy and the integrity of the parties' agreement. See the following case illustration where this principle was not followed by the conciliator.

4. The delegates at Working Group II who opposed the inclusion of the single document requirement in the Singapore Convention argued that this requirement 'would not necessarily reflect the current practice where the form and content of settlement agreements varied greatly. It was mentioned that settlement agreements might consist of more than one document including annexes, and might comprise of different forms which might not necessarily be captured in a single document. It was pointed out that introducing such a requirement would make the process rigid, putting additional burden on parties'. See Report of Working Group II (Dispute Settlement) on the Work of its 65th Session (Vienna, 12-23 September 2016), A/CN.9/896 (2016), at para. 67. Available at http://undocs.org/A/CN.9/867 (Accessed 12 May 2022).
5. See the commentary to Art. 2(2). See also Timothy Schnabel, *The Singapore Convention on Mediation: A Framework for the Cross-Border Recognition and Enforcement of Mediated Settlements*, 19 Pepp. Disp. Resol. L.J. 1 (2019), at 28.
6. See Timothy Schnabel, *The Singapore Convention on Mediation: A Framework for the Cross-Border Recognition and Enforcement of Mediated Settlements*, 19 Pepp. Disp. Resol. L.J. 1 (2019), at 28.
7. Working Group II debated whether the Singapore Convention should expressly provide that a settlement agreement might be signed by authorised representatives of a party. Working Group II came to the conclusion that the Singapore Convention should not expressly refer to authorised representatives with the understanding that this notion would be implicit in the text of the Convention. It was also stated that this issue would be addressed in the relevant applicable legislation. See Report of Working Group II (Dispute Settlement) on the Work of its 67th Session (Vienna, 2-6 October 2017), A/CN.9/929 (2017), at paras 49-51. Available at http://undocs.org /A/CN.9/929 (Accessed 12 May 2022).

Case Illustration

In *Haresh Dayaram Thakur v State of Mahrashtra*,[8] after holding meetings with the parties, the conciliator drew up the settlement agreement himself in secrecy. He then sent the settlement agreement to the High Court of Bombay in a sealed cover. The High Court confirmed the settlement agreement received from the conciliator. Following an appeal by one of the parties, the Supreme Court of India set aside both the settlement agreement and the High Court's confirmation order, holding that the conciliator had committed an illegality. Pursuant to sections 30, 61, 64, 67, 69, 70 and 72-77 of the 1996 Indian Arbitration and Conciliation Act, a settlement agreement is only effective when the parties draw up the settlement agreement or request the conciliator to prepare the same and affix their signatures to it. According to section 73(3), the settlement agreement signed by the parties is final and binding on the parties and persons claiming under them. It follows, therefore, that a successful conciliation proceeding comes to an end only when the settlement agreement signed by the parties comes into existence. The conciliator and the High Court Judge who passed the impugned order had failed to take note of the relevant provisions of the Act. The High Court Judge also failed to notice the apparent illegalities committed by the conciliator in drawing up the settlement agreement, keeping it secret from the parties and sending it to the court without obtaining their signatures.

4.06 The rationale behind the requirement of the parties' signatures on an iMSA is to guarantee that parties to an iMSA had agreed to all terms and conditions contained therein. It is no substitute that the mediator signs the iMSA and the parties, in the presence of the mediator, orally express their acceptance of the contents of the iMSA. The case below is illustrative in this regard:

Case Illustration

In *Weimann v Allphones Retail Pty Ltd (No 2)*,[9] the Federal Court of Australia addressed the issue of whether the parties reached a binding settlement agreement at the mediation evidenced by, amongst other factors, the signature of the mediator on the settlement agreement.

In this case, the parties were engaged in an extensive mediation process that lasted several days. After they reached an understanding on some of the issues at the mediation, the Chairman of the Board of Directors of the respondent made a

8. *Haresh Dayaram Thakur v State of Mahrashtra* AIR 2000 SC 2281; 2000 AIR SCW 2058.
9. *Weimann (as trustee for Weimann Family Trust (No 3)) v Allphones Retail Pty Ltd* (No. 2) (2009) 261 ALR 343.

remark: '[w]hy don't we get the mediator to sign the document'. The other party agreed. The mediator, in fact, signed the settlement agreement in the presence of the parties. However, the parties themselves never actually confirmed the settlement terms with their signatures.

The applicant, in arguing that the parties reached a binding settlement, took the position that the mediator's signature confirmed the parties' settlement. Otherwise, there would not be any point in asking the mediator to sign the settlement agreement. The court rejected this argument, on the ground that the lack of the parties' signatures on the document was an indication that the parties were not willing to be immediately bound by the terms of the settlement agreement.

Meaning of 'competent authority'

4.07 While the meaning of 'Party to the Convention' is addressed in the commentary to Article 3, the term 'competent authority' appears for the first time in Article 4(1). Though not defined within the Convention or explicitly discussed by Working Group II, the term 'competent authority' is said to refer to 'a court or any other authority empowered by the relevant state to address these issues, including an arbitral tribunal seated in that state'.[10] In the context of the New York Convention, the term 'competent authority' refers to the authority that is in charge of the enforcement and recognition of foreign arbitral awards[11] and the authority that has the jurisdiction to suspend or annul arbitral awards.[12]

Meaning of 'relief'

4.08 The Singapore Convention refers to the remedy sought as 'relief', which functionally encompasses the right of parties to the iMSA to recognise and enforce an iMSA *per* the terms of Article 3.[13] As indicated in the commentary to Article 3, the expedited enforcement mechanism of the Singapore Convention – which is functionally an exercise of recognition and enforcement of dispute resolution outcomes in the private

10. Timothy Schnabel, *The Singapore Convention on Mediation: A Framework for the Cross-Border Recognition and Enforcement of Mediated Settlements*, 19 Pepp. Disp. Resol. L.J. 1 (2019), at 28.
11. By way of example, Art. V(1) of the New York Convention states: '[r]ecognition and enforcement of the award may be refused, at the request of the party against whom it is invoked, only if that party furnishes to *the competent authority* where the recognition and enforcement is sought [...]' [*emphasis added*].
12. By way of example, Art. V(1)(e) of the New York Convention states: '[t]he award has not yet become binding on the parties, or *has been set aside or suspended by a competent authority of the country in which, or under the law of which, that award was made*' [*emphasis added*].
13. UNCITRAL Working Group II (Arbitration and Conciliation), *Settlement of Commercial Disputes, International Commercial Conciliation: Enforceability of Settlement Agreements*, Note by the Secretariat (1-5 February 2016), A/CN.9/WG.II/WP.195, at para. 49. Also see Haris Meidanis, *International Enforcement of Mediated Settlement Agreements: Two and a Half Models – Why and How to Enforce Internationally Mediated Settlement Agreements*, 85(1) Arbitration 49 (2019), at 55.

international law sense – may be administered as a 'sword' in the context of enforcement and a 'shield' in the context of recognition. In applying these metaphors, the drafters of the Convention avoided explicitly referring to the expedited enforcement mechanism of Article 3 as 'recognition' and 'enforcement' provisions.

4.09 In this way, the drafters were able to address the concerns of delegates from civil law traditions that the recognition of (international) dispute resolution outcomes is tied closely to the concept of *res judicata.* To expressly refer to an iMSA as capable of engendering such recognition in the articles of the Singapore Convention may lead to possibly discordant interpretations of private international law 'recognition' under domestic conditions. As a reflection of the functional purpose of Article 3 and to maintain consistency in drafting, the drafters of Article 4 of the Singapore Convention *do not refer* to the remedy sought under the former article by 'recognition' or 'enforcement'. Instead, the term 'relief' is used.

4.10 To illustrate, 'relief' embraces the process of homologation as the first step of enforcement of iMSAs in some civil law jurisdictions (for example, France and Belgium), as well as the process undertaken by parties of iMSAs to apply to the competent court of a signatory State to strike out proceedings[14] because those discrete issues have already been resolved at mediation and are appropriately reflected in an iMSA.[15]

What Amounts to Evidence that the Settlement Agreement Resulted from Mediation

4.11 The Singapore Convention does not apply to settlement agreements negotiated outside of a mediation process.[16] For this reason, parties seeking to enforce settlement agreements are required to produce the original iMSA signed by the parties,[17] which may be in electronic form.[18] In addition, parties are required to produce evidence that the iMSA was the outcome of a mediation process. Sensitive to the diversity in

14. Cf. *Jumaiah bte Amir and Another v Salim bin Abdul Rashid* [2019] SGHC 63.
15. Haris Meidanis, *International Enforcement of Mediated Settlement Agreements: Two and a Half Models – Why and How to Enforce Internationally Mediated Settlement Agreements*, 85(1) Arbitration 49 (2019), at 55.
16. The issue as to whether the Convention should also extend to negotiated settlement agreements without a mediator was debated in UNCITRAL Working Group II: see Report of Working Group II on the Work of its 62nd Session (2-6 February 2015), A/CN.9/832 (2015) at para. 42; UNCITRAL Working Group II (Arbitration and Conciliation), *Settlement of Commercial Disputes, International Commercial Conciliation: Enforceability of Settlement Agreements*, Note by the Secretariat (2-6 February 2016), A/CN.9/WG.II/WP.187, at para. 34; Report of Working Group II on the Work of its 64th Session (1-5 February 2016), A/CN.9/867 (2016) at para. 117. The Model Law on Mediation gives States the possibility of applying the expedited enforcement regime to settlement agreements negotiated outside of a mediation process. See footnote 5 of the Model Law on Mediation, which states: '[a] State may consider enacting this section to apply to agreements settling a dispute, irrespective of whether they resulted from mediation. Adjustments would then have to be made to relevant articles'.
17. The meaning of party (with a small 'p') to an iMSA is addressed in the commentary to Art. 1.
18. In relation to iMSAs in electronic form, see the commentary to Art. 2(2) and the discussion below on electronic communications and parties' signatures.

international practice, the drafters of the Convention refrained from setting out uniform mandatory evidential requirements.[19]

4.12 Rather, they set out three different forms of non-hierarchical evidence, any one of which will suffice as evidence that the settlement agreement resulted from mediation.[20] Article 4(1)(b) identifies three types of evidence that parties *may* produce.

1. The mediator's signature on the settlement agreement (Article 4(1)(b)(i))

4.13 An iMSA is a document between the parties, and so, as a general rule, mediators are not required to sign mediated settlement agreements (MSAs).[21] Consequently, instead of formulating it as a requirement, the Singapore Convention gives evidentiary power to the mediator's signature to prove that a settlement agreement is the result of the mediation process.[22] The rationale behind the mediator's signature on a settlement agreement is to prove the involvement of the mediator in the mediation process and it

19. Working Group II rejected the idea that the list should be exhaustive (closed) instead of illustrative (open) on the ground that 'an illustrative list would be preferable as it would not necessarily be feasible to reach out to the conciliator in various circumstances, including when the settlement agreement would need to be raised as a defence against a claim, a procedure which might take place a number of years after the conciliation. It was also highlighted that there might be costs involved, or conciliators might be hesitant, in providing attestations or signing settlement agreements'. See Report of Working Group II (Dispute Settlement) on the Work of its 67th Session (Vienna, 2-6 October 2017), A/CN.9/929 (2017), at para. 56. Available at http://undocs.org/A/CN.9/929 (Accessed 12 May 2022).
20. Working Group II debated whether there should be a hierarchy among the types of evidence provided in Art. 4(1). This proposal was rejected on the ground that 'it would be difficult to provide a hierarchy, particularly when the list was open-ended. It was further said that prescribing a hierarchy would give prevalence to certain practices to the detriment of others and could run contrary to existing laws and practices. Further, it was suggested that the proposal would be difficult to implement, for instance when the conciliation involved multiple conciliators, and might give rise to legal disputes particularly with regard to the party being obliged to demonstrate that it had made such attempts'. See Report of Working Group II (Dispute Settlement) on the Work of its 67th Session (Vienna, 2-6 October 2017), A/CN.9/929 (2017), at para. 58. Available at http://undocs.org/A/CN.9/929 (Accessed 12 May 2022).
21. Working Group II pointed out that 'in certain jurisdictions, signature by the conciliator was not common practice, for example, due to potential liability issues. In response, it was pointed out that if conciliators signed the settlement agreement, it would generally be for the purpose of certifying that he or she was involved in the conciliation, which would be unlikely to give rise to liability issues'. It was also noted that 'conciliators were usually not involved in the drafting or preparation of settlement agreements so as to respect party autonomy and to avoid any complications that might arise (for example, a conciliator by signing the settlement agreement might be called as a witness in a dispute involving the agreement)'. See Report of Working Group II (Arbitration and Conciliation) on the Work of its 63rd Session (Vienna, 7-11 September 2015), A/CN.9/861 (2015), at paras 55-56. Available at http://undocs.org/A/CN.9/861 (Accessed 12 May 2022).
22. Report of Working Group II (Dispute Settlement) on the Work of its 65th Session (Vienna, 12-23 September 2016), A/CN.9/896 (2016), at para. 73. Available at http://undocs.org/A/CN.9/896 (Accessed 12 May 2022).

'*should not be construed as an endorsement of the settlement agreement nor as an indication that the conciliator*[23] *was a party to the agreement* [*emphasis added*]'.[24]

4.14 In certain jurisdictions, and in line with the facilitative mediation model,[25] mediators maintain the practice not to sign off on a MSA on the basis that doing so may give the impression that a mediator is approving the substance of the MSA and could impinge on the overriding mediation principle of party autonomy and the perception of mediator impartiality.[26] As such, a requirement for mediators to sign an iMSA along with the parties may be contrary to local ethical guidelines for mediators. Conversely, in other jurisdictions, mediators may be required to sign MSAs in certain circumstances. By way of example, in Greece, a MSA signed by the mediator and the parties becomes enforceable by application of any party to it before the competent court.[27] Other illustrations can be found in China, India, Japan, the Philippines and Sri Lanka.

23. UNCITRAL texts use the terms 'mediator' and 'conciliator' interchangeably.
24. Report of Working Group II (Dispute Settlement) on the Work of its 65th Session (Vienna, 12-23 September 2016), A/CN.9/896 (2016), at para. 75. Available at http://undocs.org/A/CN.9/896 (Accessed 12 May 2022).
25. On mediation models, see the commentary to Art. 2(3).
26. By way of example, this approach represents much of the mediation training practice in Australia, Canada, England and Wales, and the US. However, the approach may vary according to the mediation scheme and institution.
27. Law 4512/2018 Art. 184(4). See Haris Meidanis, *International Enforcement of Mediated Settlement Agreements: Two and a Half Models – Why and How to Enforce Internationally Mediated Settlement Agreements*, 85(1) Arbitration 49 (2019). In Georgia, Art. 9(3) of the Law of Georgia on Mediation states that a mediated settlement agreement (domestic) is to be made in writing and signed by the parties and the mediator. In India, mediation is regulated under various acts. The Commercial Courts Act 2015, which provides for the constitutions of commercial courts, consists of mandatory mediation before the commencement of litigation. Section 12A(4) states that any settlement arrived at by parties during such mandatory mediation shall be made in writing and signed by the parties and the mediator. According to s. 73(4) of the Arbitration and Conciliation Act 1996, which governs all forms of conciliation in India – whether private or court-mandated, the conciliator shall authenticate the settlement agreement and furnish a copy thereof to each of the parties. In China, there are different forms of mediation available for parties to resolve disputes, including private mediation. The signing of a settlement agreement by the mediator may depend on the administering institution's rules. By way of example, Art. 25 of the Mediation Rules of Shanghai Commercial Mediation Center requires a settlement agreement to be signed by the mediator and the parties and be affixed with the seal of the institution. Art. 15(3) of the Decree No. 22/2017/ND-CP on Commercial Mediation of Vietnam also requires the signatures of the parties and the commercial mediator on a settlement agreement. In the Philippines, s. 17(b) of the Alternative Dispute Resolution Act of 2004 states that the mediator shall certify that he/she explained the contents of the settlement agreement to the parties in a language known to them. In Japan, administering institutions' rules may require the mediator to sign a settlement agreement upon request made by parties. By way of example, Art. 26(2) of the Mediation Rules of the Japan Commercial Arbitration Association provides that the mediator shall sign the settlement agreement as a witness upon the request of all parties. In Sri Lanka, s. 11(1) of the Mediation Boards Act No. 72 of 1988 states that a settlement agreement shall be signed by the Chief Mediator and the parties.

Case Illustration

In *Yan How Yee (甄巧儀) v Yu Kin Sang Paul (俞乾生) & Ors*,[28] Hong Kong's Court of First Instance was seized with the question of whether the parties reached a binding settlement agreement at the mediation. The mediator prepared the document in question, which was titled as 'settlement agreement' and signed by the parties. The mediator also signed the document as a witness. The defendants took the position that the settlement agreement was only a draft document, which had to be eventually finalised, and the defendants signed the document only as witnesses.

The court opined that the settlement agreement was a binding and enforceable legal instrument. One relevant legal consideration in reaching this conclusion was the mediator's signature on the settlement agreement as a witness. The court made the following statement, which shows the importance of the mediator's signature on a settlement agreement: '[a]s noted above, the Mediator was, at the time of the mediation, a barrister of five years' standing. Although Mr Ho gave some evidence about the lack of litigation and mediation experience of the Mediator, in my view any barrister who professes to practise as a mediator in a civil case would appreciate that it is highly likely that if parties signed on a document entitled "Settlement Agreement" in such terms, there would at least be a very high risk that such a document would create legal obligations. If the defendants' factual version were true, it would be extremely irresponsible, and hence extremely unlikely, for the Mediator not to amend the terms of the document, and then sign the document as a witness'.[29]

Point of Interest

The Singapore Convention does not require an iMSA to be signed by the mediator. The signature of a mediator is a form of evidence under Article 4 of the Singapore Convention that may prove that the mediator assisted the parties in coming to a compromise. This is, however, without prejudice to a requirement for the mediator's signature that may exist under the applicable law to the mediation process that resulted in the signing of an iMSA. As indicated previously, some States require an MSA to be signed by the mediator, including Georgia[30] and Vietnam.[31] A question might arise whether an iMSA will still be

28. *Yan How Yee (甄巧儀) v Yu Kin Sang Paul (俞乾生) & ors* [2019] 3 HKC 170.
29. *Id.*, paras 72-73.
30. Art. 9(3) of the Law of Georgia on Mediation, in relation to domestic mediated settlement agreements.
31. Art. 15(3) of the Decree No. 22/2017/ND-CP on Commercial Mediation of Vietnam.

enforceable under the Singapore Convention if it does not conform to the formal requirements of the applicable law, specifically the requirement for the mediator's signature. The answer to this question depends on whether the absence of the mediator's signature will render the iMSA 'null and void, inoperative or incapable of being performed' under the applicable law to the iMSA and for the purposes of Article 5(1)(b)(i) of the Singapore Convention.[32] Consider the following example drawn from Vietnamese law: Article 15(3) of the Decree on Commercial Mediation of Vietnam states that a written record of a successful mediation result must bear the signatures of the involved parties and the commercial mediator. Article 16 of the same Decree states that a written record of a successful mediation result shall be recognised in accordance with the civil procedure law. For the purposes of Article 5 (1)(b)(i) of the Singapore Convention, the aforementioned provisions of applicable Vietnamese law raise the issue as to whether or not the absence of the mediator's signature could render an iMSA 'null and void, inoperative or incapable of being performed under the law to which the parties have validly subjected it'. In this scenario, it seems highly unlikely that the requirements of Article 5 (1)(b)(i) of the Convention would be fulfilled, as the signature of a mediator under the Decree on Commercial Mediation of Vietnam is required for the purposes of the special enforcement procedure under Chapter XXXIII of the Code of Civil Procedure of Vietnam. Therefore, it follows that the absence of the mediator's signature ought not deprive the iMSA of its legal value under the Singapore Convention, which contains no requirement that an iMSA be signed by the mediator.

In many cases, as in the case of Vietnam, the requirement for the mediator's signature under applicable domestic law may exist as a precondition for accessing a special local enforcement procedure, the absence of which should not render the iMSA invalid for the purposes of the Singapore Convention.

Irrespective of any such requirements that may exist under the applicable law, parties to a mediation may specify that an iMSA will only be binding and valid if the mediator signs it. In this case, the absence of the mediator's signature may result in a refusal to enforce the iMSA under Article 5(1)(b)(ii) of the Singapore Convention.[33] The case below, albeit in the context of employment law, is illustrative in this regard.

32. For more on the grounds for refusing to enforce and recognise an iMSA, see the commentary to Art. 5.
33. According to this provision, the competent authority may refuse to grant relief if the iMSA is not binding, or is not final, according to its terms. For more on this ground, see the commentary to Art. 5.

Case Illustration

In *Abernethy v Dynea NZ LTD*,[34] the Employment Court of New Zealand addressed the issue of whether the parties reached a binding settlement agreement in accordance with section 149 of the Employment Relations Act 2000 of New Zealand on the basis that the settlement agreement was never signed by the mediator. According to section 149 of the Act, a mediator may, at the request of the parties to the problem and under that general authority, sign a compromise reached between them. Further, such a compromise will be enforceable as a compliance order under section 151. The plaintiff took the position that the absence of the mediator's signature, in this case, made the settlement non-binding.

Based on an analysis of the relevant factual background, the court formed the view that the parties intended to submit any oral settlement agreement reached to the section 149 procedure. This meant that any settlement reached and approved by each of the parties eventually had to be signed by the mediator. The court stated that even though such a procedure is not contained within section 149 itself, the parties had agreed to the procedure requiring the mediator's signature and, therefore, had to comply with it.[35] The court concluded that when parties agree to such a procedure, there is no binding contract until the procedure is completed. In this case, as the parties did not follow the procedure they agreed to, namely that the settlement was not approved by the plaintiff itself and was not signed by the mediator, there was no binding settlement agreement between them.[36]

2. A separate document signed by the mediator verifying that mediation was carried out in regards to the settlement agreement concerned (Article 4(1)(b)(ii))

4.15 This approach to evidencing that a mediation took place is increasingly common, and mediators frequently are subject to reporting obligations, especially in institutional settings such as courts as well as in industry and corporate settings. Some courts oblige mediators to provide certificates relating to the completion of mediations and indicating whether or not settlements were reached, but without commenting on the extent to which parties participated or refused to participate in the process.[37] This type of

34. *Abernethy v Dynea NZ Ltd* [2007] NZEmpC CC 13/07.
35. *Id.*, para. 56.
36. *Id.*, para. 58.
37. In Australia, see for example, rr 331(2)–331(3) of the Queensland Uniform Civil Procedure Rules (1999). Here the mediator can report that a party failed to attend but not on how they performed in the mediation. See also the Supreme Court of Queensland Act 1991, s. 108. Contrast with the Farm Debt Mediation Act (NSW) 1994, s. 18A; See ss 7(a) and 7(b)(1) of the UMA (2003). In Liechtenstein, according to Art. 13(1) of the Law on Mediation in Civil Law Matters (ZMG), the mediator shall document the beginning, the circumstances indicating whether the mediation has

reporting is described as minimalist as it does not involve any assessment of the process or the participants' conduct within it. The Uniform Mediation Act (UMA) in the US[38] adopts this approach, permitting reports to courts and other adjudicative bodies only in relation to 'whether the mediation occurred or has terminated, whether a settlement was reached, and attendance'.[39] Reports that go beyond these parameters cannot be considered by the body or person ruling on the dispute.[40] In France, Article 131-11 of the Civil Procedure Code imposes a duty on mediators to report to the court on the outcome of the mediation and, in particular, whether there was an agreement. The report must respect the principles of confidentiality set out in the Civil Procedure Code[41] and in the mediation agreement. These minimalist reporting requirements aim to protect the integrity of the mediation process and its associated principle of confidentiality, while at the same time fulfilling administrative tasks required in relation to the mediation. Accordingly, we suggest that this type of evidence would be acceptable in the courts of most States and would be suitable for ad hoc and institutional mediations. There is no temporal requirement in relation to the signing and issuing of such a document by the mediator; for example, it could be done at the time the iMSA is concluded or when a party seeking relief pursuant to the Convention requests it from the mediator.

3. *A formal attestation by the institution or dispute resolution service provider administering the mediation (Article 4(1)(b)(iii))*

4.16 This form of evidence creates the greatest distance between the evidential form and the mediator as it requires the attestation document to be supplied by the institution or dispute resolution provider rather than the mediator himself or herself. It also addresses the situation where a mediator is no longer available or contactable; a party seeking relief pursuant to the Singapore Convention can approach the institution to supply an attestation. It is not difficult to imagine dispute resolution providers developing standard form attestation templates for the purposes of the evidential requirement in the Singapore Convention.

---

been duly continued and the end of the mediation. The commencement of the mediation shall be deemed to be the time at which the parties have engaged the mediator to act in their dispute. The mediation shall end when a result has been achieved or one of the parties or the mediator declares that they no longer wish to continue the mediation. According to Art. 13(4), the mediator shall also, upon request of a party, issue a confirmation of the mediation and deliver it to the party for submission to the Regional Court in the event of an action being brought. The confirmation shall contain: (a) the names of the parties; (b) the subject matter of the mediation; (c) the date of commencement and termination of the mediation; (d) the signature of the mediator.

38. UMA (2003). See also the widely used US model standards: 2005 AAA/ABA/ACR Revised Model Standards of Conduct for Mediators, Standard V(A)(2), which permits mediators to report 'if required, whether parties appeared at a scheduled mediation and whether or not the parties reached a resolution'.
39. See ss 7(a) and (b)(1) of the UMA (2003).
40. See s. 7(c) of the UMA (2003).
41. Code of Civil Procedure (France) (2007), Art. 131-14.

4.17 In the unlikely event that the three above-listed default forms of evidence are not available, the competent court or authority may decide what other kinds of evidence may be acceptable as proof that the settlement agreement sought to be enforced resulted from mediation (Article 4(1)(b)(iv)). It has been suggested that a mediation agreement may be one of such documents requested by the competent authority,[42] as a matter of proof that mediation has taken place.[43] Furthermore, the case outlined below shows that the competent authority may rely on the express language used in the settlement agreement and resolutions adopted by the parties to the settlement agreement as evidence of mediation.

Case Illustration

In the Indian case of *Anuradha SA Investments LLC v Parsvanth Developers Limited,*[44] the High Court of Delhi addressed the issue of whether a settlement agreement was the result of conciliation and, therefore, subject to the enforcement provisions set out under sections 73-74 of Part III of the Arbitration and Conciliation Act 1996. In this case, the respondents took the position that the parties had already arrived at a settlement when the conciliator was introduced at the final stages of the negotiations before the signing of the settlement agreement. Therefore, the respondents argued that the parties arrived at a settlement without the assistance of the conciliator.

The court rejected the respondents' contention on the ground that the express language of the settlement agreement, as well as the resolutions passed by the respondents, indicated that the parties arrived at a settlement with the help of the conciliator. The court relied on the recitals of the settlement agreement, which contained the following stipulation: 'F. Consequently, the Promoters, the Company and the Investors have engaged in conciliation proceedings, before Mr. Piyoosh Gupta, Advocate ('Conciliator'), pursuant to Part III of the Act (as defined hereinafter) with a view to resolve the disputes with respect to the Non-Compliances. G. Pursuant to the conciliation proceedings referred to in Recital F above conducted by the Conciliator through various hearings, the Parties have by mutual consent and with the assistance of the Conciliator, arrived at a settlement in relation to the disputes that arose between them.' Further, according to a resolution passed by one of the respondents' board of

42. Report of Working Group II on the Work of its 63rd Session (7-11 September 2015), A/CN.9/861 (2015), at para. 68. It was also suggested that a Mediation Agreement could be accompanied by evidence of payment of the mediator to show that the mediation occurred.
43. Shouyu Chong and Felix Steffek, *Enforcement of International Settlement Agreements Resulting from Mediation under the Singapore Convention – Private International Law Issues in Perspective,* 31 SAcLJ 448 (2019), at para. 40.
44. *Anuradha Sa Investments Llc & Anr. v Parsvnath Developers Limited & Ors* on 20 April 2017, the High Court of Delhi at New Delhi.

directors, 'the Parties have by mutual consent and with the assistance of the Conciliator, arrived at a settlement in relation to the disputes and differences that arose between them. Consequently, the Parties are entering into a Settlement Agreement to record the terms of settlement in the manner provided in the draft Settlement Agreement placed on the table which shall be authenticated by the Conciliator'. Another respondent also adopted a similar resolution. Notably, the court also relied on various email exchanges between the representatives of the parties and the conciliator to arrive at the conclusion that the settlement agreement was reached with the help of the conciliator at the conciliation.

4.18 Article 4(1) of the Singapore Convention has a dual purpose. First, it prescribes the items that a party wishing to enforce or recognise an iMSA has to submit to the competent authority, namely, the iMSA signed by the parties and evidence of mediation. Second, Article 4(1) imposes the obligation on the competent authority to examine whether a party wishing to enforce or recognise an iMSA complied with the requirements prescribed in Article 4(1) of the Singapore Convention. This implies that the competent authority may examine whether the iMSA in issue does, in fact, result from mediation, irrespective of whether the opposing party makes such a request.[45] Article 4(4) supports this conclusion, which states that the competent authority may require additional documents '*in order to verify that the requirements of the Convention have been complied with* [*emphasis added*]'. This is to ensure that parties to an iMSA do not circumvent the requirements of the Singapore Convention, such as the requirement that only settlement agreements resulting from *mediation* fall into the scope of the Convention. By way of example, a settlement agreement may simply state that it is the result of mediation without providing any further evidence. In this case, the competent authority may ask the parties to provide other evidence that the settlement agreement is actually the result of the mediation process.

4.19 As discussed above, Article 4(4) vests with the competent authority the power to request *necessary* documentation, in order to verify that there has been compliance with the 'requirements' of the Convention.[46] Here, the term 'requirements' equates to

45. This point must be distinguished from the defences set out in Art. 5 of the Singapore Convention. See the commentary to Art. 5. The defences that are prescribed in Art. 5 of the Singapore Convention will only come into play if the iMSA at issue falls within the scope of the Singapore Convention.
46. Working Group II debated whether the competent authority's power to request additional documents would result in the introduction of additional application requirements. In response, it was pointed out that this concern could be dealt with 'by providing that the competent authority would be able to require any necessary document "only to verify that the conditions of this instrument are met"'. Eventually, Working Group II agreed that 'limiting the power of the competent authority to require documents as *necessary* in light of the conditions of the instrument constituted an acceptable safeguard' [*emphasis added*]. See Report of Working Group II (Dispute Settlement) on the Work of its 67th Session (Vienna, 2-6 October 2017), A/CN.9/929 (2017), at para. 64. Available at http://undocs.org/A/CN.9/929 (Accessed 12 May 2022).

the term 'conditions' in Article 3(b).[47] In other words, this provision cannot be used to add evidential requirements such as notarisation of the iMSA.

4.20 If the settlement agreement sought to be enforced is not drafted in an official language of the State where relief is sought, the competent authority may request that parties furnish a translation of it into that official language (Article 4(3)).

4.21 Finally, the competent court or other authority has a duty to act expeditiously in relation to requests for relief (Article 4(5)). In the absence of express timeframes, a reasonable time is to be inferred and interpreted in light of the object and purpose of the Singapore Convention, which is to facilitate the circulation of iMSAs.[48] By way of example, Georgia recently amended its legislation to implement the provisions of the Singapore Convention. The competent authority, that is to say, the Supreme Court of Georgia[49], examines the completeness of the application documents, submitted for the enforcement or recognition of an iMSA, within five days of submitting an application.[50] If the application documents are not submitted in accordance with the prescribed requirements,[51] the competent authority will give the applicant a reasonable period of time within which the applicant has to rectify the application.[52] If the applicant does not rectify the application within the prescribed period, the application shall not be reviewed.[53] If the application is accepted, the competent authority will transfer the application documents within five days of accepting the application to the other party against which the enforcement or recognition of the iMSA is sought.[54] The other party may oppose the enforcement or recognition of the iMSA within five days of receiving the application documents.[55] The competent authority will make a decision without an oral hearing within 30 days of receiving an application from the other party opposing the enforcement or recognition of the iMSA, or of the expiry of a period of five days.[56] The competent authority has the discretion to hear the parties' oral arguments if it deems necessary.[57] Finally, the decision of the competent authority shall not be appealed.[58]

47. These conditions refer to the scope of the Convention, the grounds of refusal (or absence thereof) and declarations of reservations made by a State.
48. On the object and purpose of the Convention, see the introduction to this book.
49. Art. 363^{43}(1) of the Civil Procedural Code of Georgia.
50. Art. 363^{44}(1) of the Civil Procedural Code of Georgia.
51. Art. 363^{43}(3) states that an applicant has to submit the following documents: (a) the original or a certified copy of the iMSA, and a translation of the iMSA made in the Georgian language; (b) evidence of mediation, which may include the mediator's signature on the iMSA; an attestation issued by the mediator or the administering institution; or any other evidence that can be admitted by the court.
52. Art. 363^{44}(1) of the Civil Procedural Code of Georgia.
53. *Ibid.*
54. Art. 363^{44}(3) of the Civil Procedural Code of Georgia.
55. *Ibid.*
56. Art. 363^{44}(4) of the Civil Procedural Code of Georgia.
57. *Ibid.*
58. Art. 363^{44}(6) of the Civil Procedural Code of Georgia.

Electronic Communications and Parties' Signatures

4.22 As indicated in the commentary to Article 2, Article 2(2) of the Singapore Convention establishes that iMSAs recorded in electronic form may be produced in fulfilment of the written requirement implied under Article 4(1)(a).

4.23 Further, Article 4(2) of the Singapore Convention imports the principles encompassed by Article 9(3) of the 2005 United Nations Convention on the Use of Electronic Communications in International Contracts (ECC).[59] Article 9(3) of the ECC removes obstacles to the use of electronic signatures in endorsing documents which must be signed by law to become legally enforceable.[60] It establishes a functional equivalence between electronic signatures and handwritten signatures. It is useful at this juncture to consider what may qualify as a valid electronic signature, which would be functionally equivalent to a handwritten signature.

4.24 Electronic signatures may take a variety of forms and can be administered through various technological methods. Yet neither the ECC nor the Singapore Convention refers to the term 'electronic signature', nor provides a definition for it. Therefore, the possibilities are limitless when it comes to the methodology by which a person or entity may choose to electronically sign an electronic document. Below are some non-exhaustive examples of the more frequently observed electronic signature options:[61]

(1) name or initials typed at the bottom of an electronic-mail communication by the sender;[62]
(2) digitised impression of a handwritten signature affixed to an electronic document;
(3) personalised secret pin, code or password administered to identify the sender of a request to the recipient of that request (for example, the system administered via Automated Teller Machine (ATM) cards and credit cards);
(4) personalised biometrically linked identifier (for example, a fingerprint, a voice print or a retinal scan);
(5) action of clicking on an 'I Accept' or 'I Agree' button on a webpage; or
(6) employment of a 'digital signature' created through the use of public key cryptography.

4.25 Whether an electronic signature will be recognised as a signature stands to be assessed upon the attributes of the method of its conception (Article 4(2)(a) of the

59. United Nations Convention on the Use of Electronic Communications in International Contracts (2005).
60. See Thomas J. Smedinghoff, *Article 9 – Form Requirements*, in Amelia H. Boss and Wolfgang Kilian (eds), The United Nations Convention on the Use of Electronic Communications in International Contracts – An In-Depth Guide and Sourcebook, Wolters Kluwer (2008).
61. *Id.*, at 147.
62. Consider for instance, *Rosenfeld v Zern* 2004 N.Y. Slip Op. 24143 (2004); *Shattuk v Klotzbach* 2001 Mass. Super. LEXIS 642 (11 December 2001).

Singapore Convention and Article 9(2)(a) of the ECC). Essentially, electronic signatures may be considered functionally equivalent to handwritten signatures if they can be *reliably* observed from their use in electronic communication and if they:

(1) identify the party that has initiated the signing; and
(2) discern its intention with regard to the information enclosed in that electronic communication.

4.26 It should be emphasised that there is a need to *both* identify the party *and* discern its intention. However, these two attributes do not necessarily need to be embodied in one single set of indicia or be accomplished within the same step.[63] This means that the step taken to identify the party and the step taken to discern its intention may accrue separately. To illustrate: A party to a settlement agreement may log on to a system that provides online dispute resolution services through a unique and secure process which identifies them clearly. At the end of the mediation process, a separate process may be adopted to record and indicate its intent to be bound by a resulting settlement agreement by simply clicking on an 'I Agree' button. As long as the overall method (that is, the conjunction of the identification and intent steps) yields a reliable assurance that a distinctly identifiable party pressed the 'I Agree' button, the method should sufficiently furnish the required functional equivalence to fulfil the legal signature requirement.

4.27 Finally, Article 4(2)(b) of the Singapore Convention and Article 9(3)(b) of the ECC both proffer the need to administer a reliability test. Through an evaluation of the method of signature,[64] the reliability test seeks to ensure that the security of the transaction endorsed by that electronic signature is not compromised. To test the trustworthiness of the signature's method in the context of the specific transaction it has been administered, two approaches are provided:

(1) the test for theoretical reliability (Article 4(2)(b)(i) of the Singapore Convention and Article 9(3)(b)(i) of the ECC); and
(2) the test for reliability in fact (Article 4(2)(b)(ii) of the Singapore Convention and Article 9(3)(b)(ii) of the ECC).

4.28 The test for theoretical reliability is an objective one. The Explanatory Note by the UNCITRAL Secretariat on the United Nations Convention on the Use of Electronic Communications in International Contracts elucidates the technical and commercial factors which may be considered in determining whether the electronic signature's method is reliable:

63. Thomas J. Smedinghoff, *Article 9 – Form Requirements*, in Amelia H. Boss and Wolfgang Kilian (eds), The United Nations Convention on the Use of Electronic Communications in International Contracts – An In-Depth Guide and Sourcebook, Wolters Kluwer (2008), at 150.
64. As discussed earlier in respect of Art. 4(2)(a) of the Singapore Convention and Art. 9(3)(a) of the ECC.

> Legal, technical and commercial factors that may be taken into account in determining whether the method used [...] is appropriate, include the following: (a) the sophistication of the equipment used by each of the parties; (b) the nature of their trade activity; (c) the frequency at which commercial transactions take place between the parties; (d) the kind and size of the transaction; (e) the function of signature requirements in a given statutory and regulatory environment; (f) the capability of communication systems; (g) compliance with authentication procedures set forth by intermediaries; (h) the range of authentication procedures made available by any intermediary; (i) compliance with trade customs and practice; (j) the existence of insurance coverage mechanisms against unauthorized communications; (k) the importance and the value of the information contained in the electronic communication; (l) the availability of alternative methods of identification and the cost of implementation; (m) the degree of acceptance or non-acceptance of the method of identification in the relevant industry or field both at the time the method was agreed upon and the time when the electronic communication was communicated; and (n) any other relevant factor.[65]

4.29 The test for reliability, in fact, is an alternative to the first test for theoretical reliability. It provides that regardless of the ability of parties to prove objective reliability of the method of signature, so long as they may prove that it fulfils the functions of identifying the signing party and its intentions, the method is deemed reliable 'in fact'. There is, therefore, allowance for the use of methods which may, objectively speaking, not be deemed adequately reliable in the given context, but which nevertheless may be shown under certain circumstances to establish sufficiently the identity and intention of the signing party. Drawing from Smedinghoff's observations, it is submitted that '[Article 4(2)(b)(ii) of the Singapore Convention and] Article 9(3)(b)(ii) [of the ECC] validates a signature method – regardless of its reliability in principle – whenever the method used is proven in fact to have identified the signatory and indicated the signatory's intention in respect of the information contained in the electronic communication.'[66]

Case Illustration

Jonathan (in Bullfields, a Party to the Singapore Convention) and *Tate* (in Maplewood, also a Party to the Singapore Convention) resolve their dispute online with the help of a mediator (in Bakersville). During the mediation process, they use a combination of email, text-based chat and online video communication. The resulting iMSA is recorded through an email exchange. Ten months

65. UNCITRAL, *The Explanatory Note by the UNCITRAL Secretariat on the United Nations Convention on the Use of Electronic Communications in International Contracts*, available at https://www.uncitral.org/pdf/english/texts/electcom/06-57452_Ebook.pdf (Accessed on 20 May 2019), at 162.
66. Thomas J. Smedinghoff, *Article 9 – Form Requirements*, in Amelia H. Boss and Wolfgang Kilian, The United Nations Convention on the Use of Electronic Communications in International Contracts – An In-Depth Guide and Sourcebook, Wolters Kluwer (2008), at 155.

later, Jonathan claims that Tate has not complied with the iMSA and seeks to enforce it in Maplewood. He submits the following documentation to the Maplewood Court to show he has an iMSA within the meaning of the Convention:

(1) The email correspondence between the parties and the mediator containing the settlement agreement. Both parties used their regular email addresses. It complies with the 'in writing' requirement of Article 2(2) and the party signature requirements pursuant to Article 4(2). Parties signed off on their emails by inserting the abbreviation 'Sgd' before their names.
(2) An original document signed by the mediator confirming that she mediated the dispute that led to the settlement agreement contained in the email correspondence in accordance with Article 4(1)(b)(ii).

The court may accept the evidence and suggest that the mediator's separate original document was perhaps not needed, as it was evident from the email exchange that she was acting as mediator to guide the parties towards the settlement agreement they reached (see Article 4(1)(b)(iv)).

ARTICLE 5

Grounds for Refusing to Grant Relief

1. The competent authority of the Party to the Convention where relief is sought under article 4 may refuse to grant relief at the request of the party against whom the relief is sought only if that party furnishes to the competent authority proof that:

(a) A party to the settlement agreement was under some incapacity;
(b) The settlement agreement sought to be relied upon:
  (i) Is null and void, inoperative or incapable of being performed under the law to which the parties have validly subjected it or, failing any indication thereon, under the law deemed applicable by the competent authority of the Party to the Convention where relief is sought under article 4;
  (ii) Is not binding, or is not final, according to its terms; or
  (iii) Has been subsequently modified;
(c) The obligations in the settlement agreement:
  (i) Have been performed; or
  (ii) Are not clear or comprehensible;
(d) Granting relief would be contrary to the terms of the settlement agreement;
(e) There was a serious breach by the mediator of standards applicable to the mediator or the mediation without which breach that party would not have entered into the settlement agreement; or
(f) There was a failure by the mediator to disclose to the parties circumstances that raise justifiable doubts as to the mediator's impartiality or independence and such failure to disclose had a material impact or undue influence on a party without which failure that party would not have entered into the settlement agreement.

2. The competent authority of the Party to the Convention where relief is sought under article 4 may also refuse to grant relief if it finds that:

(a) Granting relief would be contrary to the public policy of that Party; or
(b) The subject matter of the dispute is not capable of settlement by mediation under the law of that Party.

COMMENTARY

5.01 Article 5 of the Convention sets out exhaustively the possible exceptions to enforcement and recognition of international mediated settlement agreements (iMSAs) which otherwise satisfy the requirements and conditions prescribed in the Singapore Convention. The relevant court of a State *may*[1] refuse to grant relief if at least one of these grounds is proved. It appears on plain reading of Articles 5(1) and 5(2) that the relevant court has some discretion to nevertheless grant enforcement relief, although at least one of the Article 5 grounds for refusal may be proven.[2] However, it is likely that the courts would only exercise that discretion sparingly as it is widely accepted that the courts do not have an open-ended discretion to overlook the fact that at least one of the Article 5 defences is proven. For instance, if the parties were acting in an abuse of the court's process when they plead an Article 5 defence,[3] there is probably only narrow scope for the courts to exercise that discretion.[4]

5.02 An analysis of Article 5 of the Convention requires a consideration of the role that confidentiality plays in mediation and how it may impact procedures associated with the recognition and enforcement of iMSAs. Indeed, Working Group II (WG II) considered 'whether the Convention would need to address the possible contradiction that might arise between the confidential nature of mediation and the need to disclose information during the enforcement process'.[5] It was subsequently decided that this issue should be left to domestic laws to regulate and so the Singapore Convention is silent on the subject of confidentiality. Nevertheless, confidentiality remains an essential element of the law applicable to the recognition and enforcement of iMSAs and accordingly will be examined below.

---

1. It is in theory within the prerogative of the competent authority to exercise its discretion and, nevertheless, enforce the iMSA even if one or more of the Art. 5 grounds were proved. As to theories behind how such discretion may be exercised, see Jonathan Hill, *The Exercise of Judicial Discretion in Relation to Applications to Enforce Arbitral Awards under the New York Convention 1958*, 36 Oxford J. Legal Stud. 304 (2016).
2. Jonathan Hill, *The Exercise of Judicial Discretion in Relation to Applications to Enforce Arbitral Awards under the New York Convention 1958*, 36 Oxford J. Legal Stud. 304 (2016).
3. Consider *BWG v BWF* [2020] 1 SLR 1296, at [56].
4. Consider the analogous case of *BWG v BWF* [2020] 1 SLR 1296. Here the Singapore Court of Appeal suggested that the Singapore courts may have some discretion to decline to enforce an arbitration agreement, in accordance with their obligations under the New York Convention (which is brought into force in Singapore by the International Arbitration Act (Cap 143A, 2002 Rev Ed.), s. 6), if the parties are relying on a relevant arbitration agreement in an abuse of court process. In contrast, it should be noted that in the subsequent case of *6DM (S) Pte Ltd v AE Brands Korea Ltd* [2021] SGHC 257 (at [88]), the Singapore High Court ruled that there is no such discretion for the courts to decline to enforce a choice of court agreement, as this would not be in accordance with Singapore's obligations under the 2005 Hague Choice of Court Agreements Convention (which is brought into force in Singapore by the Choice of Court Agreements Act (2020 Rev Ed.), s. 12).
5. Report of Working Group II (Dispute Settlement) on the Work of its 65th Session (Vienna, 12-23 September 2016), A/CN.9/896, (2016), at paras 120-121. Available at http://undocs.org/A/CN.9/896 (Accessed 13 May 2022). See also Report of Working Group II (Dispute Settlement) on the Work of its 66th Session (New York, 6-10 February 2017), A/CN.9/901 (2017), at para. 48. Available at http://undocs.org/A/CN.9/901 (Accessed 13 May 2022).

5.03 Article 5 grounds for refusal may be categorised as follows: contract-related grounds for refusal, mediator conduct-related grounds for refusal, public policy justifications and cases where the subject matter is not capable of settlement by mediation. It should also be noted that parties relying on the defences under Article 5(1) must furnish proof that one or more of these grounds for refusal exist, while it is within the prerogative of the relevant competent authority enforcing iMSAs to refuse to grant relief on its own motion, if it finds that one of the Article 5(2) defences have been satisfied, without having the parties to the iMSA furnish proof. Nonetheless, in practice, it is quite necessary for the parties to demonstrate to the relevant competent authorities that the conditions under Article 5(2) are satisfied, if they are the ones to raise an objection under Article 5(2). This is because parties must always bear the burden of proving issues which they allege or submit in a dispute resolution forum.[6]

5.04 The commentary to Article 5 is structured as follows. It begins with an examination of the scope and dimensions of confidentiality in mediation, in particular in the context of recognition and enforcement of iMSAs. In terms of the grounds for refusal, first, contract-related grounds for refusal are addressed, followed by a focus on mediator conduct-related grounds for refusal. Next, public policy and subject matter-related grounds for refusal are analysed. Finally, four reflections are presented to close the examination of Article 5.

Confidentiality in Mediation

5.05 In this part, the role of confidentiality in mediation is considered in terms of its scope and how the principle of confidentiality is applied in the litigation context, especially in relation to attempts to enforce or challenge an iMSA.

5.06 Confidentiality is considered an essential quality of mediation as it ensures the integrity of the process and protects the interests of all mediation participants.[7]

5.07 It is widely accepted that confidentiality encourages parties to speak freely and openly in mediation. In the absence of rules of evidence and other legal safeguards, communications in mediation may extend to matters beyond those considered relevant for arbitral, judicial or tribunal proceedings to include personal, commercial and non-legal issues. Parties do not generally expect what they say and do in mediation to have the same consequences as if they occurred in a courtroom. Without the confidentiality protection, lawyers and clients might be reluctant to disclose certain information potentially useful for settlement discussions on the basis that they risk it

6. Consider *Gater Assets Ltd v Nak Naftogaz Ukrainy* [2007] EWCA Civ 988.
7. For US literature on this topic, *see* Kent Brown, *Comment, Confidentiality in Mediation: Status and Implications*, 2 J. Disp. Resol. 307 (1991); Lawrence Freedman and Michael Prigoff, *Confidentiality in Mediation: The Need for Protection*, 2 Ohio State J. Disp. Resol. 37 (1986), at 37–38. For mediation confidentiality in the French context, see Delphine Wietek, *France*, in Nadja Alexander et al. (eds), EU Mediation Law Handbook: Regulatory Robustness Ratings for Mediation Regimes, Wolters Kluwer (2017), at 339. In the context of Austria, see Christina Lenz and Martin Risak, *Austria*, in Nadja Alexander et al. (eds), EU Mediation Law Handbook: Regulatory Robustness Ratings for Mediation Regimes, Wolters Kluwer (2017), at 51.

being used against them in later proceedings. This could inhibit their negotiation conduct. Moreover, mediation conducted without comprehensive confidentiality protection can invite fishing expeditions with good catches to be made by opportunistic negotiators at the expense of vulnerable parties such as those that are unrepresented.

5.08 At the same time, there are limitations to the scope of confidentiality. The confidentiality principle in mediation reflects the tension between the integrity of this system and that of the due administration of justice. In terms of access to justice, there are competing public interests, on the one hand, of supporting out-of-court settlements through confidential mediation processes and, on the other hand, of the desirability of relevant evidence being made available to courts.[8] The integrity of the mediation process requires that confidentiality provisions do not provide safe havens for participant wrongdoing or injustice.[9] As the following paragraphs demonstrate, legal regimes around the world have established rules to achieve this balance.

The Scope of Confidentiality

5.09 Confidentiality attaches to the mediation process. Mediation agreements that initiate mediation (also called agreements to mediate) and iMSAs at the conclusion of mediation are generally not considered part of the mediation process. Subject to party arrangements to the contrary[10] and specific legislative provisions indicating otherwise, these agreements fall outside the scope of confidentiality; the fact that a party contracted to mediate, and the written terms of a mediated settlement are prima facie not protected by the confidentiality attaching to the mediation process. Parties may therefore produce as evidence before the court a mediation agreement in order to establish the terms of the mediation, including the nature of the agreed confidentiality

8. *See*, for example, the US case of *Blue Buffalo Co., Ltd. v Wilbur-Ellis Co*, in which the court ordered the production of communications from a mediation that resulted in a settlement for an in camera review, thus attempting to strike a balance between maintaining the confidentiality of mediated settlement proceedings and obtaining relevant evidence in related court proceedings: *see Blue Buffalo Co., Ltd. v Wilbur-Ellis Co.*, LLC, No. 4:14 CV 859 RWS, 2022 WL 292972, at *4-5 (E.D. Mo. 1 February 2022).
9. Hence the German phrase *Keine Flucht in die Mediation* (No escape in mediation).
10. *See* Art. 14 of the Optional Conciliation Rules, Permanent Court of Arbitration, for an example of an institutional rule which provides that all matters relating to the conciliation process, including the settlement agreement, shall be kept confidential unless disclosure is necessary for enforcement. See also the Singaporean case of *Engineering Centre of Industrial Constructions and Concrete v EFE (SEA) Pte Ltd* [2021] SGHC 01, in which the High Court rejected the defendants' attempt to rely on an alleged settlement agreement. The defendants had merely asserted that the debt had been settled and refused to give details, claiming that the settlement agreement was confidential. The court stated at [52] that this defence was 'entirely incapable of belief', especially where the defendants had not even disclosed basic details such as the date of the settlement, the quantum paid, proof and date of payment, as well as whether the settlement was oral or in writing. The court was skeptical of the sincerity of the defendants' concerns about confidentiality, noting at [54] that the defendants had not applied to seal the case file or for other court orders to maintain the confidentiality of the terms of the settlement agreement and further that they had already pleaded the terms of the settlement in a related lawsuit. For a commentary on this case, see Nadja Alexander and Shouyu Chong, *Mediation and Appropriate Dispute Resolution*, 22 SAL Ann. Rev. (2021).

provisions. Similarly, parties may submit a written iMSA in evidence before the court in order to enforce its terms.[11]

5.10 One of the major concerns for mediation parties is the possibility that something said or done in, or for the purposes of, mediation might be used to their disadvantage in subsequent civil or criminal proceedings.[12] The behaviours and communications relevant here are wide-ranging. They include information, documents, recordings or other communications created or shared in joint or private mediation sessions, observations about party behaviour and reasons for inability to settle and the fact that a party has made an offer to settle. This aspect of confidentiality involves the rights and obligations associated with protecting these mediation communications from being legally discovered or admitted in evidence in subsequent court and arbitral proceedings. It is dealt with by Article 11 of the UNCITRAL Model Law on International Commercial Mediation and International Settlement Agreements Resulting from Mediation (2018) (UNCITRAL Model Law on Mediation), is addressed in the Directive 2008/52/EC of the European Parliament and of the Council of 21 May 2008 on Certain Aspects of Mediation in Civil and Commercial Matters (EU Directive) and it is the primary focus of the Uniform Mediation Act (2001) (UMA) and also addressed in numerous domestic mediation statutes.[13]

Regulatory Approaches to Confidentiality

5.11 In terms of legal constructs, the issue of mediation confidentiality before courts can be addressed in a number of ways. These include:

(1) general duty of confidentiality,[14]
(2) without prejudice privilege,[15]

11. See, for example, *Fair v Bakhtari* (2006) 40 Cal 4th 189, 51 Cal Rptr 3d 871.
12. By way of example, Art. 7 of the EU Directive focuses solely on civil proceedings, thereby prima facie permitting the admission of mediation evidence in criminal proceedings, whereas Austrian law sets out separate regulations for mediator confidentiality in relation to civil and criminal proceedings.
13. See, for example, the Hong Kong Mediation Ordinance 2013.
14. For a statutory general duty of confidentiality, see the 2003 Austrian Civil Law Mediation Act (*Zivilrechtsmediationsgesetz*) (CMA 2003), § 18. In some jurisdictions there may also be implied or equitable duties of confidentiality – independent of express contractual commitments and legislative obligations – which arise when a person receives information which he knows or should know is confidential. Vivian Ramsay J in *Farm Assist (N° 2)* has suggested that this duty would apply to a mediator in the course of a mediation: See *Farm Assist Ltd (In Liquidation) v Secretary of State for the Environment, Food and Rural Affairs (No. 2)* [2009] EWHC 1102 (TCC), at paras 23-29 referring *inter alia* to Charles Phipps and Roger Toulson, *Confidentiality* (2nd ed.), Sweet and Maxwell (2006) at para. 15-016.
15. In Australia, see, for example, *AWA v Daniels* (1992) 7 ACSR 436; *Rajski v Tectran Corp Pty Ltd* [2003] NSW 476; *Lukies v Ripley (N° 2)* (1994) 35 NSWLR 283 for applications of without prejudice privilege to mediation. For a discussion on exceptions to without prejudice privilege, see *Quad Consulting Pty Ltd v David R Bleakley and Associates Pty Ltd* (1990–1991) 98 ALR 659; *Barry v City West Water Ltd* [2002] FCA 1214; *Capolingua v Phylum Pty Ltd* (1991) 5 WAR 137; *Williams v Commonwealth Bank* [1999] NSWCA 345; *Abriel v Australian Guarantee Corporation Ltd* [2000] FCA 1198; *Tapoohi v Lewenberg and Ors (N° 2)* [2003] VSC 410 (21 October 2003).

(3) mediation privilege,[16]
(4) prohibition on calling a witness,[17]
(5) right of refusal to testify,[18] and
(6) evidentiary exclusion.[19]

5.12 It is beyond the scope of this commentary to offer a detailed international and comparative treatment of the ways in which mediation confidentiality is regulated.[20]

In England, see *Unilever plc v Procter and Gamble* [2000] 1 WLR 2436; *Halsey v Milton Keynes General NHS Trust* [2004] EWCA Civ 576. For exceptions to the without prejudice rule in mediations, see *Brown v Patel* [2007] EWHC 625 (Ch); *Farm Assist Ltd (In Liquidation) v Secretary of State for the Environment, Food and Rural Affairs* [2008] EWHC 3079 (TCC); *Farm Assist Ltd (In Liquidation) v Secretary of State for the Environment, Food and Rural Affairs (No. 2)* [2009] EWHC 1102 (TCC). Further examples and discussion of exceptions may be found in *BNP Paribas v Mezzotero* [2004] IRLR 508 and *Ferster v Ferster* [2016] EWCA Civ 717.

In the US, see, for example, *Smith v Genstar Capital*, LLC, N C-01-3936 MMC, 2001 WL 1658315 (ND Cal Dec 20, 2001) and *Wimsatt et al v Superior Court of California* 152 Cal App 4th 137, 61 Cal Rpter 3d 200 (2007).

16. In Australia see, Alternative Dispute Resolution Act 2001 (TAS) s. 10(2). See also *Sharjade Pty Ltd v RAAF (Landings) Ex-Servicemen Charitable Fund Pty Ltd* [2008] NSWSC 1347 in relation to statutory mediation privilege. In the US, see ss 4-7 of the UMA. See the Point of Interest below.
17. In Austria, the strict duty of confidentiality placed on mediators in the CMA 2003 is reinforced by their civil procedure legislation. Mediators' confidentiality obligations are absolute – there are no exceptions and their duty of confidentiality cannot be dispensed with, modified or waived by parties. See Lenz and Risak (2017), above note 7, at 51-52. It should be noted however that the same cannot be said of parties' confidentiality obligations. Lenz and Risak (2017) at 51 note that 'Austrian civil procedure law does not include any prohibition on the use of mediation evidence as it is considered that material truth should prevail over procedural fairness. Therefore mediation evidence must be considered by the judge even if it were to be introduced into a court procedure by a breach of confidentiality.' The remedy in such cases would merely be a claim for compensation for breach of the mediation agreement's terms of confidentiality.
18. The right of refusal to testify is distinct from a prohibition on being called as a witness, according to which the person subject to the prohibition has no choice in relation to testifying. For example, while Austrian mediators are subject to a prohibition on being called as witnesses in civil proceedings as mentioned above, in criminal proceedings they have the *right* to refuse to testify – see § 157(1)3 of the Austrian Act on Criminal Procedure (*Strafprozessordnung*). In other words they have the choice to testify or not. See generally Lenz and Risak (2017), above note 7, at 52.

    In Germany, mediators and persons involved in implementing the mediation (e.g., the mediator's staff, translators, etc) have a general duty of confidentiality. This is accompanied by a right of refusal to testify in civil court proceedings (§ 383 (1) No. 6 of the Code of Civil Procedure (*Zivilprozessordnung*, ZPO)). However, mediators do not have the right to refuse to testify in criminal proceedings, unless they are lawyers by profession (§ 53 (1) No. 3 Code of Procedure for Criminal Law Matters (*Strafprozeßordnung*, StPO)). Several exceptions apply to the right of refusal to testify, see § 385 (2) ZPO and § 4 (1) (3) of the German Mediation Act (*Mediationsgesetz*, MediationsG). See Kristina Osswald and Gustav Flecke-Giammarco, *Germany*, in Nadja Alexander et al. (eds), EU Mediation Law Handbook: Regulatory Robustness Ratings for Mediation Regimes, Wolters Kluwer (2017).
19. See, for example, Art. 10 of the Model Law on International Commercial Mediation and International Settlement Agreements Resulting from Mediation 2018; s. 131 of the Evidence Act 1995 in Australia; Art. 131-14 of the French Civil Procedure Code; s. 8 of the Hong Kong Mediation Ordinance 2013; s. 9 of the Singapore Mediation Act 2017. Unlike privilege and rights of refusal to testify, evidentiary exclusions do not attach to mediation participants and therefore cannot be waived.
20. For a detailed treatment of the law on mediation confidentiality from an international, comparative perfective, see Nadja Alexander, International and Comparative Mediation: Legal

However, the Point of Interest, below, explains what the concept of mediation privilege generally refers to and examines the dimensions of mediation privilege as regulated by the UMA in the US.

Point of Interest

Mediation Privilege

The concept of privilege derives from common law systems. Essentially privilege provides a right to refuse to reveal information and, in some circumstances, to prevent others from revealing information, for the purposes of discovery or evidence, providing an exemption to the fundamental maxim that the public has a right to every person's evidence. It refers to rules which exclude evidence on the basis that it would be adverse to a fundamental principle or relationship. As privilege is a type of prerogative or right, a person who holds privilege may waive it if he or she should not wish to claim it.

Depending on the jurisdiction, privilege can include without prejudice privilege, legal professional privilege, privilege against self-incrimination, marital privilege, public interest privilege and mediation privilege. Insofar as mediation privilege exists, it takes the form of a statutory privilege, such as without prejudice privilege. While without prejudice privilege has been held to apply to mediation, it only attaches to parties and not others such as the mediator. A mediation privilege is broader in application and derives from legislative instruments, such as the UMA in the US.[21] Statutory mediation privilege is explored here with reference to the UMA. Specifically, the following aspects of statutory mediation privilege are considered: scope of the privilege, parts of the mediation covered by the privilege, the nature of communications and information subject to the privilege, holders of the privilege and the subsequent proceedings at which the privilege can be asserted.

The confidentiality provisions (sections 4-7) of the UMA are broad in scope. The privilege applies to court-ordered mediations, to mediations to which the parties agree and which are intended to be subject to privilege and to any mediation conducted by persons holding themselves out as mediators (section 4(a)). In other words, it applies prima facie to all mediations irrespective of the path taken to get to mediation. Exceptions relate to collective bargaining, for which there are

Perspectives, Kluwer Law International (2009), and the relevant country chapters in Nadja Alexander et al. (eds), EU Mediation Law Handbook: Regulatory Robustness Ratings for Mediation Regimes, Wolters Kluwer (2017).

21. For other illustrations of mediation privilege: in the US see also New Jersey Rules of Evidence r. 519 and the Texas Civil Practice and Remedies Code s. 154.053 (1991) (b) and (c) for illustrations of mediation privilege; in Australia, see the Alternative Dispute Resolution Act 2001 (TAS), s. 10(2).

long-standing and specific regulations, school mediation, mediation in which parties are residents of a youth correctional centre and mediations conducted by judges who will rule on the case (section 4(b)). In addition, parties may opt out of privilege protection in relation to all or part of a mediation provided they do so in writing and in advance of the mediation (section 3(c)).

Mediation privilege must specify not only the category of mediation but also the aspects of the mediation to which it applies, such as intake sessions, preliminary meetings, telephone conversations, emails, private meetings and follow-up sessions. The extent to which initial communications between mediator and parties before an agreement to mediate has been signed are covered by privilege may become a crucial legal point should litigation follow the mediation. In the UMA, this is addressed through the definition of mediation communication. Section 2 of the UMA provides that '"mediation communication" means a statement, whether oral or in a record or verbal or nonverbal, that occurs during a mediation or is made for purposes of considering, conducting, participating in, initiating, continuing, or reconvening a mediation or retaining a mediator'. By linking the privilege to mediation communications as defined in section 2 of the UMA, the privilege is offered a wide and flexible scope and is not limited to the period between the commencement and termination of the mediation itself.

Related to the aspects of mediation to which the privilege attaches is the question of the nature of the information and communications covered by the privilege. Again, privilege statutes differ in their approaches to this issue, some providing broad definitions followed by specific exclusions and others with narrower circumscriptions of what is included. The broad definition of communication in the UMA includes statements that are made orally, through conduct, in writing or through other recorded activity.

Privilege applies to subsequent proceedings, but the exact nature of the proceedings may vary depending on the statute. Section 4 of the UMA extends coverage to 'a proceeding' which section 2(7) defines as a legislative hearing or similar process, a judicial, arbitral, or other adjudicative process, including related pre-hearing and post-hearing motions, conferences and discovery.

A critical function of privilege statutes is the designation of who holds the right to claim or waive the privilege and otherwise exercise it in the future. Mediation parties and their representatives have an interest in knowing that information disclosed will be kept in confidence and that what transpires in mediation is not admissible in any court or arbitral proceedings that may follow. The ability of mediators to build trust and rapport with parties and to be seen as impartial is linked to the privacy and confidentiality of the process. Accordingly, mediators have a strong interest in maintaining confidentiality. Mediators are generally reluctant to provide evidence about what occurred in mediation unless they are responding to negligence, malpractice or similar claims against them.

In order for mediation privilege to offer substantial confidentiality protection, everyone with access to mediation information should hold the privilege to some extent. Section 4 of the UMA provides differentiated privileges for mediation participants. Mediation parties may refuse to disclose, and may prevent other persons from disclosing, any mediation communication. A mediator may refuse to disclose, and may prevent any other person from disclosing, his/her mediation communication. Finally, a non-party participant may refuse to disclose, and may prevent any other person from disclosing, his/her mediation communication. Parties have the broadest privilege and the ability to prevent disclosures by any mediation participant, including the mediator, while the mediator and other participants possess a privilege limited to their own communications.

In relation to a waiver of privilege, section 5 of the UMA requires an express waiver, formal and on the record, and not a waiver implied or by conduct. The intent of this provision is to protect the unintentional waiver of privilege, especially by non-lawyers. However, a person who has made representations about a mediation communication that prejudices another person in the proceeding is precluded from claiming privilege to the extent necessary for the person prejudiced to respond. Anyone intentionally using a mediation for criminal activity is also precluded from asserting the privilege.

Exceptions to Mediation Confidentiality

5.13 Across jurisdictions and legal systems, the rules applicable to the admissibility of mediation evidence in courts are subject to a variety of exceptions. As indicated previously, the use of exceptions helps courts achieve the balance between supporting mediation confidentiality to encourage the facilitation of out-of-court settlement agreements, on the one hand, and upholding the integrity of the mediation process by ensuring accountability of participants in mediation, on the other. Notably, the existence of these types of exceptions is nothing new. By way of example, in relation to without prejudice privilege, a series of tried and tested exceptions to the privilege has long been recognised.[22]

5.14 An international comparative overview of confidentiality laws reveals the following main categories of exceptions:

(1) Pre-existing information otherwise subject to discovery or equivalent procedures.[23]

22. Nadja Alexander, International and Comparative Mediation: Legal Perspectives, Kluwer Law International (2009), at 285.
23. See, for example, s. 5 of the UMA, Art. 11(5) of the MLICM and the cases *AWA v Daniels* (1992) 7 ASCR 436 and *Aird and Aird v Prime Meridian* [2006] EWCA Civ 1886. See also Scott Hughes, *The Uniform Mediation Act: To the Spoiled Go the Privileges*, 85 Marquette L. Rev. 9 (2001).

(2) Information open to the public. This exception refers to information generally available or accessible under freedom of information[24] and privacy laws.[25]

(3) Breach of duty/professional misconduct. An exception is also appropriate to allow disclosure of mediation information if a dispute arises between the mediator and any of the parties, or the professional conduct of the mediator or other participants in mediation, such as legal representatives, is challenged.[26]

(4) Threat of future violence or harm to others and communications to plan or attempt crimes or to conceal ongoing criminal activity. Provisions to this effect can be found in section 5(c) and sections 6(a)(3) and (4) of the UMA and Article 7(1)(a) of the EU Directive. However, many statutes are silent on this point, leaving it to courts to rely on general principles to imply the exception on public interest and policy grounds.

(5) Abuse of a child or vulnerable party. Mediation communications that go to show the abuse, neglect or abandonment of a vulnerable person may not be subject to confidentiality provisions. Examples can be found in section 6(a)(7) of the UMA and Article 7(1)(a) of the EU Directive.

(6) Costs determinations. In certain jurisdictions, courts have been willing to admit limited evidence from mediations in applications for costs of the mediation or proceedings to which the mediation relates. Here evidence may be adduced relating to participants' behaviour to show a lack of good faith or unreasonable behaviour in relation to the mediation.

(7) To prove the existence of a settlement agreement. Exceptions to confidentiality are often invoked by post-mediation actions seeking to prove or set aside MSAs. This exception is directly linked to the grounds for refusal in Article 5 of the Singapore Convention on Mediation. In other words, where a party seeks relief in relation to an iMSA, the veil of confidentiality may be lifted for the purposes of proving the existence of, or the terms of, that iMSA. A number of legislative illustrations of this exception follow. Article 11(3) of the Model Law on Mediation provides for disclosure and admission of evidence 'for the purposes of implementation or enforcement of a settlement agreement'. The EU Directive contains a similar exception, more narrowly worded. Article 7(1)(b) of the Directive provides an exception to the prohibition on mediator testimony 'where disclosure of *the content of the agreement* resulting from mediation is necessary in order to implement or enforce that agreement' [*emphasis added*]. In the US, this exception is expressly included in the public

24. See s. 7(a)(2) of the UMA. At the US Federal level see the Freedom of Information Act 1966 and at State level the various Open Records Acts or Open Public Records Acts such as Washington's Open Records Act (Revised Code of Washington (RCW) s. 42.56) and California Public Records Act (California Government Code §§ 6250-6276.48). In England see the Freedom of Information Act 2000 and in Australia the Freedom of Information Act 1982 (Cth) at federal level and various FOI Acts at State levels.

25. See, for example, the Privacy Act 1988 (Cth) in Australia.

26. See ss 6(a)(5) and 6(a)(6) of the UMA. However despite making provision for the exception, the UMA specifically prevents mediators from being called to give evidence in relation to professional misconduct claims against representatives or others in mediation (s. 6(c)).

interest provision, section 6(b) of the UMA. However, the UMA does not go so far as to permit courts to compel mediators to provide evidence of mediation communications in relation to such claims (section 6(c)). In other words, mediators cannot be required to provide testimony about the conduct of parties or other participants in relation to enforcing settlement agreements, but evidence from other sources may be adduced. Thus, the terms of this particular UMA exception are distinctly narrower than equivalent exceptions in other legal instruments granting mediators greater - albeit not absolute - security in relation to their confidentiality obligations.

5.15 In summary, the general principle seems to be that mediation disclosure is not ordered unless a court finds a competing public interest need of sufficient magnitude to outweigh maintaining the integrity of the mediation for participants and public confidence that mediation communications will be kept confidential. This principle is expressed in section 6(b) of the UMA which provides an exception to confidentiality protection where, in relation to evidence sought to be admitted in criminal proceedings or in relation to a claim to set aside an MSA, evidence is not otherwise available and the need for the evidence outweighs the interest in protecting confidentiality.[27] Further, the section provides for in camera determination of issues relating to confidentiality so that the benefits of confidentiality protection are not jeopardised the moment confidentiality is challenged in open court. The English Civil Procedure Rules in Part 39.2(3)(c) and (g) also provide for in camera determinations of certain types of confidential information where the court considers it necessary in the interests of justice.

5.16 Although framed broadly, Article 7 of the EU Directive provides that confidentiality is to be subject, *inter alia*, to public policy requirements and the need to establish the existence or otherwise of an iMSA; as such, this Article may also anticipate the possible use of in camera hearings.

5.17 Finally, exceptions to confidentiality are construed narrowly so that disclosure is proportional to the exception. Therefore, disclosures are permitted strictly for the purposes underlying the exception and only that part of a mediation communication necessary for applying the exception is disclosed or admitted as evidence. The principle of proportionality is enshrined in section 6(d) of the UMA.

Courts and Confidentiality

5.18 So far, mediation confidentiality has been considered from a legislative perspective. Here some reflections will be made on the approach of courts to confidentiality. Three illustrated cases below from England and the US outline the scope of confidentiality and the without prejudice rule in mediation and settlement negotiations.

27. Note limitations to this exception to confidentiality insofar as mediators cannot be compelled to give evidence about a mediation in relation, *inter alia*, to claims to set aside mediated settlements (s. 6(c)).

Case Illustrations

Illustration [A]: In the English case of *Berkeley Square Holdings v Lancer Property Asset Management Ltd,*[28] the defendants were relying on the position statements made in a mediation and expressly marked as 'without prejudice' in order to *oppose* the claims of fraud. The High Court of Justice addressed whether the defendants were precluded from relying on these statements expressly marked as without prejudice or whether the circumstances come within an exception to the without prejudice rule. The court stated that the without prejudice rule is not absolute and resort may be had to without prejudice material for several reasons. The defendants relied on three exceptions to the without prejudice rule, one of which related to the admissibility of evidence 'to show that an agreement apparently concluded between the parties during the negotiations should be set aside on the ground of misrepresentation, fraud or undue influence'.[29] The court agreed on the position argued by the defendants that '[s]ince a party to a concluded agreement can rely on the preceding WP [without prejudice] discussions to show that the agreement was reached following a fraudulent misrepresentation by the other party which undermined the agreement, so also should a party to a concluded agreement be able to rely on the preceding WP [without prejudice] discussions to show that the agreement was reached following a representation which shows that there was no fraud on the other party as alleged which would undermine the agreement'.[30] According to the court, it would be 'contrary to principle' if parties could rely on evidence to prove the invalidity of a settlement agreement but not to defend themselves from allegations of fraud. Therefore, the court admitted the without prejudice communications relied on by the defendants.

Illustration [B]: In another English case, *Motorola v Hytera China Comms,*[31] the Court of Appeal addressed the issue of admitting without prejudice statements in evidence based on the 'unambiguous impropriety' exception. In this case, *Hytera* appealed a freezing injunction, which was granted in support of substantive proceedings brought by *Motorola* in the US. The injunction was granted based on a without prejudice statement according to which 'if Motorola obtained a judgment in the US proceedings which was "unacceptable" to Hytera, then Hytera would take steps to transfer its assets away from western jurisdictions in order to make enforcement of the judgment more difficult'.[32] Justice Jacobs, in

28. *Berkeley Square Holdings and others v Lancer Property Asset Management Ltd and others* [2020] EWHC 1015 (Ch).
29. *Id.*, para. 43.
30. *Id.*, para. 51.
31. *Motorola Solutions, Inc. and another company v Hytera Communications Corp Ltd. and another company* [2021] EWCA Civ 11.
32. *Id.*, para. 3.

granting the injunction, held that such a threat amounted to 'unambiguous impropriety'. Furthermore, these statements were admissible because there was a 'good arguable case' that they were indeed made as alleged by Motorola.[33] Justice Jacobs came to this conclusion despite accepting that 'there was scope for misunderstanding what had been said at the meeting'. According to Justice Jacobs, 'this was irrelevant because what mattered was whether Motorola's evidence amounted to a good arguable case'. The Court of Appeal, among other issues, addressed whether a party seeking to rely on the 'unambiguous impropriety' exception need only establish a good arguable case of such impropriety.

The Court of Appeal came to the conclusion that the 'unambiguous impropriety' exception cannot be based on 'a good arguable case'. It was stated that '[a]lthough the unambiguous impropriety exception has been recognised, cases in which it has been applied have been truly exceptional' and 'there has been no scope for dispute about what was said, either because the statement was recorded' or 'because it was in writing'.[34] According to the Court of Appeal, '[i]f all that is needed to be shown is a good arguable case, parties engaging in settlement discussions will need to exercise care not to say anything which might be misconstrued; they will need a careful record of what has been said; there will be scope for manoeuvring to obtain an advantage in the litigation at the expense of frank discussion with a view to settlement; and evidence of statements made without prejudice will be admitted much more often than has hitherto been the case. All this runs directly counter to the policy of promoting settlement which the without prejudice rule exists to support'.[35]

The Court of Appeal made the following statement regarding the considerations for maintaining the integrity of the without prejudice rule: 'On the one hand, too demanding an evidential standard runs the risk that in some cases an abusive statement will not be admitted in evidence and that an impropriety will therefore not be exposed. On the other hand, too low a standard runs the risk that statements which were not in fact abusive (or which in fact were not even made) will be admitted in evidence when they ought not to be and that, in order to avoid this, frank discussion in settlement meetings generally will be inhibited. In weighing these considerations, the cases have firmly and rightly set their face against any erosion of the without prejudice rule, even if that means that some statements disclosing or constituting impropriety, albeit not unambiguously so, retain the protection of the rule. The policy choice is that the public interest in the settlement of litigation generally outweighs the risk of abuse of the privilege in individual cases.'[36] According to the Court of Appeal, the relevant test is the 'one

33. *Ibid.*
34. *Id.*, para. 57.
35. *Id.*, para. 60.
36. *Id.*, para. 62.

of unambiguous impropriety' and 'nothing less will do'.[37] In deciding whether or not to grant the injunction, Justice Jacobs should have asked whether 'the evidence before him established an unambiguous impropriety'.[38] The Court of Appeal eventually came to the conclusion that the evidence did not establish an unambiguous impropriety.

Illustration [C]: In the US case of *Mozer v Augustine*,[39] the appellant argued that an MSA was invalid on the ground that it was procured by 'the mediator's fraud, undue influence and failure to disclose pertinent conflicts of interests'. The Court of Appeal of California dismissed the appellant's claims on the ground that Mozer, that is to say the appellant's claims were based on confidential information. According to the court, 'Mozer identifies no statutory exception or provision in the parties' agreement that would allow a court to disregard the statutory protections afforded the mediator's communications. Rather, Mozer contends it is fundamentally unfair to apply the confidentiality statutes to protect the mediator and, by extension, to preserve an unfair settlement at her expense. Mozer's policy argument does not justify disregarding the Legislature's mandate.'[40] The appellant also relied on the information shared in a pre-mediation settlement conference. According to the appellant, such information should not be protected by the cloak of confidentiality. The court rejected this argument and stated that the 'mediation privilege is not limited to those communications made in the course of the mediation but includes communications between participants in a mediation consultation or a conference in preparation for mediation'.[41]

Securing Confidentiality and the Role of Contract

5.19 In a cross-border context, it is imperative to ensure that confidentiality provisions are effective in the relevant jurisdiction. The above examination of the law of confidentiality has shown that there are different types of confidentiality that can be regulated in different ways, depending on the jurisdiction. One of these regulatory forms is a private contract. Drafting contracts containing confidentiality provisions – particularly contracts which traverse national borders and legal cultures – requires an analysis of the applicable law on mediation confidentiality and the extent to which the relevant courts recognise contractual undertakings of this nature.

5.20 Contractual instruments such as agreements to mediate containing confidentiality provisions are limited in relation to their ability to bind non-signatories to the contract and to address public policy concerns. Nevertheless, the use of contractual terms can be a desirable form of regulating confidentiality and is often used in addition

37. *Id.*, para. 64.
38. *Id.*, para. 66.
39. *Mozer v Augustine*, 2019 Cal. App. Unpub. LEXIS 6183.
40. *Ibid.*
41. *Ibid.*

to other forms of regulation.[42] Parties and their legal representatives should consider how incorporating confidentiality provisions into mediation clauses, agreements to mediate and other relevant contractual instruments can help to secure the type of confidentiality protection they desire.[43]

5.21 Contractual provisions will not override mandatory forms of regulation and they may be subject to exercises of judicial discretion. They can, however, be useful in clarifying the existing law and parties' intentions, especially with regard to discretionary law[44] and any *gaps* in existing regulation. By way of example, the EU Directive provides for a positive duty of confidentiality only for mediators and does not require the EU Member States to regulate this duty for parties, lawyers and others who find themselves in a mediation. It is therefore up to the relevant EU Member State as to whether this gap has been legislatively regulated or not.

Guidelines for Lawyers

5.22 In analysing confidentiality rules in relation to the choice of law, lawyers and parties will find the following questions useful:

(1) *What is the scope of the confidentiality provision?* Confidentiality provisions can be broad and extend beyond considerations of admissibility of evidence of mediation communications. They may extend to rules which regulate the confidentiality of private sessions in mediation and also general duties of confidentiality that prohibit the sharing of mediation information and communications with people outside the mediation. Here the focus is on how the admissibility of evidence of mediation communications in subsequent litigation is regulated.

(2) *Who holds obligations or rights in relation to confidentiality?* Article 7 of the EU Directive requires the Member States to introduce regulations which ensure insider/court confidentiality for mediators and those involved in the administration of the mediation process, but the Directive encourages the Member States to enact even stricter rules on confidentiality.

---

42. See para. 45 of the UNCITRAL Notes on Mediation (2021), which is reproduced in Appendix G of this book. For a critique of the use of contract to safeguard confidentiality, see Alan Kirtley, *The Mediation Privilege's Transition from Theory to Implementation: Designing a Mediation Privilege Standard to Protect Mediation Participants, the Process and the Public Interest*, J. Disp. Resol. 1 (1995), at 10–11.
43. For example, the Centre for Effective Dispute Resolution (CEDR) model agreement to mediate provides an absolute bar on calling the mediator as witness.
44. For example, in France the Law regarding the organisation of the court system and civil, criminal and administrative procedure, 8 February 1995, No. 95-125 (*Loi n° 95-125* du *8 février 1995 relative à l'organisation des juridictions et à la procédure civile, pénale et administrative*), Art. 21-3 permits parties to agree to contractually exclude the application of confidentiality provisions. See Delphine Wietek, *France*, in Nadja Alexander et al. (eds), EU Mediation Law Handbook: Regulatory Robustness Ratings for Mediation Regimes, Wolters Kluwer (2017), at 339, note 207.

(3) *What is protected by confidentiality?* The protection of confidentiality can extend to verbal and non-verbal communications and to documents prepared for, and created in, the mediation. It has been shown above that the definition of mediation communication in the UMA is very broad.

(4) *To which parts of the mediation do the various obligations of confidentiality attach?* For the purposes of confidentiality, it is important to be clear about whether the mediation includes preliminary contact between parties and mediator, separate sessions and interim and follow-up contact.

(5) *Are there any exceptions to the confidentiality provisions?* In jurisdictions with legislation dedicated to mediation, it can be relatively easy to identify the exceptions to confidentiality, but in others, they may not be obvious and one may need to search through various criminal and civil procedural codes and other laws to find them. Moreover, as shown above, courts have taken inconsistent approaches to confidentiality exceptions.

CONTRACT-RELATED GROUNDS FOR REFUSAL

Article 5. Grounds for Refusing to Grant Relief

1. The competent authority of the Party to the Convention where relief is sought under article 4 may refuse to grant relief at the request of the party against whom the relief is sought only if that party furnishes to the competent authority proof that:

(a) A party to the settlement agreement was under some incapacity;
(b) The settlement agreement sought to be relied upon:
- **(i) Is null and void, inoperative or incapable of being performed under the law to which the parties have validly subjected it or, failing any indication thereon, under the law deemed applicable by the competent authority of the Party to the Convention where relief is sought under article 4;**
- **(ii) Is not binding, or is not final, according to its terms; or**
- **(iii) Has been subsequently modified;**

(c) The obligations in the settlement agreement:
- **(i) Have been performed; or**
- **(ii) Are not clear or comprehensible;**

(d) Granting relief would be contrary to the terms of the settlement agreement;

[...]

COMMENTARY

Contract-Related Grounds

5.23 Article 5(1) of the Singapore Convention contains the grounds for refusal of enforcement and recognition of iMSAs based on contract law. Upon the furnishing of proof by parties, an iMSA may be refused enforcement by a competent authority if:

(1) a party to it was under some incapacity at its conclusion,[45]
(2) it is null and void, inoperative or incapable of being performed under the applicable law,[46]
(3) it is not binding, or is not final, according to its terms,[47]
(4) it has been subsequently modified,[48]
(5) the obligations in it have been performed,[49]

45. UN Convention on International Settlement Agreements Resulting from Mediation (2019), Art. 5(1)(a).
46. *Id.*, Art. 5(1)(b)(i).
47. *Id.*, Art. 5(1)(b)(ii).
48. *Id.*, Art. 5(1)(b)(iii).
49. *Id.*, Art. 5(1)(c)(i).

(6) the obligations in it are not clear or comprehensible,[50] or
(7) granting relief would be contrary to the terms of the settlement agreement.[51]

5.24 While the discussion in this commentary proceeds on the basis that these grounds for refusal may be analysed individually, the drafters of the Singapore Convention have acknowledged that these grounds for refusal may potentially overlap with each other and that multiple grounds for refusal may be applicable to one given fact pattern.[52] Each of these grounds for refusal will be examined in turn.

Article 5(1)(a): Incapacity

5.25 An iMSA may be refused enforcement or recognition by the relevant court of a Party to the Convention if a party to the iMSA was affected by some incapacity at the point of its conclusion. This provision applies to both natural and legal persons. 'Incapacity' is a term of art which cannot be perceived in isolation. It is difficult to approach the concept of incapacity from an autonomous perspective, as there are underlying differences in its concept from within civil and common law traditions.[53] For instance, the capacity of natural persons from the perspective of legal systems classified within the civil law tradition is normally governed by the law of their nationality, while the capacity of natural persons under legal systems which draw from the common law tradition is governed by the law of their domicile. Hence, in order to meaningfully examine this ground for refusal, one must first identify the governing law of the iMSA. This will be considered below. From a general understanding of the concept, the incapacity defence under Article 5(1)(a) is relevant for consideration when parties participating in the conclusion of the iMSA are minors,[54] natural persons with intellectual disabilities or deficits, natural persons who are under the influence of drugs[55] or alcohol[56] or legal persons not validly represented.[57]

50. *Id.*, Art. 5(1)(c)(ii).
51. *Id.*, Art. 5(1)(d).
52. Natalie Y. Morris-Sharma, *The Singapore Convention: A Milestone for Mediation*, 6(2) BCDR Int'l Arb. Rev. 261 (2019), at 274.
53. Shouyu Chong and Felix Steffek, *Enforcement of International Settlement Agreements Resulting from Mediation under the Singapore Convention – Private International Law Issues in Perspective*, 31 SAcLJ 448 (2019), at para. 64. For instance, the capacity of natural persons in civil law jurisdictions is generally governed by the law of their nationality, while the capacity of natural persons in common law jurisdictions is governed by the law of their domicile: Gary Born, *International Commercial Arbitration* (2nd Ed.), Wolters Kluwer (2014), at 3489-3490.
54. See Loo Wee Ling, *Full Contractual Capacity: Use of Age for Conferment of Capacity*, Sing. J. Legal Stud. 328 (2010). The position of Singapore law, for instance, has been re-stated in *BAZ v BBA* [2018] SGHC 275, [2020] 5 SLR 266, at [178]. The French law position is stated in Arts. 1146 and 1149 of the *Code civil* (as modified by Ordinance no. 2016-131 of February, 2016, reforming the law of contract and the general regime and proof of obligations).
55. See *Chan Gek Yong v Violet Netto* [2019] 3 SLR 1218, at [39].
56. See *Resorts World At Sentosa Pte Ltd v Lee Fook Kheun* [2018] 5 SLR 1039; *Molton v Camroux* (1849) 4 Exch 17, at 19.
57. See *Alphire Group Pte Ltd v Law Chau Loon* [2020] SGCA 50. For the French law position, see Art. 1145 of the *Code civil* (as modified by Ordinance no. 2016-131 of February 2016, reforming the law of contract and the general regime and proof of obligations).

5.26 Article 5(1)(a) of the Singapore Convention was modelled after Article V(1)(a) of the New York Convention,[58] but omitting the choice of law provision (that is, the words 'under the law applicable to them').[59] Having removed the choice of law provision, it may appear on its plain reading that the drafters of the Singapore Convention may have intended for incapacity to be examined from an autonomous[60] perspective. However, elucidating the concept of 'incapacity' from an autonomous perspective could be all but a search in vain, as one has to account for the various idiosyncratic national rules on determining capacity across several jurisdictions, which point in various (sometimes opposing) directions.[61] The difficulty encountered is a result of the fact that there are fundamental differences to determine capacity under various governing laws.[62] Accordingly, it is unlikely that the drafters would have intended the concept of 'incapacity' to be read from an autonomous perspective. Rather a more nuanced interpretation of Article 5(1)(a) may have been intended.

5.27 A more useful interpretation of the deliberate omission would be that it advocates for a more expansive choice of law concept to be applied when the issue of incapacity is raised as a defence. It is possible, on the one hand, to administer the 'validation principle'.[63] The 'validation principle' is an innovative choice of law concept, which posits that parties, by virtue of their participation in international commerce, must be taken to have desired for their contractual arrangements with respect to all matters of their transaction (including the effects flowing from a *choice* of governing law) to be

58. Report of Working Group II (Dispute Settlement) on the Work of its 65th Session (30 September 2016), A/CN.9/896 (2016), at para. 85. Available at http://undocs.org/A/CN.9/896 (Accessed 25 March 2018).
59. Convention on the Recognition and Enforcement of Foreign Arbitral Awards (1958), Art. V(1)(a). Art. V(1)(a) of the New York Convention states: 'Recognition and enforcement of the [arbitral] award may be refused, at the request of the party against whom it is invoked, only if that party furnishes to the competent authority where the recognition and enforcement is sought, proof that[...] [t]he parties to the agreement referred to in Article II were, under the law applicable to them, under some incapacity, or the said agreement is not valid under the law to which the parties have subjected it or, falling any indication thereon, under the law of the country where the award was made[...].'
60. In the study of private international law, the autonomous method of interpreting terms of art found in an international instrument (e.g., a Conventional instrument) invites the interpreter to derive the meaning of that term as far as possible from within the instrument itself, independent of other external considerations. The implicit assumption is that the instrument, which is a subject of interpretation, subsists on its own as a comprehensive set of rules. See Maren Heidemann, *The Autonomous Interpretation Method in International Law with Particular Reference to the Proposed European Sales Law I*, 93 Amicus Curiae 21 (2013), at 22. This concept was first examined earlier in the commentary to Art. 1.
61. Gary Born, *International Commercial Arbitration* (2nd Ed.), Wolters Kluwer (2014), at 3489-3490.
62. *Ibid.* For instance, 'the capacity of natural persons in civil law jurisdictions is generally governed by the law of their nationality, while the capacity of natural persons in common law jurisdictions is governed by the law of their domicile'; Also see Albert Jan van den Berg, *The New York Arbitration Convention of 1958 – Towards a Uniform Judicial Interpretation*, Wolters Kluwer (1981), at 276-277.
63. *Enka Insaat ve Sanayi AS v OOO Insurance Company Chubb* [2020] UKSC 38, at paras 95 et seq.

validly concluded, enforceable and performed to their best effect.[64] To illustrate: in the mediation context, where an iMSA may have been concluded through mediation taking place across borders with the assistance of Internet technology between Jennifer Pty Ltd and Johannes AG which are incorporated in Uppland and Gotland, respectively, the parties' capacity to conclude the iMSA would be upheld owing to the validation principle where either laws of Uppland or Gotland would reach this result. This engenders a pro-enforcement bias with respect to iMSAs sought to be enforced under the Singapore Convention.

5.28 On the other hand, the competent authority may administer *renvoi* to decide if parties indeed have capacity when concluding an iMSA at the end of a mediation session. Take, for instance: if Ron (who is 20 years old) concludes an iMSA in and under the governing law of Uppland (where the age of majority is 21) but seeks to enforce it expeditiously with the assistance of the Singapore Convention in his State of ordinary residence, Gotland (where the age of majority is 18), the competent authority of Gotland may apply *renvoi* to rule that Ron has the capacity to conclude the iMSA, if the private international law rules of Uppland determine the capacity of a person by reference to the laws of his State of residence.

5.29 The validation principle has recently been re-stated and affirmed in English law by a majority decision in the English Supreme Court.[65] However, its application remains questioned in other Commonwealth jurisdictions, such as in Singapore.[66] The administration of *renvoi* has not received overwhelming judicial support at this moment in time.[67] It appears that in practice, the theory behind *renvoi* is so esoteric that it receives little support for fear of confusion. It remains to be observed if the competent authorities of States and other Parties to the Convention will apply *renvoi* when evaluating if an iMSA should be refused enforcement under the Convention, when parties plead the incapacity defence.

5.30 Three case illustrations in relation to the administration of Article 5(1)(a) of the Singapore Convention are set out below.

64. *Id.*, at paras 95-96, citing *Re Missouri Steamship Co* (1889) 42 Ch D 321.
65. *Enka Insaat ve Sanayi AS v OOO Insurance Company Chubb* [2020] UKSC 38, at paras 95 et seq. The majority of the court, consisting of Lords Hamblen and Leggat (with whom Lord Kerr agreed) ruled, '[t]his principle may apply if, in determining whether the parties have agreed on a choice of governing law, a putative governing law would render all or a part of the contract ineffective' (at para. 96), citing *Re Missouri Steamship Co* (1889) 42 Ch D 321.
66. *BNA v BNB* [2019] SGHC 142, at [52]-[66]. Vinodh Coomaraswamy J opined that the validation principle, when applied to derive the governing law of a contractual agreement, would offend the principle of effective interpretation of a contract, and is inconsistent with legal authority. See Shouyu Chong, *Choice of Law Governing a Contract Where Its Existence Is in Dispute: Clarifications from the Singapore International Commercial Court in* Lew, Solomon v Kaikhushru Shiavax Nargolwala *[2020] 3 SLR 61*, 33 SAcLJ 662 (2021), at para. 28.
67. See David Alexander Hughes, *The Insolubility of 'Renvoi' and its Consequences*, 6 J. Priv. Int'l L. 195 (2010); David McClean and Veronica Ruiz Abou-Nigm, *Morris: The Conflict of Laws* (10th Ed.), Sweet & Maxwell (2021), at para. 20-033.

Case Illustrations

Illustration [A]: *Georgina* was gifted as a child, and a high achiever by any standards. By the age of ten, she learned to code complex programs and by 17, she had started a successful sole-proprietorship offering web development services to the rich and famous in Janetwood. Unfortunately, the tech whizzes at *OurSpace Pte Ltd* (OurSpace), a company registered in Gotland, discovered that a long line of one of Georgina's codes for an anonymous celebrity blogger's website was plagiarised from them, and threatened to sue her for copyright infringement. Both parties agreed to settle this dispute at mediation. While Georgina agreed in the concluded iMSA to pay USD 30 million in licensing fees to OurSpace in her personal capacity, she refused to pay up at the end of the day. As Janetwood is a Party to the Singapore Convention, OurSpace takes the iMSA to its competent authority for enforcement against Georgina. Knowing that the age of majority in Janetwood is 21, Georgina may plead incapacity in her defence, if she were indeed below that age when she agreed to the terms of the iMSA, to avoid an enforcement action under the Singapore Convention from OurSpace.

Illustration [B]: *Miranda Pty Ltd* (Miranda) runs a manufacturing business in Lappland. It purchases raw materials from *Emily AG* (Emily), a company incorporated in Gotland. Because of a fraud perpetrated by one of its employees, Emily fails to deliver a large order of raw materials in time to Miranda, causing the latter significant losses in revenue. As both parties intend to continue their business relationship because of long-standing goodwill, they agreed to mediate their dispute, and explicitly agree in writing that California law is to apply to their iMSA. Miranda sends its Managing Director to the mediation table, while Emily sends their team of lawyers. An iMSA is concluded expeditiously. Soon after, Emily secretly transfers a large amount of its assets into Uppland, and Miranda becomes suspicious when this information was brought to its attention. As Uppland is a Party to the Singapore Convention, Miranda applies to have the iMSA enforced by the High Court of Uppland, which is its relevant competent authority for the purposes of enforcement under the Singapore Convention. Emily may plead the defence of incapacity in the High Court of Uppland (and in accordance with the relevant rules of civil or court procedure) that under California law, §664.6 of the Code of Civil Procedure of California states that a settlement agreement made outside of court is not enforceable unless it is signed by the 'litigants personally'; there is precedent in its favour, ruling that legal counsel who possess their client's authority to enter into settlement agreements on their behalf would still not have the requisite authority under California law to fulfil the capacity requirements for representatives concluding settlement agreements on behalf of parties.[68]

68. *Finney v Ford Motor Co.*, No. 17-CV-06183-JST, WL 5879730 (N.D. Cal. Nov 7 2018), at 4.

Article 5(1)(b)(i): The Settlement Agreement is Null and Void, Inoperative or Incapable of Being Performed

5.31 A competent court may refuse to enforce an iMSA if it finds that it is null and void, inoperative or incapable of being performed under the law which the parties have validly subjected it or under the law deemed applicable by the competent authority of the Contracting State.

5.32 It appears that Article 5(1)(b)(i) of the Singapore Convention was modelled after Article II (3) of the New York Convention, with the addition of a choice of law provision.[69] Thus it is incumbent on the enforcing court to make an objective determination as to the proper law[70] of the iMSA before proceeding to decide if it is null and void, inoperative or incapable of being performed; owing to the theoretical 'separation of the process of identifying the proper law of a contract, and determination by that law of the validity of the contract' persuasively posited by Briggs,[71] any concerns about whether this becomes an exercise of pulling the rug from under one's feet[72] should be allayed.

5.33 Having ascertained the proper law, the enforcing court must discern what 'null and void, inoperative or incapable of being performed' entails in its proper context. It becomes useful to consider and elucidate the individual characteristics of the terms 'null and void', 'inoperative' and 'incapable of being performed', to facilitate a better appreciation and application of this ground for refusal of relief.

69. See Interventions of Thailand and Finland, in UNCITRAL Audio Recordings: Working Group II (Arbitration and Conciliation), 64th Session, 4 February 2016, 15:00-18:00.
70. Bearing in mind that it is trite in private international law that there is 'no contract without a law': Berthold Goldman, *Les conflits de lois dans l'arbitrage international de droit privé*, Recueil de Cours 351 (1964), at 480. Also see Yock Lin Tan, *Good Faith Choice of a Law to Govern a Contract*, Sing. J. Legal Stud. 307 (2014). It bears noting that the express choice of law may not necessarily be the proper law: Tan has persuasively shown how the express choice of law theoretically only leads to a presumption that that express choice is the proper law. Furthermore, it is also worthwhile mentioning that Alexander has observed that 'research indicates that business people and lawyers typically select places and regions with which they are familiar as the basis for the governing law [of the mediation]': by extension, this observation could prove helpful in discerning the proper law of the iMSA (see Nadja Alexander, *Introducing Regulatory Robustness Ratings for Mediation Regimes in the EU*, in Nadja Alexander et al. (eds), EU Mediation Law Handbook – Regulatory Robustness Ratings for Mediation Regimes, Wolters Kluwer (2017), at 1-2).
71. Adrian Briggs, *The Formation of International Contracts*, Lloyd's Maritime and Commercial Law Quarterly 192 (1990), at 203.
72. That is, when arguing that the contract concerned is invalid, does one effectively pull the plug on any possible agreement found therein to the choice of law of *that* contract and hence the determination of the proper law? It has been argued and shown by Chong that these concerns are unfounded: see Shouyu Chong, *Choice of Law Governing a Contract Where Its Existence is in Dispute: Clarifications from the Singapore International Commercial Court in* Lew, Solomon v Kaikhushru Shiavax Nargolwala *[2020] 3 SLR 61*, 33 SAcLJ 662 (2021), at para. 28.

5.34 An iMSA that is 'null and void' is one which contains defects which subsist from the point in time when the contract is formed;[73] defects which appear subsequently will not render it null and void. For instance, an iMSA founded on illegality would be deemed null and void by an overwhelming majority of legal systems.[74] Furthermore, contingent on the proper law of the iMSA, it may be adjudged null and void if it were founded upon a lack of consent, misrepresentation,[75] fraud,[76] duress, undue influence or unconscionability:[77] this list of contractual defences is illustrative but non-exhaustive.[78] It is likely that iMSAs which were negotiated and concluded in breach of competition laws may be refused recognition and enforcement for being void.[79] Conversely, secondary obligations provisions (e.g., provisions for liquidated damages) in an international settlement agreement which may fall foul of the 'no penalty' rule under English law may not be refused enforcement under this Article 5 provision because such clauses are generally taken to be not enforceable under English contract law, rather than null and void.[80] In contrast, where the governing law is French law, it appears likely that where an iMSA may be found defective of consent leading to the

73. Shouyu Chong and Felix Steffek, *Enforcement of International Settlement Agreements Resulting from Mediation under the Singapore Convention – Private International Law Issues in Perspective*, 31 SAcLJ 448 (2019).
74. See George A. Bermann, *Recognition and Enforcement of Foreign Arbitral Awards – The Interpretation and Application of the New York Convention by National Courts*, in George A. Bermann (ed.), Recognition and Enforcement of Foreign Arbitral Awards – The Interpretation and Application of the New York Convention by National Courts, Springer (2017), at 23.
75. See Intervention of the Chair, in UNCITRAL Audio Recordings: Working Group II (Dispute Settlement), 65th Session, 16 September 2016, 09:30-12:30.
76. *Ibid.*
77. Timothy Schnabel, *The Singapore Convention on Mediation: A Framework for the Cross-Border Recognition and Enforcement of Mediated Settlements*, 19 Pepp. Disp. Resol. L.J. 1 (2019), at 44; Schnabel succinctly reports the intention of the drafters, '[This] ground for refusal encompasses various contract law concepts such as fraud and misrepresentation, and is *broad enough to cover instances in which the mediated settlement may be considered voidable* at the option of the party resisting relief' [*emphasis added*]. Also see Natalie Y. Morris-Sharma, *The Singapore Convention: A Milestone for Mediation*, 6(2) BCDR Int'l Arb. Rev. 261 (2019), at 275.
78. See Interventions of Israel, the US, and the Chair, in UNCITRAL Audio Recordings: Working Group II (Dispute Settlement), 68th Session, 5 February 2018, 15:00-18:00.
79. If, for instance, Singapore law governs the settlement agreement, see the Singapore Competition Act (Cap 50B, 2006 Rev Ed.), at s. 34(3). Where the applicable law is that of a State that is part of the EU, Art. 81 of the EC Treaty also renders anti-competitive agreements void and it is broadly worded enough to regulate MSAs (see Treaty Establishing the European Community, as amended (by the Single European Act, 1987 O.J. (L 169), consolidated text, 2002 O.J. (C 325). Articles of the EC Treaty were renumbered by the Treaty of Amsterdam Amending the Treaty on European Union, the Treaties Establishing the European Communities and Certain Related Acts, 1997 O.J. (C 340) 1. Arts 85-94 on competition policy, including State Aids, were renumbered as Arts 81-89, Art. 85 becoming Art. 81.
80. Shouyu Chong, *Another Piece of the Puzzle: Are Penalty Clauses Unenforceable or Void?* (September 2021) Paper D234 presented at the Society of Construction Law, https://www.scl.org.uk/papers/another-piece-puzzle-are-penalty-clauses-unenforceable-or-void (Accessed 6 October 2021). Also see Andrew Burrows, *A Restatement of the English Law of Contract*, OUP (2016), at 136.

remedy of *nullité*,[81] it may be refused enforcement under this ground as such contracts are taken to be void *ab initio*. Additionally, the 'null and void' ground for refusal does not cover situations where iMSAs may be rendered invalid owing to non-compliance with domestic law requirements which have been displaced by the Convention.[82] For instance, domestic laws or rules which render iMSAs void (e.g., laws regulating domestic mediation which provide that if mediation were not conducted under specified rules within the confines of specific institutions, or when localised requirements of notarisation and other kinds of formal requirements are not fulfilled, the resulting settlement agreement would be null and void) are *not caught* by Article 5(1)(b)(i).[83]

5.35 An iMSA that is 'inoperative' is one which ceases to be in force, or one which is sterile in the first place.[84] For instance, when parties to an iMSA waive rights to pursue any obligations under it in a subsequent agreement, this indicates the inoperability of that iMSA in totality,[85] as the waiver negates the force of the iMSA. In construction contracts, where the parties have failed to expressly provide for an extension of time for delays, and the employer of the services of a contractor commits an act that prevents the latter from performing their work, the contractor is not only no longer bound by the original contractual completion date, but additionally, any liquidated damages provisions binding the contractor to pay in the event of a delay is said to be rendered inoperative.[86] This applies to iMSAs which are concluded between disputing parties in a construction contract. Inoperability could also be embodied in poorly drafted iMSAs containing inherently contradictory or self-defeating terms which cancel out the obligations found within, rendering it incapable of any effect in the first place. The Singapore Convention cannot bring to life contractual terms which are ineffectual in

81. A contract governed by French law set aside for *nullité* is treated as one that is never to have existed and will be deemed void *ab initio*. See Arts 1178-1185 of the *Code civil* (as modified by Ordinance no. 2016-131 of February, 2016, reforming the law of contract and the general regime and proof of obligations).
82. See, for example, Interventions of the US, Singapore and the Chair, in UNCITRAL Audio Recordings: Working Group II (Arbitration and Conciliation), 64th Session, 4 February 2016, 15:00-18:00, https://icms.unov.org/CarbonWeb/public/uncitral/speakerslog/83bbcdba-28c4-4368-bab6- e8d17b3fbcb6; Interventions of the US, Finland and the Chair, in UNCITRAL Audio Recordings: Working Group II (Dispute Settlement), 65th Session, 15 September 2016, 14:00-1 7:00, https://icms.unov.org/CarbonWeb/public/uncitral/speakerslog/11675955-4681-4557-b4 d6- 52e0e6b28f09; and Timothy Schnabel, *The Singapore Convention on Mediation: A Framework for the Cross-Border Recognition and Enforcement of Mediated Settlements*, 19 Pepp. Disp. Resol. L.J. 1 (2019), at 44.
83. Timothy Schnabel, *The Singapore Convention on Mediation: A Framework for the Cross-Border Recognition and Enforcement of Mediated Settlements*, 19 Pepp. Disp. Resol. L.J. 1 (2019), at 44.
84. Shouyu Chong and Felix Steffek, *Enforcement of International Settlement Agreements Resulting from Mediation under the Singapore Convention – Private International Law Issues in Perspective*, 31 SAcLJ 448 (2019).
85. This is Bermann's interpretation of *Apple & Eve LLC v Yantai N. Andre Juice Co.*, 610 F. Supp. 2d 226 (E.D. N.Y., 2009), found in George A. Bermann, *Recognition and Enforcement of Foreign Arbitral Awards – The Interpretation and Application of the New York Convention by National Court*, in George A. Bermann (ed.), Recognition and Enforcement of Foreign Arbitral Awards – The Interpretation and Application of the New York Convention by National Courts, Springer (2017), at 23, footnote 68.
86. *Crescendas Bionics Pte Ltd v Jurong Primewide Pte Ltd* [2019] SGHC 04, at [353].

the first place. It is further noteworthy that in international commercial arbitration, there are precedents which have recognised that arbitration agreements may be taken to be inoperative against non-arbitrable subject matters.[87] If this principle were to be applied by analogy to international commercial mediation, where an iMSA resolves a subject matter which is not susceptible to mediation under the relevant governing law, it may be treated as inoperative.

5.36 An iMSA that is 'incapable of being performed', a concept which may allude to the frustration doctrine, is one which cannot be executed but for impossibility, or supervening events occurring *after* its conclusion.[88] Enforcement will be denied because of impossibility in cases where non-implementable clauses are found in the iMSA, owing to poor[89] drafting. An interesting illustration of such non-implementable clauses occurred in a compromise arbitration agreement between an Italian and a Syrian party, who provided that 'any dispute arising[...] shall be settled by a sole arbitrator[...] [T]he arbitrator shall be an expert in Swiss law and in the production of Arabic bread'.[90] Unfortunately, the agreement was found to be incapable of being performed because no arbitrator satisfying the conjunctive requirements could be located.[91] Alternatively, subject to its proper law, frustrating events (such as the death of a performing party whose personal performance of the obligation found in the iMSA is crucial, or if an outbreak of war prevents those obligations from being fulfilled) could suffice to render an iMSA incapable of being performed.

5.37 It bears reiterating that it is imperative for the enforcing courts, when applying the proper law of the iMSA, to interpret 'null and void, inoperative or incapable of being performed' in a judicious manner, so that the reach of the Singapore Convention is not compromised. To achieve this requires an aspiration to achieve a consistent application of a uniform set of principles across all competent authorities of States and other Parties to the Convention.

87. *Fulham Football Club (1987) Ltd v Richards* [2012] Ch. 333, at paras 35-36; *Tomolugen Holdings Ltd v Silica Investors Ltd* [2016] 1 SLR 373, at [74].
88. Shouyu Chong and Felix Steffek, *Enforcement of International Settlement Agreements Resulting from Mediation under the Singapore Convention – Private International Law Issues in Perspective*, 31 SAcLJ 448 (2019). See, for instance, *Alliance Concrete Singapore Pte Ltd v Sato Kogyo (S) Pte Ltd* [2014] 3 SLR 857 (Singapore); *Fibrosa Spolka Akcyjna v Fairbairn Lawson Combe Barbour Ltd* [1943] AC 32 (England); and consider, under French Contract Law, events of *force majeure* (see Art. 1195 of the *Code civil* (as modified by Ordinance No. 2016-131 of February, 2016, reforming the law of contract and the general regime and proof of obligations)) and grounds of *imprévision* (Eva Steiner, *French Law: A Comparative Approach*, OUP (2010), at 334-335).
89. The drafting must be so inadequate (e.g., where contradicting terms simply cancel each other out and it is impossible to objectively ascertain, according to the parties' intentions, which term should prevail over the other) that the courts are unable to give effect to any of the objective intentions of the parties, even if it goes through a generous application of the available contractual construction tools.
90. Aldo Frignani, *Interpretation and Application of the New York Convention in Italy*, in George A. Bermann (ed.), Recognition and Enforcement of Foreign Arbitral Awards – The Interpretation and Application of the New York Convention by National Courts, Springer (2017), at 568.
91. *Ibid.*

5.38 A number of case illustrations from judgments in a variety of jurisdictions are set out below.

Case Illustrations

Illustration [A]: In the case reviewed below, an MSA was found to be null and void because of illegality. Although it deals with mediation in marital relations, it may be instructive for the purposes of examining Article 5(1)(b)(i) of the Singapore Convention. In *Taiwan High Court Judgment (April 26, 2011)*,[92] the parties in dispute were married in 2000. The appellant sued for divorce in accordance with paragraph 2, Article 1052 of the Civil Code. With respect to the underlying dispute, a separation agreement was entered into by the appellant and the appellee after a mediation proceeding in 2007. Under this MSA (which is essentially a separation agreement), the parties agreed that if and when the appellee becomes eligible for applying for a ROC National Identity Card and notifies the appellant of the same, the appellant shall assist the appellee to obtain the ROC National Identity Card. Under Taiwanese law, the husband and the wife are under mutual obligations to cohabit. However, in 2009, the appellee moved to another man's residence and left the family affairs unattended without notifying the appellant. The question before the court was whether the terms under this an MSA could be enforced? Or should it instead be considered void? Essentially the question which arises is whether the appellee was entitled to separate from the appellant according to the terms of that MSA.

It is important to note here that the wife was from the Mainland Area in the People's Republic of China (Mainland Area). Paragraphs 1 and 2, Article 10 of the Act Governing Relations between the People of the Taiwan Area and the Mainland Area (Act) states that no person of the Mainland Area may enter into the Taiwan Area without permission of the competent authorities and any person of the Mainland Area who is permitted to enter into the Taiwan Area may not engage in any activity inconsistent with the purpose of the permission. Further, pursuant to subparagraph 9, paragraph 3, Article 27 of the Regulations Governing the Permission of Residence from the Dependent Relative, Long-Term Residence and Registered Permanent Residence in the Taiwan Area for the People of the Mainland Area (Regulation) as enacted prior to August 12, 2009, the residence permission may be revoked when the applicant no longer lives with the dependent relative. In other words, since the wife entered into Taiwan by marrying a Taiwanese person and later applied for long-term residency, she has to cohabit with her spouse. The MSA, which essentially is a separation agreement between husband and wife, contradicted the imperative provision as it provides for the parties to remain in Taiwan without cohabiting with their

92. 100-Jia-Shang-Geng-Yi-Zi-1.

spouse. The MSA was thus held by the High Court of Taiwan to be in clear violation of the provisions under the Act and Regulation and rendered void in accordance with Articles 71 and 72 of the Civil Code.

Under the Singapore Convention, it is likely that an iMSA that is procured in ignorance of mandatory State laws governing immigration and customs matters, just as it was involved in this case, may fall within the ambit of Article 5(1)(b)(i). Such iMSAs may be rendered null and void because of illegality.

Illustration [B]: The following is a case illustration from the US, where parties have argued that an MSA should be found null and void because of duress. In *In re Johnson,*[93] one of the parties to a settlement agreement contended that the latter should be vacated because of several defences to contract enforcement, such as duress, fraud and criminal activity. The claimant argued that he had agreed to the terms of the settlement agreement under duress because he only participated in the mediation as he was pursuing, as damages, the legal fees that he believed were rightfully his. However, the Minnesota Court of Appeal held that a party cannot rely on the fact that they are seeking damages as grounds for duress during mediation, as this would necessarily and, in reality, void most settlement agreements. Further, the Court of Appeal ruled that the party concerned failed to explain how such an argument would fit into Minnesota's definition of duress, which according to the leading precedent of *St. Louis Park Inv. Co v R.L. Johnson Inv. Co.*[94] requires coercion by means of physical force or unlawful threats that destroy one's free will. As such, the court dismissed the argument that the MSA should be rendered void for duress.

Of note to readers is that if the choice of law governing the iMSA sought to be enforced under the Singapore Convention is Minnesota law, the elements to prove duress (established by *St. Louis Park Inv. Co v R.L. Johnson Inv. Co.*) must be shown, in order to successfully plead the Article 5(1)(b)(i) defence.

Illustration [C]: *George Joseph Assets, LLC v Chenevert*[95] comes from the US, where parties have argued that the terms under an MSA should not be enforced as they are null and void because of fraud. While this case deals with the mediation of probate matters, it may be instructive for the purposes of examining Article 5(1)(b)(i) of the Singapore Convention. Following the death of her husband, the appellee was embroiled in protracted litigation with the appellants, her husband's children and a limited liability company owned by her husband's estate (GJA). In an effort to settle the litigation, they mediated their dispute and signed an MSA on 5 December 2011. As a result of the mediation, the children

93. *In re Johnson,* No. A17-1765, WL 2770527 (2018).
94. *St. Louis Park Inv. v R* 411 N.W.2d 288 (1987).
95. *George Joseph Assets, LLC v Chenevert* 557 S.W.3d 755 (2018).

agreed to convey to the appellee a parcel of commercial real estate owned by the estate of the deceased in exchange for the appellee discontinuing the lawsuit. The settlement agreement between the appellee and the children provided that she would take the property subject to any current leases, which would include a lease with one of its tenants, Excel. This meant that the appellee would be responsible for the cost of any tenant improvements. Separately, in June 2012, the appellants and Excel became involved in litigation alleging Excel's non-payment of rent, GJA's non-payment of USD 100,000 for tenant improvements and damage resulting from water penetration to the building. Four months later, in October 2012, GJA and Excel settled the lawsuits by executing a confidential settlement agreement. Under the terms of the agreement, Excel received a complete rent abatement through 31 May 2013.

On 20 November 2012, the appellants and the appellee were locked in conflict over their MSA. Believing GJA had paid USD 100,000 to Excel for tenant improvements, the appellee reimbursed the money as agreed in the MSA. The appellee testified that she expected to begin receiving rent of USD 8,666.67 per month, increasing monthly thereafter, from the Excel lease, but no such payments were made in her favour. The appellant conceded at trial that GJA had not actually paid USD 100,000 in cash to Excel and that he did not disclose to the appellee the confidential settlement agreement between GJA and Excel and their rent abatement arrangements.

Consequently, the appellee succeeded in their claim over the appellant on the basis of common-law fraud and statutory fraud under section 27.01 of the Texas Business and Commerce Code. The Texas Court found that GJA failed to notify the appellee that it did not need to be reimbursed for a USD 100,000 payment to Excel because it had never made the payment and that it had amended Excel's lease to allow for a rent abatement. This meant that the appellee's obligations flowing from the MSA, under which she was responsible for the cost of any tenant improvements, may be rendered null and void by reason of fraud.

Illustration [D]: The following is a reported case from the Polish Supreme Court, illustrating how agreements may be considered incapable of being performed. While this case does not deal specifically with an MSA (instead, an arbitration agreement is examined), the principles discerned serve as a useful analogy. In *Supreme Court (Sąd Najwyższy) Civil Chamber Decision*,[96] a case which concerned a construction contract, it was defined within the contract that its terms are to be administered by a Contract Administrator. According to its multi-tier dispute resolution clause, should a dispute concerning the performance of the contract arise, the parties are to undergo certain stages of a clearly defined

96. *Case No. V CSK 231/14* of (5 February 2015). Reported in English in the *Czech (& Central European) Yearbook of Arbitration* (2015), at 214-216.

dispute resolution process. First, the parties would have to notify the Contract Administrator of their dispute within 14 days of the time at which the dispute arose. The conciliatory commission would then examine the dispute. If the efforts of the conciliatory commission were to no avail, then an adjudicator would be appointed. In this case, A, the construction company and the claimant, sued B, the defendant, for payment of interest in accordance with the terms of the underlying contract. The Supreme Court held that it was impossible to refer the case to arbitration. This was because it found that the Contract Administrator referred to in the contract and dispute resolution clause was relieved from his duties several years earlier. There would be no other person who could be notified of the dispute between the parties and no qualified person who could initiate the dispute resolution process and the selection of arbitrators *per* the terms of the dispute resolution clause. While this case does not concern mediation, it is still highly instructive because it provides a useful example of how a privately negotiated agreement reached between parties may be viewed as incapable of being performed, for the purposes of Article 5(1)(b)(i).

Article 5(1)(b)(ii): Settlement Agreement that is not Binding, or is not Final, According to its Terms

5.39 A competent authority may refuse to enforce or recognise an iMSA if it is not binding, or is not final, *according to its terms*. This means that where there are express (or implied) terms demonstrating that the iMSA sought to be enforced or recognised is *not* a final and/or binding one, competent courts may refuse to grant relief to the party seeking its enforcement or recognition.[97] It is the drafters' intention to reverse the burden of proof as to the determination of an iMSA's binding nature. Therefore, when an iMSA is brought to a competent court for enforcement or recognition, there is an implied rebuttable presumption that a binding iMSA is sought to be enforced.[98] Consequently, the burden lies on the objecting party to prove (under an application for refusal to grant relief under Article 5(1)(b)(ii)) that its express or implied terms objectively reflect a non-binding and/or non-finalised agreement.[99]

5.40 The governing law of the indicative terms must be the proper law of the contract, which also governs the substantive obligations contained within the iMSA.[100] For the avoidance of doubt, the express (or implied) term in the iMSA which indicates its bindingness and/or finality *must not* be regarded in the same manner as dispute

97. *Ward v Keen (No 2)* [2009] WASC 369.
98. Timothy Schnabel, *The Singapore Convention on Mediation: A Framework for the Cross-Border Recognition and Enforcement of Mediated Settlements*, 19 Pepp. Disp. Resol. L.J. 1 (2019), at 42.
99. *Id.*, at 46.
100. The governing law is *not necessarily* benchmarked to the law of the State where the iMSA is brought for enforcement: Interventions of the US, Japan, Mexico and China, in UNCITRAL Audio Recordings: Working Group II (Dispute Settlement), 67th Session, 4 October 2017, 14:00-17:00.

resolution clauses (e.g., mediation clauses, arbitration clauses and exclusive jurisdiction clauses), for it embraces *all* the substantive obligations found within the iMSA. In contrast, dispute resolution clauses may be 'separable' from the substantive obligations found inside a contract (e.g., an iMSA) because the obligation to resolve disputes in the agreed manner runs parallel to all the other substantive obligations.[101] Furthermore, the fact that an iMSA only resolves a part or fraction of the parties' disputes *cannot* be used as evidence that it is not a final or binding agreement.[102] This means that settlement agreements which compromise a part or fraction of the parties' disputes may be enforceable under the Singapore Convention.

5.41 By administering Article 5(1)(b)(ii) through the lenses of the proper law of the contract, the competent courts will avoid a parochial reading of the clause. If the iMSA were governed by contract laws derived from the old and repealed sections of the French *Code civil*, the requirement of *cause* may be relevant as a matter of law,[103] under Article 1131 of the repealed *Code civil*,[104] which provided that contracts are not legally binding if there is no justification for each party's agreement.[105] For instance, Articles 1261 and 1262 of the Spanish Civil Code, which draws inspiration from the old French *Code civil*, retains the requirement of *cause* in the contract law of Spain. In contrast, if, for instance, the proper law governing the iMSA were Singapore law, it may be conceivable that an express clause declaring that an iMSA is binding and/or final may be construed as one that is, in fact, *not* binding and/or final.[106] Applying Singapore law, where sufficient contextual evidence may be adduced by the objecting party to elucidate that the iMSA, which was sought to be enforced, was conceived on the basis of a pretence or sham,[107] the competent court may in such circumstances interpret and characterise an express statement declaring its binding and/or final nature to be one that is *actually* indicative of its non-bindingness and/or non-finality. It is also noteworthy that if Singapore law were the governing law of the iMSA, those settlement agreements which are concluded in the context of social and domestic arrangements (which may also address commercial subject matters, if the parties are mediating, for

101. Nadja Alexander, *International and Comparative Mediation – Legal Perspectives*, Wolters Kluwer (2009), at 188 et seq.
102. See Interventions of the Czech Republic and Colombia, in UNCITRAL Audio Recordings: Working Group II (Dispute Settlement), 65th Session, 15 September 2016, 14:00-17:00.
103. See, for instance, under the Spanish Civil Code, Arts 1261 and 1262.
104. Art. 1131 of the *repealed Code civil* provides: 'An obligation without a cause, or based on a false cause, or an illegal cause, can have no effect.' The *Code civil* has since been modified by Ordinance No. 2016-131 of February 2016, reforming the law of contract and the general regime and proof of obligations. The requirement of *cause* has been abolished as a matter of French contract law (Irina Cvetkova, *The Abolition of the Concept of 'Causa' in French Civil Law*, 26 Bialystok Legal Stud. 91 (2021)).
105. See Eva Steiner, *French Law: A Comparative Approach*, OUP (2010), at 331.
106. See *Ye Huishi Rachel v Ng Ke Ming Jerry* [2021] SGHC 250, at [130]-[134]. Consider Hans Tjio, *When Is an Elephant a Bird?*, 18 SAcLJ 473 (2006): In this case note, Tjio interestingly observes how it has become possible in Singapore contract law that post-contractual evidence could be applied to convince a court to re-characterise a contract (i.e., applying the tools of common law contractual interpretation) which was explicitly labelled a 'sale and repurchase agreement' into a 'loan', *particularly* in situations when the contract was conceived as a form of sham, or under a pretence, in *Cheah Geok Tuan v Lie Khin Sin* [2006] 1 SLR 340.
107. See *Ye Huishi Rachel v Ng Ke Ming Jerry* [2021] SGHC 250, at [130]-[134].

instance, over a transactional dispute in a family-run business) may attract a presumption that the parties *do not intend* to create legal relations;[108] in contrast, settlement agreements concluded in the context of business and commercial arrangements engender a presumption that parties *do intend* to create legal relations.[109] These presumptions are consequential in the court's determination of whether the iMSA concluded was intended to be binding on the parties.[110]

5.42 As different legal traditions apply different nuances in the determination of whether a contract is legally binding or not, it is most sensible for the relevant competent authorities to evaluate whether an iMSA is not binding or is not final, according to its terms, with reference to the proper law of the contract.

5.43 A number of case illustrations from court judgments in Singapore, India, Australia and New Zealand are set out below.

Case Illustrations

Illustration [A]: In *Choo Ah Sam v Kieu Ka Tong*,[111] the parties had negotiated for a settlement of their dispute over some shares through an exchange of WhatsApp messages. While there was a meeting of the minds between the disputing parties, as they later proceeded to draft out the terms negotiated over WhatsApp into a document, the Singapore High Court found that there was an implied understanding between the parties that the settlement agreement would only be binding after it had been executed by the parties, namely, after the parties had signed the written settlement agreement.[112] Consequently, Justice Ang Cheng Hock found that the settlement agreement was not binding, according to its implied terms, because there was no such signature reflected on the settlement agreement.

Illustration [B]: In *Oei Hong Leong v Chew Hua Seng*,[113] the parties were at loggerheads over their stake holding in a Singapore-listed corporation and decided to meet at the home of a third party to attempt to resolve their disputes informally. The parties engaged in a brief discussion and had a friendly chat with each other at the venue, and very quickly arrived at an agreement, which was recorded (and handwritten) on a piece of paper by themselves. Essentially, the terms of the purported settlement agreement concluded would oblige one of the parties to the agreement to procure a buyer of shares in that corporation, which

108. *Gay Choon Ing v Loh Sze Ti Terence Peter* [2019] 2 SLR(R) 332, at [72], citing *Balfour v Balfour* [1919] 2 KB 571.
109. *Ibid.*, para. 72, citing *Rose and Frank Co v J R Crompton and Brothers, Ltd* [1925] AC 445.
110. *Oei Hong Leong v Chew Hua Seng* [2020] SGCA 78.
111. *Choo Ah Sam v Kieu Ka Tong* [2020] SGHC 62.
112. *Id.*, at [133].
113. *Oei Hong Leong v Chew Hua Seng* [2020] SGHC 39; *Oei Hong Leong v Chew Hua Seng* [2020] SGCA 78.

was worth more than SGD 60 million, within a month and trade them off at a premium. The Singapore High Court found that the purported settlement agreement could not be enforced, as it opined that the parties could not have intended to create legal relations with each other, when they concluded that agreement informally. This finding was affirmed by the Singapore Court of Appeal. Crucially, focusing on the unique fact pattern of the case, the courts opined that it was unlikely for the parties to have intended to bind themselves to such an onerous legal obligation (namely, to trade shares worth more than SGD 60 million within a month) under such an informal setting, with little negotiations leading up to the signing of the handwritten agreement.

Illustration [C]: In *Ye Huishi Rachel v Ng Ke Ming Jerry*,[114] the Singapore High Court found that a settlement agreement concluded between the parties, Rachel and Jerry was a sham agreement. Examining the evidence submitted by the parties in demonstrating the circumstances under which the settlement agreement was concluded, the High Court concluded that the agreement was conceived as a sham document. According to the High Court, the agreement is to be shown to investors to appease and deceive them into believing that they would pay back the money under the terms of the sham settlement agreement. Consequently, the court ruled that the settlement agreement was not enforceable, as the parties were not minded to create enforceable legal obligations under it, to begin with.

Illustration [D]: In *Mysore Cements v Svedala Barmac*,[115] the Respondent, a foreign company, contracted with the appellant, Mysore Cements Limited, for the supply and commissioning of rock crushing machines. After the failure of the machinery to crush limestone in accordance with the Respondent's assurances, the parties proceeded with conciliation proceedings. As a result, a 'Memorandum of Conciliation' recording certain terms was produced and the Respondents' representatives also gave the appellant a 'Letter of Comfort'. This 'Letter of Comfort' assured the Appellant that modification work of the crushing system will be completed by the Respondent by 30 April 1998 and further modification work will be completed by 31 August 1998. The Appellant subsequently approached the High Court of New Delhi for enforcement of a 'Letter of Comfort' and the 'Memorandum of Conciliation' through execution under the 1996 Indian Arbitration and Conciliation Act (IACA). However, the High Court dismissed the execution as the statutory requirements were not satisfied. On appeal, the Supreme Court affirmed the Delhi High Court's decision that neither one of the documents constituted a 'settlement agreement' capable of being enforced through execution under the IACA. Specifically, the court observed that the 'Letter of Comfort' did not form part of the 'Memorandum of Conciliation'. As the

114. *Ye Huishi Rachel v Ng Ke Ming Jerry* [2021] SGHC 250.
115. *Mysore Cements Ltd. v Svedala Barmac Ltd.* 2003 AIR SCW 2007.

first term inside the 'Letter of Comfort' elucidates that it was made '[i]n pursuance of' the 'Memorandum of Conciliation', the Supreme Court interpreted those words as clearly evincing the parties' intentions that the former shall not form part of the latter which, putatively, may constitute a binding instrument functioning as a settlement agreement. In this way, the court may discern that the 'Letter of Comfort' was not purposed to be binding (that is, binding on equal terms as the 'Memorandum of Conciliation') on the parties according to its terms.

Illustration [E]: There is precedent from the Supreme Court of Western Australia ruling that the constitution of a binding settlement agreement may be affected when important terms and conditions crucial to the performance of the obligations under the settlement have been omitted in its final draft. In *Ward v Keen (No 2)*,[116] the parties had different views as to whether a binding settlement agreement had been derived at the end of a mediation session. While the parties had reached a consensus that the first defendant would pay a sum of AUD 500,000 without interest in a given time frame of three months and that he could pay at his election that sum in four instalments, there was no consensus reflected in the settlement agreement as to several critical issues in relation to the payment. The court could not discern when the parties agreed that the first instalment would be paid, when the subsequent three instalments would be paid and how the agreed instalment arrangement would operate with respect to the payee's right to pay the sum of money in three months without incurring any interest liability.[117] Justice Murphy ruled, 'These matters were, in my view, objectively material in the circumstances to the constitution of a binding [settlement agreement]. They were objectively relevant to "price", and they assumed particular relevance in this matter given that judgment could be entered if payment were not made. They are matters for negotiation and agreement between the parties [at mediation], which cannot be remedied by the court employing techniques of contractual construction or by the court ascertaining the existence of implied terms.'[118] As the court found no further evidence of consensus as to those critical terms, Justice Murphy ruled that the settlement agreement was neither unambiguous nor sufficiently comprehensive to constitute a binding agreement.

Illustration [F]: The New Zealand High Court case of *Fletcher Challenge Energy Ltd v Electrical Corporation of New Zealand Ltd*[119] provides a useful contrast to *Ward v Keen (No 2)*. Although it does not deal with mediation, it provides useful insights for the mediation field. The case concerned negotiations for the acquisition of shares in a gas field and for the long-term supply of gas. There was an

116. *Ward v Keen (No 2)* [2009] WASC 369.
117. *Id.*, at para. 84.
118. *Id.*, at para. 85.
119. *Fletcher Challenge Energy Ltd v Electrical Corporation of New Zealand Ltd* [2001] 2 NZLR 219.

exchange of correspondence, a letter signed by the CEO agreeing to the deal, followed by a heads of agreement (HOA). The HOA contained a clause requiring parties to use all reasonable endeavours to complete a full agreement. A full agreement was not reached and the question was whether or not there was an enforceable agreement and, if so, whether it had been breached. The court stated that where a contract shows an intention to be bound, the court will give effect to this, provided there is agreement on essential terms. Further, a contract is not necessarily incomplete if particular terms are not agreed or remain to be agreed provided the essential terms are clear. Thus, it is possible for parties to satisfy the intention to be bound by an informal document even if a more formal agreement is contemplated. In this case, the court decided that the parties' agreement was not incomplete. While it ruled that certain terms – such as *force majeure*, minimum flow rates and a start date for gas supply – were 'not agreed' or 'to be agreed', they were not essential or necessary to make the contract binding and workable and the court could by applying contractual construction tools read in the reasonable terms if necessary.

Article 5(1)(b)(iii): Settlement Agreement that has been Subsequently Modified

5.44 A competent authority may refuse to enforce an iMSA if it has subsequently been modified. Modifications as to the iMSA's terms may take many forms: it could be as simple as requesting for a time extension to fulfil some payment obligations or it could involve further set-offs in obligations between parties which could require further negotiations. It follows that the original iMSA may be refused enforcement. It complements the provision for refusal of enforcement by reason of inoperability found in Article 5(1)(b)(i) as analysed earlier: by forming a subsequent agreement to amend its terms, effectively, parties are minded to waive their rights pursuing all specific obligations under *that* original iMSA without reference to the revised terms. Only the *final* iMSA may be enforced under the Singapore Convention. To distinguish Article 5(1)(b)(i) from Article 5(1)(b)(iii), it may be posited that the former envisions the formation of a subsequent compromise agreement, *completely bypassing* the original iMSA rendering it 'inoperable', while the latter envisions some agreed variations made to the original terms of a less-radical nature. But in any circumstance, it should nevertheless be noteworthy that the Singapore Convention does not eschew overlapping Article 5 defences, and these two defences may be applied successfully to one given factual pattern.[120]

120. Report of Working Group II (Dispute Settlement) on the Work of its 68th Session, (5-9 February 2018), A/CN.9/934 (2018), at para. 65. Available at http://undocs.org/A/CN.9/934 (Accessed 17 May 2022).

5.45 To determine if the iMSA has indeed been modified, the proper law of the original and revised iMSA should first be identified. If the governing law were Singapore law[121] or English law,[122] parties may possibly dispute the presence of any effective modification, but for want of consideration.[123] If the iMSA contains a 'no oral modifications' clause ('NOM clause'),[124] English law would dictate that it would be given full effect, such that any subsequent variations to that iMSA would be treated as *invalid*, unless it complies with the formalities set out by that NOM clause (for instance, for such variations to be documented on paper and signed by all parties involved) and estoppel is not available to the parties;[125] in other words, the Article 5(1)(b)(iii) defence would be unavailable to the parties relying on the modification made to the iMSA, if that modification does not comply with the NOM clause. Similarly, if the applicable law contains the same provisions as Article 2.1.18 of the UNIDROIT Principles of International Commercial Contracts (4th Edition, 2016),[126] any provisions setting out precisely written formalities contained in the original iMSA must be adhered to, in order for a subsequent iMSA (which modifies the terms of the original) to be deemed enforceable. Analysing party objections to iMSA enforcement with the proper law applied under Article 5(1)(b)(iii), the competent courts would administer it with the necessary nuance and avoid parochialism.

---

121. See Chee Ho Tham, *Discharge by Agreement*, in Andrew Phang (Gen Ed.), The Law of Contract in Singapore, Academy Publishing (2012) at paras 18.042 et seq.; Tham reports the state of Singapore law, '[P]arties could effect a discharge of a contract through a subsequent agreement which may take the form of [...] an exchange of mutual promises that the terms of the original contract are no longer to bind either of them.'

    Also see Pey Woan Lee, *Consideration*, in Andrew Phang (Gen Ed.), The Law of Contract in Singapore, Academy Publishing (2012), at paras 04.054-04.061.
122. See Edwin Peel, *Tritel on the Law of Contract* (15th ed.), Sweet & Maxwell (2020), at para. [3-062]; *Stead v Dawber* (1839) 10 A. & E. 57, at 66.
123. It also bears reiterating Briggs' theory, discussed above, that a finding that the putatively modified iMSA was not so modified owing to a want of consideration should not affect the determination of the proper law of that putative agreement. This is because the 'process of identifying the proper law of a contract and determination by that law of the validity of the contract [are theoretically two separate exercises]' (Adrian Briggs, *The Formation of International Contracts*, Lloyd's Maritime and Commercial Law Quarterly 192 (1990), especially at 203).
124. 'No oral modifications' clauses are commonly found in building contracts. They serve to set out for the parties the written formalities required to make a valid variation to the terms of their contractual agreement and oftentimes this excludes the possibility that the parties may vary their contract by verbal or oral agreement. An example of such a clause is observed in *Rock Advertising Ltd v MWB Business Exchange Centres Ltd* [2018] UKSC 24, at para. 2: 'This Licence sets out all of the terms as agreed between MWB and licensee. No other representations or terms shall apply or form part of this Licence. All variations to this Licence must be agreed, set out in writing and signed on behalf of both parties before they take effect.'
125. *MWB Business Exchange Centres Ltd v Rock Advertising Ltd* [2018] UKSC 24.
126. Art. 2.1.18 of the UNIDROT Principles of International Commercial Contracts (4th Ed.) (2016) provides: 'A contract in writing which contains a clause requiring any modification or termination by agreement to be in a particular form may not be otherwise modified or terminated. However, a party may be precluded by its conduct from asserting such a clause to the extent that the other party has reasonably acted in reliance on that conduct.'

Case Illustration

Martin Pty Ltd (Martin) runs a manufacturing business in Utopia. It purchases raw materials from *Zelmerlöw AB* (Zelmerlöw), a company incorporated in Ruritania. Because of a fraud perpetrated by one of its employees, Zelmerlöw failed to deliver a large order of raw materials in time to Martin, causing the latter significant losses in revenue. As both parties intend to continue their business relationship because of long-standing goodwill, they agree to mediate their dispute. Zelmerlöw agrees to set off some debts owed by Martin when the mediation is concluded and this is reflected in the iMSA that was drafted and finalised. The iMSA does not contain a NOM clause. However, two months after the conclusion of the iMSA, Zelmerlöw runs into cash flow problems. They propose to Martin for a renegotiation at the offices of the same mediation service provider of the terms of the iMSA, which Martin agrees to participate in. A second round of mediation yields the following modified terms: Zelmerlöw would pay USD 500,000 in damages to Martin, but in monthly instalments beginning one calendar year after the conclusion of the second iMSA. In the event that Martin wishes to take the iMSA into a competent authority of a Party to the Singapore Convention for enforcement, it follows that the *original* iMSA (that is, the debt set-off agreement) may be refused enforcement under Article 5(1)(b)(iii) of the Singapore Convention as it has subsequently been modified.

Article 5(1)(c)(i): Obligations in the Settlement Agreement have been Performed

5.46 A competent authority may refuse to enforce an iMSA if the obligations in the settlement agreement have been performed. This clause envisages the possibility of parties making a doubled claim. Where the obligations found in the iMSA have been discharged by performance, parties may not seek the assistance of a competent court to enforce those obligations that have already been discharged. It may generally be understood that discharge by performance occurs when those obligations stated in the iMSA have been *precisely* and *exactly* performed by the parties.[127]

5.47 Nevertheless, the competent authorities should refer to the proper law governing the iMSA before making a determination as to whether the obligations contained therein have been discharged by performance. For instance, if the governing law were Singapore or English law, there may be some exceptions to the rule on precise and exact performance which ought to be considered before the court relies on this provision to deny relief: notably, the tolerance of some *de minimis* deviations[128] and

127. Chee Ho Tham, *Discharge by Performance or Operation of Law*, in Andrew Phang (Gen Ed.), The Law of Contract in Singapore, Academy Publishing (2012), at para. 16.007.

128. *Id.*, at paras 16.009-16.011; and see *Arcos Ltd v E A Ronaasen & Son* [1933] AC 470, at 479-480. It seems that the common law position (and especially the Singapore position) recognises that

recognition of substantial discharge by performance[129] may assist the party seeking a denial of relief, owing to the performance of those obligations found in the iMSA. In contrast, the tolerance of *de minimis* deviations is generally not accepted under German contract law. As such, a nuanced approach is preferred by the competent courts, taking into consideration the proper law of the iMSA *before* exercising their prerogative to refuse relief under this limb of Article 5(1)(c)(i).

Case Illustration

In *Dalmation Nominees v Franko Marinovich*,[130] the parties had agreed to settle a land-related dispute at mediation. A settlement agreement was reached, where the plaintiff had agreed to perform some works on their property at their own cost and obtain the necessary approvals and certificates of completion of works from either a statutory authority or the Shire Engineer (also noteworthy is the clause in the settlement agreement which provided that the decision made by the Shire Engineer shall be final). The plaintiff had carried out the works envisaged by the settlement agreement and also obtained the necessary certificate of compliance and completion from the Shire Engineer. The defendant nevertheless applied to the Supreme Court of Western Australia to obtain specific performance of the works *already* certified by the Shire Engineer, claiming that the precise measurements of the plaintiff's work were not satisfied: namely that the length of an open drain which the plaintiff should construct was not exactly 2 meters wide and 1.2 meters in depth. Applying principles of Australian contract law, Justice Murray ruled that the satisfaction of the precise measurements upon a proper construing of the settlement agreement did not form the crux of the contract. Instead, the court ruled that the settlement agreement may be deemed to have been properly complied with and discharged upon receipt of the conclusive certification provided by the Shire Engineer. Hence the claim for enforcement of

'entirely precise performance in exact conformity with that which is required by the terms of a contract is impossible, and the common law pragmatically recognises this. To begin with, the common law recognises that minor shortfalls and deviations in performance from the precise requirements of the contractual terms may, nevertheless, be treated *as if* precise performance had been rendered. Therefore, although in principle, *any* deviation from the performance specified in the terms of the contract would permit the party not in default to deny that the contract had been performed, where that deviation is viewed by the courts as being "*de minimis*", the party not in default will be precluded from making such denial'. (Pearlie Koh and Andrew Phang, *Express and Implied Terms*, in Andrew Phang (Gen Ed.), The Law of Contract in Singapore, Academy Publishing (2012), at para. 6.009).

129. Consider Chee Ho Tham, *Discharge by Performance or Operation of Law*, in Andrew Phang (Gen Ed.), The Law of Contract in Singapore, Academy Publishing (2012), at paras 16.055-16.070. Also consider the criticisms directed at the substantial performance exception in *Anson's Law of Contract*, in Jack Beatson et al., Anson's Law of Contract (29th Ed.), OUP (2010), at 455.
130. *Dalmation Nominees Pty Ltd v Franko Marinovich* [1998] WASC 354.

the MSA agreement was dismissed because its terms have been performed and discharged.

Article 5(1)(c)(ii): Obligations in the Settlement Agreement are not Clear or Comprehensible

5.48 A competent authority may refuse to enforce an iMSA if it is not capable of being enforced because it is not clear and comprehensible. As Schnabel clarifies: 'If the competent authority can determine whether the mediated settlement provides for an obligation, and can adequately frame its order providing relief, then this ground for refusal does not apply; the exception is meant only to protect competent authorities from being forced to act in situations in which they truly do not know what relief to provide.'[131] Proposed by the German delegation on WG II, this provision addresses the issue of enforcing vague or insufficiently defined terms found in the iMSA.[132] If a competent authority, after applying the appropriate contractual construction techniques,[133] is unable to resolve the apparent ambiguity, it may consequently refuse to enforce the iMSA. For instance, if a party to the mediation has agreed to apologise to the other party, the obligations reflected in the written settlement agreement should be worded *precisely* to the approximate effect that 'Nicole Sdn Bhd (Nicole) shall publish [x] words in the [y] local newspaper and on their social media platforms, such as [z], as a form of apology to Chrystal Pte Ltd (Chrystal), in return for Chrystal's promise to discontinue [zz] proceedings'. To simplistically write that 'Nicole shall apologise to Chrystal' would likely be too unclear for enforcement to be possible: it is unlikely in this case for the competent authorities to be able to discern what relief it may provide to either party in the event of non-compliance.

5.49 When construing the apparently ambiguous terms, prudent legal intuition dictates that it should be imperative for the court to first discern the proper law of the contract: the conflict of laws considerations seem identical to when the competent authority is asked to refuse relief under Article 5(1)(b)(ii), as analysed above, for the court must similarly grapple with construing[134] the terms of the iMSA.

131. Timothy Schnabel, *The Singapore Convention on Mediation: A Framework for the Cross-Border Recognition and Enforcement of Mediated Settlements*, 19 Pepp. Disp. Resol. L.J. 1 (2019), at 48.
132. See Intervention of Germany, in UNCITRAL Audio Recordings: Working Group II (Dispute Settlement), 67th Session, 3 October 2017, 09:30-12:30; and Intervention of Germany, in UNCITRAL Audio Recordings: Working Group II (Dispute Settlement), 67th Session, 5 October 2017, 09:30-12:30.
133. It bears emphasis that this involves the exercise of *both* contractual interpretation and implication in general. See Mindy Chen-Wishart, *Contract Law* (5th Ed.), OUP (2015), at 392-414.
134. This is an issue of contractual construction: Michael Furmston and Gregory Tolhurst, Contract Formation – Law and Practice, OUP (2010), at para. 11.04; but for completeness, consider all of 'Chapter 11 – Certainty and Completeness'. Normally, contracts in English law may be void for uncertainty and incompleteness, Michael Furmston and Gregory Tolhurst, Contract Formation – Law and Practice, OUP (2010), at para. 11.03; citing *Whitlock v Brew* (1968) 11 CLR 445; *G Scammell & Nephew Ltd v Ouston* [1941] AC 251), hence when asked to refuse relief under

5.50 However, owing to the broad phrasing of the words 'not clear and comprehensible', it is feared that an overly generous interpretation, which is quite conceivable even with reference to the proper law of the iMSA, may arise, narrowing the legal reach of the Singapore Convention.[135] It may be possible to administer the validation principle[136] (as examined earlier[137] when the defence of incapacity was discussed) to determine if the terms of the iMSA are (or are not) clear and comprehensible. Consequently, the competent authority may consider if the iMSA would have been upheld under any of the possible applicable laws it may be subject to, beyond its proper governing law, when it is asked to refuse enforcement under Article 5(1)(c)(ii).

5.51 Two case illustrations from judgments in Singapore and India are set out below.

Case Illustrations

Illustration [A]: This illustration from the Singapore High Court may be a useful reference for competent authorities when they are presented with unclear or incomprehensible terms to construe. In *Jumaiah bte Amir v Salim bin Abdul Rashid*,[138] the parties had reached a settlement agreement after mediation with respect to a real estate deal which fell through in 2016. In the settlement agreement, Salim was given the option to purchase the disputed property at SGD 3 million if he was unable to find another party to purchase it by 31 December 2017; but if he were to successfully find a purchaser who was willing to pay more than SGD 3 million for it, he was entitled to keep the profits of the deal (that is, the difference between the sale price and SGD 3 million). In the meantime, Salim agreed to pay a monthly sum of SGD 9000 in rent to Jumaiah and Ezzad beginning from 1 August 2017 until 'the date of Completion of the sale of the Property' (the words quoted were the express terms reflected in the MSA). Salim was unsuccessful in selling the property by 31 December 2017. On 2 January 2018, he decided not to exercise his option of purchasing the property and returned vacant possession of it to Jumaiah and Ezzad on 8 January 2018. Thereafter Salim ceased making the monthly rental payments. Jumiah and Ezzad sold the property on 30 April 2018. Jumaiah and Ezzad filed a suit in the Singapore High Court to enforce Salim's alleged obligation under the settlement

Art. 5(1)(c), the competent authorities should also consider if a refusal of relief may be granted under Art. 5(1)(b)(i) as well, as the iMSA may be void, where English law is the governing law of the contract as well. The WG II anticipates such overlaps to happen (Report of Working Group II (Dispute Settlement) on the Work of its 68th Session (19 February 2018), A/CN.9/934 (2018), at para. 65. Available at http://undocs.org/A/CN.9/934 (Accessed 17 May 2022).

135. See Interventions of Canada and the Forum for International Conciliation and Arbitration (FICA), in UNCITRAL Audio Recordings: Working Group II (Dispute Settlement), 67th Session, 4 October 2017, 09:00-12:30.
136. See *Enka Insaat ve Sanayi AS v OOO Insurance Company Chubb* [2020] UKSC 38, at paras 95 et seq.
137. See para. 5.27 above.
138. *Jumaiah bte Amir and another v Salim bin Abdul Rashid* [2019] SGHC 63.

agreement to pay the monthly rental sum of SGD 9000 between January to 30 April 2018 (which was the date of Completion of the sale of the Property). Justice Choo Han Teck ruled that there was ambiguity in the term in the settlement agreement which reflected Salim's obligations to pay Jumiah and Ezzad rent until 'the date of Completion of the sale of the Property'. Had the parties intended that Salim would continue to make such payments *after* he had delivered vacant possession of the property concerned, Justice Choo thought that it should have been specifically articulated in the MSA. As the term in the settlement agreement sought to be enforced was not clearly expressed, the Singapore High Court may refuse to enforce it. The sentiment of the court is also buttressed by the rule of *contra proferentum*: that any ambiguity subsisting in contractual terms will be construed against the maker of the document. In this case, Jumaiah and Ezzad, who sought to rely on the ambiguity and benefit from it, were found by the Singapore High Court to be the 'makers' of the ambiguous terms in the settlement agreement. Consequently, the ambiguity will be construed against their favour (that is, they were unsuccessful in their claims to enforce the obligations to pay a monthly rent against Salim).

Illustration [B]: In *Mysore Cements v Svedala Barmac*,[139] the Respondent, a foreign company, contracted with the appellant, Mysore Cements Limited, for the supply and commissioning of rock crushing machines. After the failure of the machinery to crush limestone in accordance with the Respondent's assurances, the parties proceeded to conciliation proceedings. A 'Memorandum of Conciliation' recording the agreed terms between parties resulting from the conciliation was produced and the Respondents' representatives also provided the appellant with a 'Letter of Comfort'. This 'Letter of Comfort' assured the Appellant that modification work of the crushing system will be completed by the Respondent by 30 April 1998 and further modification work will be completed by 31 August 1998. The Appellant subsequently approached the High Court of New Delhi for enforcement of a 'Letter of Comfort' and the 'Memorandum of Conciliation' through execution. However, the High Court dismissed the execution under the 1996 Indian Arbitration and Conciliation Act. On appeal, the Supreme Court affirmed the Delhi High Court's decision and held that neither of the documents constituted a 'settlement agreement' capable of being enforced through execution. Specifically, the 'Memorandum of Conciliation' lacked important terms such as compensation terms. For instance, it was not stated what would follow in the case of a default of completion of the modification work. Consequently, the High Court was unable to frame a proper enforcement order for relief in the case of non-compliance with the 'Memorandum of Conciliation'. This is an illustrative example of a settlement agreement where its terms may be unenforceable because they are unclear or uncertain.

139. *Mysore Cements Ltd. v Svedala Barmac Ltd.* 2003 AIR SCW 2007.

Article 5(1)(d): Granting Relief would be Contrary to the Terms of the Settlement Agreement

5.52 Pursuant to Article 5(1)(d) of the Singapore Convention, a competent authority may refuse to enforce an iMSA if granting relief would be directly inconsistent with the terms of the settlement agreement. This reflects the importance of party autonomy at mediation: for mediation is a means to empower disputing parties to privately (that is, outside the realm of the judicial system) arrive at a resolution to their conflicts on their own terms, it would defeat the fundamental functions of mediation (and, by implication, the Singapore Convention) if iMSAs may be enforced in manners contrary to the terms reflected within.[140]

5.53 This article was initially set aside during the WG II's meetings over the course of 2017, but reappeared in the concluded Convention draft of February 2018.

5.54 First, Article 5(1)(d) applies where parties to an iMSA agree to privately opt-out[141] of the Singapore Convention's applicability – that is, if they were to agree in the express and certain terms to exclude the application of the Singapore Convention *vis-à-vis* their iMSA – the competent courts may refuse its enforcement under the Singapore Convention's terms. To enforce the iMSA under the Singapore Convention would be contrary to the terms of the settlement agreement.[142] The ability for commercial parties to expressly opt-out of a United Nations (UN) Convention is also observed in Article 6 of the UN Convention on Contracts for the International Sale of Goods (CISG).[143] Although articles of the Singapore Convention do not expressly provide that parties may, by private agreement, opt-out of its enforcement mechanism (that is, with the same degree of specificity as Article 6 of the CISG), there is no reason in principle to deny commercial parties their autonomy to exclude its application,[144] barring legislative intervention from the individual States or other Parties to the Convention, for the respective State legislatures are seized with the prerogative to elevate the status of the Singapore Convention to that of a forum mandatory law upon its ratification.

5.55 Second, according to the official report from its 68th meeting, Article 5(1)(d) may apply where the obligations in a settlement agreement would be conditional or

140. Timothy Schnabel, *The Singapore Convention on Mediation: A Framework for the Cross-Border Recognition and Enforcement of Mediated Settlements*, 19 Pepp. Disp. Resol. L.J. 1 (2019), at 48; and see Intervention of the US, in UNCITRAL Audio Recordings: Working Group II (Dispute Settlement) 65th Session, 15 September 2016, 14:00-17:00.
141. Assuming that the Singapore Convention applies by default in the jurisdiction as the Party to the Convention has not made any Art. 8 reservations.
142. Report of Working Group II (Dispute Settlement) on the Work of its 68th Session (19 February 2018), A/CN.9/934 (2018), at para. 78. Available at http://undocs.org/A/CN.9/934 (Accessed 17 May 2022).
143. Art. 6 reads, 'The parties may exclude the application of this Convention or, subject to article 12, derogate from or vary the effect of any of its provisions.'
144. See Interventions of the US, Israel and the Netherlands, in UNCITRAL Audio Recordings: Working Group II (Dispute Settlement), 68th Session, 5 February 2018, 15:00-18:00.

reciprocal, or where parties' non-performance could be justified for a variety of reasons anticipated by the iMSA.[145] It appears that parties may successfully plead this defence upon the fulfilment (or, conversely, owing to non-fulfilment) of contingent conditions (that is, conditions precedent[146] or conditions subsequent); this should also encompass the occurrence of a supervening event anticipated by a *force majeure* clause[147] contained within the iMSA.

5.56 The governing law of the indicative contingent terms must be the proper law of the iMSA; the proper law should also assist the competent authority to establish whether obligations contained within the iMSA have been discharged when an event constituting a *force majeure* occurs. However, owing to the broad phrasing of the article, it is observed that this is not the only conflict of laws consideration which arises.

5.57 As Article 5(1)(d) is generally worded, it is conceivable that jurisdictional issues may inadvertently arise when enforcement is sought under the Singapore Convention. Such a conundrum may be anticipated if the parties agree to insert a choice of forum clause prorogating and derogating jurisdictions under which the iMSA may be enforced. This is in contrast with dispute resolution provisions which may be inserted into iMSAs designating forums for the parties to proceed to resolve ambiguities in its implementation, for instance, where a valuation of assets is necessary before the obligations under the settlement may be carried out.[148] As there is no clear definition in the Singapore Convention that the 'terms of the settlement agreement' would exclude jurisdiction clauses, it may be open to the competent courts to refuse enforcement under Article 5(1)(d), but for a want of jurisdiction: enforcement could contradict that jurisdiction clause, which may be considered a '[term] of the settlement agreement'

145. Report of Working Group II (Dispute Settlement) on the Work of its 68th Session, (19 February 2018), A/CN.9/934, (2018), at para. 57. Available at http://undocs.org/A/CN.9/934 (Accessed 17 May 2022).
146. Take, for instance, sometimes parties might have agreed in their iMSA that they must return to the mediator before seeking enforcement relief from the Singapore Convention in court.
147. Edwin Peel, *Treitel on The Law of Contract* (15th Ed.), Sweet & Maxwell (2020), at para. 19-079; also see Chee Ho Tham, *Discharge by Agreement*, in Andrew Phang (Gen Ed.), The Law of Contract in Singapore, Academy Publishing (2012), at paras 18.002-18.041.
    Consider *Channel Island Ferries Ltd v Sealink UK Ltd* [1988] 1 Lloyd's Rep 323; *The Kriti Rex* [1996] 2 Lloyd's Rep 171; *RDC Concrete Pte Ltd v Sato Kogyo (S) Pte Ltd* [2007] 4 SLR(R) 413. In French law, events of *force majeure* are regulated by Art. 1195 of the *Code civil* (as modified by Ordinance no. 2016-131 of February 2016, reforming the law of contract and the general regime and proof of obligations): see Mustapha Mekki, *The French Reform of Contract Law: The Art of Redoing Without Undoing*, 10(1) J. Civil L. Stud. 224, at para. 24. It bears further note that the effect of such *force majeure* clauses on the iMSA would turn on a proper construction of that clause, in accordance with its governing law. Depending on its construction, it is possible that the parties' obligations under the iMSA may be automatically discharged (e.g., *Tsakiroglou & Co v Noblee Thorl GmbH* [1962] AC 93 (English law)) or that the *force majeure* provision could give rise to one of the parties obtaining an option to cancel the agreement (e.g., *Bank Line Ltd v Arthur Capel & Co* [1919] AC 435 (English law)). In French law, Art. 1195 of the *Code civil* sets out the consequences of *force majeure*.
148. See *Retrospect Investment (S) Pte Ltd v Lateral Solutions Pte Ltd* [2020] 1 SLR 763. Also see Nadja Alexander and Shouyu Chong, *Mediation and Appropriate Dispute Resolution*, 21 SAL Ann. Rev. 724 (2020), at para. 23.49.

broadly defined.[149] In this way, it may be applied to give effect to a valid dispute resolution clause.[150]

5.58 As a result, parties are placed at a crossroads. Being empowered to insert a jurisdiction clause in an iMSA is attractive, if one were to consider the possibilities for compromise when a deadlock occurs. Such flexibility could also be said to give rise to party autonomy to the fullest extent at the mediation table. However, there is potential for parties to abuse the insertion of dispute resolution provisions, to exploit it as a back-door method to stifle the expedited international enforcement mechanism of the Singapore Convention. This could lead to the ironic situation where disputing parties end up litigating over what was thought to be resolved at mediation. Furthermore, what is to prevent a recalcitrant party to the iMSA from frustrating the enforcement process by siphoning off its assets into the jurisdiction which has been excluded from enforcement?[151]

5.59 Intuitively, the words 'terms of the settlement agreement' under Article 5(1)(d) may be interpreted to exclude the consideration of jurisdiction agreements,[152] for it could defeat the spirit of the Convention if the converse holds true. In September 2016, during the WG II's 65th Session in Vienna, the committee reported that 'the wording [of what is now Article 5(1)(d)] was acceptable but might need further elaboration to provide a clear meaning and scope [...] as it should not inadvertently introduce defences not contemplated'.[153] There remains a serious want for clarification, as this yields a potential unintended escape route for parties to circumvent its effect.

149. See Timothy Schnabel, *The Singapore Convention on Mediation: A Framework for the Cross-Border Recognition and Enforcement of Mediated Settlements*, 19 Pepp. Disp. Resol. L.J. 1 (2019), at 49.
150. See Vakho Giorgadze, *Dispute Resolution Clauses and the Enforcement of International Mediated Settlement Agreements under the Singapore Convention on Mediation*, TDM 3 (2021); and Nadja Alexander and Shouyu Chong, *Leading the Way for the Recognition and Enforcement of International Mediated Settlement Agreements – The Singapore Convention on Mediation Act 2020*, 34 SAcLJ 1 (2022), at para. 59.
151. To clarify, this scenario is quite unlike the case where parties agree to exclude the Convention's application (i.e., they have agreed to opt out of the Convention's applicability) to their iMSA by express terms. Even in so doing, they would still be able to enforce their iMSA through other means, such as through private law remedies, within jurisdiction.
152. See Report of Working Group II (Dispute Settlement) on the Work of its 68th Session (19 February 2018) A/CN.9/934 (2018), at para. 95, where the WG II explained that parties should not be able to exploit what is Art. 5(1)(d) in its present state to resist enforcement 'based on that ground if the settlement agreement contained a *dispute resolution clause*' (emphasis added). However, they failed to consider specifically if Art. 5(1)(d) may be applied *vis-à-vis* exclusive jurisdiction agreements (i.e., parties agree to refrain from enforcement proceedings in certain jurisdictions).
153. Report of Working Group II (Dispute Settlement) on the Work of its 68th Session (19 February 2018), A/CN.9/934 (2018), at para. 98. Available at http://undocs.org/A/CN.9/934 (Accessed 17 May 2022).

Case Illustration

With respect to settlement agreements which would come into being only upon the fulfilment of some stated conditions precedent, the Australian case of *Sebastian v Rail Infrastructure Corp*[154] is instructive. Here, the parties involved had concluded a settlement agreement after a mediation of certain complaints. The parties had executed a 'Principles of Agreement' document. However, the respondent's solicitor prepared a Deed of Release which was never signed. The performance of the obligations reflected in the settlement agreement was found to be conditional upon the execution of that deed. If the condition precedent was not satisfied, there is a good argument that granting enforcement relief with respect to the settlement agreement would be contrary to its terms.

154. *Sebastian v Rail Infrastructure Corp* [2005] NSWADT 281.

MEDIATOR CONDUCT-RELATED GROUNDS FOR REFUSAL

Article 5. Grounds for Refusing to Grant Relief

1. The competent authority of the Party to the Convention where relief is sought under article 4 may refuse to grant relief at the request of the party against whom the relief is sought only if that party furnishes to the competent authority proof that:

[...]

(e) There was a serious breach by the mediator of standards applicable to the mediator or the mediation without which breach that party would not have entered into the settlement agreement; or

(f) There was a failure by the mediator to disclose to the parties circumstances that raise justifiable doubts as to the mediator's impartiality or independence and such failure to disclose had a material impact or undue influence on a party without which failure that party would not have entered into the settlement agreement.

[...]

COMMENTARY

Mediator Conduct-Related Grounds

5.60 In this commentary, the mediator conduct-related grounds for refusing to grant relief will be discussed in turn.

Article 5(1)(e) and (f): Mediator Conduct and Breach of Mediator Standards

5.61 The Convention provides two grounds for refusal related to mediator (mis-) conduct.

5.62 Article 5(1)(e) identifies the first mediator conduct-related ground for refusal as 'a serious breach by the mediator of standards applicable to the mediator or the mediation without which breach that party would not have entered into the settlement agreement'.

5.63 Article 5(1)(f) identifies the second mediator conduct-related ground for refusal as 'a failure by the mediator to disclose to the parties circumstances that raise justifiable doubts as to the mediator's impartiality or independence [where] [...] such failure to disclose had a material impact or undue influence on a party without which failure that party would not have entered into the settlement agreement'.

5.64 Before examining these provisions, it is useful to offer some background to the topic of professional mediator ethical standards.

Mediator Standards: Background

5.65 Mediation is generally conducted behind closed doors on a private and confidential basis. As a result, the risk that unethical behaviour might occur increases. Hinshaw offers a disturbing analysis of *Gary J. Karpin*, an attorney in Vermont, US, who, after being disbarred for conduct that the Professional Conduct Board described as 'so significant and wide-ranging that he is a threat to the public, the profession, the courts, and his clients',[155] moved to Arizona and established himself as a divorce mediator. After several years and multiple complaints from clients, Karpin was eventually charged with 25 counts of theft by means of material misrepresentation (for which the jury found him guilty of 23 counts) and one count of fraudulent schemes and artifices (for which the jury found him guilty).

5.66 Still in the US, in *Everett v Morgan*,[156] a consent decree was set aside when it came to light that the parties' mediator was not a mediator but a convicted felon and a friend of the ex-husband posing as a mediator. The 'mediator' not only convinced the ex-wife to discharge her attorney but also that the amount of child support due was significantly less than what she was seeking.[157]

5.67 Fraudulent cases aside, there are also instances of alleged mediator negligence, albeit it being very few. By way of example, there have been allegations of coercion,[158] undue influence,[159] bias by mediators,[160] and failure to disclose[161] and advise[162] on various matters. These cases will be examined below.

5.68 Ironically, it has often been lawyers arguing against the regulation of mediators and against setting credentialing and practice standards.[163] Bar associations and law societies historically resisted the introduction of mediator accreditation in many countries. For example, in 2012, the Bay Area Lawyers for Individual Freedom proposed legislation to the California Conference of Bar Associations (CCBA), whose work involves debating and promoting solutions to law-related issues for the benefit of

155. Art Hinshaw, *Regulating Mediators*, 21 Harv. Neg. L. Rev. 163 (2016), at 179, footnote 115.
156. *Deborah Gail Davis Morgan Everett v Charles Scotty Morgan*, No. E2007-01491-COA-R3-CV (Tenn. Ct. App. 16 January 2009).
157. Art Hinshaw, *Regulating Mediators*, 21 Harv. Neg. L. Rev. 163 (2016), at 185, footnote 170.
158. See, for example, *Pittorino v Meynert* [2002] WASC 76.
159. See, for example, *Olam v Congress Mortgage Co* 68 F Supp 2d 1110 (ND Cal 1999).
160. See, for example, *SITA v Watson Wyatt: Maxwell Batley Pt 20 Defendants* [2002] EWHC 2401/2025 (Ch).
161. See, for example, *CEATS, Inc. v Continental Airlines, Inc.*, No. 13-1529 (Fed. Cir. 24 June 2014).
162. See, for example, *Lange v Marshall*, 1981 622 S.W.2d 237.
163. While the focus is on standards of mediator conduct or practice and not on credentialing, these topics may be connected. For example, certain mediator institutions may issue mediator standards with the intention that they only apply to mediators with certain credentialing: see, for example, Australia, where the Practice Standards only apply to mediators accredited under the National Mediator Accreditation Scheme.

Californians. The proposed legislation would have established minimum qualifications for mediators, including completing 40 hours of mediation training and holding a law degree or specialised graduate degree in a field directly related to the subject matter of the mediation. It also named the State Bar of California as the certifying and regulating body.[164] The CCBA rejected the proposal. One of the bases of disapproval was by the CCBA's Committee on Alternative Dispute Resolution (ADR), which argued that requiring the State Bar to regulate non-attorneys was outside its mission and arguably beyond its regulatory jurisdiction.

5.69 Many bar associations and law societies consider mediation a specialised form of legal practice rather than a distinct, independent profession. Accordingly, it is not unusual for legal professional bodies to issue ethical and practice guidelines for their own lawyer members who mediate[165] rather than working towards shared ethical codes, such as those provided by dedicated mediation service providers and standards bodies.[166]

5.70 Since 2000, there has been a significant growth in national mediator credentialing and practice schemes around the world. These mediator schemes set assessment protocols and continuing training requirements for the formal recognition of professional mediators in that jurisdiction, uniform standards for practice and codes of conduct. National mediator credentialing and practice schemes may be legislative (e.g., in Austria and Vietnam),[167] industry- or institution-based (e.g., in Australia and Hong Kong),[168] or a combination of both (e.g., in Germany and Singapore).[169] At the same time, many countries do not have uniform mediator standards.[170] Rather,

164. See Conference of California Bar Associations, *Resolution 05-01-2012*, https://ccba.law/wp-content/uploads/Archives/Resolutions/CCBA-2012-All-Resolutions.pdf (Accessed 31 March 2022).
165. See, for example, in Australia: Queensland Law Society, *Standards of Conduct for Solicitor Mediators*, 1996; in England and Wales: Law Society Code of Practice, Civil and Commercial Mediation Accreditation Scheme, 2011.
166. See, for example, in Singapore, the Singapore International Mediation Institute (SIMI)'s Code of Professional Conduct for SIMI Mediators; in Hong Kong, see the Hong Kong Mediation Code; in Australia, see the Practice Standards of the National Mediator Accreditation System; in the US, see JAMS' Mediation Ethics Guidelines and the International Institute for Conflict Prevention and Resolution's Model Rule for the Lawyer as Third-Party Neutral; in Canada, see the ADR Institute of Canada's Code of Ethics.
167. For Austria, see Civil Law Mediation Act (*ZivMediatG*), http://mediatorenliste.justiz.gv.at//mediatoren/mediatorenliste.nsf/docs/home (Accessed 31 March 2022); and for Vietnam, see Decree No. 22/2017/ND-CP on commercial mediation, https://vanbanphapluat.co/decree-22-2017-nd-cp-commercial-mediation (Accessed 31 March 2022).
168. For Australia, see the website of the Mediator Standards Board, www.msb.org.au (Accessed 31 March 2022); for Hong Kong, see the website of the Hong Kong Mediation Accreditation Association Limited, www.hkmaal.org.hk (Accessed 31 March 2022).
169. For Germany, see Verordnung über die Aus-und Fortbildung von zertifizierten Mediatoren (*Zertifizierte-Mediatoren-Ausbildungsverordnung, ZMediatAusbV*), mediatorenliste.justiz.gv.at//mediatoren/mediatorenliste.nsf/docs/home (Accessed 31 March 2022); for Singapore see ss 2 and 7 of the 2017 Singapore Mediation Act and the website of the Singapore International Mediation Institute, www.simi.org.sg (Accessed 31 March 2022).
170. Over the years, there have also been attempts to establish national standards in England and Wales, Canada and the US, but these have not met with success. As a result, mediator standards vary according to industry, institution or the terms of the mediation agreement.

mediator standards are regulated variously by private contracts (such as mediation agreements), institutional standards (such as the standards by the Family Mediation Council in the UK) and general law.

5.71 Mediation is a still-emerging profession characterised by mediators from diverse professional, cultural and disciplinary backgrounds. The significant use of soft law in mediator standards, such as industry-based mediator practice standards and codes of ethical conduct, reflects the notion that regulation is most useful when it can be responsive to, and evolve with, the mediation profession itself. A predominantly soft law approach does not exclude the possibility of different regulatory forms for mediator standards being introduced at a future time. In Hong Kong, for example, it has been expressly recognised that the possibility of legislatively backed provisions for mediator credentialing will be revisited in the future.[171] In the EU, the EU Directive imposes an obligation on its Member States to ensure the quality of mediation through 'the development of, and adherence to, voluntary codes of conduct by mediators and organisations providing mediation services, as well as other effective quality control mechanisms concerning the provision of mediation services'.[172]

5.72 The trend towards the professionalisation of mediation at the national level has been followed by cross-border initiatives that aim to recognise or set international standards for the mediation profession. International organisations such as the Singapore International Mediation Centre (SIMC), the Japan International Mediation Center (JIMC) and the International Chamber of Commerce (ICC) select mediators from diverse countries for their panels, thereby recognising a variety of national and organisational standards for mediator competency, certification and practice. The International Mediation Institute (IMI) is a private, public-interest organisation based in the Hague that has an international panel of mediators. It works with mediator credentialing institutions around the world to establish an internationally recognised certification for professional mediators.

5.73 This overview has highlighted the dynamic nature of private, institutional, national and international systems for mediator standards. Mediator standards may be found in legislation, court practice directions, a range of instruments referred to variously as ethical codes, codes of conduct or practice standards, private mediation agreements, the general law, including case law, or, a combination of the above.[173] The

171. See the HKSAR Department of Justice Report of the Working Group on Mediation, February 2010, https://www.doj.gov.hk/eng/public/pdf/2010/med20100208e.pdf (Accessed 31 March 2022).
172. Art. 4(1) of the EU Directive.
173. On the regulation of mediator standards, see Nadja Alexander and Felix Steffek, Making Mediation Law, International Finance Corporation (2016); See also the Australian case of *Tapoohi v Lewenberg* [2003] VSC 410, at para. 46, where the court applied general law principles to the question of professional standards of mediators.

reality of regulatory diversity in relation to mediator standards aligns with the intention of the drafters of the Singapore Convention to take an inclusive approach to mediator standards and recognise the range of regulatory approaches to this topic.[174] The WG II intended that it would be up to each State's competent authority to determine the standards applicable.[175]

5.74 In this commentary, the term 'mediator standards' will be used to apply to any and all of these regulatory instruments containing such standards.

What is the Content of Mediator Standards?

5.75 In some jurisdictions, mediators' duties may differ according to their professional qualifications and affiliations so that, for example, lawyer-mediators might be held to a different standard than counsellor-mediators.[176] There is no uniformity on this point.

5.76 Generally speaking, mediator duties may include the duty to:

(1) disclose qualifications and experience relevant to mediation;
(2) disclose potential conflicts of interest;
(3) explain the process and its potential consequences for legal rights and remedies;
(4) explain participant roles;
(5) advise parties to seek independent legal advice;
(6) refrain from giving technical or legal advice about the merits of the dispute;
(7) explain the parameters of confidentiality that applies in the mediation process;
(8) be impartial and conduct a fair process;
(9) terminate the mediation process in certain circumstances;
(10) report matters relating to abuse of children or any other criminal offence; and
(11) report to courts or other institutional bodies on certain aspects of the mediation outcome.

5.77 This section focuses on four mediator duties, namely those relating to disclosure, impartiality, confidentiality and termination of mediation.

174. See Report of Working Group II on the Work of its 66th Session (6-10 February 2017), A/CN.9/901 (2017), at para. 87. Available at http://undocs.org/A/CN.9/901 (Accessed 17 May 2022).
175. See Report of Working Group II on the Work of its 67th Session (2-6 October 2017), A/CN.9/929 (2017), at para. 96. Available at http://undocs.org/A/CN.9/929 (Accessed 17 May 2022). Available at http://undocs.org/A/CN.9/929 (Accessed 31 March 2022).
176. See discussion below in relation to the regulation of mediators in Austria.

Duty of Disclosure

5.78 Mediator disclosure requirements are regularly found in codes of conduct and statements of ethical duties. These requirements are relevant to Articles 5(1)(e) and 5(1)(f) of the Singapore Convention.[177] Article 5(1)(f) expressly refers to a 'failure to disclose'. The provision effectively imposes upon mediators a duty to disclose to parties circumstances that raise justifiable doubts as to a mediator's impartiality or independence. In Article 6(5) of the UNCITRAL Model Law on Mediation,[178] the duty to disclose is positively framed; it provides for an ongoing duty of disclosure by mediators in relation to their impartiality and independence. Article 4 of the EU Directive requires the Member States to encourage mediators and service providers to adhere to codes of conduct, including on matters of disclosure. Disclosure obligations are also found in section 9 of the UMA in the US. Other examples include Cyprus,[179] Croatia,[180] Georgia[181] and the Philippines.[182]

5.79 Duties of disclosure impose a continuing obligation on mediators to communicate to the parties potential conflicts of interest and grounds for bias in relation to the mediation process. The UNCITRAL Notes on Mediation (2021) state that *from the time of appointment and throughout the mediation*, a mediator is usually required to disclose any circumstances likely to give rise to justifiable doubts as to her/his impartiality.[183] Potential conflicts of interest may arise where the mediator has, at any time prior to the mediation provided legal counselling or other services, or has had any social or professional relationship with, or financial interest in, any of the participants.[184] In certain circumstances, disclosure requirements may also require disclosure

177. In the EU, see such as Art. 2.1 of the European Code of Conduct. In Australia, see s. 3 Australian National Mediator Practice Standards and s. 5 Law Council of Australia's Ethical Guidelines for Mediators. In the US, see Art. 4 of the Michigan Supreme Court's Standards of Conduct for Mediators and s. 7(d) of the Supreme Court of South Carolina Court Annexed ADR Rules. In Singapore, see s. 3.2 of the Singapore International Mediation Institute (SIMI) Code of Professional Conduct for SIMI Mediators (2017).
178. UNCITRAL Model Law on International Commercial Mediation and International Settlement Agreements Resulting from Mediation (2018) (amending the UNCITRAL Model Law on International Commercial Conciliation, 2002) (the Model Law is reproduced in Appendix E of this book). The duty of disclosure is also found in Art. 3(6) of the UNCITRAL Mediation Rules (2021). Available at https://uncitral.un.org/sites/uncitral.un.org/files/media-documents/uncitral/en/22-01369_mediation_rules_ebook_1.pdf (Accessed 31 March 2022). The UNCITRAL Mediation Rules is reproduced in Appendix F of this book. The UNCITRAL Notes on Mediation (2021), which serve as an explanatory text of the mediation process, contain reference to the duty of disclosure. Available at https://uncitral.un.org/sites/uncitral.un.org/files/media-documents/uncitral/en/v2107071_mediation_notes.pdf at para. 34 (Accessed 31 March 2022). The UNCITRAL Notes on Mediation is reproduced in Appendix G of this book.
179. Art. 10(2) of the Law on Certain Aspects of Mediation in Civil Matters of 2012, Law No. 159(I)/2012 of Cyprus.
180. Art. 8(1) of the Mediation Act of Croatia.
181. Art. 6(1) of the Law of Georgia on Mediation.
182. S. 13 of the Alternative Dispute Resolution Act of 2004 of the Philippines.
183. Para. 34 of the UNCITRAL Notes on Mediation (2021).
184. By way of example, the UNCITRAL Notes on Mediation (2021), at para. 35, states that laws and mediation rules also often require that the mediator shall not act as a representative or counsel

of mediators' qualifications and other matters related to their competency (for instance, as in section 9 of the UMA). Disclosure requirements are closely related to issues of impartiality, independence, neutrality and fair treatment, which are said to form the core aspects of the mediator's role.[185] Article 2.1 of the European Code of Conduct makes this explicit by requiring disclosure of matters that 'affect a mediator's independence or give rise to a conflict of interests'.[186] Section 9(a)(1) of the UMA contains similar requirements.

5.80 Disclosure requirements are designed to enhance self-determination by assisting parties to make fully informed choices in relation to the selection of their mediator, to remove doubts about the fairness of the process and the person conducting it and finally to establish 'a visible, fundamental and familiar safeguard of public protection'.[187] If, after full disclosure, the parties agree to continue with the mediator, the mediation may proceed according to section 9(2)(g) of the UMA.[188] The European Code of Conduct also requires the explicit consent of the parties in this situation, in addition to a guarantee from the mediators that they are 'certain of being able to carry out the mediation with full independence and neutrality in order to guarantee full impartiality'.[189]

5.81 In their analysis of US cases alleging mediator conflict of interest or bias, *Coben* and *Thompson* found that alleged conflicts of interest were often *cured* by disclosure or knowledge.[190] In *Lehrer v Zwernemann*,[191] the plaintiff alleged, *inter alia*, misconduct, breach of contract and breach of duty based on non-disclosed conflicts of interest by the mediator defendant. In summarily dismissing the claim, the court found that the plaintiff had constructive knowledge of the non-disclosed information concerning the mediator's relationship with the legal representatives of the other party. It also found that the plaintiff was not able to show any damage from the alleged misconduct.

5.82 Another illustration is provided by Article 3 of the IMI Code of Professional Conduct (which is reproduced in Appendix H of this book), which mandates disclosure of 'anything within their knowledge that may, or may not be perceived to, materially affect their impartiality'. Further, it provides that if, at any time, the mediator feels unable to conduct the process in an impartial manner, he/she must express that

---

of a party in any arbitral, judicial or other dispute resolution proceedings in respect of the dispute that is the subject of the mediation.

185. The French Civil Procedure Code requires that court-appointed mediators guarantee their independence *vis-à-vis* the parties and the dispute, thereby bringing together notions of impartiality, disinterestedness and the absence of any conflicts of interest which could impair independence: see Art. 131-5.5 C pr civ.
186. Art. 2(1) of the European Code of Conduct.
187. See Reporter's Notes to the UMA in *Uniform Mediation Act with Prefatory Note and Comments*, National Conference of Commissioners on Uniform State Laws, Chicago: NCCUSL (2001).
188. Similar provisions can be found in Art. 5 of the International Centre for Dispute Resolution (ICDR) International Mediation Rules.
189. European Code of Conduct, Art. 2.1.
190. See James Coben and Peter Thompson, *Disputing Irony: A Systematic Look at Litigation About Mediation*, 11 Harv. Neg. L. Rev. 43 (2006), at 95.
191. See *Lehrer v Zwernemann* 14 SW 3d 775.

concern and withdraw from the mediation. The continuing nature of the disclosure obligation means that if new circumstances requiring disclosure emerge during the course of a mediation, the mediator must comply with the duty at the first practicable opportunity. To enforce this requirement, Article 3.4 of IMI's Code of Professional Conduct imposes an *ongoing* duty on a mediator to disclose all 'newly discovered interests or relationships creating an actual or perceived threat to mediator impartiality'. The parties must then renew their consent to continue with the process.

5.83 Interesting questions arise where a mediator is a partner or an associate of a legal adviser retained by either of the parties. It is generally thought that in such situations, a mediator should not commence the mediation without the fully informed consent of all parties.[192]

5.84 A specific duty of disclosure is found in Australia, where nationally accredited mediators who engage in advice-giving have an obligation to disclose to parties that they are offering a dispute resolution process which differs from the standard facilitative mediation model under the Australian National Standards. In addition, they must obtain the parties' consent in order to proceed.[193] In so far as such advisory dispute resolution processes fall within the definition of mediation pursuant to the Singapore Convention, these additional requirements in the National Standards are likely to be relevant.

5.85 In relation to mediators acting as arbitrators, and vice versa, certain arbitration and mediation rules contain provisions that a dual role is only possible with the informed consent of the parties and disclosure on the part of the mediator–arbitrator.[194]

Duty of Independence and Impartiality

5.86 The Singapore Convention expressly refers to 'impartiality' and 'independence' in Article 5(1)(f) to strengthen parties' trust in the mediator and the mediation process.

192. See *Wan Hoe Keet and another v LVM Law Chambers LLC* [2019] SGHC 103, where a lawyer had an injunction issued against him from an opposing party at litigation because he had earlier represented another client against that opposing party at a settlement negotiation in respect to the same issues. The Singapore High Court granted the injunction on the basis that there was a risk that the opposing party would be disadvantaged, owing to the confidential knowledge the lawyer possessed of the opposing party after the conclusion of the first set of settlement negotiations. The Singapore Court of Appeal overturned the injunction (*LVM Law Chambers LLC v Wan Hoe Keet* [2020] 1 SLR 1083), ruling that in order for an injunction to be granted, (a) the information which the lawyer holds against their former client has to have the necessary quality of confidence about it in order to attract an equitable duty of confidence to apply, (b) that information must have been obtained by the lawyer under circumstances which would attract that obligation of confidence, *and* (c) there is a real and sensible chance of that information be misused (at [15]).
193. See Mediator Standards Board, *National Mediator Accreditation Standards*, https://msb.org.au/themes/msb/assets/documents/practice-standards.pdf (Accessed 31 March 2022).
194. Art. 12(1) of the UNCITRAL Mediation Rules (2021) and para. 35 of the UNCITRAL Notes on Mediation (2021); Singapore Arbitration Act (Cap 10, 2002 Rev Ed.), s. 62(3); Mixed-mode arrangements involving mediation and arbitration are considered in the commentary to Art. 1(3) of the Singapore Convention.

Impartiality, often used interchangeably with the term 'neutrality', is considered to be a fundamental principle of mediation. It is found in various regulatory instruments, including the UNCITRAL Model Law on Mediation, statutes, codes of conduct, self-regulatory standards and private contracts. Accordingly, this concept is relevant to Articles 5(1)(e) and 5(1)(f). Although the terms 'independence' and 'impartiality' are expressly used in the Convention, an international comparative overview suggests that the terms 'neutrality' and 'fair treatment' are also used in domestic regulatory systems in relation to this core mediator duty.[195] For this reason, all four terms are explored here, beginning with the term 'neutrality' because, historically, it has most closely been associated with contemporary mediation.

5.87 Definitions of neutrality in the literature are wide-ranging.[196] Neutrality suggests that mediators should be free of bias and should set aside their opinions, feelings and agendas. In other words, they should not make personal judgments about the parties and their disputes. Neutrality embraces the idea that mediators ought to be disinterested outsiders with no prior knowledge of the dispute, no stake in the outcome and no relationship to the parties other than as mediators in their dispute. Neutrality may also incorporate notions of fair process and impartiality, namely that parties be treated equally and fairly in the process. Thus, neutrality covers a lot of ground and, as indicated previously, can incorporate the meaning of the terms 'impartiality' and 'independence'. In France, mediators must be able to demonstrate that they are neutral from both objective (reasonable person) and subjective (in the parties' eyes) perspectives.[197] Despite the ubiquity of the term 'neutrality', regulatory provisions increasingly fall short of defining neutrality except, as Hopt and Steffek point out,[198] through notions of impartiality and independence.[199]

5.88 A number of commentators have questioned the utility of neutrality as a concept in mediation practice, arguing, *inter alia*, that the culture, values and personal biases of the human being behind the mediator make neutrality an unattainable ideal. Astor advocates values of transparency and the maximisation of party control as more useful

195. See, generally, Klaus J. Hopt and Felix Steffek (eds), Mediation Principles and Regulation in Comparative Perspective, OUP (2013).
196. The various definitions in the text are drawn from the literature, especially Peter Tochtermann, Die Unabhängigkeit und Unparteilichkeit des Mediators, Mohr Siebeck (2008); Kevin Gibson, Leigh Thompson and Max H. Bazerman, *Shortcomings of Neutrality in Mediation*, 12 Neg. J. 71 (2016); and Bernard Mayer, Beyond Neutrality: Confronting the Crisis in Conflict Resolution, Jossey-Bass Publishers (2004).
197. See Katrin Deckert, *Mediation in France: Legal Framework and Practical Experiences*, in Klaus J. Hopt and Felix Steffek (eds), Mediation Principles and Regulation in Comparative Perspective, OUP (2013), at 498, referring to *Cass Ass plén*, 6.11.1998, JCP 1998 II 10198.
198. See Klaus J. Hopt and Felix Steffek, *Mediation: Comparison of laws, Regulatory Models, Fundamental Issues*, in Klaus J. Hopt and Felix Steffek (eds), Mediation Principles and Regulation in Comparative Perspective, OUP (2013), at 75.
199. See, for example, Art. 1(1) of the Mediation Rules of the Mediation Institute of the Stockholm Chamber of Commerce and Art. 7(1) of the Permanent Court of Arbitration (PCA) Optional Conciliation Rules.

principles than neutrality in relation to practitioners' duties.[200] Transparency highlights the need for disclosure which allows parties to decide whether disclosed information warrants the dismissal or non-appointment of a mediator. It is consistent with the approach of some of the disclosure rules discussed previously and highlights the interconnectedness between these principles. As a guiding principle, transparency maximises party control of the content and outcome of the mediation and minimises the influence of a mediator's values, beliefs and assumptions. Accordingly, it is said that transparency causes mediators to be less likely to find themselves advising parties on options for agreement and alternatives to settlement – a practice which is not without risk.[201]

5.89 'Impartiality' is a term used interchangeably with neutrality, but it has a stronger emphasis on mediator conduct than neutrality. It denotes disinterestedness, or absence of bias, in the sense of no partiality directed at either party in the conduct of the mediation process. This contrasts with the German notion of *Allparteilichkeit*, which literally means the ability to be partial to all parties rather than to one or the other. The difference between being on no one's side and on everyone's side could be significant in terms of how a mediator guides parties through a mediation process.

5.90 The European Code of Conduct for Mediators distinguishes between independence and neutrality,[202] on the one hand, and impartiality, on the other, while at the same time recognising in the final paragraph of Article 2.1 that all three concepts are connected with one another. Whereas the former concepts are linked to duties of disclosure around conflicts of interest,[203] impartiality is defined by reference to mediator conduct.[204] The idea of impartiality is also encapsulated in Article 7(3) of the UNCITRAL Model Law on Mediation which provides that mediators must treat all parties fairly and conduct the process in a fair manner.[205] This provision focuses on the behaviour of mediators in the process and, from a practitioner's point of view, may be

200. See, for example, Hilary Astor, *Mediator Neutrality: Making Sense of Theory and Practice*, 16 Soc. & Legal Stud. 22 (2007). See also, Douglas who builds on Astor's work and advocates a relational, non-absolute understanding of neutrality and self-determination grounded in the relationship between mediators and parties: Susan Douglas, *Neutrality in Mediation: A Study of Mediator Perceptions*, 8(1) QUT L. & Just. J. 139 (2008), at 150-151.
201. Hilary Astor and Christine Chinkin, Dispute Resolution in Australia, LexisNexis Butterworths (2002), at 153-154. On the risk of advice-giving by mediators, see the Australian case of *Tapoohi v Lewenberg (No 2)* [2003] VSC 410.
202. On independence of the mediation practitioners, see Donna Cooper and Rachael Field, *The Family Dispute Resolution of Parenting Matters in Australia: An Analysis of the Notion of an 'Independent' Practitioner'*, 8(1) QUT L. & Just. J. 158 (2008).
203. European Code of Conduct for Mediators, Art. 2.1.
204. *Id.*, Art. 2.2.
205. UNCITRAL Model Law on International Commercial Mediation and International Settlement Agreements Resulting from Mediation (2018) (amending the UNCITRAL Model Law on International Commercial Conciliation, 2002). The Model Law is reproduced in Appendix E of this book. A similar duty is also provided in Art. 4(2) of the UNCITRAL Mediation Rules (2021) (reproduced in Appendix F of this book), which prescribes that the mediator shall maintain fair treatment of the parties and, in so doing, shall take into account the circumstances of the case. The UNCITRAL Notes on Mediation (2021) (reproduced in Appendix G of this book) explain that fair treatment does not mean equal treatment because depending on the dispute, the mediator may need to spend more time with one party than the other (at para. 68).

more tangible and achievable than neutrality. The EU Directive defines a 'mediator' in Article 3(b) as someone who conducts mediation in an impartial manner, thus signalling impartiality as a central aspect of the mediator's role. In contrast, section 9(g) of the UMA renders mediator impartiality optional. Given the significance of the duty of impartiality in most theory, policy and practice, it is worthwhile to examine the reasons behind the decision to give this so-called duty an optional character in the UMA.[206] According to the Reporter's Notes, the drafters of the UMA were swayed by the following factors:

(1) A concern in the mediation community that common human biases such as attributional distortions of judgment could be used as a basis for an argument of bias if there was a strict and mandatory duty of impartiality.
(2) Interventionist mediators – such as those using expert advisory and wise counsel models[207] – feared a plethora of lawsuits alleging breaches of the duty of impartiality by parties who no longer wished to be bound by their agreements. Although there have been very few findings of mediator misconduct by courts, parties dissatisfied with a mediated outcome in an attempt to vitiate it or have it set aside have been prepared to claim mediator duress, undue influence, coercion, inappropriate legal advice from the mediator and other manifestations of failure to maintain impartiality.[208] In the US, however, claims of mediator misconduct appear to be on the decline.[209]
(3) The UMA drafters did not regard impartiality as a universal mediator characteristic in practice. In many non-western cultures, mediators are not disinterested outsiders to the dispute – quite the opposite, they are often sought out precisely because they know the parties and are already aware of, or even somehow involved in, the dispute. As insiders, they are active, interested and engaged.[210]

5.91 Given the broad definition of mediation in Article 2(3), these considerations may be relevant in the interpretation of mediator standards pursuant to the Singapore Convention.

---

206. UMA, see Reporter's Notes to s. 9, at 46.
207. On the diversity in mediation practice, see the commentary to Art. 2(3) of the Singapore Convention.
208. In Australia see *Tapoohi v Lewenberg (No 2)* [2003] VSC 410. In England see *SITA v Watson Wyatt: Maxwell Batley Pt 20 Defendants* [2002] EWHC 2401/2025 (Ch) where the allegation of mediator bias was raised to justify one party's refusal to mediate. In the US see the cases of *In re Young* 253 F 3d 926 (7th Cir 2001), *Patterson v Taylor* 969 P 2d 1106 (Wash Ct App 1999) and *Vitakis-Valchine v Valchine* 793 So 2d 1094 (Fla Dist Ct App 2001).
209. See James R. Coben, *Evaluating the Singapore Convention Through a U.S.-Centric Litigation Lens: Lessons Learned from Nearly Two Decades of Mediation Disputes in American Federal and State Courts*, Cardozo J. Conflict Resol. (2019), at 16.
210. See Paul Wehr and John Paul Lederach, *Mediating Conflict in Central America*, in Jacob Bercovitch (ed.), Resolving International Conflicts: The Theory and Practice of Mediation, Lynne Rienner Publishers (1996).

5.92 Section 9(g) of the UMA attempts to address these issues by allowing *fully informed* parties to accept mediators who may fall short of a strict standard of impartiality. In relation to those US States that choose to introduce section 9(g), the drafters of the UMA considered that the default nature of the provision would be balanced by the specific provisions and sanctions related to disclosure and the duty found elsewhere in section 9 to implement the principles of impartiality in its broad interpretive sense. In other words, it was thought that potential risks arising from insufficient attention to impartiality would be minimised by the strict disclosure provisions. Consistent with the nature of a model law, enacting States desiring a stricter impartiality rule are free to deviate from the UMA and enact a higher standard.

5.93 We suggest that this approach may be aligned with that of the Singapore Convention. The Convention's definition of mediation in Article 2(3) envisages that an advisory mediation model may be used. In addition, there is a strong emphasis on disclosure (Article 5(1)(f)) and a causal link that must be established between any breach of mediator standards such as impartiality (Article 5(1)(e)) or failure to disclose (Article 5(1)(f)), on the one hand, and a party's decision to enter into the iMSA, on the other. These issues are further discussed below.

5.94 Another aspect of impartiality arises in relation to the concept of *(unauthorised) practice of law*. Where mediators provide parties with legal advice or assistance in drafting terms of the settlement, they may be engaging in conduct that amounts to the practice of law, thereby attracting the application of rules regulating the legal profession.[211] In these circumstances, non-lawyer mediators may fall foul of laws restricting the practice of law to certified practitioners. This is referred to as the unauthorised practice of law. Furthermore, lawyer–mediators may find that their legal professional duties relating to confidentiality, disclosure and reporting conflict with applicable mediator rules and codes of conduct, thereby leading to a lack of clarity in this regard.[212]

5.95 The facilitative model of mediation sidesteps this difficulty.[213] As a non-interventionist model, it does not permit advice-giving by mediators and emphasises impartiality in the treatment of the parties and the conduct of the process. As indicated previously, a facilitative model of practice is prescribed by the Australian National Mediator Standards, thereby minimising the risk that mediators might be engaging in the unauthorised practice of law.

5.96 Finally, mediators who also act as arbitrators in the same dispute need to be mindful of managing differing duties of impartiality in relation to each dispute

211. See Art Hinshaw, *Regulating Mediators*, 21 Harv. Neg. L. Rev. 163 (2016), at 177.
212. See, for example, *ABA Section on Dispute Resolution*, Mediation and the Unauthorised Practice of Law (2002) Mediate.com.
213. See, for example, clause 4 of the NADRAC Model Mediation Clause (referring to the Australian standards which endorse an interest-based model) and the Resolve to Resolve Report, available at https://www.ag.gov.au/LegalSystem/AlternateDisputeResolution/Documents/NADRAC%20Publications/the-resolve-to-resolve-embracing-adr-improve-access-to-justice-september2009.pdf. (Accessed 22 May 2019).

resolution process.[214] Here we note that according to the UNCITRAL Model Law on Mediation, the mediator shall not act as an arbitrator in the same dispute unless the parties expressly agree otherwise.[215]

Duty of Confidentiality

5.97 As indicated previously, confidentiality is a central value associated with mediation.[216] The confidentiality associated with mediation is said to encourage parties to engage in a full and frank discussion of their differences with a view to finding a resolution to the conflict. Parties should not be concerned that what transpires in mediation may be used to their disadvantage in subsequent judicial, tribunal, arbitral,[217] administrative or disciplinary proceedings. Confidentiality supports mediator impartiality insofar as it prevents mediators from sharing details of the mediation with third parties and giving evidence of various kinds of mediation communications in subsequent proceedings. Confidentiality may also aid process efficiency insofar as formal documentation of the process is neither required nor desired. At the same time, it is important to recall from the earlier analysis in the commentary on Article 5 that mediation confidentiality is not absolute. It has its limitations, such as for the purpose of enforcing or challenging an iMSA.[218] This discussion builds on the previous examination of confidentiality[219] and focuses on mediator duties of confidentiality that are usually contained in instruments setting out mediator standards; they are therefore relevant to Article 5(1)(e). There is a general duty of confidentiality that prevents mediators from disclosing information from the mediation to outsiders or non-participants.[220] For example, under Article 10 of the UNCITRAL Model Law on Mediation, all information relating to the mediation proceedings has to be kept

214. The nature of information passed to arbitrators may be more restricted than that to which mediators conducting a stand-alone process are privy, especially where private mediation sessions are held. As a result, parties may be less likely to engage in open and constructive settlement discussions where they know their mediator may subsequently act as arbitrator. In addition, the integrity of arbitral awards resulting out of such mixed-mode processes may be questioned in situations where arbitrators have been privy to one party's confidential information during the private sessions of the previous mediation phase. This last point is relevant to due process rights under the New York Convention. On this issue, see Nadja Alexander, International Comparative Mediation, Kluwer Law International (2009).
215. Art. 13 of the UNCITRAL Model Law on Mediation.
216. For a discussion on confidentiality as a central mediation value, see Chapter 2. Parts of this section are drawn from Nadja Alexander, International and Comparative Mediation, Kluwer Law International (2009), at Chapter 6.
217. Note, however, the obligation of an arbitrator to disclose to all parties any material confidential information obtained during mediation where the arbitrator acts as mediator with the consent of the parties to the arbitral proceedings and the mediation does not result in a settlement of the dispute: Singapore Arbitration Act (Cap. 10), s. 63; and Singapore International Arbitration Act (Cap. 143A), s. 17.
218. See paras 5.13-5.17 above.
219. See paras 5.05-5.22 above.
220. See, for example, in Austria, Civil Mediation Act 2003, §. 18; in Portugal, Law no. 29/2013 of 19 April, Art. 5; in Slovenia, Mediation in Civil and Commercial Matters Act, Art. 11; and in Malaysia, Mediation Act 2012, s. 15.

confidential, except 'where disclosure is required under the law or for the purposes of implementation or enforcement of a settlement agreement'.[221]

5.98 In Singapore, this duty of confidentiality takes the form of legislative and contractual obligations. Section 9(1) of the Mediation Act prohibits disclosure of any mediation communication to any third parties.[222] This is subject to the exceptions listed in section 9(2), such as if the disclosure is made with the consent of the parties[223] or made to assist a law enforcement agency in the investigation of any offence under any written law.[224] Provisions on confidentiality may also be found in mediation agreements (whether express or implied), mediators' codes of conduct of professional associations and the rules of mediation service providers. Paragraph 7 of the SIMI Code of Professional Conduct[225] places SIMI Mediators under a duty to keep strictly confidential at all times any information acquired in the course of serving as a mediator in a mediation. There are exceptions to this duty where disclosure of the information is compelled by law; necessary to prevent death, serious physical harm, damage or an illegal act; required to address a complaint made against the mediator or any other disciplinary proceedings involving the mediator; or in relation to information that is already in the public domain or expressly consented to by the parties. This duty of confidentiality is extended in paragraph 8 to a prohibition against a SIMI Mediator, after a mediation, giving evidence or testimony on behalf of one of the disputing parties against another party where he has received confidential information from the other party. This prohibition does not apply if the information is no longer confidential or the parties protected by the confidentiality give consent, or the law otherwise provides.

5.99 Another duty of confidentiality deals with the flow of information within mediation, especially in relation to private sessions (also known as caucuses) between the mediator and a party. The specific duty of confidentiality is usually regulated by the mediation agreement. Generally, the mediator has a duty not to disclose information or communications from a private session without the permission of the party making the statement or sharing the information. Pursuant to Article 9 of the Model Law of Mediation, when a mediator receives information from a party, subject to a specific condition that it be kept confidential, that information cannot be disclosed to any other

221. UNCITRAL Model Law on International Commercial Mediation and International Settlement Agreements Resulting from Mediation (2018) (amending the UNCITRAL Model Law on International Commercial Conciliation, 2002) (reproduced in Appendix E of this book.), Art. 10. The duty of confidentiality is also provided for in Art. 6 of the UNCITRAL Mediation Rules (2021) (reproduced in Appendix F of this book). The UNCITRAL Notes on Mediation (2021) (reproduced in Appendix G of this book) explain that it is advisable for the parties to check the scope of confidentiality under the applicable law at the outset of the mediation. The Notes also suggest that all mediation participants should be covered by a confidentiality agreement (at paras 45-48).
222. Mediation Act 2017 (No. 1 of 2017), s. 9(1).
223. *Id.*, s. 9(2)(a).
224. *Id.*, s. 9(2)(h).
225. The SIMI Code of Professional Conduct can be downloaded from www.simi.org.sg/What-We-Offer/Mediators/Code-of-Professional-Conduct (Accessed 22 March 2019).

party to the mediation.[226] Similarly, in Singapore, the State Courts' Code of Ethics and Basic Principles on Court Mediation provides that a mediator may not reveal to any other party information which the mediator received during a private session and which the disclosing party has indicated is confidential.[227]

5.100 Finally, there are also rules about the extent to which mediators are able to testify in court as to what occurred at mediation, usually after an MSA has been concluded.[228] These are evidentiary rules and are less relevant for the purposes of Articles 5(1)(e) and 5(1)(f) which are intended to address mediator conduct which materially influences the entering into an iMSA by at least one of the parties.

Duty to Consider Termination of Mediation in Certain Circumstances

5.101 In order to preserve the integrity of mediation, mediators may be required to terminate the process in certain circumstances. This duty is contained in most mediator standards, and is therefore of relevance to the application of Article 5(1)(e) of the Singapore Convention. By way of example, Article 12 of the Model Law on Mediation provides that mediators may terminate a mediation if they are of the view that further efforts at mediation are no longer justified.[229] The UNCITRAL Notes on Mediation (2021) explain that the termination should be 'clearly and unambiguously recorded as it may constitute the starting point of subsequent procedures or it may have an impact on the running of limitation periods applicable to the claim that is the subject matter of

226. UNCITRAL Model Law on International Commercial Mediation and International Settlement Agreements Resulting from Mediation (2018) (amending the UNCITRAL Model Law on International Commercial Conciliation, 2002) (reproduced in Appendix E of this book), at Art. 9. See also Art. 5(3) of the UNCITRAL Mediation Rules (2021) (reproduced in Appendix F of this book), which states that 'when the mediator receives information concerning the dispute from a party, the mediator shall keep such information confidential, unless that party indicates that the information is not subject to the condition that it should be kept confidential, or expresses its consent to the disclosure of such information to another party to the mediation'. The UNCITRAL Notes on Mediation (2021) (reproduced in Appendix G of this book) explain that the parties may agree on how the mediator should treat information received from one party at the mediation (at para. 49). The parties may agree that the mediator may disclose any information received from one party to the other party if such disclosure may assist the parties in reaching a settlement. However, the parties are also free to adopt the opposite approach according to which any information received by the mediator from one party shall not be disclosed to the other party.
227. The State Courts' Code of Ethics and Basic Principles on Court Mediation, at para. 3.3.2.
228. See, for example, UNCITRAL Model Law on Mediation, Art. 9; and the Singapore Mediation Act 2017, ss 10 and 11.
229. For similar provisions, see the UNCITRAL Mediation Rules (2021), Art. 9; London Court of International Arbitration Mediation Procedure, Art. 6; Permanent Court of Arbitration Optional Conciliation Rules, Art. 15; the Mediation Rules of the Arbitration Institute of the Stockholm Chamber of Commerce, Art. 13; UNCITRAL Conciliation Rules (UCR), Art. 15; World Intellectual Property Organisation (WIPO) Mediation Rules, Art. 19; International Institute for Conflict Prevention and Resolution (CPR) Procedures and Clauses Mediation Procedure, Art. 6; In relation to the mediator's duty to terminate in Austria, see the Government bill (Regierungsvorlage), RV 24 BlgNR XXII.GP. See also Sascha Ferz and Ewald Filler, Mediation - Gesetzestext und Kommentar, WUV Universitätsverlag (2003), at § 17 RN 2.

the mediation'.[230] The types of situations that may lead a mediator to terminate a mediation are varied. Article 3.2 of the European Code of Conduct for Mediators identifies two such situations, namely where:

(1) a settlement is being reached that appears to the mediator as unenforceable or illegal; or
(2) the mediator considers that continuing the mediation is unlikely to result in a settlement.

5.102 More specifically, mediators may be required to terminate a mediation where they form the view that a party or its legal representative is:

(1) on a fishing expedition for information to damage the other side;
(2) just going through the motions of mediating;
(3) withholding information vital to decision-making;
(4) obstructing the conduct or progress of the mediation; or
(5) otherwise acting in bad faith;
and the behaviour of the offending party appears to the mediator to be irreversible. Another illustration is the situation where the mediator takes the view that child abuse, threats to human safety or other criminal activities are being planned or are ongoing within the parameters of the mediation.

Are the Mediator Misconduct Provisions Necessary?

5.103 Questions may arise regarding the necessity of the Convention's provisions on mediator misconduct. After all, there are very few cases of mediator misconduct. In the US, for example, Coben and Thompson note that mediator misconduct is not commonly used as a defence against enforcement of mediated settlements and that cases in which parties sue mediators for breach of their duty of care are infrequent and on the decline.[231] The low number of legal actions against mediators may be indicative of substantial compliance with mediator obligations and standards. Alternatively, it may represent a response to the lack of success in using this defence and a shift of legal strategy to other potential MSA defences. It may also reflect poor understanding on the part of users on what they can expect from mediators and a lack of effective mechanisms for user feedback.

5.104 The introductory comments to this section show that *low* misconduct does not mean *no* misconduct. Moreover, the illustrations offered earlier show how a lack of

230. The UNCITRAL Notes on Mediation (2021), para. 81.
231. See James R. Coben, *Evaluating the Singapore Convention through a U.S.-Centric Litigation Lens: Lessons Learned from Nearly Two Decades of Mediation Disputes in American Federal and State Courts*, Cardozo J. Conflict Resol. (2019), at 16-17.

clear standards in certain jurisdictions has allowed fraudulent conduct by self-proclaimed mediators to remain beyond legal reproach.[232] In applying the English law of tort to four reported judgments in jurisdictions on mediator negligence, Koo found that the proof of breach was insurmountable due to the lack of clear standards against which to measure a mediator's performance and that causation of damage was hard to establish.[233]

5.105 With the growth of commercial and investment international mediation practice, disgruntled parties will look increasingly not just to their professional advisers but to their mediators for redress. The mediator misconduct provisions in Articles 5(1)(e) and 5(1)(f) lend professional mediator standards an international visibility that until now has been absent.

5.106 Accordingly, it is essential to establish clarity on the proper standards applicable to mediators and the type of conduct that would fall below those standards. It is against this richly textured background that the grounds for refusal in Articles 5(1)(e) and 5(1)(f) are now analysed.

The Elements of the Mediator Misconduct Provisions

5.107 Article 5(1)(e) provides that a court (competent authority of a State) may choose to not enforce an iMSA where there was 'a serious breach by the mediator of standards applicable to the mediator or the mediation without which breach that party would not have entered into the settlement agreement'.[234] There are two parts to this ground for refusal. First, there must be a serious breach of the applicable mediator standards. This provision seems to apply only where a set of applicable standards can be identified.[235] The meaning of a serious breach is discussed below. Second, there must be a *causal* link between the alleged misconduct of the mediator and the decision of at least one party to enter into the resulting settlement agreement. The causal link must be positively established by the party seeking to rely on this ground for refusal. Here, analogies with areas of contract law such as misrepresentation[236] may be useful in terms of defining the meaning and scope of the causal link to be established. For example, in *Ram Niranjan v Navin Jatia* [2020] 3 SLR 982 (at [51]), the High Court of Singapore had laid out the test for setting aside settlement deeds or settlement agreements for misrepresentation:

> An actionable misrepresentation consists in a false statement of *existing or past fact* made by one party before or at the time of making the contract, which is addressed to the party misled, and which induces that party to enter into the

232. See Art Hinshaw, *Regulating Mediators*, 21 Harv. Neg. L. Rev. 163 (2016), at 179 footnote 115.
233. Anna Koo, *Exploring Mediator Liability in Negligence*, 45 Common L. World Rev. 165 (2016).
234. Art. 5(1)(e). Note that this aligns with Arts 6(4), 6(5) and 7(3) of the 2018 Model Law on International Commercial Mediation.
235. On how to determine the applicable mediator standards, see the discussion below.
236. The test in England to establish fraudulent misrepresentation is whether but for the misrepresentation, would the parties have acted differently: *BV Nederlandse Industrie Van Eiprodukten v Rembrandt Enterprises, Inc* [2018] EWHC 1857 (Comm).

contract: *Tan Chin Seng and others v Raffles Town Club Pte Ltd* [2003] 3 SLR(R) 307 at [20], citing *Anson's Law of Contract* (28th Ed, 2002) at p 237. [...] [A]n actionable misrepresentation does not operate on statements of intention.

5.108 Here, the allegation of misrepresentation was made against one of the parties and not a mediator. Nevertheless, the exploration of the relevant principles by the courts may prove useful in unpacking and analysing Article 5(1)(e) and (f).

5.109 Article 5(1)(f) contains the second mediator conduct-related ground for refusal, that '[t]here was a failure by the mediator to disclose to the parties circumstances that raise justifiable doubts as to the mediator's impartiality or independence and "such failure to disclose had a material impact or undue influence on a party" without which failure that party would not have entered into the settlement agreement'.[237] This provision seeks to establish an independent standard irrespective of the applicability of other mediator standards.[238] There are three parts to this provision. First, there must be a breach of the duty of disclosure that attaches to mediators by virtue of Article 5(1)(f). Second, this failure to disclose raises justifiable doubts as to the mediator's impartiality or independence. Finally, there must be a causal link between the alleged mediator's misconduct and the decision of at least one party to enter into the resulting settlement agreement.

5.110 As with Article 5(1)(e), the causal link must be positively established. It must be such that the mediator's conduct 'had a material impact or undue influence on a party' in order for this ground for refusal to be available for parties to plead relief from enforcement. If, for example, a party is already aware of the information that ought to have been disclosed by the mediator, then it would not seem possible to establish a causal link between the mediator's failure to disclose and the party's decision to enter into an iMSA.[239] It can be hard to see how a mediator's failure to disclose information already known to a party has undue influence or a material impact on a party's decision to settle the dispute within mediation. Specifically, a mediator's misconduct must be one in relation to her ability to be and remain impartial or independent; where real and credible doubts of this (using an objective standard)[240] can be shown, parties seeking relief from enforcement must *additionally* demonstrate that the failure to disclose amounted to undue influence[241] to accept the terms of the iMSA, or that there was some

237. Art. 5(1)(f). Note that this aligns with Arts 6(4), 6(5) and 7(3) of the 2018 Model Law on International Commercial Mediation. This second ground seems to fall within the broad scope of the first ground.
238. Timothy Schnabel, *The Singapore Convention on Mediation: A Framework for the Cross-Border Recognition and Enforcement of Mediated Settlements*, 19 Pepp. Disp. Resol. L.J. 1 (2009), at 53.
239. This issue was raised at WG II. In response to the query whether this ground would apply to the circumstances that the parties were already aware of, it was explained that 'that in such instances, non-disclosure by a conciliator should not be construed as a ground for resisting enforcement [...]'. Report of Working Group II (Dispute Settlement) on the Work of its 66th Session (New York, 6-10 February 2017), at A/CN.9/901 (2017), at para. 77, http://undocs.org/A/CN.9/901 (17 May 2022).
240. See the discussion on 'justifiable doubts' below.
241. See generally, *Chan Gek Yong v Violet Netto* [2019] 3 SLR 1218, where a party to an MSA attempted to challenge its validity owing to duress, some of which was allegedly attributed to

other material impact flowing from that specific mediator misconduct, such as a misrepresentation as to the terms of the iMSA, or an unconscionable[242] action swaying the outcome of the iMSA.

5.111 Next, the terms 'serious breach', 'justifiable doubts', 'material impact' and 'undue influence' will be explored. The causal link in the context of the concept of reliance is also examined.

Serious Breach

5.112 Article 5(1)(e) refers to a serious breach, which means that minor breaches or questionable conduct would not suffice.[243] There were initial concerns within the WG II that the inclusion of these defences could lead to ancillary disputes, especially where the standards were subjective and susceptible to varying interpretations.[244] Hence, the use of the adjective 'serious' was to highlight the *exceptional* circumstances that can be raised and to establish that the threshold should be high.[245]

---

the mediators; also see, for a case summary, Nadja Alexander and Shouyu Chong, *Singapore Case Note: What Happens when a Party to an MSA Has a Change of Heart?*, Kluwer Mediation Blog (17 October 2018), http://mediationblog.kluwerarbitration.com/2018/10/17/singapore-case-note-happens-party-msa-change-heart (Accessed 8 May 2018).

242. The definition of unconscionable action by parties to a contract during the process of contract formation which may result in the avoidance of some contractual obligations has been clarified in the Singapore Court of Appeal recently in *BOM v BOK* [2019] 1 SLR 349, at [142]-[153]. An instance of an unconscionable action which may vitiate contractual obligations may be illustrated by the facts in *BOM v BOK* [2019] 1 SLR 349: where a wife takes advantage of the immense grief suffered by her estranged husband, whose mother had passed away suddenly and violently in a murder, to compel him to sign away *the entirety* of his multi-million dollar inheritance and put it on trust in favour of their infant child, this could be viewed by the Singapore courts as an unconscionable action which engenders vitiation of contractual obligations tainted by the wife's conduct.

243. Timothy Schnabel, *The Singapore Convention on Mediation: A Framework for the Cross-Border Recognition and Enforcement of Mediated Settlements*, 19 Pepp. Disp. Resol. L.J. 1 (2009), at 40. The term 'gross misconduct' in an earlier version of this provision was removed due to concerns that the terminology was unfamiliar to civil legal traditions and might lead to uncertainties.

244. See Report of Working Group II on the Work of its 66th Session, (6-10 February 2017), A/CN.9/901 (2017), at para. 52. Available at http://undocs.org/A/CN.9/901 (Accessed 17 May 2022). In addition, concerns were expressed in relation to: '(i) misconduct by the conciliator during the conciliation process, which had an impact on its outcome, could probably be covered by other defences in the instrument'; '(ii) conciliation was a voluntary process, from which parties were free to withdraw at any time, and therefore the misconduct of the conciliator should not have an impact at the enforcement stage'; and '(iv) the court at the place of enforcement might not be best placed to consider issues pertaining to the conciliation process which, in most cases, would have taken place in a different State'. See Report of Working Group II (Dispute Settlement) on the Work of its 65th Session (Vienna, 12-23 September 2016), A/CN.9/896 (2016), at para. 106. Available at http://undocs.org/A/CN.9/896 (Accessed 17 May 2022).

245. Eunice Chua, *The Singapore Convention on Mediation: A Brighter Future for Asian Dispute Resolution*, 9(2) Asian J. Int'l L. 195 (2019), at 202.

Causal Link and the Concept of Reliance

5.113 Both Articles 5(1)(e) and 5(1)(f) use a similar wording of 'without which breach – or in Article 5(1)(f) "failure" – that party would not have entered into the settlement agreement'. This term establishes the requirement of a causal link, and it suggests an element of 'reliance' by the party that had entered into the iMSA. Here, the drafters intended that this inquiry be an objective one, that is that the link between the breach and decision to enter into an iMSA should be examined objectively such that the breach of standard in Article 5(1)(e) or the failure to disclose in Article 5(1)(f) would have caused a reasonable person to refrain from entering the settlement agreement.[246] The term 'reasonable' was not expressly included in the text as it was understood not to be easily applicable in certain legal systems. Such an approach would mean that the parties' subjective experiences are eschewed in the assessment of whether the reliance requirement is satisfied.[247] This requirement of reliance and a causal link makes the mediator misconduct provisions extraordinarily difficult to establish, especially as mediation sessions are not usually recorded.

5.114 The concept of 'reliance' is also used in other contexts in law. By way of example, in misrepresentation, the representee has to show that it had relied on the misrepresentation to enter into the contract.[248] The phrasing also calls to mind the 'but-for' test frequently used in tort law, which requires that the harm suffered by a claimant was caused by the breach of the defendant's duty, on the basis the claimant would not have suffered harm 'but for' the defendant's breach.[249] Such analogies could be drawn to illustrate the ambit of these defences.

Justifiable Doubts

5.115 Article 5(1)(f) also makes reference to the phrase 'justifiable doubts'. A similar phrase is used in Article 6(5) of the UNCITRAL Model Law on Mediation which imposes an obligation on a mediator to disclose 'any circumstances likely to give rise

246. An early version of this provision referred to 'a material breach of applicable standards by the conciliator but for which a reasonable party would not have entered into a settlement agreement'. It was pointed out that 'the word "material" would ensure that only serious (non-trivial) breach constitute grounds for refusal, the word "reasonable" would provide for objective standards, the words "applicable standards" would encompass the various standards on conduct (including fair treatment) as well as disclosure, and the "but for" phrase would ensure that the ground could be invoked only when the consent of the parties to enter into a settlement agreement had been vitiated'. See Report of Working Group II (Dispute Settlement) on the Work of its 66th Session (New York, 6-10 February 2017), A/CN.9/901 (2017), at para. 79. Available at http://undocs.org/A/CN.9/901 (Accessed 17 May 2022).
247. The word 'reasonable' was excluded from the compromise proposal because 'that word introduced subjective elements, which should be avoided, and that it was therefore not retained in the drafting proposal'. See Report of Working Group II (Dispute Settlement) on the Work of its 66th Session (New York, 6-10 February 2017), A/CN.9/901 (2017), at para. 84. Available at http://undocs.org/A/CN.9/901 (Accessed 17 May 2022).
248. See *Derry v Peek* (1889) LR 14 App Cas 337.
249. See *Barnett v Chelsea & Kensington Hospital* [1969] 1 QB 428.

to justifiable doubts as to his or her impartiality or independence'.[250] The provenance of this phrase can be traced all the way back to the UNCITRAL Arbitration Rules, which state that '[a]ny arbitrator may be challenged if circumstances exist that give rise to 'justifiable doubts' as to the arbitrator's impartiality or independence'.[251] In this context, in *Gallo v Canada*, the International Centre for Settlement of Investment Disputes (ICSID) Deputy Secretary-General, acting as the appointing authority in the case, stated that 'under the UNCITRAL Arbitration Rules doubts are justifiable ... if they give rise to an apprehension of bias that is, to the objective observer, reasonable'.[252] This coheres with Schnabel's view that justifiable doubts are 'not affected by whether the party in question subjectively doubts the mediator's independence and impartiality'.[253] Situations that might give rise to justifiable doubts as to a mediator's impartiality or independence might include a mediator's personal or business relationship with one of the parties, a mediator's financial or other interest in the outcome of the mediation and the mediator or a member of his or her firm having acted in any capacity other than mediator for one of the parties.[254]

Material Impact

5.116 Interpretation of the term 'material' has been the subject of jurisprudence in a variety of contexts. In the English case of *Decura IM Investments LLP v UBS AG*,[255] the High Court had to interpret the term 'material' in the context of determining whether a termination event had occurred under an exclusivity agreement. The court held that 'material' means 'substantial' or 'significant' within the factual matrix of the case. It is suggested that the impact on the party that has entered into the settlement agreement will need to reach a similar level. Additionally, in determining an issue of material non-disclosure of evidence in arbitration proceedings in a case related to fraudulent misrepresentation between commercial parties, the Singapore Court of Appeal has held that the test for admitting further evidence is 'that the further evidence "materially affects the basis of the earlier decision" and "the change must substantially affect a basic assumption made at the trial"'.[256] In the context of the mediator misconduct

250. Art. 3(6) of the UNCITRAL Rules on Mediation (2021) (reproduced in Appendix F of this book) also makes reference to 'justifiable doubts' in relation to 'any personal, professional, financial or other interest that may influence the outcome of the dispute'. See also para. 34 of the UNCITRAL Notes on Mediation (2021) (reproduced in Appendix G of this book).
251. 1976 UNCITRAL Arbitration Rules, Art. 10(1).
252. *Vito G. Gallo v The Government of Canada*, UNCITRAL, Decision on the Challenge to Mr. J. Christopher Thomas, QC, PCA Case No. 55798.
253. Timothy Schnabel, *The Singapore Convention on Mediation: A Framework for the Cross-Border Recognition and Enforcement of Mediated Settlements*, 19 Pepp. Disp. Resol. L.J. 1 (2019), at 42. See also for example, interventions of IAM and FICA, in Audio Recording: Working Group II, 66th Session (United Nations 2017), 10 February 2017, 10:00-13:00, https://conferences.unite.un.org/carbonweb/public/uncitral/speakerslog/f619271a-e928-400e-b6d0-08b213c54710 (Accessed 31 March 2022).
254. European Code of Conduct for Mediators, Art. 2.1.
255. [2015] EWHC 171.
256. See *BNX v BOE and another appeal* [2018] 2 SLR 215, at [98].

provisions, the impact on the party that has been induced to enter into the settlement agreement will likely need to reach a similar level.

5.117 This approach is further supported by a decision of the Court of Appeal for Ontario, where it was held that discretion was afforded to States to set aside arbitral awards for procedural impropriety under Art. 34(2) of the Model Law on International Commercial Arbitration (1985) with amendments as adopted in 2006 for the purpose of prevention of 'real unfairness and real practical injustice'. In that case, it denied setting aside the award, although the arbitrators had an ex parte meeting with a Rabbi who had previously acted as arbitrator in another dispute involving the same parties without notice to the appellant. The court held that merely any procedural impropriety was insufficient, and the relevant standard for the materiality of the procedural impropriety was 'whether the procedural error had an impact on the "reliability" of the result (i.e. the award), or to the fairness, or the appearance of the fairness of the arbitral process'.[257]

Undue Influence

5.118 'Undue influence' can refer to how a transaction may be set aside if it was procured by the influence exerted by one person on another, such that the transaction cannot 'fairly be treated the expression of [that person's] free will'.[258] In a mediation context, one may look to the US case of *Olam v Congress Mortgage Co.*[259] In that case, the 65-year-old plaintiff suffered from a number of medical conditions and submitted evidence that she was weak, dizzy and experiencing pain during the mediation. She further alleged that her lawyer, the defendants and their lawyers pressured her into reaching a settlement at 1 am in the morning in a mediation that continued for 15 hours. After a detailed and considered judgment, the court held that there was insufficient evidence of undue influence to justify setting aside the contract. While this was a case involving undue influence between parties to a settlement agreement, it is suggested that this case could be illustrative of the extent of influence required to prove mediator misconduct under Article 5(1)(f).

5.119 Concerns were raised in WG II in relation to terms such as 'material impact' and 'undue influence', which, they said, were unfamiliar in their legal traditions and could introduce uncertainties.[260]

---

257. See *Popack v Lipszyc* 2016 ONCA 135.
258. See *Royal Bank of Scotland plc v Etridge (No 2)* [2001] UKHL 41. At least under English law, there are various classes of undue influence.
259. See *Olam v Congress Mortgage* Co 68 F Supp 2d 1110 (ND Cal 1999) at 1139–51.
260. See Report of Working Group II on the Work of its 66th Session (6-10 February 2017), A/CN.9/901 (2017), at para. 72. Available at http://undocs.org/A/CN.9/901 (Accessed 17 May 2022). In response to these concerns, it was pointed out that 'the introduction of those terms in the compromise proposal was an attempt to incorporate more objective standards with a higher threshold, balancing the different views expressed in the Working Group on the need for such a provision in the instrument. It was stated that while those terms might be novel, the enforcing authorities would not have much difficulty in interpreting them'. Report of Working Group II

Case Illustrations

Illustrations from a number of cases involving allegations of misconduct against mediators in Australia, Singapore and the US are presented in this case illustration series.

Illustration [A]: In Singapore, *Chan Gek Yong v Violet Netto* [2019] 3 SLR 1218 offers an illustration of an allegation against co-mediators which was not substantiated by the evidence. Here, the plaintiff, Mdm Chan, sued her former lawyer, Violet Netto, for professional negligence. The parties participated in mediation which resulted in a signed MSA. Nevertheless, *one week* after signing the MSA, Mdm Chan informed the court at a pre-trial conference that she intended to proceed with her pending civil suits against Violet Netto, seemingly ignoring her obligations under the MSA. Despite this, Violet Netto began issuing the cheques needed to fulfil their payment obligations under the terms of the MSA. At the same time, Violet Netto filed countersuits to strike out Mdm Chan's pending civil suits. Contrary to the agreement, however, Mdm Chan continued to pursue the civil claim against Violet Netto. In the litigation that followed, Mdm Chan sought to argue in court that the MSA she signed was invalid for a large platter of reasons. One of her noteworthy contentions was that she felt pressured by the co-mediators.

As reported in the judgment, Mdm Chan alleged that the co-mediators 'persuaded and urged her to accept the amount offered by the defendants as it was almost the end of the one-day mediation session. The mediators further said that if the mediation failed, [they] would have to go back to Court for trial'. The reported judgment further states that Mdm Chan maintained that she 'understood this to mean that she would have to incur further costs to continue the [pending suits]. She also stated that there was no time for her to consider the Settlement Agreement before signing it' (at paragraph 52).

Mediators will immediately recognise the standard mediator intervention of reality testing and ensuring mediating parties are aware of the implications and/or costs of pursuing alternatives to settlement, such as going to trial.

After considering all the arguments and evidence, Justice Tan opined that there was 'no reason for anyone to feel pressured by [the mediators' actions]' (at paragraph 57). As the mediators were merely conveying words of advice founded upon facts and logical consequences of Mdm Chan's ultimate decision to agree or disagree with the negotiated terms, it demands a tremendous stretch of the imagination to interpret those words as undue pressure.

(Dispute Settlement) on the Work of its 66th Session (New York, 6-10 February 2017), A/CN.9/901 (2017), at paras 74-75. Available at http://undocs.org/A/CN.9/901 (Accessed 17 May 2022).

Second, Justice Tan ruled that no undue pressure had been applied on Mdm Chan by the mediators, though she alleged that she was pressed to endorse the MSA 'as it was already late in the day [and hence] she had no time to consider the [terms of the] Settlement Agreement' (at paragraph 58). It appears to be the court's view that circumstantial time pressures should not invalidate MSAs. His Honour opined that Mdm Chan could simply have requested more time if she needed it to consider the terms of the MSA before she endorsed it with her signature. There was also no actual pressure by the mediators, as she admitted that they had not forced her to endorse the MSA against her volition.

This case demonstrates several points. First, it shows that prima facie MSAs are to be honoured. Second, parties need to take reasonable care to read and ensure they understand an MSA before signing it. In this case, it is notable that Mdm Chan was unrepresented. Third, where parties are legally represented in mediation, lawyers should explain the meaning of the MSA's terms to their clients and explain the consequence of breach of the MSA. Although not directly addressed in the judgment, this point is consistent with the tenor of the Court's reasoning and would be consistent with case law in Australia and other jurisdictions. Lastly, evidence of the shift in a party's position (here, Mdm Chan) after the signing of the MSA is, in itself, not evidence of undue influence, intimidation or the like.

For mediators, this point will be of note: reality testing by mediators is an indispensable part of the mediation process. At the same time, and as a matter of best practice, mediators are encouraged to be sensitive to the conflict dynamics between parties as they shift throughout the mediation and to be on high alert for signs of potential discomfort or dissatisfaction by a party. For example, in relation to unrepresented parties, mediators may consider including in the mediation agreement a clause recommending that parties obtain professional advice and additionally remind parties of this option during the mediation, perhaps at the start of the mediation and again before signing off on an MSA. It may also be helpful for mediators to reflect on how they frame their reality testing to ensure they make clear that their role is to assist the parties in assessing the consequences of both reaching a particular settlement and also pursuing an alternative strategy outside the mediation room – highlighting that the choice is always theirs.

Illustration [B]: In *Tapoohi v Lewenberg & Ors (No 2)*,[261] the Supreme Court of Victoria, Australia, considered it arguable that a mediator owes a duty of care to the disputants. This concerned litigation between two legally represented sisters

261. [2003] VSC 410. This case illustration is adapted from Alan Limbury, *Mediation Lessons from the Cases: Part 2*, Kluwer Mediation Blog (22 February 2019), http://mediationblog.kluwerarbitration.com/2019/02/22/mediation-lessons-from-the-cases-part-2/ (Accessed 31 March 2022).

over the estate of their deceased mother. Mrs Tapoohi attended by telephone. The mediator was an experienced senior counsel and mediator. Handwritten Terms of Settlement were executed and faxed to Mrs Tapoohi, who faxed back a signed copy. The settlement contemplated payment by Mrs Tapoohi of AUD 1.4 million for certain real estate and transfer by her of certain shares for AUD 1.00 (one dollar). Following the mediation, it later became apparent that the AUD 1.00 figure had undesirable tax consequences for Mrs Tapoohi. Her sister refused to change the price, so Mrs Tapoohi commenced fresh court proceedings seeking to set aside the settlement, saying it was subject to an express oral term that the parties would seek taxation advice before concluding any settlement.

Mrs Tapoohi later added a claim against her solicitors that they had advised her to sign the Terms because they were subject to the express oral term and were not binding upon her. Alternatively, if the settlement was binding, she had suffered loss and damage due to the solicitors' breach of their retainer or negligent advice. More than two years after bringing the initial proceedings, Mrs Tapoohi discontinued the second proceedings against her sister and thereafter pursued only her solicitors.

The solicitors claimed that if the Terms of Settlement were binding, the damage suffered by Mrs Tapoohi was due to breaches by her barrister and by the mediator of duties they owed to her in contract and in tort. Hence, if the solicitors were liable to pay damages to her, they were entitled to contributions from the barrister and the mediator. The mediator then applied to strike out the solicitors' claim, submitting that it had no arguable basis. The solicitors and the mediator provided sworn affidavits as to what happened at the mediation. The judge noted that a number of important allegations were vigorously disputed by the mediator, saying:

> For the purposes of an application such as this I must approach the matter on the basis that the facts most favourable to the claim will be established. This means that, in the event of conflict, I must prefer the affidavits filed on behalf of the solicitors.

The barrister also sought to strike out the solicitors' claim but did not pursue that application.

In determining whether to strike out the claim against the mediator, the judge examined in detail the solicitors' evidence as to the conduct of the mediation, summarised below. The solicitors for both sisters verbally agreed to appoint the mediator and so informed him. The mediator then wrote to the parties confirming his nomination and proposing a preliminary conference, saying:

> I confirm that the aim of the Mediation Conference is to assist the parties in reaching a settlement of their dispute by the involvement of an impartial mediator. It is not the role or function of a mediator to impose a settlement on the parties. It is up to the parties to arrive at their own resolution of the dispute. The purpose of the mediator is to assist the parties to define the issues, eliminate obstacles to successful communication, explore settlement alternatives, and generally work with the parties to achieve a negotiated resolution.

The solicitors for Mrs Tapoohi confirmed his appointment 'to act as mediator in the proceedings'.

On several occasions during the mediation, it was made clear to the mediator that any agreement reached would need to be subject to getting proper tax advice. After approximately nine hours, the parties reached an agreement in principle. The mediator told everyone to return to the main room so that they could get something down for the parties to sign, saying forcefully:

> 'You have got to stay, you have got to do the terms of settlement tonight.' 'No, we are doing it now. We are signing up tonight as that is the way that I do it, that's how I conduct mediations.' 'Given the acrimony between these two sisters we must go away with something that is written. It is in the interests of all the parties to sign up tonight.'

The mediator then dictated the Terms. There had been no discussion as to the price to be paid for the shares. The mediator suggested AUD1.00 as nominal consideration. Her solicitor took this as recognition that the Terms were not binding because of the need to obtain tax advice. Nobody noticed that this requirement was not included in the Terms.

The solicitors pleaded the doubtful proposition that: 'the Parties retained the mediator for reward to act for them and advise them as a mediator at the Mediation' and that it was implied in the mediation agreement that the mediator would: '(a) exercise all the due care and skill of a senior barrister specialising in commercial litigation and related matters; (b) exercise all the due care and skill of a senior expert mediator; (c) reasonably protect the interests of the Parties; (d) not act in a manner patently contrary to the interests of the Parties, or any of them; (e) act impartially as between the Parties; (f) carry out his instructions from the Parties by all proper means; and further or alternatively (g) not coerce or induce the Parties into settling the Earlier Proceeding when, at the relevant time or times, there was a real and substantial risk that settlement would be contrary to the interests of the Parties, or any of them'.

The judge dismissed the mediator's application to strike out or dismiss the solicitors' claim for contribution, holding that it was arguable that the mediator owed duties to the disputants in both contract and in tort, saying:

> I have reached the conclusion that it is not beyond argument that some at least of the breaches of the contractual and tortious duties might be made out. I consider that it is possible that a court could find that there was such a breach constituted by the imposition of undue pressure upon resistant parties, at the end of a long and tiring mediation, to execute an unconditional final agreement settling their disputes where it was apparent that they, or one of them, wanted to seek further advice upon aspects of it, or where it was apparent that the agreement was not unconditional, or where the agreement was of such complexity that it required further consideration. I emphasise that it is not for me to conclude that any of these things occurred in the present case and I do not do so. It is sufficient that I conclude, as I do, that on the evidence before me such a contention is not plainly hopeless.

In the absence of any reported judgment, it appears Mrs Tapoohi's claim against the solicitors and their claim for contribution against the mediator did not proceed to trial. In the result, it remains to be judicially decided whether mediators do owe a duty in contract or tort to disputants, especially where, as here, no Mediation Agreement was entered into.

What are the lessons for mediators? One advantage for mediators in having a Mediation Agreement is that the mediator may expressly exclude liability to the parties. That might have been useful in this case. It frequently happens in mediation that settlement is reached only after a very long day when everyone is exhausted. In the case under consideration, it took nine hours to reach an agreement in principle. It is not clear how much longer it took to write the Terms and have them executed. Where the parties are legally represented, the mediator can usefully hover behind them as they write, occasionally suggesting some language or the need to address a topic, but not in a way that could be understood as telling them what to do.

Illustration [C]: In *Robert Samuel McCosh v David A R Williams*,[262] the New Zealand Court of Appeal considered the conduct of a mediator, after the conclusion of the mediation, in attempting to help the parties resolve a fresh dispute over the terms of settlement signed on the mediation day. The mediation concerned a 'bitterly contested' dispute between a father and three daughters over their entitlements to a dairy farming property. The Settlement Agreement required the father to transfer 21,530 shares to the daughters. Shortly after the mediation, a dispute broke out between the daughters and their father as to whether the number of shares the daughters were to receive should be 59,430, taking into account a bonus issue a year earlier.

262. [2003] NZCA 192. This case illustration is adapted from Alan Limbury, *Mediation Lessons from the Cases: Part 1*, Kluwer Mediation Blog (22 February 2019), http://mediationblog.kluwerarbitration.com/2018/12/22/mediation-lessons-from-the-cases-part-1/ (Accessed 31 March 2022).

It appears the daughters were unaware of the bonus issue at the time of the mediation and the father did not draw attention to it. The daughters invoked a clause of the Settlement Agreement, which provided:

> In the event of any dispute between the parties in relation to the interpretation or implementation of this Agreement, that dispute shall be submitted to [the mediator] for summary determination and his decision will be final...

Despite objections by the father that the mediator had no jurisdiction to do so, the mediator issued a 'Summary Determination', declaring that the reference to 21,530 shares in the Settlement Agreement 'as amplified and interpreted by this separate binding determination' should be interpreted as meaning 56,954 shares. The father did not transfer any additional shares and, relying on the mediator's Summary Determination, the daughters sued their father for the balance of 35,424 shares. Those proceedings were settled.

The father then sued the mediator, alleging the mediator lacked jurisdiction to make the Summary Determination, acting in a negligent and misleading manner in doing so. The father claimed legal costs and expenses in relation to the litigation with his daughters, travelling expenses, interest on the value of the shares while they were 'frozen' and NZD 25,000 for 'trauma, worry, stress and the upset suffered of ongoing litigation with [the] daughters for a three-year period', including aggravated damages.

The Court of Appeal found that, under the Settlement Agreement, the mediator could make a summary determination only as to the interpretation of the meaning of the words of that agreement or as to the implementation of the mechanics of putting it into effect. The mediator had exceeded his jurisdiction because changing the number of shares from 21,530 to 56,954 was a rectification of the agreement. However, the mediator had not been negligent in undertaking the task of giving a summary determination and had not been misleading. Further, because the daughters would probably have sued their father for the additional shares even if the mediator had declined to adjudicate, the mediator was not liable to pay anything to the father, who was ordered to contribute towards the mediator's costs. So the mediator escaped liability but no doubt suffered the stress and strain of the proceedings, all because he tried to help the parties resolve their dispute in the way he thought they had intended when they signed the Settlement Agreement.

In the first instance, the High Court Judge did not need to determine the jurisdiction issue because he accepted the mediator's argument that an exclusion clause in the Mediation Agreement, signed before the mediation began, protected the mediator from liability. It read:

> The parties jointly and severally release, discharge and indemnify the Mediator in respect of all liability of any kind whatsoever (whether involving negligence or not) which may be alleged to arise in connection with or to result from or to relate in any way to this mediation.

By contrast, the Court of Appeal commented that the exclusion clause applied only in relation to acts and omissions of the mediator when acting as a mediator. The actions complained of were, instead, taken by the mediator after the mediation had concluded by the execution of the Settlement Agreement and were purportedly done in pursuance of the Settlement Agreement. Clear and unambiguous language would be required for an exclusion clause to be effective beyond the scope of the mediation process.

The lesson for mediators here would be to broaden their exclusion of liability clauses. As a consequence of this case, mediators have sensibly amended their usual form of mediation agreement to include a broader exclusion of liability, along the following lines:

> The disputants jointly and severally release, discharge and indemnify the Mediator in respect of all liability of any kind whatsoever (whether involving negligence or not) which may be alleged to arise in connection with or to result from or to relate in any way to the mediation or to any arbitration or expert determination by the Mediator or to any subsequent act or failure to act pursuant to any settlement of the dispute.

Mediators may safely adjudicate within the mediation or afterwards if the parties agree. However, their safety comes from excluding, in the mediation agreement (by clear and unambiguous language) all potential liability for whatever might be done, consciously or inadvertently, before, during or after the mediation and whether having anything to do with the mediation or not. Substantial professional indemnity insurance cover in the widest terms is also a good idea.

Illustration [D]: *Lange v Marshall*[263] is a divorce case, but the allegations of mediator misconduct are also relevant to cases that fall under the Singapore Convention. In this case, the defendant acted as a mediator in the petition for a divorce of a husband and wife. The defendant helped negotiate a settlement which was then signed by both parties and filed with the court, together with a petition for dissolution. However, before the judgment was entered, the wife had second thoughts about the settlement and sought legal counsel. The husband did the same and the mediator withdrew from the case. The matter was taken off a submission from the court, and ten months later, both parties entered into a new settlement which was more favourable to the wife. The wife then sued the mediator, alleging that he had failed to inquire and advise as to her husband's financial state, negotiate a better settlement for her, advise on the possibility of

263. *Lange v Marshall*, 1981 622 S.W.2d 237.

achieving a better settlement through litigation and disclose fully and fairly her rights as to marital property, custody and maintenance. Eventually, the Missouri Court of Appeal did not find the mediator liable because they held that even if the defendant had been negligent, the plaintiff still could not prove that she had sustained any damage as a proximate result of the defendant's negligence.

Illustration [E]: *Pohlman v Pohlman*[264] is also a divorce case that involves allegations about the mediator's misconduct that are pertinent to the Singapore Convention. In this case, the mediation lasted 6.5 hours and resulted in a settlement agreement. The plaintiff alleged that she suffered duress during the mediation at the hands of the mediator and her counsel, as neither of them let her leave the room until she signed the settlement agreement. Ultimately the court did not grant the plaintiff the relief she sought and the MSA remained intact. However, the dissenting opinion of Judge Elizabeth L. Gleicher in the Court of Appeal's decision remains of particular interest. The dissenting opinion reads as follows:

> The circumstances surrounding mediation as described by both Jody and James reflect that the process was coercive and violent. Forcing someone to stay in a room until she signs a document is a form of abuse. I recognize that the behaviors of the mediator and counsel do not necessarily provide Jody with grounds to disavow the settlement agreement. Here, however, James's averments suggest a coordinated effort in which he participated to overcome Jody's will. If proven, I cannot envision why this concert of action would be legally insufficient to invalidate the agreement. Further, I suggest that the evidence may show that had screening been done and Jody's status monitored throughout the process as required by the court rule, the mediation procedure may have terminated before she signed the agreement.

Illustration [F]: In the Australian case of *Collins v State of Queensland,*[265] the applicant (Mr Collins) challenged the validity of a settlement deed on several grounds, including an alleged conflict of interest on the part of the mediator who had a professional association with the respondent. The respondent admitted that the mediator previously had acted as a lawyer in matters for it and against it and as a mediator in matters in which it was a party. The respondent did not disclose this fact to the applicant. However, the respondent denied that the applicant was under a special disadvantage. The Supreme Court of Queensland did not find any conflict of interest on the part of the mediator and deemed: 'Mr Collins has failed to demonstrate any conflict of interest on the part of the mediator. There was no suggestion, for example, that the latter was in some way dependent on the respondent for work or that the outcome of the mediation

264. *Pohlman v Pohlman*, 2020 Mich. App. LEXIS 798, *1, 2020 WL 504775 (Mich. Ct. App. 30 January 2020).

265. *Collins v State of Queensland* [2020] QSC 154, (2020) 61 Fam LR 160.

could conceivably affect his livelihood. (Indeed, there was no evidence that he was currently available to perform the respondent's work or that it was considering him for briefing.) And it is perfectly clear that he was not the respondent's choice; it was only at Mr Collins' urging that Ms Freeleagus [the solicitor of the respondent] agreed to his appointment. There was nothing in the circumstance of the mediator's having taken briefs from the respondent in the past which should have caused anyone involved a concern about conflict of interest. The fact that Mr Collins might have chosen differently had he known of the past briefing of the mediator does not mean that anyone concerned in the mediation was obliged to convey it to him.'[266]

Illustration [G]: In the US case of *Mozer v Augustine*,[267] the appellant challenged the validity of a settlement agreement based on several grounds, including the mediator's failure to disclose an alleged conflict of interest with the respondent. The respondent's claim was based on rule 3.855(b) of the California Rules of Court, according to which a court-appointed mediator was required to disclose certain business, financial or personal affiliations that could undermine the mediator's impartiality. To support this alleged breach of a standard of mediator conduct, the appellant relied on the following factual allegations: the mediator and the respondent's counsel had contributed to the same charities; an associate of the respondent's counsel wrote a positive profile about the mediator on the Internet; the respondent litigated cases in which the mediator served as the bench officer and the mediator had appointed the respondent to serve as a conservator in a high profile conservatorship matter; and the respondent had participated in another unrelated matter which the mediator had mediated. The Court of Appeal of California stated that none of the professional contacts the appellant identified came close to a past or present business or financial relationship that would require disclosure.

How to Determine the Applicable Standards ('Proper Standard')?

5.120 At mediation, the applicable standards governing the mediator's conduct are a fundamental element of the forum. The applicable standard may be determined in a number of ways. The preferred method in determining the applicable standard is to peruse the mediation agreement for the standard expressly chosen by the parties.[268]

266. *Ibid.*, para. 38.
267. *Mozer v Augustine*, 2019 Cal. App. Unpub. LEXIS 6183, 2019 WL 4439664 (Cal. App. 2d Dist. 17 September 2019).
268. Cf. *Vita Food Products Inc v Unus Shipping Co Ltd* [1939] AC 277 (PC, Nova Scotia), at 289-290.

Case Illustration

The SIMC model mediation clause reads:[269]

> All disputes, controversies or differences arising out of or in connection with this contract, including any question regarding its existence, validity or termination, shall be first referred to mediation in Singapore in accordance with the Mediation Rules of the Singapore International Mediation Centre for the time being in force.

Examining the mediation clause, it is evident that parties agreeing to it would have expressly chosen the Mediation Rules of the SIMC to apply at mediation. The applicable mediation standards may be discerned from perusing the Mediation Rules of the SIMC (this has been reproduced in Appendix F of this book).

Where Choice of Standard Fails

5.121 In line with the respect for party autonomy in the alternative dispute resolution forums, if the choice of the parties is made *bona fide* and complies with the laws of the jurisdiction regulating private law agreements, the applicable standard would be so determined.[270] However, there are situations where the choice of standard fails:

(1) if the parties made the choice *mala fides*;
(2) if the parties made a choice that is not legal under the governing law, for instance:
  (a) where multiple choices[271] of standards have been elected to apply simultaneously,
  (b) where the chosen standard has latent ambiguities or is intrinsically inadequate, or
  (c) where there is a lack of clarity as to which standard was chosen;
(3) if the parties choose a standard that does not exist; or
(4) if the parties fail to make any choice at all in their mediation agreement.

269. Sourced from the SIMC webpage on 26 September 2018. For the latest information on SIMC, please go to http://simc.com.sg.
270. Cf. Tiong Min Yeo, *The Effective Reach of Choice of Law Agreements*, 20 SAcLJ 723 (2008), at para. 3.
271. In principle, where parties make multiple coexisting or alternative choices of standards, the choices would be invalid and unenforceable. As the standards governing a mediation are so fundamental to its process (e.g., how a mediator should conduct herself, how the mediator may or may not engage parties in private sessions, how a mediator should proceed with drafting a settlement agreement, in what circumstances should the mediator terminate the mediation or recuse herself, etc.), they must subsist from the point in time where the terms of reference for the mediation session (e.g., the mediation agreement) are conceived, and cannot linger indeterminately between multiple possibilities. Cf. *Dubai Electricity Co and ors v Islamic Republic of Iran Shipping Lines (The Iran Vojdan)* [1984] 2 Lloyd's Rep 380, at 385; and *Shanghai Turbo Enterprises Ltd v Liu Ming* [2018] SGHC 172, at [27] et seq.

5.122 In such cases, the determination of the proper standard will be left to the governing law of the dispute. There are namely two methods which the governing law may proffer:

(1) legislation or regulations that may govern how the choice of proper standards at mediation may be determined and prioritised; or, in the alternative,
(2) a fallback rule that the proper standard shall be the one which serves as the closest and most real connection with the transaction, the parties at mediation and all other circumstances which become apparent at mediation.

Consider the following scenarios.

Case Illustrations

Illustration [A]: The *Mediationsgesetz* (German Mediation Act) (Act of July 21, 2012) (hereinafter referred to as 'MediationsG') has codified the basic standards governing mediations taking place in Germany.[272] § 2 MediationsG sets forth the elementary principles of the procedure and the tasks of the mediator, while § 3(1) provides that the 'mediator must disclose any and all circumstances which can interfere with his independence and neutrality'. Furthermore, §§ 3(2) to 3(4) list certain limitations of practice and clarify under which scenarios a mediator is prevented from acting in a case. Where an express choice of mediation standards for a mediation occurring in Germany does not meet the basic requirements of the MediationsG, the prevailing legislative standards would be prioritised.

Illustration [B]: *Kylie Pte Ltd*[273] (Kylie) and *Jason Sdn Bhd*[274] (Jason) have agreed to settle a commercial dispute at mediation at the Utopia International Mediation Centre. Kylie and Jason decided to draft their post-dispute mediation clause without legal assistance, and they mistakenly (but in good faith) decided to select *both* the Mediation Rules of the SIMC and the Mediators' Rules and Code of Ethics of the Malaysian Mediation Centre as governing rules and standards at the mediation. While Kylie and Jason were able to conclude an iMSA, Jason's representatives were unhappy with some remarks made by the mediator, Dannii, who is an accredited mediator at the Utopia International Mediation Centre. While those remarks do not run contrary to the Mediation Rules of the SIMC, they may suggest a violation of a rule in the Mediators' Rule and Code of Ethics of the Malaysian Mediation Centre. If the iMSA were disputed in the High Court of

272. Kristina Osswald and Gustav Flecke-Giammarco, *Germany*, in Nadja Alexander et al. (eds), EU Mediation Law Handbook – Regulatory Robustness Ratings for Mediation Regimes, Wolters Kluwer (2017), at 362.
273. 'Pte Ltd' is an abbreviation used by private limited companies in countries such as Singapore.
274. Sendirian Berhad (Sdn Bhd) is a suffix used in countries such as Malaysia to identify a private limited company.

Utopia, it is likely that the court would not enforce the express choice made of the two different standards.[275] The court may prioritise the Utopian general law, legislation, national codes of mediator conduct, or other regulatory instruments, which serve to inform parties of the standards expected of mediators at mediation.[276] If there are no such laws, national standards or instruments, the court may rule that the proper standard governing the mediation be the one which serves as the closest and most real connection with the transaction, the parties at mediation and other circumstances which become apparent at mediation. This includes the Mediation Rules of the Utopia International Mediation Centre, with which Dannii is accredited.

275. Cf. *Dubai Electricity Co and ors v Islamic Republic of Iran Shipping Lines (The Iran Vojdan)* [1984] 2 Lloyd's Rep 380; and *Shanghai Turbo v Liu Ming* [2018] SGHC 172, at [27] et seq.
276. Recall *Tapoohi v Lewenberg & Ors (No. 2)* [2003] VSC 410 examined above, where in the absence of clearly applicable standards, the court looked to the general law to suggest that the mediator owed duties to the disputants in both contract and in tort.

PUBLIC POLICY AND SUBJECT MATTER-RELATED GROUNDS FOR REFUSAL

Article 5. Grounds for Refusing to Grant Relief

[...]
2. The competent authority of the Party to the Convention where relief is sought under article 4 may also refuse to grant relief if it finds that:

(a) Granting relief would be contrary to the public policy of that Party; or
(b) The subject matter of the dispute is not capable of settlement by mediation under the law of that Party.

COMMENTARY

Public Policy and Subject Matter Grounds

5.123 Article 5(2) sets out the public policy and subject matter-related grounds for refusal of iMSAs. They will be discussed in turn in this commentary. It is observed that different jurisdictions would adopt differing approaches to the application of the public policy and subject matter grounds for refusal. However, it is common ground that there should be a cautious and restrictive application of these defences, especially in the context of enforcement of *commercial* iMSAs. This is because the enforcement of mediation outcomes in this context centres around the fulfilment of party compromises over *commercial* disputes negotiated at arm's length, and in most cases, these issues may be said to seldom affect the public interest.[277] Nonetheless, it is accepted that the Singapore Convention's definition of '*commercial*' includes disputes of the investor-State category in which public interest issues frequently feature.[278] It is also worth further noting that the take-up rate for mediation provisions in international investment agreements is, at the time of writing, gradually increasing.[279]

5.124 The disputing parties' autonomy to decide how their disputes may be resolved, through mediation and negotiation, is generally recognised to be prioritised and paramount, even though it has, in theory, to be balanced with some overarching considerations of policy and justice. This is why it is accepted that iMSAs which resolve commercial disputes should generally be enforced, as long as there is no violation of

277. See Yun Zhao, *The Singapore Mediation Convention: A Version of the New York Convention for Mediation?*, 17(3) J. Priv. Int'l L. (2021), 538, 547.
278. Nadja Alexander and Shouyu Chong, *The Singapore Convention on Mediation: Origins and Application to Investor-State Disputes*, in Mahdev Mohan and Chester Brown (eds), The Asian Turn in Foreign Investment, CUP (2021), at 340-360.
279. Romesh Weeramantry et al., *Conciliation and Mediation in Investor-State Dispute Settlement Provisions: A Quantitative and Qualitative Analysis*, 37 ICSID Rev. (2022).

any fundamental provisions by the domestic laws (which are usually mandatory in nature) of the competent authority. For instance, where mediation is applied to resolve cross-border construction disputes, it is expected by industry stakeholders that the resulting negotiated iMSA is worth its weight in gold, in order to ensure continuity and a move towards completion, especially in complex infrastructure projects.[280] The precise considerations which the competent authorities need to undertake when they are asked to refuse enforcement of iMSAs by reason of public policy or that the subject matter in dispute is not capable of resolution by mediation under the law of the State are discussed below.

5.125 Finally, it is within the prerogative of the relevant competent authority enforcing iMSAs to refuse to grant relief, if it finds that one of Article 5(2) defences has been satisfied, *without* having the parties to the iMSA furnish proof. This is in contrast with Article 5(1) defences, under which the relevant competent authority may refuse enforcement *upon furnishing of proof by parties* that these defences may apply. Nonetheless, in practice, it is quite necessary for the parties to demonstrate to the relevant competent authorities that the conditions under Article 5(2) are satisfied.

Article 5(2)(a): Public Policy as a Ground for Refusal

5.126 Pursuant to Article 5(2)(a), a competent authority may refuse to enforce an iMSA that is contrary to the public policy of the State in which enforcement is sought. It should be emphasised that the public policy exception must be considered in the context of prevailing private international law principles, which contemplates consideration of *both* domestic and international principles.[281] The domestic public policy of the State in which enforcement is sought must be considered 'in a manner that is consistent, insofar as possible, with the objectives of the Convention and the public policies and interests of other Contracting States'.[282] Consequently, the competent authority should only under *highly exceptional circumstances* refuse to enforce iMSAs

280. Shouyu Chong, *The Singapore Convention on Mediation – Its Impact on International Construction Disputes*, in Renato Nazzini (ed.), Construction Arbitration and Alternative Dispute Resolution – Theory and Practice Around the World, Informa Law (2021).

281. Nadja Alexander and Shouyu Chong, *An Introduction to the Singapore Convention on Mediation – Perspectives from Singapore*, 22(4) Nederlands-Vlaams tijdschrisft voor Mediation en conflict management 37 (2018), at 48; and Shouyu Chong and Felix Steffek, *Enforcement of International Settlement Agreements Resulting from Mediation under the Singapore Convention – Private International Law Issues in Perspective*, 31 SAcLJ 448 (2019). Also consider Gary Born, International Commercial Arbitration (2nd Ed.), Wolters Kluwer (2014), at 3652, which is cited by Timothy Schnabel, *The Singapore Convention on Mediation: A Framework for the Cross-Border Recognition and Enforcement of Mediated Settlements*, 19 Pepp. Disp. Resol. L.J. 1 (2019), at 54.

282. Gary Born, International Commercial Arbitration (2nd Ed.), Wolters Kluwer (2014), at 3655; although taken out of context (i.e., Born's words refer to the New York Convention), the phrasing of the words apply with equal logical force to the Singapore Convention as well. See *Renusagar Power Co. Ltd v General Electric Co* [1994] AIR 860, at para. 63.

by reason of public policy,[283] for it is trite that in the realm of private international law, the public policy exception functions as an 'escape mechanism'.[284]

5.127 Administering Article 5(2)(a) *purely* on the basis of the public policy of that enforcement forum's national laws may be imprudent. Doing so may lead to unpredictable outcomes. The unpredictability arises from the fact that public policy varies from country to country,[285] and a deluge of anomalous outcomes is likely to ensue if an unchecked recourse to the forum's domestic public policy were prevalent.[286]

5.128 For completeness, a broad consideration of which kinds of iMSAs may be refused enforcement by competent authorities on public policy grounds can be considered. It is fairly uncontroversial that iMSAs procured by (or in furtherance of) corruption and bribery should be refused enforcement for being contrary to public

283. Timothy Schnabel, *The Singapore Convention on Mediation: A Framework for the Cross-Border Recognition and Enforcement of Mediated Settlements*,19 Pepp. Disp. Resol. L.J. 1 (2019), at 54; Shouyu Chong and Felix Steffek, *Enforcement of International Settlement Agreements Resulting from Mediation under the Singapore Convention – Private International Law Issues in Perspective*, 31 SAcLJ 448 (2019); see also Tiong Min Yeo, *Statute and Public Policy in Private International Law: Gambling Contracts and Foreign Judgments*, 9 Sing. YB Int'l L. 133 (2005). The Singapore Court of Appeal has described exceptional circumstances as those which would 'shock the conscience' or be 'clearly injurious to the public good or ... wholly offensive to the ordinary reasonable and fully informed member of the public', or violate 'the forum's most basic notion of morality and justice' (*PT Asuransi Jasa Indonesia (Persero) v Dexia Bank SA* [2007] 1 SLR(R) 597, at [59]). In contrast, consider the Chinese case of *USA Prods v Women Travel* [1997] SPC 35 (Chinese Zuigao Fayuan), where the court denied the recognition of an arbitral award under the New York Convention's public policy limb because the contract in dispute was one for the performance of heavy metal music, which was repugnant to Chinese domestic public policy. Also consider *Telnikoff v Matusevitch* 347 Md 561 (Md Ct App 1997), where a Maryland Court of Appeal denied the recognition of an English judgment which awarded damages for defamation, as it thought that the English defamation laws were contrary to a domestic public policy which protects free speech as enshrined in the Constitution of the US. The courts in *USA Prods* and *Telnikoff* have adopted, in the authors' view, parochial views of public policy when recognising and enforcing foreign judgments and arbitral awards.
284. Consider *IPCO Nigeria Ltd v Nigerian National Petroleum Corp* [2005] EWHC 726, at para. 13, where in the context of refusing to enforce arbitral awards under the New York Convention by reason of the relevant public policy exception, Peter Gross J warned that 'considerations of public policy, if relied upon to resist enforcement of an [arbitral] award, should be approached with extreme caution ... [the public policy exception] was not intended to furnish an open-ended escape route for refusing enforcement of New York Convention awards'.
285. Pierre Mayer and Audley Sheppard, *Final ILA Report on Public Policy as a Bar to Enforcement of International Arbitral Awards*, 19 Arb. Int'l 249 (2003), at 254. Also consider as a useful illustration the Hong Kong case of *Gao HaiYan and another v Keeneye Holdings Ltd and another* [2011] HKCFI 240, [2011] 3 HKC 157 (Court of First Instance). In the Court of First Instance, Justice Reyes (at para. 96) makes a useful observation about the public policy defence in the context of an international arbitration across the Chinese and Hong Kong jurisdictions: 'Before the Xian Intermediate Court as the court of supervisory jurisdiction, the Respondents accused the Arbitration Panel[...] of bias. The Xian Court rejected the submission. That does not prevent the Hong Kong Court from considering the question of bias from the viewpoint of Hong Kong public policy. This is because Hong Kong public policy may well be different from public policy in Xian. The Hong Kong Court is not bound by a finding of the Xian Court relating to Xian public policy.'
286. Ilias Bantekas, An Introduction to International Arbitration, CUP (2015), at 242-245.

policy.[287] It is highly unlikely that courts will enforce iMSAs while ignoring 'palpable and indisputable illegality'.[288] Therefore, iMSAs procured by duress may also be refused enforcement.[289] National security is a valid public policy concern for the purposes of this article.[290] There may be precedent from the English Court of Appeal lending support to refusal of enforcement by reason of public policy if the iMSA procured enforces obligations which were initially conceived under undue influence.[291] However, it appears that iMSAs procured in violation of trade sanctions (or similar world trade regulations) *may* be enforced.[292]

5.129 Accordingly, it is the prerogative of the competent authorities to determine if their domestic public policy has been contravened for the purposes of administering Article 5(2)(a) of the Singapore Convention. At the same time, the object, purpose and reach of the Singapore Convention are best fulfilled where courts judiciously consider *only* those public policies identified by the forum as sufficiently 'international'.[293]

Case Illustrations

Illustration [A]: It is useful to consider *Daiichi Sankyo Company Limited v Malvinder Mohan Singh.*[294] In this decision, the High Court of New Delhi exercised its discretion on public policy grounds to refuse to enforce an

287. These are serious wrongdoings, and there may be more equally serious ones, such as drug trafficking, prostitution (see *Re Macartney* [1921] 1 Ch 522), paedophilia etc.: Gary Born, International Commercial Arbitration (2nd Ed.), Wolters Kluwer (2014), at 3673-3674. Also see *Soleimany v Soleimany* [1999] QB 785, [1999] 3 All ER 847; and contrast with *Westacre Investments Inc v Jugoimport-SDPR Holding Co.* [1998] 4 All ER 570, at 593, affirmed by the English Court of Appeal in [1999] 2 Lloyd's Rep. 65.
288. *Westacre Investments Inc v Jugoimport-SDPR Holding Co.* [1998] 4 All ER 570, at 593, affirmed by the English Court of Appeal in [1999] 2 Lloyd's Rep. 65.
289. Consider *Re Meyer* [1971] P 298.
290. Timothy Schnabel, *The Singapore Convention on Mediation: A Framework for the Cross-Border Recognition and Enforcement of Mediated Settlements*, 19 Pepp. Disp. Resol. L.J. 1 (2019), at 54. See, also, Report of Working Group II (Dispute Settlement) on the Work of its 68th Session (5-9 February 2018), A/CN.9/934 (2018), at para. 67. Available at http://undocs.org/A/CN.9/934 (Accessed 17 May 2022); and Intervention of Israel, in UNCITRAL Audio Recordings: Working Group II (Dispute Settlement), 68th Session, 5 February 2018, 15:00-18:00.
291. See *Israel Discount Bank of New York v Hadjipateras* [1984] 1 WLR 137. However, this decision may be criticised because the undue influence vitiating factor is traditionally understood as a purely domestic form of public policy: the decision by the English Court of Appeal had inexplicably elevated its status. Furthermore, the soundness of the court's decision may be questioned for conflating the issues arising from the *underlying cause of action from the initial avenue of dispute resolution* with the issues arising from *enforcing those dispute resolution outcomes*.
292. See Gary Born, *International Commercial Arbitration* (2nd Ed.), Wolters Kluwer (2014), at 3674-3676.
293. Consider Gabriel Michael Wilner, *Choice of Forum and Public Policy: Some Indications of the Development in United States Law of a Distinct 'International' Public Policy*, 2 N.C.J. Int'l L. & Comm. Reg. 29 (1977).
294. *Daiichi Sankyo Company Limited v Malvinder Mohan Singh and ors.* O.M.P. (EFA) (Comm.) (6/2016).

international arbitral award, as it bound young children (aged between eight and 12 years old when the arbitration was conducted) to be jointly and severally liable for damages amounting to *greater than €490 million* awarded by an arbitral tribunal seated in Singapore.[295] The rendering of such an exorbitant sum of damages against minors would have been offensive in the eyes of the public policies of both domestic and international standards, hence the court severed from enforcement the parts of the arbitral award which went against the minors' favour. Similar considerations may likely apply when iMSAs binding young children jointly and severally to pay an exorbitant amount in damages are sought to be enforced under the Singapore Convention.

Illustration [B]: This case was discussed earlier in the commentary of Article 5(1)(b)(i). Only the important facts are repeated here. In *Taiwan High Court Judgment (April 26, 2011)*,[296] the parties were married in 2000. However, they subsequently filed for divorce. A separation agreement was entered into after a mediation proceeding in 2007, under which the parties agreed that if and when the appellee becomes eligible for applying for a ROC National Identity Card and notifies the appellant of the same, the appellant shall assist the appellee to obtain the ROC National Identity Card. In 2009, the appellee moved to another man's residence and left the family affairs unattended without notifying the appellant. This was in breach of Taiwanese immigration law, which imposes an obligation on the appellee, who was from the Mainland Area in the People's Republic of China - and whose purpose for entering into the Taiwan Area was for marriage - to cohabit with the appellant. It is conceivable that if a settlement agreement runs contrary to State law and could perpetuate a serious illegality (e.g., the breach of immigration laws), it may not be enforced under the Singapore Convention on public policy grounds.

Article 5(2)(b): Subject Matter of the Dispute is not Capable of Settlement by Mediation

5.130 Article 5(2)(b) of the Singapore Convention provides that the competent authority may refuse to enforce iMSAs if the subject matter of the dispute is not capable

295. Also see *BAZ v BBA and others and other matters* [2018] SGHC 275, [2020] 5 SLR 266, especially at [169] et seq., for a deeper perusal of the facts of this case. Here, the Singapore High Court ruled on an application to set aside the arbitral award. Interestingly (and unusually so), the judgment of the New Delhi enforcement proceedings, which were concurrently initiated with the setting aside proceedings in Singapore, was delivered first, before the setting aside proceedings were concluded. If the Singapore judgment had been delivered before the New Delhi proceedings were concluded, the public policy issue raised in the New Delhi court may be rendered moot, as the Singapore High Court ruled to set aside the award against the children for public policy reasons. Justice Belinda Ang ruled (at [180]): 'All in all, such an award against the Minors that saddles them with legal liability for an amount exceeding S$720m shocks the conscience, and it violates Singapore's most basic notion of justice to find the Minors liable under a contract that was entered into when they were only between three to eight years old at the material time. At the time of the arbitration, they were only between eight at 12 years old.'

296. 100-Jia-Shang-Geng-Yi-Zi-1.

of settlement by mediation under the law of that State. This clause was modelled after Article V(2)(a) of the New York Convention, with respect to the cross-border enforcement of international commercial arbitral awards.[297] So some lessons may be drawn from how the New York Convention is applied with respect to this subject matter defence. An analogy from Article II(1) of the New York Convention[298] may also be drawn, as identical standards and considerations are applied.[299] However, caution should be exercised in applying the case law from international commercial arbitration, with respect to the setting aside of arbitral awards at the seat by reason of subject matter non-arbitrability.[300] This analogy would not work in practice as iMSAs are not regulated by a 'seat', unlike in international commercial arbitration.[301]

5.131 Parties seeking to avoid enforcement under this provision in the Convention should demonstrate to the competent authority that the subject matter of the dispute resolved by their iMSA is not susceptible to mediation under the relevant governing law. As Schnabel notes, some international disputes may be subject to forum mandatory adjudication processes.[302] For instance, according to South Korean law, some intellectual property disputes may not be capable of settlement at mediation, for it is the orthodox view that such disputes fall within the exclusive jurisdiction of other more competent and specialised dispute resolution authorities under the Korean Intellectual Property Office.[303] Yet, in practice, this should be a seldom-invoked ground for refusal, owing to the many methods for reframing issues and disputes at mediation to address a range of commercial and other interests, needs and priorities.

5.132 Here, even though the choice of law provided by the article appears to trigger the *lex fori* (that is, law of the forum) of the competent authority, the court should interpret it with similar private international law considerations as the 'public policy'

297. Convention on the Recognition and Enforcement of Foreign Arbitral Awards (1958), Art. V(2)(a) reads, '[r]ecognition and enforcement of an arbitral award may also be refused if the competent authority in the country where recognition and enforcement is sought finds that[...] [t]he subject matter of the difference is not capable of settlement by arbitration under the law of that country[...]'.
298. Convention on the Recognition and Enforcement of Foreign Arbitral Awards (1958), Art. II(1) reads, 'Each Contracting State shall recognise an agreement in writing under which the parties undertake to submit to arbitration all or any differences which have arisen or which may arise between them in respect of a defined legal relationship, whether contractual or not, concerning a subject matter capable of settlement by arbitration.'
299. Gary Born, International Commercial Arbitration (2nd Ed.), Wolters Kluwer (2014), at 3696; Albert Jan van den Berg, The New York Arbitration Convention of 1958 – Towards a Uniform Judicial Interpretation, Kluwer (1981), at 359. Cf. Timothy Schnabel, *The Singapore Convention on Mediation: A Framework for the Cross-Border Recognition and Enforcement of Mediated Settlements*, 19 Pepp. Disp. Resol. L.J. 1 (2019), at 54-55.
300. See, for instance, *Westbridge Ventures II Investment Holdings v Anupam Mittal* [2021] SGHC 244.
301. Nadja Alexander and Shouyu Chong, *Leading the Way for the Recognition and Enforcement of International Mediated Settlement Agreements – The Singapore Convention on Mediation Act 2020*, 34 SAcLJ 1 (2022), at para. 19.
302. *Ibid.*
303. See Gyooho Lee, Keon-Hyung Ahn and Hacques de Werra, *Euro-Korean Perspectives on the Use of Arbitration and ADR Mechanisms for Solving Intellectual Property Disputes*, 30 Arb. Int'l 91, (2014), at 104.

exception, just as it has been analysed earlier. This is another exceptional 'escape mechanism' defence.[304] While the enforcing court may consider under its own domestic rules that certain subject matter areas are not susceptible to mediation (for instance, some jurisdictions may consider tax or certain kinds of intellectual property disputes in the commercial setting as not capable of being resolved at mediation), they ought to additionally consider the extent to which the subject matter concerned has a sufficient nexus to the forum. In private international law disputes, Born has persuasively argued with the support of precedents – albeit in the context of international commercial arbitration, but this may be justifiably analogised to the international commercial mediation context – that the courts should, as far as possible, not practice parochialism in respect to the 'subject matter' exception, but consider the law of closest-connection to the dispute when enforcing dispute resolution outcomes stemming from Convention obligations.[305] In this way, competent authorities ought to avoid simply imposing their domestic rules upon all iMSAs which come before them and give due consideration to the international nature of iMSAs.

Case Illustration

Under the laws of Gotland, commercial tax disputes are subject matters that are not capable of settlement at mediation. The competent authority of Gotland is presented with an iMSA that was concluded in Uppland, of which the choice of law for that settlement points to the laws of Ruritania. Under the laws of Uppland and Ruritania, tax disputes may be resolved at mediation. If the mediated dispute has *no connection* whatsoever to Gotland, the competent courts of Gotland should not refuse to grant enforcement relief owing to their Convention obligations and prioritise the enforcement of the iMSA.[306]

304. Shouyu Chong and Felix Steffek, *Enforcement of International Settlement Agreements Resulting from Mediation under the Singapore Convention – Private International Law Issues in Perspective,* 31 SAcLJ 448 (2019); Nadja Alexander and Shouyu Chong, *An Introduction to the Singapore Convention on Mediation – Perspectives from Singapore,* 22(4) Nederlands-Vlaams tijdschrisft voor Mediation en conflictmanagement 37 (2018), at 49; and Timothy Schnabel, *The Singapore Convention on Mediation: A Framework for the Cross-Border Recognition and Enforcement of Mediated Settlements,* 19 Pepp. Disp. Resol. L.J. 1 (2019), at 55.
305. Gary Born, International Commercial Arbitration (2nd Ed.), Wolters Kluwer (2014), at 3702.
306. *Id.*, at 606 and 3700.

FOUR REFLECTIONS ON ARTICLE 5

5.133 In closing the discussion on Article 5, we offer four observations: first in relation to the role confidentiality plays in recognition and enforcement procedures; second, the discretion of the competent authority; third, in relation to the burdens of proof *vis-à-vis* parties in respect to enforcement of iMSAs; and fourth, in relation to the exhaustiveness of the provisions in Article 5.

5.134 First, an observation on mediation confidentiality. Confidentiality is a hallmark of the mediation process. It can provide a kind of safety net to encourage parties to engage in a full and frank exchange during mediation without fear of evidence of mediation communications being admitted into subsequent litigation proceedings. At the same time, the parties will not be permitted to hide behind the cloak of confidentiality to avoid legal accountability for conduct during the mediation. For this reason, there is a clear legislative and jurisprudential precedent for exceptions to mediation confidentiality as this commentary has set out. Moreover, there is a long history of exceptions to the *without prejudice privilege*, which has been expressly applied to mediation situations.

5.135 Second, as previously indicated, the relevant competent authority of a Party to the Convention *may* refuse to grant enforcement relief if one or more of the grounds for refusal under Article 5 is proved. In other words, it appears on the plain reading of Article 5 that the competent authorities of States and other Parties to the Convention possess residual discretion to enforce iMSAs even if one or more of the grounds for refusal is proved.[307] This wording appears to be drawn from the New York Convention and reflects the stance taken in international commercial arbitration.[308] Following the conventional practice in arbitration, it is likely that such discretion is to be exercised within narrow circumstances. Hill has eloquently proposed, albeit in the arbitration context, '[A]s a general rule, if a defence to enforcement [...] is established, enforcement will be (and should be) refused. [However, to] this general principle, there is a limited number of exceptions [...], which are based on intelligible legal principles, rather than the court's perception of what would be fair in all the circumstances.'[309] There is fertile ground for deeper investigation (going beyond the analogy with arbitration) into the exercise of judicial discretion in relation to applications to enforce iMSAs under the Convention, as more examples of iMSA enforcement (or challenges to its enforcement) under the Convention are reported in the years after it came into force in September 2020.

5.136 Next, it was mentioned earlier in the commentary of Article 5(1)(b)(ii) about how the burdens of proof in respect to the enforcement of iMSAs have been reversed,

307. Timothy Schnabel, *The Singapore Convention on Mediation: A Framework for the Cross-Border Recognition and Enforcement of Mediated Settlements*, 19 Pepp. Disp. Resol. L.J. 1 (2019), at 42.
308. See Julian Lew, Loukas Mistelis and Stefan Kröll, *Comparative International Commercial Arbitration*, Kluwer Law International (2003), at para. [26-68].
309. Jonathan Hill, *The Exercise of Judicial Discretion in Relation to Applications to Enforce Arbitral Awards under the New York Convention 1958*, 36 Oxford J. Legal Stud. 304 (2016), at 333.

if it falls to become enforced under the ambit of the Singapore Convention. We hope to take this observation further. In the past, parties in many jurisdictions would need to prove the bindingness of their iMSA if they sought its enforcement – sometimes through processes of notarisation or court approval. Under the Singapore Convention, so long as Article 4 formality requirements are satisfied, an iMSA will be presumed to be binding on parties, unless the objecting party is able to prove that this is not so according to its terms to rebut that presumption (that is, Article 5(1)(b)(ii)), or if any of the other Article 5 defences are available. The implications of such a reversal of burden are wide: iMSAs covered by the Convention would become prima facie enforceable instruments and the onus lies on the party that wishes to excuse themselves from the obligations contained therein to plead to the competent courts that an Article 5 defence is available. It follows that Article 5(1) (which includes the contract-related and mediator conduct-related grounds for refusal) is worded in a way that stringently manages *when* the relevant competent authorities may consider the issue of Article 5 defences, to the exception of the public policy and subject matter defences (which falls under the ambit of Article 5(2)). The availability of these defences falling under Article 5(1) are contingent upon the furnishing of proof by the objecting party,[310] further galvanising the effect of the reversal of burdens of proof which the Singapore Convention has on iMSAs falling within its scope. Owing to the inherent powers of courts to regulate matters as to public policy and subject matters amenable to their jurisdiction, the competent courts may consider on their own accord the defences falling under Article 5(2) without an objecting party's pleading[311] – but as analysed earlier in the commentary of Articles 5(2)(a) and 5(2)(b), these defences serve as exceptional escape mechanisms and should be sparingly invoked unless egregious[312] circumstances exist.

5.137 Finally, in relation to the grounds for a refusal to enforce iMSAs set out in Article 5 of the Singapore Convention, it has been understood that they are intended to be exhaustive.[313] However, it is conceivable that this position may be challenged if we scrutinise Article 6, which specifically addresses parallel enforcement proceedings, in

310. To recall, Art. 5(1) essentially provides, 'The competent authority of the Party to the Convention where relief is sought under article 4 may refuse to grant relief *at the request of the party against whom the relief is sought* ***only*** *if that party furnishes to the competent authority proof* [...]' (emphasis, bold and underline added).
311. Timothy Schnabel, *The Singapore Convention on Mediation: A Framework for the Cross-Border Recognition and Enforcement of Mediated Settlements*, 19 Pepp. Disp. Resol. L.J. 1 (2019), at 42. Of course, parties remain free to plead for the public policy or subject matter defences to apply.
312. Take, for example, *Daiichi Sankyo Company Limited v Malvinder Mohan Singh and ors.* (2016) O.M.P. (EFA) (Comm.) (6/2016), where young children were found jointly and severally liable to pay an exorbitant multi-million dollar sum of money in damages: such a factual scenario represents the degree of egregiousness which should exist in order for courts to yield their inherent powers under the public policy exception.
313. See, for example, interventions of Canada, Norway, and the Chair in UNCITRAL Audio Recordings: Working Group II (Arbitration and Conciliation), 63rd Session, 10 September 2015, 9:30-12:30, https://icms.unov.org/CarbonWeb/public/uncitral/speakerslog/ba60b99e-4f4c-4070-a244-1566055d7948 (Accessed 21 May 2019); and Timothy Schnabel, *The Singapore Convention on Mediation: A Framework for the Cross-Border Recognition and Enforcement of Mediated Settlements*, 19 Pepp. Disp. Resol. L.J. 1 (2019), at 42.

light of the principles of recognition of foreign judgments in private international law.[314] We will examine this in detail in the commentary of Article 6.

314. Art. 6 provides that the relevant competent authority of a Party to the Convention may adjourn enforcement proceedings if the same iMSA were to be brought to the competent authority of *another* Party to the Convention for enforcement *and* parties challenge its enforceability by – possibly – seeking to prove the same Art. 5 ground for refusal of enforcement in both jurisdictions. Can the second competent authority refuse to grant enforcement relief of the iMSA on the basis of the first forum's refusal? There may be a case for such a refusal, if we consider the principle of recognition of foreign judgments in private international law: that is, the former court may recognise the latter's judgment – in respect to the discrete Art. 5 question that has been litigated – under its private international law rules, and administer the Convention accordingly. If refusal is possible, there could be an unspoken ground for refusal not articulated by the drafting of Art. 5 of the Convention which necessitates further indulgence.

ARTICLE 6

Parallel Applications or Claims

If an application or a claim relating to a settlement agreement has been made to a court, an arbitral tribunal or any other competent authority which may affect the relief being sought under article 4, the competent authority of the State where such relief is sought may, if it considers it proper, adjourn the decision and may also, on the request of a party, order the other party to give suitable security.

COMMENTARY

6.01 Article 6 of the Singapore Convention addresses the case where parties to an international mediated settlement agreement (iMSA) apply under Article 4 of the Convention to the competent authorities of two or more Contracting Parties to the Convention for the recognition or enforcement of the iMSA in parallel proceedings.[1] Where the recognition or enforcement proceedings are challenged in the first forum,[2] the second (and later) forum(s) may, if it considers proper, adjourn their recognition or enforcement proceedings. Additionally, upon the request of a party to the iMSA, the adjourning forum may order the other party to furnish security.

Case Illustration

Natalie's Bakes AB[3] (Natalie) and *Tate Confections Pty Ltd*[4] (Tate) have concluded a settlement agreement after a mediation session. The iMSA falls within the scope of the Convention's application *per* Article 1, and easily satisfies the Article 4 evidential requirements for reliance on settlement agreements.

1. Shouyu Chong and Nadja Alexander, *An Implied Ground for Refusal to Enforce iMSAs under the Singapore Convention on Mediation: The Effect of Article 6*, Kluwer Mediation Blog (17 February 2019).
2. The challenge may be on Art. 5 grounds. Alternatively, the challenge may be in respect of the non-fulfilment of the Art. 4 requirements regarding the evidence of mediation taking place.
3. 'AB' is the abbreviation of *Aktiebolag* which is used in company names in countries such as Sweden to denote private limited companies.
4. 'Pty Ltd' is an abbreviation used by proprietary limited companies in countries such as Australia.

Unfortunately, Tate fails to comply with the terms of the iMSA. Natalie, knowing that Tate has liquid assets in Sugarstone and SpiceCastle (which we shall assume are Parties to the Singapore Convention), applies to the High Courts of both States (which are the relevant competent courts) to enforce the iMSA under the Singapore Convention's enforcement mechanism. However, Tate challenges the enforcement – first in Sugarstone and subsequently in SpiceCastle. In the High Court of Sugarstone, Tate claims that the iMSA should be void[5] because it was conceived based upon a fraudulent misrepresentation by Natalie. Tate submits the same arguments in their defence in the High Court of SpiceCastle. Applying Article 6, the High Court of SpiceCastle may adjourn enforcement proceedings if it considers proper, in view of parallel proceedings taking place in the High Court of Sugarstone.

6.02 The rule in Article 6 is straightforward, but the practical effect of its application is less clear. Referring to the illustration above, there is a need to consider what an adjourning court may do should a challenge lodged in the first forum succeed.[6] A settlement agreement – which is essentially a *contractual agreement* concluded between two parties – that has been refused enforcement in one jurisdiction may, in theory, be enforced in another. From a private law perspective, the judicial vitiating of contractual obligations in one forum does not extinguish those obligations extraterritorially. Therefore, the adjourning forum may not simply apply Article 5(1)(b)(i)[7] to refuse the recognition and enforcement of the challenged iMSA, as its obligations nevertheless subsist. What follow-up powers may the adjourning court(s) possess?

The Scope of Article 6

6.03 Article 6 of the Singapore Convention covers three broad categories of claims and applications:

(1) an application or claim about the substance of the iMSA;
(2) an application or claim about the annulment of the iMSA; and
(3) parallel enforcement proceedings in several jurisdictions.[8]

5. United Nations Convention on International Settlement Agreements Resulting from Mediation (2019), Art. 5(1)(b)(i).
6. That is, if Tate were to successfully prove that the settlement agreement it had entered into was tainted by fraudulent misrepresentation, and therefore should be rendered 'null and void', it would fall within the Art. 5(1)(b)(i) defence.
7. That is, the provision which allows the competent authority of a State to refuse recognition or enforcement of a settlement agreement because it is an instrument that is null and void, inoperative or incapable of being performed.
8. Report of Working Group II (Dispute Settlement) on the Work of its 65th Session (Vienna, 12-23 September 2016), A/CN.9/896 (2016), at para. 124. Available at http://undocs.org/A/CN.9/896 (Accessed 13 May 2022).

6.04 Article 6 of the Singapore Convention relates to any claim or application that 'may affect' the enforcement and recognition process of an iMSA. This is in contrast to Article VI of the New York Convention, which only covers instances when the award is being challenged in the jurisdiction of origin.

6.05 Furthermore, Article 6 of the Singapore Convention states that a parallel application is to be made to 'a court, an arbitral tribunal or any other competent authority'. By comparison, Article VI of the New York Convention refers to a competent authority of the country 'in which, or under the law of which, that award was made'. Reference to a court, an arbitral tribunal or any other competent authority indicates that Article 6 not only regulates parallel enforcement proceedings in two jurisdictions, but the provision also covers the cases that involve substantive disputes. By way of example, a party to an iMSA may bring a claim against the other party, based on a dispute resolution clause of the iMSA. At the same time, the other party may start the enforcement process in another jurisdiction under the Singapore Convention. In this case, the competent authority under Article 6 has to address whether the parallel dispute that involves substantive claims justifies the suspension of the enforcement proceedings under Article 6 of the Singapore Convention. The competent authority may uphold party autonomy and adjourn the enforcement process if the requirements for enforcing the dispute resolution clause of the iMSA are met.[9]

Case Illustrations

Illustration [A]: *Natalie* and *Tate* signed a settlement agreement after the conclusion of a successful mediation. The settlement agreement contains a dispute resolution clause, according to which any dispute that arises out of the settlement agreement, including the questions of its validity, shall be resolved by an ad hoc arbitration under the arbitration rules of UNCITRAL. Tate fails to comply with the terms of the settlement agreement. As a result, Natalie commences the enforcement process of the settlement agreement in Sugarstone, a Contracting Party to the Singapore Convention. In parallel, Tate decides to trigger the dispute resolution clause of the settlement agreement, as they consider the settlement agreement invalid. The competent authority in Sugarstone has to address whether the parallel arbitration process regarding the invalidity of the settlement agreement justifies the suspension of the enforcement process under the Singapore Convention.

Illustration [B]: The US case of *Smith v Smith*[10] represents an illustration, albeit in the context of family law of a court staying the enforcement process of a settlement agreement. This case involved a matrimonial action, which resulted

9. See Vakhtang Giorgadze, *Dispute Resolution Clauses and the Enforcement of International Mediated Settlement Agreements under the Singapore Convention on Mediation*, TDM 3 (2021).
10. *Smith v Smith*, 178 A.D.3d 980, 112 N.Y.S.3d 580, 2019 N.Y. App. Div. LEXIS 9059, 2019 NY Slip Op 09051, 2019 WL 6884765 (N.Y. App. Div. 2d Dep't 18 December 2019).

in a settlement agreement. The settlement agreement contained a dispute resolution provision, according to which the parties had to mediate any disputes under the settlement. The plaintiff commenced a civil action and asked the court to hold the defendant in civil contempt for his failure to comply with the support obligations under the settlement agreement. The defendant filed a motion to dismiss the action, on the ground that the parties were obliged to mediate any disputes under the settlement. The Appellate Division of the Supreme Court of New York agreed with the defendant that the parties had to attend mediation and opined: '[a] matrimonial settlement is a contract subject to principles of contract interpretation. Here, the parties' stipulation of settlement contained an unambiguous mediation clause requiring the parties to resolve their dispute through mediation'. The court went on and explained that the lower court should have stayed any further proceedings in this case while the mediation session was pending.

An Implied Ground for Refusal to Enforce iMSAs under the Singapore Convention on Mediation: The Effect of Article 6?

6.06 Article VI of the New York Convention may be considered for guidance: it is similarly worded and was the basis for Article 6 of the Singapore Convention.[11] Article VI of the New York Convention[12] facilitates the application of Article V(1)(e) of the New York Convention,[13] which stipulates that a court may refuse recognition and enforcement of a foreign arbitral award if it 'has not yet become binding on the parties, or has been set aside or suspended by a competent authority of the country'.

Case Illustration

Drawing from the earlier case illustration, if *Natalie* and *Tate* are dealing with an arbitral award, Tate will:

11. Report of Working Group II (Dispute Settlement) on the Work of its 68th Session (New York, 5-9 February 2018), A/CN.9/934 (2018), at para. 68. Available at http://undocs.org/A/CN.9/934 (Accessed 13 May 2022).
12. Convention on the Recognition and Enforcement of Foreign Arbitral Awards (1958). Art. VI provides, 'If an application for the setting aside or suspension of the award has been made to a competent authority referred to in article V(1)(e), the authority before which the award is sought to be relied upon may, if it considers it proper, adjourn the decision on the enforcement of the award and may also, on the application of the party claiming enforcement of the award, order the other party to give suitable security.'
13. Art. V(1)(e) of the New York Convention provides, 'Recognition and enforcement of the award may be refused, at the request of the party against whom it is invoked, only if that party furnishes to the competent authority where the recognition and enforcement is sought, proof that: ... [t]he award has not yet become binding on the parties, or has been set aside or suspended by a competent authority of the country in which, or under the law of which, that award was made.'

(1) first apply to set aside the arbitral award at the seat of the arbitration;
(2) then proceed to the jurisdictions where Natalie has applied to enforce the award to apply for an adjournment of enforcement proceedings.

If the setting aside application in the courts at the seat is successful, the adjourning courts would refuse to recognise or enforce the foreign arbitral award on the basis of Article V(1)(e).

6.07 The significant difference here between the New York Convention and the Singapore Convention is that the Singapore Convention does not make provisions for what the court may do once a challenge to the recognition or enforcement of an iMSA in a parallel proceeding succeeds. This leads to an interesting possibility: can Article 6 of the Singapore Convention be read in a way that creates an implied ground for refusal of recognition or enforcement of iMSAs outside the scope of Article 5? This implied defence is founded upon the fact that the iMSA sought to be enforced has already been refused enforcement by the courts of another State. In other words, this implied defence is buttressed by private international law principles of recognition of foreign judgments.[14] Consequently, the adjourning forum has to give effect (by applying the principles of recognition in the private international law sense) to the first forum's judgment ruling finally and conclusively on the *specific issue* in respect of how the challenged iMSA may be refused enforcement on Article 5 grounds.

6.08 Such an implied defence would need to be restricted to settlement agreements that have been refused enforcement because of succeeding defences which stem from private law vitiating factors (for instance, incapacity of parties, terms which are null and void, inoperability and incapability of performance etc.) and mediator misconduct. It should be emphasised that the proposed implied defence would not apply to iMSAs that were refused enforcement on public policy grounds or because their subject matter may not be susceptible to mediation. This is because the legal test administered to adjudicate whether these grounds for refusal are available are likely to be particular to the domestic laws in each State.[15] It may be possible for an iMSA to be enforceable in one State, but for the courts of another to refuse enforcement on public policy grounds.[16]

6.09 Therefore, an implied ground for refusal of enforcement could conceivably be read into Article 6 of the Singapore Convention. This may be buttressed by trite private international law principles of recognition of foreign judgments (that is, particularly of a court judgment that determines finally and conclusively if an iMSA may be refused

14. Shouyu Chong and Felix Steffek, *Enforcement of International Settlement Agreements Resulting from Mediation under the Singapore Convention – Private International Law Issues in Perspective*, 31 SAcLJ 448 (2019).
15. Cf. *BAZ v BBA and others and other matters* [2018] SGHC 275, [2020] 5 SLR 266, at [50].
16. Consider *Gao HaiYan and another v Keeneye Holdings Ltd and another* [2011] HKCFI 240, [2011] 3 HKC 157 (Court of First Instance). This judgment was eventually reversed by the Court of Appeal in *Gao HaiYan and another v Keeneye Holdings Ltd and another* [2011] HKCA 459, [2012] 1 HKC 335, [2012] 1 HKLRD 627.

enforcement in that jurisdiction). The competent authority of the adjourning State should recognise the first forum's ruling on the issue of how a party may satisfy Article 5 grounds for refusal of enforcement of the iMSA. Although, in some jurisdictions,[17] courts do not recognise foreign court judgments and require parties to sue afresh in relation to the discrete issues adjudged under their private international law, it is certainly arguable that the competent authorities of Parties to the Convention are – nonetheless – bound by their Convention obligations to recognise a *particular* judgment of the court which has determined whether an iMSA may be refused enforcement.

6.10 A different view is espoused by Stute and Wansac who note that 'there is a plausible argument that the Singapore Convention's signatories, by [expressly] excluding such a non-enforcement ground, sought to eliminate any *res judicata* effect for enforcement litigation arising from mediated settlement agreements'. They have instead proposed in a footnote that '[a] possible textual hook for parties seeking a *res judicata* effect of a non-enforcement decision in other jurisdictions could rely on the Singapore Convention Article 5(2)'s exception for public policy or not being "capable of settlement by mediation under the law of that Party"'.[18]

6.11 On the public policy point, there is no precedent to characterise an iMSA that has been refused enforcement by the competent authority (or authorities) of one State as one that would lead to a contravention of public policy, as the public policy exception would only apply under highly exceptional (and also egregious) circumstances.[19] It would also appear illogical to refuse to enforce an iMSA which has been refused enforcement in another State by reason of its subject matter being incapable of being settled by mediation, as the fact of refusal of enforcement has no direct link to the question of whether the resolved subject matter in the iMSA is capable of being settled by mediation.

---

17. According to Adrian Briggs, the Netherlands is one of such jurisdictions: see Adrian Briggs, *Recognition of Foreign Judgments: A Matter of Obligation*, 129 L. Q. Rev. 87 (2013), at note 18. In Asia, it is reported that the courts of Thailand would also require parties to sue afresh: Poomintr Sooksripaisarnkit, *Country Report: Kingdom of Thailand*, in Adeline Chong (ed.), Recognition and Enforcement of Foreign Judgments in Asia, Asian Business Law Institute (2017), at para. 21. However the report on Thailand may be cast in doubt as it has failed to consider recent judicial precedents (such as *Supreme Court decision no. 6565/2544* (2001 A.D.)) which have ruled that Thai courts may recognise and enforce foreign judgments under specified conditions; see Tosaporn Leepuengtham, *Cross-border Enforcement of IP Rights in Thailand*, in Paul Torremans (ed.), Research Handbook on Cross-Border Enforcement of Intellectual Property, Elgar (2014), at 105-106.
18. David Stute and Alexis Wansac, *The Singapore Convention: Not much There, There*, 3 ITA Rev. 32 (2021), 52-53.
19. See the analysis on Art. 5(2)(a) in the commentary on 'Article 5(2)(a): Public Policy as a Ground for Refusal'. The cases of *BAZ v BBA* [2018] SGHC 275, [2020] 5 SLR 266, and *Daiichi Sankyo Company Limited v Malvinder Mohan Singh and ors.* O.M.P. (EFA) (Comm.) (6/2016) are illustrative.

Case Illustration

Following the earlier illustration, *Natalie's Bakes AB* (Natalie) and *Tate Confections Pty* Ltd (Tate) have concluded an iMSA after a mediation session. The settlement agreement falls within the scope of the Convention's application *per* Article 1 and satisfies the Article 4 evidential requirements for reliance on settlement agreements. Tate fails to comply with the terms of the iMSA.

Natalie, knowing that Tate has liquid assets in Sugarstone and SpiceCastle (which we shall assume are Parties to the Singapore Convention), applies to the High Courts of both States (which are the relevant competent courts) to enforce the iMSA under the Singapore Convention's enforcement mechanism. However, Tate challenges the enforcement, first in Sugarstone and second, in SpiceCastle. In the High Court of Sugarstone, Tate claims that the iMSA should be void[20] because it was conceived based upon a fraudulent misrepresentation by Natalie. Tate submits the same arguments in its defence in the High Court of SpiceCastle. Applying Article 6, the High Court of SpiceCastle may adjourn enforcement proceedings if it considers proper, in view of parallel proceedings taking place in the High Court of Sugarstone. If Tate successfully proves a fraudulent misrepresentation in the High Court of Sugarstone, and the court issues a final and conclusive judgment ruling that the iMSA is void and refuses to enforce it because Article 5(1)(b)(i) was proven, Tate may subsequently proceed to the High Court of SpiceCastle, apply to lift the Article 6 adjournment, and apply to have the foreign judgment from the first court recognised. Consequently, it is likely that the iMSA will be refused enforcement as well in SpiceCastle.

6.12 It is likely that Article 6 has been worded as such to respect the autonomy of the States to the Convention, and their respective competent authorities, to respond to decisions of the competent courts and other authorities in other States in a manner most consistent with their interpretation of the Singapore Convention read with their domestic laws on recognising foreign judgments.

20. United Nations Convention on International Settlement Agreements Resulting from Mediation, Art. 5(1)(b)(i).

ARTICLE 7

Other Laws or Treaties

This Convention shall not deprive any interested party of any right it may have to avail itself of a settlement agreement in the manner and to the extent allowed by the law or the treaties of the Party to the Convention where such settlement agreement is sought to be relied upon.

COMMENTARY

7.01 Article 7 of the Singapore Convention preserves the existing obligations of Contracting Parties pursuant to other laws and treaties, particularly in regard to the rights associated with international mediated settlement agreements (iMSAs) and other kinds of settlement agreements. It is, in effect, a 'more favourable right' provision drafted into the Convention.[1] For instance, where States are bound by subsisting bilateral or multilateral arrangements governing how iMSAs arising from investor-State disputes may be enforced, the Singapore Convention will be administered in a way that does not interfere with those subsisting obligations, but only to such a degree that the relevant laws would authorise.[2] Article 7 of the Singapore Convention mirrors Article VII(1) of the New York Convention.

7.02 Additionally, Article 7 preserves the rights of parties to the iMSA to elect to enforce it as a contract or other type of enforceable instrument (such as an arbitral award) in accordance with the domestic laws of States which are Signatories to the Convention, outside of the scope of the Convention. By way of illustration, in India, an iMSA might be enforceable under Part III of the Arbitration and Conciliation Act, 1996 if the parties to the iMSA specifically designate the Arbitration and Conciliation Act,

1. Report of Working Group II (Dispute Settlement) on the Work of its 67th Session (Vienna, 2-6 October 2017), A/CN.9/929 (2017), at para. 19. Available at http://undocs.org/A/CN.9/929 (Accessed 19 April 2022).
2. Shouyu Chong and Felix Steffek, *Enforcement of International Settlement Agreements Resulting from Mediation under the Singapore Convention – Private International Law Issues in Perspective*, 31 SAcLJ 448 (2019), at para. 23.

1996 as the applicable law.[3] Section 74 of the Act prescribes that the settlement agreement shall have the same status and effect as an arbitral award on agreed terms. In *Anuradha SA Investments LLC v Parsvanth Developers Limited*,[4] the preamble of the settlement agreement expressly referred to the Arbitration and Conciliation Act, 1996 as the governing law of the settlement agreement. In addition, the settlement agreement made reference to section 74 of the same Act and stated that the settlement agreement should be enforceable as an arbitral award on agreed terms. In this case, one party was from India and the other party was domiciled outside India. The court opined that the settlement agreement was subject to section 74 of the Arbitration and Conciliation Act, 1996. Assuming that India ratifies the Singapore Convention,[5] parties may have different paths open to them to enforce an iMSA if the governing law of the iMSA is Indian law: namely as an iMSA under the Singapore Convention or as an arbitral award on agreed terms under the Arbitration and Conciliation Act, 1996. Therefore, iMSAs that might be enforceable under section 74 of the Arbitration and Conciliation Act, 1996 arguably are *not* excluded from the scope of the Singapore Convention by virtue of Article 1(3)(b) of the Singapore Convention, because such iMSAs are merely *treated* as awards on agreed terms as per section 74, rather than being *recorded* as awards as envisaged by Article 1(3)(b) of the Singapore Convention.[6] Similarly, in the US state of New Jersey, an iMSA might be enforceable under the International Arbitration, Mediation, and Conciliation Act (the New Jersey Act). The New Jersey Act applies to international disputes when at least one of the parties is a non-resident to the US.[7] The term 'arbitration' includes all forms of alternative dispute resolution processes, including mediation and conciliation.[8] Further, a settlement agreement is treated as an arbitral award under this Act, the enforcement of which is subject to the New York Convention.[9] As with the case illustration from India above, so in relation to the New Jersey legislation, Article 1(3)(b) of the Singapore Convention will not apply to exclude an iMSA from its scope. Again, this is because those settlement agreements are merely *treated* as arbitral awards under the New Jersey Act; they have not been *recorded* as awards as envisaged under Article 1(3)(b) of the Singapore Convention.

7.03 It is important to note that the Singapore Convention does not prohibit States from adopting domestic legislation on the enforcement and recognition of settlement agreements that are otherwise excluded from the scope of application of the Singapore Convention. For example, a State can adopt a law on the enforcement and recognition

3. Gracious Timothy Dunna and Jatan Rodrigues, *Chapter 14: Cross-Border Enforcement of International Mediated Settlement Agreements and the Singapore Convention*, in Gracious Timothy (ed.), Conciliation and Mediation in India, Kluwer Law International (2021), 369-406.
4. *Anuradha Sa Investments Llc & Anr. v Parsvnath Developers Limited*, The High Court of Delhi at New Delhi, 20 April 2017.
5. At the time of writing, India has not ratified the Singapore Convention.
6. Art. 1(3)(b) of the Singapore Convention prescribes that the Convention does not apply to settlement agreements that have been *recorded* and are enforceable as an arbitral award.
7. S 4(a).
8. S 3.
9. Ss 3 and 8.

of settlement agreements similar to the terms of the Singapore Convention, irrespective of whether settlement agreements are the result of a mediation process. This would not be done in breach of their Convention obligations. This is specifically envisaged by the drafters of the Singapore Convention who drafted the Model Law on International Commercial Mediation in parallel.[10]

Case Illustrations

Illustration [A]: *Sam's Chocolates Pte Ltd*[11] (Sam) and *Terence Supplies Sdn Bhd*[12] (Terence) have concluded an iMSA in Utopia, which is a party to the Lugano Convention.[13] They endeavour to enforce the iMSA in Dystopia, which is also a party to the Lugano Convention. Both Utopia and Dystopia are parties to the Singapore Convention. The iMSA may be enforced in accordance with Article 58 of the Lugano Convention,[14] if the relevant conditions have been fulfilled. All of Utopia's and Dystopia's obligations under the Singapore Convention shall not serve to impede the administration of the relevant settlement agreement under the Lugano Convention for Sam or Terence.

Illustration [B]: *Evan Group Corporation* (Evan) and *Peters Corp Berhad*[15] (Peters) are State-sponsored investors from Whiteville and Blackdale, respectively. Whiteville and Blackdale have signed an Economic Partnership Agreement (EPA), which expressly covers investment activity engaged between Evan and Peters. The EPA contains a detailed dispute resolution clause: the first level of dispute resolution would be mediation at the Greyland International Mediation Centre, situated in a neutral jurisdiction, Greyland. If mediation fails, or if an iMSA was produced but its terms were dishonoured, there is a *mandatory* provision for the constitution of a third-party tribunal of esteemed legal professionals who would be in charge of arbitrating the dispute. It is assumed that

10. See footnote 5 of the Model Law on International Commercial Mediation. The Model Law is reproduced in Appendix E of this book. See also the drafting history of Art. 7 of the Singapore Convention, which shows that States have the flexibility to enact domestic legislation on the enforcement of settlement agreements that are otherwise excluded from the scope of the Singapore Convention. Report of Working Group II (Dispute Settlement) on the Work of its 67th Session (Vienna, 2-6 October 2017), A/CN.9/929 (2017), at para. 19. Available at http://undocs.org/A/CN.9/929 (Accessed 19 April 2022).
11. 'Pte Ltd' is an abbreviation used by private limited companies in countries such as Singapore.
12. Sendirian Berhad (Sdn Bhd) is a suffix used in countries such as Malaysia to identify a private limited company.
13. Convention on Jurisdiction and the Recognition and Enforcement of Judgments in Civil and Commercial Matters, L339 (21 December 2007) (the Lugano Convention).
14. Art. 58 of the Lugano Convention states: 'A settlement which has been approved by a court in the course of proceedings and is enforceable in the State bound by [the Lugano] Convention in which it was concluded shall be enforceable in the State addressed under the same conditions as authentic instruments. The court or competent authority of a State bound by [the Lugano] Convention where a court settlement was approved shall issue, at the request of any interested party, a certificate using the standard form in Annex V to this Convention.'
15. Berhad is a suffix used in countries such as Malaysia to identify a public limited company.

Whiteville and Blackdale are also Parties to the Singapore Convention. If Evan endeavours to enforce a settlement agreement against Peters which has dishonoured the terms of the agreement in Whiteville and/or Blackdale, compliance with the EPA must be prioritised over their obligations under the Singapore Convention. This means that the iMSA should be enforced via the *mandatory* constitution of a third-party tribunal in accordance with the EPA, instead of through the enforcement mechanism of the Singapore Convention.

'any interested party of any right'

7.04 A plain reading of Article 7 of the Singapore Convention suggests that the provision can only be relied upon by a party who seeks the enforcement or recognition of an iMSA. The other party does not appear to have a possibility to rely on more favourable defences that may exist in the State where enforcement or recognition is sought. Reference can be made to Article VII(1) of the New York Convention, which has been interpreted to refer to a party seeking enforcement or recognition.[16]

16. UNCITRAL Secretariat Guide on the Convention on the Recognition and Enforcement of Foreign Arbitral Awards (New York, 1958) (2016), at 290.

ARTICLE 8

Reservations

1. A Party to the Convention may declare that:

(a) It shall not apply this Convention to settlement agreements to which it is a party, or to which any governmental agencies or any person acting on behalf of a governmental agency is a party, to the extent specified in the declaration;
(b) It shall apply this Convention only to the extent that the parties to the settlement agreement have agreed to the application of the Convention.

2. No reservations are permitted except those expressly authorized in this article.
3. Reservations may be made by a Party to the Convention at any time. Reservations made at the time of signature shall be subject to confirmation upon ratification, acceptance or approval. Such reservations shall take effect simultaneously with the entry into force of this Convention in respect of the Party to the Convention concerned. Reservations made at the time of ratification, acceptance or approval of this Convention or accession thereto, or at the time of making a declaration under article 13 shall take effect simultaneously with the entry into force of this Convention in respect of the Party to the Convention concerned. Reservations deposited after the entry into force of the Convention for that Party to the Convention shall take effect six months after the date of the deposit.
4. Reservations and their confirmations shall be deposited with the depositary.
5. Any Party to the Convention that makes a reservation under this Convention may withdraw it at any time. Such withdrawals are to be deposited with the depositary, and shall take effect six months after deposit.

COMMENTARY

8.01 Article 8 of the Singapore Convention provides for two reservations. Article 8(2) expressly dictates that no further reservations are permitted. Articles 8(3) and 8(4) provide for the procedure for reservations to be lodged and the timeframe for when they would enter into force with respect to the lodging States to the Convention. Article 8(5) provides that States to the Convention which have lodged reservations may withdraw them at any time: they must lodge a withdrawal notice and deposit it at the depositary. The withdrawal will come into force six months after the notice has been deposited at the depositary. The commentary addresses the following topics: meaning of 'Party', meaning and function of a 'reservation', a procedure for making reservations, effect of reservations, acceptance of objections to reservations, the first reservation, the second reservation, meaning and function of a depositary and withdrawal of a reservation.

Meaning of 'Party'

8.02 The meaning of Party (with a capital P) to the Convention is examined in the commentary to Article 3.

Meaning and Function of a 'Reservation'

8.03 A 'reservation' is defined as:

> a unilateral statement, however phrased or named, made by a State, when signing, ratifying, acceding to, accepting or approving a treaty, whereby it purports to exclude or to vary the legal effect of certain provisions of the treaty in their application to that State.[1]

8.04 A reservation is to be distinguished from a declaration; in practice, the two are often confused. According to the Commentary of the International Law Commission (ILC) to the Vienna Convention on the Law of Treaties 1969 (VCLT):

> ...States, when signing, ratifying, acceding to, accepting or approving a treaty, not infrequently make declaration as to their understanding of some matter or as to their interpretation of a particular provision. Such a declaration may be a mere clarification of the State's position or it may amount to a reservation, according as it does or does not vary or exclude the application of the terms of the treaty as adopted.

8.05 Declarations do not seek to change or modify a State's treaty obligations, unlike a reservation; rather, they are attempts to explain to other parties what the State understands its obligations to be.[2] States may also make unilateral statements that are neither reservations nor declarations and these are often declarations of political opinion or intention on matters relating to the treaty but not its specific provisions.[3] Differentiating among these three categories is key because they each have different legal effects: the applicability of the VCLT and actual treaty relationships between Parties to the Convention may turn on whether a statement is a reservation, an interpretive declaration or a unilateral statement.[4]

---

1. Vienna Convention on the Law of Treaties 1969 (VCLT), Art. 2(1)(d).
2. Edward T. Swaine, *Treaty Reservations*, in Duncan B. Hollis (ed.), The Oxford Guide to Treaties, OUP (2014), at 279.
3. *Id.*, at 280.
4. *Ibid.*

8.06 In practice, States have also been known to propose changes to their obligations under the guise of making a 'declaration' or issuing an 'understanding'[5] (when in substance proposing a reservation or amendment). States may do this because the treaty prohibits or restricts reservations (as in the case of this Convention), to avoid opening to other States the capacity to object, to avoid possible negative consequences such as reputational effects, or genuinely in consideration of their position as within the treaty's provisions.[6]

8.07 Only two types of reservations are permitted under Articles 8(1) and 8(2) of the Singapore Convention. A reservation may enable a State to participate in a multilateral treaty in which the State would otherwise be unwilling or unable to participate.[7]

Procedure for Making Reservations

8.08 Reservations may be made at any time under the Singapore Convention, pursuant to Article 8(3). If a reservation is made at the time of signature, it will take effect simultaneously with the entry into force of the Convention, but is subject to ratification, acceptance or approval.[8] If it is made after the entry into force of the Convention, it will take effect six months after the deposit.

8.09 Reservations are to be deposited with the depositary. Annex 6 of the Treaty Handbook, 2012, by the UN Treaty Section Office of Legal Affairs, provides a model instrument of reservation.

Effect of Reservations

8.10 The legal effects of a reservation are set out in VCLT Article 19(1):

(a) Modifies for the reserving State the provisions of the treaty to which the reservation relates to the extent of the reservation; and
(b) Modifies those provisions to the same extent for such other party in its relations with the reserving State.

8.11 The legal effects in Article 19(1) follow directly from the consensual basis of the relations between parties to a treaty. A reservation operates reciprocally between the reserving State and any other party, so that it modifies the treaty for both of them in their mutual relations to the extent of the reserved provision.[9]

5. *Ibid.*
6. *Ibid.*
7. UN Office of Legal Affairs, *Treaty Handbook* (Rev. Ed.) (2012), at para. 3.5.1.
8. The meaning of the terms 'ratification', 'acceptance' and 'approval' are examined in the commentary to Art. 11.
9. Commentary of the International Law Commission (ILC) to the VCLT, Art. 19(1), Yearbook of the International Law Commission, Vol. II (1966), at para 1.

8.12 A reservation does not, however, modify the provisions of the treaty for the other parties,[10] since they have not accepted it as a term of the treaty in their mutual relations.[11]

Case Illustration

By way of illustration, on 23 July 2008, Kazakhstan deposited a reservation to paragraph 24(1) of the International Convention for the Suppression of the Financing of Terrorism (ICSFT).[12] No objections to the reservation were received by the depositary, the Secretary-General, within one year of the date of the deposit of the reservation. Consistent with the terms of the ICSFT, after one year, the Secretary-General accepted the reservation for deposit.

The terms of the reservation are, 'The Republic of Kazakhstan does not consider itself bound by the provisions of article 24, paragraph 1 of the [ICSFT].' Article 24(1) is a dispute resolution clause referring parties to the negotiation, arbitration and, in the last resort, the International Court of Justice, in the event of a dispute on the interpretation or application of the ICSFT.

Cabo Verde is also a party to the ICSFT. The effect of Kazakhstan's reservation on Cabo Verde is that, between these two States, Article 24(1) does not apply between them, that is, if there is a dispute between Cabo Verde and Kazakhstan on the interpretation of the ICSFT, they are not bound to the dispute resolution procedures in Article 24(1). However, if there is a similar dispute between Cabo Verde and Nauru (also a party to the ICSFT), both Cabo Verde and Nauru remain bound by Article 24(1) because Kazakhstan's reservation does not alter the other States' legal obligations to the ICSFT.

Acceptance of and Objections to Reservations

8.13 Under VCLT Article 20(1), '[a] reservation expressly authorised by a treaty does not require any subsequent acceptance by the other contracting States unless the treaty so provides'. This would apply to the Singapore Convention, which permits only the two reservations set out in Article 8(1), read in conjunction with Article 8(2). The effect of this is that the reservation enters into force either simultaneously with the entry into force of this Convention or after six months following the deposit of the declaration, as provided for in Article 8(3). Other treaties may require the acceptance of a reservation, and this is provided for in VCLT Articles 20(2)-(4).

10. VCLT, Art. 21(2).
11. ILC to the VCLT (1966), above note 9.
12. International Convention for the Suppression of the Financing of Terrorism, C.N.526.2008. TREATIES-5 (Depositary Notification) (9 December 1999).

8.14 Generally, States have the right to object to reservations and may oppose the entry into force of the treaty between themselves and the author of the reservation,[13] or render the relevant provision to which the reservation applies as non-applicable between the two States to the extent of the reservation.[14] Typically, such objections relate to reservations interpreted as against the 'object and purpose' of the treaty.[15] Given that only two types of reservations are allowed under the Singapore Convention, objections to reservations are unlikely to arise (though this is provided for in VCLT Articles 20-22) because any reservation made other than the ones set out in Article 8(1) will likely be rejected by the depositary.

The First Reservation: Exclusion of Application of the Convention to Government

8.15 In Article 8(1)(a), the first reservation permits Contracting Parties to the Singapore Convention to exclude the Convention's applicability to international mediated settlement agreements (iMSAs) to which they are a party, or to which any governmental agencies or any person acting on behalf of a governmental agency is a party. It should be noted that by default, the Convention will apply to iMSAs to which States or their governmental agencies (or any person acting on their behalf) are a party, so long as it satisfies the requirements as to scope elucidated in Articles 1 and 2 (as examined in the earlier commentaries).[16] Essentially, this reservation may be made if Contracting Parties to the Convention wish to carve out immunities for their respective government or governmental agencies insofar as the Convention is concerned, possibly for national security or fundamental public policy reasons. State-owned enterprises may *not* be excluded under this reservation.[17]

8.16 UNCITRAL's Working Group II (WG II) adopted the view that an outright exclusion of governmental agencies was undesirable as it is, in this day and age, commonplace for government entities to participate in commercial ventures - such as infrastructure investments, research and development in intellectual property rights and defence contracts - and it may be prudent for them to turn to mediation in the event disputes arise in any one of those ventures.[18] For this reason, it was agreed by WG II that the decision of whether such an exclusion should apply to the Singapore Convention was best left to the States of the Convention, who may make a reservation

13. ILC Guide to Practice on Reservations to Treaties (2011), at paras 2.6.2, 2.6.6.
14. VCLT, Arts 20(4)(b), 21(3).
15. VCLT, Art. 19(c).
16. See Timothy Schnabel, *The Singapore Convention on Mediation: A Framework for the Cross-Border Recognition and Enforcement of Mediated Settlements*, 19(1) Pepp. Disp. Resol. L.J. 1 (2019), at 55.
17. See, for example, intervention of Singapore, in Audio Recording: Working Group II, 63rd Session (United Nations 2015), 8 September 2015, 09:30-12:30, http://www.uncitral.org/uncitral/audio/meetings.jsp. (Accessed 20 May 2019).
18. Report of Working Group II (Arbitration and Conciliation) on the Work of its 63rd Session (Vienna, 7-11 September 2015), A/CN.9/861 (2015), at para. 46; Eunice Chua, *The Singapore Convention on Mediation: A Brighter Future for Asian Dispute Resolution*, Asian J. Int'l L. (2 January 2019), at 9.

in accordance with Article 8 to whichever extent they see fit. In other words, States may, in accordance with Article 8, lodge targeted reservations, defining at their indulgence the scope within which they wish the Convention to be administered in their courts.[19] Again, this is emblematic of the model of consensus-based treaty-making. It is, for instance, possible that States to the Convention may choose to exclude one of the three types of entities (that is, State, government agencies or person acting on behalf of a governmental agency), or perhaps more specifically, a governmental agency operating over a particular industry, such as the defence sector.

Case Illustrations

By way of illustration, Belarus made a reservation under Article 8(1)(a) upon the signature of the Singapore Convention, which reads as follows:

> 'In accordance with the article 8 of the Convention the Republic of Belarus shall not apply this Convention to settlement agreements to which it is a party, or to which any governmental agencies or any person acting on behalf of a governmental agency is a party.'

Saudi Arabia made a reservation under Article 8(1)(a) upon the ratification of the Singapore Convention, which reads as follows:

> 'The Kingdom of Saudi Arabia hereby declares that the Convention shall not apply to settlement agreements to which it or any of its governmental agencies is a party, or any person acting on behalf of those governmental agencies.'

Georgia made the following reservation:

> 'The following reservations shall be taken into consideration upon ratification of the United Nations Convention on International Settlement Agreements Resulting from Mediation:
>
> a) Georgia declares that this Convention shall not apply to settlement agreements to which it is a party, or to which any governmental agencies or any person acting on behalf of governmental agency is a party [...].'[20]

8.17 Irrespective of whether a State makes a reservation under Article 8(1)(a), the delegates at WG II confirmed that the Singapore Convention does not have any impact on the public international law aspect of State liability and State immunity.[21] Public international law distinguishes two aspects of State immunity – immunity from

19. Timothy Schnabel, *The Singapore Convention on Mediation: A Framework for the Cross-Border Recognition and Enforcement of Mediated Settlements*, 19(1) Pepp. Disp. Resol. L.J. 1 (2019), at 55.
20. Georgia has also made the reservation under Art. 8(1)(b). See the Case Illustration following para. 8.21.
21. Report of Working Group II (Dispute Settlement) on the Work of its 65th Session (Vienna, 12-23 September 2016), A/CN.9/896 (2016), at para. 61. Reference was made to Art. 2(6) of the Hague Convention of 30 June 2005 on Choice of Court Agreements (HCCCA) which states: '[n]othing

adjudication and immunity from execution.[22] By way of example, Article 5 of the United Nations Convention on Jurisdictional Immunities of States and Their Property (2004) captures both aspects of sovereign immunity and prescribes that a State enjoys immunity, in respect of itself and its property, from the jurisdiction of the courts of another State. Considering the scope of the Singapore Convention, immunity from execution is of relevance in the enforcement of iMSAs, as a party to an iMSA may be barred from executing the iMSA against the property that enjoys sovereign immunity. Generally, there are two exceptions to immunity from execution: when a State consents to execution and when the property against which enforcement is sought is in use or intended for use by that State for commercial purposes.[23] While sovereign immunity is considered part of customary international law,[24] the norms of State immunity are normally formulated in the domestic law of a State, which are relied upon in deciding whether particular property enjoys sovereign immunity in the State where enforcement is sought. By way of example, in England, State immunity is regulated by the State Immunity Act 1978 and in the US – by the Foreign Sovereign Immunities Act (FSIA) of 1976. The case below is illustrative as to what constitutes property, which is in use or intended for use by a State for commercial purposes.

Case Illustrations

In the English case of *Orascom Telecom Holding SAE v The Republic of Chad*,[25] the Queen's Bench Division of the Commercial Court addressed the issue of whether Chad's borrower's account, held at Citibank in London, was used or intended to be used for commercial purposes and therefore, whether the execution of an unpaid arbitration award against the bank account in question was allowed under the State Immunity Act 1978.

in this Convention shall affect privileges and immunities of States or of international organisations, in respect of themselves and of their property.' The Working Group II noted that issues relating to sovereign immunity would not need to be regulated under the Singapore Convention. The Working Group II made reference to the United Nations Convention on Jurisdictional Immunities of States and Their Property (2004). It was noted that the issues of State immunity should be left to be decided by the enforcing authority on the basis of the applicable rules on foreign State immunity. See Report of Working Group II (Arbitration and Conciliation) on the Work of its 63rd Session (Vienna, 7-11 September 2015), A/CN.9/861 (2015), at para. 45.

22. Xiaodong Yang, *State Immunity in International Law*, Cambridge University Press (2012), 34-35.
23. By way of example, s. 13(2)(b) of the State Immunity Act 1978 (UK) states: the property of a State shall not be subject to any process for the enforcement of a judgment or arbitration award or, in an action *in rem*, for its arrest, detention or sale. Section 13(3) states that subs. (2) does not prevent the giving of any relief or the issue of any process with the written consent of the State concerned; and any such consent (which may be contained in a prior agreement) may be expressed so as to apply to a limited extent or generally; but a provision merely submitting to the jurisdiction of the courts is not to be regarded as a consent for the purposes of this subsection. Also, s. 13(4) states that subs. (2)(b) does not prevent the issue of any process in respect of property which is for the time being in use or intended for use for commercial purposes.
24. Xiaodong Yang, *State Immunity in International Law*, Cambridge University Press (2012), 35.
25. [2008] 2 Lloyd's Rep 396.

The arbitration award in question originated from an ICC arbitration between Orascom and the Chad national telecommunication company. Even though Chad itself was not a party to the arbitration agreement that formed the basis of the award, Chad joined the arbitration proceedings and accepted the jurisdiction of the tribunal. According to the final award, Chad had to pay substantial sums in excess of GBP 3.7m. After Chad refused to comply with the award, Orascom applied for a third-party debt order against an account held by Chad at Citibank in London.

Chad held multiple accounts at Citibank in London to secure the payment of the USD 300m loan issued by the World Bank to Chad for the construction of an oil pipeline. The World Bank required Chad's oil revenue to be transferred into Chad's accounts held at Citibank so that Chad could meet its repayment obligations towards the World Bank. The remaining funds could be transferred into Chad's borrower's account. Orascom asserted that the borrower's account was in use or intended to be used for commercial purposes and therefore, Chad could not rely on State immunity. Chad relied on a document signed by the Chad Ambassador to England, which stated that the borrower's account was not used for commercial purposes.

In the judgment, the court emphasised the fact that the State Immunity Act 1978 substantially eased the principle of sovereign immunity both in respect of the bringing of a suit and the enforcement of judgments and awards. With respect to the question of State immunity from execution, the court opined that such execution was possible against property, which was in use or intended for use for commercial purposes. The court explained that 'commercial purposes' referred to the purposes of commercial transactions, which were any contract for the supply of goods or services, and any loan or other transaction for the provision of finance and any guarantee or indemnity in respect of any such transaction or of any other financial obligation. According to the court, such transactions would still fall into the category of commercial transactions even if they were entered into or engaged upon by a State in the exercise of sovereign authority. The borrower's account was established for the purposes of a commercial transaction, specifically to receive the proceeds of a contract for the supply of goods or services. Therefore, the court allowed the execution of the award against Chad's borrower's account.

In the US case of *Crystallex Int'l Corp. v Bolivarian Republic of Venez.*,[26] Crystallex sought to enforce a judgment in the amount of USD 1.2b against the Bolivarian Republic of Venezuela, by executing on a property, specifically shares of common stock, nominally owned by an oil company Petróleos de Venezuela,

26. *Crystallex Int'l Corp. v Bolivarian Republic of Venez.* 333 F. Supp. 3d 380, 2018 U.S. Dist. LEXIS 138978 (D. Del. 9 August 2018).

S.A. (PDVSA). Crystallex alleged that PDVSA was the alter ego company of Venezuela, and therefore, PDVSA's property could be used for the execution of Venezuela's debt. The court explained that a judgment could be executed against property of a foreign State if the property was used for a commercial activity. For the court, the property in question must be used for a commercial activity at the time the writ of execution was issued. The court went on to explain situations when the property is used for a commercial activity:

> 'Property is used for a commercial activity in the United States when the property in question is put into action, put into service, availed or employed *for* a commercial activity, not in connection with a commercial activity or in relation to a commercial activity. The Foreign Sovereign Immunities Act (FSIA), 28 U.S.C.S. § 1602 et seq., defines a commercial activity as either a regular course of commercial conduct or a particular commercial transaction or act. The commercial character of an activity shall be determined by reference to the nature of the course of conduct or particular transaction or act, rather than by reference to its purpose. 28 U.S.C.S. § 1603(d). Because the FSIA provides that the commercial character of an act is to be determined by reference to its nature rather than its purpose, the question is not whether the foreign government is acting with a profit motive or instead with the aim of fulfilling uniquely sovereign objectives. Rather, the issue is whether the particular actions that the foreign state performs are the type of actions by which a private party engages in trade and traffic or commerce [*emphasis added*].'[27]

The court found that the property in question was used for a commercial activity because Venezuela, through PDVSA, used the shares to appoint directors, approve contracts and pledge assets as security for PDVSA's debt. The court also stated that 'once a foreign state has used property in commerce, that property continues to satisfy the commercial use requirement unless that property becomes "cordoned off for use of the [foreign state] in its sovereign capacity"', which was not the case in the present dispute.

The Second Reservation: Selection of an Opt-In Regime

8.18 The second reservation in Article 8(1)(b) permits Contracting Parties to the Singapore Convention to reverse the default application of this Convention by providing for an opt-in regime instead.[28] If a State to the Convention makes the second reservation, obligations under the Convention would only apply in that State if the parties to an iMSA have expressly agreed that the Convention would apply as such,

27. *Ibid.*
28. It is noteworthy that the Convention applies as default law, except to the extent which parties to an iMSA have positively and clearly in a private arrangement agreed to opt out from its applicability. If parties choose to opt out of the Convention, Art. 5(1)(d) would facilitate that choice and effectively take the iMSA out of the Singapore Convention's enforcement scope: Timothy Schnabel, *The Singapore Convention on Mediation: A Framework for the Cross-Border Recognition and Enforcement of Mediated Settlements*, 19(1) Pepp. Disp. Resol. L.J. 1 (2019), at 56.

thereby 'opting-in' to its regime. If a State to the Convention makes the second reservation, the opt-in regime will *only* apply in respect of the competent authority where relief is sought; it has no reciprocal effect on the treatment of iMSAs in other jurisdictions.[29] The inclusion of this reservation was the fruit of a compromise within WG II in order for it to progress through negotiations in the Convention's final drafts.[30]

8.19 Some commentators have suggested that, to the extent that States make use of the second reservation, it may have the effect of limiting the application of the Singapore Convention.[31] Their reasoning is based on empirical research which indicates that mediating parties will be unlikely to modify the status quo of non-application by taking a supplementary step to opt in to a novel, untried and untested legal framework (*see* Point of Interest below).[32] As Schnabel observes, '[A]s arbitration does not have an opt-in requirement for awards to be enforceable, imposing such a requirement in this Convention would make mediation less attractive by comparison.'[33] A different view is that the second reservation promotes the principle of party autonomy,[34] in that it gives parties a choice as to whether the Convention is to apply to their iMSAs.[35]

29. See Timothy Schnabel, *The Singapore Convention on Mediation: A Framework for the Cross-Border Recognition and Enforcement of Mediated Settlements*, 19(1) Pepp. Disp. Resol. L.J. 1 (2019), at 58. The question of reciprocity in this context is but a red herring. There is never a need for other competent authorities to evaluate whether iMSAs are attributable to a State making the reservation to begin with, as there is no such thing as a seat of mediation: see the discussion in the commentary to Art. 1 under 'The Absence of a Seat in Mediation'.
30. Eunice Chua, *The Singapore Convention on Mediation: A Brighter Future for Asian Dispute Resolution*, 9(2) Asian J. Int'l L. 195 (2 January 2019), at 203.
31. Nadja Alexander and Shouyu Chong, *An Introduction to the Singapore Convention on Mediation – Perspectives from Singapore*, 22(4) Nederlands-Vlaams tijdschrift voor Mediation en conflict management 37 (2018), at 50-51; Shouyu Chong and Felix Steffek, *Enforcement of International Settlement Agreements Resulting from Mediation under the Singapore Convention – Private International Law Issues in Perspective*, 31 SAcLJ 443 (2019); Timothy Schnabel, *The Singapore Convention on Mediation: A Framework for the Cross-Border Recognition and Enforcement of Mediated Settlements*, 19(1) Pepp. Disp. Resol. L.J. 1 (2019), at 58; and Eunice Chua, *The Singapore Convention on Mediation: A Brighter Future for Asian Dispute Resolution*, 9(2) Asian J. Int'l L. 195 (2019), at 203. Also see intervention of the American Bar Association (ABA), in Audio Recording: Working Group II, 64th Session (United Nations 2016), 3 February 2016, 15:00-18:00, http://www.uncitral.org/uncitral/audio/meetings.jsp (Accessed 20 May 2019); and interventions of China, Pakistan and the US, in Audio Recording: Working Group II, 65th Session (United Nations 2016), 22 September 2016, 09:30-12:30, http://www.uncitral.org/uncitral/audio/meetings.jsp (Accessed 20 May 2019).
32. Nadja Alexander and Shouyu Chong, *An Introduction to the Singapore Convention on Mediation – Perspectives from Singapore*, 22(4) Nederlands-Vlaams tijdschrift voor Mediation en conflict management 37 (2018), at 50-51. On the status quo bias, see Daniel Watkins, *A Nudge to Mediate: How Adjustments in Choice Architecture Can Lead to Better Dispute Resolution Decisions*, 4 The Am. J. Med. 1 (2010), at 14 et seq.; and Nadja Alexander, *Nudging Users Towards Cross-Border Mediation: Is It Really about Harmonised Enforcement Regulation?*, 7(2) Contemp. Asia Arb. J. 405 (2014), at 410. Cf intervention of the ABA, in Audio Recording: Working Group II, 64th Session (United Nations 2016), 3 February 2016, 15:00-18:00, http://www.uncitral.org/uncitral/audio/meetings.jsp (Accessed 20 May 2019).
33. Timothy Schnabel, *The Singapore Convention on Mediation: A Framework for the Cross-Border Recognition and Enforcement of Mediated Settlements*, 19(1) Pepp. Disp. Resol. L.J. 1 (2019), at 57.
34. Respect for party autonomy is an important feature in the practice of private international law: see Alex Mills, Party Autonomy in Private International Law, CUP (2018).
35. Report of Working Group II (Arbitration and Conciliation) on the Work of its 66th Session (New York, 6-10 February 2017), A/CN.9/901 (2017), at para. 37. It is noteworthy that Schnabel

8.20 To overcome the cognitive bias favouring the maintenance of the status quo, it has been suggested that mediators, aware of a real possibility that parties may need to take their iMSAs into an opt-in jurisdiction for enforcement, are well-placed to bring to the parties' attention the availability of the Singapore Convention's expedited enforcement mechanism.[36] There is in theory no specific formulation of what words or phrases may be used to discern or indicate the parties' intentions to opt in to the Convention.[37] As long as the intention to opt in is objectively evident from the terms of the iMSA, it is likely that the competent authorities would interpret the same. However, this approach must be balanced with the caveats on mediator misconduct expressed in Articles 5(1)(e) and 5(1)(f) of the Convention, as analysed in the commentary to Article 5: it bears reminding that mediators must adhere to the ethical practice standards applicable to them should they provide parties with such advice.

8.21 In any event, if States or other Parties to the Singapore Convention have made the second reservation in an abundance of caution, it is noteworthy that this reservation may be withdrawn at a subsequent time, in accordance with the procedure set out in Article 8(5) of the Convention (discussed below).

Case Illustration

By way of illustration, Georgia made the following reservation:

> 'The following reservations shall be taken into consideration upon ratification of the United Nations Convention on International Settlement Agreements Resulting from Mediation:
>
> [...]
>
> b) Georgia hereby declares that this Convention shall apply only to the extent that the parties to the settlement agreement have agreed to the application of the Convention.'

---

observed, 'Some delegations argued that the desire for a mediated settlement to be enforceable could not be assumed across cultures.' (Timothy Schnabel, *The Singapore Convention on Mediation: A Framework for the Cross-Border Recognition and Enforcement of Mediated Settlements*, 19(1) Pepp. Disp. Resol. L.J. 1 (2019), at 56).

36. Shouyu Chong and Felix Steffek, *Enforcement of International Settlement Agreements Resulting from Mediation under the Singapore Convention – Private International Law Issues in Perspective*, 31 SAcLJ 448 (2019). Also see Report of Working Group II (Arbitration and Conciliation) on the Work of its 66th Session (New York, 6-10 February 2017), A/CN.9/901 (2017), at para. 37. Available at http://undocs.org/A/CN.9/901 (Accessed 12 May 2022). Schnabel also notes the possibility that 'the disputing parties would not [need] to opt in via the mediated settlement itself; they could also opt in at an earlier stage of the process as well, such as in an agreement to mediate.' (Timothy Schnabel, *The Singapore Convention on Mediation: A Framework for the Cross-Border Recognition and Enforcement of Mediated Settlements*, 19(1) Pepp. Disp. Resol. L.J. 1 (2019), at 58).
37. Timothy Schnabel, *The Singapore Convention on Mediation: A Framework for the Cross-Border Recognition and Enforcement of Mediated Settlements*, 19(1) Pepp. Disp. Resol. L.J. 1 (2019), at 57.

Iran also made a declaration upon signature, which captures both reservations under Article 8(1)(a) and (b):

> 'The Government of the Islamic Republic of Iran seizes the opportunity at this moment of signing "the United Nations Convention on International Settlement Agreements Resulting from Mediation", to place on the record its "understanding" in relation to provisions of the Convention, bearing in mind that the main objective for submitting this declaration is the avoidance of eventual future interpretation of the following articles in a manner incompatible with the original intention and previous positions or in disharmony with national laws and regulations of the Islamic Republic of Iran.
>
> It is the understanding of the Islamic Republic of Iran as well as reservations that:
>
> (1) the Islamic Republic of Iran has no obligation to apply this Convention to settlement agreements to which it is a party, or to which any governmental agencies or any person acting on behalf of a governmental agency is a party, to the extent specified in the declaration;
> (2) The Islamic Republic of Iran will apply this Convention only to the extent that the parties to the settlement agreement have agreed to the application of the Convention;
> (3) The Islamic Republic of Iran may have the choice to make reservations upon ratification;
> (4) The Islamic Republic of Iran, in accordance with the relevant provisions of the Convention, reserves the right to adopt laws and regulations to co-operate with the States.'

Point of Interest

Behavioural Science and the Impact of Opt-In and Opt-Out Provisions

Knowledge from the behavioural sciences[38] is increasingly applied in the regulation of dispute resolution. Research indicates that when faced with an

38. Studies carried out in behavioural sciences suggest that people are more likely to choose a pre-selected option, otherwise known as a default. See Jon M. Jachimowicz, Shannon Duncan, Elke U. Weber and Eric J. Johnson, *When and Why Defaults Influence Decisions: A Meta-analysis of Default Effects,* 3(2) Behav. Pub. Pol'y 159 (2019). By way of example, Johnson and Goldstein's study compared the uptake of organ donation signup in countries where organ donation was the default option (opt-out option) to countries where people specifically had to opt in to the organ donation program (opt-in option). The difference was dramatic, as more than 90 per cent of people participated in organ donation in countries with the opt-out option, while only less than 28 per cent of people participated in countries with the opt-in option. See Eric J. Johnson and Daniel Goldstein, *Do Defaults Save Lives?,* 302 Science 1338 (2003). In another study by Brigitte C. Madrian and Dennis F. Shea, employees were 50% more likely to take part in a retirement pension program with a default participation option. See Brigitte C. Madrian and Dennis F. Shea, *The Power of Suggestion: Inertia in 401(k) Participation and Savings Behavior,* 116(4) Q. J. Econ. 1149 (2001).

opportunity to opt out of mediation, most dispute resolution users have the tendency to remain with the default process – in this case, mediation.[39] Conversely, when presented with the choice to opt into a mediation process, most dispute resolution users would similarly follow the path of least resistance, choosing to remain with the default process such as litigation or arbitration, but not with mediation. In both situations, parties have the same dispute resolution options made available to them. However, depending on the framing of the options made available, the forum for dispute resolution ultimately engaged by the parties is likely to vary significantly: more users would ultimately end up in mediation if it were set as the default option, compared to when the parties could choose to opt into mediation. This is one example of how carefully framed regulatory provisions influence the behaviour of disputants and their legal advisers.

In Singapore, a presumption was introduced in 2012 that parties would resort to alternative dispute resolution processes[40] at the earliest stages of dispute. This presumption provides a useful illustration of how such interdisciplinary insights from the perspective of the behavioural sciences may be integrated into the design of triggering mechanisms for alternative dispute resolution, successfully leading to increased traffic into mediation.[41]

Meaning and Function of 'Depositary'

8.22 The meaning and function of 'depositary' are examined in the commentary to Article 10. The 'depositary' has the responsibility to accept reservations, objections and communications.

39. Daniel Watkins, *A Nudge to Mediate: How Adjustments in Choice Architecture Can Lead to Better Dispute Resolution Decisions*, 4 Am. J. Med. 1 (2010), at 19 et seq. See also Maurits Barendrecht and Berend R. de Vries, *Fitting the Forum to the Fuss with Sticky Defaults: Failure in the Market for Dispute Resolution Services?*, 7 Cardozo J. Conflict Resol. 83 (2005).
40. See Joyce Low and Dorcas Quek Anderson, *Introducing a 'Presumption of ADR' for Civil Matters in the Subordinate Courts*, Singapore Law Gazette (May 2012). The Chief Justice of the Supreme Court of Singapore has very succinctly reported of the presumption: 'Under this initiative, civil cases in the State Courts [of Singapore] are automatically referred to the most suitable mode of ADR – whether it is mediation, neutral evaluation or arbitration under the Law Society Arbitration Scheme – unless the parties choose to opt out of the ADR process.' (Sundaresh Menon, *Mediation and the Rule of Law*, The Law Society Mediation Forum (10 March 2017), at 22).
41. Sundaresh Menon, *Mediation and the Rule of Law*, The Law Society Mediation Forum (10 March 2017), at 17 and 22-23; Andrew B.L. Phang, *Alternative Dispute Resolution and Regional Prosperity – A View from Singapore*, Address by Judge of Appeal Justice Andrew Phang, Supreme Court of Singapore at the China-ASEAN Justice Forum (11 September 2014); and K.C. Vijayan, *Number of Mediation Cases Filed Hits Record High*, The Straits Times (28 January 2017). Also noteworthy is the continuing improvement of the Singapore State Courts' user satisfaction rates since the presumption of alternative dispute resolution was introduced: from 92 per cent in 2013 to 96 per cent in 2015.

Withdrawal of Reservation

8.23 Article 8(5) makes clear that there are no set periods within which reservations are to be withdrawn, and Parties to the Singapore Convention are free to withdraw their reservations at any time. Such withdrawals take effect six months after depositing the same with the depositary.

ARTICLE 9

Effect on Settlement Agreements

The Convention and any reservation or withdrawal thereof shall apply only to settlement agreements concluded after the date when the Convention, reservation or withdrawal thereof enters into force for the Party to the Convention concerned.

COMMENTARY

9.01 Article 9 functions as a transitional provision. It establishes explicitly that this Convention applies only to the relevant settlement agreements concluded after the date when the Convention comes into force for the Party to the Convention. The purpose of Article 9 (and Article 16 on denunciation) is to enhance legal certainty for parties to mediated settlement agreements by making clear when the Convention would have an effect on such settlement agreements.[1] The effect of Article 9 may be illustrated through the following examples.

Case Illustrations

Let us assume that the Convention comes into force for Solas State on 1 July 2020 and for Dorak State on 1 April 2020. *Janet* and *Hussin* have concluded a relevant international mediated settlement agreement (iMSA) for the purposes of enforcement under the Convention.

Illustration [A]: If the iMSA was concluded on 1 June 2020, Janet and Hussin may only enforce the terms of their iMSA in Dorak and not Solas.

Illustration [B]: If the iMSA were concluded on 1 June 2022, and Solas and Dorak had decided to withdraw from the Convention in order to sign on to a later-negotiated Convention relating to the same subject matter, with the

1. Report of the United Nations Commission on International Trade Law on the Work of its 51st Session (25 June-13 July 2018), A/73/17 (2018), at para. 41. Available at https://undocs.org/A/73/17 (Accessed 13 May 2022).

withdrawal taking effect on 31 May 2022, then Janet and Hussin may not enforce the terms of their iMSA under the Convention in Solas or Dorak. However, either party could enforce in another State that had ratified the Convention, for example, Amber State, assuming there was a reason to do so, such as the location of assets that could potentially be accessed as part of the enforcement proceedings.

ARTICLE 10
Depositary

The Secretary-General of the United Nations is hereby designated as the depositary of this Convention.

COMMENTARY

10.01 Article 10 designates the Secretary-General of the United Nations (UN) as the depositary of the Convention.

Role and Functions of the Depositary

10.02 The depositary of a treaty plays an essential procedural role in the smooth operation of a multilateral treaty.[1] Its functions are international in character, and the depositary is under an obligation to act impartially in its performance.[2]

10.03 In the case of a treaty adopted within an international organisation, the usual practice is to designate the competent organ of the organisation as depositary.[3] It is, therefore, the usual practice that this Convention, adopted by the General Assembly of the UN, would designate the Secretary-General of the UN as the depositary. The Secretary-General is, on a worldwide basis, the principal depositary of treaties.[4]

10.04 Unless a treaty otherwise provides, the functions of a depositary include preparing certified copies of the original text and transmitting them to the States entitled to become parties to the treaty; receiving any signatures to the treaty and any instruments and notifications relating to it, as well as reservations, objections and

1. Commentary of the International Law Commission (ILC) to the Vienna Convention on the Law of Treaties (1969) (VCLT), Art. 71(1), Yearbook of the International Law Commission, Vol. II, (1966). The VCLT concerns the international law of treaties concluded between states. The work of the ILC is considered as teachings of 'highly qualified publicists', pursuant to Art. 38(1)(d) of the Statute of the International Court of Justice, in interpreting international law.
2. VCLT (1969), Art. 71(1).
3. ILC Commentary to the VCLT (1966), Art. 71(1).
4. Summary of Practice of the Secretary-General as Depositary of Multilateral Treaties Chap. I, ST/LEG/7/Rev.1 (1994), at para. 1.

communications; examining whether a signature, an instrument or a reservation is in conformity with the provisions of the treaty; and informing the States entitled to become parties to the treaty when the number of signatures or of instruments of ratification, accession, acceptance or approval required for the entry into force of the treaty has been received or deposited.[5] It bears emphasis that the role of a depositary is primarily administrative in nature.[6] It is therefore not, for instance, the prerogative of a depositary to scrutinise reservations substantively. The depositary's task is confined to receiving and disseminating such instruments.

10.05 The depositary also ensures that only eligible entities, that is, those to which the treaty is open to, sign or express consent to be bound. Where the status of particular entities is unclear, for instance, whether they are to be regarded as sovereign States, the Secretary-General has sought directives from the General Assembly and other UN organs.[7]

5. VCLT (1969), Art. 72(1).
6. See Reservations to the Convention on the Prevention and Punishment of the Crime of Genocide, Advisory opinion, ICJ GL No 12, [1951] ICJ Rep 15, ICGJ 227 (ICJ 1951), 28 May 1951, United Nations; International Court of Justice.
7. Arancha Hinojal-Oyarbide and Annebeth Rosenboom, *Managing the Process of Treaty Formation: Depositaries and Registration*, in Duncan Hollis (ed.), The Oxford Guide to Treaties, OUP (2014), at 259 and 264.

ARTICLE 11

Signature, Ratification, Acceptance, Approval, Accession

1. This Convention is open for signature by all States in Singapore, on 1 August 2019, and thereafter at United Nations Headquarters in New York.
2. This Convention is subject to ratification, acceptance or approval by the signatories.
3. This Convention is open for accession by all States that are not signatories as from the date it is open for signature.
4. Instruments of ratification, acceptance, approval or accession are to be deposited with the depositary.

COMMENTARY

11.01 Article 11 lists the ways in which a State may become a Party to this Convention, the period over which the Convention is open for signature and accession, as well as the deposit of instruments of ratification, approval or accession.

Meaning of 'Signature'

11.02 Article 11(2) expressly states that the Convention is *subject to* 'ratification', 'acceptance' or 'approval' by the signatories. This means that the 'signature' in Article 11(1) refers to a 'simple signature', pursuant to which a signing State does not undertake positive legal obligations under the Convention upon signature but indicates the State's intention to take steps to express its consent to be bound by the Convention at a later date. In contrast, the 'definitive signature' typically refers to a signature that indicates consent to be bound.[1] Nevertheless, the 'simple signature' does create an obligation, in the period between signature and ratification, acceptance or approval to, in good faith, refrain from acts that would defeat the object and purpose of the treaty.[2]

1. UN Office of Legal Affairs, *Treaty Handbook* (Rev. Ed.) (2012), at para. 3.1.4.
2. *Id.*, at 3.1.3; Vienna Convention on the Law of Treaties (1969) (VCLT), Art. 18. See the introduction for further commentary on the 'object and purpose' of the treaty and the principle of *pacta sunt servanda.*

For States that have participated in treaty negotiations, a 'simple signature' can be a useful means of marking the conclusion of those negotiations.[3] In effect, there is almost no State practice that would help clarify the content of the signing obligation, and there is relatively little judicial precedent.[4]

11.03 The result of expressing a State's consent to be bound by ratification, acceptance, approval or accession is nevertheless the same, whichever method is adopted by a State endeavouring to become a Party to this Convention. The State has the autonomy to choose the method it deems most expedient for itself.

11.04 Each of the terms 'ratification', 'acceptance' and 'approval' in Article 11(2) refer to the international act whereby a State establishes on its international plane its consent to be bound by a treaty.[5] Domestic legislation of many States contains specific requirements for the submission of treaties, and the form requirements to be fulfilled, in internal law, before competent organs of the State may proceed to the international act establishing the State's consent to be bound. Often categorised into 'monist' and 'dualist' approaches, these will be elaborated upon below. Since there is often a tendency to confuse international and internal procedures, the definition of the terms here lays 'heavy emphasis'[6] on purely the international act to which the terms 'ratification', 'acceptance', 'approval' and 'accession' relate.

Meaning of 'Ratification'

11.05 The term 'ratification' denotes the 'definitive confirmation of a willingness to be bound',[7] usually available only to States that have signed a treaty. It involves a two-faceted process, comprising both an internal and international element: (1) the introduction of the treaty into the internal legal order of the State through the completion of an 'instrument of ratification'; and (2) the notification of this act of ratification at an international level through an exchange of such instruments or providing them to a depositary.[8] The interval between the signature and ratification of a treaty affords the relevant governmental departments of a State an opportunity to scrutinise the advantages and disadvantages of the treaty without the same time pressure faced by its treaty negotiators.[9] The requirement of ratification thus serves the purpose of allowing States to deliberate over their decisions to accept the treaty, thereby ensuring a greater likelihood of compliance with treaty obligations. While ratification is discretionary, it has been observed that it is the general practice of

3. Curtis A. Bradley, *Treaty Signature*, in Duncan B. Hollis (ed.), The Oxford Guide to Treaties, OUP (2014), at 211.
4. *Id.*, at 213.
5. VCLT (1969), Art. 2(1)(b).
6. Commentary of the International Law Commission (ILC) to the VCLT, Art. 2(1)(b), Yearbook of the International Law Commission, Vol. II (1966), at 189.
7. George Korontzis, *Making the Treaty*, in Duncan B. Hollis (ed.), The Oxford Guide to Treaties, OUP (2014), at 197.
8. *Ibid.*
9. Arnold McNair, *The Law of Treaties*, Clarendon Press (1961), at 133-134.

democratic governments to sign a treaty only if they intend to make an effort in good faith to ratify it in due course.[10]

Meaning of 'Acceptance' and 'Approval'

11.06 The terms 'acceptance' or 'approval', though not identical, are usually used interchangeably to designate a form of expression of consent to be bound by a State which has opted not to use the 'ratification' process. At the international level, acceptance and approval are usually treated as equivalent either to ratification or accession.[11] According to the International Law Commission (ILC), 'on the international plane "acceptance" is an innovation which is more one of terminology than of method'.[12]

Meaning of 'Accession'

11.07 In Article 11(3), the term 'accession' refers to the process by which States which have not participated in the negotiation and signature of the treaty may subsequently become parties.[13] As in the case of the Convention, treaties typically provide for a certain period during which they can be signed; thereafter, they are open only to accession. Generally, a State may only accede to a treaty if the treaty itself permits accession or if the parties otherwise agree.[14] At the internal level, the procedure for accession remains the same as ratification, though, at the international level, an instrument of accession differs from one of ratification because the State concerned did not previously sign the treaty.[15]

Significance of Monist and Dualist Approaches

11.08 Following the commentary at 11.04 above, monist and dualist approaches to international law play a part in determining the effect of an international convention on domestic laws. International conventions are not necessarily *effective* under internal law unless and until they are incorporated into the domestic law of the relevant State. A monist perspective is that both international and domestic laws are naturally integrated within a single system (hence, 'monism'). Once a country has signed and ratified an international agreement, the terms of the agreement are automatically

10. Frank Berman and David Bentley, *Treaties and Other International Instruments – IV Ratification, Accession and Approval, Treaty Succession*, in Sir Ivor Roberts (ed.), Satow's Diplomatic Practice (7th Ed.), Book VII, OUP (2016), at 634.
11. *Id.*, at 199.
12. Commentary of the ILC to the VCLT, Yearbook of the International Law Commission, Vol. II (1966), at 198.
13. George Korontzis, *Making the Treaty*, in Duncan B. Hollis (ed.), The Oxford Guide to Treaties, OUP (2014), at 200.
14. Anthony Aust, *Modern Treaty Law and Practice* (2nd Ed.), Cambridge University Press (2007), at 110.
15. *Ibid.*

binding and effective on a domestic level and override any pre-existing and/or conflicting national law.

11.09 Conversely, in dualist legal systems, the distinction between international and national law is emphasised such that States are obliged to transpose international law, such as that contained in international treaties, into domestic law. This may be done, for example, by enacting legislation, applying decisions of treaty bodies on the interpretation and context of international treaties, or through litigation of transnational issues, using the choice of law principles, where the other relevant legal system is a monist State.[16] Both monists and dualists, however, accept that some international law, such as peremptory norms and international custom, is automatically binding, irrespective of a State's consent or domestic legal order.[17]

11.10 In practice, numerous monist jurisdictions adopt a mixed monist-dualist approach insofar as the legislature is involved in ratification, so that ratification becomes a legislative act. As a result, treaties can have the same effect as legislation, and a treaty such as the Convention may become effective in international and the domestic law of a signatory State simultaneously.

11.11 For international treaties to have effect in dualist jurisdictions, they must be implemented separately through legislation passed by the domestic legislature.[18] Some jurisdictions adopt neither a pure monist nor dualist approach, and often have different ways to implement treaties depending on the type of treaty concerned.

11.12 Timothy Schnabel, who proposed and negotiated the Singapore Convention on behalf of the US, proposed that the US adopt a monist approach, which he refers to as 'self-execution'.[19] Schnabel explains that this has been the most common approach taken by the US for private law treaties. By deeming the Convention to be self-executing, it would 'apply directly in US courts without the need for any implementing legislation'.[20] He further suggests that the fact that Working Group II (WG II) prepared both a Convention and a Model Law, the latter containing, *inter alia*, corresponding terms to the Convention, is indicative of the intent of the WG II to draft a multilateral treaty suitable for self-execution. States would have the option of choosing the Model Law path, which would necessarily involve enacting domestic laws, or alternatively the Convention approach, which would be suitable for self-execution.[21]

16. Dinah Shelton, *Chapter 1: Introduction* 2, in Dinah Shelton (ed.), International Law and Domestic Systems: Incorporation, Transformation and Persuasion, OUP (2011).
17. *Ibid.*
18. In Australia, see *Bradley v Commonwealth* (1973) 128 CLR 557; in Singapore, see *Kong Hoo (Pte) Ltd and another v Public Prosecutor* [2019] 1 SLR 1131, at [92]; in the United Kingdom, see *R v Bow Street Metropolitan Stipendiary Magistrate*, ex parte *Pinochet* [2000] 1 AC 61, at 81.
19. Timothy Schnabel, *Implementation of the Singapore Convention: Federalism, Self-Execution, and Private Law Treaties*, 30 Am. Rev. Int'l Arb. 265 (2020) https://ssrn.com/abstract=3320823.
20. *Ibid.* See the text to note 64 of Schnabel's article.
21. *Ibid.*

ARTICLE 12

Participation by Regional Economic Integration Organizations

1. A regional economic integration organization that is constituted by sovereign States and has competence over certain matters governed by this Convention may similarly sign, ratify, accept, approve or accede to this Convention. The regional economic integration organization shall in that case have the rights and obligations of a Party to the Convention, to the extent that that organization has competence over matters governed by this Convention. Where the number of Parties to the Convention is relevant in this Convention, the regional economic integration organization shall not count as a Party to the Convention in addition to its member States that are Parties to the Convention.

2. The regional economic integration organization shall, at the time of signature, ratification, acceptance, approval or accession, make a declaration to the depositary specifying the matters governed by this Convention in respect of which competence has been transferred to that organization by its member States. The regional economic integration organization shall promptly notify the depositary of any changes to the distribution of competence, including new transfers of competence, specified in the declaration under this paragraph.

3. Any reference to a 'Party to the Convention', 'Parties to the Convention', a 'State' or 'States' in this Convention applies equally to a regional economic integration organization where the context so requires.

4. This Convention shall not prevail over conflicting rules of a regional economic integration organization, whether such rules were adopted or entered into force before or after this Convention: (a) if, under article 4, relief is sought in a State that is member of such an organization and all the States relevant under article 1(1) are members of such an organization; or (b) as concerns the recognition or enforcement of judgments between member States of such an organization.

COMMENTARY

12.01 Article 12 sets out the procedural requirements to be fulfilled before a regional economic integration organisation (REIO) may become a Party to the Convention. Article 12(4) establishes an order of precedence, in the event the REIO has rules conflicting with this Convention, on matters relating to the recognition or enforcement of judgments.

Possible Forms of REIOs as Parties

12.02 Articles 12(1) to 12(3) establish how a REIO may become a Party to this Convention. There are two scenarios pursuant to which a REIO and its constituent Member States may become Parties to the Convention: (1) if the REIO has exclusive external competence over the subject matter of the Convention, it will alone become a Party to the Convention, binding its constituent Member States by virtue of the agreement which constitutes the REIO; (2) the REIO and its constituent Member States may both become Parties. This second scenario will materialise if the REIO and its constituent Member States enjoy concurrent external competence over the subject matter of the Convention (that is, joint competence) or if they have shared or mixed competence for the Convention as a whole (that is, some matters fall within the purview of the Member States while others within the external competence of the REIO). Article 12(1) provides that REIOs have the same rights and obligations as a Contracting State *to the extent* that it possesses such external competence. Article 12(2) provides that a REIO must notify the depositary of the matters for which it possesses external competence, as well as of any variations in this regard.

12.03 Article 12(2) exemplifies the competence-based approach that has been the basis of practice in multilateral conventions since the United Nations (UN) Convention on the Law of the Sea, which required a declaration of competence as a condition for REIO participation.[1]

Examples of REIOs

12.04 The European Union (EU) and its predecessor, the European Community (EC), are both examples of REIOs. For some time, the EC was the primary, if not only, example of a REIO. The Treaty of Lisbon has since supplanted the EC with the EU, whose competence is not limited to economic matters,[2] but extends also to matters

1. UN Convention on the Law of the Sea Annex IX, (10 December 1982), Art. 5(1), cited in: Marise Cremona, *Who Can Make Treaties? The European Union*, in Duncan B. Hollis (ed.), The Oxford Guide to Treaties, OUP (2014), at 120.
2. Duncan B. Hollis, *Initial Decisions on Treaty-Making*, in Duncan B. Hollis (ed.), The Oxford Guide to Treaties, OUP (2014), at 665. Commenting on this Convention specifically, Meidanis explains that the adoption of an international convention on mediation falls into the EU's competence according to Art. 3(2) of the Treaty of the Functioning of the European Union (TFEU), which provides that: 'The Union shall also have exclusive competence for the conclusion of an

such as the conservation of marine biological resources under a common fisheries policy and concluding international agreements under certain circumstances.[3] The EU is party to approximately forty treaties which include a declaration of competence by the EU, all of them multilateral.[4] The EU is not a party to the New York Convention, which is open to a Member of the UN, a State which becomes a member of a specialised agency of the UN, a party to the Statute of the International Court of Justice or any other State invited by the UN General Assembly.[5] The EU has permanent observer status at the UN but does not fall within the aforementioned categories. No REIOs are signatories to the New York Convention.

Reconciling Conflicting Rules of REIOs

12.05 Article 12(4) is a 'give-way' clause providing *specifically* for REIOs and their constituent Member States, that where provisions in this Convention were to conflict with those of the REIO, the latter's rules will be prioritised no matter if they were in force before or after the former.

12.06 Under Article 12(4)(a), any conflicting REIO rules will prevail if relief is sought in a Member State of a REIO and all States relevant under Article 1(1) are Member States of the REIO (that is to say, none of the factors qualifying the mediated settlement as 'international' are connected to a State outside the REIO). This means that if a non-REIO State is relevant to the determination of whether the iMSA is 'international', then Article 12(4)(a) will not be applicable. For example, if the EU and all its Member States are parties to the Convention, the Convention would still apply (notwithstanding any contrary EU rules), if the subject matter of the iMSA is most closely connected with a non-EU Member State.

12.07 In relation to Article 12(4)(b), the recognition or enforcement rules of foreign judgments between the Member States of REIOs will prevail over the provisions of this Convention. This means that if an iMSA is brought into a Member State for enforcement and that State issues judgment allowing or denying that enforcement, the other Member States of the REIO may be obliged to recognise that judgment *per* their internal

international agreement when its conclusion is provided for in a legislative act of the Union or is necessary to enable the Union to exercise its internal competence, or in so far as its conclusion may affect common rules or alter their scope.' To support his point, the commentator refers to Opinion 1/2003 on the relevant competence of the EC in relation to the Lugano Convention, namely 'judicial cooperation in civil and commercial matters', an area closely linked to mediation: Haris Meidanis, *Singapore Convention Series: A Plea for The Adoption of the Singapore Convention by the EU*, Kluwer Mediation Blog (30 March 2019), http://mediationblog.kluwerarbitration.com/2019/03/20/singapore-convention-series-a-plea-for-the-adoption-of-the-singapore-mediation-convention-by-the-eu/?print=print (Accessed 14 May 2019).

3. TFEU (2007), above note 2, Art. 3.
4. Marise Cremona, *Who Can Make Treaties? The European Union*, in Duncan B. Hollis (ed.), The Oxford Guide to Treaties, OUP (2014), at 120.
5. Convention on the Recognition and Enforcement of Foreign Arbitral Awards (1958), Art. VIII.

recognition rules of foreign judgments;[6] the iMSA may not be enforced *de novo* in the other Member States, as those internal rules should prevail.

12.08 In response to a question of the operation of Article 12(4)(b), UNCITRAL Working Group II explained that subparagraph (b):

> would ensure that when a party invoking a settlement agreement in a court of a member State of the REIO was not granted relief under the convention, such a judgment by the court would circulate within the REIO while that party would no longer be able to rely on the settlement agreement in a court of another member State of the REIO.[7]

It was also pointed out that, in practice, this would require a party to seek relief in only one Member State of the REIO.[8]

Case Illustration

Article 12(4)(b), read with Articles 4 and 5 of the Convention, may apply, for example, between two Member States of the EU, should the EU sign, ratify, accept, approve or accede to this Convention as a REIO. The EU, as a REIO, has prescribed recognition and enforcement rules of foreign judgments among its Member States.

Pursuant to Article 36(1) of the EU Regulation (EU) No 1215/2012 of the European Parliament and of The Council of 12 December 2012 (commonly referred to as the 'Brussels I Recast Regulation'), 'a judgment in a Member State shall be recognised in the other Member States without any special procedure being required'. Article 39 provides that, 'a judgment given in a Member State which is enforceable in that Member State shall be enforceable in the other Member States without any declaration of enforceability being required'. The Regulation does not apply to arbitration, perhaps arguably because the European Convention on International Commercial Arbitration of 1961 and the New York Convention have well-established rules on recognition and enforcement in arbitration.

The application of the Brussels I Recast Regulation suggests that, where there is a conflict between it and the Convention (particularly Articles 4 and 5), the Regulation would take precedence on issues of recognition and enforcement, above Articles 4 and 5 of the Convention.

---

6. Timothy Schnabel, *The Singapore Convention on Mediation: A Framework for the Cross-Border Recognition and Enforcement of Mediated Settlements*, 19(1) Pepp. Disp. Resol. L.J. 1 (2019), at 59.
7. Report of Working Group II on the Work of its 68th Session (5-9 February 2018), A/CN.9/934 (2018), at paras 104-107.
8. *Ibid.*

One commentator suggests that if the EU, or all the EU Member States, becomes a Party (or Parties) to this Convention, the international enforcement of iMSAs in the EU will be based on the same legislation and that this will diminish or eliminate the imbalances caused by divergent national laws on iMSAs within the EU, thus creating a welcoming environment for mediation in the EU.[9]

9. Haris Meidanis, *International Enforcement of Mediated Settlement Agreements: Two and a Half Models – Why and How to Enforce Internationally Mediated Settlement Agreements*, 85(1) Arbitration 49 (2019).

ARTICLE 13

Non-unified Legal Systems

1. If a Party to the Convention has two or more territorial units in which different systems of law are applicable in relation to the matters dealt with in this Convention, it may, at the time of signature, ratification, acceptance, approval or accession, declare that this Convention is to extend to all its territorial units or only to one or more of them, and may amend its declaration by submitting another declaration at any time.
2. These declarations are to be notified to the depositary and are to state expressly the territorial units to which the Convention extends.
3. If a Party to the Convention has two or more territorial units in which different systems of law are applicable in relation to the matters dealt with in this Convention:

(a) Any reference to the law or rule of procedure of a State shall be construed as referring, where appropriate, to the law or rule of procedure in force in the relevant territorial unit;
(b) Any reference to the place of business in a State shall be construed as referring, where appropriate, to the place of business in the relevant territorial unit;
(c) Any reference to the competent authority of the State shall be construed as referring, where appropriate, to the competent authority in the relevant territorial unit.

4. If a Party to the Convention makes no declaration under paragraph 1 of this article, the Convention is to extend to all territorial units of that State.

COMMENTARY

13.01 This article applies to State Parties that comprise two or more territorial units with different legal systems applicable to matters relating to this Convention. Article 13 sets out declarations they may make on the effect of this Convention on their territorial units and the presumption which will apply in the event no such declaration is made.

Significance of Territorial Units

13.02 Article 13 addresses the potential issues that may result from some States comprising two or more territorial units, each with their own judicial system, including countries comprising federated States, such as the US and Canada. This also applies to the People's Republic of China, which includes the Special Administrative Regions of Macau and Hong Kong.

13.03 Though all territorial units situated within a Contracting State may apply the same legal tradition (for example, the common law), it does not necessarily entail that they administer the same systems of law. For example, in countries that have a federal system, such as Australia, each Australian state may have different legislation governing similar aspects of the law, even though all her States fall under the common law tradition.[1] When these countries decide to become Parties to the Convention, issues will arise, necessitating a determination on whether references are to be made to the State as a whole (that is, 'State' in the international sense) or to only a specific territorial unit within that State. The solution is provided for in Article 13(3), which establishes that where different systems of law are applicable within those territorial units with respect to any issue addressed by the Convention, the Convention shall be interpreted as being administered either to the State in the international sense or to the relevant territorial unit, where it is appropriate to do so.

13.04 Article 13(1) provides that States comprising two or more territorial units have the prerogative (at the time of signature, ratification, acceptance, approval or accession) to declare that the Convention may extend to all its territorial units or only to one or a number of them and may amend their declaration by submitting a separate declaration at any time. To be abundantly clear, when a State does not extend the Convention's terms to a territorial unit, it means that the competent authorities in that unit do not have to apply the Convention when relief is sought from it. However, this does not mean that the Convention's scope does not extend to the parties whose place

1. Take the *Moçambique* Rule, which is a common law rule in private international law that subsists in many jurisdictions associated with the common law tradition, for instance: *British South Africa Co v Companhia de Moçambique* [1893] AC 602. The rule proffers that courts have 'no jurisdiction to entertain an action for (1) the determination of the title to, or the right to the possession of, any immovable situate out of [the state] (foreign land), or (2) the recovery of damages for trespass to such immovable' (Albert Van Dicey, *A Digest of the Law of England with Reference to the Conflict of Laws*, The Boston Book Co. (1896), at 214–215). In other words, when courts are asked to make a determination as to private law rights associated with an immovable piece of property – for example, a piece of real estate – they would not have the requisite subject matter jurisdiction to do so if that piece of property is located outside of the territorial limits of the state in which the court sits. There are some well-defined exceptions to this rule, for example, where parties are enforcing personal obligations ancillary to the real property in dispute. In Australia, the *Moçambique* Rule has been abolished by legislation in the state of New South Wales (see s. 3 of the Jurisdiction of Courts (Foreign Land) Act 1989 (NSW)). However, the *Moçambique* Rule is good law in the common law of other Australian States, which have not enacted legislation to repeal its applicability.

of business is situated within that territorial unit.[2] In other words, if a mediated settlement agreement, which involves a party which has its place of business in such a territorial unit, is brought to a competent authority for the purposes of this Convention to be enforced, that settlement agreement will be covered by this Convention, so long as it satisfies the criteria as to scope – established by Articles 1 and 2 – and form – established by Article 4 – as examined in the earlier commentaries.

13.05 Article 13(2) provides that the declaration should state explicitly the territorial units to which the Convention extends. To ensure clarity, Article 13(4) provides that if a Party to the Convention makes no specific declaration under Article 13(1), the Convention shall prima facie extend to all territorial units which comprise that State.

13.06 Article 13 also applies in the context of amendments under Article 15.[3] In other words, States can rely on Article 13 to decide whether and how to apply amendments to the Convention under Article 15 to their territorial units.

---

2. Timothy Schnabel, *The Singapore Convention on Mediation: A Framework for the Cross-Border Recognition and Enforcement of Mediated Settlements*, 19(1) Pepp. Disp. Resol. L.J. 1 (2019), at 59.
3. Report of the United Nations Commission on International Trade Law on the Work of its 51st Session (25 June-13 July 2018), A/73/17 (2018), at para. 46. Available at https://undocs.org/A/73/17 (Accessed 13 May 2022).

ARTICLE 14

Entry into Force

1. This Convention shall enter into force six months after the deposit of the third instrument of ratification, acceptance, approval, or accession.
2. When a State ratifies, accepts, approves or accedes to this Convention after the deposit of the third instrument of ratification, acceptance, approval or accession, this Convention shall enter into force in respect of that State six months after the date of the deposit of its instrument of ratification, acceptance, approval or accession. The Convention shall enter into force for a territorial unit to which this Convention has been extended in accordance with article 13 six months after the notification of the declaration referred to in that article.

COMMENTARY

14.01 Article 14 serves a key function present in any treaty, as it sets out the timeline and procedure by which the Convention becomes legally binding, that is, has entered into force. It also addresses the applicable timeline for the entry into force of the Convention for territorial units referred to in Article 13.

Timeline for Entry into Force

14.02 Article 14 specifies when the Singapore Convention will enter into force. The Convention's entry into force will take place six months after the deposit of the third instrument of ratification, acceptance, approval or accession. The United Nations Treaty Collection provides a model instrument for ratification, acceptance or approval.[1] The meaning of the terms 'ratification', 'acceptance' and 'approval' is examined in the commentary to Article 11. Qatar became the third State to ratify the

1. UN Treaty Collection, *Model Instruments*, https://treaties.un.org/doc/source/modelinstruments/model_instrument_of_ratification_acceptance_or_approval-English.pdf (Accessed 11 May 2019). UNCITRAL has also prepared the Accession Kit for States intending to become Parties to the Convention on International Settlement Agreements Resulting from Mediation (the 'Singapore Convention on Mediation'). Available at https://uncitral.un.org/sites/uncitral.un.org/files/media-documents/uncitral/en/singapore_convention_accession_kit.pdf (Accessed 13 May 2022).

Singapore Convention on 12 March 2020 and the Convention entered into force on 12 September 2020.

Procedure for Entry into Force

14.03 There are two steps to the procedure:

(1) first, a minimum of three instruments is required to be deposited; and
(2) second, a period of six months following the third deposit is to pass before the Convention enters into force.

14.04 The requirement for the deposit of three instruments is similar to that in Article XII(1) of the New York Convention.[2] Some members of UNCITRAL Working Group II expressed that the number of ratifications required for entry into force should be higher (ten, for instance), while some held the view that three was sufficient. It was eventually agreed, after discussions and for the purpose of achieving consensus, that the deposit of three instruments would be sufficient.[3] While the Convention would enter into force six months after the deposit of the third instrument, the New York Convention entered into force on the ninetieth day after the deposit of the third instrument.

14.05 Similar rules for entry into force are laid down for territorial units to which the Convention has been extended in accordance with Article 13(1).

2. Convention on the Recognition and Enforcement of Foreign Arbitral Awards (1958). Art. XII(1) provides, 'This Convention shall come into force on the ninetieth day following the date of deposit of the third instrument of ratification or accession.'
3. Report of Working Group II on the Work of its 68th Session (5-9 February 2018), A/CN.9/934 (2018), at paras 104-107. Available at http://undocs.org/A/CN.9/934 (Accessed 13 May 2022).

ARTICLE 15

Amendment

1. Any Party to the Convention may propose an amendment to the present Convention by submitting it to the Secretary-General of the United Nations. The Secretary-General shall thereupon communicate the proposed amendment to the Parties to the Convention with a request that they indicate whether they favour a conference of Parties to the Convention for the purpose of considering and voting upon the proposal. In the event that within four months from the date of such communication at least one third of the Parties to the Convention favour such a conference, the Secretary-General shall convene the conference under the auspices of the United Nations.
2. The conference of Parties to the Convention shall make every effort to achieve consensus on each amendment. If all efforts at consensus are exhausted and no consensus is reached, the amendment shall, as a last resort, require for its adoption a two-thirds majority vote of the Parties to the Convention present and voting at the conference.
3. An adopted amendment shall be submitted by the depositary to all the Parties to the Convention for ratification, acceptance or approval.
4. An adopted amendment shall enter into force six months after the date of deposit of the third instrument of ratification, acceptance or approval. When an amendment enters into force, it shall be binding on those Parties to the Convention that have expressed consent to be bound by it.
5. When a Party to the Convention ratifies, accepts or approves an amendment following the deposit of the third instrument of ratification, acceptance or approval, the amendment shall enter into force in respect of that Party to the Convention six months after the date of the deposit of its instrument of ratification, acceptance or approval.

COMMENTARY

15.01 Article 15 establishes the procedure for States to propose an amendment. It sets out the procedural requirements for the proposal, discussion, adoption and entry into force of an amendment.

Procedure and Requirements for Amendment

15.02 In order for an amendment to be passed, a Conference must be convened by the Secretary-General of the United Nations (UN), in accordance with Article 15(1). Next, Article 15(2) provides that while the first priority of the Conference should be to achieve a consensus on each proposed amendment, the success of the amendment's adoption would ultimately depend on whether the minimum threshold of a two-thirds majority vote of the parties to the Convention present and voting at the Conference is achieved.

15.03 Article 15 mirrors the substantive principles in Article 40 of the Vienna Convention on the Law of Treaties (VCLT),[1] which keep to the formal model of consent-based treaty-making, under which explicit consent is required of an individual State with the intention to be bound by the amendment. Treaties differ on the number of instruments required to be deposited before the adopted amendment enters into force and typically this number is counter-balanced by the majority required to adopt the amendment. For example, amendments to the UN Framework Convention on Climate Change are normally adopted by consensus but as a last resort, by a three-quarters majority of the 194 parties to the Convention. The adopted amendment does not enter into force unless three-quarters of the 194 parties to the Convention have accepted it.[2] Amendments to the International Covenant on Civil and Political Rights may be adopted by a majority of the parties present and voting but do not enter into force without approval by the UN General Assembly and acceptance by two-thirds of the Covenant's parties.[3] In comparison, the New York Convention does not contain a provision relating to amendments.

Effect of an Amendment

15.04 The procedural requirements for the entry into force of the amendment follow those set out in Article 14(1) of the Convention.

15.05 Pursuant to Article 15(4), when the amendment comes into force, it shall only bind States *that have expressed consent to be bound by it*. This is consistent with VCLT Article 40(3). While this may mean that different States may have different legal obligations arising from the Convention (if only some but not all States deposit instruments in response to the adopted amendment), the safeguard contained within Article 15(2) is that only amendments that are agreed upon by consensus or a majority will be adopted. At the minimum, there is an agreement that the amendment may exist, but not necessarily an agreement for it to be binding on the States that choose not to deposit instruments in response to the adopted amendment. This is typical and consistent with the consent-based model of multilateral treaty-making.

1. Vienna Convention on the Law of Treaties (1969).
2. UN Framework Convention on Climate Change (9 May 1992), Art. 15(4).
3. The International Covenant on Civil and Political Rights (19 December 1966), Art. 51(2).

Case Illustration

For example, under the Rome Statute of the International Criminal Court, any amendment to certain articles of the Statute would enter into force:

> for those State Parties which have accepted the amendment one year after the deposit of their instruments of ratification or acceptance. In respect of a State Party which has not accepted the amendment, the Court shall not exercise its jurisdiction regarding a crime covered by the amendment ....[4]

On 14 December 2017, the Assembly of State Parties to the Statute adopted an amendment to Article 8 of the Statute.[5] In brief, the amendment relates to, in the context of the definition of 'war crimes' in the Statute, weapons 'the primary effect of which is to injure by fragments which in the human body escape detection by X-rays'. On 2 April 2019, Luxembourg deposited an instrument of ratification in respect of the amended Article 8. Assuming no other parties to the Rome Statute deposit instruments of ratification or acceptance, the amendment will take effect for Luxembourg only on 2 April 2020. Hypothetically, this means if a war crime is committed using the weapon as described in the amended Article 8 and the requisite one year has passed, the International Criminal Court will have jurisdiction to prosecute nationals of Luxembourg but not any other parties to the Rome Statute who have not ratified or accepted the amendment.

4. Rome Statute of the International Criminal Court (17 July 1998), Art. 121(5).
5. Amendment to the Rome Statute of the International Criminal Court, Adoption of Amendment to Art. 8, C.N. 125.2018.TREATIES-XVIII.10 (Depository Notification) (8 March 2018).

Article 16

Denunciations

1. A Party to the Convention may denounce this Convention by a formal notification in writing addressed to the depositary. The denunciation may be limited to certain territorial units of a non-unified legal system to which this Convention applies.
2. The denunciation shall take effect twelve months after the notification is received by the depositary. Where a longer period for the denunciation to take effect is specified in the notification, the denunciation shall take effect upon the expiration of such longer period after the notification is received by the depositary. The Convention shall continue to apply to settlement agreements concluded before the denunciation takes effect.

COMMENTARY

16.01 Article 16 sets out the procedural requirement for denunciations and the effect of a notification of denunciation.

Procedural Requirement for Denunciation

16.02 Article 16 of this Convention provides that States may denounce the Convention through a notification process, namely a notice in writing addressed to the depositary. The denunciation may be confined to a number of territorial units of a non-unified legal system to which the Convention is applicable. The denunciation takes effect 12 months after the date on which the above-mentioned notice is received by the depositary. If the written notice provides for a longer period of time for the denunciation to take effect, it shall take effect when the longer period of time specified has elapsed.

Effect of Notification of Denunciation in Interim Period

16.03 During the interim period between the notification of denunciation and the end of the 12 months specified in Article 16(2), the legal obligations of all States, including the denunciating State, continue unabated.[1]

16.04 Once the denunciation takes effect, the treaty is considered terminated with respect to the denunciating State. However, this termination does not 'affect any right, obligation or legal situation of the parties created through the execution of the treaty prior to'[2] the date that the termination takes effect. Further, the termination does not 'impair the duty of any State to fulfil any obligation embodied in the treaty to which it would be subject under international law independently of the treaty'[3] which is an implicit reference to the application of customary international law.

16.05 Denunciation or termination will not affect the Convention's continuation in force for the remaining States, given that there is no minimum number of required States specified in this Convention.[4]

Denunciations Generally

16.06 A fundamental tenet of treaty participation is the principle of *pacta sunt servanda*, which basically prescribes that '[e]very treaty in force is binding upon the parties to it and must be performed by them in good faith'.[5] Over time, a State party who has consented to being bound by a treaty may find that its obligations under that treaty have grown to be inconsistent with its own national or political interests. In such a circumstance, the State is faced with four different options: (1) refuse to observe particular elements of the treaty; (2) encourage amendments to the treaty; (3) threaten withdrawal from the treaty to instigate change; or (4) withdraw from the treaty altogether.[6]

16.07 Electing to refuse to comply with treaty obligations generally constitutes a breach. Hence, like in most international agreements, Article 16 offers a State Party to the Convention a mechanism to withdraw unilaterally from the Convention without requiring the consent of other State Parties.

---

1. Laurence R. Helfer, *Terminating Treaties*, in Duncan B. Hollis (ed.), The Oxford Guide to Treaties, OUP (2014), at 641.
2. *Id.*, at 640; Vienna Convention on the Law of Treaties (1969) (VCLT), Art. 70(1)(b).
3. Laurence R. Helfer, *Terminating Treaties*, in Duncan B. Hollis (ed.), The Oxford Guide to Treaties, OUP (2014), at 640; VCLT (1969), Art. 43.
4. Laurence R. Helfer, *Terminating Treaties*, in Duncan B. Hollis (ed.), The Oxford Guide to Treaties, OUP (2014), at 635; VCLT (1969), Art. 55.
5. VCLT, Art. 26. See the introduction for further commentary on the principle of *pacta sunt servanda.*
6. Nicola Christine Port, David Fuhr and Jessica Simonoff, *Article XIII*, in Herbert Kronke et al. (eds), Recognition and Enforcement of Foreign Arbitral Awards: A Global Commentary on the New York Convention, Kluwer Law International (2010), at 533.

16.08 Notwithstanding, taking a drastic step like denunciation would, in all likelihood, be rare. This is because the Convention has in place certain mechanisms which allow a State to avoid results inimical to its national interests without resorting to denunciation. For instance, States may articulate reservations under Article 8 upon joining or at any time thereafter. This pre-empts the need for future denunciations by affording States the flexibility to circumscribe the reach of the Convention and avoid from the outset provisions which they deem objectionable.

Case Illustration

Twelve States, including Australia, Canada, the United Kingdom and France, submitted instruments of denunciation to the Constitution of the United Nations (UN) Industrial Development Organisation. Copies of these instruments of denunciation are available in the UN Treaty Collection.

Denunciations occur for a variety of reasons, ranging from signalling a challenge to disfavoured international legal rules, to joining a later-negotiated agreement relating to the same subject matter.

Appendix A: A Comparison Table on the Enforcement of an iMSA under the Singapore Convention and Enforcement of a Consent Arbitral Award under the New York Convention

	Singapore Convention	*New York Convention*
Enforcement.	Yes. Article 3(1) of the Singapore Convention provides a direct enforcement mechanism for iMSAs.	Yes. Article III of the New York Convention provides a direct enforcement mechanism for foreign arbitral awards. Regarding the limitations on the enforcement of consent arbitral awards under the New York Convention, see commentary to Article 1.
Recognition.	Yes. Even though the Singapore Convention does not expressly mention the term 'recognition', Article 3(2) provides a functional description of the process of recognition.	Yes. Article III imposes the obligation on Contracting States to the New York Convention to recognise foreign arbitral awards. Regarding the preclusive effect of consent arbitral awards, see the commentary to Article 3.

	Singapore Convention	*New York Convention*
Rules of procedure of the State where enforcement/ recognition is sought.	Yes. Article 3(1) – (2) of the Singapore Convention prescribes that each Contracting Party shall enforce and recognise iMSAs in accordance with its rules of procedure.	Yes. Article III of the New York Convention prescribes that each Contracting State shall recognise foreign arbitral awards as binding and enforce them in accordance with its rules of procedure.
Prohibition of imposing different conditions in relation to domestic and international awards/iMSAs.	No. There is no provision restricting Contracting Parties to the Singapore Convention imposing more onerous conditions and higher fees on the enforcement and recognition of iMSAs than they impose on the recognition and enforcement of domestic mediated settlements.	Yes. Article III of the New York Convention states that there shall not be imposed substantially more onerous conditions or higher fees or charges on the recognition or enforcement of arbitral awards to which this Convention applies than are imposed on the recognition or enforcement of domestic arbitral awards.
Enforcement of an agreement to submit disputes to mediation/arbitration.	No. The Singapore Convention does not prescribe an enforcement regime for an agreement to mediate.	Yes. Article II enforces an agreement to arbitrate that is made in writing.
Commercial nature.	Yes. The Singapore Convention only applies to commercial iMSAs.The definition of the term 'commercial' does not depend on the domestic law of a Contracting Party to the Singapore Convention.	No. Article I(1) of the New York Convention states that it applies to foreign arbitral awards. However, according to Article I(3), Contracting States can make a reservation and declare that they apply the New York Convention only to awards that are considered 'commercial' according to their domestic laws.

	Singapore Convention	*New York Convention*
Seat.	No. The Singapore Convention does not provide a seat of mediation.	Yes. A seat of arbitration determines the 'foreign' nature of arbitral awards under Article I(1) of the New York Convention. Also, Article V(1)(e) contains a ground for refusing to enforce an award if that award was set aside or suspended in the jurisdiction where the award was made.
A supervisory court with exclusive jurisdiction over a set-aside procedure.	No. The Singapore Convention does not provide a concept of seat. As a result, no court has exclusive jurisdiction to set aside an iMSA. However, an iMSA may provide for a dispute resolution clause for the resolution of disputes arising out of the iMSA.	Yes. A seat of arbitration determines a court with exclusive jurisdiction to set aside an award. Article V(1)(e) of the New York Convention contains a reference to the seat of arbitration.
Contractual defences to enforcement and recognition.	Yes. Article 5(1)(a) – (d) of the Singapore Convention contains grounds for refusing to grant relief that are contractual in nature.	No. The New York Convention does not provide such grounds. The only contractual defence in the New York Convention is found in Article V(1)(a), which relates to the invalidity of the arbitration agreement.

	Singapore Convention	*New York Convention*
Defences relating to ethical standards.	Yes. Article 5(1)(e) – (f) of the Singapore Convention expressly provides two novel grounds for refusing to enforce iMSAs relating to mediators' misconduct.	Yes. Even though the New York Convention does not expressly provide a defence relating to arbitrators' misconduct, a party has the possibility to raise this defence under the public policy ground according to Article V(2)(b). However, the standard of review under the New York Convention may be different as compared to the Singapore Convention.
Possibility to opt out by parties.	Yes. Parties to an iMSA can opt out of the application of the Singapore Convention.	No. The New York Convention does not contain such a possibility.
Items that shall be submitted to the competent authority for enforcement and recognition.	Two items shall be submitted to the competent authority according to Article 4: (1) the iMSA signed by the parties; (2) evidence of mediation.	Two items shall be submitted to the competent authority according to Article IV: (1) The duly authenticated original award; (2) The original agreement to arbitrate.
More favourable regime.	Yes. According to Article 7, a party to an iMSA can avail itself of a more favourable regime that may exist in the enforcing State.	Yes. According to Article VII, a party can avail itself to a more favourable regime in the enforcing State.

	Singapore Convention	*New York Convention*
Reciprocity reservation.	No. iMSA can be enforced in a Contracting Party to the Singapore Convention irrespective of whether the iMSA was signed in a Contracting Party to the Singapore Convention.	Yes. The Contracting States to the New York Convention have the possibility of making a reservation under Article I(3) and declaring that they apply the New York Convention only to awards made in another Contracting State to the New York Convention.
Reservation on enforcement against States.	Yes. A Contracting Party can make a reservation under Article 8(1)(a) and declare that it shall not apply this Convention to settlement agreements to which it is a party, or to which any governmental agencies or any person acting on behalf of a governmental agency is a party, to the extent specified in the declaration.	No. The New York Convention does not provide such a possibility.
Opt-in reservation.	Yes. A Contracting Party can make a reservation under Article 8(1)(b) and declare that it shall apply this Convention only to the extent that the parties to the settlement agreement have agreed to the application of the Convention.	No. The New York Convention does not provide such a possibility.

Appendix B: United Nations Convention on International Settlement Agreements Resulting from Mediation*

Preamble

The Parties to this Convention,

Recognizing the value for international trade of mediation as a method for settling commercial disputes in which the parties in dispute request a third person or persons to assist them in their attempt to settle the dispute amicably,
Noting that mediation is increasingly used in international and domestic commercial practice as an alternative to litigation,
Considering that the use of mediation results in significant benefits, such as reducing the instances where a dispute leads to the termination of a commercial relationship, facilitating the administration of international transactions by commercial parties and producing savings in the administration of justice by States,
Convinced that the establishment of a framework for international settlement agreements resulting from mediation that is acceptable to States with different legal, social and economic systems would contribute to the development of harmonious international economic relations,
Have agreed as follows:

Article 1. Scope of application

1. This Convention applies to an agreement resulting from mediation and concluded in writing by parties to resolve a commercial dispute ("settlement agreement") which, at the time of its conclusion, is international in that:
   (a) At least two parties to the settlement agreement have their places of business in different States; or
   (b) The State in which the parties to the settlement agreement have their places of business is different from either:

 The text reproduced here is valid at the time of reproduction [23 February 2022]. The Convention is available at https://uncitral.un.org/sites/uncitral.un.org/files/media-documents/EN/Texts/UNCITRAL/Arbitration/mediation_convention_v1900316_eng.pdf.

        (i) The State in which a substantial part of the obligations under the settlement agreement is performed; or
        (ii) The State with which the subject matter of the settlement agreement is most closely connected.

2. This Convention does not apply to settlement agreements:
    (a) Concluded to resolve a dispute arising from transactions engaged in by one of the parties (a consumer) for personal, family or household purposes;
    (b) Relating to family, inheritance or employment law.
3. This Convention does not apply to:
    (a) Settlement agreements:
        (i) That have been approved by a court or concluded in the course of proceedings before a court; and
        (ii) That are enforceable as a judgment in the State of that court;
    (b) Settlement agreements that have been recorded and are enforceable as an arbitral award.

Article 2. Definitions

1. For the purposes of article 1, paragraph 1:
    (a) If a party has more than one place of business, the relevant place of business is that which has the closest relationship to the dispute resolved by the settlement agreement, having regard to the circumstances known to, or contemplated by, the parties at the time of the conclusion of the settlement agreement;
    (b) If a party does not have a place of business, reference is to be made to the party's habitual residence.
2. A settlement agreement is "in writing" if its content is recorded in any form. The requirement that a settlement agreement be in writing is met by an electronic communication if the information contained therein is accessible so as to be useable for subsequent reference.
3. "Mediation" means a process, irrespective of the expression used or the basis upon which the process is carried out, whereby parties attempt to reach an amicable settlement of their dispute with the assistance of a third person or persons ("the mediator") lacking the authority to impose a solution upon the parties to the dispute.

Article 3. General principles

1. Each Party to the Convention shall enforce a settlement agreement in accordance with its rules of procedure and under the conditions laid down in this Convention.
2. If a dispute arises concerning a matter that a party claims was already resolved by a settlement agreement, a Party to the Convention shall allow the party to invoke the settlement agreement in accordance with its rules of procedure and

under the conditions laid down in this Convention, in order to prove that the matter has already been resolved.

Article 4. Requirements for reliance on settlement agreements

1. A party relying on a settlement agreement under this Convention shall supply to the competent authority of the Party to the Convention where relief is sought:
   (a) The settlement agreement signed by the parties;
   (b) Evidence that the settlement agreement resulted from mediation, such as:
      (i) The mediator's signature on the settlement agreement;
      (ii) A document signed by the mediator indicating that the mediation was carried out;
      (iii) An attestation by the institution that administered the mediation; or
      (iv) In the absence of (i), (ii) or (iii), any other evidence acceptable to the competent authority.
2. The requirement that a settlement agreement shall be signed by the parties or, where applicable, the mediator is met in relation to an electronic communication if:
   (a) A method is used to identify the parties or the mediator and to indicate the parties' or mediator's intention in respect of the information contained in the electronic communication; and
   (b) The method used is either:
      (i) As reliable as appropriate for the purpose for which the electronic communication was generated or communicated, in the light of all the circumstances, including any relevant agreement; or
      (ii) Proven in fact to have fulfilled the functions described in subparagraph (a) above, by itself or together with further evidence.
3. If the settlement agreement is not in an official language of the Party to the Convention where relief is sought, the competent authority may request a translation thereof into such language.
4. The competent authority may require any necessary document in order to verify that the requirements of the Convention have been complied with.
5. When considering the request for relief, the competent authority shall act expeditiously.

Article 5. Grounds for refusing to grant relief

1. The competent authority of the Party to the Convention where relief is sought under article 4 may refuse to grant relief at the request of the party against whom the relief is sought only if that party furnishes to the competent authority proof that:
   (a) A party to the settlement agreement was under some incapacity;
   (b) The settlement agreement sought to be relied upon:

   (i) Is null and void, inoperative or incapable of being performed under the law to which the parties have validly subjected it or, failing any indication thereon, under the law deemed applicable by the competent authority of the Party to the Convention where relief is sought under article 4;
   (ii) Is not binding, or is not final, according to its terms; or
   (iii) Has been subsequently modified;

(c) The obligations in the settlement agreement:
   (i) Have been performed; or
   (ii) Are not clear or comprehensible;

(d) Granting relief would be contrary to the terms of the settlement agreement;

(e) There was a serious breach by the mediator of standards applicable to the mediator or the mediation without which breach that party would not have entered into the settlement agreement; or

(f) There was a failure by the mediator to disclose to the parties circumstances that raise justifiable doubts as to the mediator's impartiality or independence and such failure to disclose had a material impact or undue influence on a party without which failure that party would not have entered into the settlement agreement.

2. The competent authority of the Party to the Convention where relief is sought under article 4 may also refuse to grant relief if it finds that:
   (a) Granting relief would be contrary to the public policy of that Party; or
   (b) The subject matter of the dispute is not capable of settlement by mediation under the law of that Party.

Article 6. Parallel applications or claims

If an application or a claim relating to a settlement agreement has been made to a court, an arbitral tribunal or any other competent authority which may affect the relief being sought under article 4, the competent authority of the Party to the Convention where such relief is sought may, if it considers it proper, adjourn the decision and may also, on the request of a party, order the other party to give suitable security.

Article 7. Other laws or treaties

This Convention shall not deprive any interested party of any right it may have to avail itself of a settlement agreement in the manner and to the extent allowed by the law or the treaties of the Party to the Convention where such settlement agreement is sought to be relied upon.

Article 8. Reservations

1. A Party to the Convention may declare that:
   (a) It shall not apply this Convention to settlement agreements to which it is a party, or to which any governmental agencies or any person acting on

behalf of a governmental agency is a party, to the extent specified in the declaration;

(b) It shall apply this Convention only to the extent that the parties to the settlement agreement have agreed to the application of the Convention.

2. No reservations are permitted except those expressly authorized in this article.
3. Reservations may be made by a Party to the Convention at any time. Reservations made at the time of signature shall be subject to confirmation upon ratification, acceptance or approval. Such reservations shall take effect simultaneously with the entry into force of this Convention in respect of the Party to the Convention concerned. Reservations made at the time of ratification, acceptance or approval of this Convention or accession thereto, or at the time of making a declaration under article 13 shall take effect simultaneously with the entry into force of this Convention in respect of the Party to the Convention concerned. Reservations deposited after the entry into force of the Convention for that Party to the Convention shall take effect six months after the date of the deposit.
4. Reservations and their confirmations shall be deposited with the depositary.
5. Any Party to the Convention that makes a reservation under this Convention may withdraw it at any time. Such withdrawals are to be deposited with the depositary, and shall take effect six months after deposit.

Article 9. Effect on settlement agreements

The Convention and any reservation or withdrawal thereof shall apply only to settlement agreements concluded after the date when the Convention, reservation or withdrawal thereof enters into force for the Party to the Convention concerned.

Article 10. Depositary

The Secretary-General of the United Nations is hereby designated as the depositary of this Convention.

Article 11. Signature, ratification, acceptance, approval, accession

1. This Convention is open for signature by all States in Singapore, on 7 August 2019, and thereafter at United Nations Headquarters in New York.
2. This Convention is subject to ratification, acceptance or approval by the signatories.
3. This Convention is open for accession by all States that are not signatories as from the date it is open for signature.
4. Instruments of ratification, acceptance, approval or accession are to be deposited with the depositary.

Article 12. Participation by regional economic organizations

1. A regional economic integration organization that is constituted by sovereign States and has competence over certain matters governed by this Convention may similarly sign, ratify, accept, approve or accede to this Convention. The

regional economic integration organization shall in that case have the rights and obligations of a Party to the Convention, to the extent that that organization has competence over matters governed by this Convention. Where the number of Parties to the Convention is relevant in this Convention, the regional economic integration organization shall not count as a Party to the Convention in addition to its member States that are Parties to the Convention.

2. The regional economic integration organization shall, at the time of signature, ratification, acceptance, approval or accession, make a declaration to the depositary specifying the matters governed by this Convention in respect of which competence has been transferred to that organization by its member States. The regional economic integration organization shall promptly notify the depositary of any changes to the distribution of competence, including new transfers of competence, specified in the declaration under this paragraph.
3. Any reference to a 'Party to the Convention', 'Parties to the Convention', a 'State' or 'States' in this Convention applies equally to a regional economic integration organization where the context so requires.
4. This Convention shall not prevail over conflicting rules of a regional economic integration organization, whether such rules were adopted or entered into force before or after this Convention: (a) if, under article 4, relief is sought in a State that is member of such an organization and all the States relevant under article 1, paragraph 1, are members of such an organization; or (b) as concerns the recognition or enforcement of judgments between member States of such an organization.

Article 13. Non-unified legal systems

1. If a Party to the Convention has two or more territorial units in which different systems of law are applicable in relation to the matters dealt with in this Convention, it may, at the time of signature, ratification, acceptance, approval or accession, declare that this Convention is to extend to all its territorial units or only to one or more of them, and may amend its declaration by submitting another declaration at any time.
2. These declarations are to be notified to the depositary and are to state expressly the territorial units to which the Convention extends.
3. If a Party to the Convention has two or more territorial units in which different systems of law are applicable in relation to the matters dealt with in this Convention:
   (a) Any reference to the law or rule of procedure of a State shall be construed as referring, where appropriate, to the law or rule of procedure in force in the relevant territorial unit;
   (b) Any reference to the place of business in a State shall be construed as refer-ring, where appropriate, to the place of business in the relevant territorial unit;

(c) Any reference to the competent authority of the State shall be construed as referring, where appropriate, to the competent authority in the relevant territorial unit.

4. If a Party to the Convention makes no declaration under paragraph 1 of this article, the Convention is to extend to all territorial units of that State.

Article 14. Entry into force

1. This Convention shall enter into force six months after deposit of the third instrument of ratification, acceptance, approval, or accession.
2. When a State ratifies, accepts, approves or accedes to this Convention after the deposit of the third instrument of ratification, acceptance, approval or accession, this Convention shall enter into force in respect of that State six months after the date of the deposit of its instrument of ratification, acceptance, approval or accession. The Convention shall enter into force for a territorial unit to which this Convention has been extended in accordance with article 13 six months after the notification of the declaration referred to in that article.

Article 15. Amendment

1. Any Party to the Convention may propose an amendment to the present Convention by submitting it to the Secretary-General of the United Nations. The Secretary-General shall thereupon communicate the proposed amendment to the Parties to the Convention with a request that they indicate whether they favour a conference of Parties to the Convention for the purpose of considering and voting upon the proposal. In the event that within four months from the date of such communication at least one third of the Parties to the Convention favour such a conference, the Secretary-General shall convene the conference under the auspices of the United Nations.
2. The conference of Parties to the Convention shall make every effort to achieve consensus on each amendment. If all efforts at consensus are exhausted and no consensus is reached, the amendment shall, as a last resort, require for its adoption a two-thirds majority vote of the Parties to the Convention present and voting at the conference.
3. An adopted amendment shall be submitted by the depositary to all the Parties to the Convention for ratification, acceptance or approval.
4. An adopted amendment shall enter into force six months after the date of deposit of the third instrument of ratification, acceptance or approval. When an amendment enters into force, it shall be binding on those Parties to the Convention that have expressed consent to be bound by it.
5. When a Party to the Convention ratifies, accepts or approves an amendment following the deposit of the third instrument of ratification, acceptance or approval, the amendment shall enter into force in respect of that Party to the Convention six months after the date of the deposit of its instrument of ratification, acceptance or approval.

Article 16. Denunciations

1. A Party to the Convention may denounce this Convention by a formal notification in writing addressed to the depositary. The denunciation may be limited to certain territorial units of a non-unified legal system to which this Convention applies.
2. The denunciation shall take effect twelve months after the notification is received by the depositary. Where a longer period for the denunciation to take effect is specified in the notification, the denunciation shall take effect upon the expiration of such longer period after the notification is received by the depositary. The Convention shall continue to apply to settlement agreements concluded before the denunciation takes effect.

Appendix C: List of States That Have Signed the Convention

In order of signing:

1. Singapore
2. Afghanistan
3. Belarus[1]
4. Benin
5. Brunei Darussalam
6. Chile
7. China
8. Colombia
9. Congo
10. Democratic Republic of the Congo
11. Eswatini
12. Fiji
13. Georgia[2]
14. Grenada
15. Haiti
16. Honduras
17. India
18. Iran (Islamic Republic of)[3]
19. Israel
20. Jamaica
21. Jordan
22. Kazakhstan[4]
23. Lao People's Democratic Republic
24. Malaysia
25. Maldives
26. Mauritius
27. Montenegro
28. Nigeria
29. North Macedonia
30. Palau
31. Paraguay
32. The Philippines
33. Qatar
34. Republic of Korea
35. Samoa
36. Saudi Arabia[5]
37. Serbia
38. Sierra Leone
39. Sri Lanka
40. Timor-Leste
41. Turkey
42. Uganda
43. Ukraine
44. United States of America
45. Uruguay
46. Venezuela (Bolivarian Republic of)
47. Ecuador
48. Gabon
49. Armenia
50. Chad
51. Guinea-Bissau
52. Rwanda
53. Ghana
54. Brazil
55. Australia

1. Reservation made upon signature:

'In accordance with article 8 of the Convention, the Republic of Belarus shall not apply this Convention to settlement agreements to which it is a party, or to which any governmental agencies or any person acting on behalf of a governmental agency is a party.'

2. Reservation made upon ratification:

'The following reservations shall be taken into consideration upon ratification of the United Nations Convention on International Settlement Agreements Resulting from Mediation

a) Georgia declares that this Convention shall not apply to settlement agreements to which it is a party, or to which any governmental agencies or any person acting on behalf of governmental agency is a party;
b) Georgia hereby declares that this Convention shall apply only to the extent that the parties to the settlement agreement have agreed to the application of the Convention.'

3. Declaration made upon signature:

'The Government of the Islamic Republic of Iran seizes the opportunity at this moment of signing 'the United Nations Convention on International Settlement Agreements Resulting from Mediation', to place on the record its 'understanding' in relation to provisions of the Convention, bearing in mind that the main objective for submitting this declaration is the avoidance of eventual future interpretation of the following articles in a manner incompatible with the original intention and previous positions or in disharmony with national laws and regulations of the Islamic Republic of Iran.

It is the understanding of the Islamic Republic of Iran as well as reservations that:

- the Islamic Republic of Iran has no obligation to apply this Convention to settlement agreements to which it is a party, or to which any governmental agencies or any person acting on behalf of a governmental agency is a party, to the extent specified in the declaration;
- The Islamic Republic of Iran will apply this Convention only to the extent that the parties to the settlement agreement have agreed to the application of the Convention;
- The Islamic Republic of Iran may have the choice to make reservations upon ratification;
- The Islamic Republic of Iran, in accordance with the relevant provisions of the Convention, reserves the right to adopt laws and regulations to co-operate with the States.'

4. Reservations made upon ratification:

'1. In accordance with article 8, paragraph 1 (a) of the Convention, the Republic of Kazakhstan does not apply this Convention to settlement agreements to which it is a party, or to which any governmental agencies or any person acting on behalf of a governmental agency is a party.

2. In accordance with article 8, paragraph 1 (b) of the Convention, the Republic of Kazakhstan shall apply this Convention only to the extent that the parties to the settlement agreement have agreed to the application of the Convention.'

5. Reservation made upon ratification:

'The Kingdom of Saudi Arabia hereby declares that the Convention shall not apply to settlement agreements to which it or any of its governmental agencies is a party, or any person acting on behalf of those governmental agencies.'

Appendix D: List of States That Have Ratified the Convention

In order of ratification:

1. Singapore
2. Fiji
3. Qatar
4. Saudi Arabia
5. Belarus
6. Ecuador
7. Honduras
8. Turkey
9. Georgia
10. Kazakhstan

Appendix E: UNCITRAL Model Law on International Commercial Mediation and International Settlement Agreements Resulting from Mediation, 2018 (amending the UNCITRAL Model Law on International Commercial Conciliation, 2002)*

Section 1 – General provisions

Article 1. Scope of application of the Law and definitions

1. This Law applies to international commercial[1] mediation[2] and to international settlement agreements.
2. For the purposes of this Law, "mediator" means a sole mediator or two or more mediators, as the case may be.
3. For the purposes of this Law, "mediation" means a process, whether referred to by the expression mediation, conciliation or an expression of similar import, whereby parties request a third person or persons ("the mediator") to assist them in their attempt to reach an amicable settlement of their dispute arising

1. The term "commercial" should be given a wide interpretation so as to cover matters arising from all relationships of a commercial nature, whether contractual or not. Relationships of a commercial nature include, but are not limited to, the following transactions: any trade trans- action for the supply or exchange of goods or services; distribution agreement; commercial representation or agency; factoring; leasing; construction of works; consulting; engineering; licensing; investment; financing; banking; insurance; exploitation agreement or concession; joint venture and other forms of industrial or business cooperation; and carriage of goods or passengers by air, sea, rail or road.
2. In its previously adopted texts and relevant documents, UNCITRAL used the term "conciliation" with the understanding that the terms "conciliation" and "mediation" were interchangeable. In preparing this Model Law, the Commission decided to use the term "mediation" instead in an effort to adapt to the actual and practical use of the terms and with the expectation that this change will facilitate the promotion and heighten the visibility of the Model Law. This change in terminology does not have any substantive or conceptual implications.

out of or relating to a contractual or other legal relationship. The mediator does not have the authority to impose upon the parties a solution to the dispute.

Article 2. Interpretation

1. In the interpretation of this Law, regard is to be had to its international origin and to the need to promote uniformity in its application and the observance of good faith.
2. Questions concerning matters governed by this Law which are not expressly settled in it are to be settled in conformity with the general principles on which this Law is based.

Section 2 – International commercial mediation

Article 3. Scope of application of the section and definitions

1. This section applies to international[3] commercial mediation.
2. A mediation is "international" if:
   (a) The parties to an agreement to mediate have, at the time of the conclusion of that agreement, their places of business in different States; or
   (b) The State in which the parties have their places of business is different from either:
      (i) The State in which a substantial part of the obligations of the commercial relationship is to be performed; or
      (ii) The State with which the subject matter of the dispute is most closely connected.
3. For the purposes of paragraph 2:
   (a) If a party has more than one place of business, the place of business is that which has the closest relationship to the agreement to mediate;
   (b) If a party does not have a place of business, reference is to be made to the party's habitual residence.
4. This section also applies to commercial mediation when the parties agree that the mediation is international or agree to the applicability of this section.
5. The parties are free to exclude the applicability of this section.
6. Subject to the provisions of paragraph 7 of this article, this section applies irrespective of the basis upon which the mediation is carried out, including agreement between the parties whether reached before or after a dispute has arisen, an obligation established by law, or a direction or suggestion of a court, arbitral tribunal or competent governmental entity.
7. This section does not apply to:

3. States wishing to enact this section to apply to domestic as well as international mediation may wish to consider the following changes to the text:

   Delete the word "international" in paragraph 1 of articles 1 and 3; and
   Delete paragraphs 2, 3 and 4 of article 3, and modify references to paragraphs accordingly.

(a) Cases where a judge or an arbitrator, in the course of judicial or arbitral proceedings, attempts to facilitate a settlement; and
(b) [...].

Article 4. Variation by agreement

Except for the provisions of article 7, paragraph 3, the parties may agree to exclude or vary any of the provisions of this section.

Article 5. Commencement of mediation proceedings[4]

1. Mediation proceedings in respect of a dispute that has arisen commence on the day on which the parties to that dispute agree to engage in mediation proceedings.
2. If a party that has invited another party to mediate does not receive an acceptance of the invitation within 30 days from the day on which the invitation was sent, or within such other period of time as specified in the invitation, the party may elect to treat this as a rejection of the invitation to mediate.

Article 6. Number and appointment of mediators

1. There shall be one mediator, unless the parties agree that there shall be two or more mediators.
2. The parties shall endeavour to reach agreement on a mediator or mediators, unless a different procedure for their appointment has been agreed upon.
3. Parties may seek the assistance of an institution or person in connection with the appointment of mediators. In particular:
   (a) A party may request such an institution or person to recommend suitable persons to act as mediator; or
   (b) The parties may agree that the appointment of one or more mediators be made directly by such an institution or person.
4. In recommending or appointing individuals to act as mediator, the institution or person shall have regard to such considerations as are likely to secure the appointment of an independent and impartial mediator and, where appropriate, shall take into account the advisability of appointing a mediator of a nationality other than the nationalities of the parties.

4. The following text is suggested for States that might wish to adopt a provision on the suspension of the limitation period:

   Article X. Suspension of limitation period

   When the mediation proceedings commence, the running of the limitation period regarding the claim that is the subject matter of the mediation is suspended.

   Where the mediation proceedings have terminated without a settlement agreement, the limitation period resumes running from the time the mediation ended without a settlement agreement.

5. When a person is approached in connection with his or her possible appointment as mediator, he or she shall disclose any circumstances likely to give rise to justifiable doubts as to his or her impartiality or independence. A mediator, from the time of his or her appointment and throughout the mediation proceedings, shall without delay disclose any such circumstances to the parties unless they have already been informed of them by him or her.

Article 7. Conduct of mediation

1. The parties are free to agree, by reference to a set of rules or otherwise, on the manner in which the mediation is to be conducted.
2. Failing agreement on the manner in which the mediation is to be conducted, the mediator may conduct the mediation proceedings in such a manner as the mediator considers appropriate, taking into account the circumstances of the case, any wishes that the parties may express and the need for a speedy settlement of the dispute.
3. In any case, in conducting the proceedings, the mediator shall seek to maintain fair treatment of the parties and, in so doing, shall take into account the circumstances of the case.
4. The mediator may, at any stage of the mediation proceedings, make proposals for a settlement of the dispute.

Article 8. Communication between mediator and parties

The mediator may meet or communicate with the parties together or with each of them separately.

Article 9. Disclosure of information

When the mediator receives information concerning the dispute from a party, the mediator may disclose the substance of that information to any other party to the mediation. However, when a party gives any information to the mediator, subject to a specific condition that it be kept confidential, that information shall not be disclosed to any other party to the mediation.

Article 10. Confidentiality

Unless otherwise agreed by the parties, all information relating to the mediation proceedings shall be kept confidential, except where disclosure is required under the law or for the purposes of implementation or enforcement of a settlement agreement.

Article 11. Admissibility of evidence in other proceedings

1. A party to the mediation proceedings, the mediator and any third person, including those involved in the administration of the mediation proceedings, shall not in arbitral, judicial or similar proceedings rely on, introduce as evidence or give testimony or evidence regarding any of the following:
   (a) An invitation by a party to engage in mediation proceedings or the fact that a party was willing to participate in mediation proceedings;

(b) Views expressed or suggestions made by a party in the mediation in respect of a possible settlement of the dispute;
(c) Statements or admissions made by a party in the course of the mediation proceedings;
(d) Proposals made by the mediator;
(e) The fact that a party had indicated its willingness to accept a proposal for settlement made by the mediator;
(f) A document prepared solely for purposes of the mediation proceedings.

2. Paragraph 1 of this article applies irrespective of the form of the information or evidence referred to therein.
3. The disclosure of the information referred to in paragraph 1 of this article shall not be ordered by an arbitral tribunal, court or other competent governmental authority and, if such information is offered as evidence in contravention of paragraph 1 of this article, that evidence shall be treated as inadmissible. Nevertheless, such information may be disclosed or admitted in evidence to the extent required under the law or for the purposes of implementation or enforcement of a settlement agreement.
4. The provisions of paragraphs, 1, 2 and 3 of this article apply whether or not the arbitral, judicial or similar proceedings relate to the dispute that is or was the subject matter of the mediation proceedings.
5. Subject to the limitations of paragraph 1 of this article, evidence that is otherwise admissible in arbitral or judicial or similar proceedings does not become inadmissible as a consequence of having been used in mediation.

Article 12. Termination of mediation proceedings

The mediation proceedings are terminated:

(a) By the conclusion of a settlement agreement by the parties, on the date of the agreement;
(b) By a declaration of the mediator, after consultation with the parties, to the effect that further efforts at mediation are no longer justified, on the date of the declaration;
(c) By a declaration of the parties addressed to the mediator to the effect that the mediation proceedings are terminated, on the date of the declaration; or
(d) By a declaration of a party to the other party or parties and the mediator, if appointed, to the effect that the mediation proceedings are terminated, on the date of the declaration.

Article 13. Mediator acting as arbitrator

Unless otherwise agreed by the parties, the mediator shall not act as an arbitrator in respect of a dispute that was or is the subject of the mediation proceedings or in respect of another dispute that has arisen from the same contract or legal relationship or any related contract or legal relationship.

Article 14. Resort to arbitral or judicial proceedings

Where the parties have agreed to mediate and have expressly undertaken not to initiate during a specified period of time or until a specified event has occurred arbitral or judicial proceedings with respect to an existing or future dispute, such an undertaking shall be given effect by the arbitral tribunal or the court until the terms of the undertaking have been complied with, except to the extent necessary for a party, in its opinion, to preserve its rights. Initiation of such proceedings is not of itself to be regarded as a waiver of the agreement to mediate or as a termination of the mediation proceedings.

Article 15. Binding and enforceable nature of settlement agreements

If the parties conclude an agreement settling a dispute, that settlement agreement is binding and enforceable.

Section 3 – International settlement agreements[5]

Article 16. Scope of application of the section and definitions

1. This section applies to international agreements resulting from mediation and concluded in writing by parties to resolve a commercial dispute ("settlement agreements").[6]
2. This section does not apply to settlement agreements:
   (a) Concluded to resolve a dispute arising from transactions engaged in by one of the parties (a consumer) for personal, family or household purposes;
   (b) Relating to family, inheritance or employment law.
3. This section does not apply to:
   (a) Settlement agreements:
      (i) That have been approved by a court or concluded in the course of proceedings before a court; and
      (ii) That are enforceable as a judgment in the State of that court;
   (b) Settlement agreements that have been recorded and are enforceable as an arbitral award.
4. A settlement agreement is "international" if, at the time of the conclusion of the settlement agreement:[7]
   (a) At least two parties to the settlement agreement have their places of business in different States; or

5. A State may consider enacting this section to apply to agreements settling a dispute, irrespective of whether they resulted from mediation. Adjustments would then have to be made to relevant articles.
6. A State may consider enacting this section to apply only where the parties to the settlement agreement agreed to its application.
7. A State may consider broadening the definition of "international" settlement agreement by adding the following subparagraph to paragraph 4: "A settlement agreement is also 'international' if it results from international mediation as defined in article 3, paragraphs 2, 3 and 4."

   (b) The State in which the parties to the settlement agreement have their places of business is different from either:
      (i) The State in which a substantial part of the obligations under the settlement agreement is to be performed; or
      (ii) The State with which the subject matter of the settlement agreement is most closely connected.
5. For the purposes of paragraph 4:
   (a) If a party has more than one place of business, the relevant place of business is that which has the closest relationship to the dispute resolved by the settlement agreement, having regard to the circumstances known to, or contemplated by, the parties at the time of the conclusion of the settlement agreement;
   (b) If a party does not have a place of business, reference is to be made to the party's habitual residence.
6. A settlement agreement is "in writing" if its content is recorded in any form. The requirement that a settlement agreement be in writing is met by an electronic communication if the information contained therein is accessible so as to be useable for subsequent reference.

Article 17. General principles

1. A settlement agreement shall be enforced in accordance with the rules of procedure of this State, and under the conditions laid down in this section.
2. If a dispute arises concerning a matter that a party claims was already resolved by a settlement agreement, the party may invoke the settlement agreement in accordance with the rules of procedure of this State, and under the conditions laid down in this section, in order to prove that the matter has already been resolved.

Article 18. Requirements for reliance on settlement agreements

1. A party relying on a settlement agreement under this section shall supply to the competent authority of this State:
   (a) The settlement agreement signed by the parties;
   (b) Evidence that the settlement agreement resulted from mediation, such as:
      (i) The mediator's signature on the settlement agreement;
      (ii) A document signed by the mediator indicating that the mediation was carried out;
      (iii) An attestation by the institution that administered the mediation; or
      (iv) In the absence of (i), (ii) or (iii), any other evidence acceptable to the competent authority.
2. The requirement that a settlement agreement shall be signed by the parties or, where applicable, the mediator, is met in relation to an electronic communication if:

(a) A method is used to identify the parties or the mediator and to indicate the parties' or mediator's intention in respect of the information contained in the electronic communication; and

(b) The method used is either:

(i) As reliable as appropriate for the purpose for which the electronic communication was generated or communicated, in the light of all the circumstances, including any relevant agreement; or

(ii) Proven in fact to have fulfilled the functions described in subparagraph (a) above, by itself or together with further evidence.

3. If the settlement agreement is not in an official language of this State, the competent authority may request a translation thereof into such language.
4. The competent authority may require any necessary document in order to verify that the requirements of this section have been complied with.
5. When considering the request for relief, the competent authority shall act expeditiously.

Article 19. Grounds for refusing to grant relief

1. The competent authority of this State may refuse to grant relief at the request of the party against whom the relief is sought only if that party furnishes to the competent authority proof that:

(a) A party to the settlement agreement was under some incapacity;

(b) The settlement agreement sought to be relied upon:

(i) Is null and void, inoperative or incapable of being performed under the law to which the parties have validly subjected it or, failing any indication thereon, under the law deemed applicable by the competent authority;

(ii) Is not binding, or is not final, according to its terms; or

(iii) Has been subsequently modified;

(c) The obligations in the settlement agreement:

(i) Have been performed; or

(ii) Are not clear or comprehensible;

(d) Granting relief would be contrary to the terms of the settlement agreement;

(e) There was a serious breach by the mediator of standards applicable to the mediator or the mediation without which breach that party would not have entered into the settlement agreement; or

(f) There was a failure by the mediator to disclose to the parties circumstances that raise justifiable doubts as to the mediator's impartiality or independence and such failure to disclose had a material impact or undue influence on a party without which failure that party would not have entered into the settlement agreement.

2. The competent authority of this State may also refuse to grant relief if it finds that:

(a) Granting relief would be contrary to the public policy of this State; or
(b) The subject matter of the dispute is not capable of settlement by mediation under the law of this State.

Article 20. Parallel applications or claims

If an application or a claim relating to a settlement agreement has been made to a court, an arbitral tribunal or any other competent authority which may affect the relief being sought under article 18, the competent authority of this State where such relief is sought may, if it considers it proper, adjourn the decision and may also, on the request of a party, order the other party to give suitable security.

Appendix F: Mediation Rules*

UNCITRAL Mediation Rules (2021)

Article 1 – Application of the Rules

1. Where parties have agreed that disputes between them shall be submitted to mediation under the UNCITRAL Mediation Rules, these Rules shall apply. The Rules may apply irrespective of the basis, whether contractual or not, upon which the mediation is carried out.
2. Mediation under the Rules is a process, whether referred to by the term mediation, conciliation or an expression of similar import, whereby parties request a third person or persons ("the mediator") to assist them in their attempt to reach an amicable settlement of their dispute. The mediator shall not have the authority to impose upon the parties a solution to the dispute.
3. The parties to a mediation shall be presumed to have referred to the Rules in effect on the date of commencement of the mediation, unless the parties have agreed to apply a particular version of the Rules.
4. The parties may agree to exclude or vary any provision of the Rules at any time.
5. Where any provision of these Rules is in conflict with a provision of the law applicable to the mediation from which the parties cannot derogate, including any applicable instrument or court order, that provision of law shall prevail.

Article 2 – Commencement of mediation

1. Mediation in respect of a dispute that has arisen shall be deemed to have commenced on the day on which the parties to that dispute agree to engage in mediation, unless otherwise agreed.
2. If a party that invited another party to mediate does not receive an acceptance of the invitation within 30 days from the day on which the invitation was sent by any means that provides for a record of its transmission, or within such

other period of time as specified in the invitation, the party may elect to treat this as a rejection of the invitation to mediate.

Article 3 – Number and appointment of mediators

1. There should be one mediator, unless otherwise agreed. Where there is more than one mediator, the mediators shall act jointly.
2. The parties should endeavour to appoint a mediator by agreement, unless a different appointment procedure applies. They may agree to replace a mediator at any time.
3. The parties may seek the assistance of an institution or person for appointing a mediator.
4. In recommending or selecting individuals to act as mediator, the institution or person shall have regard to:
   (a) The professional expertise and qualifications of the prospective mediator, experience as a mediator and ability to conduct the mediation;
   (b) Any relevant accreditation and/or certification awarded to the prospective mediator by a recognized professional mediation standards body;
   (c) The availability of the mediator; and
   (d) Such considerations as are likely to secure the appointment of an independent and impartial mediator.
5. If the parties have different nationalities, the institution or person, in consultation with the parties, may also take into account the advisability of appointing a mediator of a nationality other than the nationalities of the parties. In addition, the institution or person, in selecting, shall take into consideration geographical diversity and gender of the candidates.
6. When a person is approached in connection with a possible appointment as mediator, that person shall disclose any circumstances likely to give rise to justifiable doubts as to his or her impartiality or independence, including the disclosure of details of any personal, professional, financial or other interest that may influence the outcome of the dispute. A mediator, from the time of appointment and throughout the mediation, shall, without delay, disclose to the parties any such circumstance s as they arise.
7. Prior to accepting the appointment, the prospective mediator shall ensure his or her availability to conduct the mediation diligently and efficiently.
8. In the event the mediator cannot perform her or his functions, the parties shall appoint a substitute mediator pursuant to the procedure mentioned in paragraphs 2, 3, 4, and 5. Paragraph 6 and 7 shall apply to the newly appointed mediator.

Article 4 – Conduct of mediation

1. The parties may agree on the manner in which the mediation is to be conducted. Otherwise, the mediator may determine the conduct of the mediation in consultation with the parties, taking into account the circumstances of

the case, any wishes that the parties may express and the need for a speedy settlement of the dispute.

2. The mediator shall maintain fair treatment of the parties and, in so doing, shall take into account the circumstances of the case.
3. In order to facilitate the conduct of the mediation:
   (a) The parties and the mediator may convene a meeting at an early stage to agree on the organization of the mediation;
   (b) The parties, or the mediator with the consent of the parties, may arrange for administrative assistance by a suitable institution or person; and
   (c) The parties, or the mediator with the consent of the parties, may appoint experts.
4. In conducting the mediation, the mediator may, in consultation with the parties and taking into account the circumstances of the dispute, utilize any technological means as he or she considers appropriate, including to communicate with the parties and to hold meetings remotely.
5. A party may be represented or assisted by a person or persons of its choice. The name, address and function of such persons shall be communicated to all parties and to the mediator in advance of the mediation or without delay. This communication shall also indicate the scope of authority and whether the purpose of the appointment is for representation or assistance.

Article 5 – Communication between the parties and the mediator

1. The mediator may meet or communicate with the parties together or with each of them separately.
2. At any stage of the mediation, the parties may submit information concerning the dispute, such as statements describing the general nature of the dispute, the points at issue, and any supporting document or additional information deemed appropriate. The information may also include a description of the goals, interests, needs and motivations of the parties as well as any relevant documents.
3. When the mediator receives information concerning the dispute from a party, the mediator shall keep such information confidential, unless that party indicates that the information is not subject to the condition that it should be kept confidential, or expresses its consent to the disclosure of such information to another party to the mediation.

Article 6 – Confidentiality

Unless otherwise agreed by the parties, all information relating to the mediation, including, if relevant, the settlement agreement, shall be kept confidential by those involved in the mediation, except where disclosure is required by the law or as referred to under article 8, paragraph 4.

Article 7 – Introduction of evidence in other proceedings

1. Unless otherwise agreed by the parties, a party to the mediation, the mediator and any third person, including those involved in the administration of the mediation shall not, in arbitral, judicial or other dispute resolution proceedings, rely on, introduce as evidence or give evidence regarding any of the following:
   (a) An invitation by a party to engage in mediation or the fact that a party was willing to participate in mediation;
   (b) Views expressed, or suggestions made by a party in the mediation in respect of a possible settlement of the dispute;
   (c) Statements or admissions made by a party in the course of the mediation;
   (d) Proposals made by the mediator or the parties;
   (e) The fact that a party had indicated its willingness to accept a proposal (or parts thereof) for settlement made by the mediator or the parties; and
   (f) A document prepared primarily for purposes of the mediation.
2. Paragraph 1 applies irrespective of the form of the information or evidence referred to therein.
3. Paragraphs 1 and 2 apply whether or not the arbitral, judicial, or other dispute resolution proceedings relate to the dispute that is or was the subject matter of the mediation.
4. Subject to the limitations of paragraph 1, evidence that is otherwise admissible in arbitral, judicial, or other dispute resolution proceedings does not become inadmissible as a consequence of having been used or disclosed in the mediation.

Article 8 – Settlement agreement

1. Once the parties agree on the terms of a settlement to resolve all or part of the dispute through mediation, they should prepare and sign a settlement agreement. If requested by the parties and if the mediator deems it appropriate, the mediator may provide support to the parties in preparing the settlement agreement.
2. Unless otherwise agreed by the parties, the mediator or the mediation institution may sign or stamp the settlement agreement or provide other evidence that the agreement resulted from mediation.
3. The requirement that a settlement agreement shall be signed by the parties is met in relation to an electronic communication if:
   (a) A method is used to identify the parties and to indicate the parties' intention in respect of the information contained in the electronic communication;
   (b) The method is used either:
      (i) As reliable as appropriate for the purpose for which the electronic communication was generated or communicated, in the light of all the circumstances, including any relevant agreement; or

   (ii) Proven in fact to have fulfilled the functions described in subparagraph (a) above, by itself or together with further evidence.

4. By signing the settlement agreement, the parties agree that the settlement agreement can be used as evidence that it results from mediation, and that it can be relied upon for seeking relief under the applicable law.

Article 9 – Termination of mediation

The mediation shall terminate:

(a) By the signing of the settlement agreement by the parties, on the date of the agreement or such other date as agreed by the parties in the settlement agreement;
(b) By a declaration of the parties to the mediator to the effect that the mediation is terminated, on the date of the declaration;
(c) By a declaration of a party to the other party and the mediator, if appointed, to the effect that it no longer wishes to pursue mediation, on the date of the declaration;
(d) By a declaration of the mediator, after consultation with the parties, to the effect that further efforts at mediation are no longer justified, on the date of the declaration;
(e) By a declaration of the mediator, after consultation with the parties, in the situation referred to in article 11, paragraph 5, on the date of the declaration; or
(f) At the expiration of any mandatory period in the applicable international instrument, court order or mandatory statutory provision, or as agreed upon by the parties.

Article 10 – Arbitral, judicial, or other dispute resolution proceedings

1. Mediation may take place under the Rules at any time regardless of whether arbitral, judicial, or other dispute resolution proceedings have been already initiated.
2. Where the parties have agreed to mediate and have also expressly undertaken not to initiate, during a specified period of time or until a specified event has occurred, arbitral, judicial or other dispute resolution proceedings with respect to an existing or future dispute, such an undertaking shall be complied with, except to the extent necessary for a party, in its opinion, to preserve its rights. Initiation of such proceedings is not of itself to be regarded as waiver of the agreement to mediate or as a termination of the mediation.

Article 11 – Costs and deposit of costs

1. The method for fixing the costs of mediation should be agreed upon by the parties and the mediator as early as possible in the mediation. Upon termination of the mediation, the mediator shall fix the costs of the mediation, which

shall be reasonable in amount and give written notice thereof to the parties. The term "costs" includes only:

(a) The fees of the mediator;
(b) The travel and other expenses of the mediator;
(c) The cost of expert advice requested by the mediator with the agreement of the parties;
(d) The cost of any assistance provided pursuant to article 3, paragraph 3, and article 4, paragraph 3, of the Rules; and
(e) Any other expenses that may have been accrued out of the mediation, including in relation to translation and interpretation services.

2. Unless otherwise agreed by the parties, the costs, referred to in paragraph 1, are borne equally by the parties and, in the case of multiparty mediation, they are shared pro rata. All other expenses incurred by a party are borne by that party.
3. The mediator, upon appointment, may request each party to deposit an equal amount as an advance for the costs referred to in paragraph 1, unless otherwise agreed by the parties and the mediator.
4. During the course of the mediation, the mediator may request supplementary deposits in an equal amount from each party, unless otherwise agreed by the parties and the mediator.
5. If the required deposits under paragraph s 3 and 4 are not paid in full by all parties within a reasonable period set by the mediator, the mediator may suspend the mediation or may declare the termination of the mediation, in accordance with article 9, subparagraph (e).
6. Upon termination of the mediation and if deposits were received, the mediator shall render an accounting to the parties of the deposits received and return any unexpended funds to the parties.

Article 12 – Role of the mediator in other proceedings

1. Unless otherwise agreed by the parties, the mediator shall not act as an arbitrator in respect of the dispute that was or is the subject of the mediation and of a dispute that has arisen from the same or a related contract or legal relationship.
2. The mediator shall not act as a representative or counsel of a party in any arbitral, judicial or other dispute resolution proceedings in respect of the dispute that was or is the subject of the mediation and of a dispute that has arisen from the same or a related contract or legal relationship.
3. The parties shall not present the mediator as a witness in any such proceedings.

Article 13 – Exclusion of liability

Save for intentional wrongdoing, the parties waive, to the fullest extent permitted under the applicable law, any claim against the mediator based on any act or omission in connection with the mediation.

Annex

Model mediation clauses

Mediation only

Any dispute, controversy or claim arising out of or relating to this contract, or the breach, termination, or invalidity thereof, shall be submitted to mediation in accordance with the UNCITRAL Mediation Rules.

Note: The parties should consider adding:

(a) The year of adoption of the version of the Rules;
(b) The parties agree that there will be one mediator, appointed by agreement of the parties [within 30 days of the mediation agreement], and if the parties cannot agree, the mediator shall be selected by [relevant selecting authority];
(c) The language of the mediation shall be ...;
(d) The location of mediation shall be ....

Multi-tiered clause

Any dispute, controversy or claim arising out of or relating to this contract, or the breach, termination, or invalidity thereof, shall be submitted to mediation in accordance with the UNCITRAL Mediation Rules.

Note: Parties should consider adding:

(a) The selecting authority shall be (name of institution or person);
(b) The language of the mediation shall be ...;
(c) The location of mediation shall be....

If the dispute, or any part thereof, is not settled within [(60) days] of the request to mediate under these Rules, the parties agree to resolve any remaining matters by arbitration in accordance with the UNCITRAL Arbitration Rules.

Note: Parties should consider adding:

(a) The appointing authority shall be (name of institution or person);
(b) The number of arbitrators shall be (one or three);
(c) The place of arbitration shall be (town and country);
(d) The language of the arbitration shall be....

Model declaration of disclosure

No circumstances to disclose

To the best of my knowledge, there are no circumstances, past or present, likely to give rise to justifiable doubts as to my impartiality or independence.

I shall promptly notify the parties of any such circumstances that may subsequently come to my attention during this mediation.

Circumstances to disclose

Attached is a statement of (a) my past and present professional, business and other relationships with the parties and (b) any other relevant circumstances. [*Include statement.*] I confirm that those circumstances do not affect my independence and impartiality. I shall promptly notify the parties of any such further relationships or circumstances that may subsequently come to my attention during this mediation.

Model statement of availability

I confirm, on the basis of the information presently available to me, that I can devote the time necessary to conduct this mediation.

SIMC Mediation Rules*

1. Application of Rules

1.1. These Mediation Rules (the "Rules") shall apply to all mediations administered by the Singapore International Mediation Centre ("SIMC") save that where a media tion is administered pursuant to the Arb-Med-Arb Protocol between the Singapore International Arbitration Centre ("SIAC") and SIMC (the "AMA Protocol"), these Rules shall be modified as necessary to be consistent with the terms of the AMA Protocol.

1.2. The parties may at any time agree to modify the provisions of the Rules, subject to the agreement of the mediator and SIMC.

2. Commencement of Mediation

2.1. Any party or parties wishing to commence mediation under the Rules shall submit a written request for mediation in the form set out in *Appendix B* (the "Request") together with the applicable filing fee set out in *Appendix B*.

2.2. A copy of the Request should be sent to all other parties to the mediation.

3. Agreement to Mediate[1]

3.1. If the Request is made pursuant to an agreement to mediate at SIMC, evidence of such an agreement shall be attached to the Request.

3.2. If the request is made pursuant to an agreement to mediate at SIMC, SIMC will acknowledge receipt of the Request in writing. The date on which SIMC

* © Singapore International Mediation Centre (SIMC). Reproduced with permission of SIMC. The text reproduced here is valid at the time of reproduction [10 March 2022]. The Rules are available at http:// simc.com.sg/mediation-rules/.

1. For cases administered pursuant to the AMA Protocol, Rules 3.1 to 3.5 will be modified by the AMA Protocol.

acknowledges such receipt shall be deemed to be the date of the filing of the Request and the date of commencement of mediation.

3.3. If the Request is not made pursuant to an agreement to mediate at SIMC, SIMC will promptly contact the parties regarding the proposal for mediation, and may assist the parties in considering the proposal. The mediation shall be deemed to commence on the date on which SIMC sends written confirmation to the parties that an agreement to mediate has been reached.

3.4. In the event of any doubt as to the existence of an agreement to mediate at SIMC, SIMC may request further information from the parties or take such other steps as may be appropriate.

4. Appointment of Mediator

4.1. The parties may jointly nominate a mediator to conduct the mediation for confirmation by SIMC. The nomination may be from SIMC's Panel of Mediators or from any other panel.

4.2. Where the parties are unable to agree on a mediator to be nominated within 10 days from the date of commencement of the mediation, SIMC shall appoint a mediator from SIMC's Panel of Mediators. SIMC may also nominate a mediator from the panel of one of its partner organisations, in the event that there is no suitable mediator from the SIMC panel.

4.3. In confirming or appointing a mediator, SIMC shall consider the prospective mediator's attributes, including but not limited to nationality, language, skills, qualifications, areas of expertise, experience, and the prospective mediator's availability.

4.4. The parties may nominate more than one mediator or request SIMC to appoint more than one mediator, in accordance with the provisions of the Rules. Where appropriate, SIMC may propose to the parties that there be more than one mediator. References to "mediator" under these Rules will then be deemed as reference to "mediators".

4.5. Before confirmation or appointment, a prospective mediator shall make a written declaration of his or her acceptance, availability, impartiality and independence, and shall also immediately disclose to the parties any known actual or potential conflicts of interest which could reasonably raise any question of his or her impartiality and independence.

4.6. Any party may object to the appointment of the mediator on the basis of any disclosed actual or potential conflict, or choose to waive the conflict.

4.7. If any party has valid objections to the appointment of the mediator, the party shall notify SIMC and all the other parties in writing as soon as possible and SIMC may within five business days of receipt of notification of the objections, appoint another mediator.

4.8. SIMC may replace the mediator in the course of the mediation if a conflict arises or in exceptional circumstances raised by the mediator or any of the parties.

5. Fees and Costs[2]

5.1. The party or parties filing a Request shall pay SIMC a non-refundable filing fee, as set out in *Appendix B*.
5.2. Following commencement of the mediation, SIMC shall request all parties to pay one or more deposits to cover SIMC's administrative fees, as set out in Appendix B, the mediator's fees, and other expenses of SIMC and the mediator.
5.3. SIMC may stay or terminate the mediation if any requested deposit is not paid.
5.4. Upon termination of the mediation, SIMC shall fix the total costs of the mediation and reimburse the parties for any excess payment or bill the parties for any balance required pursuant to the Rules.
5.5. All deposits requested and costs fixed by SIMC shall be borne equally by the parties, except where they have agreed otherwise in writing.
5.6. Any party is free to pay the unpaid balance of any deposits and costs should another party fail to pay its share.
5.7. Any other expenditure incurred by the respective parties shall remain the responsibility of that party, unless otherwise agreed by the parties.

6. Conduct of Mediation

6.1. SIMC will, in consultation with the parties, determine the location of the mediation and may engage in the following in order to facilitate the achievement of full settlement at mediation:
(a) Appointing a suitable mediator;
(b) Assisting parties with entering into a mediation agreement;
(c) Organising the exchange of any pertinent information and documents;
(d) Arranging a suitable venue and date for mediation;
(e) Providing administrative and logistical support; and
(f) Providing case-management services.
6.2. The parties may, by agreement, determine the language(s) in which the mediation is to be conducted and shall inform SIMC of their agreement within such time as SIMC may specify. Absent any agreement between the parties, SIMC will determine the language(s) of the mediation in consultation with the mediator.
6.3. The parties shall inform SIMC of the names of their representatives and advisors attending the mediation within such time as SIMC may specify.
6.4. At least 10 days, or such other time as the mediator may specify, before the scheduled mediation, the parties shall submit to SIMC and exchange statements of their cases and any relevant documents.
6.5. Where appropriate, SIMC may arrange for a pre-mediation conference to discuss the manner and procedure for the conduct of the mediation,

2. For cases administered pursuant to the AMA Protocol, Rules 5.1 and 5.2 will be modified by the AMA Protocol.

including setting relevant timelines. For the avoidance of doubt, the pre-mediation conference may take place in person, by teleconference, or any other electronic means.

6.6. In determining the manner and procedure for the conduct of the mediation, the mediator shall give due respect to the wishes of the parties and be fair and impartial.

6.7. The mediator may communicate with the parties orally, in writing, in person, electronically, or otherwise, and may do so jointly or separately, before and during the scheduled mediation, and, in the event that there is no full settlement during the scheduled mediation, for a period of time after the scheduled mediation in order to facilitate the achievement of a full settlement.

6.8. The mediator may obtain expert advice or assistance in technical matters with the parties' consent and the parties shall bear any expenses incurred in this regard.

6.9. All parties shall act in good faith to prepare for the mediation and in the course of participating in the mediation.

7. Termination of Mediation

7.1. The mediation commenced pursuant to the Rules shall terminate upon:
   (a) the signing by the parties of a written settlement agreement; or
   (b) the issuance of written confirmation of termination by SIMC after the occurrence of the earliest of:
      (i) any party giving written notice of withdrawal to SIMC, the mediator and the other parties;
      (ii) the mediator giving written notice to SIMC and the parties that the mediation should be terminated;
      (iii) SIMC giving written notice to the parties that any time limit set for the mediation, including any extension thereof, has expired; or
      (iv) SIMC giving written notice to the parties that any payment by one or more parties pursuant to the Rules has not been made for more than 14 days after the due date for payment.

8. Settlement Agreement

8.1. Any settlement agreement reached in the course of mediation shall be in writing and signed by or on behalf of the parties.

8.2. For the avoidance of doubt, a settlement agreement may take the form of an electronic record, and be signed by electronic signature.

8.3. Where any settlement agreement has been reached, the mediator shall promptly notify SIMC of the same, and provide SIMC with a copy of such agreement.

8.4. A settlement agreement may be recorded substantially in the format set out in *Appendix C*.

9. Confidentiality

9.1. Subject to any agreement between the parties, the Singapore Mediation Act 2017, and any other applicable law:
(a) The mediation shall be private and confidential; and
(b) Any settlement agreement between the parties shall not be disclosed save where it is necessary for the purposes of its implementation or enforcement.

9.2. No communications made in the mediation, including any information disclosed and views expressed in relation to any proposal for settlement, shall be used in any judicial, arbitration, or similar proceedings, unless required by applicable law.

9.3. The mediator shall not give testimony in any judicial, arbitration or similar proceedings concerning any aspect of the mediation under the Rules, unless required by applicable law or unless all of the parties and the mediator agree otherwise in writing.

9.4. No persons other than the parties, their representatives, their advisors, and the mediator may attend the mediation, save with the permission of the parties and the mediator.

9.5. There shall be no transcript or formal record of the mediation, save for that which may be necessary to record any settlement agreement.

10. General Provisions

10.1. The mediator, SIMC and its employees shall not be liable to any person for any act or omission in connection with the mediation, unless there is fraudulent or wilful misconduct.

ICC Mediation Rules*

Article 1 Introductory Provisions

1 The Mediation Rules (the "Rules") of the International Chamber of Commerce (the "ICC") are administered by the ICC International Centre for ADR (the "Centre"), which is a separate administrative body within the ICC.

2 The Rules provide for the appointment of a neutral third party (the "Mediator") to assist the parties in settling their dispute.

3 Mediation shall be used under the Rules unless, prior to the confirmation or appointment of the Mediator or with the agreement of the Mediator, the parties agree upon a different settlement procedure or a combination of settlement procedures. The term "mediation" as used in the Rules shall be deemed to cover such settlement procedure or procedures and the term "Mediator" shall

* © International Chamber of Commerce (ICC). Reproduced with permission of ICC. The text reproduced here is valid at the time of reproduction [9 March 2022]. The Rules are available at https://iccwbo.org/dispute-resolution-services/mediation/mediation-rules/.

be deemed to cover the neutral who conducts such settlement procedure or procedures. Whatever settlement procedure is used, the term "Proceedings" as used in the Rules refers to the process beginning with its commencement and ending with its termination pursuant to the Rules.

4 All of the parties may agree to modify any of the provisions of the Rules, provided, however, that the Centre may decide not to administer the Proceedings if, in its discretion, it considers that any such modification is not in the spirit of the Rules. At any time after the confirmation or appointment of the Mediator, any agreement to modify the provisions of the Rules shall also be subject to the approval of the Mediator.

5 The Centre is the only body authorized to administer Proceedings under the Rules.

Article 2 Commencement Where there is an Agreement to Refer to the Rules

1 Where there is an agreement between the parties to refer their dispute to the Rules, any party or parties wishing to commence mediation pursuant to the Rules shall file a written Request for Mediation (the "Request") with the Centre. The Request shall include:

a. the names, addresses, telephone numbers, email addresses and any other contact details of the parties to the dispute and of any person(s) representing the parties in the Proceedings;
b. a description of the dispute including, if possible, an assessment of its value;
c. any agreement to use a settlement procedure other than mediation, or, in the absence thereof, any proposal for such other settlement procedure that the party filing the Request may wish to make;
d. any agreement as to time limits for conducting the mediation, or, in the absence thereof, any proposal with respect thereto;
e. any agreement as to the language(s) of the mediation, or, in the absence thereof, any proposal as to such language(s);
f. any agreement as to the location of any physical meetings, or, in the absence thereof, any proposal as to such location;
g. any joint nomination by all of the parties of a Mediator or any agreement of all of the parties as to the attributes of a Mediator to be appointed by the Centre where no joint nomination has been made, or, in the absence of any such agreement, any proposal as to the attributes of a Mediator;
h. a copy of any written agreement under which the Request is made.

2 Together with the Request, the party or parties filing the Request shall pay the filing fee required by the Appendix hereto in force on the date the Request is filed.

3 The party or parties filing the Request shall simultaneously send a copy of the Request to all other parties, unless the Request has been filed jointly by all parties.

4 The Centre shall acknowledge receipt of the Request and of the filing fee in writing to the parties.
5 Where there is an agreement to refer to the Rules, the date on which the Request is received by the Centre shall, for all purposes, be deemed to be the date of the commencement of the Proceedings.
6 Where the parties have agreed that a time limit for settling the dispute pursuant to the Rules shall start running from the filing of a Request, such filing, for the exclusive purpose of determining the starting point of the time limit, shall be deemed to have been made on the date the Centre acknowledges receipt of the Request or of the filing fee, whichever is later.

Article 3 Commencement Where there is No Prior Agreement to Refer to the Rules

1 In the absence of an agreement of the parties to refer their dispute to the Rules, any party that wishes to propose referring the dispute to the Rules to another party may do so by sending a written Request to the Centre containing the information specified in Article 2(1), subparagraphs a)-g). Upon receipt of such Request, the Centre will inform all other parties of the proposal and may assist the parties in considering the proposal.
2 Together with the Request, the party or parties filing the Request shall pay the filing fee required by the Appendix hereto in force on the date the Request is filed.
3 Where the parties reach an agreement to refer their dispute to the Rules, the Proceedings shall commence on the date on which the Centre sends written confirmation to the parties that such an agreement has been reached.
4 Where the parties do not reach an agreement to refer their dispute to the Rules within 15 days from the date of the receipt of the Request by the Centre or within such additional time as may be reasonably determined by the Centre, the Proceedings shall not commence.

Article 4 Place and Language(s) of the Mediation

1 In the absence of an agreement of the parties, the Centre may determine the location of any physical meeting of the Mediator and the parties or may invite the Mediator to do so after the Mediator has been confirmed or appointed.
2 In the absence of an agreement of the parties, the Centre may determine the language(s) in which the mediation shall be conducted or may invite the Mediator to do so after the Mediator has been confirmed or appointed.

Article 5 Selection of the Mediator

1 The parties may jointly nominate a Mediator for confirmation by the Centre.
2 In the absence of a joint nomination of a Mediator by the parties, the Centre shall, after consulting the parties, either appoint a Mediator or propose a list of Mediators to the parties. All of the parties may jointly nominate a Mediator

from the said list for confirmation by the Centre, failing which the Centre shall appoint a Mediator.

3 Before appointment or confirmation, a prospective Mediator shall sign a statement of acceptance, availability, impartiality and independence. The prospective Mediator shall disclose in writing to the Centre any facts or circumstances which might be of such a nature as to call into question the Mediator's independence in the eyes of the parties, as well as any circumstances that could give rise to reasonable doubts as to the Mediator's impartiality. The Centre shall provide such information to the parties in writing and shall fix a time limit for any comments from them.

4 When confirming or appointing a Mediator, the Centre shall consider the prospective Mediator's attributes, including but not limited to nationality, language skills, training, qualifications and experience, and the prospective Mediator's availability and ability to conduct the mediation in accordance with the Rules.

5 Where the Centre appoints a Mediator, it shall do so either on the basis of a proposal by an ICC National Committee or Group, or otherwise. The Centre shall make all reasonable efforts to appoint a Mediator having the attributes, if any, which have been agreed upon by all of the parties. If any party objects to the Mediator appointed by the Centre and notifies the Centre and all other parties in writing, stating the reasons for such objection, within 15 days of receipt of notification of the appointment, the Centre shall appoint another Mediator.

6 Upon agreement of all of the parties, the parties may nominate more than one Mediator or request the Centre to appoint more than one Mediator, in accordance with the provisions of the Rules. In appropriate circumstances, the Centre may propose to the parties that there be more than one Mediator.

Article 6 Fees and Costs

1 The party or parties filing a Request shall include with the Request the non-refundable filing fee required by Article 2(2) or Article 3(2) of the Rules, as set out in the Appendix hereto. No Request shall be processed unless accompanied by the filing fee.

2 Following the receipt of a Request pursuant to Article 3, the Centre may request that the party filing the Request pay a deposit to cover the administrative expenses of the Centre.

3 Following the commencement of the Proceedings, the Centre shall request the parties to pay one or more deposits to cover the administrative expenses of the Centre and the fees and expenses of the Mediator, as set out in the Appendix hereto.

4 The Centre may stay or terminate the Proceedings under the Rules if any requested deposit is not paid.

5 Upon termination of the Proceedings, the Centre shall fix the total costs of the Proceedings and shall, as the case may be, reimburse the parties for any excess payment or bill the parties for any balance required pursuant to the Rules.
6 With respect to Proceedings that have commenced under the Rules, all deposits requested and costs fixed shall be borne in equal shares by the parties, unless they agree otherwise in writing. However, any party shall be free to pay the unpaid balance of such deposits and costs should another party fail to pay its share.
7 A party's other expenditure shall remain the responsibility of that party, unless otherwise agreed by the parties.

Article 7 Conduct of the Mediation

1 The Mediator and the parties shall promptly discuss the manner in which the mediation shall be conducted.
2 After such discussion, the Mediator shall promptly provide the parties with a written note informing them of the manner in which the mediation shall be conducted. Each party, by agreeing to refer a dispute to the Rules, agrees to participate in the Proceedings at least until receipt of such note from the Mediator or earlier termination of the Proceedings pursuant to Article 8(1) of the Rules.
3 In establishing and conducting the mediation, the Mediator shall be guided by the wishes of the parties and shall treat them with fairness and impartiality.
4 Each party shall act in good faith throughout the mediation.

Article 8 Termination of the Proceedings

1 Proceedings which have been commenced pursuant to the Rules shall terminate upon written confirmation of termination by the Centre to the parties after the occurrence of the earliest of:
   a. the signing by the parties of a settlement agreement;
   b. the notification in writing made to the Mediator by any party, at any time after it has received the Mediator's note referred to in Article 7(2), that such party has decided no longer to pursue the mediation;
   c. the notification in writing by the Mediator to the parties that the mediation has been completed;
   d. the notification in writing by the Mediator to the parties that, in the Mediator's opinion, the mediation will not resolve the dispute between the parties;
   e. the notification in writing by the Centre to the parties that any time limit set for the Proceedings, including any extension thereof, has expired;
   f. the notification in writing by the Centre to the parties, not less than seven days after the due date for any payment by one or more parties pursuant to the Rules, that such payment has not been made; or

g. the notification in writing by the Centre to the parties that, in the judgment of the Centre, there has been a failure to nominate a Mediator or that it has not been reasonably possible to appoint a Mediator.

2 The Mediator shall promptly notify the Centre of the signing of a settlement agreement by the parties or of any notification given to or by the Mediator pursuant to Article 8(1), subparagraphs b)-d), and shall provide the Centre with a copy of any such notification.

Article 9 Confidentiality

1 In the absence of any agreement of the parties to the contrary and unless prohibited by applicable law:
  a. the Proceedings, but not the fact that they are taking place, have taken place or will take place, are private and confidential;
  b. any settlement agreement between the parties shall be kept confidential, except that a party shall have the right to disclose it to the extent that such disclosure is required by applicable law or necessary for purposes of its implementation or enforcement.

2 Unless required to do so by applicable law and in the absence of any agreement of the parties to the contrary, a party shall not in any manner produce as evidence in any judicial, arbitral or similar proceedings:
  a. any documents, statements or communications which are submitted by another party or by the Mediator in or for the Proceedings, unless they can be obtained independently by the party seeking to produce them in the judicial, arbitral or similar proceedings;
  b. any views expressed or suggestions made by any party within the Proceedings with regard to the dispute or the possible settlement of the dispute;
  c. any admissions made by another party within the Proceedings;
  d. any views or proposals put forward by the Mediator within the Proceedings; or
  e. the fact that any party indicated within the Proceedings that it was ready to accept a proposal for a settlement.

Article 10 General Provisions

1 Where, prior to the date of the entry into force of the Rules, the parties have agreed to refer their dispute to the ICC ADR Rules, they shall be deemed to have referred their dispute to the ICC Mediation Rules, unless any of the parties objects thereto, in which case the ICC ADR Rules shall apply.

2 Unless all of the parties have agreed otherwise in writing or unless prohibited by applicable law, the parties may commence or continue any judicial, arbitral or similar proceedings in respect of the dispute, notwithstanding the Proceedings under the Rules.

3 Unless all of the parties agree otherwise in writing, a Mediator shall not act nor shall have acted in any judicial, arbitral or similar proceedings relating to the

dispute which is or was the subject of the Proceedings under the Rules, whether as a judge, an arbitrator, an expert or a representative or advisor of a party.

4 Unless required by applicable law or unless all of the parties and the Mediator agree otherwise in writing, the Mediator shall not give testimony in any judicial, arbitral or similar proceedings concerning any aspect of the Proceedings under the Rules.

5 The Mediator, the Centre, the ICC and its employees, the ICC National Committees and Groups and their employees and representatives shall not be liable to any person for any act or omission in connection with the Proceedings, except to the extent such limitation of liability is prohibited by applicable law.

6 In all matters not expressly provided for in the Rules, the Centre and the Mediator shall act in the spirit of the Rules.

Centre for Effective Dispute Resolution (CEDR) Model Mediation Procedure*

1. What is mediation?

Mediation is a flexible process conducted confidentially in which a neutral person actively assists the parties in working towards a negotiated agreement of a dispute or difference, with the parties in ultimate control of the decision to settle and the terms of resolution. The principal features of mediation are that it:

- involves a neutral third party to facilitate negotiations;
- is quick to set up and is inexpensive, and, in most circumstances, is without prejudice and confidential;
- involves party representatives with sufficient authority to settle;
- is flexible, enabling the process to be designed and managed by the Mediator to suit the parties, in consultation with them;
- puts the parties in control (unlike litigation/arbitration);
- enables the parties to devise solutions which are not possible in an adjudicative process such as litigation or arbitration, and which may benefit all the parties, particularly if there is the possibility of a continuing relationship between them;
- can be used in both domestic and cross-border disputes, two-party and multi-party disputes, and whether or not litigation or arbitration has been commenced.

Many commercial and government contracts now require parties to use mediation in accordance with CEDR's Model Mediation Procedure. While mediation is essentially flexible, the Model Procedure set out in this document, taken with the CEDR

* © Centre for Effective Dispute Resolution (CEDR). Reproduced with permission of CEDR. The text reproduced here is valid at the time of reproduction [9 March 2022]. The text it available at https://www.cedr.com/wp-content/uploads/2020/01/CEDR-Model-Mediation-Procedure.pdf.

Model Mediation Agreement, will give sufficient certainty to enable the process to be set up and used.

Any contemplated or existing litigation or arbitration in relation to the dispute may be started or continued despite the mediation, unless the parties agree or a Court orders otherwise. If settlement terms cannot be agreed through mediation, the parties can revert to litigation or arbitration.

2. Referral to mediation

Referral of a dispute to a mediator or to CEDR for mediation may be as a result of:

- voluntary referral by all parties;
- referral by one party who asks CEDR to secure the involvement of other parties into a mediation;
- responding to a Pre-action Protocol, Court Rules, a Court Order or a recommendation by a judge before trial or appeal;
- the provisions of an ADR clause in a commercial or government contract requiring the use of mediation as a step in the parties' agreed dispute resolution process;
- the provisions for use of mediation within an industry or public sector policy framework.

Parties referring a case to CEDR are encouraged to include a copy of any appropriate document or agreement as per above with the referral.

3. Choosing the mediator

The parties may choose their own mediator directly or from any CEDR panel of mediators, or may ask CEDR to nominate one or to recommend names from whom they can choose one to act as the mediator for a dispute in accordance with the wishes of the parties or under contractual agreement or the provisions of any relevant Court Order. Where there is a contractual or court requirement for the parties to act under the auspices of CEDR, CEDR will appoint a mediator where the parties fail to agree on a name within 14 days of notice of the dispute.

CEDR will only nominate or appoint a mediator who, in its view, possesses the relevant skills and experience to mediate the dispute for the parties effectively, and who will comply with the CEDR Code of Conduct for Third Party Neutrals ('the Code'). Any nominated mediator and all other parties to the mediation will be required to confirm immediately to CEDR if there is any matter which might prevent the nominated mediator from complying with the Code in relation to the mediation of the dispute, such as a conflict of interest. CEDR or the mediator will then notify all the parties of any such matter immediately it is disclosed to them.

If required by any of the parties or the Court, or under the published terms of any CEDR dispute resolution scheme, CEDR will appoint a mediator to be used in relation to a dispute, subject always to that mediator not being prevented from complying with the Code in relation to the mediation of that dispute. As part of CEDR's role to develop the field and its professionalism, the parties may be asked by CEDR to approve the appointment of an observer mediator to attend a mediation at no cost to the parties, provided that the observer mediator also appropriately complies with the Code in respect of the mediation. The identity of any observer mediator proposed to attend the mediation will be made known in advance of the mediation to the parties, who are free to object to any such nomination or decline any such appointment.

The mediator's signature on the mediation agreement binds any observer mediator to its terms. In appropriate cases CEDR may recommend, or the parties agree, the use of co-mediators or the appointment of a neutral expert to advise the mediator on technical matters. If co-mediators are chosen by the parties, all references to the mediator in a document are taken to indicate the plural. CEDR recommends however, that documents related to the process be adapted to refer to the Mediator in the plural and that both mediators be signatories to the Mediation Agreement. The circumstances in which a co-mediator may be appropriate are:

- The number of parties or number of attendees within a party is such that it would be of benefit to have co-mediators
- Where a specific technical expertise is required.
- The varying nationalities and cultural backgrounds of the parties. This is separate to the potential need for a translator.
- Personal preference of the parties

4. Preparing for the mediation

CEDR or the mediator, when agreed or appointed, will make the necessary arrangements for the mediation as required or agreed by the parties or under the terms of any scheme, including:

- drafting the agreement for mediation, submitting it for approval by the parties and preparing the final form for signature, incorporating any agreed amendments if requested;
- compiling names and roles of attendees for the circulation of a participants' form before the mediation takes place;
- facilitating agreement as to the date, start time and providing venue arrangements for the mediation when necessary;
- organising exchange of case summaries and document bundles between the parties and the mediator when requested;
- setting up any pre-mediation meetings agreed by the parties and the mediator if requested.

The parties will:

- agree the appointment of the mediator or a process to select or appoint the mediator;
- agree with CEDR the date, venue and start time for the mediation;
- agree the terms of the mediation agreement;
- pay CEDR's fees and expenses as agreed under CEDR's Terms and Conditions of business;

- each prepare and exchange a case summary for the mediation in respect of their approach to the dispute at the mediation and endeavour to agree with all other parties what documents are needed for the mediation;
- send to the mediator directly, or to the location indicated by CEDR, a copy of their case summary and a copy of the bundle of documents at the earliest convenience, usually no less than one week before the date set for the mediation, making clear:
  - whether case summaries have or have not yet been exchanged;
  - whether or not and when CEDR or the mediator is to effect exchange; and
  - whether all or any part of any case summary or documentation is intended to be confidential for CEDR and the mediator only.

    (Late submission of documents might call into question that party's good faith involvement in the mediation process, and have detrimental effects on the prospects of success of any mediation;)
- notify the mediator and CEDR of the names and roles of all those attending the mediation on their behalf, so that CEDR can inform all parties and the mediator in advance of the mediation;
- ensure that a lead negotiator with full authority to settle the dispute attends the mediation to sign the mediation agreement and any potential settlement agreement;
- alternatively notify the mediator, CEDR and (unless very good reason exists to the contrary) the other parties of any limitation on authority to settle, for instance lack of legal capacity, or the need for ministerial committee, court approval, or board ratification, in which case the lead negotiator will need to have power to recommend acceptance of any settlement. Late disclosure of limited authority to settle can call into question that party's good faith involvement in the mediation process, and have detrimental effects on the prospects of success of any mediation.

The mediator will:

- ensure at all times that the Code is complied with in respect of the mediation of the dispute, reporting any conflict of interest or other relevant matter, if any, to CEDR and (subject to any question of confidentiality or privilege) the parties, immediately it emerges;
- attend any pre-mediation meetings on terms and agenda agreed by the parties, or proposed by the mediator;
- read each case summary and document bundle submitted in advance of the mediation by the parties;
- make contact with a representative of each of the parties before the mediation to assist in preparation for the mediation and discuss issues arising.

5. Documentation

Documentation intended to be treated as confidential by the mediator or CEDR (such as a counsel's opinion, an undisclosed expert report, a draft proof of evidence or a confidential briefing for the mediator) must be clearly marked as such, and will not be circulated further without express authority.

One of the advantages of mediation is that its success is not dependent on exhaustive disclosure of documents. Bundles can usually be relatively limited in size, containing only key documents, and case summaries can be quite brief, and can, to advantage, be prepared jointly by the parties. The parties can ask CEDR to effect simultaneous exchange of case summaries if required.

While documents brought into existence for the purpose of the mediation, such as case summaries, are clearly privileged from later production in other proceedings, the fact that a document which is otherwise disclosable in proceedings is produced for the first time during the mediation does not normally confer privileged status on it. The parties must take legal advice on such matters if they arise.

6. The mediation agreement

The agreement to mediate provides the essential legal basis for the mediation. Its signatories (the parties to the dispute, the mediator and CEDR) all agree by signing it that the mediation is to be conducted consistent with both this CEDR Model Mediation Procedure and the Code.

A draft mediation agreement will be sent for approval to the parties as part of the preparation process for the mediation, and any proposed amendments can then be discussed and inserted if agreed by all. The mediation agreement will normally be signed at the beginning of the mediation day on behalf of each of the parties and the mediator, having been pre-signed on behalf of CEDR. Upon appointment of the mediator by the parties (or by CEDR) any pre-mediation contact between the parties, CEDR staff and CEDR mediator, will observe the mediation agreement's terms as to confidentiality, regardless of whether the agreement has already been signed or not.

7. The mediation

It is normal for each of the parties to have a private room for confidential consultations on their own and with the mediator during the mediation. There should also be a further room large enough for all parties to meet with the mediator jointly.

The mediator will chair and take responsibility for determining the procedure at the mediation, in consultation with the parties.

The likely procedure will comprise:

- preliminary meetings with each of the parties when they arrive at the venue;
- a joint meeting of all attending the mediation, at which each of the parties will normally be invited to make an oral presentation;
- a mix of further private meetings and joint meetings (which may involve all or some of each party's team), as proposed by the mediator and agreed by the parties.

Professional advisers, particularly lawyers, can and usually do attend the mediation. Such advisers play an important role in the exchange of information and opinion on fact, evidence and law; in supporting their clients (particularly individuals) in the negotiations; in advising clients on the implications of settlement; and in drawing up the settlement agreement and any consent order.

No verbatim recording or transcript should be made of the mediation by the parties or the mediator in any form, but participants can make their own private notes which will not be disclosable to anyone else, including in any subsequent litigation or arbitration.

Mediations can last beyond a normal working day and it is important that the key people attending for each of the parties remain present or, at worst, available by telephone or video conference for so long as the mediation continues. Any time constraints should be reported to CEDR or the mediator as soon as known, as any unexpected departure can be detrimental to the progress of the mediation and perceived as disrespectful by other parties.

8. Confidentiality in relation to the mediation

The CEDR Model Mediation Agreement provides that what happens at the mediation is to be treated as confidential by the parties, the mediator and CEDR, including the terms of settlement, unless otherwise agreed by the parties in writing. However, the fact that the mediation is to take place or has taken place is not normally made confidential, as one or other of the parties may wish to claim credit for agreeing to engage in the process or it may have been directed from a public court. If it is desired to make the fact that the mediation is taking place confidential also, the agreement can be amended.

As the mediation is held under the auspices of CEDR, and CEDR is a party to the mediation agreement, CEDR is also bound to keep confidential information which the mediator may share with CEDR for the purposes of case reports or queries regarding professional conduct. Apart from where the parties agree in writing to consent to disclosure of what would normally be confidential, there may be rare circumstances in which the confidentiality of the mediation process cannot be preserved, such as where:

- the mediator or any party or their representative is required by law to make disclosure;
- the mediator reasonably considers that there is a serious risk of significant harm to the life or safety of any person if the information in question is not disclosed; or
- the mediator reasonably considers that there is a serious risk of being personally subject to criminal proceedings unless the information in question is disclosed.

Such questions might arise in relation to duties under the Proceeds of Crime Act 2002 or related legislation or under any other legislation. Legal representatives (who may themselves be under a comparable duty of disclosure in their own capacity) must take full responsibility for advising their clients of the implications of disclosure in relation to any such matters at a mediation.

9. Conclusion of the mediation

The mediation may end in a number of ways:

- by settlement of the dispute in whole or part, when all agreed matters must be written down and signed by the parties to be binding;
- by an 'in principle settlement' of the dispute with an agreement to draft binding terms after the mediation day;
- by the mediator advising the parties that a settlement, for the time being, at least, cannot be reached;
- by one or more parties leaving the mediation before settlement is achieved;
- by an agreed adjournment for such time and on such terms as the parties and the mediator agree;
- by withdrawal of the mediator in accordance with the mandatory and optional circumstances set out in the Code;
- by production of a document of summary or recommendations from a mediator, if requested by all parties and agreed by the mediator.

The mediator will facilitate the drawing up of any settlement agreement, though the drafting is normally done by the lawyers representing each of the parties. Where proceedings have not been started in respect of the dispute, the settlement agreement will (if so intended and drafted) be a contract enforceable by legal action. Where proceedings have been issued in relation to the dispute, it is normal for a Consent Order to be agreed either at or after the mediation and later lodged with the relevant tribunal to end the proceedings on the terms agreed. Parties should agree who will be responsible for lodging the Consent Order.

Where the mediation does not end in complete settlement, the mediator may make contact with the parties thereafter to see whether further progress might be possible. Many disputes which do not settle at the mediation settle later, usually as a result of what occurred or was learned at the mediation. Where the mediator agrees to stay in contact with the parties after a mediation, the provisions of the mediation agreement should be taken to continue to apply to those communications with and/or including the mediator.

In the event that a settlement is not reached, the mediator if requested and if agreed by each of the parties and the mediator, may produce a non-binding opinion or recommendation in an effort to take the matter forward.

CEDR endeavours to make contact with all parties after every mediation to obtain their feedback on both the process itself and, in particular, the mediator. Any feedback obtained regarding the mediator will be given in full to the mediator as part of the mediator's continuing learning and development and CEDR's quality assurance.

10. Complaints

Any formal complaint about CEDR or any mediator nominated by CEDR should follow the procedure set out on the CEDR website at http://www.cedr.com/complaints.

Appendix G: UNCITRAL Notes on Mediation*

Introduction

Purpose of the Notes

1. The Notes list and briefly describe matters relevant to mediation. Prepared with a focus on international mediation, they are intended to be used in a general and universal manner by mediation practitioners and parties to a dispute.
2. Given the flexibility that characterizes mediation, procedural styles, practices and methods to foster a settlement between parties vary. Each approach has its own merit. Therefore, the Notes do not seek to promote any particular practice as best practice.
3. The Notes seek to assist parties in better understanding mediation including the wide and flexible range of possible outcomes. The parties and the mediator may use or refer to the Notes at their discretion and to the extent they see fit, and need not adopt or provide reasons for not adopting any particular element of the Notes. The Notes do not impose any legal requirements binding upon the parties or the mediator and are not suitable to be used as mediation rules.

Main features of mediation

4. Mediation is an efficient and cost-effective dispute settlement mechanism. It allows parties to prevent or settle a dispute taking their interests into account and avoiding a win/lose outcome.
5. Mediation can be used for solving a wide range of disputes. Its use results in significant benefits, such as facilitating the administration of international transactions by parties and reducing the instances where a dispute leads to the termination of a commercial relationship.

Non-adjudicatory process

6. Mediation is not formal and in contrast to any adjudicative proceedings, it does not rely on complex rules of form and procedure. Indeed, the manner in which a mediation process unfolds is not legally predetermined.
7. In successful mediation, the parties frequently shift from an adversarial ("one party against the other") to a solution-oriented ("both parties against the problem") mindset. Even if the parties do not reach a settlement agreement, the process can still allow them to gain a better understanding of the issues at stake and overcome unrealistic expectations.

Flexible process

8. Mediation is a flexible process, which allows parties to tailor it as they wish, taking also into account their needs as well as the circumstances of the case. As a result, mediation is usually less time and resources consuming than adjudication.
9. The parties focus on their underlying concerns and interests. They can resolve potential misunderstandings and develop the basis for a longer-term business relationship.

Voluntary process based on party autonomy

10. Mediation relies on party autonomy. Indeed, the parties retain full control of their participation in a mediation. Unless mandatory requirements apply under a relevant source of law, the parties are usually free to:
    - Agree on the mediator
    - Agree on the conduct of the mediation procedure
    - Determine the scope of issues to be submitted to mediation
    - Develop their own solutions
    - Solve their dispute holistically or agree on a partial solution, and/or
    - Terminate the mediation at any time
11. The following chart provides an overview of the mediation steps.

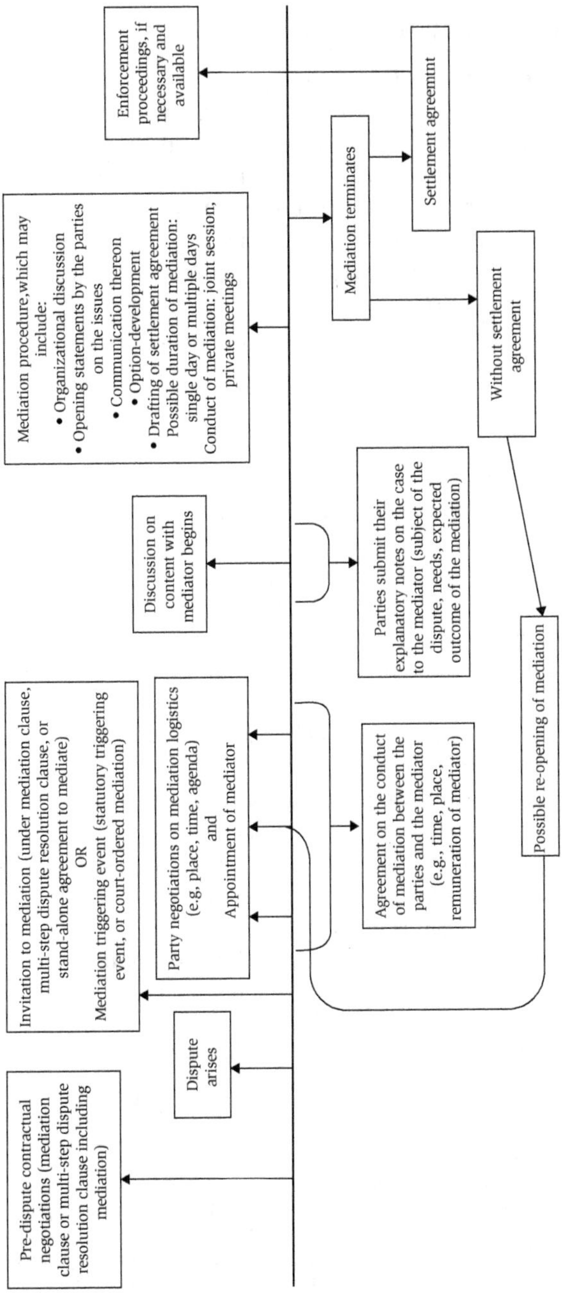
Pre-dispute contractual negotiations (mediation clause or multi-step dispute resolution clause including mediation)
Dispute arises
Invitation to mediation (under mediation clause, multi-step dispute resolution clause, or stand-alone agreement to mediate)
OR
Mediation triggering event (statutory triggering event, or court-ordered mediation)
Party negotiations on mediation logistics (e.g, place, time, agenda)
and
Appointment of mediator
Agreement on the conduct of mediation between the parties and the mediator (e.g., time, place, remuneration of mediator)
Discussion on content with mediator begins
Parties submit their explanatory notes on the case to the mediator (subject of the dispute, needs, expected outcome of the mediation)
Mediation procedure,which may include:
• Organizational discussion
• Opening statements by the parties on the issues
• Communication thereon
• Option-development
• Drafting of settlement agreement
Possible duration of mediation: single day or multiple days
Conduct of mediation: joint session, private meetings
Mediation terminates
Settlement agreemnt
Without settlement agreement
Possible re-opening of mediation
Enforcement proceedings, if necessary and available

Legal framework

Singapore Convention on Mediation

12. The United Nations Convention on International Settlement Agreements resulting from Mediation ("Singapore Convention on Mediation" or "Convention"), adopted by the General Assembly on 20 December 2018,[1] applies to international settlement agreements resulting from mediation, concluded by parties to resolve a commercial dispute, as defined in the Convention.[2] It provides a uniform and efficient framework for the enforcement of international settlement agreements resulting from mediation and for allowing parties to invoke such agreements. It ensures that a settlement reached by par-ties becomes binding and enforceable in accordance with a simplified and streamlined procedure.

Mediation laws

13. Mediation laws, such as those modelled on the UNCITRAL Model Law on International Commercial Mediation and International Settlement Agreements Resulting from Mediation (the "Model Law on Mediation") usually define mediation as a process where parties are assisted by a third person or persons in their attempt to negotiate and reach an amicable settlement of their dispute. The mediator is to assist the parties in their communication so that they can find a solution, and has no authority to impose a solution on the parties.
14. Essentially, mediation laws seek to strike a balance between protecting the integrity of the mediation process, for example, by ensuring that the mediator would make the necessary disclosures, while also providing maximum flexibility by preserving party autonomy. The laws are designed to accommodate procedural differences. Therefore, they usually include default provisions on the mediation procedure. They often focus on domestic mediation, and include provisions on access to mediation, the establishment of mediation institutions or organizations, the appointment and accreditation of mediators and the protection of confidentiality.

1. General Assembly resolution 73/198 of 20 December 2018.
2. Article 1(1) of the Convention reads as follows: "This Convention applies to an agreement resulting from mediation and concluded in writing by parties to resolve a commercial dispute ("settlement agreement") which, at the time of its conclusion, is international in that: (a) At least two parties to the settlement agreement have their places of business in different States; or (b) The State in which the parties to the settlement agreement have their places of business is different from either: (i) The State in which a substantial part of the obligations under the settlement agreement is performed; or (ii) The State with which the subject matter of the settlement agreement is most closely connected."

Mediation rules

15. The parties may agree to use a set of mediation rules. Such rules usually determine the procedural framework of the mediation. They also contain model mediation clauses that can be easily adopted by the parties in their commercial contracts. For example, the UNCITRAL Mediation Rules are a set of procedural rules, that can be used without an institution administering the mediation, and that parties are free to modify and adapt as they wish. Parties can also decide to have the proceedings administered by an institution. Most institutional rules also give parties a high degree of flexibility.

List of matters for possible consideration in organizing a mediation

1. Commencement of the mediation

(a) Various basis
(b) Agreement of the parties
(c) Invitation to mediate
(d) Date of commencement of the mediation
(e) Institutional support

2. Selection and appointment of a mediator

(a) How to select and appoint a mediator
(b) Availability, skills and background
(c) Ethical requirements

3. Preparatory steps

(a) Terms of reference, fees and other costs
(b) Administrative assistance
(c) Parties' attendance and representation
(d) Addressing confidentiality
(e) Determining the location and the timing of the mediation
(f) Agreeing on the language of the mediation

4. Conduct of the mediation

(a) Role of the mediator
(b) Initial consultations
(c) Submissions and supporting documents
(d) Mediation sessions and active negotiations

5. Settlement agreement

(a) Settlement proposals
(b) Drawing up the settlement agreement
(c) Enforceability

6. *Termination of the mediation*

Annotations

1. *Commencement of the mediation*

(a) Various basis

16. Mediation can be used successfully at different stages of a dispute, either before or during any arbitral, judicial or other dispute resolution proceedings.
17. Mediation can be carried out based on an agreement between the parties whether reached before or after a dispute has arisen (see below, paras. 19–22). Mediation often represents the last possible attempt to find a solution to settle a dispute before formal proceedings are initiated, or after they are concluded (for example, for the purposes of enforcement of an arbitral award or a judgment).
18. Mediation can also be carried out based on an obligation established by an international instrument or by law, or by a direction or suggestion of a court, arbitral tribunal or competent governmental entity.

(b) Agreement of the parties

Pre-dispute agreement

19. It is advisable for the parties to include in their contract a mediation clause. Such a clause usually provides that the parties will seek to solve any dispute under the contract through mediation. Par-ties usually tailor the mediation clause to their needs. They may choose to refer to a set of mediation rules (see above, para. 15). Further, they may indicate the language of mediation and the place of any mediation (see below, paras. 52–54).
20. A pre-dispute mediation clause can be included in a contract either as a simple clause, as part of a multi-tiered dispute resolution clause where mediation is one of the initial tiers, or in a clause which provides that mediation shall proceed concurrently with arbitral, judicial or other dispute resolution proceedings. In the case of a multi-tiered clause, it is advisable for the parties to determine periods during which they must comply with certain actions as part of the multi-tiered process, indicating steps regarding both timing and the process.

Agreement to mediate an existing dispute

21. If there is no pre-existing agreement to mediate, a party can request mediation at any stage, even if arbitral, judicial or other dispute resolution proceedings are ongoing.
22. Where a mediation takes place during arbitral or court proceedings, the arbitration or litigation may be stayed to allow time for conducting the

mediation, unless prohibited by the applicable law. In certain cases, the parties may agree to proceed concurrently with mediation and arbitration or litigation.

(c) Invitation to mediate

23. The party that wishes to commence a mediation usually sends an invitation to mediate to the other party or parties.
24. At this preliminary stage, subject to any agreed or mandatory procedure, it is useful to indicate the following in the invitation to mediate:
    (i) A brief outline of the subject matter of the dispute;
    (ii) Any contract or other legal instrument out of or in relation to which the dispute arises or, in the absence of such contract or instrument, a brief description of the relevant relationship;
    (iii) The identification of the basis for the mediation such as whether the invitation is made under a mediation agreement or on a different basis;
    (iv) The applicable mediation rules, if any, or mediation procedure; and
    (v) A period after which if no acceptance of the invitation is received, the party may elect to treat this as a rejection of the invitation to mediate.

(d) Date of commencement of the mediation

25. It is advisable for the parties to determine the date of commencement of the mediation for several reasons, including that this date marks the starting point of the obligation of confidentiality.
26. The commencement date is often the day on which the parties to the dispute agree to engage in the mediation.

(e) Institutional support

27. The parties may consider referring their disputes to a mediation institution. Mediation institutions may handle mediation generally or be specialized in certain types of disputes, such as construction, infrastructure or intellectual property disputes, or a certain mode of settlement, such as online dispute resolution.
28. The availability, nature and cost of institutional support vary depending on the institution. Support may include:
    (i) Providing guidance on the organization of the mediation (for example on procedural steps and costs);
    (ii) Helping select and appoint a mediator;
    (iii) Assisting with administrative and logistical matters (for example, reserving conference facilities and translation services);
    (iv) Providing data protection or cybersecurity measures (in particular for online mediation); and
    (v) Certifying that a mediation took place.

2. Selection and appointment of a mediator

(a) How to select and appoint a mediator

29. After the parties have agreed to engage in a mediation, they usually proceed with the selection and appointment of the mediator. The parties may agree on a mediator or on a procedure for appointing the mediator. The advantage of the parties first seeking to mutually agree on a mediator is that this approach respects the consensual nature of mediation and provides the parties with greater control and autonomy, and therefore confidence in the mediation process.
30. Generally, the practice is to appoint a single mediator in order to allow for a speedy and inexpensive process. Sometimes, the parties appoint two or more mediators, for example, in cases where:
    (i) Special expertise is needed in more than one area if the dispute is complex (in which case the parties may also choose to appoint an expert instead);
    (ii) A single mediator may not be sufficiently familiar with the law and trade usages, languages or cultures with which an international transaction is connected; or
    (iii) Multiple parties are involved.
31. Certain sets of mediation rules provide for the involvement of an appointing authority when the parties cannot agree on a mediator. In these cases, the parties may request an institution or a person to recommend a suitable mediator or to directly appoint the mediator.[3] In recommending or appointing an individual to act as mediator in international mediation, the appointing institution or person may consider whether it is necessary to choose a mediator of a nationality other than the nationalities of the parties and should strive to respect geographical diversity and gender.

(b) Availability, skills and background

32. When selecting a prospective mediator, the parties may con-sider the following elements:
    (i) Availability;
    (ii) Training and experience in the field of mediation and ability to conduct the mediation;
    (iii) Background such as nationality and legal tradition;
    (iv) Any relevant accreditation and/or certification awarded by a recognized professional mediation standards body; and
    (v) Professional expertise and qualifications, including expertise in the subject matter in controversy, languages and technical skills.

---

3. For example, the UNCITRAL Mediation Rules foresee in article 3(3) that the parties can refer to an institution or a person for the selection of a mediator, which the parties may subsequently appoint.

(c) Ethical requirements

33. A mediator usually shall be independent and impartial, and shall not have any professional, financial or other interest in the dispute and its outcome.
34. From the time of appointment and throughout the mediation, a mediator is usually required to disclose any circumstances likely to give rise to justifiable doubts as to her/his impartiality. If the parties have been informed of potential conflicts of interests and have given their informed consent to appoint the mediator, the mediator can proceed with the mediation.
35. Many jurisdictions do not allow the mediator to act as an arbitrator or judge in a dispute that was or is the subject of the mediation or for another dispute that has arisen from the same or any related contract or legal relationship, unless otherwise agreed by the parties. Laws and mediation rules also often require that the mediator shall not act as a representative or counsel of a party in any arbitral, judicial or other dispute resolution proceedings in respect of the dispute that is the subject of the mediation.

3. Preparatory steps

(a) Terms of reference, fees and other costs

36. Once a mediator is selected by the parties, the appointment of the mediator should be confirmed. The parties may send an appointment letter to the mediator. It is also common for the parties and the mediator to sign terms of reference which cover various elements of the mediation and mediators' involvement in the process. The terms of reference may contain an outline of the dispute, relevant rules determining the conduct of the mediation, such as the ethical standards applicable to the mediator and relevant disclosure obligations as well as the parties' agreement regarding confidentiality (see below, paras. 45–51).
37. The parties and the mediator should agree at the outset on the determination and allocation of the fees of the mediator and the mediation costs. The fee of the mediator may or may not be dependent on the outcome of the mediation or the amount in dispute. Furthermore, regardless of the outcome, the parties should agree from the outset that the mediator will be paid. The costs of mediation usually include:
    (i) The fees of the mediator;
    (ii) The fees of the institution administering the mediation, if any;
    (iii) The expenses incurred by the mediator, such as for travel, accommodation, administrative and techno-logical support, if not directly covered by the parties;
    (iv) The expenses occurred by experts, if any; and
    (v) Other expenses including translation and interpretation costs.
38. The mediator may require the parties to deposit an amount as an advance for costs and may suspend the mediation until such a deposit is paid. Mediation rules often have provisions regarding these matters, including whether the

deposit should be made in equal amounts by the parties and the consequences of the failure of a party to make the required payment.[4] Where the mediation is administered by a mediation institution, the institution's services may include fixing the amount of the deposit as well as holding, managing and accounting for deposits. If the mediation institution does not offer such services, the parties or the mediator will have to make necessary arrangements, for example, with a bank or other external provider. In any case, it is useful to clarify matters, such as the type and the location of the account in which the deposit will be kept, how the deposit will be managed and whether interest on the deposit will accrue.

39. Regulatory restrictions may have an impact on the handling of deposits of costs, such as restrictions in professional and ethical codes, financial regulations relating to the identity of beneficiaries and restrictions on trade or payment.
40. Allocation of costs is usually agreed by the parties or provided for in the applicable mediation rules. Generally, if no allocation method is agreed upon, costs in respect of the mediation are borne by the parties in equal shares.[5] In multiparty proceedings, an agreement on "equally sharing costs" would need to be further specified.

(b) Administrative assistance

41. The mediator may need administrative support to facilitate the conduct of the mediation. The parties, or the mediator with the con-sent of the parties, may arrange for administrative assistance by a suitable person or institution.

(c) Parties' attendance and representation

42. If a party has a limitation on the authority to settle (for example, where any settlement will need to be approved by a board of directors, a ministerial committee or an insurer), the party should, at the outset, inform the mediator and the other parties of this limitation. This allows the mediator to discuss these issues with the parties in advance of the mediation. Producing a power of attorney may be required.
43. Participants in the mediation may include persons who can assist in the resolution of the dispute.
44. It is common, particularly in international disputes, for a counsel to assist parties in some or all parts of the mediation process. Legal representation is not required in all cases as negotiation between the parties is generally interest-based and not limited to legal considerations. Participation by counsel is recommended where there is a need to discuss the party's legal rights and obligations, analyse the legal implications of offers and options for settlement, and draft the settlement agreement.

4. See, for example, article 11, paragraphs 3 to 5 of the UNCITRAL Mediation Rules.
5. See, for example, article 11, paragraph 2 of the UNCITRAL Mediation Rules.

(d) Addressing confidentiality

45. It is advisable for the parties to consider at the outset of the mediation the extent to which they wish the mediation to remain confidential, and to check the applicable law and rules to ensure that the confidentiality obligations are clearly spelled out and sufficiently safeguarded. The parties should consider agreeing on how confidentiality should be dealt with, covering the following aspects.

The mediator and those involved in the mediation

46. The mediator is generally expected to keep the mediation, including any information related to, or obtained during, the mediation, confidential. The duty of confidentiality usually not only applies to the mediator but also to others involved in the mediation (such as those representing or assisting the parties as well as those providing administrative support). It is advisable that all those involved in the mediation should be covered by a confidentiality agreement.

Between the parties

47. The parties may agree on the desired confidentiality regime to the extent not precluded by the applicable law. They may determine the extent to which the mediation itself and any information exchanged or disclosed during the mediation should remain confidential.
48. An agreement on confidentiality may cover one or more of the following matters: *(a)* the material or information that is to be kept confidential (for example, the fact that the mediation is taking place, the identity of the parties and the mediator, written and oral communications, the content of the settlement); *(b)* measures for maintaining the confidentiality of such information and the duration of the obligation on confidentiality; *(c)* circumstances in which confidential information may be disclosed in whole or in part to the extent necessary to protect a legal right; and *(d)* other circumstances in which such disclosure might be permissible (for example, information in the public domain, or disclosures required by law or a regulatory body).

Between the parties and the mediator during the mediation

49. The parties should agree on how the mediator will deal with the information received from a party during the mediation. For example, the understanding could be that the mediator may disclose the substance of that information to any other party to the mediation where such disclosure is likely to assist the parties in resolving their dispute. However, when a party gives information to

the mediator, subject to a request that it remains confidential, such information shall not be disclosed to any other party to the mediation.[6]

Admissibility of evidence in other proceedings

50. Any documents prepared primarily for the mediation, any suggestions made regarding the settlement, or any admissions made by a party in the mediation should not be admissible as evidence in arbitral, judicial or other dispute resolution proceedings.
51. The inadmissibility of evidence in other proceedings is to ensure that no party has a disadvantage resulting from her/his openness regarding substantive information or views expressed to bring the parties closer to settlement. The inadmissibility of communications and information exchanged in the mediation as evidence and the inability to call a mediator as a witness in any post-mediation procedure should cover all subsequent proceedings that relate to the dispute that is or was the subject matter of the mediation. Nevertheless, such information usually may be disclosed or admitted as evidence if required under the law or for the purposes of implementation or enforcement of a settlement agreement.

(e) Determining the location and the timing of the mediation

52. The parties should determine, at the outset, where the mediation will take place. When deciding on meeting locations, the following may be considered:
    (i) The convenience and neutrality of the location for the parties and the mediator, including travel to the location;
    (ii) The availability and cost of support services; and
    (iii) Whether the venue includes separate rooms for each party and a large room for holding joint meetings with all parties.
53. Mediation can also be conducted fully or partially online, limiting the contact between the parties and the mediator to virtual meetings. In these cases, the determination of the applicable law may be affected, and thus predetermination of the law applicable to the mediation process and the settlement agreement might be of particular importance.
54. The parties can determine the timing, including agreeing on a timetable and time frame for the mediation, so as to be able to be properly prepared.

(f) Agreeing on the language of the mediation

55. The parties normally also agree on the language or languages in which the mediation will be conducted. When multiple languages are to be used during the mediation, the parties and the mediator need to decide whether the

6. See, for example, article 9 of the Model Law on Mediation.

languages are to be used interchangeably without any translation or interpretation, or whether some documents and communications (or some relevant sections thereof) need to be translated into all languages.

4. Conduct of the mediation

(a) Role of the mediator

56. In general, the role of mediators is to build trust between the parties and in the process so as to reach a settlement of the dispute. Mediators aim, at the outset, to create a safe, neutral and supportive atmosphere for effective negotiation. Mediators apply varying degrees of influence in accordance with the parties' expectations, the circumstances of the case and different practices. The neutral status of mediators makes them uniquely qualified to react to parties' allegations and arguments and aids the parties in assessing the credibility of their positions. Mediators also assist the parties in identifying and prioritizing their needs and interests, leading to informed negotiations and tailor-made solutions to the dispute.
57. Mediators have a variety of methodological techniques and tools at their disposal to overcome deadlocks and move the process forward. Throughout the mediation, mediators assist the parties and provide guidance on the discussions, often helping the parties to think innovatively, thereby empowering them to consider a range of possible outcomes and find solutions, including creative or otherwise suitable solutions, which might not be available in court or arbitration.

(b) Initial consultations

58. Once a mediator is appointed, the parties and the mediator typically hold a preparatory meeting (which can take place in person or remotely, for example, through a conference call), during which the parties and the mediator work out the best arrangements for the case, including the procedural conduct (the parties may choose from the variety of rules available and adapt them to their needs)[7] and logistical matters. Such initial consultations are intrinsic to the consensual nature of mediation and are normally undertaken with respect to most organizational decisions addressed in the Notes, in particular those covered under Note 3 (Preparatory steps). If the parties have agreed on these matters before the mediation starts, or even in a pre-dispute mediation agreement, the parties may then confirm their decisions.
59. Further, the initial consultations help to clarify the parties' expectations on the conduct of the mediation and allow the parties to assess whether the mediator's approach, methods and style fit to the dispute at stake, and to

7. See, for example, article 7, paragraph 1 of the Model Law on Mediation. Examples of the "set of rules" that may be agreed upon by the parties to organize the conduct of the mediation include the UNCITRAL Mediation Rules and rules of mediation institutions.

assess the reasonableness of the fees and costs involved. Therefore, initial consultations are crucial, even in an institutional mediation where logistical issues might have already been taken care of.

60. If the parties have not agreed on a procedure to be followed by the mediator or on a set of mediation rules to govern the mediation, the mediator and the parties can design the procedure together. The parties may leave it to the discretion of the mediator to determine how the mediation should be conducted, subject to mandatory provisions of any applicable law. In particular, at an early stage, the parties may occasionally have difficulties agreeing on procedural matters, and may request the mediator to decide on those matters. Some mediators consider that engaging the parties on routine procedural matters is a first and necessary step to establish confidence in the process.
61. The parties should seek to clarify various questions at an early stage of the mediation, including whether the mediation constitutes a bar to initiate arbitral, judicial or other dispute resolution proceedings. They may also consider questions regarding the legal framework for the conclusion, implementation and enforcement of a settlement agreement.

(c) Submissions and supporting documents

62. The parties are free to agree on how the information on their case should be provided to the mediator and in what form. As part of the mediation process, the parties usually exchange short papers (sometimes called position papers, mediation statements, briefs or case summaries).
63. If any such written summary is prepared, it is usually meant to be used only in mediation with a view to finding a settlement and it is not meant to be used in any further litigation. The summary may be submitted by each party or jointly, and it would usually contain:
    (i) The dispute history;
    (ii) An explanation of the issues; and
    (iii) What the party seeks to obtain in mediation.
64. The parties may agree on documents to be provided that will support their arguments or clarify the dispute. Such documentation may include contracts and correspondence, as well as any other relevant information.
65. The parties and the mediator may consider whether it would be helpful to agree on practical details such as the form in which the information will be conveyed (for example, in hard copy, electronic form or through a shared platform), including their format (for example, specific electronic format, with search features).
66. The use of electronic means of communication can make the mediation more expeditious and efficient. However, it is advisable to consider whether all parties have access to, or are familiar with, such means. The parties and the mediator may need to consider issues of compatibility, storage, access, data security as well as related costs when deciding on electronic means of

communication. The parties and the mediator also need to ensure that electronic communications are adequately protected.

(d) Mediation sessions and active negotiations

67. A solid understanding of key facts and possible outcomes should emerge from the mediation process. To that end, the mediator usually organizes one or several meetings, in person or remotely by using, for example, an appropriate platform that allows for joint and private meetings (referred to as 'mediation sessions'). It may be advisable for the mediator, in consultation with the parties, to deter-mine the time to be allocated to the mediation sessions.
68. Such mediation sessions may be held with all parties present or may be held separately with each party alone (often referred to as caucus) or a combination of both joint and private meetings. For example, a mediator may start with a joint meeting where the parties discuss their views on the dispute and then caucus with the parties separately. Ex parte communications are not prohibited and, on the contrary, are considered useful in mediation. However, the mediator is expected to maintain a fair treatment of the parties and to disclose to any other party that an ex parte communication is taking place. Fair treatment does not mean equal treatment, as a mediator may need to spend more time with one party than the other. It is recommended that the parties participate in mediation sessions.
69. The number of mediation sessions and their duration depend on the complexity of the issues and can be adjusted to the case and the approach favoured by the mediator and the parties. For exploring the issues and identifying a lasting and sustainable solution, taking the necessary time is critical.
70. In complex mediations, more attention is required regarding the organization of mediation sessions. Following the prior and express consent by the parties, interested stakeholders and/or experts may be invited to attend and participate as necessary. The issue of maintaining confidentiality in such cases needs to be addressed, for example by confidentiality agreements.

5. Settlement agreement

(a) Settlement proposals

71. The mediator cannot impose a settlement on the parties, but she/he will assist the parties in reaching an amicable settlement of their dispute. Settlement proposals can be made directly between the parties or through the mediator.
72. The mediator may, if requested by the parties, recommend terms of settlement.

(b) Drawing up the settlement agreement

73. If the parties agree to settle their dispute, they will prepare a settlement agreement. Depending on the applicable law, the mediator may, if so requested, assist the parties in preparing the settlement agreement, for example by providing a summary of the agreed terms. Usually, settlement agreements are made in writing; it is advisable for the parties to check how this requirement can be satisfied.[8]
74. The settlement agreement should be clearly worded, for example, the conditions of performance should be unambiguously identifiable.
75. When agreeing on the law applicable to the settlement agreement, and when considering the place where the obligations in the settlement agreement are connected to, the parties may keep in mind the legal consequences attached thereto, as well as more generally the legal framework, including the Singapore Convention on Mediation.

(c) Enforceability

76. Generally, the parties comply voluntarily with the obligations set forth in the settlement agreement. Nevertheless, the parties should consider any requirement as to the form (including language requirements), content, filing, registering or delivering of the settlement agreement set forth by the applicable mediation law, the relevant law at the place(s) of enforcement and the applicable mediation rules.
77. If necessary, the settlement agreement may be enforced in accordance with the procedure of the State in which enforcement is sought. Such procedure varies in different jurisdictions.
78. States that are party to the Singapore Convention on Mediation and States that have enacted legislation based on the Model Law on Mediation presumably follow the enforcement procedure defined therein. While drafting the settlement agreement, the parties may take note of the relevant provisions and requirements under the Singapore Convention on Mediation and the Model Law on Mediation.[9] A list of reservations made by State Parties under article 8 of the Convention can be found on the UNCITRAL website.[10]

---

8. For example, article 16, paragraph 6 of the Model Law on Mediation provides as follows: "A settlement agreement is 'in writing' if its content is recorded in any form. The requirement that a settlement agreement be in writing is met by an electronic communication if the information contained therein is accessible so as to be useable for subsequent reference."
9. See, in particular, articles 4 and 5 of the Convention and articles 18 and 19 of the Model Law.
10. Under article 8(1)(a) of the Singapore Convention on Mediation, a State Party may declare that it shall not apply the Convention to settlement agreements to which it is a party, or to which any governmental agencies or any person acting on behalf of a governmental agency is a party, to the extent specified in the declaration; under article 8(1)(b) of the Singapore Convention on Mediation, a State Party may declare that it shall apply this Convention only to the extent that the parties to the settlement agreement have agreed to the application of the Convention.

79. It is advisable that the parties state their understanding that the settlement agreement can be used as evidence that resulted from mediation, and that it can be relied upon for seeking relief under the applicable legal framework.

6. Termination of the mediation

80. After the parties have engaged in mediation, the mediation is usually terminated by:
    (i) The conclusion of a settlement agreement by the parties, on the date of the agreement, or such other date as agreed by the parties in the settlement agreement;
    (ii) By a declaration of the mediator, after consultation with the parties, if the required deposits are not paid in full by all parties within a reasonable period set by the mediator, on the date of the declaration;
    (iii) A declaration of the mediator, after consultation with the parties to the effect that further mediation efforts are no longer justified on the date of the declaration;
    (iv) A declaration of the parties addressed to the media-tor to the effect that the mediation proceedings are terminated, on the date of the declaration;
    (v) A declaration of a party to the other party or parties and the mediator, if appointed, to the effect that the mediation proceedings are terminated as to that party, on the date of the declaration; or
    (vi) At the expiration of a defined period in the applicable international instrument, court order or mandatory statutory provision, or as agreed upon at the outset by the parties.
81. It is advisable that any termination be clearly and unambiguously recorded as it may constitute the starting point of subsequent procedures or it may have an impact on the running of limitation periods applicable to the claim that is the subject matter of the mediation.

Appendix H: International Mediation Institute (IMI) Code of Professional Conduct*

The IMI Code of Professional Conduct ("the Code") provides users of mediation services with a concise statement of the ethical standards they can expect from IMI Certified Mediators.
Users who believe the standards established in this Code have not been met may activate the IMI Professional Conduct Assessment Process.

DEFINITIONS

For the purposes of this Code, Mediation is defined as a process in which a third-party (the IMI Certified Mediator) assists parties in engaging in a dialogue oriented toward managing or resolving a dispute.

An IMI Certified Mediator (also called a Mediator in this Code) is one:

- whose competency in the practice of mediation has been certified by IMI, and
- who is authorized by IMI to use the IMI name and logo, and
- whose Profile is included on the IMI web portal at: http://www.IMImediation.org

1. MEDIATOR APPOINTMENT

1.1. Entitlement to use the title "IMI Certified Mediator" and the IMI logo

In the event that an IMI Certified Mediator fails to maintain IMI requirements for certification, or no longer qualifies as an IMI Certified Mediator, use of the title IMI Certified Mediator and use of the IMI name and logo will end, and the Mediator's Profile will no longer be included on the IMI web portal.

1.2. Promotion of Mediators' services

Subject to applicable laws and to regulations governing professional practice, Mediators will present and promote their practice truthfully and accurately. They may quote freely from, and link to, their Profile on the IMI web portal and they are free to replicate that Profile, or extracts from it, for their own professional purposes.

1.3. Appointment

1.3.1 Before the mediation begins, Mediators will inform the parties of their relevant background and experience.

1.3.2 Mediators will advise parties that they will be invited to offer the Mediator feedback on the process at any stage, including offering written feedback at the conclusion of the mediation.

1.3.3 Mediators will, prior to appointment, conduct reasonable inquiries to determine if any pre-existing relationship or interest in the subject matter of the dispute creates a real or perceived conflict of interest. The mediator will disclose any such interests and obtain the parties' consent to continue. Regardless of party consent, if the mediator thinks that the relationship or interest poses a threat to the mediator's ability to conduct the mediation impartially, the mediator shall decline the appointment.

2. DILIGENCE

Mediators may accept an assignment to act as Mediator in any situation in which they are competent to serve in that capacity. Mediators should ensure that they have the requisite time, energy and procedural and subject matter expertise to competently meet the reasonable expectations of the parties.

3. IMPARTIALITY

3.1 Mediators will always conduct mediation in an impartial manner, avoiding bias or prejudice in favor or against any party. Bias or favoritism can result from several sources: mediator reaction to a mediation participant's personal characteristics, background or values; mediator personal, professional or financial interests in the subject matter of the dispute; or preexisting relationships with any mediation participant. If at any time a Mediator feels unable to conduct the process in an impartial manner, (s)he will express that concern and withdraw from the mediation.

3.2 Mediators will not accept an appointment without first disclosing anything within their knowledge that may, or may be perceived to, materially affect their impartiality. This duty to disclose is a continuing obligation throughout the mediation process.

3.3 The existence of relationships or interests potentially affecting, or appearing to affect, a Mediator's impartiality will not automatically imply unfitness to act as a mediator provided these circumstances have been fully disclosed and addressed to the satisfaction of the parties and the Mediator.

3.4 The duty to disclose perceived or actual threats to Mediator impartiality is ongoing. Newly discovered interests or relationships creating an actual or perceived threat to Mediator impartiality must be disclosed and parties must renew their consent to proceed with the process.

3.5 Following any such disclosures, if any party raises an objection, the Mediator will withdraw from the mediation.

3.6 After accepting appointment, and until the mediation process ends, Mediators will not enter into financial, business, professional, family or social relationships or acquire financial or personal interests that are likely to create an actual or perceived threat to mediation impartiality. In the case of perceived threats, mediators may proceed after full disclosure and party consent.

3.7 Within 12 months following the end of a mediation, Mediators will not represent in an advisory capacity or accept employment with any party to a mediation in the same or a substantially related matter, unless all parties to the mediation expressly consent to that representation after full disclosure. Acting as a neutral in other dispute resolution proceedings (e.g. as a mediator or arbitrator) that may involve some or all of the parties will not be considered a representation in an advisory capacity for the purposes of this clause.

4. MEDIATION PROCESS

4.1. Procedure

Mediators will endeavor to ensure that the parties to the mediation and their advisers understand the characteristics of the mediation process, their roles as parties and advisers, and the role of a mediator, as well as the enforceability of any resulting agreement. The Mediator will ensure that before the mediation begins, the parties have understood and agreed to the terms and conditions which will govern the mediation including those relating to Mediator and party obligations to respect Mediator confidentiality. It is best practice for those terms to be contained in a written Agreement to Mediate, unless the parties or the circumstances dictate otherwise.

4.2. Fairness and Integrity of the process

4.2.1 Mediators will explain the mediation process to the parties and their advisers, and be satisfied that they consent to the process being used and to the Mediator selected (unless applicable law, court rules or contract require use of a particular process and/or mediator). Mediators will ensure that all parties are aware that they have an equal opportunity to engage in pre-mediation private communications with the Mediator.

4.2.2 Mediators will conduct the process with attention to procedural fairness to all parties. The Mediator will take particular care to ensure that all parties have adequate opportunities to be heard, to be involved in the process and to have the opportunity to seek and obtain legal or other counsel before finalizing any resolution.

4.2.3 Mediators will take reasonable steps to prevent any misconduct that might invalidate an agreement reached in mediation or create or aggravate a hostile environment. Mediators will endeavor to ensure that the parties have reached agreement of their own volition and knowingly consent to any resolution.

4.3. Termination of the process

4.3.1 The Mediator will ensure the parties understand that they may withdraw from the mediation at any time by informing the Mediator of that preference (unless applicable law, court rules or contract require otherwise).

4.3.2 Mediators shall withdraw from a mediation if a negotiation among the parties appears to be moving toward an unconscionable or illegal outcome. An unconscionable outcome is one which is the product of undue pressure, exploitation or duress. An unconscionable outcome reflects one party's exploitation of an existing power imbalance to the degree that the resulting agreement 'shocks the conscience' and violates accepted legal and cultural norms of fairness.

4.4. Feedback

Unless inappropriate in the circumstances, Mediators will, at the conclusion of a mediation, invite the parties and advisers and any co-mediators or assistant mediators, to complete an IMI Feedback Request Form and return it to the Mediator or to the Reviewer indicated by the Mediator in his/her IMI Profile to assist in the preparation of the Mediator's Feedback Digest.

4.5. Fees

4.5.1 Mediators will, before accepting appointment, agree with the parties how their fees and expenses will be calculated, and how they will be paid by the parties (and if shared between the parties, in what proportions). Mediators who withdraw from a case will return to the parties any fees already paid relating to the period following withdrawal.

4.5.2 Mediators will not suggest to the parties that their remuneration should be based on, or related to, the outcome of the mediation.

5. CONFIDENTIALITY

5.1.1 Mediators will keep confidential all information acquired in the course of serving as a mediator in a mediation unless:

- compelled to make a disclosure by law or by some governmental agency having appropriate authority and jurisdiction, or
- arising under paragraph 5.1, in which event the recipients of the confidential information shall themselves be bound to maintain the confidentiality, or

- the specific information comes into the public domain (otherwise than as a result of a disclosure by the Mediator), or
- the parties release the Mediator from the confidentiality restriction, or as necessary to defend the Mediator from any proceedings or charges for which (s)he risks incurring any liability, or
- disclosure is necessary to prevent death or imminent bodily harm or severe damage to an identifiable third party or to prevent the commission of illegal and morally objectionable acts. Before using or disclosing such information, if not otherwise required to be disclosed by law, Mediators should make a good faith effort to persuade the party, and/or the party's counsel or other advisers, to act in such a way that would remedy the situation.

5.1.2 The Mediator may, however, disclose having previously served as a mediator in a mediation involving one or more of the parties, provided none of the details of that case are disclosed.

5.1.3 Mediators will discuss confidentiality with the parties before or at the beginning of the mediation and obtain their consent to any communication or practice by the Mediator that involves the disclosure of confidential information.

5.1.4 At no time following the end of a mediation will Mediators adduce evidence or testify on behalf of one of the parties in making or defending a claim against another party to the same mediation where they have acquired confidential information from the other party, unless all that information is no longer confidential or unless the party protected by the confidentiality gives consent.

6. PROFESSIONAL CONDUCT ISSUES AND COMPLAINTS

6.1 An IMI Certified Mediator may consult his/her Reviewer about any professional or ethical dilemmas.

6.2 A party to a mediation who believes there has been a lack of compliance with this Code may activate the IMI Professional Conduct Assessment Process.

Table of Cases

Cases from Australian Courts

Cases from Belgium Courts

Cases from Bermuda Courts

Cases from Bulgarian Courts

Cases from Canadian Courts

Cases from EU Courts

Cases from French Courts

Cases from Georgian Courts

Cases from German Courts

Cases from Hong Kong (SAR) Courts

Cases from Indian Courts

Cases from Ireland Courts

Cases from Italian Courts

Cases from Malaysian Courts

Cases from New Zealand Courts

Cases from People's Republic of China Courts

Cases from Polish Courts

Cases from Portuguese Courts

Cases from Singapore Courts

Cases from Taiwan (the Republic of China) Courts

Cases from Thai Courts

Cases from UK Courts

Cases from US Courts

Cases from International Courts

Table of Treaties, Legislation and Other Legal Instruments

International and Regional Conventions and Treaties

Domestic Legislation

Australia

Austria

Bermuda

Canada

Croatia

Cyprus

UK Arbitration Act 1996, s 52, **2.15 Point of Interest**
UK Foreign Limitation Periods Act 1984, **3.15**
UK Civil Procedure Rules (1998), Part 83, **3.25 Point of Interest**
UK Civil Procedure Rules (1998), r 1, **2.42**
UK Civil Procedure Rules (1998), r 39, **3.25 Point of Interest, 5.15**
UK Civil Procedure Rules (1998), r 40, **3.25 Point of Interest**
UK Civil Procedure Rules (1998), r 44, **2.42**
UK Contracts (Rights of Third Parties) Act 1999, s 1, **1.26 Point of Interest**
UK Freedom of Information Act 2000, **5.14**
UK Practice Direction to the Pre-action Protocols, **2.42**
UK State Immunity Act 1978, **8.17 Case Illustrations**
UK State Immunity Act 1978, Art. 13, **8.17**

The United States of America

California Code of Civil Procedure, § 664.6, **5.30 Case Illustrations**
California Code of Civil Procedure, § 1297.401, **1.56**
California Government Code, **5.14**
California Rules of Court, **2.42**
Florida Statutes 2008, s 44, **2.42**
Minnesota General Rules of Practice, r 114, **2.42**
New Jersey International Arbitration, Mediation, and Conciliation Act, **7.02**
New Jersey Rules of Evidence, r 519, **5.12 Point of Interest**
North Carolina General Statute, § 1-567.84, **1.56**
Ohio Revised Code, § 2712.87, **1.56**
Oregon Revised Statutes, § 36.546, **1.56**
Revised Code of Washington (RCW), s 42.56, **5.14**
Texas Business and Commerce Code, s 27, **5.38 Case Illustrations**
Texas Civil Practice and Remedies Code, § 154.021, **2.42**
Texas Civil Practice and Remedies Code, § 154.053, **5.12 Point of Interest**
Texas Civil Practice and Remedies Code, § 172.211, **1.56**
US Foreign Sovereign Immunities Act (1976), **8.17, 8.17 Case Illustrations**
US Freedom of Information Act 1966, **5.14**
US Uniform Mediation Act, **2.19, 5.10, 5.12, 5.12 Point of Interest, 5.22**
US Uniform Mediation Act, Art. 2, **5.12 Point of Interest**
US Uniform Mediation Act, Art. 3, **2.33, 5.12 Point of Interest**
US Uniform Mediation Act, Art. 4, **5.11, 5.12 Point of Interest**
US Uniform Mediation Act, Art. 5, **5.11, 5.12 Point of Interest, 5.14**
US Uniform Mediation Act, Art. 6, **5.11, 5.12 Point of Interest, 5.14, 5.15, 5.17**
US Uniform Mediation Act, Art. 7, **4.15, 5.11, 5.12 Point of Interest, 5.14**
US Uniform Mediation Act, Art. 9, **5.78, 5.79, 5.80, 5.90, 5.92**

Turkey (Republic of Türkiye)

Turkey Law on Mediation in Civil Disputes No. 6325, Art. 2, **2.34, 2.52**
Turkey Law on Mediation in Civil Disputes No. 6325, Art. 6, **2.52**
Turkey Law on Mediation in Civil Disputes No. 6325, Art. 18, **1.06**

Others (including mediation rules and codes of conduct)

Index

A

C

D

M

R

S

GLOBAL TRENDS IN DISPUTE RESOLUTION

1. Nadja Alexander (ed.), *Global Trends in Mediation,* Second Edition, 2006 (ISBN 978-90-411-2571-2).
2. Giuseppe De Palo and Mary B. Trevor (eds), *Arbitration and Mediation in the Southern Mediterranean Countries*, 2007 (ISBN 978-90-411-2684-9).
3. Lars Kirchhoff, *Constructive Interventions – Paradigms, Process and Practice of International Mediation*, 2008 (ISBN 978-90-411-2685-6).
4. Nadja Alexander, *International and Comparative Mediation: Legal Perspectives*, 2009 (ISBN 978-90-411-2684-9).
5. Ewald A. Filler, *Commercial Mediation in Europe: An Empirical Study of the User Experience*, 2012 (ISBN 978-90-411-3116-4).
6. Ian Macduff (ed.), *Essays on Mediation: Dealing with Disputes in the 21st Century*, 2016 (ISBN 978-90-411-8366-8).
7. Nadja Alexander, Sabine Walsh and Martin Svatos (eds), *EU Mediation Law Handbook: Regulatory Robustness Ratings for Mediation Regimes*, 2017 (ISBN 978-90-411-5859-8).
8. Nadja Alexander, Shouyu Chong and Vakhtang Giorgadze, *The Singapore Convention on Mediation: A Commentary*, Second Edition, 2022 (ISBN 978-94-035-28 25-0).
9. Anna Howard, *EU Cross-Border Commercial Mediation: Listening to Disputants – Changing the Frame; Framing the Changes*, 2021 (ISBN 978-94-035-1753-7).
10. Lenka Holá, Martina Urbanová, Miloš Večeřa, David Fiedor and Jan Holas, *Mediation in the Reflection of Law and Society: European Perspectives*, 2022 (ISBN 978-94-035-4214-0).
11. Gracious Timothy Dunna (ed.), *Conciliation and Mediation in India*, 2022 (ISBN 978-94-035-2015-5).

www.ingramcontent.com/pod-product-compliance
Lightning Source LLC
LaVergne TN
LVHW020002031026
849161LV00023B/830
* 9 7 8 9 4 0 3 5 2 8 2 5 0 *